Book 2

Literature & Comprehension

Writing Skills

Language Arts

Lesson Guide

Book Staff and Contributors

Kristen Kinney-Haines *Director, Primary Literacy*
Beth Zemble *Director, Alternative Learning Strategies; Director, English Language Arts*
Marianne Murphy *Senior Content Specialist*
Alane Gernon-Paulsen *Content Specialist*
Anna Day *Director, Instructional Design for Language Arts and History/Social Studies*
Frances Suazo *Senior Instructional Designer*
Cheryl Howard *Instructional Designer*
Karen Ingebretsen, Anne Vogel *Text Editors*
Suzanne Montazer *Creative Director, Print and ePublishing*
Sasha Blanton *Art Director, Print and ePublishing*
Carol Leigh *Print Visual Designer*
Stephanie Shaw Williams *Cover Designer*
Joshua Briggs, Kandee Dyczko *Writers*
Amy Eward *Senior Manager, Writers*
Susan Raley *Senior Manager, Editors*
Deanna Lacek *Project Manager*
David Johnson *Director, Program Management Grades K–8*

Maria Szalay *Executive Vice President, Product Development*
John Holdren *Senior Vice President, Content and Curriculum*
David Pelizzari *Vice President, K^{12} Content*
Kim Barcas *Vice President, Creative*
Laura Seuschek *Vice President, Assessment and Research*
Christopher Frescholtz *Senior Director, Program Management*

Lisa Dimaio Iekel *Director, Print Production and Manufacturing*
Ray Traugott *Production Manager*

Credits

All illustrations © K12 unless otherwise noted
Cover: Waterlily, leungchopan/Shutterstock.com; lily leaf © Videowokart/Dreamstime.com;
orange koi © Eric IsselTe/Fotolia.com

About K12 Inc.

K12 Inc. (NYSE: LRN) drives innovation and advances the quality of education by delivering state-of-the-art digital learning platforms and technology to students and school districts around the world. K12 is a company of educators offering its online and blended curriculum to charter schools, public school districts, private schools, and directly to families. More information can be found at K12.com.

978-1-60153-211-4

Printed by Bradford & Bigelow, Newburyport, MA, USA, August 2020.

Contents

Literature & Comprehension

Writing Skills

K¹² Language Arts Green

General Overview

K¹² Language Arts Green lays a strong foundation for beginning readers and writers. A well-balanced Language Arts program provides instruction on getting words off the page (reading) as well putting words on the page (writing). According to the National Reading Panel, a comprehensive reading program includes fluency, text comprehension, spelling, vocabulary, and writing skills. Language Arts Green provides this instruction through six separate-yet-related programs.

You will spend about two hours a day working with Language Arts Green. The tables describe the programs, the time you can expect to spend on them, and the overarching Big Ideas that are covered.

Program	Daily Lesson Time (approximate)	Online/Offline
K¹² Language Arts PhonicsWorks Advanced	50 minutes in Days 1–90 30 minutes in Days 91–180	Each lesson: 15–30 minutes offline, 15–20 minutes online
Big Ideas		

- Readers must understand that print carries meaning and there is a connection between letters and sounds.
- Fluent readers blend sounds represented by letters into words.
- Breaking words into syllables helps us read and spell unfamiliar words.
- Good readers practice reading grade-level text with fluency.
- Reading sight words helps young readers read complete sentences and short stories.

Program	Daily Lesson Time (approximate)	Online/Offline
K¹² Language Arts Green Literature & Comprehension	45 minutes	All offline

Big Ideas

- *Read Aloud*   Students follow along as a proficient reader models fluent, expressive reading; what good readers think about as they read; and how good readers use strategies to understand text.
- *Shared Reading*   Students practice the reading behaviors of proficient readers with the support of a proficient reader.
- *Guided Reading*   A proficient reader helps students preview and prepare for reading, and then students use the skills and strategies of proficient readers to read texts.
- *Fluency*   The ability to decode text quickly, smoothly, and automatically allows readers to focus on comprehension.
- *Comprehension*   Comprehension requires readers to actively think, ask themselves questions, and synthesize information to make meaning from their reading.
- *Analysis*   Readers must pay careful attention to language and literary elements to appreciate the underlying meaning or message of an author's work.
- *Enjoyment*   To develop a lifelong love of reading, new readers should independently read for their own enjoyment.

Program	Daily Lesson Time (approximate)	Online/Offline
K¹² Language Arts Green Spelling	15 minutes (Days 91–180 only)	Each unit: 4 offline lessons, 1 online review

Big Ideas

- Spelling represents sounds, syllables, and meaningful parts of words.
- The spelling of all English words can be explained by rules or patterns related to word origins.
- Students benefit from spelling instruction that gradually builds on previously mastered concepts of letter–sound relationships.
- Engaging spelling activities help students develop spelling skills needed for both writing and reading.
- Spelling ability correlates to reading comprehension ability.

Program	Daily Lesson Time (approximate)	Online/Offline
K¹² Language Arts Green Vocabulary	15 minutes	All online

Big Ideas

- Vocabulary words are words we need to know to communicate and understand.
- A *speaking vocabulary* includes the words we know and can use when speaking.
- A *reading vocabulary* includes the words we know and can read with understanding.
- A *listening vocabulary* includes the words we know and understand when we hear them.
- A *writing vocabulary* includes the words we know and understand when we write.
- The more we read, the more our vocabulary grows.
- Early learners acquire vocabulary through active exposure (by talking and listening, being read to, and receiving explicit instruction).

Program	Daily Lesson Time (approximate)	Online/Offline
K¹² Language Arts Green Writing Skills	15 minutes (Days 91–180 only)	Each unit (approximately): 4 offline lessons, 1 online lesson

Big Ideas

Composition

- Developing writers should study models of good writing.
- Writing can be broken out into a series of steps, or a process, that will help developing writers become more proficient.
- All writers revise, and revision is best performed in discrete tasks.

Grammar, Usage, and Mechanics (GUM)

- Using different kinds of sentences helps writers and speakers express their ideas accurately.
- A noun is a basic part of speech. Understanding nouns gives students a basic vocabulary for building sentences and understanding how language works.
- Recognizing and using action verbs helps writers make their work specific and interesting to readers.
- The use of descriptive adjectives can turn an ordinary piece of writing into one that enables the audience to form clear mental pictures of a scene.

Program	Daily Lesson Time (approximate)	Online/Offline
K¹² Language Arts Green Handwriting	10 minutes	All offline

Big Ideas
• Instruction in posture, pencil grip, and letter formation improves students' handwriting skills. • Proper modeling of letter formation is imperative for developing handwriting skills. • Students who have formal instruction in handwriting are more engaged in composition writing.

Structure

PhonicsWorks, Literature & Comprehension, Spelling, Vocabulary, Writing Skills, and Handwriting are independent programs that work together to give students a complete, well-balanced education in Language Arts.

1. **PhonicsWorks Advanced** Students review basic letter–sound correspondences before moving into more advanced patterns. Through careful reading, rereading, and writing of words, students develop fluency to later aid in comprehension.

2. **Literature & Comprehension** Students learn and later apply a wide variety of reading and comprehension strategies as they participate in read-aloud, shared-reading, and guided-reading activities with texts that cover a wide variety of genres. Activities emphasize deeper comprehension and analysis of text while developing a love of literature. Students also study how language is used in reading selections, providing a foundation for Writing Skills instruction in the second half of the year.

3. **Spelling** In the second half of the year, students learn to focus on spelling patterns that are necessary to be fluent, proficient readers, writers, and spellers.

4. **Vocabulary** Students increase their vocabulary by learning the meanings of groups of related words. Vocabulary skills help students read and compose written material.

5. **Writing Skills** Beginning in the second half of the year, students learn about grammar, usage, and mechanics and learn about and use writing strategies as they write a variety of compositions.

6. **Handwriting** For the first half of the year, students practice handwriting at a pace that meets their needs. For the second part of the year, students may continue to practice handwriting skills as they complete written work in other programs.

First-grade students grow and change quite a bit over the course of a year. As students begin first grade, they learn by doing. By the end of the year, students are thinking more abstractly, and they are able to process information a little differently. Students also learn to read and write more fluently as they progress through first grade. K[12] Language Arts Green accommodates the changing needs of students by adapting the instruction in several programs.

► **Phonics instructional time decreases** as students become more knowledgeable about sounds and letters and have increased reading fluency.
► **Literature lessons progress** from an adult reading aloud to students to having students read more independently.
► **Spelling instruction increases** as students become ready to learn about and apply spelling patterns.
► **Writing instruction increases** after students master the basics of handwriting and are ready to learn about how to put words and thoughts together.

To accommodate these changing needs, K[12] Language Arts Green is a bit different from the first part of the year to the last.

Days 1–90	
PhonicsWorks Advanced	**50 minutes**
Literature & Comprehension	**45 minutes**
Vocabulary	**15 minutes**
Handwriting	**10 minutes**

Days 91–180	
PhonicsWorks Advanced	**30 minutes**
Literature & Comprehension	**45 minutes**
Spelling	**15 minutes**
Vocabulary	**15 minutes**
Writing Skills	**15 minutes**
Handwriting	**⊕ OPTIONAL 10 minutes**

PhonicsWorks lesson time decreases.

Spelling instruction using *K[12] Spelling Handbook* begins.

Writing Skills instruction addressing composition and grammar, usage, and mechanics begins.

Students practice handwriting on their own or as they complete assigned work in other programs.

You will be notified in Advance Preparation 10 days before the Spelling and Writing Skills programs begin. When you see the notification, you should

1. Unpack the materials for these programs and preview them before the lessons begin on Day 91.

2. Review the Spelling program overview at the front of the *K¹² Spelling Handbook* and the Writing Skills program overview at the front of this Lesson Guide.

3. View the online program introductions in Unit 1, Lesson 1, of the Spelling and Writing Skills programs.

Flexible Lesson Planning

A key aspect of K¹² is the flexibility we offer students. Doing things that work best for them is vital to students' mastery. The structure of K¹² Language Arts Green, with the separate programs, allows you to work on one skill at a time, which gives you flexibility. You will be able to

▸ **Find content more easily.** The descriptive titles in the lesson lists online and in the Lesson Guide allow you to find lessons and activities quickly.

▸ **Manage progress more easily.** You can track progress, mastery, and attendance by program so you can see at a glance how a student is progressing in each. This tracking will allow you to better customize your schedule to meet students' needs.

▸ **Pace work appropriately for students.** The focused lessons enable you to identify skills that students need to spend more or less time on and make adjustments. You can decide the pace that works best for students in each program. For example, a student may work through two Vocabulary lessons at a time but need to spend some extra time on Phonics.

▸ **Control your own schedule.** You can arrange lessons to meet your needs.

TIP Get to know the different lesson types and then set up your lesson schedule in the best way for you and your students.

How to Work Through a Lesson

Preview and Prepare

1. **Prepare in advance.** Schedule time to plan at the beginning of each week and before each school day. You may want to look ahead at any assessments or writing assignments so you know what students are working toward in each unit.

2. **Check the Lesson Guide or the online lesson** to see the lesson plan and read any instructions for completing the lesson.

3. **Complete Advance Preparation** before you begin a lesson. Look for Advance Preparation in the Lesson Guide or the online lesson.

4. **Preview the Lesson Guide** so you are prepared to teach the offline activities. You may also want to preview the online lesson and the word lists for Vocabulary.

5. **Gather the materials** listed in the Lesson Guide or the online lesson before you begin. You should always have paper and pencil available in addition to any other materials that are listed.

6. **Set up the workspace** for offline activities or move students to the computer to complete online activities.

TIP You might want to check the materials and Advance Preparation for the week in addition to reviewing them before each lesson so you know of any materials or tasks that may require some extra time or planning. For example, you may need to plan a trip to the library to get a book or go to the craft store for special materials.

Where to Begin?

For programs with both offline and online components, there is more than one way to begin a lesson. Either way will get you where you need to go.

Beginning Online   If you begin from the online lesson, the lesson screens will walk you through what you need to do, including gathering materials and moving offline if necessary.

- If the lesson begins with online activities, students will need to come to the computer and complete them.
- If the lesson begins with offline activities, gather the materials listed and begin the activities described in the lesson plan with students when you're ready.

Beginning Offline   You may choose to begin a lesson by first checking the lesson plan for the day in the Lesson Guide. The table on the first page of the lesson plan will indicate whether the lesson begins with online or offline activities.

- If the lesson begins with online activities, students will need to move to the computer and complete them.
- If the lesson begins with offline activities, gather the materials listed and begin the activities described in the lesson plan with students when you're ready.

After you've completed a unit or two in a particular program, you'll be familiar with the pattern of the units and lessons, and you'll know exactly where and how to begin.

Complete Activities with Students

Offline Activities   During offline activities, you will work closely with students away from the computer. Follow the instructions in the Lesson Guide for completing these activities.

Online Activities   Online activities take place at the computer. At first, you may need to help students learn how to navigate and use the online activities. You may also need to provide support when activities cover new or challenging content. Eventually, students will complete online activities with minimal support from you.

Work with Students to Complete Assessments

Offline Assessments   Students will complete offline assessments in Phonics, Literature & Comprehension, Writing Skills, and Spelling. After students complete the assessments offline, you will need to enter assessment scores in the Online School.

Online Assessments   Students will complete online assessments, called Unit Checkpoints, in Vocabulary. Because these assessments are all online, the computer will score them for you. You do not need to enter these assessment scores in the Online School.

Track Progress in Portfolios

K[12] recommends keeping students' work samples in a portfolio as a record of their progress. A simple folder, large envelope, or three-ring binder would work. Place offline assessments, Activity Book pages, and handwriting samples in the portfolio. Look back through the portfolio monthly and at the end of the year with students. Celebrate their progress and achievements.

How to Use This Book

K[12] Language Arts Lesson Guide contains information that will be extremely helpful to you as you prepare to begin K[12] Language Arts Green and on a daily basis as you work through the programs. Here is what the Lesson Guide contains and how you should use it.

What Is in the Lesson Guide	What You Should Do with It
Overviews of each of the programs included in K[12] Language Arts Green, including instructional philosophies, materials, and unit and lesson structure for the programs	• **Read the overviews** of the programs as you prepare to begin K[12] Language Arts Green. • **Refer back to the overview** information if you have questions as you work through the programs.
Glossary of key terms used in Literature & Comprehension and Writing Skills	• **Use the glossary** any time you need to look up a keyword used in Literature & Comprehension or Writing Skills.
Lesson plans for teaching • Literature & Comprehension lessons • Writing Skills lessons	• **Scan the unit and lesson overviews** for the lessons you will be working on each day. • **Follow the instructions** in the lesson plans to complete the activities with students. • **Use the answer keys** to check students' work on Activity Book pages and offline assessments.

Following are examples of the unit overview, lesson overview, and activity instructions that you will see in the lesson plans for teaching a Literature & Comprehension or Writing Skills lesson.

Unit Overview

There is one unit overview page per unit.

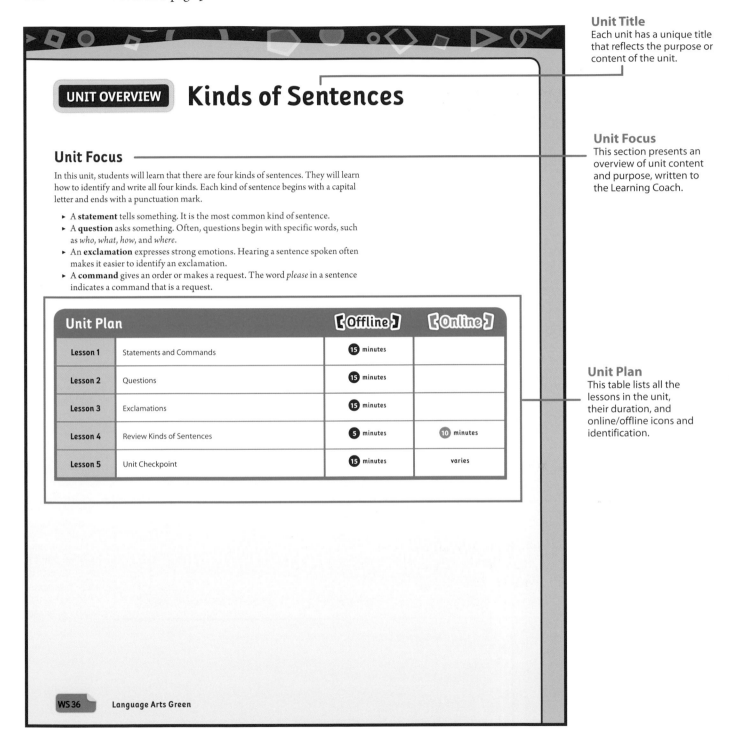

UNIT OVERVIEW **Kinds of Sentences**

Unit Focus

In this unit, students will learn that there are four kinds of sentences. They will learn how to identify and write all four kinds. Each kind of sentence begins with a capital letter and ends with a punctuation mark.

▸ A **statement** tells something. It is the most common kind of sentence.
▸ A **question** asks something. Often, questions begin with specific words, such as *who*, *what*, *how*, and *where*.
▸ An **exclamation** expresses strong emotions. Hearing a sentence spoken often makes it easier to identify an exclamation.
▸ A **command** gives an order or makes a request. The word *please* in a sentence indicates a command that is a request.

Unit Plan		〖Offline〗	〖Online〗
Lesson 1	Statements and Commands	15 minutes	
Lesson 2	Questions	15 minutes	
Lesson 3	Exclamations	15 minutes	
Lesson 4	Review Kinds of Sentences	5 minutes	10 minutes
Lesson 5	Unit Checkpoint	15 minutes	varies

WS 36   **Language Arts Green**

Unit Title
Each unit has a unique title that reflects the purpose or content of the unit.

Unit Focus
This section presents an overview of unit content and purpose, written to the Learning Coach.

Unit Plan
This table lists all the lessons in the unit, their duration, and online/offline icons and identification.

Lesson Overview

Each Literature & Comprehension and Writing Skills lesson has a lesson overview page.

Lesson Title
The title indicates the lesson topic.

Lesson Overview Table
This table has an overview of the lesson's activities, their approximate times, and whether they take place offline or online.

This section of the lesson overview page includes Advance Preparation, Big Ideas, and Content Background, if any, that you need to know.

Advance Preparation
This information is what you need to prepare before beginning the lesson.

Big Ideas
Students will work toward these major organizing ideas in Language Arts.

Content Background
You might need this information to help you better understand the content you will be teaching.

Program Name
This banner identifies the section of the book. Each program has its own banner color, so you can easily flip to a section if you know the color: orange for Literature & Comprehension and purple for Writing Skills.

Materials
This box lists all materials needed for the lesson and indicates whether they are Supplied or Also Needed.

Synopsis
In Literature & Comprehension lessons, this section gives a brief summary of the reading selection.

Keywords
The definitions of teaching terminology specific to the lesson are here.

Page Number
Each page number is preceded by an abbreviation corresponding to the section of the book you are in.
LC = Literature & Comprehension
WS = Writing Skills

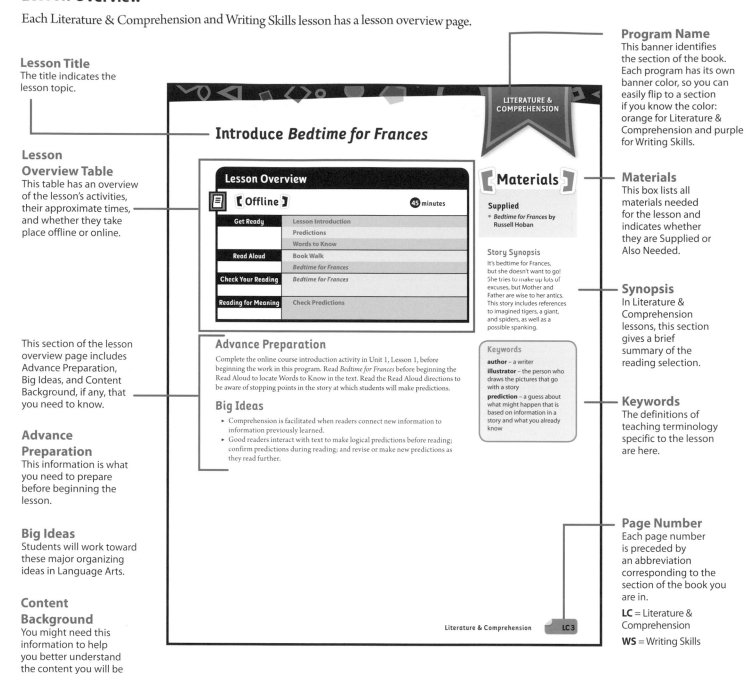

Introduce *Bedtime for Frances*

LITERATURE & COMPREHENSION

Lesson Overview

〖 Offline 〗 45 minutes

Get Ready	Lesson Introduction
	Predictions
	Words to Know
Read Aloud	Book Walk
	Bedtime for Frances
Check Your Reading	*Bedtime for Frances*
Reading for Meaning	Check Predictions

Materials

Supplied
● *Bedtime for Frances* by Russell Hoban

Story Synopsis
It's bedtime for Frances, but she doesn't want to go! She tries to make up lots of excuses, but Mother and Father are wise to her antics. This story includes references to imagined tigers, a giant, and spiders, as well as a possible spanking.

Keywords
author – a writer
illustrator – the person who draws the pictures that go with a story
prediction – a guess about what might happen that is based on information in a story and what you already know

Advance Preparation

Complete the online course introduction activity in Unit 1, Lesson 1, before beginning the work in this program. Read *Bedtime for Frances* before beginning the Read Aloud to locate Words to Know in the text. Read the Read Aloud directions to be aware of stopping points in the story at which students will make predictions.

Big Ideas

▶ Comprehension is facilitated when readers connect new information to information previously learned.
▶ Good readers interact with text to make logical predictions before reading; confirm predictions during reading; and revise or make new predictions as they read further.

Literature & Comprehension   LC 3

Activity Instructions

Lesson plans in the Literature & Comprehension and Writing Skills sections of the Lesson Guide include detailed instructions for each activity.

Program Name
This banner identifies the section of the book. Literature & Comprehension has an orange banner and Writing Skills has a purple banner.

Activity Type
These labels tell you what kind of activity you are working on.

Activity Description
This text describes what will happen in the activity. For offline activities, it provides step-by-step instructions. Answers are in magenta text.

Objectives
These learning goals indicate what students should be able to do as a result of the lesson.

Activity Book Page Answer Key
A miniature version of the Activity Book page is included in the Lesson Guide, with answers to help you check students' work.

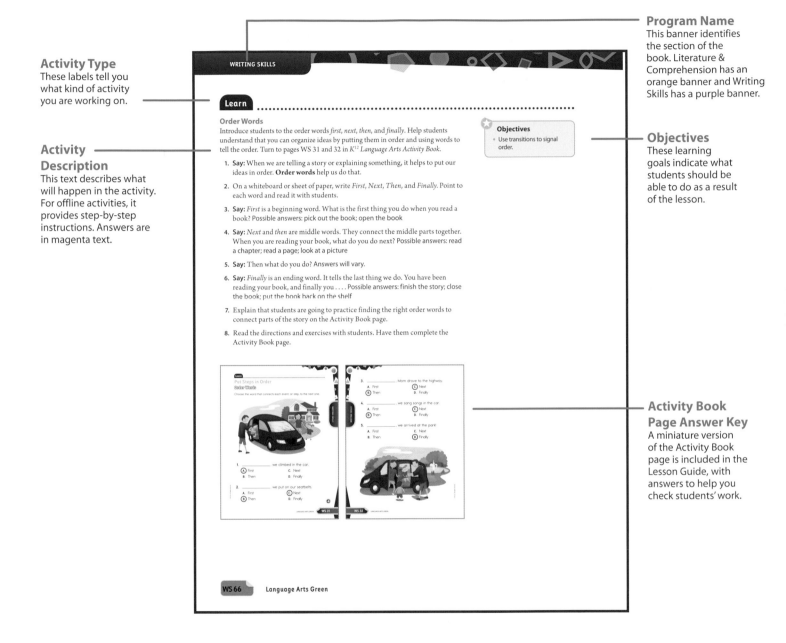

Look for Icons

The lesson plans contain icons to help you quickly see key elements as you work through the lesson. Look for these icons as you use the lesson plans.

Icon	Description
🖥 〖Online〗	Shows that an activity is online.
📄 〖Offline〗	Shows that an activity is offline.
(TIP)	Tips offer additional advice to help you explain the content.
✏	This pencil appears next to activities that provide students with the opportunity to practice their handwriting.
🎖	This blue ribbon indicates that you have reached a milestone that should be rewarded, usually by adding a sticker to the My Accomplishments chart.
⊕ OPTIONAL:	Indicates that an activity is optional.
Reading Aid	Shows that you will use a Reading Aid from the Activity Book with this activity.

(TIP) Use a bookmark or a sticky note to mark the lesson that you are working on in Literature & Comprehension and in Writing Skills. These markers will help you quickly find the page you need each day.

My Accomplishments Chart

Research shows that rewarding students for quality work can increase their motivation. To help you reward students, you will receive a My Accomplishments chart and sticker sheet for use throughout K[12] Language Arts Green. This chart gives students a tangible record of their progress and accomplishments throughout Literature & Comprehension, Spelling, Vocabulary, and Writing Skills. There is also extra space that you can use to track progress for other accomplishments, like reading additional books, if you wish.

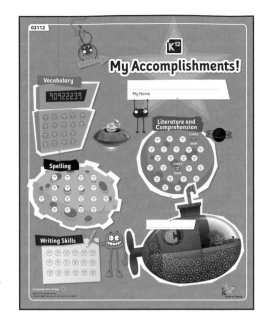

Help students proudly display and share their accomplishments with others by placing the chart somewhere visible, such as on the refrigerator or wall. Throughout the lessons, look for the reward icon 🏅, which indicates when and where students should place a sticker on the chart. Encourage students to set goals and watch their stickers accumulate. Praise students to help them understand the connection between their own growing skill set and the My Accomplishments chart. (For specific information about how to use the chart in each program, see the My Accomplishments Chart section in the following individual program overviews.)

K[12] My Journal

Research demonstrates that emerging writers are more motivated and become more confident when writing about self-selected topics. Journal writing allows young writers to explore and express themselves in a nonthreatening environment and make connections to their present knowledge. You will receive *K[12] My Journal* for use throughout K[12] Language Arts Green. Students will use the journal as they complete some lessons in Literature & Comprehension and Writing Skills, but they can also use the journal to write on their own. The journal has three sections that you will use as you work through lessons or on your own.

▶ **Thoughts and Experiences** has pages with space for drawing and writing and other pages for just writing. You will be directed to use these pages in some Literature & Comprehension lessons, but you can also encourage students to write in this section at any time.

▶ **Ideas** has some prompts to help students start writing. You can use the pages in this section at any time.

▶ **Writing Skills** has prompts that students will use to freewrite and make connections to the things that they learn as they complete the lessons in Writing Skills.

K¹² Language Arts PhonicsWorks Advanced Overview

The PhonicsWorks materials are separate from the K¹² Language Arts Green materials, so you will not find PhonicsWorks lesson plans in *K¹² Language Arts Lesson Guide* or activity pages in *K¹² Language Arts Activity Book*. Please refer to the PhonicsWorks Advanced Kit for all phonics materials.

K¹² Language Arts Green Literature & Comprehension Overview

Program	Daily Lesson Time (approximate)	Online/Offline
K¹² Language Arts Green Literature & Comprehension	45 minutes	All offline

Structure and Materials	
24 units that vary in length and structure, depending on the number and length of literary selections • 18 units of fiction, nonfiction, and poetry • 2 Reader's Choice units • 4 Checkpoints (2 Mid-Semester Checkpoints and 2 Semester Checkpoints)	**Materials** • *K¹² Language Arts Lesson Guide* • *K¹² Language Arts Activity Book* • *K¹² Language Arts Assessments* • *K¹² Classics for Young Readers, Volume A* • *K¹² My Journal* • Literature & Comprehension Support Materials • 10 Story Cards • 4 *K¹² World* nonfiction magazines: *Earth and Sky, People and Places of the Past, The Science of Inventing, Critter and Creature Stories* • 18 trade books

Philosophy

K¹² Language Arts Literature & Comprehension includes four effective instructional approaches to reading: read aloud, shared reading, guided reading, and independent reading. Each approach contributes to students' skill level and ability to apply specific reading strategies.

Read Aloud

What Is It? The **Learning Coach reads aloud to students** from carefully selected texts of various genres. The texts have features that lend themselves to modeling what good readers do. While reading aloud, the **Learning Coach will model** the following behaviors for students: fluent, expressive reading; what good readers think about as they read; and how good readers use strategies to understand text.

Why We Do It Reading aloud engages students in an enjoyable experience that promotes a love of reading. It is an opportunity to share quality literature that is too challenging for students to read independently. Listening to stories helps students build vocabulary knowledge and develop a sense of story structure.

What Does It Look Like? The Learning Coach and students sit together so that everyone can see the text and pictures or illustrations. While reading aloud, the Learning Coach tracks with his or her finger so students can follow along. While reading, the Learning Coach models the behaviors of a good reader by doing some or all of the following:

- ▶ Emphasize Words to Know in the text.
- ▶ Use the pictures or illustrations to help determine word meanings (if appropriate).
- ▶ Stop to ask questions or have students make predictions.

Shared Reading

What Is It? Shared reading is an interactive reading experience that happens when **students join in the reading of a text** while guided by a proficient reader (in this case, the Learning Coach). Students must be able to clearly see the text and follow along as the Learning Coach points to the words. Students gradually assume more responsibility for the reading as their skill level and confidence increases.

Why We Do It Shared reading gives students a chance to practice the reading behaviors of proficient readers with the support of a proficient reader. Through shared reading, students develop an awareness of the relationship between the spoken and printed word. They learn print concepts and conventions, and they are exposed to early reading strategies such as word-by-word matching. They learn where to focus their attention as they read. They also acquire a sense of story structure and the ability to predict while being exposed to the process of reading extended texts. Shared reading also familiarizes students with a collection of texts that they can use for independent reading and as resources for word study and writing.

What Does It Look Like? As in read-aloud activities, the Learning Coach and students sit together so everyone can see the text and the pictures or illustrations. The Learning Coach reads aloud, tracking with his or her finger so students can follow along. Students chime in to read parts of the story that they are familiar with. While reading, the Learning Coach will

- ▶ Model the behaviors of a good reader, as in read-aloud activities.
- ▶ Stop to discuss questions with students during the reading.
- ▶ Reread texts to examine features (for example, the use of quotation marks for dialogue or the author's use of descriptive language in the text).
- ▶ Give students specific tasks to allow them to participate in the reading (for example, reading a character's quotations or reading a section expressively).

Guided Reading

What Is It?   In guided reading, students read books specifically selected to challenge them and give them problem-solving opportunities. The Learning Coach introduces the new book to students and provides instruction that will support and enable **students to read the text themselves**. In guided reading, the Learning Coach's focused instruction helps students develop the decoding and comprehension strategies necessary to move on to texts at the next level of difficulty.

Why We Do It   Guided reading gives students the chance to apply strategies they already know to read a new text. During these Learning Coach-supported lessons, students also acquire and practice new reading strategies as they problem solve and read for meaning. While the Learning Coach provides assistance, the ultimate goal is for students to read independently. Through shared reading, students have learned how print works and how to monitor their understanding of text. Guided reading is the natural next step during which students learn to apply problem-solving strategies when they encounter difficulties decoding and understanding text.

What Does It Look Like?   The **Learning Coach guides students through a preview** of a text to prepare **students to read it on their own.** As in read-aloud activities, the Learning Coach and student sit together so that everyone can see the text and the pictures or illustrations. To prepare for reading, the Learning Coach will preview with students by doing some or all of the following:

- Look at pictures or illustrations and discuss what they show about the text.
- Examine words and phrases in the text and discuss what they mean (for example, find the words *Frog* and *Toad* and talk about why they have capital letters).
- Scan the pages to find information (for example, what the character says he likes).
- Practice reading certain words or phrases.
- Make predictions based on the information in the text.
- Model strategies for reading (for example, using pictures to determine word meaning).

After previewing with the Learning Coach, **students will read the text aloud. If** necessary, the **Learning Coach may offer support** by doing one of the following:

- Read aloud to students.
- Read aloud as students chime in.
- Take turns reading aloud (alternate pages or sections with students).

Independent Reading

What Is It?   When students do independent reading, they often choose their own books from a wide range of reading materials and read on their own for an extended block of time. During independent reading, students need to read books at a level just right for them, called their *independent level*. Independent reading is introduced in K[12] Language Arts Orange.

Approaches to Reading in K[12] Language Arts Green

In K[12] Language Arts Green Literature & Comprehension, students move from read aloud to shared reading to guided reading over the course of the year.

When in Program	Reading Approach	Learning Coach Responsibilities
First Third (Units 1–8)	**Read Aloud**	• Read to students. • Model reading strategies. • Discuss readings with students.
Second Third (Units 9–16)	**Shared Reading**	• Read with students; have students chime in and read parts of the selections. • Model reading strategies. • Discuss readings with students.
Last Third (Units 17–24)	**Guided Reading**	• Model reading strategies. • Preview selections to prepare students to read. • Support students as they read. • Discuss readings with students.

TIP   Look in the first lesson of the first unit of this program in the Online School for more information about the different approaches to reading in K[12] Language Arts Green.

Overview of Literature & Comprehension Lessons

Materials

The following materials are supplied for Literature & Comprehension:

K¹² Language Arts Lesson Guide

K¹² Language Arts Activity Book

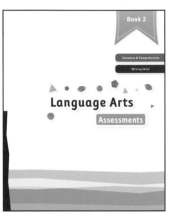

K¹² Language Arts Assessments

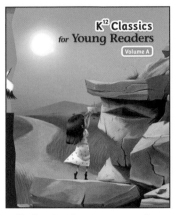

K¹² Classics for Young Readers, Volume A

K¹² World: Earth and Sky

K¹² World: People and Places of the Past

K¹² World: The Science of Inventing

K¹² World: Critter and Creature Stories

K¹² My Journal

Literature & Comprehension Support Materials

Story Cards

The following trade books are also supplied:

- ▸ *A Picture for Harold's Room* by Crockett Johnson
- ▸ *Amelia Bedelia* by Peggy Parish
- ▸ *And I Mean It, Stanley* by Crosby Bonsall
- ▸ *Bedtime for Frances* by Russell Hoban
- ▸ *Danny and the Dinosaur* by Syd Hoff
- ▸ *Frog and Toad Are Friends* by Arnold Lobel
- ▸ *Harry and the Lady Next Door* by Gene Zion
- ▸ *Listen, My Children: Poems for First Graders*
- ▸ *Little Bear* by Else Holmelund Minarik
- ▸ *Here Comes the Parade!* by Tony and Lauren Dungy
- ▸ *Owl at Home* by Arnold Lobel
- ▸ *Ready . . . Set . . . Read!: The Beginning Reader's Treasury*
- ▸ *Sylvester and the Magic Pebble* by William Steig
- ▸ *Tales of Amanda Pig* by Jean Van Leeuwen
- ▸ *The First Thanksgiving* by Linda Hayward
- ▸ *The Legend of the Bluebonnet* by Tomie dePaola
- ▸ *Weather: Poems for All Seasons*
- ▸ *Who Will Be My Friends?* by Syd Hoff

You should always have paper and pencils available. You will also need the following general materials to complete Activity Book pages:

- ▸ crayons or colored pencils
- ▸ glue
- ▸ scissors (Safety note: When students are working with scissors, please supervise them to make sure they use their scissors safely and stay seated.)

Additional materials, ranging from index cards to library books, may be needed for certain lessons.

Using the Activity Book

Keep in mind that students will write in and tear out pages from the Activity Book; you may want to store loose Activity Book pages in a three-ring binder. Remember to build students' portfolios with completed Activity Book pages.

You will find some special pages in the Activity Book for use with lessons that include shared-reading or guided-reading activities. When one of these pages is to be used, you will see the Reading Aid icon **Reading Aid** in the Lesson Guide. The Reading Aid is designed so that the Learning Coach can easily follow instructions for reading activities while simultaneously using one of the texts for reading.

TIP Look for instructions in Advance Preparation and tips within activities for saving and gathering materials that get used in more than one lesson.

Using the Journal

As students complete Literature & Comprehension lessons, they will occasionally use *K¹² My Journal* to record thoughts and ideas related to their work. You will be directed to turn to Thoughts and Experiences in the journal and then follow the instructions in the Lesson Guide for completing the journal activity. Thoughts and Experiences has pages with room for drawing and writing and pages for just writing.

Students may also write in their journal on their own. They may use pages in Thoughts and Experiences or in Ideas for writing on their own. The Ideas section has prompts to help students start writing. The Writing Skills section will be used in the Writing Skills lessons.

TIP Any time you are directed to use the journal in a lesson, you can print additional journal pages from the online lesson.

Using Support Materials

Literature & Comprehension Support Materials include posters (both wall-size and 8 ½ x 11 inches), bookmarks, and materials for completing book report projects.

The posters are included as a visual reminder for both you and students of different strategies readers use to improve their reading and comprehension. You may choose to hang the wall-size posters where you and students can easily refer to them during lessons. Take-along versions of the posters are provided in 8 ½ x 11-inch size. Additionally, two of the four bookmarks contain the reading and comprehension strategies.

A third bookmark has an inspirational quote on it, and the fourth provides room for students to write the names of books they have read. You may choose to give students the bookmarks one at a time as a motivational tool or reward, or you can give all of them to students at once. These are simply resources for to assist students in their journey to becoming independent readers.

Finally, Literature & Comprehension Support Materials include instructions, templates, and scoring aids for completing book report projects. Students will complete two book report projects as part of the Reader's Choice units in Literature & Comprehension. Encourage students to complete additional projects as they read books on their own.

Lesson Structure

Literature & Comprehension consists of daily 45-minute lessons that build in a sequence designed to meet new readers' needs and that are developmentally appropriate for an early reader's growing comprehension abilities. The number of lessons in a unit will vary, and the lessons themselves will have different combinations of activities, but the activities will include prereading, reading, and postreading instruction.

The following chart is an overview of how activities might be sequenced in lessons. As you can see, you work with students to prepare for the reading and then use one of the reading strategies to read with students. After reading, you will check students' comprehension before beginning a deeper analysis of the reading selection.

[Offline] **45** minutes

Day 1 Lesson Overview

Get Ready
- Lesson Introduction
- Main Ideas
- Words to Know

Read (Aloud, Shared, or Guided)
- Book Walk
- "Women in Space"

Check Your Reading "Women in Space"

Reading for Meaning Main Ideas in "Women in Space"

Day 2 Lesson Overview

Get Ready
- Lesson Introduction
- Finding Facts
- Words to Know

Read (Aloud, Shared, or Guided)
- Book Walk
- "Women in Space"

Reading for Meaning Facts in "Women in Space"

Looking at Language Exclamation Marks and Periods

Making Connections My Favorite Astronaut

➕ **OPTIONAL: Beyond the Lesson** Learn More About Outer Space

The activities shown are an example of what you might see in the lessons for this program. Not every lesson will contain all these activities. In some lessons, you may read a selection more than once.

Lesson Activities

Lesson plans in the Literature & Comprehension section of this Lesson Guide include detailed instructions for each activity. Literature & Comprehension activity types include the following:

- **Get Ready (Offline)**   The Get Ready activities prepare students for that day's reading selection and lesson. They include instructions to help students build background knowledge and strategies needed for comprehension, and Words to Know, which are words from the selection that students should become familiar with.

- **Read Aloud, Shared Reading, Guided Reading (Offline)**   The Learning Coach and students complete prereading activities (Book Walk) and then read the selection using read-aloud, shared-reading, or guided-reading strategies. These activities might have a Reading Aid, which is a special kind of Activity Book page designed to help the Learning Coach.

- **Check Your Reading (Offline)**   The Learning Coach asks students questions to show general comprehension of the reading selection. Students will answer the questions orally. In most cases, these questions require students to know what happened in the selection.

- **Reading for Meaning (Offline)**   The Learning Coach works with students to help them develop a deeper understanding of the reading selection through application of comprehension strategies and analysis of the selection. These activities often have an Activity Book page to complete.

- **Looking at Language (Offline)**   The Learning Coach models thought processes by talking to students as they interact with the written text. These activities might have a Reading Aid, which is a special kind of Activity Book page designed to help the Learning Coach.

- **Making Connections (Offline)**   Students will apply information and strategies learned from lessons to the reading selection. These activities often involve students making a connection between and among texts or between the text and themselves or the larger world. These activities may or may not have an Activity Book page.

- **OPTIONAL Beyond the Lesson (Offline)**   These activities are for students who have extra time and interest in exploring the reading selection further. These activities are not required and can be skipped.

- **Peer Interaction (Offline)**   The Learning Coach will lead a discussion with students about a reading selection. Ideally, students should discuss their reading with their peers.

- **Semester Review (Offline)**   Students will review skills from the semester to prepare for the Semester Checkpoint.

- **Mid-Semester and Semester Checkpoints (Offline)**   Students will apply the skills learned in the program as they read fiction, nonfiction, and poetry selections.

- **More Practice (Online)**   After each Checkpoint, suggestions are provided for activities to help review and practice areas in which students may need extra work.

My Accomplishments Chart

Rewards in Literature & Comprehension are tied to completing units. When students complete a unit, have them add a sticker for that unit to the My Accomplishments chart.

Reader's Choice Units

Throughout K[12] Language Arts Green Literature & Comprehension, Planning and Progress in the Online School will alert you to an approaching Reader's Choice unit (Units 4 and 16). These units are designed to give students an opportunity to choose books to read while fine-tuning their comprehension skills. Research indicates that providing opportunities for choice enhances performance and motivates early readers.

In each of the two Reader's Choice units, you and your students will have a bank of six texts to choose from. K[12] suggests that you discuss the possible texts with students to guarantee that they will engage with texts that interest them. Reader's Choice units are 11 lessons each. There are two important differences from other units in the program.

1. **You will need to acquire these texts on your own, through a library or bookstore.** To help you choose a text for a Reader's Choice unit, K[12] includes a brief synopsis of the story and information about grade and interest level.

2. Once you have selected the text, you will be prompted to *print* the accompanying lesson guide and activity pages. **These pages are not provided in this Lesson Guide or the Activity Book.**

To keep students engaged, deepen comprehension, and develop public speaking capabilities, they are required to complete a book report project as part of each Reader's Choice unit. Literature & Comprehension Support Materials include detailed instructions for creating, grading, and presenting a book report project.

K¹² Language Arts Green Spelling Overview

Program	Daily Lesson Time (approximate)	Online/Offline
K¹² Language Arts Green Spelling	15 minutes (Days 91–180 only)	Each unit: 4 offline lessons, 1 online review
Structure and Materials		
18 units with 5 lessons each	**Materials** • *K¹² Spelling Handbook*	

The Spelling materials are separate from the K¹² Language Arts Green materials, so you will not find Spelling lesson plans in *K¹² Language Arts Lesson Guide* or activity pages in *K¹² Language Arts Activity Book*. Please refer to *K¹² Spelling Handbook* for all materials related to the program.

K¹² Language Arts Green Vocabulary Overview

Program	Daily Lesson Time (approximate)	Online/Offline
K¹² Language Arts Green Vocabulary	15 minutes	All online
Structure and Materials		
18 units with 10 lessons each	**Materials** • *K¹² Language Arts Vocabulary Word Lists* Online Book	

Vocabulary is entirely online. Students will work through the online lessons with your supervision. You can access the word lists for all the units from the online lessons.

K¹² Language Arts Green Writing Skills Overview

Program	Daily Lesson Time (approximate)	Online/Offline
K¹² Language Arts Green Writing Skills	15 minutes (Days 91–180 only)	Each unit (approximately): 4 offline lessons, 1 online lesson

Structure and Materials	
18 units with 5 lessons each • 9 GUM units • 8 Composition units • 1 optional Composition unit	**Materials** • *K¹² Language Arts Lesson Guide* • *K¹² Language Arts Activity Book* • *K¹² Language Arts Assessments* • *K¹² My Journal* • 10 Story Cards

Philosophy

Learning to express one's ideas in writing is a fundamental requirement of an educated person. K¹² Language Arts Green Writing Skills takes a two-pronged approach to fulfilling this need. Grammar, Usage, and Mechanics (GUM) lessons teach students the nuts and bolts of communicating in standard written English. Composition lessons teach students how to think about, plan, organize, and write organized communications in a variety of forms. Writing Skills includes alternating units of GUM and Composition.

Grammar, Usage, and Mechanics (GUM)

What Is It?   The grammar, usage, and mechanics lessons give students practice in learning about sentences and the parts of speech that make up sentences; in using subjects, verbs, and pronouns correctly; and in discovering how capitalization and punctuation marks aid in conveying the message of sentences.

Why We Do It   While it is true that knowing grammar does not make someone a good writer, understanding how grammar works makes writing easier. When students know things like what a complete sentence is, what kind of punctuation is used within a sentence and at the end of a sentence, and which words need capital letters, they can spend their time focusing on ideas. When the focus is on ideas, not on mechanics, writing becomes more fluent and expressive.

Composition

What Is It? In composition lessons, students practice to become more fluent and expressive writers. In these lessons, students learn to write in a variety of forms. They start by using a journal to encourage fluid and creative thought. They use freewriting techniques and build upon their ideas to learn more structured forms. They learn to write sentences and to connect those sentences to form a group of related ideas into a paragraph. They will write short narrative and informative compositions as well as create basic explanatory texts. They will write a response to literature and practice basic presentation skills.

Why We Do It Research shows that daily writing practice is essential for the developing writer. The lessons are based on a process-writing model of instruction. Research demonstrates that engaging in a variety of prewriting techniques (such as freewriting) and planning activities helps novice writers learn to transform their ideas into organized writing. Throughout each unit, students will practice skills in discrete steps, and they will ultimately write a polished piece of writing, ready to be "published" or shared. Students will learn that the writing process is not a straight line forward and that writing always means rewriting for improvement. As you help students through these lessons, encourage them to express their thoughts and ideas. Student writing is not adult writing. Expect errors in basic sentence structure, but encourage students to express their thoughts in written form.

Overview of Writing Skills Lessons

Materials

The following materials are supplied for Writing Skills:

K¹² Language Arts Lesson Guide

K¹² Language Arts Activity Book

K¹² Language Arts Assessments

K¹² My Journal

Story Cards

You should always have paper and pencils available for students. You might sometimes also need the following general materials to complete the Activity Book pages:

- 3½ x 5-inch index cards
- crayons or colored pencils
- glue
- scissors (Safety note: When students are working with scissors, please supervise students to make sure they use their scissors safely and stay seated.)

Keeping a Writing Portfolio

Students will write in and tear out pages of the Activity Book, so periodically place some of the Activity Book pages in a student writing portfolio. In addition, save students' graphic organizers, drafts, and published compositions in the portfolio to keep track of their growth as writers. Consult the portfolio regularly and keep it as a record to share with teachers. Share the work with students so that they can see the progress they have made and celebrate it. Remember that student writing is not adult writing. Do not expect perfection, but rather look for progress over time and clarity of thought and intent.

The Activity Book contains pages with examples of different types of writing or other kinds of materials that students will refer to over the course of a unit. Look for tips in the Lesson Guide alerting you to store these materials for further use. Be sure to keep these pages in a safe place so you can easily find them and refer to them.

Using the Journal

As students complete Writing Skills lessons, they will freewrite about topics and ideas in Writing Skills of *K¹² My Journal.* You will find specific instructions in the Lesson Guide to help students get started and to encourage their writing. Students may use Thoughts and Experiences and Ideas of the journal to write on their own.

TIP You can print additional copies of the journal pages used in the Writing Skills lessons from the online lessons.

Lesson Structure

Writing Skills consists of 18 units. The units alternate: Odd-numbered units are about grammar, usage, and mechanics (GUM), and even-numbered units are about composition.

All units are five lessons long, with each lesson taking about 15 minutes to complete. Although the GUM and Composition units look similar, there are several key differences:

- Composition units begin with a freewriting activity, using the journal on Day 1.
- GUM units include an online review lesson on Day 4. Composition units are entirely offline.
- GUM units end with a Unit Checkpoint on Day 5. Composition units end with a Write Now activity, which is a writing assignment.

Day 1 Lesson Overview

GUM	Composition
【 **Offline** 】 **15** minutes	【 **Offline** 】 **15** minutes
Get Ready Learn Try It	Get Ready Try It: Freewrite (Journal)

Days 2–3 Lesson Overview

GUM	Composition
【 **Offline** 】 **15** minutes	【 **Offline** 】 **15** minutes
Get Ready Learn Try It	Get Ready Learn Try It

Day 4 Lesson Overview

GUM	Composition
【 **Online** 】 **10** minutes	【 **Offline** 】 **15** minutes
Review	Get Ready Learn Try It ⊕ **OPTIONAL:** Peer Interaction
【 **Offline** 】 **5** minutes	
Try It: Journal	

Day 5 Lesson Overview

GUM	Composition
【 **Offline** 】 **15** minutes	【 **Offline** 】 **15** minutes
Unit Checkpoint	Get Ready Learn Write Now
【 **Online** 】 varies	【 **Online** 】 varies
More Practice	More Practice

Lesson Activities

Lesson plans in the Writing Skills section of this Lesson Guide include detailed descriptions or instructions for each activity. Writing Skills lessons include the following types of activities:

▸ **Get Ready (Offline)**   The Get Ready is a short activity to prepare students for the new skills that they will learn in the lesson. Often the Get Ready draws on students' previous knowledge or builds background knowledge in preparation for the new skill. Sometimes students will preview examples of different types of writing or work with other kinds of examples as part of the Get Ready.

▸ **Learn (Offline)**   Students learn a new skill. The examples and tips in the Lesson Guide provide the Learning Coach with the information needed to explain the new skill. Often the Learn is accompanied by an Activity Book page that contains an explanation of the new skill and an example that students can refer to as they progress through the program.

▸ **Try It (Offline)**   Students practice using the new skill that they have learned by completing a page in the Activity Book. Sometimes students will freewrite in their journal or continue to work on a piece of writing that they started earlier.

▸ **Review (Online)**   Each odd-numbered unit includes an online activity to provide students with an opportunity to review and practice the grammar, usage, and mechanics (GUM) skills they have learned in that unit. Students will also have several days to review the GUM skills learned throughout the semester before completing the Semester Checkpoint.

▸ **Unit and Semester Checkpoints (Offline)**   Each GUM unit ends with an offline Unit Checkpoint, which tests the skills that students have learned in the unit. An offline Semester Checkpoint covers the GUM skills learned in the entire semester.

▸ **Write Now (Offline)**   Each Composition unit ends with a writing assignment. Students complete the assignment that they have been planning, drafting, and revising throughout the unit. The Learning Coach evaluates that writing on a three-point scale for purpose and content, structure and organization, and grammar and mechanics. Sample papers (available online) help the Learning Coach evaluate the strength of the writing and areas in which students can improve.

▸ **More Practice (Online)**   After each Checkpoint or Write Now, suggestions are provided for activities to help review and practice areas in which students may need extra work, along with links to access these materials.

▸ **Peer Interaction (Offline)**   Some composition assignments include Peer Interaction, in which students share their writing with a peer or anyone else willing to give feedback. If time allows, students can benefit from this interaction by using the feedback to revise their work.

My Accomplishments Chart

Rewards in GUM units of Writing Skills are tied to completing Unit Checkpoints. Each time students score 80 percent or higher on a Unit Checkpoint, have them add a sticker for that unit to the My Accomplishments chart. If students score lower than 80 percent, review each Checkpoint exercise with them and work with them to correct any exercises they missed.

Rewards in the Composition units of Writing Skills are tied to completing the Write Now assignments in each unit. When students' writing achieves "meets objectives" in all three categories on the grading rubric, have them add a sticker for that unit to the My Accomplishments chart. If students' work scores "does not meet objectives" in any category, help them review and revise their work to achieve "meets objectives."

K¹² Language Arts Green Handwriting Overview

Program	Daily Lesson Time (approximate)	Online/Offline
K¹² Language Arts Green Handwriting	10 minutes	All offline
Big Ideas		

- Instruction in posture, pencil grip, and letter formation improves students' handwriting skills.
- Proper modeling of letter formation is imperative for developing handwriting skills.
- Students who have formal instruction in handwriting are more engaged in composition writing.

Philosophy

K¹² supplies handwriting practice workbooks for students in kindergarten through grade 3. It is important for students to practice at a pace that suits students' fine motor skills development.

Overview of Handwriting Lessons

Lesson Structure

K[12] Handwriting is entirely offline. In each lesson, you will work with students for 10 minutes. (You may want to set a timer for 10 minutes; many students enjoy the Handwriting program, so it's easy to lose track of time and do too much in one day.)

Students should complete as many workbook pages as they can, picking up where they left off during the previous Handwriting lesson and continuing from there. They are not expected to complete a set number of pages during the 10-minute lessons. Be sure to monitor students' writing time so you can help them develop good letter formation habits.

Depending on students' pace, the workbook may take up to one full semester to complete. Move as quickly or as slowly as students need. When students have completed the workbooks, have them continue to practice their handwriting each day. Look for the Handwriting icon throughout the Lesson Guide. This icon indicates that the associated activity provides a perfect opportunity to practice proper handwriting, and if students pay careful attention to their handwriting, this time can also count as Handwriting time.

K¹² Language Arts Green Keywords

Literature and Comprehension

alliteration – the use of words with the same or close to the same beginning sounds

author – a writer

author's purpose – the reason the author wrote a text: to entertain, to inform, to express an opinion, or to persuade

autobiography – the story of a person's life written by that person

biography – the story of someone's life written by another person

brainstorming – an early step in writing that helps a writer come up with as many ideas about a topic as possible

caption – writing under a picture that describes the picture

cause – the reason something happens

character – a person or animal in a story

compare – to explain how two or more things are alike

comprehension – understanding

connection – a link readers make between themselves, information in text, and the world around them

context – the parts of a sentence or passage surrounding a word

context clue – a word or phrase in a text that helps you figure out the meaning of an unknown word

contrast – to explain how two or more things are different

decode – to sound out a word

detail – a piece of information in a text

dialogue – the words that characters say in a written work

draft – an early effort at a piece of writing, not the finished work

drama – another word for *play*

effect – the result of a cause

fable – a story that teaches a lesson and may contain animal characters

fact – something that can be proven true

fairy tale – a folktale with magical elements

fantasy – a story with characters, settings, or other elements that could not really exist

fiction – make-believe stories

first-person point of view – the telling of a story by a character in that story, using pronouns such as *I*, *me*, and *we*

folktale – a story passed down through a culture for many years that may have human, animal, or magical characters

genre – a category for classifying literary works

glossary – a list of important terms and their meanings that is usually found in the back of a book

graphic organizer – a visual tool used to show relationships between key concepts; formats include webs, diagrams, and charts

illustration – a drawing

illustrator – the person who draws the pictures that go with a story

imagery – language that helps readers imagine how something looks, sounds, smells, feels, or tastes

infer – to use clues and what you already know to make a guess

inference – a guess you make using the clues in a text and what you already know

informational text – text written to explain and give information on a topic

legend – a story that is passed down for many years to teach the values of a culture; a legend may or may not contain some true events or people

line – a row of words in a poem

literal level – a reference to text information that is directly stated

literal recall – the ability to describe information stated directly in a text

literature – made-up stories, true stories, poems, and plays

main character – an important person, animal, or other being who is central to the plot

main idea – the most important idea in a paragraph or text

moral – the lesson of a story, particularly a fable

narrative – text genre that tells a story; a narrative text usually includes characters, setting, and plot

narrator – the teller of a story

news – information about, or report of, recent events

nonfiction – writings about true things

opinion – something that a person thinks or believes, but which cannot be proven to be true

personification – giving human qualities to something that is not human
Example: The thunder shouted from the clouds.

plot – what happens in a story

point of view – the perspective a story is told from

predictable text – text written with rhyme, rhythm, and repetition

prediction – a guess about what might happen that is based on information in a story and what you already know

print features – formatting that draws attention to words in text, such as bold type, underlining, and capital letters

prior knowledge – things you already know from past experience

problem – an issue a character must solve in a story

realistic fiction – a made-up story that has no magical elements

retelling – using your own words to tell a story that you have listened to or read

rhyme – when two or more words have the same ending sounds
Example: cat and *hat* rhyme

rhythm – a pattern of accented and unaccented syllables; a distinctive beat

scriptal information – things you already know from past experience

self-correct – to correct an error without prompting while reading text aloud

self-monitor – to notice if you do or do not understand what you are reading

self-question – to ask questions of yourself as you read to check your understanding

sensory language – language that appeals to the five senses

sequence – order

setting – when and where a story takes place

simile – a comparison between two things using the words *like* or *as*
Example: He was as quiet as a mouse.

solution – how a character solves a problem in a story

stanza – a group of lines in a poem

story events – the things that happen in a story; the plot

story structure elements – components of a story; they include character, setting, plot, problem, and solution

summarize – to tell in order the most important ideas or events of a text

summary – a short retelling that includes only the most important ideas or events of a text

supporting detail – a detail that gives more information about a main idea

table of contents – a list at the start of a book that gives the titles of the book's stories, poems, articles, chapters, or nonfiction pieces and the pages where they can be found

text feature – part of a text that helps a reader locate information and determine what is most important; some examples are the title, table of contents, headings, pictures, and glossary

text structure – the organizational pattern of a text, such as cause and effect, compare and contrast, and chronological order

theme – the author's message or big idea

time line – a line showing dates and events in the order that they happened

tone – the author's feelings toward the subject and/or characters of a text

topic – the subject of a text

visual text support – a graphic feature that helps a reader better understand text, such as a picture, chart, or map

visualize – to picture things in your mind as you read

Writing Skills (Composition)

audience – a writer's readers

body (of a friendly letter) – the main text of a friendly letter

book report – a piece of writing that gives information, a summary, and an opinion about a book

book review – a piece of writing that gives an opinion about a book and tells about it

brainstorming – before writing, a way for the writer to come up with ideas

chronological order – a way to organize that puts details in time order

closing (of a friendly letter) – the part of the friendly letter that follows the body
Example: Your friend or *Love*

coherence – of writing, the smooth connection of ideas in a paragraph or essay

command – a kind of sentence that gives an order or makes a request

comparison – a look at how two things are alike

complete sentence – a group of words that tells a complete thought

concluding sentence – the last sentence of a paragraph; often summarizes the paragraph

conclusion – the final paragraph of a written work

conjunction – a word used to join parts of a sentence, such as *and*, *but*, and *or*

content – the information or ideas in a piece of writing

contrast – a look at how two things are different

declarative sentence – a group of words that makes a statement

definition – a statement that tells what a word means

description – writing that uses words that show how something looks, sounds, feels, tastes, or smells
Example: The sky is a soft, powdery blue, and the golden sun feels warm on my face.

detail – a fact or description that tells more about a topic

dialogue – the words spoken between people

dictionary – a reference work made up of words with their definitions, in alphabetical order

drafting – of writing, the stage or step in which the writer first writes the piece

encyclopedia – a reference work made up of articles on many topics, usually in alphabetical order

example – a specific instance of something, used to illustrate an idea

exclamation – a kind of sentence that shows strong feeling

exclamatory sentence – a group of words that shows strong feeling

experience story – a story about something that happened to the writer

fact – a statement that can be proven true

feedback – information given to help improve a piece of writing

fiction – a story created from the imagination; fiction is not documentation of fact

focus – the direction or emphasis of a piece of writing; writing with a focus sticks to the main idea and does not include lots of ideas that are unrelated

freewriting – a way for a writer to pick a topic and write as much as possible about it within a set time limit

friendly letter – a kind of letter used to share thoughts, feeling, and news

graphic – a picture, photograph, map, diagram, or other image

graphic organizer – a visual device, such as a diagram or chart, that helps a writer plan a piece of writing

greeting – the part of a letter that begins with the word *Dear* followed by a person's name; also called the salutation

heading – the first part of a letter that has the writer's address and the date

how-to paper – a paragraph or essay that explains how to do or make something

imperative sentence – a group of words that gives a command or makes a request

interrogative sentence – a group of words that asks a question

introductory sentence – the first sentence in a piece of writing

journal – a notebook where a writer regularly records experiences and ideas

logical order – a way to organize that groups details in a way that makes sense

main idea – the most important point of the paragraph

narrative – a kind of writing that tells a story

news – information about, or report of, recent events

nonfiction – writing that presents facts and information to explain, describe, or persuade; for example, newspaper articles and biographies are nonfiction

opinion – a statement of belief that cannot be proven true; the opposite of a fact

order of importance – a way to organize that presents details from least to most important, or from most to least important

K¹² Language Arts Green Keywords

Writing Skills (Composition) *continued*

order words – words that connect ideas or a series of steps, or create a sequence, such as *first, next, later, finally*

organization – of a piece of writing, the way the ideas are arranged

outline – an organized list of topics in an essay

paragraph – a group of sentences about one topic

paraphrase – to restate information in one's own words

personal narrative – an essay about a personal experience of the writer

plagiarism – using another person's words without giving that person credit as a source

plot – what happens in a story; the sequence of events

point of view – the perspective from which a story is told

presentation – an oral report, usually with visuals

prewriting – the stage or step of writing in which a writer chooses a topic, gathers ideas, and plans what to write

proofreading – the stage or step of the writing process in which the writer checks for errors in grammar, punctuation, capitalization, and spelling

publishing – the stage or step of the writing process in which the writer makes a clean copy of the piece and shares it

purpose – the reason for writing

question – a kind of sentence that asks something

quotation – a report of the exact words spoken or written by a person; usually placed within quotation marks

reason – a statement that explains why something is or why it should be

reference – a work that contains useful information for a writer, such as an encyclopedia, a dictionary, or a website

research – to find information through study rather than through personal experience

revising – the stage or step of the writing process in which the writer rereads and edits the draft, correcting errors and making changes in content or organization that improve the piece

rubric – the criteria used to evaluate a piece of writing

sentence – a group of words that tells a complete thought

sentence combining – to join two sentences that have similar parts into one sentence

sequence – the order in which things happen

setting – where and when a literary work takes place

showing language – words used to create pictures in the reader's mind, rather than words that merely tell what happened
Example: The sun blazed on the street, and my bare feet sizzled like a frying egg each time I took a step.
[as opposed to] The sun was hot, and my bare feet burned each time I took a step.

signature – the end of a letter where the writer writes his or her name

source – a provider of information; a book, a historical document, online materials, and an interviewee are all sources

speaker tag – the part of a dialogue that identifies who is speaking

statement – a kind of sentence that tells something

story map – a kind of a graphic organizer that helps a writer plan a story

structure – the way a piece of writing is organized

style – the words the writer chooses and the way the writer arranges the words into sentences

summarize – to restate briefly the main points of a text

supporting details – the sentences that give information about the main idea or topic sentence

time order – the arrangement of ideas according to when they happened

topic – the subject of a piece of writing

topic sentence – the sentence that expresses the main idea of the paragraph

transition – a word or phrase that connects ideas

visual – a graphic, picture, or photograph

visual aid – a graphic, picture, photograph, or prop used in a presentation

website – a place on the Internet devoted to a specific organization, group, or individual

writing process – a series of five steps (which can be repeated) to follow during writing: prewriting, drafting, revising, proofreading, and publishing

Writing Skills (GUM)

action verb – a word that shows action

adjective – a word that describes a noun or a pronoun

article – the adjective *a, an*, or *the*

command – a kind of sentence that gives an order or makes a request

common noun – a word that names any person, place, or thing

contraction – a shortened word or words where an apostrophe replaces missing letters

demonstrative adjective – one of four describing words—*this, that, these, those*—that point out an object or objects

exclamation – a kind of sentence that shows strong feeling

future tense – a form of a verb that names an action that will happen later

indefinite pronoun – the form of a pronoun that refers to an unnamed person or group

irregular verb –a verb that does not add *–d* or *–ed* to the present form to make the past and the past participle

noun – a word that names a person, place, or thing

past tense – the form of the verb that tells what already has happened

personal pronoun – a word that takes the place of a noun

plural – more than one of something

possessive noun – the form of a noun that shows ownership

possessive pronoun – the form of a pronoun that shows ownership

predicate – the verb or verb phrase in a sentence

present tense – the verb form that tells what is happening now

pronoun – a word that takes the place of one or more nouns

proper noun – a word that names a specific person, place, or thing

question – a kind of sentence that asks something

sentence – a group of words that tells a complete thought

singular – one of something

statement – a kind of sentence that tells something

subject – a word or words that tell whom or what the sentence is about

verb – a word that shows action

words in a series – a list of words in a sentence that are separated by commas

Literature & Comprehension

Colonial Times

Unit Focus

In this unit, students will hear the story of the Pilgrims and explore colonial life in America. This unit follows the shared-reading instructional approach (see the instructional approaches to reading in the introductory lesson for this program). In this unit, students will

- Learn why it's important to preview text and think about our prior knowledge related to a text before reading.
- Explore cause-and-effect relationships.
- Make inferences.
- Learn about the use of descriptive language in poetry.
- Explore rhyme and rhythm in poetry.
- Practice identifying main idea and supporting details.
- Learn how the verbs in a story can indicate when a story happens.
- Identify text clues that help determine the order in which events happen.
- Explore how visual elements in a nonfiction article can help a reader remember and better understand the article.
- Learn how nonfiction articles can be written to compare and contrast information.

Unit Plan

Offline

45 minutes a day

Lesson 1	Explore *The First Thanksgiving* (A)	
Lesson 2	Explore *The First Thanksgiving* (B)	
Lesson 3	Explore "Thanksgiving Day"	
Lesson 4	Introduce "Digging into Jamestown"	
Lesson 5	Explore "Digging into Jamestown"	
Lesson 6	Introduce "Colonial Kids"	
Lesson 7	Explore "Colonial Kids"	
Lesson 8	Your Choice	

Explore *The First Thanksgiving* (A)

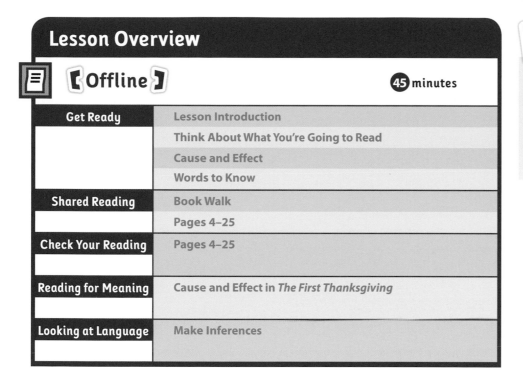

Lesson Overview

[Offline] **45** minutes

Get Ready	Lesson Introduction
	Think About What You're Going to Read
	Cause and Effect
	Words to Know
Shared Reading	Book Walk
	Pages 4–25
Check Your Reading	Pages 4–25
Reading for Meaning	Cause and Effect in *The First Thanksgiving*
Looking at Language	Make Inferences

Advance Preparation

Before beginning the Shared Reading, read pages 4–25 of *The First Thanksgiving* to locate Words to Know in the text. Preview pages LC 139 and 140 in *K¹² Language Arts Activity Book* to prepare the materials for Looking at Language.

Big Ideas

- ▶ Previewing text helps readers call up prior knowledge they will need to help them understand what they will be reading.
- ▶ Activating prior knowledge provides a framework for a reader to organize and connect new information to information previously learned; readers that activate prior knowledge before reading are more likely to understand and recall what they read.
- ▶ Comprehension is facilitated when readers connect new information to information previously learned.
- ▶ Comprehension entails an understanding of the organizational patterns of text.
- ▶ Good readers use prior knowledge and text clues to infer, or draw conclusions about what is implied but not directly stated in text.

[Materials]

Supplied

- *The First Thanksgiving* by Linda Hayward
- *K12 Language Arts Activity Book*, pp. LC 137–140

Story Synopsis

In 1620, a brave group of people set sail for the New World on the *Mayflower* so they can practice the religion of their choice, not that of their king. After an arduous nine-week journey across the Atlantic Ocean, this hardy group finally reaches the shores of America. What adventures await them?

Keywords

cause – the reason something happens

effect – the result of a cause

inference – a guess you make using the clues in a text and what you already know

prior knowledge – things you already know from past experience

visual text support – a graphic feature that helps a reader better understand text, such as a picture, chart, or map

 **45** minutes

Work **together** with students to complete Get Ready, Shared Reading, Check Your Reading, Reading for Meaning, and Looking at Language activities.

Get Ready

Lesson Introduction
Prepare students for listening to and discussing *The First Thanksgiving*.

1. Tell students that you are going to read *The First Thanksgiving*, a story about the Pilgrims.

2. Explain that before you read the story, you will get ready by discussing how

   ▸ We get our brain ready to read by previewing a text and thinking about the subject of the text we will be reading.
   ▸ One thing can cause another thing to happen.
   ▸ An event can cause someone to do something.

 Objectives
- Identify examples of cause and effect.
- Activate prior knowledge by previewing text and/or discussing topic.
- Build vocabulary through listening, reading, and discussion.
- Use new vocabulary in written and spoken sentences.
- Increase concept and content vocabulary.

Think About What You're Going to Read
Introduce the idea of previewing text to get ready to read.

1. Explain to students that good readers preview text before reading by looking at the cover, title, table of contents (if the book has one), and pictures of a book. We do this before we read to think about what we already know about the subject we'll be reading about.

2. Tell students that what we already know is our **prior knowledge**. When we preview a text, we call up our prior knowledge to help get our brain ready to read.

3. Tell students that our brain is like a file cabinet that has drawers filled with information. When we preview text, we open the drawers in our brain that are filled with information, or prior knowledge, related to what we will be reading.

4. Explain that when we read, our brain connects the new information we learn to the prior knowledge that we already have filed away. This makes it easier for us to understand and remember what we read.

5. Provide an example that demonstrates how thinking about prior knowledge can help readers better understand what they read. Answers to questions may vary.
   Say: Let's do an experiment to show how your prior knowledge can help you understand what you read. Imagine that the first sentence of a story says, "Sam jumped all over Dad as soon as he came home from work."

   ▸ What do you think the story might be about?

   Say: You can't be sure what the story is about because you don't have enough information. You haven't called up your prior knowledge related to the story. But now I'm going to ask you a couple of questions that will help you to open the file drawers in your brain related to the story.

- ▸ Do you have a dog? If so, what is your dog like?
- ▸ What are some things that dogs do when they're excited?

6. Explain that calling up readers' prior knowledge about dogs makes it easier to know what's going on in a story that starts off with, "Sam jumped all over Dad as soon as he came home from work."

- ▸ What is Sam? a dog
- ▸ Why does Sam jump all over Dad? He's excited to see Dad.

7. Tell students that before they read a story, they should always ask themselves what they already know about the subject. This will help them to open the file drawers in their brain and get ready to take in new information.

Cause and Effect

Explore cause and effect and have students practice identifying examples. Turn to page LC 137 in *K¹² Language Arts Activity Book*.

1. Explain to students that doing one thing can make another thing happen. The thing that you do is called the **cause**, and the thing that happens is called the **effect**.
   Cause: You slam the door. → **Effect:** The door makes a loud noise.
   Cause: The grass is getting really tall. → **Effect:** Mom mows the lawn.

2. Have students practice identifying cause-and-effect relationships, using visual examples.

3. Have students study the pictures on the Activity Book page.

4. Have them match a cause on the left with its effect on the right by drawing a line to connect the events.

5. Have students describe each cause-and-effect relationship.

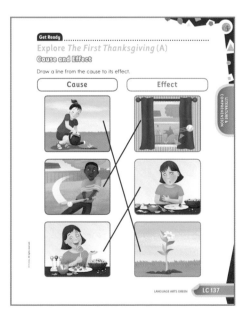

Words to Know

Before reading *The First Thanksgiving*, go over Words to Know with students.

1. Read aloud each word or phrase and have students repeat it.

2. Ask students if they know what each word or phrase means.

   ▸ If students know a word's or phrase's meaning, have them define it and use it in a sentence.

   ▸ If students don't know a word's or phrase's meaning, read them the definition and discuss the word or phrase with them.

arrest – to hold someone for breaking the law
declare – to announce
post – to make someone stand in a particular place, usually to guard something
search party – a group of people who go to look for someone or something
spring – a place where water rises up from under the ground
stuffy – not having any fresh air to breathe

Shared Reading

Book Walk

Prepare students for reading by taking them on a Book Walk of *The First Thanksgiving*. **Scan the book together up to page 25** and ask students to make predictions about the story.

1. Have students look at the picture on the cover. Point to and read aloud the **book title**.

   ▸ What do you think the book is about? Answers will vary.

2. Remind students that important information about a book can be found on the title page.

3. Have students locate the **title page** in *The First Thanksgiving*. Have them study what's on the page.

   ▸ What information do we find on the title page of this book? book title; picture from story; name of author; name of illustrator

4. Tell students that the story you're going to read is about some of the first people from England to come to America

5. Explain that you are now going to look through the book and ask questions that will help them call up their prior knowledge related to the subject of the book. This will help them get their brain ready to read.

   ▸ What do you already know about the people we call the Pilgrims? Answers will vary.

Objectives
- Identify purpose of and information provided by informational text features.
- Activate prior knowledge by previewing text and/or discussing topic.
- Make predictions based on text, illustrations, and/or prior knowledge.
- Read and respond to texts representing a variety of cultures, time periods, and traditions.

6. Turn to the first page of the story. Tell students that the picture shows the Pilgrims putting things on the ship that they will sail to America.

   ▸ What do you think you would need to bring on a long voyage across an ocean? Answers will vary.

7. Turn to pages 16 and 17.
   ▸ What do you think this picture shows? the Pilgrims arriving in America

8. Turn to pages 18 and 19.
   ▸ Who do you think these people are? Indians; Native Americans

---

Pages 4–25

It's time to read aloud pages 4–25.

1. Have students sit next to you so that they can see the pictures and words while you read aloud.

2. Remind students to listen for things that cause other things to happen.

3. **Read aloud the story through page 25.** Track with your finger so students can follow along. Emphasize Words to Know as you come to them. If appropriate, use the pictures to help show what each word means.

Check Your Reading

Pages 4–25

Check students' comprehension of *The First Thanksgiving*.

1. Have students retell *The First Thanksgiving* in their own words to develop grammar, vocabulary, comprehension, and fluency skills.

2. Ask students the following questions.

   ▸ What is the name of the ship on which the Pilgrims sailed to America? the *Mayflower*
   ▸ What is it like living on the *Mayflower*? Possible answers: stuffy; cold, damp; no water; no toilet; worms in bread
   ▸ How long does it take the Pilgrims to get to America? nine weeks
   ▸ What does the search party see and find when they go ashore? Indians, corn, baskets, a spring   What does the search party take back to the *Mayflower*? freshwater
   ▸ What things do the Pilgrims look for to choose a place to live? a harbor, freshwater, fields for planting
   ▸ What do the Pilgrims name their settlement? New Plymouth

 TIP If students have trouble responding to a question, help them locate the answer in the text or pictures.

> ⭐ **Objectives**
> - Retell or dramatize a story.
> - Answer questions requiring literal recall of details.
> - Identify important details and/or events of a story.
> - Identify important details in informational text.

Reading for Meaning

Cause and Effect in *The First Thanksgiving*

Explore cause and effect with students.

Objectives
- Describe cause-and-effect relationships in text.

1. Remind students that doing one thing can cause, or make, another thing happen.

2. Ask the following questions to check students' ability to recognize cause-and-effect relationships.

   ▸ What caused the Pilgrims to meet in secret when they lived in England? The king declared that everybody had to belong to his religion.
   ▸ The Pilgrims were not allowed to practice their religion. They were spied on and their leaders were arrested. What did the Pilgrims decide to do because of these things? leave England, come to America.
   ▸ What was the effect of deciding to come to America? What did the Pilgrims give up? They gave up their houses and friends. They had to say good-bye to England.
   ▸ Why is the *Mayflower* so crowded? The ship is small, and there are over a hundred passengers.
   ▸ What happens when the Indians see the Pilgrims' search party? They are afraid, and they run away.
   ▸ What is the effect of the bad weather during the first winter at New Plymouth? It slows down building houses.
   ▸ How do the Pilgrims know the Indians are watching them? The Pilgrims see the smoke from the Indians' campfires.
   ▸ The Pilgrims know that the Indians are watching them. What is the effect of this? The Pilgrims post a guard day and night.

Looking at Language

Make Inferences

Reread pages 4–25 of *The First Thanksgiving* with a focus on making inferences. Gather the Reading Aid on pages LC 139 and 140 in *K¹² Language Arts Activity Book*.

Objectives
- Read aloud grade-level text with appropriate expression, accuracy, and rate.
- Make inferences based on text and/or prior knowledge.
- Support inferences with evidence from text and/or prior knowledge.
- Demonstrate understanding by thinking aloud.
- Distinguish texts that describe events from long ago from those that describe contemporary events.
- Distinguish between text and visual text supports.
- Interpret information from visual text supports: graphs, tables, charts, cartoons.

1. Have students explain the kinds of information a reader uses to make inferences.

2. If students don't recall the type of information that a reader uses to make inferences, remind them that **inferences** are logical guesses based on

   ▸ The words and pictures of a story
   ▸ The reader's prior knowledge learned from past experiences

3. Tell students that **they will read aloud pages 4–25 with you**. As you read aloud together, you will stop at certain points to discuss the clues that help you make inferences.

4. Explain that when readers make inferences, you can't see what they're doing because everything is happening in their mind. Tell students that you will share your thoughts out loud so they can learn what goes on in the mind of a good reader while making an inference.

5. Refer to the Reading Aid.

Reading Aid Tear out the Reading Aid for this reading selection. Follow the instructions for folding the page, and then use the page as a guide as you reread the selection with students.

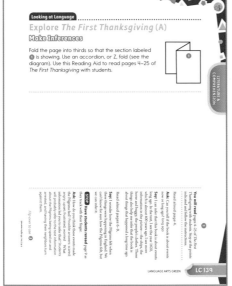

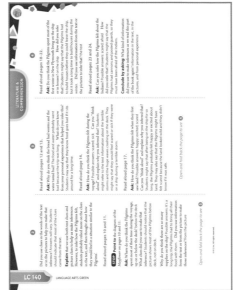

Explore *The First Thanksgiving* (B)

Lesson Overview

Offline		45 minutes
Get Ready	Lesson Introduction	
	Review Cause and Effect	
	Review What You've Read	
	Words to Know	
Shared Reading	Book Walk	
	Pages 26–48	
Check Your Reading	Pages 26–48	
Reading for Meaning	Cause and Effect in *The First Thanksgiving*	
Looking at Language	Make Inferences	
Making Connections	Cause and Effect: Pilgrims in America	

Materials

Supplied

- *The First Thanksgiving* by Linda Hayward
- *K¹² Language Arts Activity Book,* pp. LC 137, 141–144

Story Synopsis

After barely surviving a harsh winter, the Pilgrims begin a friendly relationship with their Indian neighbors. The Indians teach the Pilgrims many things, such as how to hunt deer and plant corn. After working hard all summer, the Pilgrims have a bountiful harvest and give thanks by inviting their neighbors to a great feast.

There is a brief reference to death and burials.

Keywords

cause – the reason something happens

effect – the result of a cause

inference – a guess you make using the clues in a text and what you already know

Advance Preparation

Before beginning the Shared Reading, read pages 26–48 of *The First Thanksgiving* to locate Words to Know in the text. Have students gather completed page LC 137 (Cause and Effect) in *K¹² Language Arts Activity Book.* Preview pages LC 141 and 142 to prepare the materials for Looking at Language.

Big Ideas

- Previewing text helps readers call up prior knowledge they will need to help them understand what they will be reading.
- Activating prior knowledge provides a framework for a reader to organize and connect new information to information previously learned; readers that activate prior knowledge before reading are more likely to understand and recall what they read.
- Comprehension entails an understanding of the organizational patterns of text.
- Good readers use prior knowledge and text clues to infer, or draw conclusions about what is implied but not directly stated in text.

[Offline] 45 minutes

Work **together** with students to complete Get Ready, Shared Reading, Check Your Reading, Reading for Meaning, Looking at Language, and Making Connections activities.

Get Ready

Lesson Introduction

Prepare students for listening to and discussing *The First Thanksgiving*.

1. Tell students that you are going to finish reading *The First Thanksgiving*.

2. Explain that before you read the story, you will get ready by

   ▸ Reviewing cause-and-effect relationships
   ▸ Reviewing what happened in pages 4–25

Review Cause and Effect

Review cause and effect, and have students practice giving examples.

1. Ask to students to explain cause and effect.

2. If students have trouble answering, remind them that

   ▸ Doing one thing can make another thing happen.
   ▸ The thing that you do is called the **cause**, and the thing that happens is called the **effect**.

3. Have students give an example of a cause and its possible effect.

   ▸ If students have trouble giving examples, suggest as a cause, such as "It's raining." Then have students name some possible effects.

4. Have students give an example of an effect and what might have caused it.

   ▸ If students have trouble giving examples, suggest as an effect, such as "The cookies are burnt." Then have students name some possible causes.

5. If student continue to have trouble giving examples, gather completed page LC 137 (Cause and Effect) in *K¹² Language Arts Activity Book*.

6. Have students describe each cause-and-effect relationship on the Activity Book page.

Objectives

- Activate prior knowledge by previewing text and/or discussing topic.
- Identify examples of cause and effect.
- Retell or dramatize a story.
- Build vocabulary through listening, reading, and discussion.
- Use new vocabulary in written and spoken sentences.
- Increase concept and content vocabulary.

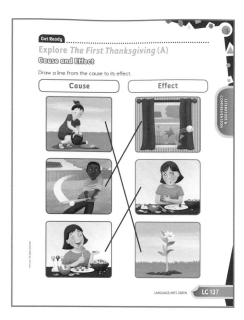

Review What You've Read

Before reading pages 26–48 of *The First Thanksgiving*, review what students have read so far in the story.

1. Have students retell the important events of pages 4–25.

2. Tell students that you will read the next part of the book beginning with page 26.

Words to Know

Before reading *The First Thanksgiving*, go over Words to Know with students.

1. Read aloud each word or phrase and have students repeat it.

2. Ask students if they know what each word or phrase means.

   ▸ If students know a word's or phrase's meaning, have them define it and use it in a sentence.

   ▸ If students don't know a word's or phrase's meaning, read them the definition and discuss the word or phrase with them.

bleak – gloomy; hopeless
governor – the person who is in charge of a settlement
settlement – a new place where people live
survive – to stay alive
time of plenty – a period of time when there is a lot of something, such as food
wilderness – an area of land in its natural state, where no people live

Shared Reading

Book Walk

Prepare students by taking them on a Book Walk of *The First Thanksgiving*. Scan pages 26–48 of the book together and ask students to make predictions about this part of the story.

1. Read aloud the **book title**.

2. Read aloud the **name of the author and illustrator**.

3. Look through the book beginning with page 26. Have students scan the **pictures**.

4. Remind students that previewing text helps activate their prior knowledge.

5. Tell them that asking questions about their related experiences is a good way to activate their prior knowledge. Answers to questions may vary.

   ▸ What have you learned about the Pilgrims that you didn't already know?
   ▸ Have you ever moved? What was it like? How did it make you feel to be in a new place?
   ▸ What do you think will happen in this part of the story?

Objectives

- Activate prior knowledge by previewing text and/or discussing topic.
- Make predictions based on text, illustrations, and/or prior knowledge.
- Read and respond to texts representing a variety of cultures, time periods, and traditions.

Pages 26–48

It's time to read aloud the rest of the story.

1. Have students sit next to you so that they can see the pictures and words while you read aloud.

2. Remind students to listen for things that cause other things to happen.

3. **Read aloud the story beginning with page 26.** Track with your finger so students can follow along. Emphasize Words to Know as you come to them. If appropriate, use the pictures to help show what each word means.

Check Your Reading

Pages 26–48

Check students' comprehension of this part of *The First Thanksgiving*.

1. Have students retell pages 26–48 of *The First Thanksgiving* in their own words to develop grammar, vocabulary, comprehension, and fluency skills.

Objectives

- Retell or dramatize a story.
- Answer questions requiring literal recall of details.
- Identify important details and/or events of a story.
- Identify important details in informational text.

2. Ask students the following questions.

  ▸ Who is Samoset? an Indian who walks into the settlement and welcomes the Pilgrims

  ▸ What are some of the things the Indians teach the Pilgrims? Possible answers: how to survive in the wilderness; how to hunt deer; how to plant corn; how to put fish in the ground before planting crops

  ▸ Why do the Pilgrims want to have a feast? because they are happy that they have so much food this year

  ▸ Why do they invite their Indian friends? because the Indians helped them learn how to live in America; because they are their friends

TIP If students have trouble responding to a question, help them locate the answer in the text or pictures.

Reading for Meaning

Cause and Effect in *The First Thanksgiving*

Explore cause and effect with students.

Objectives
- Describe cause-and-effect relationships in text.

1. Remind students that doing one thing can cause another thing to happen. The thing that happens is called the effect.

2. Ask the following questions to check students' ability to recognize cause-and-effect relationships.

  ▸ Why are only half of the Pilgrims alive by the end of the first winter? because many of them got sick and died

  ▸ What causes Squanto to live with the Pilgrims? He likes them.

  ▸ What was the effect of the Indians putting fish in the ground when they plant their seed? The soil is richer.

  ▸ What is the effect of the Pilgrims and the Indians signing a treaty? There is peace; they do not harm each other.

  ▸ How do the Pilgrims feel when the *Mayflower* sails back to England in April? sad   Why don't any of the Pilgrims leave with the *Mayflower*? They all want to stay in America.

  ▸ What causes the Pilgrims' fields to be full of good things to eat in the fall? the hard work the Pilgrims did all summer

  ▸ Why are the Pilgrims worried when Massasoit shows up for the feast with ninety Indians? They don't know how they will feed so many people.   What does Massasoit do? He sends his men into the forest to get five deer.

  ▸ What is the effect of more and more people from England coming to America? The town of Plymouth gets bigger and bigger.

  ▸ What happens when the children of the Pilgrims grow up? They have children of their own; they have harvest feasts, too.

  ▸ Why is Thanksgiving Day never forgotten? because President Lincoln made it a national holiday

Looking at Language

Make Inferences

Reread pages 26–48 of *The First Thanksgiving* with a focus on making inferences. Gather the Reading Aid on pages LC 141 and 142 in *K¹² Language Arts Activity Book*.

1. Have students explain the kinds of information a reader uses to make inferences.

2. If students don't recall the type of information that a reader uses to make inferences, tell them that inferences are guesses. However, they are not wild guesses. They are logical guesses based on the following information:

   ▶ The words and pictures of a story
   ▶ The reader's prior knowledge learned from past experiences

3. Tell students that **they will read aloud pages 26–48 with you**. As you read aloud together, you will stop at certain points to have them practice making inferences.

4. Refer to the Reading Aid.

Reading Aid Tear out the Reading Aid for this reading selection. Follow the instructions for folding the page, and then use the page as a guide as you reread the selection with students.

Objectives

- Read aloud grade-level text with appropriate expression, accuracy, and rate.
- Make inferences based on text and/or prior knowledge.
- Support inferences with evidence from text and/or prior knowledge.
- Demonstrate understanding by thinking aloud.

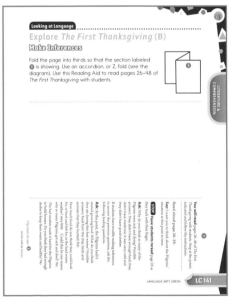

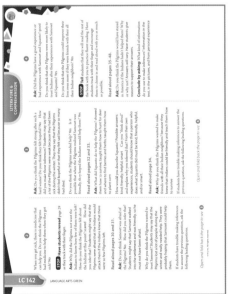

Making Connections

 Cause and Effect: Pilgrims in America

Check students' understanding of cause-and-effect relationships in the story. Turn to pages LC 143 and 144 in *K¹² Language Arts Activity Book*.

1. Tell students they are going to fill out a chart that shows cause-and-effect relationships in *The First Thanksgiving*.

2. Read aloud each column heading.

3. Read aloud the first row heading and the answers that are already in the chart.

   ▶ Have students tell you what caused the Pilgrims to live in houses instead of on the ship. Help students write their answer in the chart.

4. Read aloud the next row heading and help students write their answers in the chart.

   ▶ If students have trouble with an answer, help them refer back to the book.

5. Repeat Step 4 until the chart is complete.

6. Ask the follow questions to help students evaluate information in the chart and to encourage discussion.

   ▶ How would you describe the Pilgrims? Possible answers: hard-working; brave   Why do you describe them that way? Answers will vary. Have students provide examples from the book to support their answers.

   ▶ Do you think that the Pilgrims could have survived without help from the Indians? Why or why not? Answers will vary. Have students provide examples from the book to support their answers.

   ▶ Would you want to live like the Pilgrims? Why or why not? Answers will vary. Have students provide examples from the book and their own lives to support their answers.

Objectives

- Demonstrate understanding through graphic organizers.
- Describe cause-and-effect relationships in text.
- Compare and contrast elements within informational texts.
- Evaluate information in print and/or electronic and visual media.
- Make connections with text: text-to-text, text-to-self, text-to-world.

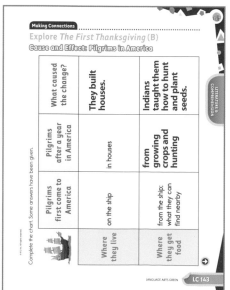

Explore "Thanksgiving Day"

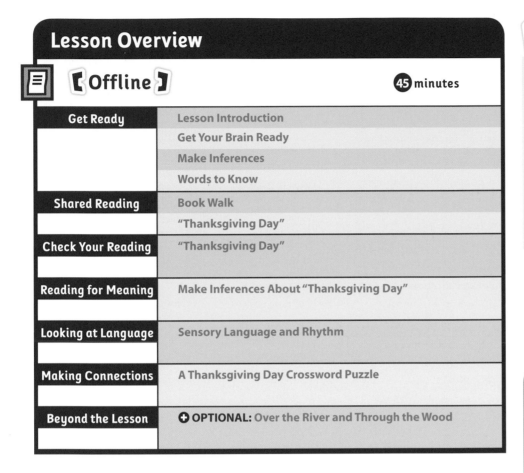

Lesson Overview

[Offline]   **45** minutes

Get Ready	Lesson Introduction
	Get Your Brain Ready
	Make Inferences
	Words to Know
Shared Reading	Book Walk
	"Thanksgiving Day"
Check Your Reading	"Thanksgiving Day"
Reading for Meaning	Make Inferences About "Thanksgiving Day"
Looking at Language	Sensory Language and Rhythm
Making Connections	A Thanksgiving Day Crossword Puzzle
Beyond the Lesson	⊕ OPTIONAL: Over the River and Through the Wood

Materials

Supplied

- *Listen, My Children: Poems for First Graders*, p. 19
- *K¹² My Journal*, pp. 2–53
- *K¹² Language Arts Activity Book*, pp. LC 145–147

Also Needed

- crayons

Poetry Synopsis

Lydia Maria Child pens a well-known Thanksgiving Day poem about going "over the river and through the wood."

Keywords

inference – a guess you make using the clues in a text and what you already know

prior knowledge – things you already know from past experience

rhythm – a pattern of accented and unaccented syllables; a distinctive beat

sensory language – language that appeals to the five senses

visualize – to picture things in your mind as you read

Advance Preparation

Before beginning the Shared Reading, read "Thanksgiving Day" to locate Words to Know in the text. Preview pages LC 145 and 146 in *K¹² Language Arts Activity Book* to prepare the materials for Looking at Language.

Big Ideas

▶ Activating prior knowledge provides a framework for a reader to organize and connect new information to information previously learned; readers that activate prior knowledge before reading are more likely to understand and recall what they read.

▶ Good readers use prior knowledge and text clues to infer, or draw conclusions about what is implied but not directly stated in text.

▶ The use of imagery and sensory language creates detailed pictures in the reader's mind, so the reader can understand and appreciate the ideas and feelings the writer conveys.

▶ Readers who visualize, or form mental pictures, while they read have better recall of text than those who do not.

▶ During shared-reading activities, students learn more about how print works.

[Offline] 45 minutes

Work **together** with students to complete offline Get Ready, Shared Reading, Check Your Reading, Reading for Meaning, Looking at Language, Making Connections, and Beyond the Lesson activities.

Get Ready

Lesson Introduction

Prepare students for reading and discussing "Thanksgiving Day."

1. Tell students that you are going to read the poem "Thanksgiving Day." While this text was originally written as a poem, many people are more familiar with it as a song.

2. Explain to students that before you read the poem, you will get ready by

   ▸ Having them get their brain ready to read by drawing a picture
   ▸ Discussing how to make inferences
   ▸ Having them practice reading aloud a line from the poem that is repeated in every stanza

Objectives

- Activate prior knowledge by previewing text and/or discussing topic.
- Make inferences based on text and/or prior knowledge.
- Support inferences with evidence from text and/or prior knowledge.
- Build vocabulary through listening, reading, and discussion.
- Use new vocabulary in written and spoken sentences.

Get Your Brain Ready

Help students get their brain ready to read. Gather *K¹² My Journal* and have students turn to the next available page for **drawing and writing** in Thoughts and Experiences.

1. Tell students that **good readers get their brain ready to read by thinking about the topic** they will read about. This makes it easier for us to learn new information because our brain can connect the new information to what we already know about a topic.

2. Explain that students will get their brain ready by drawing a picture of something they like to do on Thanksgiving Day.

3. Discuss what students like to do on Thanksgiving Day. In their journal, have them draw a picture of what they like to do.

4. If students don't celebrate Thanksgiving, have them think about another special day they celebrate with their family. Have them draw a picture of what they do on that special day.

5. Have students dictate a sentence that describes their picture. Write the sentence under the picture and have students read aloud the sentence with you.

   ▸ If students are ready to write on their own, allow them to do so.

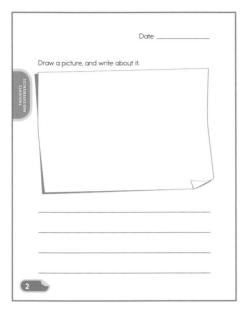

Make Inferences

Explore making inferences with students.

1. Tell students that good readers are able to **infer**, or figure out, things in a poem that the poet does not say directly. Good readers think about **clues in the poem and their own prior knowledge from past experience** to make an inference.

2. Tell students to listen for clues to figure out what a poem is about. **Read aloud** the following poem.

   Fluffy likes to purr and wiggle.
   My furry friend makes me giggle.

   ▸ What is Fluffy? a cat or kitten
   ▸ What clues in the poem helped you figure this out? *purr, furry*
   ▸ What do you know from your own experiences that helped you figure this out? Students should say that they know cats purr and that they have fur.

Words to Know

Before reading "Thanksgiving Day," go over Words to Know with students.

1. Read aloud each word and have students repeat it.

2. Ask students if they know what each word means.

   ▸ If students know a word's meaning, have them define it and use it in a sentence.
   ▸ If students don't know a word's meaning, read them the definition and discuss the word with them.

first-rate – the best
sleigh – a sled, usually pulled by a horse, that is used to carry people over snow
spring – to jump or bounce
spy – to see

Shared Reading

Book Walk

Prepare students for reading by taking them on a Book Walk of "Thanksgiving Day." Scan the poem together, and ask students to make predictions. Answers to questions may vary.

1. Turn to the **table of contents** in *Listen, My Children*. Help students find the selection and turn to that page.

2. Point to and read aloud the **title of the poem** and the **name of the poet**.

   ▸ What do you think the poem is about?

3. Have students look at the **picture**.

   ▸ Do you know what Thanksgiving Day is?
   ▸ What are your favorite things to eat on Thanksgiving Day?
   ▸ Do you see relatives who live far away?
   ▸ If you don't celebrate Thanksgiving, do you have another special holiday that you celebrate with your family?

4. Point to and have students practice reading aloud the first occurrence of the following line from the poem: "Over the river and through the wood . . . ."

5. Tell students that they will hear this line repeated at the beginning of each stanza in the poem. Invite them to **chime in and read this line aloud with you** every time it appears.

Objectives

- Make predictions based on text, illustrations, and/or prior knowledge.
- Activate prior knowledge by previewing text and/or discussing topic.
- Read and discuss poetry.

"Thanksgiving Day"

It's time to read aloud the poem.

1. Have students sit next to you so that they can see the pictures and words while you read aloud.

2. Tell students to listen carefully to see if they can figure out some things that the poet doesn't say directly.

3. Remind students to chime in and read aloud the first line of each stanza, which they practiced during the Book Walk.

4. **Read aloud the entire poem**. Track with your finger so students can follow along. Emphasize Words to Know as you come to them. If appropriate, use the picture to help show what a word means.

Check Your Reading

"Thanksgiving Day"

Check students' comprehension of "Thanksgiving Day."

1. Have students retell "Thanksgiving Day" in their own words to develop grammar, vocabulary, comprehension, and fluency skills.

2. Ask students the following questions.

   ▶ Where is the person in the poem going? to Grandfather's house
   ▶ Why is the person in the poem visiting Grandfather? to eat Thanksgiving dinner
   ▶ What "stings the toes / And bites the nose"? the wind
   ▶ What does the person in the poem spy when she gets to the house? Grandmother's cap
   ▶ What desserts are mentioned at the end of the poem? pudding, pumpkin pie

 If students have trouble responding to a question, help them locate the answer in the text.

> **Objectives**
> • Retell or dramatize a story.
> • Answer questions requiring literal recall of details.

Reading for Meaning

Make Inferences About "Thanksgiving Day"

Explore making inferences about "Thanksgiving Day."

1. Remind students that good readers are able to **infer**, or figure out, things in a poem that the author does not say directly. Good readers use **clues from the poem and what they know from their own experiences** to make inferences.

2. Check students' ability to make inferences by asking the following questions.

   ▶ What does the person in the poem ride in to get to Grandfather's house? a sleigh   What clue in the poem helped you figure this out? The poem says *the horse knows the way to carry the sleigh*.

   ▶ What is the weather like outside? cold   How do you know? The poem mentions snow and the wind.

   ▶ What is the horse wearing that makes noise? bells   The poem does not directly state that the horse is wearing bells. What clue in the poem helped you figure this out? *Hear the bells ring*

   ▶ Where does Grandfather live? on a farm   How did you use prior knowledge, or what you already know, to figure this out? Students should say that a *barn-yard gate* is found on a farm, so Grandfather must live on one.

   ▶ What does the person in the poem mean when she says that they "seem to go / Extremely slow / It is so hard to wait!"? She's excited to get to Grandfather's house, so it seems to take a long time to get there. What do you know from personal experience that helped you figure this out? Students may say that when they're excited about going somewhere special, they can't wait to get there.

   ▶ What does the person in the poem like to eat? pudding, pumpkin pie How did you figure this out? The person in the poem wants to know if the pudding is done yet, and says "Hurrah!" for pumpkin pie.

Objectives

- Make inferences based on text and/or prior knowledge.
- Support inferences with evidence from text and/or prior knowledge.

Looking at Language ....

Sensory Language and Rhythm

Reread "Thanksgiving Day" with a focus on sensory language and rhythm. Gather the Reading Aid on pages LC 145 and 146 in *K¹² Language Arts Activity Book*.

1. Remind students that poets carefully choose the words in their poems. They often use descriptive words and phrases that help you imagine pictures in your head. Poets may also use words that can help you imagine how something sounds or feels.

2. Explain that descriptive language makes a poem more interesting and helps you visualize what the poet wants you to imagine. And when you visualize, you're more likely to understand and remember what you read.

3. Tell students that poets may also write the words in a poem so that there is a distinctive beat or rhythm to the poem.

4. Tell students that they will **read the poem aloud with you**. You will stop after each stanza to discuss the descriptive language and rhythm of the poem.

5. Refer to the Reading Aid.

Reading Aid Tear out the Reading Aid for this reading selection. Follow the instructions for folding the page, and then use the page as a guide as you reread the selection with students.

Objectives
- Identify author's use of sensory language.
- Use visualizing to aid understanding of text.
- Identify the effects of rhyme and rhythm.
- Respond to poetic devices of rhyme, rhythm, and/or alliteration.
- Read aloud grade-level text with appropriate expression, accuracy, and rate.

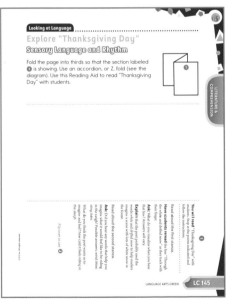

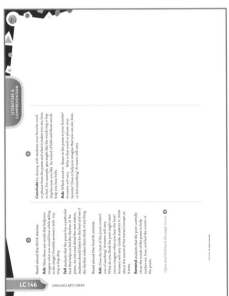

Making Connections ....

A Thanksgiving Day Crossword Puzzle

Check students' understanding of words used in the poem "Thanksgiving Day." Turn to page LC 147 in *K¹² Language Arts Activity Book*.

1. Tell students they will use words from the poem "Thanksgiving Day" to complete a crossword puzzle.

2. Point to and read aloud each word in the word box on the Activity Book page to familiarize students with the words they will be using.

3. Explain that the words fit in either a row or a column in the puzzle.

4. Point to the first picture and have students identify what word the picture represents.

5. Write the word in the appropriate row or column in the crossword puzzle.

6. Repeat Steps 4 and 5 for each picture until the crossword puzzle is complete.

7. When finished, ask students to explain how each of the words in the crossword puzzle is used in the poem. For example, students could say that a *horse* pulls the *sleigh*.

Objectives
- Build vocabulary through listening, reading, and discussion.
- Use new vocabulary in written and spoken sentences.

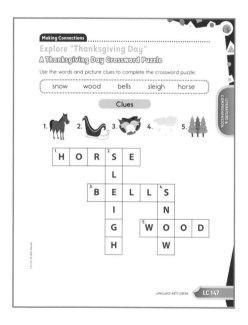

Beyond the Lesson

⊕ OPTIONAL: **Over the River and Through the Wood**

This activity is OPTIONAL. It is intended for students who have extra time and would enjoy learning a Thanksgiving song. Feel free to skip this activity.

1. Explain to students that the poem "Thanksgiving Day" can be sung as a song.

2. Read aloud the first stanza from the poem and then have students repeat the words.

3. Sing the first stanza of the poem and then have students join in.

   ► If you are unfamiliar with the song, search the Internet for "Over the River and Through the Wood" to find an audio or video clip of the tune. Be sure to locate a traditional version, which has an easy-to-recognize beat.

4. Help students hear the rhythm of the song by clapping on the beat.

5. Ask students what the rhythm of the song reminds them of. Answers will vary; help students recognize that the beat is similar to the clip-clop sound a horse makes when it runs or trots.

Objectives
- Identify the effects of rhyme and rhythm.
- Respond to poetic devices of rhyme, rhythm, and/or alliteration.

Introduce "Digging into Jamestown"

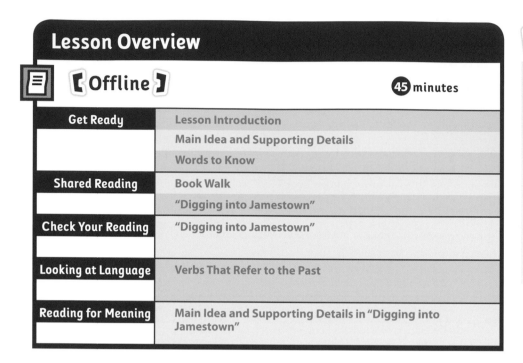

Lesson Overview		
[Offline]		**45** minutes
Get Ready	Lesson Introduction	
	Main Idea and Supporting Details	
	Words to Know	
Shared Reading	Book Walk	
	"Digging into Jamestown"	
Check Your Reading	"Digging into Jamestown"	
Looking at Language	Verbs That Refer to the Past	
Reading for Meaning	Main Idea and Supporting Details in "Digging into Jamestown"	

Advance Preparation

Before beginning the Shared Reading, read "Digging into Jamestown" to locate Words to Know in the text. Cut out and tape together the sentence strip on page LC 149, and preview pages LC 151 and 152 in *K¹² Language Arts Activity Book* to prepare the materials for Looking at Language.

Big Ideas

- ▶ Previewing text helps readers call up prior knowledge they will need to help them understand what they will be reading.
- ▶ Activating prior knowledge provides a framework for a reader to organize and connect new information to information previously learned; readers that activate prior knowledge before reading are more likely to understand and recall what they read.
- ▶ Comprehension is facilitated when readers connect new information to information previously learned.
- ▶ Comprehension entails an understanding of the organizational patterns of text.
- ▶ During shared-reading activities, students learn more about how print works.

Materials

Supplied

- "Digging into Jamestown," *K¹² World: People and Places of the Past*, pp. 2–15
- *K¹² Language Arts Activity Book*, pp. LC 149–152

Also Needed

- scissors, adult
- tape, clear

Story Synopsis

Modern-day archaeologists uncover clues about America's early history by digging into Jamestown, one of the first English settlements in the New World.

Keywords

irregular verb – a verb that does not add –*d* or –*ed* to the present form to make the past and the past participle

main idea – the most important idea in a paragraph or text

past tense – the form of the verb that tells what has already happened

prior knowledge – things you already know from past experience

supporting detail – a detail that gives more information about a main idea

verb – a word that shows action

〔 Offline 〕 45 minutes

Work **together** with students to complete Get Ready, Shared Reading, Check Your Reading, Looking at Language, and Reading for Meaning activities.

Get Ready ....

Lesson Introduction

Prepare students for listening to and discussing "Digging into Jamestown."

1. Tell students that you are going to read "Digging into Jamestown," a nonfiction article about one of the first English settlements in the New World.

2. Explain that before you read the article, you will get ready by discussing

   ▸ The style of writing called nonfiction
   ▸ Main idea and supporting details

⭐ Objectives

- Identify the main idea and supporting details.
- Build vocabulary through listening, reading, and discussion.
- Use new vocabulary in written and spoken sentences.
- Increase concept and content vocabulary.

Main Idea and Supporting Details

Explore main idea and supporting details in nonfiction text.

1. Remind students that texts about real things are called **nonfiction**, or **informational text**.

2. Explain that in nonfiction texts, most paragraphs have a **main idea**. The main idea is what the paragraph is mostly about. Most of the other sentences in a paragraph give information, or **details**, about the main idea.

3. **Read aloud** the following paragraph and then model how to determine the main idea.

   Native Americans used the elm tree for many things. They used the bark of the elm tree to build houses and make canoes. They sat under the elm tree to keep cool in the summer. They used the dried branches of the elm tree for firewood.

   Say: This paragraph gives information about how Native Americans used elm trees in different ways. So I think the main idea is "Native Americans used the elm tree for many things." I can make sure that this is the main idea by checking whether most of the other sentences give details about how Native Americans used the elm tree.

   ▸ Does the sentence "They used the bark of the elm tree to build houses and make canoes" talk about how Native Americans used the elm tree? Yes
   ▸ Does the sentence "They sat under the elm tree to keep cool in the summer" talk about how Native Americans used the elm tree? Yes
   ▸ Does the sentence "They used the dried branches of the elm tree for firewood" talk about how Native Americans used the elm tree? Yes

   Say: The other sentences give details about how Native Americans used elm trees. So I can confirm that "Native Americans used the elm tree for many things" is the main idea of the paragraph. We call the details that give information about how Native Americans used the elm tree **supporting details**.

4. Tell students the main idea and supporting details are like a table: The table top is the main idea, and the legs are the details that support it, or hold it up.

5. **Read aloud** the following paragraph and then have students practice identifying the main idea and supporting details.

   Dogs bark for many reasons. They bark when they are scared. They bark when they are playing with people or other dogs. Sometimes they bark just to say, "Hey, I like this!"

   ▸ What do you think is the main idea of the paragraph? Possible answers: the reasons dogs bark; dogs bark for many reasons; why dogs bark.

   ▸ Do the other sentences in the paragraph give details about why dogs bark? Yes

   ▸ What are some of the details about why dogs bark? They bark when they are scared; they bark when they are playing with people or other dogs; they bark to say they like something.

6. Tell students that when they read nonfiction texts, they should look for main ideas and supporting details.

Words to Know

Before reading "Digging into Jamestown," go over Words to Know with students.

1. Read aloud each word or phrase and have students repeat it.

2. Ask students if they know what each word or phrase means.

   ▸ If students know a word's or phrase's meaning, have them define it and use it in a sentence.

   ▸ If students don't know a word's or phrase's meaning, read them the definition and discuss the word or phrase with them.

archaeologist – a scientist who digs up and studies objects and ruins from long ago
artifact – an object made by people long ago
copper – a reddish-brown metal; it is used for electrical wires and water pipes
dig – a project to find and dig up things from long ago
fort – a strong building that protects people against attack
goods – things that people trade or sell
New World – another name for the part of the world that includes North America, Central America, and South America; used during the time of European exploration
settler – a person who goes to live in a new area

Shared Reading

Book Walk

Prepare students by taking them on a Book Walk of "Digging into Jamestown." Scan the magazine article together and ask students to make predictions about the text.

1. Turn to the **table of contents** in *K¹² World: People and Places of the Past*. Help students find the selection and turn to that page.

2. Point to and read aloud the **title of the article**.

   ▶ What do you think the article is about? Answers will vary.

3. Point to and read aloud any headers, captions, or other features that stand out.

4. Have students look at the **pictures of the article**.

   ▶ What do you think the article might tell us about Jamestown and the people that lived there? Answers will vary.

5. Remind students that thinking about their prior knowledge will help them connect new information they learn to things that they already know. This makes it easier to understand and remember new information. Explain that the next questions will help them open the file drawers in their brain that have their prior knowledge related to the article.

   ▶ What do you already know about some of the first English people to come to America? Answers will vary; if students need prompting, suggest that they think about what they learned about the Pilgrims by reading *The First Thanksgiving*.

   ▶ Did you ever find something old in your home, such an old watch or piece of jewelry? Whom did it belong to first? How did it end up with your family? If students can't think of anything, tell them about a time when you found something, and then tell the story of whom it belonged to and how it was handed down in your family.

Objectives

- Make predictions based on text, illustrations, and/or prior knowledge.
- Activate prior knowledge by previewing text and/or discussing topic.
- Read and respond to texts representing a variety of cultures, time periods, and traditions.

"Digging into Jamestown"

It's time to read aloud the article.

1. Have students sit next to you so that they can see the pictures and words while you read aloud.

2. Tell students to listen carefully to hear the main idea and supporting details of each paragraph.

3. **Read aloud the entire article.** Track with your finger so students can follow along. Emphasize Words to Know as you come to them. If appropriate, use the pictures to help show what each word means.

Check Your Reading

"Digging into Jamestown"
Check students' comprehension of "Digging into Jamestown."

1. Have students retell "Digging into Jamestown" in their own words to develop grammar, vocabulary, comprehension, and fluency skills.

   ▶ **Tell students to use the pictures in the article** to help them with their retelling.

2. Ask students the following questions.

   ▶ Where did the Jamestown settlers come from? England
   ▶ Why did the fort have to be rebuilt? The first one burned down.
   ▶ What do archaeologists do during a dig? They look for things that people from the past left behind.
   ▶ Why didn't the settlers bring much food with them? They hoped to trade with the Native Americans.
   ▶ What kind of bones did the archaeologists find at Jamestown? fish; deer; raccoon   What did finding these bones tell the archaeologists? the kinds of animals the people ate

TIP Tell students that the terms *Indians* and *Native Americans* both refer to the groups of people that were living in the New World when Europeans arrived. Older texts often use *Indians*, while texts written more recently use the term *Native Americans*.

Objectives
- Retell a story using various media.
- Use illustrations to aid understanding of text.
- Identify important details and/or events of a story.
- Identify important details in informational text.

Looking at Language

Verbs That Refer to the Past
Reread "Digging into Jamestown" with a focus on action words that indicate when the story is happening. Gather the sentence strip that you prepared and the Reading Aid on pages LC 151 and 152 in *K¹² Language Arts Activity Book*.

1. Tell students that we can find clues in an article that tell us when the events of the article are happening—now or in the past.

2. Point to the sentence strip. Tell students that as you read aloud the sentence, they should think about when the event discussed is happening—now or in the past.

3. Track with your finger as you read aloud the sentence.

   ▶ When is the event taking place in the sentence "The men start building a fort."—now or in the past? now

4. Tell students that you are going to change the sentence. Then, write *–ed* at the end of the word *start*.

5. Track with your finger as you read aloud the changed sentence.

   ▶ When is the event happening in the sentence "The men start building a fort."—now or in the past? in the past
   ▶ Which word in each sentence helped you figure out when the event is happening? *start; started*

Objectives
- Identify verbs in sentences.
- Recognize the past tense of verbs.
- Recognize and use the past tense of irregular verbs.
- Read aloud grade-level text with appropriate expression, accuracy, and rate.

6. Explain that the clues that tell us when events happen are action words, or **verbs**. We can tell that a sentence is about an event that is happening now because of verbs such as *start*. We were able to make the sentence tell about something that happened in the past by changing *start* to *started*.

7. Explain that sometimes it's easy to figure out which words are the verbs that tell us something happened in the past. We know that if we see a *–d* or *–ed* at the end of the verb, the action is in the past.
   Say: Think about the sentence "The settlers store food for the winter."

   ▸ How would we change this sentence so that it's describing something that happened in the past? *The settlers stored food for the winter.*
   ▸ Which word do we change? *store*   What do we change it to? *stored*

8. Tell students that some verbs are not as easy to recognize because we don't just add a *–d* or *–ed*. We change the way the verb is spelled so it looks like a completely new word.
   Say: Think about the sentence "The settlers come from England."

   ▸ If we want the sentence to describe something that happened in the past, do we say, "The settlers comed from England?" *No*   What's the correct way to change the sentence? *The settlers came from England.*

9. Explain that instead of adding a *–d* to the end of *come*, we change the way the verb is spelled to *came*.

10. Tell students that **they will read aloud the story with you**. You will stop at certain points to discuss the verbs that let us know when the story is happening and how the spelling of some of those verbs changes when referring to the past.

11. Refer to the Reading Aid.

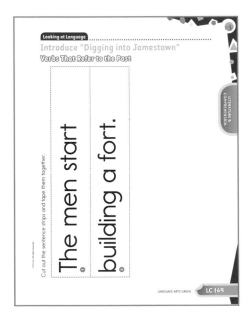

Reading Aid Tear out the Reading Aid for this reading selection. Follow the instructions for folding the page, and then use the page as a guide as you reread the selection with students.

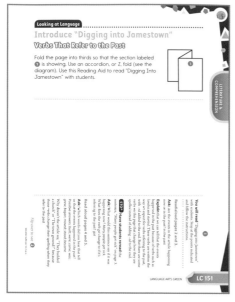
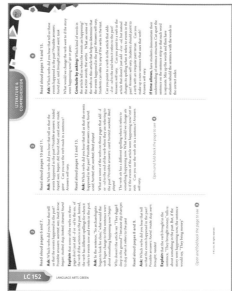

Reading for Meaning

Main Idea and Supporting Details in "Digging into Jamestown"
Check students' understanding of main idea and supporting details.

1. Remind students that the **main idea** of a paragraph is what a paragraph is mostly about. Most of the other sentences in a paragraph give information, or supporting details, about the main idea.

2. Turn to page 3 of the article and **read aloud** the second paragraph on the page.

   ▸ What is the main idea of this paragraph? The settlers had a tough time.
   ▸ Name two details in this paragraph that support the main idea "The settlers had a tough time." Possible answers: The weather was bad; many people got sick; the fort burned down and had to be rebuilt; there wasn't enough food; many people died.

3. Turn to page 4 and **read aloud** the first paragraph on the page.

   ▸ What is the main idea of this paragraph? Possible answers: The settlers started a new town; the settlers started a town called Jamestown; the settlers built a town.
   ▸ Name two details in this paragraph that support the main idea "The settlers started a new town." Possible answers: They built a church; they built places to store food; they built houses.

Objectives
- Identify the main idea.
- Identify the main idea and supporting details.

4. Turn to page 6 and **read aloud** the second paragraph on the page.

   ▸ What is the main idea of this paragraph? Archaeologists looked for clues.
   ▸ Name two details in this paragraph that support the main idea "Archaeologists looked for clues." Possible answers: They studied old papers to learn about where Jamestown might have been; they started a dig; they dug deep in the ground; they looked for things the settlers had left behind.

5. Turn to page 8 and **read aloud** the third paragraph on the page.

   ▸ What is the main idea of this paragraph? Possible answers: The settlers had to bring almost everything with them; the settlers brought lots of things with them; the settlers brought things they needed with them.
   ▸ Name two details in this paragraph that support the main idea "The settlers had to bring almost everything with them." Possible answers: There were no stores in America; they brought money; they brought dishes; they brought tools.

Explore "Digging into Jamestown"

Lesson Overview

[Offline] **45** minutes

Get Ready	Lesson Introduction
	Sequence of Events
	Words to Know
Shared Reading	Book Walk
	"Digging into Jamestown": Sequence
Reading for Meaning	Sequence in "Digging into Jamestown"
Making Connections	What Would Archaeologists Find?
Beyond the Lesson	⊕ OPTIONAL: A Jamestowne Scavenger Hunt

[Materials]

Supplied

- "Digging into Jamestown," *K¹² World: People and Places of the Past*, pp. 2–15
- *K¹² Language Arts Activity Book*, pp. LC 153–155

Keywords

informational text – text written to explain and give information on a topic

sequence – order

Advance Preparation

Preview pages LC 153 and 154 in *K¹² Language Arts Activity Book* to prepare the materials for the Shared Reading.

Big Ideas

- ▸ Previewing text helps readers call up prior knowledge they will need to help them understand what they will be reading.
- ▸ Activating prior knowledge provides a framework for a reader to organize and connect new information to information previously learned; readers that activate prior knowledge before reading are more likely to understand and recall what they read.
- ▸ Comprehension entails an understanding of the organizational patterns of text.
- ▸ Comprehension is facilitated by an understanding of physical presentation (for example, headings, subheads, graphics, and other features).

[Offline] ⏱ minutes

Work **together** with students to complete Get Ready, Shared Reading, Reading for Meaning, Making Connections, and Beyond the Lessons activities.

Get Ready

Lesson Introduction

Prepare students for listening to and discussing "Digging into Jamestown."

1. Tell students that you are going to reread "Digging into Jamestown."

2. Explain that before you read the article, you will get ready by reviewing sequence, or the order of events, in nonfiction text.

Sequence of Events

Explore sequence of events.

1. Remind students that the order in which things happen in a story or article is called the **sequence**. Words and phrases like *first*, *next*, and *soon after* help tell the sequence.

2. Explain that there may be other signals that help us determine the order of events. Authors may use words and phrases such as *last week*, *yesterday*, and *today*. They may also refer to seasons or years, which allows a reader to determine a sequence of events that happen over a long period of time.

3. Have students practice identifying a sequence of events. Tell students to listen for words that tell the order in which things happen and then **read aloud** the following paragraph.

   In February, Petra decided that she would plant daisies in her garden once spring arrived. In the first week of April, Petra bought a packet of daisy seeds. The next week, she planted the seeds. At the beginning of May, Petra started to see little green sprouts.

   Say: This is the sequence: Petra decided to plant daisies. She bought seeds. She planted the seeds. She saw sprouts appear.

4. Reread the sequence and then ask the following questions.

   ▶ What did Petra do first? decided to plant daisies in her garden
   Which word signals the time when Petra decided to plant daisies? *February*
   ▶ What did Petra do next? bought seeds   How do you know that she bought the seeds after she decided to plant daisies? because *the first week of April* comes after February
   ▶ What did Petra do after she bought the seeds? planted them
   ▶ What happened last? Petra saw little green sprouts.

Words to Know

Before reading "Digging into Jamestown," go over Words to Know with students.

1. Read aloud each word or phrase and have students repeat it.

2. Ask students if they know what each word or phrase means.

   ▶ If students know a word's or phrase's meaning, have them define it and use it in a sentence.
   ▶ If students don't know a word's or phrase's meaning, read them the definition and discuss the word or phrase with them.

archaeologist – a scientist who digs up and studies objects and ruins from long ago
artifact – an object made by people long ago
copper – a reddish-brown metal; it is used for electrical wires and water pipes
dig – a project to find and dig up things from long ago
fort – a strong building that protects people against attack
goods – things that people trade or sell
New World – another name for the part of the world that includes North America, Central America, and South America; used during the time of European exploration
settler – a person who goes to live in a new area

Shared Reading

Book Walk

Prepare students by taking them on a Book Walk of "Digging into Jamestown." Scan the magazine article together to revisit the text.

1. Turn to the **table of contents** in *K¹² World: People and Places of the Past*. Help students find the selection and turn to that page.

2. Point to and read aloud the **title of the article**.

3. Have students look at the **pictures of the article**.

4. Tell students that as they look through the article, they should think about what they learned the first time they read the article. The information they learned from the first time they read the article is now stored in the file cabinet in their brain and is part of their **prior knowledge**.

5. Explain that thinking about their prior knowledge about the Jamestown settlement before they reread the article will help them remember even more information when they reread it.

6. Point to the pictures on pages 2 and 3.

   ▶ What was Jamestown? a fort; a settlement   Who used to live there? people from England; settlers

7. Point to the pictures of archaeologists at the dig on pages 6 and 7.

   ▶ What are these archaeologists doing? Possible answers: digging; looking for clues or artifacts; looking for things the settlers left behind

Objectives

- Activate prior knowledge by previewing text and/or discussing topic.
- Use illustrations to aid understanding of text.
- Read and respond to texts representing a variety of cultures, time periods, and traditions.
- Identify sequence of events in informational text.
- Read aloud grade-level text with appropriate expression, accuracy, and rate.

8. Point to the pictures of the men on pages 10 and 11.

   ▸ Who are these men? a settler and an Indian, or Native American
   What are the men doing? trading

   ▸ Why did settlers and Native Americans trade goods? because the settlers
   couldn't bring everything they needed with them

"Digging into Jamestown": Sequence

It's time to reread the article. Tell students that they will reread "Digging into Jamestown" with a focus on the sequence of events. Gather the Reading Aid on pages LC 153 and 154 in *K¹² Language Arts Activity Book*.

1. Remind students that we can tell the order of events in an article when we see words and phrases such as *first*, *next*, *last*, and even *soon after*. We call these **signal words** because they signal when things happen.

2. Explain that time periods such as *yesterday* or *last week*, and even specific years, can also help us figure out the order of events.

3. Tell students that when an article has most of the important events organized in the order in which they happened, we say that the article is organized **in sequence**.

4. Have students sit next to you so that they can see the pictures and words while you read aloud the article.

5. Tell students that **they will read aloud the article with you**. As you read aloud together, you will stop at certain points to discuss clues in the text that indicate the sequence in which things happened.

6. Refer to the Reading Aid.

Reading Aid Tear out the Reading Aid for this reading selection. Follow the instructions for folding the page, and then use the page as a guide as you reread the selection with students.

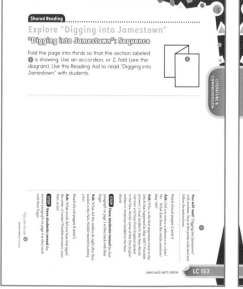
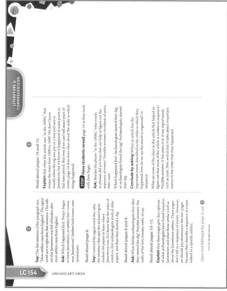

Reading for Meaning

Sequence in "Digging into Jamestown"
Check students' understanding of sequence.

1. Have students retell "Digging into Jamestown" in their own words to develop grammar, vocabulary, comprehension, and fluency skills.

2. Remind them that the order in which things happen in an article is called the **sequence**.

3. Ask the following questions.

   ▶ What happened in the New Word in 1607? A boat with settlers from England landed.
   ▶ What is the first thing the settlers did? built Fort James
   ▶ What are some of the things the settlers built after they built the fort? Possible answers: a new fort (after the old one burned down); Jamestown; a church; places to store food; houses
   ▶ What happened after new settlers started to build towns near Jamestown? People moved to the new towns.
   ▶ What finally became of Jamestown? It became a farm.
   ▶ What happened in Jamestown 300 years after it became a farm? Archaeologists started a dig there.

4. Turn to pages 14 and 15 and point out the illustrations that show the sequence of events related to the tag that archaeologists found.

   ▶ Archaeologists found an old tag from England in the ground at Jamestown. When was the tag put on a box? in the 1600s
   ▶ What was the next thing that happened to the tag? Someone put it on a ship that was going to Jamestown.
   ▶ When did the archaeologists find the box with the tag? hundreds of years later
   ▶ What was the last thing that happened to the tag? Astronauts took it with them into space.

Objectives
- Retell or dramatize a story.
- Identify sequence of events in informational text.
- Use illustrations to aid understanding of text.

Making Connections

What Would Archaeologists Find?

Check students' ability to make inferences about and comparisons between their lives and those of the Jamestown settlers. Turn to page LC 155 in *K¹² Language Arts Activity Book*.

1. Explain that the Jamestown settlers probably never imagined that after hundreds of years, archaeologists would dig up artifacts from their lives.

   ▸ What were some of the artifacts that archaeologists found? Accept any item mentioned in the article.

2. Tell students that you want them to imagine that it's hundreds of years from now and their neighborhood is buried just like Jamestown was. Archaeologists want to learn about how the people in the students' town or city lived. So they start a dig.

   ▸ What kinds of artifacts do you think archaeologists would find if they were to dig up your neighborhood hundreds of years from now? Answers will vary.

3. Look at the chart on the Activity Book page with students. Explain that they will complete the chart to compare artifacts from the Jamestown dig to what archaeologists might find at a future dig in the students' neighborhood.

4. Point to and read aloud the first row heading "Kinds of buildings." Have students dictate the kinds of buildings found at the Jamestown dig; write them in the box under the heading "Jamestown."

5. Have students think about the kinds of building that are in their neighborhood. Have them dictate the kinds of buildings they think archaeologists would find in a dig of their neighborhood. Write them in the box under the heading with the name of their town or city.

   ▸ If students have trouble thinking of buildings, suggest that they look out a window and tell you what buildings they see. Ask them to think about what buildings they see when they are riding around or walking in their neighborhood.

6. Repeat Steps 4 and 5 for the remaining rows.

7. Ask the following questions to encourage discussion about how students' lives are the same as and different from the lives of the Jamestown settlers. Answers to questions may vary.

▶ Would archaeologists find some of the same kinds of buildings in your neighborhood as they found in Jamestown? Yes Which buildings might be the same? Possible answers: houses; churches; shops

▶ Do you think that archaeologists would find a fort if they were to dig up your neighborhood? probably not Why did the Jamestown settlers build a fort? Possible answers: for protection; because they were scared of the Native Americans Why don't you have a fort in your neighborhood like the Jamestown settlers did?

▶ What kinds of tools would archaeologists find in both your neighborhood and Jamestown? Would kind of tools would they find in your neighborhood but not in Jamestown? Why didn't the Jamestown settlers have those tools?

▶ What kinds of foods would be the same? Which would be different?

▶ Why do you think some of the foods would be different? Where did the settlers get most of their food? Where does most of your food come from? the grocery store

▶ Are there any other artifacts that might be the same at the Jamestown dig and a dig of your neighborhood? Are there any artifacts that would be different? Do you think archaeologists would find a well in your neighborhood? Why or why not?

▶ Based on what you've learned, would you rather live in the Jamestown settlement or in your neighborhood? Why?

TIP The amount of time students need to complete this activity will vary. Students need only work for the remaining time of the lesson. If students have more they would like to do, they can complete it at a later time.

Making Connections

Explore "Digging into Jamestown"

What Would Archaeologists Find?

Fill in the chart. Compare artifacts from Jamestown to artifacts that might be found in your neighborhood.

Place	Jamestown	My neighborhood
Kinds of buildings	fort; church; houses; shops	Answers will vary.
Kinds of tools	sewing tools; axes; arrowheads; fish hooks	Answers will vary.
Kinds of food	fish; beans; turtles; oysters; deer; raccoons	Answers will vary.
Other artifacts	wells; armor; coins; pots; jugs; dishes; metal tag	Answers will vary.

LANGUAGE ARTS GREEN   LC 155

Beyond the Lesson

⊕ OPTIONAL: A Jamestowne Scavenger Hunt

This activity is OPTIONAL. It is intended for students who have extra time and would enjoy learning more about the Jamestown archaeological dig. Feel free to skip this activity. Answers to questions may vary.

1. Tell students that the archaeological dig at the site of Jamestown is still happening, and new artifacts are often found at the dig.

2. Explain that you will visit a website with information about the Jamestown settlement and the archaeological dig to find out about recent finds.

3. Go to www.historicjamestowne.org.

4. Help students locate the link at the top of the Web page "The Dig" and click the link.

5. On the Web page "The Dig," point out the question at the top that says, "Where are We Digging Now?" Have students look at the various features on the Web page.

   ▸ What kind of information do you think we will find on this Web page? Possible answers: where the archaeologists are digging; what kinds of things have been found lately

   ▸ Can you find a picture that shows something about the dig? What does the picture show?

6. Direct students' attention to the video on the Web page.

   ▸ What is this? a video   What do you think the video will be about?

7. Have students watch the video.

   ▸ What did you find out from the video?
   ▸ Based on the pictures and video, what kinds of things do you think archaeologists might find while they dig this year?

8. Direct students' attention to the links located to the right of the video. Read the links that say "What Have We Found?" and "Featured Finds."

   ▸ What do you think we'll find if we click on these links? more information about what archaeologists have found at the dig

9. Have students click the link "What Have We Found?"

Objectives

- Distinguish between text and visual text supports.
- Locate information using features of text and electronic media.
- Interpret information provided by features of text and electronic media.
- Recognize and/or respond to visual media.
- Identify forms of mass media.

10. Have students point to the text on this page, and then read it aloud to them.

   ▸ Did you learn something new?

11. Point to the map on the Web page.

   ▸ What is this? a map   What does the map show? the site of the fort and the river

12. Help students further explore the Historic Jamestowne website. Suggest that they return to the Web page "The Dig" and click the link "Featured Finds."

   ▸ What are some of the artifacts listed on the "Featured Finds" Web page? Which of the items did you find most interesting? Why?
   ▸ What other interesting things did you find while exploring the Historic Jamestowne website?

TIP Most of the discussion questions have no right or wrong answers. This is because of the ongoing nature of the archaeological dig at Jamestown. The website will be updated at times, based on new discoveries at the dig.

Introduce "Colonial Kids"

Lesson Overview

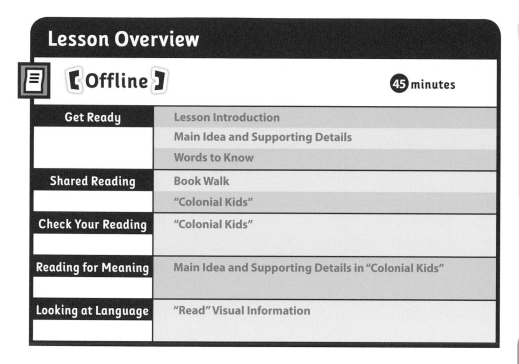

[Offline] · **45** minutes

Get Ready	Lesson Introduction
	Main Idea and Supporting Details
	Words to Know
Shared Reading	Book Walk
	"Colonial Kids"
Check Your Reading	"Colonial Kids"
Reading for Meaning	Main Idea and Supporting Details in "Colonial Kids"
Looking at Language	"Read" Visual Information

Advance Preparation

Before beginning the Shared Reading, read "Colonial Kids" to locate Words to Know in the text. Preview pages LC 157 and 158 in *K¹² Language Arts Activity Book* to prepare the materials for Looking at Language.

Big Ideas

▶ Previewing text helps readers call up prior knowledge they will need to help them understand what they will be reading.

▶ Activating prior knowledge provides a framework for a reader to organize and connect new information to information previously learned; readers that activate prior knowledge before reading are more likely to understand and recall what they read.

▶ Comprehension entails an understanding of the organizational patterns of text.

▶ Comprehension is facilitated by an understanding of physical presentation (for example, headings, subheads, graphics, and other features).

▶ Comprehension is enhanced when information is presented through more than one learning modality; learning modalities are visual (seeing), auditory (hearing), and kinesthetic (touching).

Materials

Supplied

- "Colonial Kids," *K¹² World: People and Places of the Past*, pp. 16–27
- *K¹² Language Arts Activity Book*, pp. LC 157–158

Article Synopsis

Learn interesting facts about children in colonial America, including how they worked and played, the food they ate, and clothes they wore.

Keywords

main idea – the most important idea in a paragraph or text

supporting detail – a detail that gives more information about a main idea

visual text support – a graphic feature that helps a reader better understand text, such as a picture, chart, or map

[Offline] 45 minutes

Work **together** with students to complete Get Ready, Shared Reading, Check Your Reading, Reading for Meaning, and Looking at Language activities.

Get Ready

Lesson Introduction

Prepare students for listening to and discussing "Colonial Kids."

1. Tell students that you are going to read "Colonial Kids," a nonfiction article about some of the first children to settle in the American colonies.

2. Explain that before you read the article, you will get ready by reviewing main idea and supporting details.

Objectives

- Identify the main idea and supporting details.
- Build vocabulary through listening, reading, and discussion.
- Use new vocabulary in written and spoken sentences.
- Increase concept and content vocabulary.

Main Idea and Supporting Details

Review main idea and supporting details.

1. Have students explain main idea and supporting details.

2. If students have trouble recalling, remind them that the **main idea** is what a paragraph is mostly about. Most of the other sentences in a paragraph give information, or **supporting details**, about the main idea.

3. **Read aloud** the following paragraph and then have students practice identifying the main idea and supporting details.

Native Americans used pumpkins for many things. They used long strips of dried pumpkin to make mats. They roasted slices of pumpkin over a fire for food. They put pumpkin flowers in stews. They used dried pumpkin shells as bowls.

   ► What do you think is the main idea of the paragraph? different ways Native Americans used pumpkins
   ► Do the other sentences in the paragraph give details about how Native Americans used pumpkins? Yes
   ► What are some of the supporting details about how Native Americans used pumpkins? They used long strips of dried pumpkin to make mats; they roasted slices of pumpkin over a fire for food; they put pumpkin flowers in stews; they used dried pumpkin shells as bowls.

4. Remind students that when they read nonfiction texts, they should look for main ideas and supporting details.

Words to Know

Before reading "Colonial Kids," go over Words to Know with students.

1. Read aloud each word or phrase and have students repeat it.

2. Ask students if they know what each word or phrase means.

   ▸ If students know a word's or phrase's meaning, have them define it and use it in a sentence.
   ▸ If students don't know a word's or phrase's meaning, read them the definition and discuss the word with them.

canvas – a type of strong, rough cloth
colonial – a word that describes the people or things in a colony
colony – a region ruled by a faraway country
New World – another name for the part of the world that includes North America, Central America, and South America; used during the time of European exploration
Pilgrim – an early English settler in America who came to have religious freedom
poppet – a doll
porridge – a soft food made by boiling grains in milk or water until thick
settler – a person who goes to live in a new area

Shared Reading

Book Walk

Prepare students by taking them on a Book Walk of "Colonial Kids." Scan the magazine article together and ask students to make predictions about the text. Answers to questions may vary.

1. Turn to the **table of contents** in *K¹² World: People and Places of the Past*. Help students find the selection and turn to that page.

2. Point to and read aloud the **title of the article**.

   ▸ What do you think the article is about?

3. Point to and read aloud any headers, captions, or other features that stand out.

4. Have students look at the **pictures of the article**.

5. Remind students that thinking about their **prior knowledge** will help them connect new information they learn to things they already know. This makes it easier to remember new information.

   ▸ What do you think the article might tell us about the children who lived in colonies in the New World?
   ▸ What do you already know about what it was like to be a settler in the New World? Answers may vary; if students need prompting, suggest they think about what they learned about the Pilgrims when they read *The First Thanksgiving* and the early settlers in "Digging into Jamestown."
   ▸ Do you have chores? What are they? What kinds of chores do you think colonial children had to do?
   ▸ What is your favorite game to play? Do you think colonial children played this game? Why or why not?

Objectives

- Make predictions based on text, illustrations, and/or prior knowledge.
- Activate prior knowledge by previewing text and/or discussing topic.
- Read and respond to texts representing a variety of cultures, time periods, and traditions.

"Colonial Kids"

It's time to read aloud the article.

1. Have students sit next to you so that they can see the pictures and words while you read aloud.

2. Tell students to listen carefully to hear the main idea and supporting details of each paragraph.

3. **Read aloud the entire article.** Track with your finger so students can follow along. Emphasize Words to Know as you come to them. If appropriate, use the pictures to help show what each word means.

Check Your Reading

"Colonial Kids"

Check students' comprehension of "Colonial Kids."

1. Have students retell "Colonial Kids" in their own words to develop grammar, vocabulary, comprehension, and fluency skills.

   ▶ Tell students to **use the pictures in the article** to help them with their retelling.

2. Ask students the following questions.

   ▶ What is the name of the pouch a colonial girl would tie around her waist? a pocket
   ▶ What were colonial clothes made out of? wool; canvas
   ▶ When did colonial children eat their main meal of the day? in the middle of the day
   ▶ Who taught colonial children, and where did they teach them? parents; at home
   ▶ Why did colonial children do most of their learning at night? because they had to work during the day
   ▶ What kind of work, or chores, did colonial girls do? work in garden; cook; sew
   ▶ What kind of work, or chores, did colonial boys do? farm work; hunting; fishing; making things from wood

 If students have trouble responding to a question, help them locate the answer in the text or pictures.

Objectives
- Retell or dramatize a story.
- Use illustrations to aid understanding of text.
- Identify important details in informational text.

Reading for Meaning

Main Idea and Supporting Details in "Colonial Kids"
Check students' understanding of main idea and supporting details.

Objectives
- Identify the main idea.
- Identify the main idea and supporting details.

1. Remind students that the **main idea** of a paragraph is what a paragraph is mostly about. Most of the other sentences in a paragraph give information, or **supporting details**, about the main idea.

2. Turn to page 19 and **read aloud** the second paragraph on the page.

   ▸ What is the main idea of this paragraph? Clothes were made of thick, sturdy fabrics.

   ▸ Name two details in this paragraph that support the main idea "Clothes were made of thick, sturdy fabrics." Possible answers: Some were made of warm sheep's wool; others were made of thick canvas.

3. Turn to page 20 and **read aloud** the second paragraph on the page.

   ▸ What is the main idea of this paragraph? Women and girls cooked the food.

   ▸ Name two details in this paragraph that support the main idea "Women and girls cooked the food." Possible answers: They put it in a heavy clay or metal pot; they put the pot over burning coals.

4. Turn to page 25 and **read aloud** the paragraph.

   ▸ What is the main idea of this paragraph? Boys did farm work with their fathers.

   ▸ Name two details in this paragraph that support the main idea "Boys did farm work with their fathers." Possible answers: They planted seeds; they weeded fields; they gathered crops; they helped take care of the farm animals.

5. Turn to page 27 and **read aloud** the third paragraph on the page.

   ▸ What is the main idea of this paragraph? Colonial children played some of the same games that boys and girls play today.

   ▸ Name two details in this paragraph that support the main idea "Colonial children played some of the same games that boys and girls play today." Possible answers: Colonial children played tic-tac-toe; they played checkers; they played hide-and-seek; they played leapfrog.

Looking at Language

"Read" Visual Information

Reread "Colonial Kids" with a focus on visual elements and the additional information they provide in a nonfiction article. Gather the Reading Aid on pages LC 157 and 158 in *K¹² Language Arts Activity Book*.

1. Have students look at the visual elements in "Colonial Kids."

2. Point out the photograph of the ship on page 17 and explain that one feature we often find in nonfiction articles is photographs.

   ▶ What other features does this nonfiction article have besides the words on the page and photographs? Possible answers: a map; illustrations; illustrations with labels

3. Explain that it's often easier for us to remember information when we have visuals that we see, such as illustrations, along with the words we read. Also, visuals that we see in an article may have extra information that gives us a better understanding of the information in an article.

4. Explain that, in addition to reading and figuring out information from the words on the page, in a way, we also "read" and figure out information from visuals.

5. Tell students that **they will aloud the article with you**. As you read aloud together, you will stop at certain points to discuss the visuals and the information they contribute to the article.

6. Refer to the Reading Aid.

Objectives

- Read aloud grade-level text with appropriate expression, accuracy, and rate.
- Distinguish texts that describe events from long ago from those that describe contemporary events.
- Distinguish between text and visual text supports.
- Interpret information from visual text supports: graphs, tables, charts, cartoons.

Reading Aid   Tear out the Reading Aid for this reading selection. Follow the instructions for folding the page, and then use the page as a guide as you reread the selection with students.

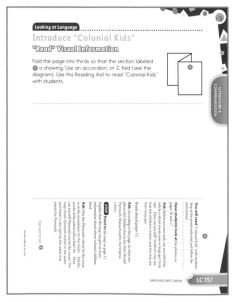

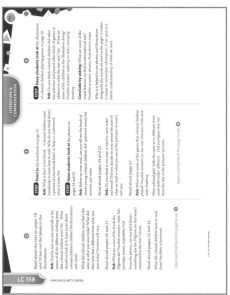

Explore "Colonial Kids"

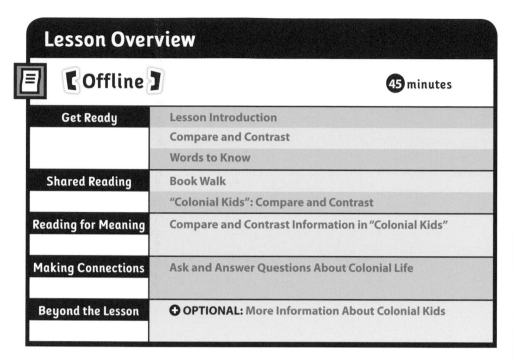

Lesson Overview

[Offline] **45** minutes

Get Ready	Lesson Introduction
	Compare and Contrast
	Words to Know
Shared Reading	Book Walk
	"Colonial Kids": Compare and Contrast
Reading for Meaning	Compare and Contrast Information in "Colonial Kids"
Making Connections	Ask and Answer Questions About Colonial Life
Beyond the Lesson	⊕ OPTIONAL: More Information About Colonial Kids

[Materials]

Supplied

- "Colonial Kids," *K¹² World: People and Places of the Past*, pp. 16–27
- *K¹² Language Arts Activity Book*, pp. LC 159–162

Keywords

compare – to explain how two or more things are alike
contrast – to explain how two or more things are different
prior knowledge – things you already know from past experience

Advance Preparation

Preview pages LC 159 and 160 in *K¹² Language Arts Activity Book* to prepare the materials for the Shared Reading.

Big Ideas

- ► Previewing text helps readers call up prior knowledge they will need to help them understand what they will be reading.
- ► Activating prior knowledge provides a framework for a reader to organize and connect new information to information previously learned; readers that activate prior knowledge before reading are more likely to understand and recall what they read.
- ► Comprehension entails an understanding of the organizational patterns of text.
- ► During shared-reading activities, students learn more about how print works.
- ► Readers must focus on the specific language of a text to aid in interpretation.
- ► Comprehension entails asking and answering questions about the text.

 **45** minutes

Work **together** with students to complete Get Ready, Shared Reading, Reading for Meaning, Making Connections, and Beyond the Lessons activities.

Get Ready

Lesson Introduction

Prepare students for listening to and discussing "Colonial Kids."

1. Tell students that you are going to reread "Colonial Kids."

2. Explain that before you reread the article, you will get ready by discussing how an author can write an article to explain how things are alike and different.

Objectives

- Compare and contrast elements within informational texts.
- Build vocabulary through listening, reading, and discussion.
- Use new vocabulary in written and spoken sentences.
- Increase concept and content vocabulary.

Compare and Contrast

Introduce text organized to compare and contrast.

1. Tell students authors can organize information in an article in different ways.

   ▸ The author might organize information according to the order in which events happen. Texts like this are written **in sequence**.

   ▸ The author might point out problems and then talk about the ways that people are trying to solve those problems. We say that texts like this are organized by **problem and solution**.

2. Explain that most of "Colonial Kids" describes things that were alike and different for colonial boys and girls. We say that texts like these are written to **compare and contrast**.

3. Tell students that when we compare things, we tell how they are alike, or the same. When we contrast things, we tell how things are different.

4. Explain that two things can be alike in some ways and different in other ways. **Say:** I'm going to read a paragraph written to compare and contrast dogs and cats. Then I will tell how they are alike and different according to the paragraph.

   Read aloud: Dogs and cats both have four legs and are covered with fur. Dogs bark, and cats meow. Dogs like to run, and cats like to climb trees. Dogs and cats make good pets.

   Say: Dogs and cats are alike in these ways: They have four legs; they are covered with fur; they make good pets. Dogs and cats are different in these ways: Dogs bark, and cats meow; dogs like to run, and cats like to climb trees.

5. Have students practice identifying how things are alike and different in a paragraph written to compare and contrast. **Read aloud** the following paragraph.

Frankie and Freddie are brothers. They both have red hair, green eyes, and lots of freckles. Frankie's favorite thing to do is play soccer. Freddie's favorite thing to do is paint pictures. Frankie likes scary movies, and Freddie likes funny movies. Both Frankie and Freddie like to eat hot dogs.

   ▶ How are Frankie and Freddie alike? They both have red hair, green eyes, and freckles. They both like hot dogs.
   ▶ How are Frankie and Freddie different? Frankie likes soccer and scary movies; Freddie likes painting and funny movies.

6. Tell students that they should look for words such as *same*, *both*, and *different* when they read a nonfiction article. If they hear those words, there's a good chance that the article is organized to compare and contrast.

Words to Know

Before reading "Colonial Kids," go over Words to Know with students.

1. Read aloud each word or phrase and have students repeat it.

2. Ask students if they know what each word or phrase means.

   ▶ If students know a word's or phrase's meaning, have them define it and use it in a sentence.
   ▶ If students don't know a word's or phrase's meaning, read them the definition and discuss the word with them.

canvas – a type of strong, rough cloth
colonial – a word that describes the people or things in a colony
colony – a region ruled by a faraway country
New World – another name for the part of the world that includes North America, Central America, and South America; used during the time of European exploration
Pilgrim – an early English settler in America who came to have religious freedom
poppet – a doll
porridge – a soft food made by boiling grains in milk or water until thick
settler – a person who goes to live in a new area

Shared Reading

Book Walk

Prepare students by taking them on a Book Walk of "Colonial Kids." Scan the magazine article together to revisit the text.

1. Turn to the selection.

2. Point to and read aloud the **title of the article**.

3. Have students look at the **pictures of the article**.

4. Remind students that thinking about their prior knowledge about colonial children before they reread the article will help them remember even more information when they read it again.

5. Ask the following questions to help students think about what they already know about colonial kids.

   ▶ Who did the cooking in a colonial home? the women and girls   Who did the farm work? the men and boys; the boys and their fathers

   ▶ Who taught colonial children to read? their parents   Why did children do their learning at night? They had to work during the day.

"Colonial Kids": Compare and Contrast

It's time to reread the article. Tell students that they will reread "Colonial Kids" with a focus on how the author wrote the article to compare and contrast. Gather the Reading Aid on pages LC 159 and 160 in *K¹² Language Arts Activity Book*.

1. Remind students that an author can organize the information in an article in different ways. "Colonial Kids" describes things that were the same and different about colonial boys and girls, so it is organized to compare and contrast.

2. Tell students that **they will read aloud the story with you**. As you read aloud together, you will stop at certain points to talk about how the author compares and contrasts information.

3. Have students sit next to you so that they can see the pictures and words while you read aloud the article.

4. Refer to the Reading Aid.

Objectives

- Activate prior knowledge by previewing text and/or discussing topic.
- Read and respond to texts representing a variety of cultures, time periods, and traditions.
- Compare and contrast elements within informational texts.
- Make connections with text: text-to-text, text-to-self, text-to-world.
- Read aloud grade-level text with appropriate expression, accuracy, and rate.

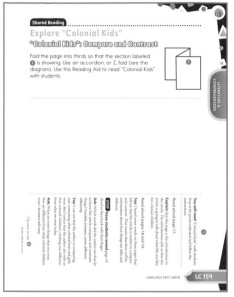
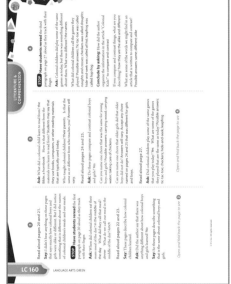

Reading for Meaning

Compare and Contrast Information in "Colonial Kids"

Check students' understanding of text written to compare and contrast.

1. Have students retell "Colonial Kids" in their own words to develop grammar, vocabulary, comprehension, and fluency skills.

2. Remind them that when we compare things, we say how they are alike. When we contrast things, we say how they are different.

3. Turn to pages 18 and 19. Have students look at the illustrations to refresh their memory.

4. Ask the following questions to have students compare and contrast colonial children's clothing.

   ▶ What kind of underclothes did colonial boys and girls wear that was the same? stockings, garters

   ▶ What kind of underclothes did colonial boys and girls wear that was different? Accept any answer that matches what's indicated in the illustrations.

   ▶ What kind of outer clothing did colonial boys and girls wear that was the same? shoes

   ▶ What kind of outer clothing did colonial boys and girls wear that was different? Accept any answer that matches what's indicated in the illustrations.

Objectives

- Retell or dramatize a story.
- Compare and contrast elements within informational texts.

5. Turn to pages 24 and 25. Have students look at the pictures to refresh their memory.

6. Ask the following questions to have students compare and contrast colonial children's chores.

   ▸ Colonial boys and girls had to work. Does this make them alike or different? alike
   ▸ What kind of chores did the young boys and girls do that was the same? carried water and wood; took care of chickens
   ▸ What kind of chores did older girls do? Possible answers: worked in the garden; cooked; took care of younger children; sewed
   ▸ What kind of chores did older boys do? Possible answers: did farm work; planted seeds; weeded fields, gathered crops; took care of farm animals; hunted and fished; made things out of wood

Making Connections

Ask and Answer Questions About Colonial Life

Check students' ability to ask questions about colonial life and identify the relevant text(s) in which they can find the answers. Turn to pages LC 161 and 162 in *K¹² Language Arts Activity Book.*

1. Explain to students that when we have questions about a topic, we may need to look for answers in more than one text.

2. Tell students that they have now learned a lot about colonial life by reading several texts on the topic. Because all the texts in this unit are about colonial life, the answer to questions students have could be in one of those texts or in more than one of those texts.

3. **Say:** If a reader has questions about a topic, it's helpful for that person to think about the most likely place to find the answer. For example, if I have questions about why the Pilgrims came to the New World, the best place to find the answer would probably be *The First Thanksgiving.*

   ▸ If you have questions about the kinds of games that colonial children played, what text from this unit would be the best place to find answers? the article "Colonial Kids"

4. Tell students that they will practice thinking of questions and figuring out the most likely text(s) that would have the answers.

5. Look at the chart with students and explain that they will think of a question related to each category listed in the first column. Then they will tell you which text or texts they think would have the answer to that question.

6. Point to and read aloud the first row heading "Name of settlement." Explain that the chart already has a question for that category and lists the texts that would have the answer. This is to help students understand how to complete the chart.

Objectives

- Generate questions and seek information from multiple sources to answer questions.
- Identify relevant sources of information.
- Demonstrate understanding through graphic organizers.

7. Have students tell you the names of the settlements they read about in this unit. Record what they dictate in the first row under the column "Answer."

   ▸ If students are unsure of the answer, refer back to the texts listed for that row, and help students find the answer.

8. Point to and read aloud the second row heading "Food" and the question for the category. Have students tell you the titles of texts from the unit that have information on what colonists ate and some examples of food items given in those texts.

   ▸ If students are unsure of the answer, refer back to the texts and help students find examples of the kinds of foods the colonists ate.

9. Point to and read aloud the third row heading "Clothes." Have students tell you a question for that category, the texts that have information that could answer the question, and then an answer to the question. Record the information students dictate in the appropriate boxes.

10. Repeat Step 9 until the chart is complete.

 Due to the length of time of the lesson, it is recommended that students dictate answers for this activity and not write on their own. The amount of time students need to complete this activity will vary. Students need only work for the remaining time of the lesson.

Reward: Add a sticker for this unit on the My Accomplishments chart to mark successful completion of the unit.

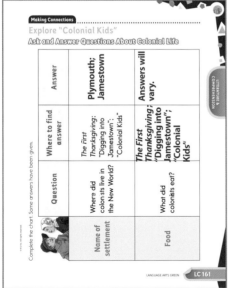

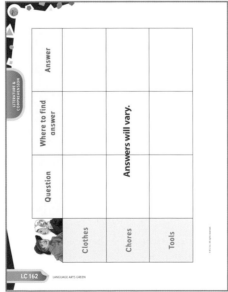

Beyond the Lesson

⊕ OPTIONAL: More Information About Colonial Kids

This activity is OPTIONAL. It is intended for students who have extra time and would enjoy learning more about children living in American during colonial times. Feel free to skip this activity.

1. Go to a library and look for one of the following books about colonial children.

   ▸ *Colonial Kids: An Activity Guide to Life in the New World* by Laurie Carlson
   ▸ *. . . If You Sailed on the Mayflower in 1620* by Ann McGovern and Anna DiVito
   ▸ *Samuel Eaton's Day: A Day in the Life of a Pilgrim Boy* by Kate Waters and Russ Kendall
   ▸ *Sarah Morton's Day: A Day in the Life of a Pilgrim Girl* by Kate Waters and Russ Kendall

2. Lead a Book Walk and then read aloud the book.

3. Have students tell how the book and the article "Colonial Kids" are alike and different.

4. Ask students what new things they learned about colonial children.

5. Ask them to tell which selection is their favorite and why.

Objectives

- Make connections with text: text-to-text; text-to-self; text-to-world.
- Compare and contrast two texts on the same topic.

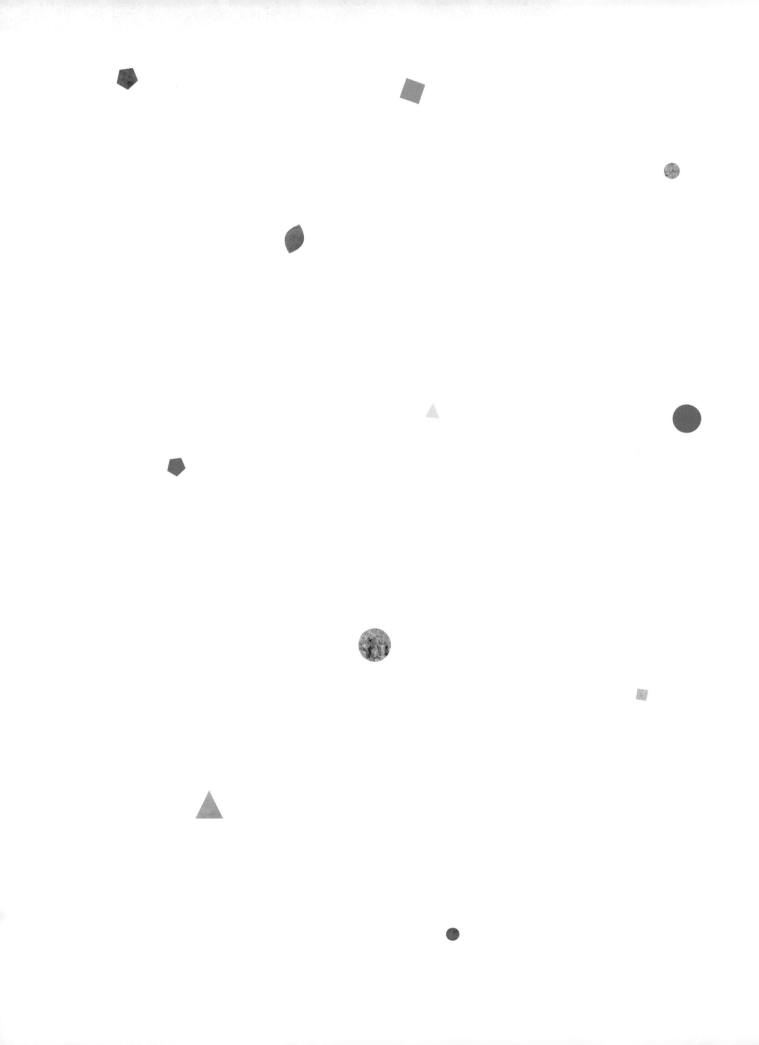

Family Fun

Unit Focus

In this unit, students will hear entertaining stories about families. This unit follows the shared-reading instructional approach (see the instructional approaches to reading in the introductory lesson for this program). In this unit, students will

▶ Explore the types of connections readers make to text.
▶ Learn strategies that can help to clear up confusion while reading a story.
▶ Explore characteristics of fiction stories.
▶ Explore how punctuation clues and knowledge of characters influence our expression when we read stories aloud.
▶ Review the story structure elements of character, setting, problem and solution.
▶ Practice making inferences.
▶ Compare and contrast characters in stories.
▶ Practice retelling a story in order to check their understanding.

Unit Plan

【Offline】

Lesson 1	Explore *Here Comes the Parade!* (A)	45 minutes a day
Lesson 2	Explore *Here Comes the Parade!* (B)	
Lesson 3	Explore *Here Comes the Parade!* (C)	
Lesson 4	Explore *Tales of Amanda Pig* (A)	
Lesson 5	Explore *Tales of Amanda Pig* (B)	
Lesson 6	Explore *Tales of Amanda Pig* (C)	
Lesson 7	Your Choice	

Explore *Here Comes the Parade!* (A)

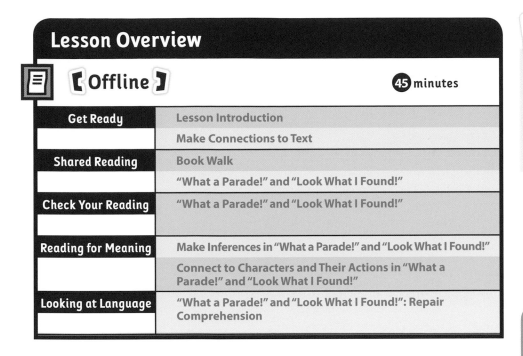

Lesson Overview

[Offline]   45 minutes

Get Ready	Lesson Introduction
	Make Connections to Text
Shared Reading	Book Walk
	"What a Parade!" and "Look What I Found!"
Check Your Reading	"What a Parade!" and "Look What I Found!"
Reading for Meaning	Make Inferences in "What a Parade!" and "Look What I Found!"
	Connect to Characters and Their Actions in "What a Parade!" and "Look What I Found!"
Looking at Language	"What a Parade!" and "Look What I Found!": Repair Comprehension

Materials

Supplied

- *Here Comes the Parade!* by Tony and Laura Dungy
- *K¹² Language Arts Activity Book*, pp. LC 163–164

Story Synopsis

Justin, Jordan, and Jade are enjoying a parade with Mom, Dad, Jason, and Jalen when Justin finds a wallet on the ground.

Keywords

character – a person or animal in a story

connection – a link readers make between themselves, information in text, and the world around them

problem – an issue a character must solve in a story

setting – when and where a story takes place

solution – how a character solves a problem in a story

Advance Preparation

Preview pages LC 163 and 164 in *K¹² Language Arts Activity Book* to prepare the materials for Looking at Language.

Big Ideas

- Comprehension is facilitated when readers connect new information to information previously learned.
- An awareness of story structure elements (setting, characters, plot) provides readers a foundation for constructing meaning when reading new stories and writing their own stories.
- Comprehension requires the reader to self-monitor understanding.
- Verbalizing your thoughts while modeling a reading strategy allows students to see what goes on inside the head of an effective reader; it makes visible the normally hidden process of comprehending text.
- Comprehension strategies can be taught through explicit instruction.
- Shared reading allows students to observe and practice the reading behaviors of proficient readers.

Offline 45 minutes

Work **together** with students to complete Get Ready, Shared Reading, Check Your Reading, Reading for Meaning, and Looking at Language activities.

Get Ready

Lesson Introduction

Prepare students for listening to and discussing "What a Parade!" and "Look What I Found!" in *Here Comes the Parade!*

1. Tell students that you are going to read "What a Parade!" and "Look What I Found!" in *Here Comes the Parade!*

2. Explain that before you read the story you will get ready by discussing how we can make connections to the characters and events that happen in a story.

Objectives

- Make connections with text: text-to-text, text-to-self, text-to-world.

Make Connections to Text

Explore making connections to text with students.

1. Tell students that good readers think about what a story reminds them of as they're reading. This is called **making a connection**. As they read, good readers make connections to things they have learned before, their prior knowledge, and their personal experiences.

2. Explain that readers who make connections to a story while they read are better able to understand and remember what they read. This is because these readers make reading a more active experience.

   ▸ When readers think, "This story reminds me of a time when I . . . " or "This character reminds me of . . . ," they are connecting the text to themselves and their personal experiences.
   ▸ When readers think, "This story reminds me of another story I've read," they are connecting the text to another text.
   ▸ When readers think, "This story reminds me of something I heard about," they are connecting to the text to the world around them.

3. Have students practice connecting to text. **Read aloud** the following short story.

   Christa always liked it when Aunt Georgia came to visit. They would pack a lunch and have a picnic at the park. After lunch, Christa would climb into a swing and Aunt Georgia would push her until she was flying high in the air. Then, they would race all the way home to bake a batch of Christa's favorite cookies.

4. Ask the following questions. Answers to questions may vary.

   ▸ What does this story remind you of?
   ▸ Is the character Christa anything like you?
   ▸ Have you ever met anyone like Christa?
   ▸ Does the story make you think of your favorite aunt or someone else in your family? How are they alike?

▸ What parts in the story remind you of something that has happened in your own life?

▸ What does this story remind you of in the real world?

Shared Reading

Book Walk

Prepare students for reading by taking them on a Book Walk of *Here Comes the Parade!* Scan the stories "What a Parade!" and "Look What I Found!" together and ask students to make predictions about the story. Answers to questions may vary.

1. Have students look at the picture on the cover. Point to and read aloud the **book title**.

   ▸ What do you think the book will be about?

2. Read aloud the **names of the author and the illustrator**.

3. Read aloud the story titles on the **contents** page. Explain to students that in this lesson, they will read "What a Parade!" and "Look What I Found!"

4. Have students look at the **pictures in "What a Parade!" and "Look What I Found!"**

   ▸ Have you ever been in a situation in which somebody kept bothering you while you were trying to do something? What happened?

   ▸ Do you ever make up stories? What kinds of stories do you like to tell?

Objectives

- Activate prior knowledge by previewing text and/or discussing topic.
- Make predictions based on text, illustrations, and/or prior knowledge.
- Read and listen to a variety of texts for information and pleasure independently or as part of a group.

"What a Parade!" and "Look What I Found!"

It's time to read aloud "What a Parade!" and "Look What I Found!"

1. Have students sit next to you so that they can see the pictures and words while you read aloud.

2. Tell students to listen for parts of the story that remind them of things in their lives or other stories they know.

3. **Read aloud the entire story.** Track with your finger so students can follow along.

Check Your Reading

"What a Parade!" and "Look What I Found!"
Check students' comprehension of "What a Parade!" and "Look What I Found!"

1. Have students retell "What a Parade!" and "Look What I Found!" in their own words to develop grammar, vocabulary, comprehension, and fluency skills.

2. Ask students the following questions.

   ▸ Where does the story take place? Possible answers: outside, in a town, at a parade

   ▸ Who are the characters in the story? Justin, Jordan, Jade; students may include Mom, Dad, Jalen, and Jason

   ▸ What was Justin worried about seeing at the parade? clowns

   ▸ What did Justin see on the ground? a wallet

   ▸ What was in the wallet? a ton of money

TIP If students have trouble responding to a question, help them locate the answer in the text or pictures.

Objectives
- Retell or dramatize a story.
- Identify setting.
- Identify character(s).
- Answer questions requiring literal recall of details.

Reading for Meaning

Connect to Characters and Their Actions in "What a Parade!" and "Look What I Found!"
Check students' ability to make connections to text.

1. Remind students that making connections to the text helps readers better understand and remember a story.

2. Ask the following questions. Answers to questions may vary.

   ▸ Does anything in this story remind you of anything in your own life?

   ▸ Justin has two brothers and two sisters. Do they remind you of anybody you know?

   ▸ Have you ever been to a parade with family or friends?

   ▸ Jordan and Jade are excited for the parade. Justin is nervous. Have you ever felt like Jordan and Jade? When? Have you ever felt like Justin? When?

   ▸ Does Justin, Jordan, or Jade remind you of anyone you know? Who? Why do these characters remind you of this person?

   ▸ Have you ever found something that didn't belong to you? What did you find? What did you do with it?

Objectives
- Make connections with text: text-to-text, text-to-self, text-to-world.
- Make inferences based on text and/or prior knowledge.

Make Inferences in "What a Parade!" and "Look What I Found!"
Explore making inferences based on text and pictures with students.

1. Remind students that readers can make inferences, or guesses, about things that the author doesn't state directly in the text.

   ▶ What kinds of information, or clues, do we use to make inferences? **clues in the text and pictures; information from a reader's personal experience**

2. If students don't recall the type of information that a reader uses to make inferences, tell them that inferences are guesses. However, inferences are not wild guesses. They are logical guesses based on the following information:

   ▶ The words and pictures of a story
   ▶ The reader's prior knowledge learned from past experience

3. Ask the following questions to help students practice making inferences. Answers to questions may vary.

   ▶ Why were Justin, Jade, and Jordan standing a few rows in front of their parents at the parade?
   ▶ Why were Jalen and Jason with their parents?
   ▶ Which brother is older: Jordan or Justin?
   ▶ Why was Justin looking down at the ground instead of up at the parade?
   ▶ How do Justin, Jade, and Jordan feel about finding a wallet?

Looking at Language

"What a Parade!" and "Look What I Found!": Repair Comprehension
It's time to reread the story. Tell students that they will reread "What a Parade!" and "Look What I Found!" in *Here Comes the Parade!* with a focus on what to do if they don't understand which character is speaking aloud. Gather the Reading Aid on pages LC 163 and 164 in *K¹² Language Arts Activity Book.*

1. Remind students that sometimes when we're reading, we realize that we're confused because we don't understand something in the story. In "What a Parade!" and "Look What I Found!" all the characters often speak. It's easy to lose track of who is speaking.

2. Explain that there are strategies we can use to help us if we're confused about who is speaking.

   ▶ Sometimes all we need to do is go back and reread a part of the story more slowly and carefully.
   ▶ Sometimes it's helpful to ask ourselves a question about which character is speaking.
   ▶ Other times it's helpful to think about our prior knowledge. If we can connect something we already know about the characters to something in the story, it can help us figure out who is speaking.

3. Tell students that when good readers do these things, you can't see what they're

Objectives

- Repair comprehension using strategies: reread, use prior knowledge, self-question.
- Recognize quotations in dialogue.
- Demonstrate understanding by thinking aloud.
- Demonstrate one-to-one correspondence (voice-to-print).
- Read aloud grade-level text with appropriate expression, accuracy, and rate.

doing, because it's happening in their head.

4. Explain that you will show students how to use these strategies by saying your thoughts out loud. That way, they can learn what goes on in the head of a good reader.

5. Have students sit next to you so that they can see the pictures and words while you read aloud.

6. Tell students that **they will read aloud the story with you**. As you read aloud together, you will stop at certain points to show students how to use strategies to help them be clear about which character is speaking.

7. Refer to the Reading Aid.

Reading Aid Tear out the Reading Aid for this reading selection. Follow the instructions for folding the page, and then use the page as a guide as you reread the selection with students.

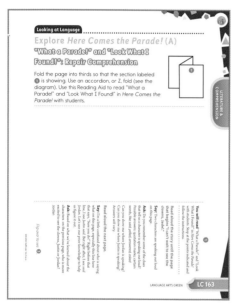
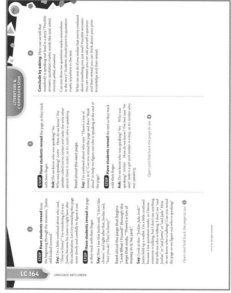

Explore *Here Comes the Parade!* (B)

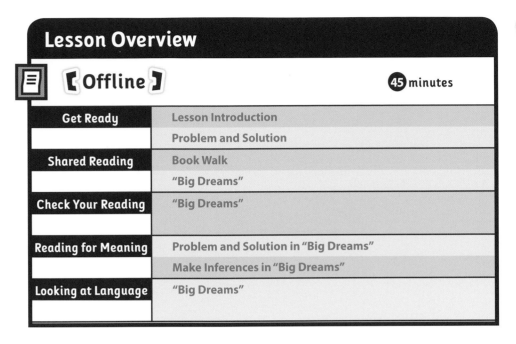

Lesson Overview

[Offline]   **45** minutes

Get Ready	Lesson Introduction
	Problem and Solution
Shared Reading	Book Walk
	"Big Dreams"
Check Your Reading	"Big Dreams"
Reading for Meaning	Problem and Solution in "Big Dreams"
	Make Inferences in "Big Dreams"
Looking at Language	"Big Dreams"

Materials

Supplied

- *Here Comes the Parade!* by Tony and Lauren Dungy
- *K¹² Language Arts Activity Book*, pp. LC 165–166

Also Needed

- whiteboard (optional)

Story Synopsis

In "Big Dreams," Justin, Jordan, and Jade talk about what they could do with all the money inside the wallet Justin found.

Advance Preparation

Preview pages LC 165 and 166 in *K¹² Language Arts Activity Book* to prepare the materials for Looking at Language.

Big Ideas

- ▸ Exposing readers to a wide variety of genres provides them with a wide range of background knowledge and increases their vocabulary.
- ▸ Good readers use prior knowledge and text clues to infer, or draw conclusions about, what is implied but not directly stated in text.
- ▸ Repeated rereading leads to increased fluency.
- ▸ During shared-reading activities, students learn more about how print works.
- ▸ Shared reading allows students to observe and practice the reading behaviors of proficient readers.

Keywords

character – a person or animal in a story

infer – to use clues and what you already know to make a guess

inference – a guess you make using the clues in a text and what you already know

problem – an issue a character must solve in a story

setting – when and where a story takes place

solution – how a character solves a problem in a story

[Offline] **45** minutes

Work **together** with students to complete Get Ready, Shared Reading, Check Your Reading, Reading for Meaning, and Looking at Language activities.

Get Ready ···

Lesson Introduction

Prepare students for listening to and discussing "Big Dreams" in *Here Comes the Parade!*

1. Tell students that you are going to read "Big Dreams" in *Here Comes the Parade!*

2. Explain that before you read the story you will get ready by discussing characters, setting, and how characters solve problems.

Objectives
- Identify character(s).
- Describe story structure elements—problem and solution.

Problem and Solution

Review character, setting, and problem and solution with students to reinforce knowledge of story structure elements.

1. Ask students to explain what characters and setting are.

2. If students have trouble explaining these story structure elements, remind them that

   ▸ A **character** is a person or animal in a story.
   ▸ The **setting** is where and when a story takes place.

3. Remind students that an important part of a story is **problem and solution**. Characters in a story usually have a problem that they try to solve throughout the story.

4. Have students think about "What a Parade!" and "Look What I Found!" in *Here Comes the Parade!*

   ▸ Who are the characters in "What a Parade!" and "Look What I Found!"? Justin, Jordan, and Jade. Students may include Mom, Dad, Jalen, and Jason.
   ▸ Justin wants to watch the parade, but he has a problem. What is his problem? Justin is worried about seeing the clowns.

Shared Reading

Book Walk

Prepare students for reading by taking them on a Book Walk of *Here Comes the Parade!* Scan the story "Big Dreams" together and ask students to make predictions about the story.

1. Have students look at the picture on the cover. Point to and read aloud the **book title**.

2. Read aloud the names of the **author** and the **illustrator**.

3. Read aloud the story titles on the Contents page. Explain to students that in this lesson, they will read "Big Dreams."

4. Have students look at the **look at the pictures in "Big Dreams."**

   ▸ What do you think might happen in this chapter? Answers may vary.

Objectives

- Activate prior knowledge by previewing text and/or discussing topic.
- Make predictions based on text, illustrations, and/or prior knowledge.
- Read and listen to a variety of texts for information and pleasure independently or as part of a group.

"Big Dreams"

It's time to read the story aloud.

1. Have students sit next to you so that they can see the pictures and words while you read aloud.

2. Tell students to listen carefully for things in the story that are fantasy and could not happen in real life.

3. **Read aloud the entire story.** Track with your finger so students can follow along.

Check Your Reading

"Big Dreams"

Check students' comprehension of "Big Dreams."

1. Have students retell "Big Dreams" in their own words to develop grammar, vocabulary, comprehension, and fluency skills.

2. Ask students the following questions.

   ▸ Who asks to keep the wallet?" Justin
   ▸ What does Justin want to do with the money? buy a new football and a new Ducks shirt
   ▸ What does Jade think about buying with the money? a new bracelet and nail polish
   ▸ What was Jordan thinking about using the money for? a new phone or some new games
   ▸ What does Justin think they should do with the wallet? keep it
   ▸ What does Jordan think they should do with the wallet? try and find the owner of the wallet
   ▸ What does Jade think they should do with the wallet? ask their Mom and Dad for help

Objectives

- Retell or dramatize a story.
- Answer questions requiring literal recall of details.

TIP If students have trouble responding to a question, help them locate the answer in the text or pictures.

Reading for Meaning

Problem and Solution in "Big Dreams"

Explore the story structure element of problem and solution with students.

1. Remind students that characters in stories often have problems that they try to solve.

2. Ask the following questions.

   ▸ What problem do Justin, Jordan, and Jade have in "Big Dreams"? They can't decide what to do with the wallet.

   ▸ Why don't they return the wallet? They don't know who it belongs to; they each have things they'd like to buy with the money in the wallet.

   ▸ How do they decide to solve their problem? They ask Mom and Dad for help.

Objectives

- Describe story structure elements—problem and solution.
- Make inferences based on text and/or prior knowledge.
- Use illustrations to aid understanding of text.
- Describe character(s).

Make Inferences in "Big Dreams"

Explore making inferences based on text and pictures with students.

1. Remind students that readers can make inferences, or guesses, about things that the author doesn't state directly in the text.

   ▸ What kinds of information, or clues, do we use to make inferences? clues in the text and pictures; information from a reader's personal experience

2. Ask the following questions to help students practice making inferences. Answers to questions may vary.

   ▸ Who do you think the wallet belongs to, a grown-up or a kid? Why?

   ▸ Jordan thinks about what he would do with the money, but he doesn't say it to his brother and sister. Why?

   ▸ Why does Jordan think they should try and find the owner of the wallet?

Looking at Language

"Big Dreams": Read with Expression

It's time to reread the story. Tell students that they will reread "Big Dreams" in *Here Comes the Parade!* with a focus on reading with expression. Gather the Reading Aid on pages LC 165 and 166 in *K¹² Language Arts Activity Book.*

1. Tell students that there are many clues in a story that help determine how to read with expression.

Objectives

- Identify sentences that are exclamations.
- Recall uses of capital letters.
- Recognize questions.
- Read aloud grade-level text with appropriate expression, accuracy, and rate.

2. Point to the exclamation mark at the end of the book title, *Here Comes the Parade!*

   ▶ What is this punctuation mark called? an exclamation mark
   ▶ How do we read a sentence that ends with an exclamation mark? Possible answers: with stress; with a lot of expression; with excitement

3. Write the question "Can I sit with you?" on a whiteboard or sheet of paper. Point to the question mark.

   ▶ What is this punctuation mark called? a question mark

4. Read the question aloud. Emphasize the rise in your voice at the end of the question.

   ▶ What did you notice about how I read the question? Guide students to recognize that your voice rises at the end of a question.

5. Tell students that in addition to punctuation marks, our knowledge of the characters and story events can influence our expression.

   ▶ When Justin says, "I don't think I like clowns," how do you think Justin is feeling? Possible answers: nervous, worried, scared If Justin is feeling nervous about seeing clowns in the parade, how do you think he would say, "I don't think I like clowns"? Answers will vary.

6. Tell students that **they will read aloud the story with you**. As you read aloud together, you will stop at certain points to discuss things in the text that influence how we read with expression.

7. Refer to the Reading Aid.

Reading Aid Tear out the Reading Aid for this reading selection. Follow the instructions for folding the page, and then use the page as a guide as you reread the selection with students.

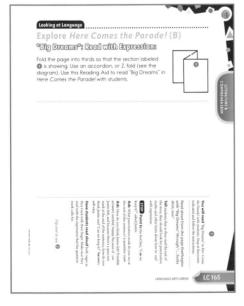
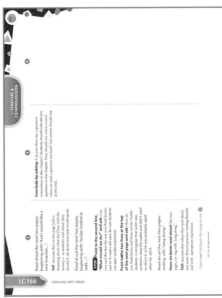

Explore *Here Comes the Parade!* (C)

Lesson Overview

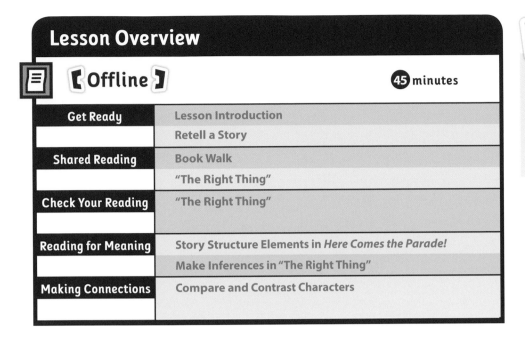

[Offline]   **45** minutes

Get Ready	Lesson Introduction
	Retell a Story
Shared Reading	Book Walk
	"The Right Thing"
Check Your Reading	"The Right Thing"
Reading for Meaning	Story Structure Elements in *Here Comes the Parade!*
	Make Inferences in "The Right Thing"
Making Connections	Compare and Contrast Characters

Big Ideas

▶ An awareness of story structure elements (setting, characters, plot) provides readers a foundation for constructing meaning when reading new stories and writing their own stories.

▶ Good readers use prior knowledge and text clues to infer, or draw conclusions about, what is implied but not directly stated in text.

▶ During shared-reading activities, students learn more about how print works.

Materials

Supplied

- *Here Comes the Parade!* by Tony and Lauren Dungy
- *K¹² Language Arts Activity Book*, p. LC 167

Story Synopses

Justin, Jordan, and Jade ask Mom and Dad for help. On their way to the Lost-and-Found, Justin bumps into a sad clown who has lost his wallet. When they realize the wallet Justin found is the clown's wallet, the clown offers a reward. Mom tells the clown it was the right thing to do, so the clown gives them balloons instead. As a result, Justin is no longer nervous about clowns. Now, they're his favorite part of the parade.

Keywords

compare – to explain how two or more things are alike

contrast – to explain how two or more things are different

graphic organizer – a visual tool used to show relationships between key concepts; formats include webs, diagrams, and charts

[Offline] 45 minutes

Work **together** with students to complete Get Ready, Shared Reading, Check Your Reading, Reading for Meaning, and Making Connections activities.

Get Ready

Lesson Introduction

Prepare students for listening to and discussing "The Right Thing" in *Here Comes the Parade!*

1. Tell students that you are going to read "The Right Thing" in *Here Comes the Parade!*

2. Explain that before you read this story, you will get ready by discussing how retelling a story can help readers check that they understand what they read.

Objectives
- Retell or dramatize a story.
- Retell a story naming plot, setting, character(s), problem, and solution.

Retell a Story

Revisit how to retell a story.

1. Remind students that **retelling means using your own words to tell a story** that you have listened to or read. Retelling a story is a good way to check that you understand what you have read.

2. Explain that when we retell a story, it is important to mention the characters; the setting; how characters solve problems; and important events that happen in the beginning, middle, and end of the story.

3. Have students revisit the pictures in "What a Parade," "Look What I Found!," and "Big Dreams."

4. Ask students to retell the story of the first three chapters of *Here Comes the Parade!* Remind them to mention all the things in Step 2. Be sure students retell events from the beginning, middle and end of the story in the correct order. Have students use the pictures from the story as a guide.

Possible answer: At the beginning of the story, Justin, Jordan, and Jade are excited for the parade to start. They stand a few rows ahead of their mom, dad, and baby brother and sister, Jason and Jalen. Justin says he's nervous about seeing the clowns.

In the next chapter, Justin is looking down at the ground instead of up at the parade because he's nervous about the clowns. He sees a wallet on the ground and picks it up. It is a funny looking wallet, with polka dots and stripes. He shows Jordan and Jade. They see it is full of money.

In the next chapter, Justin and Jalen talk about what they would do with all of the money. Jordan thinks about what he would do, but decides that they can't keep the wallet and that they should ask Mom and Dad for help trying to find the owner.

5. If students make errors in the order of events, or overlook important events, help them look back at the story to determine the sequence of the important events in the story.

Shared Reading

Book Walk

Prepare students for reading by taking them on a Book Walk of *Here Comes the Parade!* Scan the story "The Right Thing" together and ask students to make predictions about the stories.

1. Have students look at the picture on the cover. Point to and read aloud the **book title**.

2. Read aloud the names of the **author** and the **illustrator**.

3. **Have students read aloud** the story titles on the Contents page. Explain to students that in this lesson, they will read "The Right Thing."

4. Have students **look at the pictures in "The Right Thing."**

   ▸ What do you think might happen in in this chapter? Answers will vary.

"The Right Thing"

It's time to read aloud "The Right Thing."

1. Have students sit next to you so that they can see the pictures and words while you read aloud.

2. Tell students to listen for characters, setting, and how the characters solve their problems.

3. Tell students that **they will read aloud the stories with you**. As you read aloud together, you will stop at certain points to review punctuation and text features that influence our expression when we read aloud.

4. **Read aloud "The Right Thing."** Track with your finger so students can follow along. Encourage students to read with expression.

5. Stop at the page that begins "Justin gasped." Ask the following questions.
   ▸ Is the next sentence ("What does it look like?") asking something or telling something? asking something   What do we call a sentence that asks something? a question
   ▸ How should your voice sound when you read a question out loud? It should rise at the end.
   ▸ Turn the page. What do you notice about the sentence on this page? It ends with an exclamation point.   Look at the next page. What do you see there? more exclamation points   How do you think Justin says those sentences? He shouts them; he's excited.

Objectives

- Make predictions based on text, illustrations, and/or prior knowledge.
- Activate prior knowledge by previewing text and/or discussing topic.
- Read and listen to a variety of texts for information and pleasure independently or as part of a group.
- Read aloud grade-level text with appropriate expression, accuracy, and rate.
- Recognize questions.
- Recall uses of capital letters..

Check Your Reading

"The Right Thing"

Check students' comprehension of "The Right Thing."

1. Have students retell "The Right Thing" in their own words to develop grammar, vocabulary, comprehension, and fluency skills.

2. Ask students the following questions to check their comprehension of "The Right Thing."

   ▶ What is the problem Justin, Jordan, and Jade have? They found a wallet full of money and they aren't sure what to do with it.

   ▶ How do they solve their problem? They ask Mom and Dad for help. Dad shows them a Lost and Found booth.

   ▶ Who does Justin run into on the way to Lost and Found? a clown

   ▶ Why is the clown sad? He lost his wallet.

   ▶ Why did the clown want to reward Justin? Justin was honest and returned the wallet with all of the money in it.

   ▶ What did Mom say about the reward money? They didn't need it; doing the right thing made Mom and Dad proud, and that was all the reward they needed.

   ▶ What did the clown give Justin, Jordan, and Jade instead? balloons

   ▶ How does Justin feel about clowns at the end of the story? Clowns are his favorite part of the parade now.

TIP If students have trouble responding to a question, help them locate the answer in the text or pictures.

Objectives

- Retell or dramatize a story.
- Answer questions requiring literal recall of details
- Identify setting.
- Identify character(s).
- Identify the narrator of a text.

Reading for Meaning

Story Structure Elements in *Here Comes the Parade!*

Check students' ability to identify setting, characters, and problem and solution.

1. Remind students that story characters often have a problem that they try to solve.

2. Ask the following questions.

   ▸ What is the setting of *Here Comes the Parade!*? a city street; a parade
   ▸ Who are the characters in *Here Comes the Parade!*? Justin, Jordan, Jade, Mom, Dad, Jalen, Jason, and a clown
   ▸ Justin has two problems in this story. What is the problem he has in "What a Parade!"? Justin is nervous about the clowns in the parade.
   ▸ What is the second problem Justin has? He found a wallet full of money.
   ▸ Does he solve his problems? Yes   How do you know? At the end of the story, the wallet has been returned to the owner and Justin thinks clowns are the best part of the parade.

Objectives
- Identify setting.
- Identify character(s).
- Describe story structure elements—problem and solution.
- Make connections with text: text-to-text, text-to-self, text-to-world.
- Make inferences based on evidence from the text and/ or prior knowledge.

Make Inferences in "The Right Thing"

Explore making inferences based on text and pictures with students.

1. Remind students that they can infer things an author doesn't say directly by thinking about clues in the text and pictures. Ask the following questions.

2. Look at the picture on the page that begins with, "Justin gasped."

   ▸ What is Justin thinking about while the clown is talking? Possible answers: He's thinking about the wallet he found; he's thinking about the money in the wallet.
   ▸ Turn the page. Look at the pictures. How does Justin feel about finding the clown? Answers will vary; suggest he is happy to find the clown, because he's smiling in the picture.

3. Look at the pictures on the page that begins with, "Dad looked in the wallet."

   ▸ Why do you think Dad looked in the wallet? He thought there would be a photo of the wallet's owner in it.
   ▸ Look at the next page. How does the clown feel? Answers will vary; suggest he is grateful that he found the wallet and wants Justin to know it, because he offers him some money as a reward.

4. Tell students to look at the picture on the last page of the story.

   ▸ What can you tell by looking at the expressions on Jordan, Jade, and Justin's face? They like each other, they had a fun time at the parade.   How can you tell? They look happy; they're laughing.

Making Connections

Compare and Contrast Characters

Check students' understanding of how the characters are alike and different in *Here Comes the Parade!* Turn to page LC 167 in *K¹² Language Arts Activity Book*.

1. Tell students that this kind of graphic organizer is called a Venn diagram. It can be used to show how things are alike and how they are different.

2. Explain to them that they will use it to show how Justin and Jordan are alike in some ways and different in other ways.

3. Ask students to name things that describe only Jordan, and write these attributes in the left circle of the Venn diagram. Possible answers: oldest brother; likes clowns; wants to return the wallet

   ▶ If students are ready to write on their own, allow them to do so.

4. Ask students to name things that describe Justin, and write these attributes in the right circle of the Venn diagram. Possible answers: younger brother; does not like clowns, wants to keep the wallet

5. Ask students to name things that describe **both** Jordan and Justin. Write these attributes in the center of the Venn diagram, where the circles overlap. Possible answers: have younger siblings, wants to do the right thing; happy they returned the wallet

6. Ask the following questions to encourage comparison of the characters and discussion.

   ▶ How are the characters alike?
   ▶ How are the characters different?
   ▶ Are you like Justin in any way?
   ▶ Are you like Jordan in any way?
   ▶ Do the characters remind you of anybody you know?
   ▶ Does the book remind you of any other stories that you know?

Objectives

- Demonstrate understanding through graphic organizers.
- Compare and contrast story structure elements within a text.
- Make connections with text: text-to-text, text-to-self, text-to-world.s

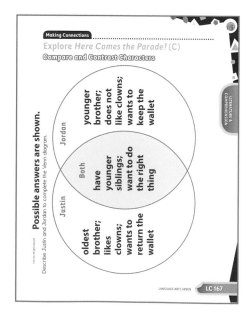

Explore *Tales of Amanda Pig* (A)

Lesson Overview

[Offline] — **45** minutes

Get Ready	Lesson Introduction
	Problem and Solution
	Words to Know
Shared Reading	Book Walk
	"Amanda's Egg" and "The Very Long Trip"
Check Your Reading	"Amanda's Egg" and "The Very Long Trip"
Reading for Meaning	Problem and Solution in "Amanda's Egg" and "The Very Long Trip"
Looking at Language	"Amanda's Egg": Questions
Beyond the Lesson	⊕ OPTIONAL: Another Egg for Breakfast

Advance Preparation

Before beginning the Shared Reading, read "Amanda's Egg" and "The Very Long Trip" to locate Words to Know in the text. Cut out and tape together the sentence strips on page LC 169, and preview pages LC 171 and 172 in *K¹² Language Arts Activity Book* to prepare the materials for Looking at Language.

Big Ideas

► An awareness of story structure elements (setting, characters, plot) provides readers a foundation for constructing meaning when reading new stories and writing their own stories.
► To understand and interpret a story, readers need to understand and describe characters and what they do.
► Good readers use prior knowledge and text clues to infer, or draw conclusions about what is implied but not directly stated in text.
► During shared-reading activities, students learn more about how print works.

Materials

Supplied
- *Tales of Amada Pig* by Jean Van Leeuwen
- *Here Comes the Parade!* by Tony and Lauren Dungy
- *Ready . . . Set . . . Read! The Beginning Reader's Treasury*, p. 98 (optional)
- *K¹² Language Arts Activity Book*, pp. LC 169–172

Also Needed
- scissors, adult
- tape, clear

Story Synopses

In "Amanda's Egg," Amanda isn't very interested in eating an unappetizing egg for breakfast. In "The Very Long Trip," Amanda and her brother, Oliver, pretend to fly a plane to visit their grandmother on a rainy day.

Keywords

character – a person or animal in a story
infer – to use clues and what you already know to make a guess
inference – a guess you make using the clues in a text and what you already know
problem – an issue a character must solve in a story
setting – when and where a story takes place
solution – how a character solves a problem in a story

 **45 minutes**

Work **together** with students to complete Get Ready, Shared Reading, Check Your Reading, Reading for Meaning, Looking at Language, and Beyond the Lesson activities.

Get Ready

Lesson Introduction

Prepare students for listening to and discussing "Amanda's Egg" and "The Very Long Trip" in *Tales of Amanda Pig*.

1. Tell students that you are going to read "Amanda's Egg" and "The Very Long Trip" in *Tales of Amanda Pig*.

2. Explain that before you read the story you will get ready by reviewing

   ▸ How characters solve problems
   ▸ How we sometimes make inferences to help us figure out things in a story that the author doesn't say directly

> **Objectives**
> - Describe story structure elements—problem and solution.
> - Make inferences based on text and/or prior knowledge.

Problem and Solution

Explore the story structure element of problem and solution.

1. Remind students that a character in a story usually needs to solve a problem. There can be more than one character in a story that needs to solve a problem.

2. Have students recall the book *Here Comes the Parade!* to help them think about how a character finds a **solution** to a **problem**. If necessary, show students the pictures from the book.

3. Remind students that in the beginning of the book, Justin has two problems: he's nervous about seeing the clowns in the parade, and he's found a wallet full of money. After asking Mom and Dad for help, Justin and Dad head to the Lost and Found, but Justin bumps into a clown. The clown is sad, and Justin asks why. The clown tells Justin that he lost his wallet. After the clown describes the wallet, Justin realizes the wallet he found is the clown's missing wallet. The clown is grateful and offers some money as a reward for being honest and returning the wallet. Mom tells the clown they don't need a reward, and the clown gives them balloons instead. After this experience, Justin decides clowns are his favorite part of the parade.

   ▸ What are Justin's problems in *Here Comes the Parade!*? He is nervous about seeing clowns, and he found a wallet full of money and doesn't know how to find the owner.

   ▸ How are Justin's problems solved? He returns the wallet to its owner, a clown. The clown is grateful and gives Justin a balloon. This makes Justin happy, and clowns no longer make him nervous.

4. Explain that sometimes we can make **inferences** related to a character's problem. For example, we can infer that Justin was afraid of clowns but now he isn't. First he was nervous about seeing clowns, but by the end of the book he said the clowns were his favorite part of the day.

5. Tell students that as they read stories, they should listen for characters' problems and what the characters do to solve their problems. They should also listen for clues about what they can infer about characters and their problems.

Words to Know

Before reading "Amanda's Egg" and "The Very Long Trip," go over Words to Know with students.

1. Read each word aloud and have students repeat it.

2. Ask students if they know what each word means.

   ▶ If students know a word's meaning, have them define it and use it in a sentence.
   ▶ If students don't know a word's meaning, read them the definition and discuss the word with them.

takeoff – when an airplane leaves the ground and begins to fly in the air
engine – a motor
screwdriver – a tool for turning a screw

Shared Reading

Book Walk

Prepare students for reading by taking them on a Book Walk of *Tales of Amanda Pig*. Scan the stories "Amanda's Egg" and "The Very Long Trip" together and ask students to make predictions about the stories. Answers to questions may vary.

1. Have students look at the picture on the cover. Point to and read aloud the **book title**.

   ▶ What do you think the stories in this book are about?

2. Read aloud the names of the **author** and the **illustrator**.

3. Read aloud the story titles on the **Contents** page. Explain to students that in this lesson, they will read "Amanda's Egg" and "The Very Long Trip."

4. Have students **look at the pictures in "Amanda's Egg" and "The Very Long Trip."**

   ▶ Do you ever have to eat something that you don't like? What is it?
   ▶ Do you ever pretend to go places? Where do you pretend to go?

Objectives

- Activate prior knowledge by previewing text and/or discussing topic.
- Make predictions based on text, illustrations, and/or prior knowledge.
- Build vocabulary through listening, reading, and discussion.
- Use new vocabulary in written and spoken sentences.
- Read and listen to a variety of texts for information and pleasure independently or as part of a group.

"Amanda's Egg" and "The Very Long Trip"

It's time to read aloud "Amanda's Egg" and "The Very Long Trip."

1. Have students sit next to you so that they can see the pictures and words while you read aloud.

2. Tell students to listen for information about how the characters solve their problems.

3. **Read aloud both stories.** Track with your finger so students can follow along. Emphasize Words to Know as you come to them. If appropriate, use the pictures to help show what each word means.

Check Your Reading

"Amanda's Egg" and "The Very Long Trip"

Check students' comprehension of "Amanda's Egg" and "The Very Long Trip."

1. Have students retell "Amanda's Egg" in their own words to develop grammar, vocabulary, comprehension, and fluency skills.

2. Ask students the following questions.

   ▸ Where does "Amanda's Egg" take place? in the kitchen
   ▸ What time of day is it? morning   How do you know? The family is eating breakfast.
   ▸ Who are the characters in this story? Amanda; Oliver; Mother; Father

3. Have students retell "The Very Long Trip" in their own words to develop grammar, vocabulary, comprehension, and fluency skills.

4. Ask students the following questions.

   ▸ Where does "The Very Long Trip" take place? in Amanda's house
   ▸ What kind of day is it? What is the weather like? rainy
   ▸ Who are the characters in "The Very Long Trip"? Amanda; Oliver; Mother; Grandmother
   ▸ Why don't Amanda and Oliver want to do puzzles? because all the puzzles have pieces missing
   ▸ Why can't Amanda and Oliver go to Grandmother's house? It's raining too hard.

TIP If students have trouble responding to a question, help them locate the answer in the text or pictures.

Objectives
- Retell or dramatize a story.
- Identify setting.
- Identify character(s).
- Answer questions requiring literal recall of details.

Reading for Meaning

Problem and Solution in "Amanda's Egg" and "The Very Long Trip"
Check students' ability to identify characters' problems and how they try to
solve them.

Objectives
- Describe story structure elements—problem and solution.
- Make inferences based on text and/or prior knowledge.
- Describe character(s).

1. Remind students that characters in stories have problems to solve, and that
   sometimes we can make inferences to better understand the character and
   the problem.

2. Ask the following questions.

   ▸ What is the problem in the story "Amanda's Egg"? Amanda doesn't want
     to eat her egg.

   ▸ Do you think Amanda likes eggs? No   How can you tell? Her mother tells
     her to eat it several times, but she doesn't eat it.

   ▸ What do Father and Oliver ask before they leave the table? They ask to
     be excused.

   ▸ Why do you think Amanda doesn't just get up and leave the table?
     She hasn't been excused.

   ▸ Why do you think Amanda tells Mother that her egg is cold? She probably
     hopes that her mother won't make her eat it after all.

   ▸ What are some things Mother does to try to get Amanda to eat her egg?
     She tells Amanda that eggs make you big and strong. She tells Amanda
     that she'll close her eyes and count to 10, and when she opens her eyes,
     Amanda's egg will be gone.

   ▸ Why do you think Mother tells Amanda that Father and Oliver are playing
     in the pile of leaves outside? She thinks that Amanda would like to play in
     the leaves, so she might eat her egg in order to be excused.

   ▸ What is Amanda's and Oliver's problem in the story "The Very Long
     Trip"? It's raining and there's not much to do.

   ▸ Whom do Amanda and Oliver want to visit? Grandmother

   ▸ Do you think Amanda likes Grandmother? Yes   Why do you think this?
     What do you know from personal experience that helps you figure this
     out? Students might say that they like to visit people whom they like.

   ▸ How do Amanda and Oliver solve their problem of nothing to do on a
     rainy day? They pretend to fly an airplane to Grandmother's house.

Looking at Language

"Amanda's Egg": Questions

Tell students that they will reread "Amanda's Egg" with a focus on questions. Gather the sentence strip that you prepared and the Reading Aid on pages LC 171 and 172 in *K¹² Language Arts Activity Book*.

1. Point to the question on the sentence strip.

   ▶ What do you see at the end of the sentence? a question mark

2. Track with your finger as you read aloud the question. Emphasize the rise in your voice at the end of the question.

   ▶ What did you notice about how I read the question? Your voice goes up at the end.

3. Explain that when somebody asks a question, one way we can tell that it's a question is that we can hear the person's voice rise at the end of the question.

4. Have students **read aloud the question with you** as they track with their finger. Make sure that they use the correct emphasis at the end of the question.

5. Tell students that they will **read aloud the story with you**. As you read aloud together, you will stop at certain points to discuss questions and how to read questions with the correct emphasis.

6. Refer to the Reading Aid.

Objectives

- Recognize questions.
- Recognize that a question ends with a question mark.
- Read aloud grade-level text with appropriate expression, accuracy, and rate.

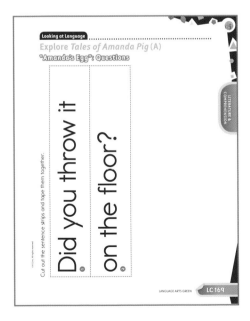

Reading Aid Tear out the Reading Aid for this reading selection. Follow the instructions for folding the page, and then use the page as a guide as you reread the selection with students.

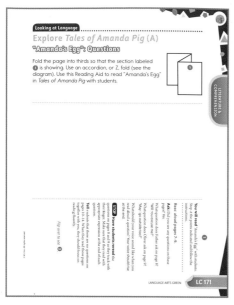
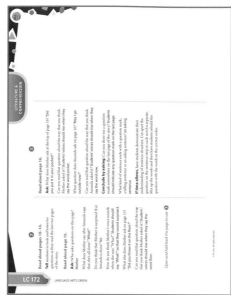

Beyond the Lesson

⊕ OPTIONAL: Another Egg for Breakfast

This activity is OPTIONAL. It is intended for students who have extra time and would enjoy reading a poem about another character who has to eat an egg for breakfast. Feel free to skip this activity. Gather *Ready . . . Set . . . Read!*

1. Remind students that the problem in "Amanda's Egg" was that Amanda didn't want to eat an egg for breakfast.

2. Tell students you are going to read a poem about another character who has to eat an egg for breakfast.

3. Gather *Ready . . . Set . . . Read!* Turn to the table of contents and have students help you locate "Soft-Boiled Egg" in the Poems section. Turn to that page.

4. Read aloud the title of the poem and the poet's name.

5. Have students look at the picture and describe what they see.

6. Read aloud the poem.

   ▸ Why doesn't the poet want to eat the egg? He doesn't like how it slides or how it is soft inside.

   ▸ Do you think the poet will eat the egg anyway? Why or why not? Answers will vary.

   ▸ What do you do when you don't want to eat something? Answers will vary.

7. Have students tell how the poem and "Amanda's Egg" are alike and different.

8. Ask students whether they like the poem or story better and why.

Objectives

- Listen to and discuss poetry.
- Compare and contrast story structure elements across texts.

Explore *Tales of Amanda Pig* (B)

Lesson Overview

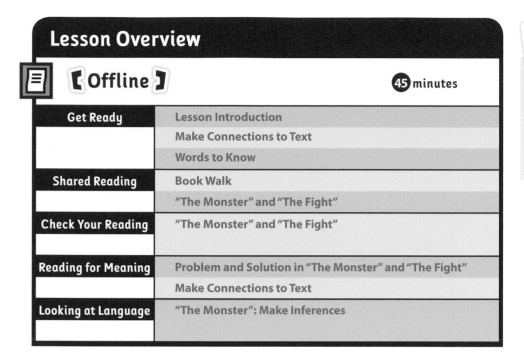

[Offline] **45** minutes

Get Ready	Lesson Introduction
	Make Connections to Text
	Words to Know
Shared Reading	Book Walk
	"The Monster" and "The Fight"
Check Your Reading	"The Monster" and "The Fight"
Reading for Meaning	Problem and Solution in "The Monster" and "The Fight"
	Make Connections to Text
Looking at Language	"The Monster": Make Inferences

Advance Preparation

Before beginning the Shared Reading, read "The Monster" and "The Fight" to locate Words to Know in the text. Preview pages LC 173 and 174 in *K¹² Language Arts Activity Book* to prepare the materials for Looking at Language.

Big Ideas

- ▸ Comprehension is facilitated when readers connect new information to information previously learned.
- ▸ Good readers use prior knowledge and text clues to infer, or draw conclusions about what is implied but not directly stated in text.
- ▸ Shared reading allows students to observe and practice the reading behaviors of proficient readers.

Materials

Supplied

- *Tales of Amada Pig* by Jean Van Leeuwen
- *K¹² Language Arts Activity Book*, pp. LC 173–174

Story Synopses

Amanda's father helps her deal with a scary hallway clock so she can go to bed in "The Monster." In "The Fight," Amanda and Oliver have a nasty quarrel but end up having fun while playing Monster House.

Keywords

connection – a link readers make between themselves, information in text, and the world around them

infer – to use clues and what you already know to make a guess

inference – a guess you make using the clues in a text and what you already know

problem – an issue a character must solve in a story

solution – how a character solves a problem in a story

[Offline] 45 minutes

Work **together** with students to complete Get Ready, Shared Reading, Check Your Reading, Reading for Meaning, and Looking at Language activities.

Get Ready

Lesson Introduction

Prepare students for listening to and discussing "The Monster" and "The Fight" in *Tales of Amanda Pig*.

1. Tell students that you are going to read "The Monster" and "The Fight" in *Tales of Amanda Pig*.

2. Explain that before you read these two stories, you will get ready by reviewing how we can connect to characters and events that happen in a story.

> **Objectives**
> - Make connections with text: text-to-text, text-to-self, text-to-world.
> - Build vocabulary through listening, reading, and discussion.
> - Use new vocabulary in written and spoken sentences.

Make Connections to Text

Explore the types of connections readers make to text.

1. Remind students that good readers use their prior knowledge and personal experiences to connect to text.

2. Explain that **making a connection** can help readers better understand a story or a character in a story. For example, if you've ever been scared by something and then you read a story in which a character gets scared, this connection can help you to understand how that character feels.

3. Tell students that when they read a story, they might notice that

   ▸ The story reminds them of another story.
   ▸ The story reminds them of a movie or TV show that they've seen.
   ▸ The characters in the story make them think of characters in another story.
   ▸ The characters in the story remind them of people they know.

4. Give examples of the type of connection a reader could make.
   Say: The story "Light-foot and Quick-foot" might remind a reader of pets they've had that bite each other when they play. Or it might remind a reader of a story or movie that has characters who fight with each other.

5. Tell students about a connection that you make to "Light-foot and Quick-foot."
   Say: The story "Light-foot and Quick-foot" reminds me of . . . ."

   Complete the sentence with a personal connection to the story.

6. Remind students about the story "Amanda's Egg." Amanda sits at the breakfast table for a long time because she doesn't want to eat her egg. Finally, she eats the egg so that she can go outside and play in the leaves with her father and brother.

7. Ask the following questions about "Amanda's Egg." Answers to questions may vary.

   ▸ Do any parts of the story remind you of something that has happened in your own life?
   ▸ Are the characters like you in any way—are there foods that you don't like to eat, do you like to play outside, do you like to play with members of your family?
   ▸ Does this story make you think about another story, or maybe a movie or something you've seen on TV?
   ▸ Do the characters in the story make you think about characters in another story, or somebody you know?

Words to Know

Before reading "The Monster" and "The Fight," go over Words to Know with students.

1. Read aloud each word and have students repeat it.

2. Ask students if they know what each word means.

   ▸ If students know a word's meaning, have them define it and use it in a sentence.
   ▸ If students don't know a word's meaning, read them the definition and discuss the word with them.

stamp – to clomp; to put your feet down hard while you walk
relief – the feeling of not having the pain or worry that you had before

Shared Reading

Book Walk

Prepare students for reading by taking them on a Book Walk of *Tales of Amanda Pig*. Scan the stories "The Monster" and "The Fight" together and ask students to make predictions about the stories.

1. Have students look at the picture on the cover. Point to and read aloud the **book title**.

2. Read aloud the **names of the author and the illustrator**.

3. Have students read aloud the story titles on the **contents** page. Explain to students that in this lesson, they will read "The Monster" and "The Fight."

Objectives

- Make predictions based on text, illustrations, and/or prior knowledge.
- Activate prior knowledge by previewing text and/or discussing topic.
- Read and listen to a variety of texts for information and pleasure independently or as part of a group.

4. Have students look at the **pictures in "The Monster" and "The Fight."**
   Answers to questions may vary.

   ▸ What do you think might happen in these stories?
   ▸ Have you ever imagined that you saw a monster or something scary at night? What did it look like? What did you do?
   ▸ Do you like to play pretend? What do you like to pretend to do or be?

"The Monster" and "The Fight"
It's time to read aloud "The Monster" and "The Fight."

1. Have students sit next to you so that they can see the pictures and words while you read aloud.

2. Tell students to listen carefully for things in the stories that remind them of other stories and their own lives.

3. Remind students to listen for how the characters solve problems.

4. **Read aloud both stories.** Track with your finger so students can follow along. Emphasize Words to Know as you come to them. If appropriate, use the pictures to help show what each word means.

Check Your Reading

"The Monster" and "The Fight"
Check students' comprehension of "The Monster" and "The Fight."

1. Have students retell "The Monster" in their own words to develop grammar, vocabulary, comprehension, and fluency skills.

2. Ask students the following questions to check their comprehension of the story.

   ▸ What is the setting of "The Monster"? Where does it take place?
     in Amanda's house; upstairs
   ▸ Who are the characters in "The Monster"? Amanda; Father; Oliver; Mother
   ▸ What does Amanda think turns into a monster at night? a clock

3. Have students retell "The Fight" in their own words to develop grammar, vocabulary, comprehension, and fluency skills.

4. Ask students the following questions to check their comprehension of the story.

   ▸ Who are the two most important characters in "The Fight"? Amanda and Oliver
   ▸ What does Amanda want to do at the beginning of the story? play house
   ▸ What does Oliver want to play? monsters
   ▸ Why does Oliver slam the door to Amanda's room? Possible answers: because he and Amanda had a fight; because he's mad

TIP If students have trouble responding to a question, help them locate the answer in the text or pictures.

Objectives
- Retell or dramatize a story.
- Identify setting.
- Identify character(s).
- Answer questions requiring literal recall of details.

Reading for Meaning

Problem and Solution in "The Monster" and "The Fight"
Check students' ability to identify characters' problems and how they solve them.

1. Remind students that characters solve problems in stories.

2. Ask the following questions.

   ▸ What is Amanda's problem in the beginning of "The Monster"? She can't go upstairs because there's a monster in the hall.
   ▸ Who helps Amanda solve her problem? Father
   ▸ What does Father take out of the closet? a flashlight, a cooking pot, Halloween masks, and an umbrella
   ▸ What is Father's plan? to scare away the monster by making lots of noise and shining a light in its eyes
   ▸ Does Father's plan work? Yes   How do you know? Amanda sees that the monster is just a clock after all.
   ▸ What new problem does Amanda have at the end of the story? She's worried that the clock might look like a monster again.
   ▸ What does Father do to solve this problem? He puts the flashlight, cooking pot, Halloween masks, and umbrella next to Amanda's bed just in case.
   ▸ What problem do Amanda and Oliver have at the beginning of "The Fight"? They don't want to play the same game; Amanda wants to play house, and Oliver wants to play monsters.
   ▸ What do Amanda and Oliver try first to solve their problem? They play by themselves.   Does it solve their problem? No   How do you know? It isn't any fun to play alone.
   ▸ What do Oliver and Amada try next to solve their problem? They play both games at the same time; they play Monster House.   Does this solve their problem? Yes   How do you know? Amanda and Oliver play together.

Make Connections to Text
Check students' ability to connect text to themselves and the world around them.

1. Remind students that making connections to a story helps readers better understand the story.

2. Ask the following questions. Answers to questions may vary.

   ▸ Does any part of "The Monster" remind you of something in your own life?
   ▸ Do you ever imagine that you see something scary in the dark? How does that make you feel? How do you think Amanda feels when she thinks she sees a monster?
   ▸ Amanda and Oliver don't want to play the same game in "The Fight." Does this ever happen to you and your brother or sister, or a friend?
   ▸ Do you have a brother, sister, or friend whom you sometimes fight with, like Oliver and Amanda?
   ▸ Oliver likes to play monsters. Does this remind you of any games that you like to play?

Objectives
- Describe story structure elements—problem and solution.
- Make connections with text: text-to-text, text-to-self, text-to-world.

▸ Do any of the characters in the stories make you think of someone you know or of characters in another story? Whom do you think of, and why?

▸ Does "The Fight" remind you of any other stories you know? Students may mention "Light-foot and Quick-foot." If they do not make this connection, discuss elements of "Light-foot and Quick-foot" that are similar to "The Fight."

Looking at Language

"The Monster": Make Inferences

Reread "The Monster" with a focus on making inferences. Gather the Reading Aid on pages LC 173 and 174 in *K¹² Language Arts Activity Book*.

1. Have students explain the kinds of information a reader uses to make inferences.

2. If students don't recall the type of information that a reader uses to make inferences, tell them that **inferences** are guesses. However, they are not wild guesses. They are logical guesses based on the following information:

   ▸ The words and pictures of a story
   ▸ The reader's prior knowledge learned from experience
   ▸ The reader's prior knowledge of similar stories they've read

3. Tell students that **they will read aloud "The Monster" with you**. As you read aloud together, you will stop at certain points to discuss the clues that help you make inferences.

4. Refer to the Reading Aid.

Reading Aid   Tear out the Reading Aid for this reading selection. Follow the instructions for folding the page, and then use the page as a guide as you reread the selection with students.

Objectives

- Read aloud grade-level text with appropriate expression, accuracy, and rate.
- Make inferences based on text and/or prior knowledge.
- Support inferences with evidence from text and/or prior knowledge.
- Use illustrations to aid understanding of text.

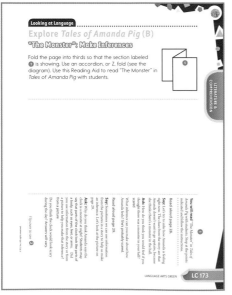
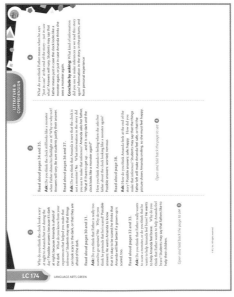

Explore *Tales of Amanda Pig* (C)

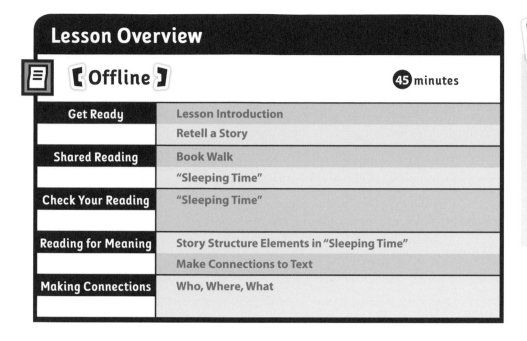

Lesson Overview

Offline   **45** minutes

Get Ready	Lesson Introduction
	Retell a Story
Shared Reading	Book Walk
	"Sleeping Time"
Check Your Reading	"Sleeping Time"
Reading for Meaning	Story Structure Elements in "Sleeping Time"
	Make Connections to Text
Making Connections	Who, Where, What

Big Ideas

► An awareness of story structure elements (setting, characters, plot) provides readers a foundation for constructing meaning when reading new stories and writing their own stories.

► Comprehension is facilitated when readers connect new information to information previously learned.

► Comprehension requires the reader to self-monitor understanding.

Materials

Supplied

• *Tales of Amada Pig* by Jean Van Leeuwen

• *K¹² Language Arts Activity Book*, pp. LC 175–178

Also Needed

• glue stick

• scissors, round-end safety

Story Synopsis

Amanda isn't sleepy, so she puts her tired mother to bed instead in "Sleeping Time."

Keywords

connection – a link readers make between themselves, information in text, and the world around them

retelling – using your own words to tell a story that you have listened to or read

self-monitor – to notice if you do or do not understand what you are reading

story structure elements – components of a story; they include character, setting, plot, problem, and solution

[Offline] ⏱ 45 minutes

Work **together** with students to complete Get Ready, Shared Reading, Check Your Reading, Reading for Meaning, and Making Connections activities.

Get Ready

Lesson Introduction

Prepare students for listening to and discussing "Sleeping Time" in *Tales of Amanda Pig*.

1. Tell students that you are going to read "Sleeping Time" in *Tales of Amanda Pig*.

2. Explain that before you read the story, you will get ready by discussing how retelling a story can help readers check that they understand what they read.

Objectives
- Retell or dramatize a story.
- Retell a story naming plot, setting, character(s), problem, and solution.

Retell a Story

Revisit how to retell a story.

1. Remind students that **retelling means using your own words to tell a story** that you have listened to or read. Retelling a story is a good way to check that you understand what you have read.

2. Explain that when we retell a story, it is important to mention the characters; the setting; how characters solve problems; and important events that happen in the beginning, middle, and end of the story.

3. Turn to page 28 in *Tales of Amanda Pig* and have students revisit the pictures in "The Monster."

4. Ask students to retell the story "The Monster." Remind them to mention all the things in Step 2. Be sure students retell events from the beginning, middle and end of the story in the correct order. Have students use the pictures from the story as a guide.
   Possible answer: At the beginning of the story, Amanda can't go upstairs because she says there's a monster in the hall; Father goes upstairs to have her show it to him.
   Then Father comes up with a plan to scare the monster; he gets some things out of the closet, and then he and Amanda stamp up the stairs while making lots of noise; Father shines a flashlight in the monster's eyes; Amanda realizes the monster really is just a clock, and she feels better.
   At the end of the story, Amanda gets into bed and says she's worried the clock might look like a monster again; Father leaves the pot, flashlight, masks, and umbrella by her bed "just in case."

5. If students make errors in the order of events, or overlook important events, help them look back at the story to determine the sequence of the important events in the story.

Shared Reading

Book Walk

Prepare students for reading by taking them on a Book Walk of *Tales of Amanda Pig*. Scan the story "Sleeping Time" together and ask students to make predictions about the story.

1. Have students point to and read aloud the **book title**.

2. Read aloud the **names of the author and the illustrator**.

3. Have students read aloud the story titles on the **contents** page. Explain to students that in this lesson, they will read "Sleeping Time."

4. Have students look at the **pictures in "Sleeping Time."** Answers to questions may vary.

   ► What do you think might happen in this story?
   ► Are you always sleepy when it's your bedtime, or are you sometimes wide awake?
   ► What do you do in bed while you wait to fall asleep?

Objectives

- Make predictions based on text, illustrations, and/or prior knowledge.
- Activate prior knowledge by previewing text and/or discussing topic.
- Read and listen to a variety of texts for information and pleasure independently or as part of a group.

"Sleeping Time"

It's time to read aloud "Sleeping Time."

1. Have students sit next to you so that they can see the pictures and words while you read aloud.

2. Remind students to listen carefully for things in the story that are important to mention when they retell the story.

3. Tell them to think about things in the story that remind them of other stories and things in their own life.

4. **Read aloud the story.** Track with your finger so students can follow along.

Check Your Reading

"Sleeping Time"
Check students' comprehension of "Sleeping Time."

Objectives
- Retell or dramatize a story.
- Answer questions requiring literal recall of details.

1. Have students retell "Sleeping Time" in their own words to develop grammar, vocabulary, comprehension, and fluency skills.

2. Ask students the following questions.

   ▶ Why does Amanda tell Mother to pretend she's the little girl and get into her bed? because Amanda isn't sleepy, but Mother is
   ▶ What does Amanda do after Mother climbs into bed? She tells Mother a story and sings her a song.
   ▶ What does Amanda give Mother to hug while she's in bed? her rabbit
   ▶ How does Amanda's room feel to her after Mother falls asleep? quiet; empty; a little bit cold
   ▶ Why does Amanda wake up Mother? It's her turn to go to bed.
   ▶ Why doesn't Mother want to get out of bed? She's nice and cozy.

TIP If students have trouble responding to a question, help them locate the answer in the text or pictures.

Reading for Meaning

Story Structure Elements in "Sleeping Time"
Check students' ability to identify setting, characters, and problem and solution.

Objectives
- Identify setting.
- Identify character(s).
- Describe story structure elements—problem and solution.
- Make connections with text: text-to-text, text-to-self, text-to-world.

1. Remind students that story characters often have a problem that they try to solve.

2. Ask the following questions.

   ▶ What is the setting of "Sleeping Time"? Amanda's bedroom
   ▶ Who are the characters in "Sleeping Time"? Amanda and Mother
   ▶ What is Amanda's problem? It's bedtime, but she isn't sleepy.
   ▶ What does Amanda do to solve her problem? She pretends Mother is the little girl instead and puts her to bed, and then she tells Mother a story and sings her a song.
   ▶ Does this solve Amanda's problem? Yes   How do you know? Amanda wakes up Mother and tells her it's her turn to get into bed to sleep.

Make Connections to Text
Check students' ability to connect text to themselves and the world around them.

1. Remind students that making connections to the text helps readers better understand a story.

2. Ask the following questions. Answers to questions may vary.

   ▸ What parts in "Sleeping Time" remind you of something in your own life?
   ▸ Amanda tells a story and sings a song to help Mother fall asleep. Have you ever done this? Has anyone ever done this for you?
   ▸ Amanda pretends she's the mother. Have you ever pretended to be a mother or father?
   ▸ Does either of the characters in the story remind you of someone you know? Whom do you think of and why?
   ▸ Does "Sleeping Time" remind you of any other story you've read? Students might say *Bedtime for Frances*. If not, remind them of the story *Bedtime for Frances* and ask them if the stories are similar in any way.

Making Connections

Who, Where, What
Check students' understanding of story structure elements and their ability to retell a story. Turn to pages LC 175–178 in *K¹² Language Arts Activity Book* and gather the glue stick and scissors.

1. Tell students they are going to complete a story map for "Sleeping Time."

2. Have students cut out the pictures on page LC 175.

3. Point to and read aloud the story title in the center of the map on page LC 177.

4. Point to the "Characters" box and read aloud the label. Have students pick out the picture that represents the characters and glue it into the box.

5. Repeat Step 4 for the "Setting" box.

6. Have students organize the pictures of the story's events in the order in which they happen and then glue them into the correct "Plot" boxes.

7. Read the first sentence starter on page 178 and write what students dictate. Possible answers: Amanda isn't sleepy, so she reads and sings to Mother; Amanda isn't sleepy so she puts Mother to bed instead.

   ▸ If students are ready to write on their own, allow them to do so.

8. Repeat Step 7 for the second sentence starter. Answers will vary.

9. Have students retell the story, using the story map as a guide.
   Possible answer: At the beginning of the story, Amanda isn't sleepy, so she pretends Mother is a little girl and puts her to bed instead.
   Then Amanda tells Mother a story and sings her a song; she gives Mother her rabbit to hug in bed; Mother falls asleep.
   At the end of the story, Amanda wakes up Mother and says it's her turn to be put to bed; Amanda gets into bed with the rabbit; Mother tucks Amanda in and says good-night.

Objectives
- Sequence pictures illustrating story events.
- Demonstrate understanding through graphic organizers.
- Retell a story naming plot, setting, character(s), problem, and solution.
- Retell a story using various media.
- Make connections with text: text-to-text, text-to-self, text-to-world.
- Self-monitor comprehension of text.

10. Guide students to think about their retellings. Answers to questions may vary.

   ▸ Did your retelling include the important characters?
   ▸ Did it include most of the important things that happened, and in the right order?
   ▸ Do you think that you understand the story?
   ▸ Was it easier for you to retell the story with or without the pictures in the story map to help you?

 TIP If students forgot to mention characters or important events in their retelling, have them retell the story again as you ask questions such as "Who are the characters in the story? What did they do?" If students don't think they understand the story, reread the story aloud, pausing to let students ask questions as you read.

Reward: Add a sticker for this unit on the My Accomplishments chart to mark successful completion of the unit.

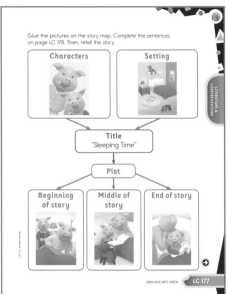

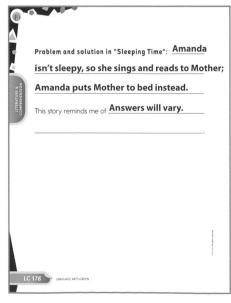

Amazing Americans

Unit Focus

In this unit, students will read articles and a poem about people who have served America in different ways. This unit follows the shared-reading instructional approach (see the instructional approaches to reading in the introductory lesson for this program). In this unit, students will

- ▶ Identify characteristics of nonfiction texts.
- ▶ Learn to recognize pronouns and the words they replace.
- ▶ Use clues in a text to identify the sequence of events.
- ▶ Learn the difference between facts and opinions, and practice identifying them in text.
- ▶ Learn how periods make it easier to understand text because they separate the ideas.
- ▶ Identify text clues that let readers know that the events described happened in the past.
- ▶ Explore how to draw a conclusion, and identify evidence that supports that conclusion.
- ▶ Summarize the information in an article.
- ▶ Practice comparing and contrasting information in a text.

Unit Plan ⌈Offline⌉

Lesson 1	Introduce "Marvelous Mount Rushmore"	45 minutes a day
Lesson 2	Explore "Marvelous Mount Rushmore"	
Lesson 3	Introduce "George Washington: American Hero"	
Lesson 4	Explore "George Washington: American Hero"	
Lesson 5	Explore "Washington"	
Lesson 6	Introduce "Women of the White House"	
Lesson 7	Explore "Women of the White House"	
Lesson 8	Your Choice	

Introduce "Marvelous Mount Rushmore"

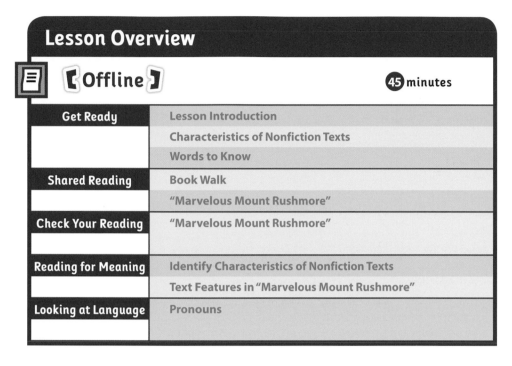

Lesson Overview

Offline — 45 minutes

Get Ready	Lesson Introduction
	Characteristics of Nonfiction Texts
	Words to Know
Shared Reading	Book Walk
	"Marvelous Mount Rushmore"
Check Your Reading	"Marvelous Mount Rushmore"
Reading for Meaning	Identify Characteristics of Nonfiction Texts
	Text Features in "Marvelous Mount Rushmore"
Looking at Language	Pronouns

Advance Preparation

Before beginning the Shared Reading, read "Marvelous Mount Rushmore" to locate Words to Know in the text. Preview pages LC 179 and 180 in *K¹² Language Arts Activity Book* to prepare the materials for Looking at Language.

Big Ideas

▸ Exposing readers to a wide variety of genres provides them with a wide range of background knowledge and increases their vocabulary.
▸ Nonfiction texts differ from fiction texts in that they describe real or true things in life, rather than things made up by the author.
▸ During shared-reading activities, students learn more about how print works.

Materials

Supplied
- "Marvelous Mount Rushmore," *K¹² World: People and Places of the Past*, pp. 28–39
- *K¹² Language Arts Activity Book*, pp. LC 179–180
- Story Card F

Article Synopsis

It took great vision and scores of determined workers to carve Mount Rushmore National Memorial from solid rock.

Keywords

author's purpose – the reason the author wrote a text: to entertain, to inform, to express an opinion, or to persuade

fact – something that can be proven true

genre – a category for classifying literary works

informational text – text written to explain and give information on a topic

nonfiction – writings about true things

pronoun – a word that takes the place of one or more nouns

topic – the subject of a text

visual text support – a graphic feature that helps a reader better understand text, such as a picture, chart, or map

(Offline) **45** minutes

Work **together** with students to complete Get Ready, Shared Reading, Check Your Reading, Reading for Meaning, and Looking at Language activities.

Get Ready

Lesson Introduction

Prepare students for listening to and discussing "Marvelous Mount Rushmore."

1. Tell students that you are going to read "Marvelous Mount Rushmore," a nonfiction article about the well-known national memorial.

2. Explain that before you read the article, you will get ready by

   ▶ Reviewing characteristics of nonfiction texts
   ▶ Learning how to anticipate what we will find in an article based on what we know about nonfiction articles

Objectives

- Identify the topic.
- Identify characteristics of different genres.
- Identify the author's purpose.
- Identify features of informational text.
- Increase concept and content vocabulary.
- Build vocabulary through listening, reading, and discussion.
- Use new vocabulary in written and spoken sentences.

Characteristics of Nonfiction Texts

Review the genre of nonfiction. Gather Story Card F.

1. Remind students that the people, places, and events in **nonfiction** texts are real, not made up. This kind of writing is also called **informational text**.

2. Nonfiction texts are about real things, so they are filled with **facts**. A fact is something that is true and real. We can prove that facts are true.

3. Remind students that every nonfiction text has a **topic**. The topic is what the text is mostly about. Good readers can figure out the topic by thinking about the title of a text and asking, "What is this text mostly about?"

4. The **author's purpose**, or reason for writing a nonfiction text, is usually to inform, or tell, readers facts about someone or something.

5. Good readers use their **prior knowledge** (what they already know) about the characteristics of nonfiction texts to figure out what they will find in informational texts such as nonfiction magazine articles.

6. Have students look at the picture on Story Card F.

   Say: Imagine that the title of a nonfiction article is "Fun at Westside Park," and this is a picture from the article. I can use my prior knowledge of nonfiction texts to predict the kind of information I will find in the article. I can guess that the article will have a topic. I would expect the article to include facts about the park and a map that shows where it is.

   ▶ What do you think the topic of the article "Fun at Westside Park" might be? Possible answers: Westside Park; fun things to do at Westside Park

   ▶ Based on what you know about nonfiction texts, what other kinds of pictures do you think you'd find in an article with the title "Fun at Westside Park"? Answers will vary; if students have trouble answering, suggest that they might expect to find pictures of the things you would see at the park, such as a basketball court, a playground, water fountains, and picnic tables.

   ▶ Why do you think an author would write an article called "Fun at Westside Park"? to inform readers; to tell facts about the park

---

Words to Know

Before reading "Marvelous Mount Rushmore," go over Words to Know with students.

1. Read aloud each word or phrase and have students repeat it.

2. Ask students if they know what each word or phrase means.

   ▶ If students know a word's or phrase's meaning, have them define it and use it in a sentence.

   ▶ If students don't know a word's or phrase's meaning, read them the definition and discuss the word or phrase with them.

carve – to make something by cutting

chisel – a metal tool with a sharp edge, used to shape stone, wood, or metal

dangle – to hang loosely

Declaration of Independence – a document that declared the American colonies' freedom from England

dedicate – to open a monument, building, park, or other place to public use

dynamite – a very powerful explosive

jackhammer – a large tool for drilling rock

memorial – something built as a reminder of a person or event

president – a person who is the head of a country, company, or other organization

sculptor – an artist who makes works of art from stone, clay, wood, or another material

sculpture – a work of art, made by carving stone, clay, wood, or another material

Shared Reading

Book Walk

Prepare students for reading by taking them on a Book Walk of "Marvelous Mount Rushmore." Scan the magazine article together and ask students to make predictions about the article.

1. Turn to the **table of contents** in *K¹² World: People and Places of the Past*. Help students find the selection and turn to that page.

2. Point to and read aloud the **title of the article**.

3. Have students look at the **pictures of the article**.

   ▸ Based on the title of the article, the pictures, and your prior knowledge of nonfiction texts, what do you think this article is mostly about? Possible answers: facts about Mount Rushmore; how Mount Rushmore was made

   ▸ What kind of information do you think you will find in this article? Possible answers: when and how the sculpture on Mount Rushmore was made; who the people shown on the sculpture are

4. Remind students that different kinds of features help show ideas that are in a nonfiction article.

5. Turn to page 29 and point to the map.

   ▸ What kind of text feature is this? a map   What kind of information do we find in maps? where places are located

6. Turn to page 31 and point to the portraits of the presidents. Explain that these pictures, called portraits, are paintings of three of the presidents that are on Mount Rushmore.

7. Turn to page 35 and have students look at the pictures. Tell students that these pictures, called photographs, show how workers carved Mount Rushmore.

8. Turn to page 38 and point to the graphic showing the scale of the Lincoln sculpture.
   Say: Each yellow outline stands for the height of a child. So this picture helps us understand the size of the faces on Mount Rushmore.

9. Tell students that when they read nonfiction text, they should pay attention to the features such as pictures, maps, and diagrams to learn more information about the topic.

Objectives

- Activate prior knowledge by previewing text and/or discussing topic.
- Make predictions based on text, illustrations, and/or prior knowledge.
- Identify purpose of and information provided by informational text features.
- Read and listen to a variety of texts for information and pleasure independently or as part of a group.

"Marvelous Mount Rushmore"

It's time to read aloud the article.

1. Have students sit next to you so that they can see the pictures and words while you read aloud.

2. Tell students to listen for what the article is mostly about and for clues to the author's purpose for writing the article.

3. **Read aloud the entire article.** Track with your finger so students can follow along. Emphasize Words to Know as you come to them. If appropriate, use the pictures to help show what each word means.

Check Your Reading

"Marvelous Mount Rushmore"

Check students' comprehension of "Marvelous Mount Rushmore."

1. Have students retell "Marvelous Mount Rushmore" in their own words to develop grammar, vocabulary, comprehension, and fluency skills.

   ▸ Tell students to include **key details** in their retelling, such as where Mount Rushmore is located and why the memorial was created.

2. Ask students the following questions.

   ▸ Who first had the idea to carve a big sculpture into a mountain? Doane Robinson
   ▸ In what state is Mount Rushmore located? South Dakota
   ▸ How many faces are carved into Mount Rushmore? four
   ▸ Why did the sculptor choose Thomas Jefferson to be one of the faces on Mount Rushmore? because Thomas Jefferson wrote the Declaration of Independence
   ▸ About how many people worked to make Mount Rushmore? 400
     What did the workers have to do to get to work at Mount Rushmore? climb 700 steps
   ▸ What did blasters use to blow away big pieces of the rock? dynamite

 If students have trouble responding to a question, help them locate the answer in the text or pictures.

Objectives
- Retell or dramatize a story.
- Identify important details in informational text.
- Answer questions requiring literal recall of details.

Reading for Meaning

Identify Characteristics of Nonfiction Texts

Explore characteristics of nonfiction texts with students.

1. Remind students that nonfiction texts have certain characteristics that are different from what we find in fiction stories.

   ▸ What are some things we might find in a nonfiction article? Possible answers: a topic; the author's purpose; facts; pictures; maps

2. Ask the following questions.

   ▸ What kind of writing is "Marvelous Mount Rushmore"? nonfiction, or informational, text   How can you tell? What makes it a nonfiction text instead of a fiction text? It's about something real; it's not a made-up story; it tells facts about something.

   ▸ What is the topic of "Marvelous Mount Rushmore"? What is the article mostly about? Possible answers: facts about Mount Rushmore; how the sculpture was made

   ▸ Why did the author write the article? Possible answers: to inform readers; to teach readers about Mount Rushmore

   ▸ Is anything in the article made up? No   Why not? It's a nonfiction text about real things.

Text Features in "Marvelous Mount Rushmore"

Remind students that nonfiction texts have many kinds of text features.

1. Turn to page 29 and point to the map.

   ▸ What is this called? a map
   ▸ What does this map show? where you can find Mount Rushmore

2. Turn to page 31 and point to the diagram of the presidents' faces at the bottom of the page.

   ▸ What does this picture show? the first three presidents' faces that were carved into Mount Rushmore and where each one appears

3. Point to the picture above the portraits of the presidents on page 31.

   ▸ Why do you think the author included this picture in the article? Possible answers: to show what Mount Rushmore looked like before it was carved; to show the reader how the sculptor had to use his imagination to see what to carve

4. Turn to pages 32 and 33 and point to the picture of Gutzon Borglum.

   ▸ What does this picture show? the sculptor making a model of the sculpture
   ▸ What do you notice about the model? It doesn't look exactly like Mount Rushmore; it shows more than just the presidents' faces.

Objectives
- Identify characteristics of different genres.
- Distinguish fiction text from nonfiction text.
- Identify the topic.
- Identify the author's purpose.
- Identify features of informational text.
- Interpret information from visual text supports: graphs, tables, charts, cartoons.

5. Turn to page 36 and have students look at both pictures.

   ▶ What do these pictures help the reader better understand? Possible answers: how the workers carved the rock; how the workers had to sit in special chairs; what it might have been like to help make the sculpture

6. Turn to page 37 and point to the picture.

   ▶ What does this picture show? how the workers had to climb lots of stairs to get to the top of Mount Rushmore
   ▶ Why do you think the author included this picture? to help readers understand how tall Mount Rushmore is; to help readers understand what the workers had to do to get to their job

7. Turn to page 38 and point to the picture.

   ▶ What does each yellow figure stand for in this picture? the height of one child
   ▶ What do the pictures of children standing on top of each other show? how big and tall the faces are on Mount Rushmore

Looking at Language

Pronouns

Reread "Marvelous Mount Rushmore" with a focus on pronouns. Gather the Reading Aid on pages LC 179 and 180 in *K¹² Language Arts Activity Book*.

1. Explain to students that you are going to read aloud the first paragraph from "Marvelous Mount Rushmore" two ways. Tell them that they should listen for the difference in the two ways you read.

2. **Read aloud** the first paragraph of the article as it is written in the text.

3. **Read aloud** the paragraph in the following way:

   In the 1920s, Doane Robinson worked for the state of South Dakota. Doane Robinson came up with a big idea.

4. Ask the following questions.

   ▶ What was different when I read the paragraph the second time? Guide students to recognize that you repeated the name *Doane Robinson*.
   ▶ Which way do you think sounds better? Answers will vary.

5. Tell students that authors often use words such as *he*, *she*, and *them* in place of names. This makes a text sound better because names in the text are not being repeated.

6. Explain that in the first paragraph of "Marvelous Mount Rushmore," the author used the word *he* in the second sentence instead of repeating the name *Doane Robinson*.

7. Remind students that words that can be used in place of names, such as *he*, *she*, and *them*, are called **pronouns**.

Objectives
- Recall what a pronoun is.
- Recognize pronouns.
- Identify pronouns.
- Read aloud grade-level text with appropriate expression, accuracy, and rate.

8. Explain that sometimes a reader can get confused about whom or what a pronoun is referring to. This could happen with an article such as "Marvelous Mount Rushmore" because the article talks about many people—Doane Robinson, Gutzon Borglum, George Washington, Thomas Jefferson, Theodore Roosevelt, and Abraham Lincoln.

9. Tell students that **they will reread pages 28–35 of the article aloud with you**. As you reread together, you will stop at certain points to discuss the pronouns and whom or what the pronouns are referring to.

10. Refer to the Reading Aid.

Reading Aid Tear out the Reading Aid for this reading selection. Follow the instructions for folding the page, and then use the page as a guide as you reread the selection with students.

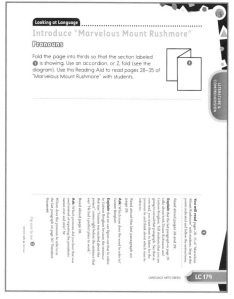

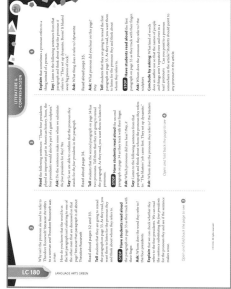

Explore "Marvelous Mount Rushmore"

Lesson Overview

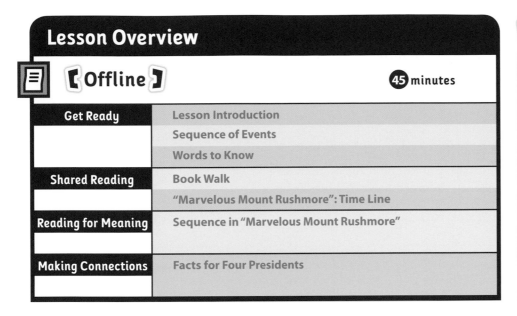

[Offline] **45** minutes

Get Ready	Lesson Introduction
	Sequence of Events
	Words to Know
Shared Reading	Book Walk
	"Marvelous Mount Rushmore": Time Line
Reading for Meaning	Sequence in "Marvelous Mount Rushmore"
Making Connections	Facts for Four Presidents

Advance Preparation

Preview pages LC 181 and 182 in *K¹² Language Arts Activity Book* to prepare the materials for the Shared Reading.

Big Ideas

▸ Comprehension entails an understanding of the organizational patterns of text.
▸ Repeated rereading leads to increased fluency.
▸ Shared reading allows students to observe and practice the reading behaviors of proficient readers.

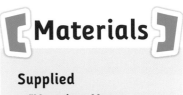

Materials

Supplied

● "Marvelous Mount Rushmore," *K¹² World: People and Places of the Past*, pp. 28–39
● *K¹² Language Arts Activity Book*, pp. LC 181–185

Also Needed

● index cards (4)
● glue stick
● scissors, round-end safety
● crayons (optional)

Keywords

chronological order – a way to organize that puts details in time order
fact – something that can be proven true
sequence – order
time line – a line showing dates and events in the order that they happened

⟦ Offline ⟧ 🕙 minutes

Work **together** with students to complete Get Ready, Shared Reading, Reading for Meaning, and Making Connections activities.

Get Ready

Lesson Introduction

Prepare students for listening to and discussing "Marvelous Mount Rushmore."

1. Tell students that you are going to reread "Marvelous Mount Rushmore."

2. Explain that before you reread the article, you will get ready by discussing sequence of events and words that tell us the order in which things happen.

Sequence of Events

Review sequence and time-order words.

1. Remind students that the order in which things happen in a story or article is called the **sequence**. Words such as *first*, *next*, and *last* help tell the sequence.

2. Explain that many nonfiction texts also include the years in which certain events happened. Paying attention to the years mentioned in a text is another way to identify the sequence, or order, in which things happen.

3. Have students practice identifying the sequence of events in a short paragraph. **Say:** Listen for years and words that tell the order in which things happen.

Margaret bought an old house in 2010. First, she painted it. Next, she got a new rug for the living room. The last thing she did was put a swimming pool in the backyard. The house looked brand-new by 2012.

- ► When did Margaret buy the old house? 2010
- ► What was the first thing she did after she bought the house? painted the house.
- ► What was the last thing Margaret did to fix up the house? put a swimming pool in the backyard.
- ► When did the house look brand-new? 2012

Objectives
- Identify sequence of events in informational text.
- Build vocabulary through listening, reading, and discussion.
- Use new vocabulary in written and spoken sentences.
- Increase concept and content vocabulary.

Words to Know

Before reading "Marvelous Mount Rushmore," go over Words to Know with students.

1. Read aloud each word or phrase and have students repeat it.

2. Ask students if they know what each word or phrase means.

   ► If students know a word's or phrase's meaning, have them define it and use it in a sentence.

   ► If students don't know a word's or phrase's meaning, read them the definition and discuss the word or phrase with them.

carve – to make something by cutting

chisel – a metal tool with a sharp edge, used to shape stone, wood, or metal

dangle – to hang loosely

Declaration of Independence – a document that declared the American colonies' freedom from England

dedicate – to open a monument, building, park, or other place to public use

dynamite – a very powerful explosive

jackhammer – a large tool for drilling rock

memorial – something built as a reminder of a person or event

president – a person who is the head of a country, company, or other organization

sculptor – an artist who makes works of art from stone, clay, wood, or another material

sculpture – a work of art, made by carving stone, clay, wood, or another material

Shared Reading

Book Walk

Prepare students for reading by taking them on a Book Walk of "Marvelous Mount Rushmore." Scan the magazine article together to revisit the text.

1. Turn to the **table of contents** in *K¹² World: People and Places of the Past*. Help students find the selection and turn to that page.

2. Point to and read aloud the **title of the article**.

3. Have students look at the **pictures of the article**.

   ► Whose faces are on Mount Rushmore? George Washington's; Thomas Jefferson's; Theodore Roosevelt's; Abraham Lincoln's

   ► Why did the sculptor choose George Washington to be one of the presidents on Mount Rushmore? George Washington was the first great American hero and the first president of the United States.

Objectives

- Activate prior knowledge by previewing text and/or discussing topic.
- Read and listen to a variety of texts for information and pleasure independently or as part of a group.
- Identify sequence of events in informational text.
- Identify chronological order.
- Create and/or interpret a time line.
- Read aloud grade-level text with appropriate expression, accuracy, and rate.

"Marvelous Mount Rushmore": Time Line

It's time to reread the article. Tell the students that they will reread "Marvelous Mount Rushmore" with a focus on the years when important events happened. Gather the Reading Aid on pages LC 181 and 182 in *K¹² Language Arts Activity Book* and the index cards.

1. Remind students that we can tell the order of events in an article when we see **signal words** such as *first, next, then,* and even *soon*. We call them *signal words* because they signal the order in which things happen.

2. Explain that we can also tell the sequence of events when an article mentions years. When an article mentions years and describes the events that happened in those years, we can determine the **chronological order** of the events. This means we can figure out the time order in which events happened.

3. Tell students that they will **read aloud the article with you**. As you read aloud together, you will stop at certain points to discuss the major events described in the article and the years when those events happened.

4. Explain that as you come across years listed in the article, you will write each year on an index card along with information about the events that happened in that year. You will use the index cards to build a time line after reading the article.

   ▸ If students are ready to write on their own, allow them to do so.

5. Refer to the Reading Aid.

Reading Aid Tear out the Reading Aid for this reading selection. Follow the instructions for folding the page, and then use the page as a guide as you reread the selection with students.

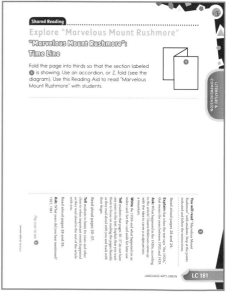
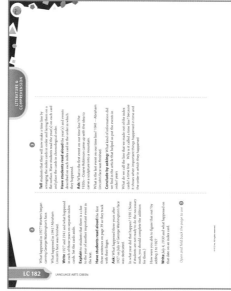

Reading for Meaning

Sequence in "Marvelous Mount Rushmore"
Check students' understanding of sequence and time-order words.

1. Remind students that the order in which things happen is called the **sequence**. Words like *first*, *next*, *then*, and *last* help tell the sequence.

2. Turn to pages 34 and 35. Reread these two pages to refresh students' memory about the order in which workers did things to carve the faces out of Mount Rushmore. Make sure students review the pictures while you read.

3. Have students retell the sequence of events using time-order, or signal, words. Possible answer: First, the workers used dynamite to blast away big pieces of rock. Next, workers drilled tiny holes into the rock. Then, sculptors used chisels to carve out a face. Last, workers used jackhammers to make the rock smooth.

   ► Which step came first? blasting the rock with dynamite
   ► Which step came last? smoothing the rock

4. Remind students that articles sometimes include years to help tell the sequence of events.

   ► When did men and women start working on Mount Rushmore? 1927
   ► When was the first face on Mount Rushmore dedicated? Possible answers: three years later; 1930
   ► When was the last face on Mount Rushmore finished? 1941

Objectives
- Identify sequence of events in informational text.
- Use time-order words.

Making Connections

 Facts for Four Presidents
Check students' understanding of facts about the presidents depicted on Mount Rushmore. Turn to pages LC 183–185 in *K¹² Language Arts Activity Book* and gather the glue stick and scissors.

1. Remind students that a fact is something that is true and can be proven. Have students think about facts they learned about the four presidents carved on Mount Rushmore.

2. Have students read aloud and follow the instructions at the top of the Activity Book page.

3. Have students cut out the pictures of the presidents on page LC 183 and glue them in the correct places on the drawing of Mount Rushmore on page LC 185.

   ► If students can't recall the correct places of the presidents, have them refer to the pictures in the article.

4. Have students write a fact about each president in the bubble above that person's picture.

   ► If students are not ready to write on their own, allow them to dictate their answers to you.

Objectives
- Respond to text through art, writing, and/or drama.
- Follow two- or three-step written directions.
- Identify facts in informational text.

5. Ask the following questions.

  ▸ Who was the first president of the United States? George Washington
    Point to the picture of George Washington. Students should point to the
    first face on the drawing of Mount Rushmore.

  ▸ Which president helped protect special places such as the Grand Canyon?
    Theodore Roosevelt   Point to the picture of Theodore Roosevelt.
    Students should point to the third face from the left on the drawing of
    Mount Rushmore.

  ▸ Why do you think Gutzon Borglun chose these four presidents to carve
    into Mount Rushmore? Answers will vary. Students may indicate that these
    presidents were all very important, or that these presidents all did great
    things for the United States.

6. If students enjoy coloring and time allows, have them color the drawing of
   Mount Rushmore.

LITERATURE &
COMPREHENSION

Introduce "George Washington: American Hero"

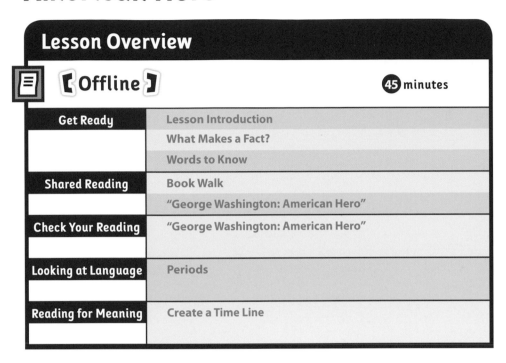

Lesson Overview		
【 Offline 】		**45** minutes
Get Ready	Lesson Introduction	
	What Makes a Fact?	
	Words to Know	
Shared Reading	Book Walk	
	"George Washington: American Hero"	
Check Your Reading	"George Washington: American Hero"	
Looking at Language	Periods	
Reading for Meaning	Create a Time Line	

Advance Preparation

Before beginning the Shared Reading, read "George Washington: American Hero" to locate Words to Know in the text. Preview pages LC 189 and 190 in *K¹² Language Arts Activity Book* to prepare the materials for Looking at Language.

Big Ideas

- ▸ Comprehension entails an understanding of the organizational patterns of text.
- ▸ Nonfiction texts differ from fiction texts in that they describe real or true things in life, rather than things made up by the author.
- ▸ Repeated rereading leads to increased fluency.
- ▸ During shared-reading activities, students learn more about how print works.

【 Materials 】

Supplied

- "George Washington: American Hero," *K¹² World: People and Places of the Past*, pp. 40–51
- *K¹² Language Arts Activity Book*, pp. LC 187–193

Also Needed

- glue stick
- scissors, round-end safety

Article Synopsis

Who could foresee that George Washington— plantation owner, horseman, and surveyor—would lead an army, help win freedom for America, and reluctantly become the first president of the newly formed United States?

Keywords

chronological order – a way to organize that puts details in time order

fact – something that can be proven true

sequence – order

time line – a line showing dates and events in the order that they happened

Literature & Comprehension LC 579

[Offline] **45** minutes

Work **together** with students to complete Get Ready, Shared Reading, Check Your Reading, Looking at Language, and Reading for Meaning activities.

Get Ready

Lesson Introduction

Prepare students for reading and discussing "George Washington: American Hero."

1. Tell students that you are going to read the nonfiction article "George Washington: American Hero," which is about the first president of the United States.

2. Explain that before you read the article, you will get ready by discussing

   ▸ What makes a fact
   ▸ How the events of an article can be told in the order in which they happened

Objectives

- Identify facts in informational text.
- Distinguish fact from opinion.
- Build vocabulary through listening, reading, and discussion.
- Use new vocabulary in written and spoken sentences.
- Increase concept and content vocabulary.

What Makes a Fact?

Explore how to identify the facts in nonfiction text.

1. Tell students that a **nonfiction article is a text about something real**. Nonfiction text is also known as **informational text**.

2. Nonfiction articles are filled with facts. A **fact** is something that you can prove is true. If you can't prove something is true, it can't be called a fact. It's important to recognize facts so that we can know if information is true or not.

3. Ask students the following questions about facts. Answers to questions may vary.

   ▸ What day is it? The day is a fact. You can prove what day it is.
   ▸ Where were you born? Your place of birth is a fact. You can prove where you were born.
   ▸ Are some tomatoes red? Yes, this is a fact. You can prove that some tomatoes are red.

4. Explain to students that the facts in some nonfiction articles are told in **time order**. For example, an article about a person's life would tell facts about events in the person's life in the order that they happened.

5. Read the following paragraph to have students practice identifying facts and the order in which the facts happened.
Say: Listen carefully to hear the facts in a paragraph.

Marvin Shultz was born in Boston, Massachusetts, in 1972. He went to college to study history in 1990. After he graduated from college, he moved to Chicago, Illinois. Then, he got a job as a history professor. Marvin thought that being a history professor was the best job in the world.

6. Ask students the following questions to check their understanding of facts.

   ▸ Is it a fact that Marvin Shultz was born in Boston? Yes   Why is it a fact? because you can prove it's true

   ▸ What did Marvin do right after he graduated from college? He moved to Chicago.   Marvin can prove that he moved to Chicago. What do we call something that you can prove is true? a fact

   ▸ Marvin got a job as a history professor. Is this a fact? Yes   How can you tell? You can prove it's true.

   ▸ Is it a fact that being a history professor is the best job in the world? No Why not? Possible answers: You can't prove it; you might think that a different job is better.

Words to Know

Before reading "George Washington: American Hero," go over Words to Know with students.

1. Read aloud each word and have students repeat it.

2. Ask students if they know what each word means.

   ▸ If students know a word's meaning, have them define it and use it in a sentence.

   ▸ If students don't know a word's meaning, read them the definition and discuss the word with them.

colony – a region ruled by a faraway country
general – a high-ranking officer in the army, air force, or marine corps
gentleman – a man with good manners; an honorable man
government – a system for ruling a country, state, or other area
inherit – to receive a person's belongings or money after that person has died
plantation – a large farm where crops are grown to be sold
surveyor – someone whose job it is to explore land, take measurements, and make maps

Shared Reading

Book Walk

Prepare students by taking them on a Book Walk of "George Washington: American Hero." Scan the magazine article together and ask students to make predictions about the text. Answers to questions may vary.

1. Turn to the **table of contents** in *K¹² World: People and Places of the Past.* Help students find the selection and turn to that page.

2. Point to and read aloud the **title of the article**.

3. Have students look at the **pictures of the article**.

   ▸ What do you think the article is about?
   ▸ Do you know who George Washington is? If so, name a fact, or something you know to be true, about George Washington.

4. Point to and read aloud any **headers, captions, or other features** that stand out.

   ▸ What do you think the article might tell us about George Washington?

Objectives

- Make predictions based on text, illustrations, and/or prior knowledge.
- Activate prior knowledge by previewing text and/or discussing topic.
- Read and listen to a variety of texts for information and pleasure independently or as part of a group.

"George Washington: American Hero"

It's time to read aloud the article.

1. Have students sit next to you so they can see the pictures and words while you read aloud the article.

2. Tell students to pay attention to the facts in the article so they can identify true things about George Washington's life.

3. **Read aloud the entire article.** Track with your finger so students can follow along. Emphasize Words to Know as you come to them. If appropriate, use pictures to help show what each word means.

Check Your Reading

"George Washington: American Hero"
Check students' comprehension of "George Washington: American Hero."

1. Have students retell the article in their own words to develop grammar, vocabulary, comprehension, and fluency skills.

2. Ask students the following questions.

   ▸ Where was George Washington born? Virginia; the English colony of Virginia
   ▸ What was George's first job? surveyor; he measured land   Who helped him to get that job? his brother, Lawrence
   ▸ What was the name of George's wife? Martha
   ▸ What is the name of the plantation where George and Martha lived? Mount Vernon
   ▸ What was George's job in the American Army? general; the top general
   ▸ How many years did George and his soldiers fight the British Army? eight
   ▸ What was George's job beginning in 1789? president; the first president of the United States

TIP If students have trouble responding to a question, help them locate the answer in the text or pictures.

Objectives
- Retell or dramatize a story.
- Answer questions requiring literal recall of details.
- Identify facts in informational text.

Looking at Language

Periods
Reread the article with a focus on how periods help readers understand text. Turn to the paragraphs on pages LC 187 and 188 and gather the Reading Aid on pages LC 189 and 190 in *K¹² Language Arts Activity Book*.

1. Explain to students that you will read the sample paragraphs to demonstrate the effect of periods. Then, **they will reread aloud with you** part of the article, focusing on periods and how they separate the ideas in a text.

2. Refer to the Reading Aid.

Objectives
- Read aloud grade-level text with appropriate expression, accuracy, and rate.
- Recognize that a statement ends with a period.

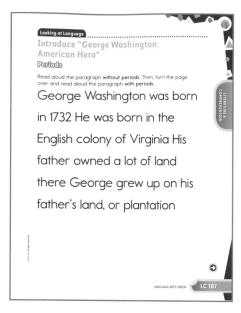

Introduce "George Washington: American Hero"

Periods

Read aloud the paragraph **without periods**. Then, turn the page over and read aloud the paragraph **with periods**.

George Washington was born in 1732 He was born in the English colony of Virginia His father owned a lot of land there George grew up on his father's land, or plantation

LITERATURE & COMPREHENSION

LANGUAGE ARTS GREEN   LC 187

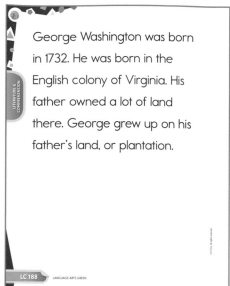

LITERATURE & COMPREHENSION

George Washington was born in 1732. He was born in the English colony of Virginia. His father owned a lot of land there. George grew up on his father's land, or plantation.

LC 188   LANGUAGE ARTS GREEN

Reading Aid   Tear out the Reading Aid for this reading selection. Follow the instructions for folding the page, and then use the page as a guide as you reread the selection with students.

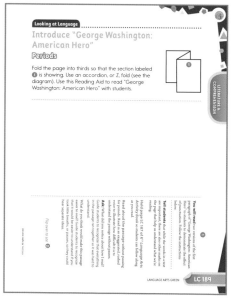

Introduce "George Washington: American Hero"

Periods

Fold the page into thirds so that the section labeled ❶ is showing. Use an accordion, or Z, fold (see the diagram). Use this Reading Aid to read "George Washington: American Hero" with students.

LITERATURE & COMPREHENSION

LANGUAGE ARTS GREEN   LC 189

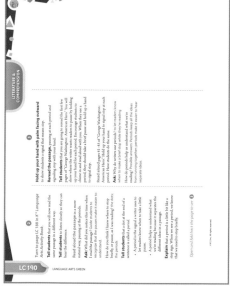

LITERATURE & COMPREHENSION

LC 190   LANGUAGE ARTS GREEN

Reading for Meaning

Create a Time Line
Check students' ability to identify the order in which events happened.

1. Tell students that the events in nonfiction articles are sometimes written in the order in which they happened in real life.

   ▸ Did George join the Virginia army before or after he became president of the United States? **before**
   ▸ When did George become president of the United States? **Possible answers: after the war against England ended; in 1789**

2. Tell students that they will create a **time line** to show the order in which events in George Washington's life happened. Turn to pages LC 191–193 in *K¹² Language Arts Activity Book* and gather the glue stick and scissors.

   ▸ Point to and read aloud the dates and information found in each fact box on page LC 191.
   ▸ Have students cut out the fact boxes and then have them lay out the boxes in the order in which the events happened.
   ▸ Help students glue the fact boxes in chronological order to the time line on page LC 193.
   ▸ Read aloud the date and the information in each box on the completed George Washington time line.

TIP Refer back to the article if students have trouble recalling the order in which things happened.

Objectives
- Identify chronological order.
- Identify facts in informational text.
- Create and/or interpret a time line.

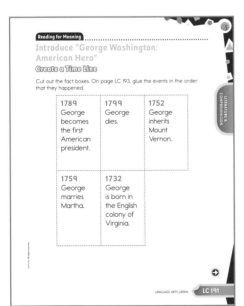

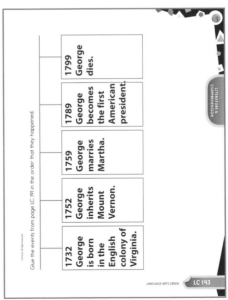

Explore "George Washington: American Hero"

Lesson Overview

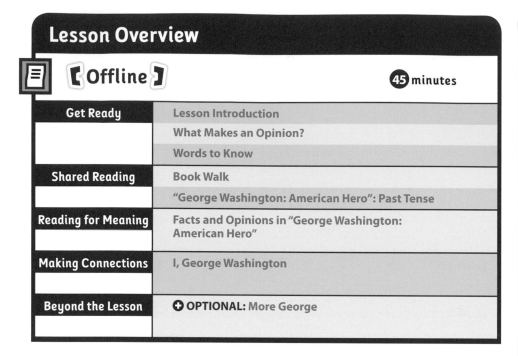

Offline · 45 minutes

Get Ready	Lesson Introduction
	What Makes an Opinion?
	Words to Know
Shared Reading	Book Walk
	"George Washington: American Hero": Past Tense
Reading for Meaning	Facts and Opinions in "George Washington: American Hero"
Making Connections	I, George Washington
Beyond the Lesson	⊕ OPTIONAL: More George

Big Ideas

▸ Repeated rereading leads to increased fluency.
▸ During shared-reading activities, students learn more about how print works.
▸ Readers must focus on the specific language of a text to aid in interpretation.

Materials

Supplied

- "George Washington: American Hero," *K¹² World: People and Places of the Past*, pp. 40–51
- *K¹² Language Arts Activity Book*, pp. LC 195–197

Also Needed

- household objects—red flower or picture of red flower; yarn; hole punch
- scissors, round-end safety

Keywords

fact – something that can be proven true

opinion – something that a person thinks or believes, but which cannot be proven to be true

verb – a word that shows action

[Offline] ⏱ 45 minutes

Work **together** with students to complete offline Get Ready, Shared Reading, Reading for Meaning, Making Connections, and Beyond the Lesson activities.

Get Ready ....

Lesson Introduction

Prepare students for reading and discussing "George Washington: American Hero."

1. Tell students that you are going to reread the article "George Washington: American Hero."

2. Explain that before you read the article, you will get ready by discussing how to tell if a statement is a fact or an opinion.

> **Objectives**
> - Identify opinions.
> - Distinguish fact from opinion.
> - Build vocabulary through listening, reading, and discussion.
> - Use new vocabulary in written and spoken sentences.
> - Increase concept and content vocabulary.

What Makes an Opinion?

Explore how to identify opinions. Gather the red flower or picture of a red flower.

1. Show students the red flower. Then make the following statements to introduce the difference between a fact and an opinion.

   ▶ This flower is red
   ▶ Red is the prettiest color.

2. Tell students that it is a **fact** that the flower is red. We can look at it and know that it's true. "Red is the prettiest color" is an **opinion**. An opinion is something that a person feels, or believes. You cannot prove it to be true. While one person may feel that red is the prettiest color, someone else may think that green is the prettiest.

3. Tell students that nonfiction articles are filled with facts. But sometimes authors of nonfiction articles make statements that are opinions, or feelings, about the subject. It's important to know the difference between a fact and opinion so that we can distinguish what is true from what somebody feels or believes.

4. Ask students if the following statements are facts or opinions.

   ▶ There are seven days in a week. fact
   ▶ I think that Saturday is the best day of the week. opinion

5. Point out that we can prove that there are seven days in a week, so this is a fact. However, some people may not believe that Saturday is the best day of the week, so it is an opinion.

6. Explain that certain words are clues that a statement is an opinion. These words include *think*, *believe*, and *feel*. Also, a phrase such as *some people say* is another hint that a statement is an opinion.

7. Read the following paragraph to have students practice identifying facts and opinions.
   Say: Listen carefully to hear the facts and opinions in a paragraph.

   Mr. Chekov has a rose garden. He grows red, white, and yellow roses. Mr. Chekov believes that the red roses smell the best but the yellow roses are the prettiest.

8. Ask students the following questions to check their understanding facts and opinions.

   ▸ Mr. Chekov has a rose garden. Is this a fact or an opinion? a fact   Why is it a fact? because you can prove it's true
   ▸ Mr. Chekov believes that red roses smell the best. Is this a fact or Mr. Chekov's opinion? Mr. Chekov's opinion   Why is it an opinion? Possible answers: because you can't prove it's true; because someone might think a different color rose smells better; because it has the word believes
   ▸ Mr. Chekov can prove he grows red, white, and yellow roses. What do we call something that you can prove is true? a fact
   ▸ Is it a fact that yellow roses are the prettiest roses? No   Why not? Possible answers: You can't prove it; you could say that a different-color rose is prettier.

Words to Know
Before reading "George Washington: American Hero," go over Words to Know with students.

1. Read aloud each word and have students repeat it.

2. Ask students if they know what each word means.

   ▸ If students know a word's meaning, have them define it and use it in a sentence.
   ▸ If students don't know a word's meaning, read them the definition and discuss the word with them.

colony – a region ruled by a faraway country
general – a high-ranking officer in the army, air force, or marine corps
gentleman – a man with good manners; an honorable man
government – a system for ruling a country, state, or other area
inherit – to receive a person's belongings or money after that person has died
plantation – a large farm where crops are grown to be sold
surveyor – someone whose job it is to explore land, take measurements, and make maps

Shared Reading

Book Walk

Prepare students by taking them on a Book Walk of "George Washington: American Hero." Scan the magazine article together to revisit the text.

1. Turn to the selection.

2. Point to and read aloud the **title of the article**.

3. Have students look at the **pictures of the article**.

4. Point to the map of George Washington's birthplace on page 41 and read aloud the caption.

   ► What does this map show? where George Washington was born
   ► George Washington was born in the Virginia colony. Is this a fact? Yes
   ► Why is it a fact? because you can prove that it is true

Objectives

- Activate prior knowledge by previewing text and/or discussing topic.
- Read and listen to a variety of texts for information and pleasure independently or as part of a group.
- Read aloud grade-level text with appropriate expression, accuracy, and rate.
- Distinguish texts that describe events from long ago from those that describe contemporary events.
- Recognize the past tense of verbs.

"George Washington: American Hero": Past Tense

Reread "George Washington: American Hero" with a focus on words that indicate that events happened in the past.

1. Have students to listen to the following sentences:

   My brother plays basketball.
   My brother played basketball.

2. Ask students the following questions.

   ► Which sentence tells us something that already happened, or happened in the past? *My brother played basketball.*
   ► Which word in the sentence is a clue that this already happened? *played*

3. Explain to students that authors use certain words to let us know that events have already happened. Some examples are action words, or **verbs**, in the past tense, such as *played*, *rode*, and *studied*. Other clues are words and phrases that indicate a time in the past, such as *last year* and *a long time ago*, and dates in the past, such as the year *2005*.

4. Tell students that **they will reread the article aloud with you**. As you reread together, you will stop at certain points to discuss the clues in the text that let us know that the events happened in the past.

5. **Read aloud** the first paragraph.

   ► Which words did the author use that let us know these events happened in the past? *was; owned; grew*
   ► What year did this paragraph mention? 1732   Does the year 1732 tell us that the events in the article are happening now or happened in the past? in the past

6. **Read aloud** the second paragraph.

   ▸ Which words did the author use that let us know these events happened in the past? *was; said; liked; grew*

7. Explain that action words, or verbs, that end in *−d* or *−ed* are clues that the events in the article happened in the past. Tell students that the verbs *owned* and *liked* in the paragraphs you just read are examples of this.

8. **Read aloud** the rest of the article. Pause at the end of each page to discuss the clues such as past tense verbs and years that indicate the events happened in the past.

9. Ask the following questions.

   ▸ Are the events of this article happening now or in the past? *in the past*
   ▸ What clues did the author use that let us know these events happened in the past? *Possible answers: verbs that end in −d or −ed; dates in the past; words such as was and rode*

Reading for Meaning

Facts and Opinions in "George Washington: American Hero"
Check students' understanding of facts and opinions.

Objectives
- Retell or dramatize a story.
- Identify facts in informational text.
- Identify opinions.
- Distinguish fact from opinion.

1. Have students retell the article in their own words to develop grammar, vocabulary, comprehension, and fluency skills.

2. Remind students that a fact is something you can prove is true. If a statement tells what somebody feels or believes, it is an opinion.

3. Ask the following questions.

   ▸ The article says that George rode horses. Is this a fact or an opinion? *fact* How do you know? *You can prove it; it's true.*
   ▸ The article says that some people thought George was the *best* horse rider in America. Is this a fact or an opinion? *opinion* How do you know? *The article says that some people thought it; you can't prove it.*

4. Read the following statements and have students identify each statement as a fact or an opinion.

   ▸ George Washington was a great hero. *opinion*
   ▸ George and Martha lived on a plantation called Mount Vernon. *fact*
   ▸ George and his soldiers were the bravest men in the land. *opinion*
   ▸ Americans won the war against England in 1783. *fact*
   ▸ George was the first president of the United States. *fact*

TIP If students are confused as to whether a statement is a fact or an opinion, pause and explain the answer.

Making Connections

I, George Washington

Check students' understanding of events in George Washington's life. Turn to pages LC 195–197 in *K¹² Language Arts Activity Book* and gather the scissors, hole punch, and yarn.

1. Tell students that they are going to plan and perform a short speech as if they were George Washington.

2. Point to and read aloud the first sentence starter on page LC 195.

3. Help students write their answer to complete the fact.

4. Continue to read aloud each sentence starter and help students write their answer.

5. Have students cut out the mask on page LC 197. Then, help them punch a hole on each side of the mask and attach pieces of yarn to the holes.

6. Help students put on the mask and tie the yarn behind their head. If you think it will be difficult for students to speak with the mask on, you may cut off the bottom of the mask so that the mask ends below the students' nose.

7. Have students use the completed Activity Book page as a script as they give a speech, pretending to be George Washington. Ideally, students should perform their speech for an audience of peers, but if necessary, they can perform their speech for you.

Objectives

Objectives

- Respond to text through art, writing, and/or drama.
- Identify facts in informational text.
- Speak audibly and clearly to express thoughts, feelings, and ideas.
- Stay on topic when speaking.
- Share work with an audience.

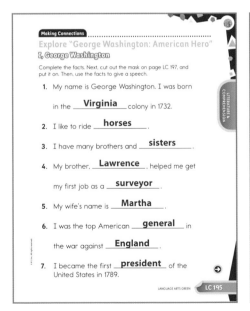

Beyond the Lesson

⊕ OPTIONAL: More George

This activity is OPTIONAL. It is intended for students who have extra time and show an interest in learning more about George Washington. Feel free to skip this activity.

1. Go to a library and look for a copy of *A Picture Book of George Washington* by David A. Adler.

2. Lead a Book Walk and then read aloud the book.

   ▸ Be sure to read aloud the dates and events on the time line.

3. Ask students to tell how the book and the article are alike and different.

4. Ask students what new facts they learned about George Washington.

   ▸ Verify that students are identifying facts, not opinions.

5. Help students locate opinions in the book.

6. Ask them to tell whether they like the book or the article better and why.

Objectives

- Compare and contrast two texts on the same topic.
- Identify facts in informational text.
- Identify opinions.
- Make connections with text: text-to-text, text-to-self, text-to-world.

Explore "Washington"

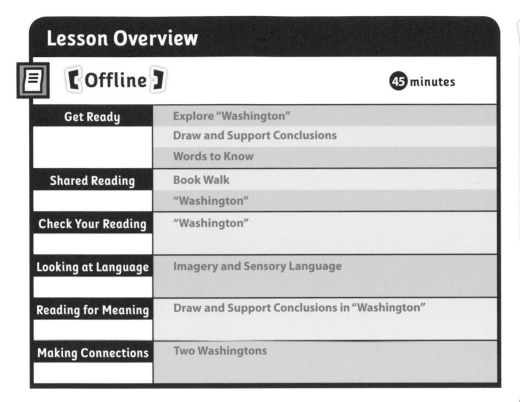

Lesson Overview

[Offline]   45 minutes

Get Ready	Explore "Washington"
	Draw and Support Conclusions
	Words to Know
Shared Reading	Book Walk
	"Washington"
Check Your Reading	"Washington"
Looking at Language	Imagery and Sensory Language
Reading for Meaning	Draw and Support Conclusions in "Washington"
Making Connections	Two Washingtons

Advance Preparation

Before beginning the Shared Reading, read "Washington" to locate Words to Know in the text. Preview pages LC 199 and 200 in *K¹² Language Arts Activity Book* to prepare the materials for Looking at Language.

Big Ideas

- Poems are different from prose in structure and content. They are generally organized in lines and often contain rhymes.
- Good readers use prior knowledge and text clues to infer or draw conclusions about what is implied but not directly stated in text.
- Readers must focus on the specific language of a text to aid in interpretation.
- The use of imagery and sensory language creates detailed pictures in the reader's mind, so the reader can understand and appreciate the ideas and feelings the writer conveys.

Materials

Supplied

- *Listen, My Children: Poems for First Graders*, p. 21
- "George Washington: American Hero," *K¹² World: People and Places of the Past*, pp. 40–51
- *K¹² Language Arts Activity Book*, pp. LC 199–201

Poetry Synopsis

This biographical and patriotic poem tells of George Washington's early days and how he eagerly responded to the call to help defend his country.

Keywords

compare – to explain how two or more things are alike

contrast – to explain how two or more things are different

graphic organizer – a visual tool used to show relationships between key concepts; formats include webs, diagrams, and charts

imagery – language that helps readers imagine how something looks, sounds, smells, feels, or tastes

sensory language – language that appeals to the five senses

 **Offline** **45** minutes

Work **together** with students to complete Get Ready, Shared Reading, Check Your Reading, Looking at Language, Reading for Meaning, and Making Connections activities.

Get Ready

Lesson Introduction

Prepare students for listening to and discussing "Washington."

1. Tell students that you are going to read a poem called "Washington."

2. Explain that before you read the poem, you will get ready by discussing how to draw and support a conclusion.

Draw and Support Conclusions

Explore how to draw and support a conclusion.

1. Remind students that sometimes a poet doesn't tell us everything in the words of a poem. Good readers listen and look for clues in the words and pictures to help them figure out things that are not directly stated.

2. Explain that along with the words and pictures of a poem, good readers think about what they know from personal experience to help them figure out things that the poet doesn't say directly. When readers do this, they **draw a conclusion**. A conclusion is based on the words you read and the pictures you see, along with your knowledge learned through personal experience.

3. Tell students to think about what the poet doesn't say directly. **Read aloud** the following poem.

    Rain, rain, go away,
    Come again some other day.
    Sun, sun, come and stay,
    Be my friend like yesterday.

    ▶ How do you think the poet is feeling? What feelings does the poet want you to think about? Possible answers: feeling sad; feeling bored; feeling restless   What do you know from your own experience that helped you draw this conclusion? Answers will vary; students might say that rain makes them sad, bored, or restless because they can't go outside and play.
    ▶ What do you think the weather was like before it rained? sunny; no rain   How did you figure that out, or draw that conclusion? The poet says the sun was a friend yesterday, so it must have been sunny.
    ▶ How do you think the poet feels about the sun? The poet likes it.   What words in the poem helped you draw that conclusion? The poet says the sun is a friend.

4. Tell students that as they listen to poetry, they should use the words and pictures and their own experience to draw conclusions.

Objectives

- Draw conclusions using text, illustrations, and/or prior knowledge.
- Support conclusions with evidence from text and/or prior knowledge.
- Build vocabulary through listening, reading, and discussion.
- Use new vocabulary in written and spoken sentences.

Words to Know

Before reading "Washington," go over Words to Know with students.

1. Read aloud each word and have students repeat it.

2. Ask students if they know what each word means.

   ▸ If students know a word's meaning, have them define it and use it in a sentence.
   ▸ If students don't know a word's meaning, read them the definition and discuss the word with them.

bugle – a kind of musical instrument that is shaped like a trumpet but doesn't have valves to press
slender – thin
strife – trouble
summons – an order; a notice to appear

Shared Reading

Book Walk

Prepare students by taking them on a Book Walk of "Washington." Scan the poem together and ask students to make predictions about the poem.

1. Turn to the **table of contents** in *Listen, My Children*. Help students find "Washington" and turn to that page.

2. Point to and read aloud the **title of the poem** and the **name of the poet**.

3. Have students look at the **picture of George Washington**.

   ▸ What do you think the poem is about? What is the topic?
   George Washington
   ▸ What are some things you already know about George Washington?
   Answers will vary.

Objectives
- Make predictions based on text, illustrations, and/or prior knowledge.
- Activate prior knowledge by previewing text and/or discussing topic.
- Read and discuss poetry.

"Washington"

It's time to read aloud the poem.

1. Have students sit next to you so that they can see the pictures and words while you read aloud.

2. Tell students to think about conclusions they can draw from the information in the poem.

3. **Read aloud the entire poem.** Track with your finger so students can follow along. Emphasize Words to Know as you come to them.

Check Your Reading

"Washington"

Check students' comprehension of "Washington."

1. Have students tell what "Washington" is about in their own words to develop grammar, vocabulary, comprehension, and fluency skills.

2. Ask students the following questions.

   ▸ What did Washington do by a river when he was a boy? play; fish
   ▸ What kind of man did Washington grow up to be? What did he look like? strong; slender; tall
   ▸ What happened when the bugles blew? What did Washington hear? He heard the bugles call his name.
   ▸ What did Washington do after he heard the bugles call his name? Possible answers: He said he knew his country needed him; he answered "Coming!"; he marched away.
   ▸ How did Washington feel about America? He loved it.

TIP If students have trouble responding to a question, help them locate the answer in the text.

Objectives
- Retell or dramatize a story.
- Answer questions requiring literal recall of details.

Looking at Language

Imagery and Sensory Language

Reread "Washington" with a focus on imagery and sensory language. Gather the Reading Aid on pages LC 199 and 200 in *K¹² Language Arts Activity Book*.

1. Remind students that poets carefully choose the words in their poems. They often use descriptive words and phrases that help you imagine pictures in your head. Poets may also use words that can help you imagine how something looks, sounds, or feels.

2. Explain that descriptive language makes a poem more interesting and helps you visualize what the poet wants you to imagine. Also, when you visualize, you're more likely to understand and remember what you read.

3. Tell students that **they will read the poem aloud with you**. You will stop after each stanza to discuss the descriptive language.

4. Refer to the Reading Aid.

Objectives
- Identify author's use of sensory language.
- Identify author's use of imagery and descriptive language.
- Use visualizing to aid understanding of text.
- Read aloud grade-level text with appropriate expression, accuracy, and rate.

Reading Aid Tear out the Reading Aid for this reading selection. Follow the instructions for folding the page, and then use the page as a guide as you reread the selection with students.

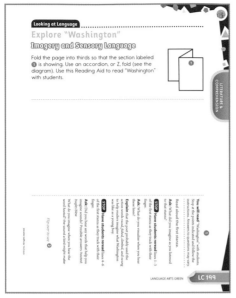
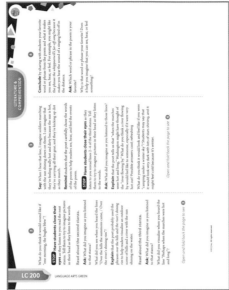

Reading for Meaning

Draw and Support Conclusions in "Washington"
Check students' ability to draw and support conclusions.

1. Remind students that good readers are able to use clues in the words and pictures to help them figure out things that the poet doesn't say directly. They also use their personal experience and prior knowledge to draw conclusions.

2. Remind students that they have a lot of prior knowledge about George Washington because of the article "George Washington: American Hero." This knowledge will help them draw conclusions about the poem "Washington."

3. The poet says that George Washington played by the river, raced rabbits, fished, climbed, and swung.

   ▸ What does this tell us about George Washington? What conclusions can you draw? He liked to play outside; he was healthy; he liked to have fun. How did you figure that out, or draw that conclusion? Answers will vary; students might say they know from personal experience that you have to be healthy to do these things, or that doing these things are fun, or that these are activities that take place outside.

> **Objectives**
> - Draw conclusions using text, illustrations, and/or prior knowledge.
> - Support conclusions with evidence from text and/or prior knowledge.

4. **Read aloud** the second stanza of the poem.

   ▶ What does it mean when the poet says Washington heard "the bugles called his name" and he "knew that his country needed him"? Washington joined the army and fought for his country.   Does the poet say directly that Washington was a soldier in the army? No   How did you draw that conclusion? What clues from the poem and your prior knowledge helped you figure that out? Answers will vary; students might say they used their prior knowledge from the article "George Washington: American Hero" to recall that Washington joined the army, and that he was the top general when America fought to be free from England.

5. The poet says that Washington "marched away / For many a night and many a day."

   ▶ What does that mean? Possible answers: George Washington was a soldier for a long time; Washington fought in the war against England for a long time.   How did you draw that conclusion? What helped you figure that out? Answers will vary; students might say they know that soldiers march. They may refer to their knowledge from the nonfiction article that Washington was a soldier and fought in a war against England for a long time.

6. **Read aloud** the last two lines of the poem.

   ▶ The poet says that George Washington "loved America all his life!" What ideas in the poem and your prior knowledge of George Washington support this statement? Answers may vary; students might say that you must love your country if you're willing to fight in a war, or that George Washington became the first president of the United States even though he didn't want to do it, which shows he cared about America very much.

Making Connections

 Two Washingtons

Check students' ability to compare and contrast characteristics of the poem "Washington" by Nancy Boyd Turner and the article "George Washington: American Hero." Gather *K¹² World: People and Places of the Past*. Turn to page LC 201 in *K¹² Language Arts Activity Book*.

1. Tell students that the poem "Washington" and the article "George Washington: American Hero" are both about the same topic—George Washington. However, the two texts are very different from each other.

2. Explain to students they are going to fill out a chart about these two texts to see how they are alike and different.

3. Point to and read aloud the title of each column on the Activity Book page.

4. Point to and read aloud the characteristic "Type of text."

Objectives
- Compare and contrast two texts on the same topic.
- Demonstrate understanding through graphic organizers.
- Make connections with text: text-to-text, text-to-self, text-to-world.

5. Help students write their answers for the poem and the article in the boxes under the titles for those texts.

6. Repeat Steps 4 and 5 for each remaining row in the chart. Students may refer to the article as needed to answer the questions.

7. Ask the following questions. Answers to questions may vary.

   ▸ How are the poem and the article alike? They are both about Washington. They both tell things that Washington believed.

   ▸ How are the poem and the article different? Students may refer to any of the differences indicated in the chart.

   ▸ Do you think the poem would be better if it included dates, as the article does? Why or why not?

   ▸ Did you learn something about Washington from the poem? If so, what did you learn?

   ▸ Which text did you like best, and why?

Introduce "Women of the White House"

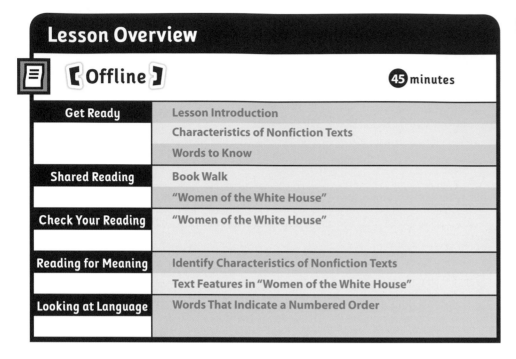

Lesson Overview

[Offline] 45 minutes

Get Ready	Lesson Introduction
	Characteristics of Nonfiction Texts
	Words to Know
Shared Reading	Book Walk
	"Women of the White House"
Check Your Reading	"Women of the White House"
Reading for Meaning	Identify Characteristics of Nonfiction Texts
	Text Features in "Women of the White House"
Looking at Language	Words That Indicate a Numbered Order

[Materials]

Supplied
- "Women of the White House," *K¹² World: People and Places of the Past*, pp. 52–61
- *K¹² Language Arts Activity Book*, pp. LC 203–204
- Story Card A

Also Needed
- whiteboard (optional)
- index cards (10)

Article Synopsis
It's been said that behind every great man there stands a great woman, and the First Ladies of the White House are proof of this.

Keywords

author's purpose – the reason the author wrote a text: to entertain, to inform, to express an opinion, or to persuade

fact – something that can be proven true

genre – a category for classifying literary works

informational text – text written to explain and give information on a topic

nonfiction – writings about true things

topic – the subject of a text

visual text support – a graphic feature that helps a reader better understand text, such as a picture, chart, or map

Advance Preparation

Before beginning the Shared Reading, read "Women of the White House" to locate Words to Know in the text. Write the words for the ordinal numbers *first* through *tenth* on index cards, one per card, and preview pages LC 203 and 204 in *K¹² Language Arts Activity Book* to prepare the materials for Looking at Language.

Content Background

An ordinal number is a number that indicates a position in a numbered order. Some examples of ordinal numbers are *first*, *third*, *tenth*, and *fifteenth*.

Big Ideas

► Nonfiction texts differ from fiction texts in that they describe real or true things in life, rather than things made up by the author.
► Exposing readers to a wide variety of genres provides them with a wide range of background knowledge and increases their vocabulary.
► Comprehension is facilitated by an understanding of physical presentation (for example, headings, subheads, graphics, and other features).

[Offline] 45 minutes

Work **together** with students to complete Get Ready, Shared Reading, Check Your Reading, Reading for Meaning, and Looking at Language activities.

Get Ready

Lesson Introduction

Prepare students for listening to and discussing "Women of the White House."

1. Tell students that you are going to read "Women of the White House," a nonfiction article about several of the First Ladies who have lived there.

2. Explain that before you read the article, you will get ready by

   ▶ Reviewing characteristics of nonfiction texts
   ▶ Practicing how to anticipate what you will find in an article based on what you already know about nonfiction articles

Characteristics of Nonfiction Texts

Review the genre of nonfiction. Gather Story Card A.

1. Remind students that **nonfiction**, or **informational**, texts are about real people and events. They are filled with **facts**.

2. Have students explain what a topic of a nonfiction text is.

   ▶ If students have trouble explaining what a topic is, remind them that the **topic** is what a text is mostly about.

3. Ask students to explain what usually is the author's purpose, or reason for writing a nonfiction text.

   ▶ If students need a reminder, tell them that the **author's purpose** for writing a nonfiction text is usually to inform, or tell, the reader facts about someone or something.

4. Tell students that since they have now read many nonfiction texts, they should have a lot of prior knowledge about what they will find in informational texts, such as nonfiction magazine articles.

Objectives

- Identify the topic.
- Identify characteristics of different genres.
- Identify the author's purpose.
- Identify features of informational text.
- Build vocabulary through listening, reading, and discussion.
- Use new vocabulary in written and spoken sentences.
- Increase concept and content vocabulary.

5. Have students practice figuring out the topic of a nonfiction article by having them look at the picture on Story Card A.

 ▸ If you saw this picture in a nonfiction article, what would you expect, or guess, the article to be about? Answers will vary; students might say they'd expect the article to be about Thanksgiving, foods Americans eat, dinnertime, or a special meal. What prior knowledge did you use to come up with you answer? Answers will vary; be sure students support their thinking with examples.

 ▸ Imagine that the topic of the article with this picture is "American holidays." Based on what you know about nonfiction texts and the topic, what other pictures do you think might be in the article? Answers will vary; if students have trouble answering, suggest they might expect to see pictures of people celebrating the Fourth of July, Valentine's Day, or New Year's Eve.

 ▸ Why do you think an author would write an article called "American Holidays"? to inform readers; to tell facts or teach readers about holidays that Americans celebrate

---

Words to Know

Before reading "Women of the White House," go over Words to Know with students.

1. Read aloud each word or phrase and have students repeat it.

2. Ask students if they know what each word or phrase means.

 ▸ If students know a word's or phrase's meaning, have them define it and use it in a sentence.

 ▸ If students don't know a word's or phrase's meaning, read them the definition and discuss the word or phrase with them.

auditorium – a large room used for performances, meetings, or other events
column – a series of articles in a newspaper or magazine, usually written by the same person
concert – a public performance by one or more musicians
construction – the act of building something
defend – to protect; to keep safe
First Lady – the wife of the leader of a country
hostess – a woman who entertains guests
lecture – a talk on a certain subject, presented to an audience or class
memorial – something built as a reminder of a person or event
wilderness – an area of land that is in its natural state, with few or no people living on it

Shared Reading

Book Walk

Prepare students for reading by taking them on a Book Walk of "Women of the White House." Scan the magazine article together and ask students to make predictions about the article.

1. Turn to the **table of contents** in *K¹² World: People and Places of the Past*. Help students find the selection and turn to that page.

2. Remind students that magazine articles have features that help readers better understand the information in the article.

3. Point to and read aloud the **title of the article**.

4. Have students look at the **pictures of the article**. Remind them that pictures help show ideas that are in the text.

   ▸ Based on the title of the article, the pictures, and your prior knowledge of nonfiction texts, what do you think this article is mostly about? facts about some of the women who have lived in the White House

   ▸ What do you think the article will tell us about women who have lived in the White House? Answers will vary. Students may mention information such as the women's names, when they lived in the White House, and important things they did.

   ▸ Based on what you know about nonfiction magazine articles, what kinds of features do you think you'll find in the article? Possible answers: a title; headings; pictures; photographs; captions; important words in bold print

5. Turn to page 54 and point to the heading. Remind students that articles can be broken up into sections, and a heading tells what a section is about. An article's headings can help readers figure out where to find certain information.
   Say: This heading tells readers that this section of the article is about Abigail Adams when she lived in the new White House. If I want to find information about Abigail Adams, this is the section I would look in.

6. Point to the caption next to the framed picture of the White House on page 54.

   ▸ What is this called? a caption
   ▸ What kind of information do we find in a caption? information about the picture that it is near

7. Point to the word *wilderness* on page 54. Remind students that some words in the article are darker, or bold, so that we will notice them. This word is bold because it's an important word in the article. We can find out what this word means in the glossary at the back of the magazine, on pages 62–64.
   Say: Let's read the definition for the word *wilderness*: an area of land that is in its natural state, with few or no people living on it. Can you make up a sentence using the word *wilderness*? Answers will vary. If students are not using the word correctly, give an example sentence that uses the word correctly and discuss the sentence to clear up any misunderstanding.

Objectives

- Activate prior knowledge by previewing text and/or discussing topic.
- Make predictions based on text, illustrations, and/or prior knowledge.
- Identify characteristics of different genres.
- Read and listen to a variety of texts for information and pleasure independently or as part of a group.

"Women of the White House"

It's time to read aloud the article.

1. Have students sit next to you so that they can see the pictures and words while you read aloud.

2. Tell students to listen for what the article is mostly about and clues to the author's purpose for writing the article.

3. **Read aloud the entire article.** Track with your finger so students can follow along. Emphasize Words to Know as you come to them. If appropriate, use the pictures to help show what each word means.

Check Your Reading

"Women of the White House"

Check students' comprehension of "Women of the White House."

1. Have students retell "Women of the White House" in their own words to develop grammar, vocabulary, comprehension, and fluency skills.

   ► Tell students to include **key details** in their retelling, such as the names of the First Ladies mentioned in the article and things that they did.

2. Ask students the following questions.

   ► Who is a First Lady? the president's wife
   ► Martha Washington was the wife of the first president. Why didn't she live in the White House? It hadn't been built yet.
   ► Why didn't Abigail Adams like living in the White House? It wasn't finished yet.
   ► Why did Dolley Madison take important things out of the White House? She wanted to protect them from English soldiers.
   ► How did Eleanor Roosevelt help Marian Anderson? She found a place where Marian could sing.
   ► Eleanor Roosevelt spoke to many people, and they listened to her through this device. What did people use so they could listen to Eleanor speak? a radio
   ► Eleanor also communicated with people in her column called "My Day." Where did Eleanor's column appear? in the newspaper

 If students have trouble responding to a question, help them locate the answer in the text or pictures.

> ### Objectives
> - Retell or dramatize a story.
> - Identify facts in informational text.
> - Identify forms of mass media.
> - Answer questions requiring literal recall of details.

Reading for Meaning

Identify Characteristics of Nonfiction Texts
Explore characteristics of nonfiction texts with students.

1. Remind students that nonfiction texts have certain characteristics, such as a topic and an author's purpose.

2. Ask the following questions.

   ▶ What kind of writing is "Women of the White House"? nonfiction; informational text   How can you tell the article is a nonfiction text and not a fiction text? It tells facts about real people; it's not a made-up story.
   ▶ What is the topic of "Women of the White House"? What is the article mostly about? First Ladies
   ▶ Why did the author write the article? to inform readers

Objectives
- Distinguish fiction text from nonfiction text.
- Identify the topic.
- Identify characteristics of different genres.
- Identify the author's purpose.
- Identify features of informational text.
- Identify purpose of and information provided by informational text features.

Text Features in "Women of the White House"
Remind students that nonfiction texts have many kinds of text features.

1. Turn to page 52 and point to the title of the article.

   ▶ What is this called? a title
   ▶ What does the title of an article usually tell the reader? what the article is about; the topic of the article

2. Point to the picture of the White House on pages 52 and 53.

   ▶ Why do you think the article has a picture of the White House? Possible answers: to show what the White House looks like; to show where the president and First Lady of the United States live

3. Turn to page 55 and point to the word *hostess*.

   ▶ Why is this word darker than the other words on the page? It's an important word.   Where can a reader find out what this word means? in the back of the magazine; in the glossary

4. Turn to page 55 and point to the mannequin wearing a gown.

   ▶ What does this picture show? a gown Abigail Adams wore
   ▶ How does this picture help the reader? It shows the kind of clothes Abigail wore when she lived in the White House.

5. Point to the drawing of Dolley Madison and the wagon on page 57.

   ▶ Why do you think the author included this drawing in the article? to help readers better understand how Dolley Madison saved important things by putting them in a wagon before the White House was set on fire

6. Point to the portrait of George Washington on page 57.

   ▸ Why do you think the author included a painting of George Washington on this page? to show one of the important things that Dolley Madison saved from the fire

7. Turn to page 58. Point to and read aloud the section heading.

   ▸ What would a reader expect to learn about by reading this section? things Eleanor Roosevelt did

8. Point to the picture of Eleanor Roosevelt on page 58.

   ▸ What is Eleanor doing in this picture? giving one of her radio talks

9. Point to the picture at the bottom of page 60.

   ▸ What does this picture show? how Eleanor used to visit with American soldiers
   ▸ Where is she sitting? outside the White House

Looking at Language

Words That Indicate a Numbered Order

Reread "Women of the White House" with a focus on words that indicate a numbered order. Gather the index cards that you prepared and the Reading Aid on pages LC 203 and 204 in *K¹² Language Arts Activity Book*.

1. Tell students that we can tell the arrangement, or order of things, with words such as *first, second, third*, and *fourth*. These words are related to numbers. For example, if a person is in the number one position in a line, we say that he or she is *first*.

   ▸ What word would we use for the number two position in a line?
   second   What about the number three position? *third*

2. Explain that the United States has had many presidents and First Ladies. So we often use words such as *first, second*, and *third* to indicate the order in which these men and women served as president and First Lady.

3. Tell students that the words *first, second*, and *third* are spelled differently than the numbers they are related to, *one, two*, and *three*. However, beginning with *fourth*, the words have something in common as to how they are spelled.

4. Write the words *four* and *fourth* on a whiteboard or sheet of paper.

   ▸ What do you notice about how the words *four* and *fourth* are spelled? They're the same except that *fourth* has the letters –*th* at the end.

5. Write the words *five* and *fifth* on the whiteboard or paper.

   ▸ What do you notice about how the words *five* and *fifth* are spelled? They're close to the same except that *fifth* has the letters –*fth* at the end.

Objectives
- Identify and use ordinal numbers, *first* through *tenth*.
- Make inferences based on text and/or prior knowledge.
- Read aloud grade-level text with appropriate expression, accuracy, and rate.
- Demonstrate one-to-one correspondence (voice-to-print).

6. Write the word *six* on the whiteboard or paper.

   ▶ What do you think we would add to the word *six* to indicate something in the number six position of a line? the letters *–th*

7. Tell students that **they will read aloud the article with you**. As you read aloud together, you will stop at certain points to discuss words that indicate the order of things.

8. Refer to the Reading Aid.

Reading Aid Tear out the Reading Aid for this reading selection. Follow the instructions for folding the page, and then use the page as a guide as you reread the selection with students.

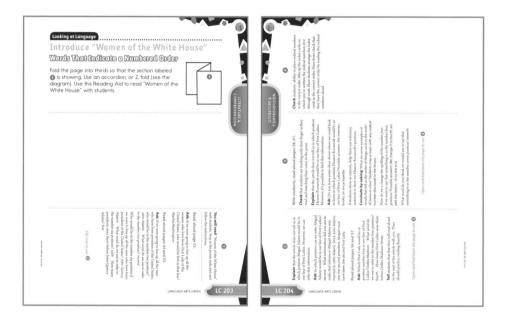

TIP If students are confused by the use of the ordinal number *first* and the use of the word *first* in the term *First Lady*, explain the following. The word *first* can be used to indicate the number one position when things are lined up or put in order, such as the first person in a line. However, the word *first* can also refer to the best or most important thing or person. So the term *First Lady* is a title that refers to the president's wife because she could be considered the "most important" woman in the country.

Explore "Women of the White House"

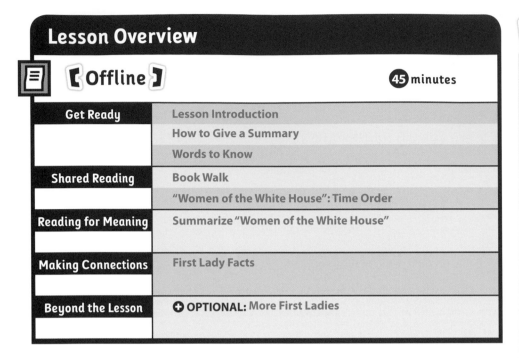

Lesson Overview

[Offline] **45** minutes

Get Ready	Lesson Introduction
	How to Give a Summary
	Words to Know
Shared Reading	Book Walk
	"Women of the White House": Time Order
Reading for Meaning	Summarize "Women of the White House"
Making Connections	First Lady Facts
Beyond the Lesson	⊕ OPTIONAL: More First Ladies

Materials

Supplied

- "George Washington: American Hero," *K¹² World: People and Places of the Past*, p. 41
- "Women of the White House," *K¹² World: People and Places of the Past*, pp. 52–61
- *K¹² Language Arts Activity Book*, pp. LC 205–211
- *K¹² My Journal*, pp. 2–53 (optional)

Also Needed

- tape, clear
- glue stick
- scissors, round-end safety

Keywords

self-monitor – to notice if you do or do not understand what you are reading

sequence – order

summarize – to tell in order the most important ideas or events of a text

summary – a short retelling that includes only the most important ideas or events of a text

Advance Preparation

Preview pages LC 205 and 206 in *K¹² Language Arts Activity Book* to prepare the materials for the Shared Reading.

Big Ideas

- ▶ Comprehension entails an understanding of the organizational patterns of text.
- ▶ Comprehension requires the reader to self-monitor understanding.
- ▶ Comprehension is facilitated by an understanding of physical presentation (for example, headings, subheads, graphics, and other features).

〖 Offline 〗 **45** minutes

Work **together** with students to complete Get Ready, Shared Reading, Reading for Meaning, Making Connections, and Beyond the Lesson activities.

Get Ready

Lesson Introduction
Prepare students for listening to and discussing "Women of the White House."

1. Tell students that you are going to reread "Women of the White House."

2. Explain that before you read the article, you will get ready by discussing how to give a summary of a nonfiction text.

> ### Objectives
> - Summarize a story.
> - Increase concept and content vocabulary.
> - Build vocabulary through listening, reading, and discussion.
> - Use new vocabulary in written and spoken sentences.

How to Give a Summary
Reinforce how to give a summary of a text.

1. Remind students that a **summary** is a very short retelling of the most important ideas or events of a text. A summary should answer questions such as "Who did what?" or "Why did this happen?"

2. Remind students that when we give a summary, we use our own words. We can use our own words to give a summary of a paragraph in a magazine article, a section, or the whole article.

3. Tell students that summarizing is important because it helps readers

   ► Check that they understand what they've read.
   ► Understand how a text is organized.
   ► Remember what they've read.

4. Have students practice giving a summary of a text. Turn to page 41 in *K¹² World: People and Places of the Past*. Read aloud the first paragraph of the article "George Washington: American Hero."
   Say: This is how I would give a summary of this paragraph: "George Washington was born in Virginia in 1732. He grew up on a big farm." I used my own words to tell the most important things in the paragraph.

5. Have students practice giving a summary of a text. Read aloud the second paragraph on page 41.

   ► How would you summarize this paragraph? Remember to use your own words to tell the most important things in the paragraph. Possible answer: When George was young, he was strong and active. He was good at riding horses.

Words to Know

Before reading "Women of the White House," go over Words to Know with students.

1. Read aloud each word or phrase and have students repeat it.

2. Ask students if they know what each word or phrase means.

   ▸ If students know a word's or phrase's meaning, have them define it and use it in a sentence.
   ▸ If students don't know a word's or phrase's meaning, read them the definition and discuss the word or phrase with them.

auditorium – a large room used for performances, meetings, or other events
column – a series of articles in a newspaper or magazine, usually written by the same person
concert – a public performance by one or more musicians
construction – the act of building something
defend –to protect; to keep safe
First Lady – the wife of the leader of a country
hostess – a woman who entertains guests
lecture – a talk on a certain subject, presented to an audience or class
memorial – something built as a reminder of a person or event
wilderness – an area of land that is in its natural state, with few or no people living on it

Shared Reading

Book Walk

Prepare students for reading by taking them on a Book Walk of "Women of the White House." Scan the magazine article together to revisit the text.

1. Turn to the selection.

2. Point to and read aloud the **title of the article**.

3. Have students look at the **pictures of the article**.

   ▸ What is the wife of a president called? the First Lady
   ▸ Who was the first First Lady? Martha Washington
   ▸ Where do the president and the First Lady of the United States live? the White House

Objectives

- Activate prior knowledge by previewing text and/or discussing topic.
- Read and listen to a variety of texts for information and pleasure independently or as part of a group.
- Identify sequence of events in informational text.
- Use time-order words.
- Read aloud grade-level text with appropriate expression, accuracy, and rate.

"Women of the White House": Time Order

It's time to reread the article. Tell students that they will reread "Women of the White House" with a focus on the time order of the important events. Gather the Reading Aid on pages LC 205 and 206 in *K¹² Language Arts Activity Book*.

1. Remind students that we can find many clues in a text that tell when events happened and the order in which they happened. Some of these clues include

   ▸ Signal words, such as *first*, *next*, and *last*
   ▸ Years, such as *2010*
   ▸ Phrases that indicate periods of time, such as *a few hours later* and *10 years after*

2. Remind students that when an article has most of the important events organized in the order in which they happened, we say that the article is organized **in sequence**.

3. Have students sit next to you so that they can see the pictures and words while you read aloud the article.

4. Tell students that **they will read aloud the article with you**. As you read aloud together, you will stop at certain points to discuss clues in the text that indicate when important events happened and the order of those events.

5. Refer to the Reading Aid.

Reading Aid Tear out the Reading Aid for this reading selection. Follow the instructions for folding the page, and then use the page as a guide as you reread the selection with students.

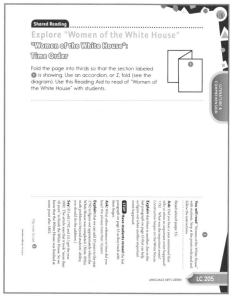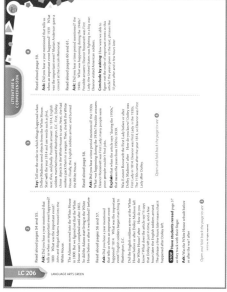

Reading for Meaning

Summarize "Women of the White House"
Check students' ability to summarize a text.

1. Remind students that a **summary** is a short retelling of the most important ideas or events of a text. A summary does not include very many details. A good way to do a summary is to answer the question "Who did what?"

2. Explain that doing a summary after reading part or all of a text is a good way to check that you understand what you've read.

3. Read aloud the section on Martha Washington and then have students give a summary of the First Lady in that section. Example summary: Martha Washington was the first First Lady, but she never lived in the White House because it wasn't built yet.

4. Read aloud the section on Abigail Adams and then tell students to give a summary of the First Lady in that section. Example summary: Abigail Adams was the first First Lady to live in the White House. Abigail was a good hostess and invited important people to the White House. She was the mother of another president.

5. Read aloud the section on Dolley Madison and then tell students to give a summary of the First Lady in that section. Example summary: Dolley Madison was the First Lady during a war. She saved many important objects in the White House before English soldiers burned it down.

6. Read aloud the section on Eleanor Roosevelt and then have students to give a summary of the First Lady in that section. Example summary: Eleanor Roosevelt was the First Lady when it was a tough time in America and during a big war. She tried to give people hope by talking to them on the radio and writing in a newspaper. Eleanor helped people, and she visited American soldiers.

7. Ask the following questions. Answers to questions may vary.

   ▶ Were you able to answer the question "Who did what?" for each section of the article?
   ▶ Do you think you understand the article?

TIP If students don't think they understand the article, reread the article aloud, pausing to let students ask you questions as you read.

Objectives
- Summarize a story.
- Self-monitor comprehension of text.

Making Connections

 First Lady Facts

Check students' ability to name important facts about the First Ladies in "Women of the White House." Turn to pages LC 207–211 in *K¹² Language Arts Activity Book* and gather the glue stick, scissors, and tape.

1. Tell students they are going to write facts about each First Lady in "Women of the White House" to make a fact cube.

   ▸ What text feature will help us find information about each First Lady mentioned in the article? headings
   ▸ Where in the article should we look for information about Abigail Adams? the section with the heading "Abigail Adams's New House"
   ▸ What is the heading of the section that has information about Eleanor Roosevelt? "Eleanor Roosevelt Does It All"

2. Have students cut out the pictures of the First Ladies. Students should match each First Lady's picture to her name and then glue the picture next to the name on the fact cube template.

3. Help students write at least one fact about each First Lady on the fact cube.

   ▸ If students are not able to write in the small spaces of the cube face, allow them to dictate the facts to you while you do the writing.

4. Have students cut out their fact cube, fold it, and glue or tape it together.

   ▸ If students will be completing the Beyond the Lesson activity, do not do this step until students have gathered facts about two additional First Ladies.

5. Ask the following questions.

   ▸ Which First Ladies lived in the White House during a war? Dolley Madison and Eleanor Roosevelt
   ▸ How do you think Dolley Madison felt when the English soldiers were marching close to the White House? Answers will vary.
   ▸ Who is your favorite First Lady? Why? Answers will vary.

 Reward: Add a sticker for this unit on the My Accomplishments chart to mark successful completion of the unit.

Making Connections

Explore "Women of the White House"

First Lady Facts

Cut out each First Lady's picture, and glue it next to her name on the shape. Write one fact for each First Lady. Cut out the shape, and fold along the lines. Glue or tape the tabs.

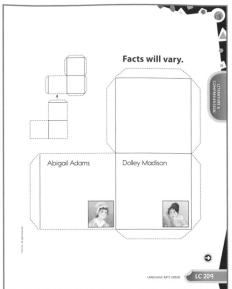

Facts will vary.

Abigail Adams

Dolley Madison

Facts will vary.

Martha Washington

Eleanor Roosevelt

Beyond the Lesson ....

⊕ OPTIONAL: More First Ladies

This activity is OPTIONAL. It is intended for students who would like to learn about other First Ladies of the United States. Feel free to skip this activity. Gather *K¹² My Journal* and turn to the next available page for **writing** in Thoughts and Experiences

1. Go to http://www.whitehouse.gov/about/first-ladies or http://www.ourwhitehouse.org/fstladyfacts.html, or conduct a search for "first ladies facts" on the Internet.

2. Help students read biographies of at least two First Ladies.

3. In their journal, help students record interesting facts about the First Ladies they learned about during their search.

4. If students have not yet completed the fact cube, have them write the names of First Ladies of their choice on the blank sides of the fact cube, along with one fact for each.

5. Ask students to tell how the First Ladies they read about are alike and different from the First Ladies in the article "Women of the White House."

Animal Antics

Unit Focus

In this unit, students will explore different types of animal tales, including fables and stories that explain why animals have certain characteristics. This unit follows the guided-reading instructional approach (see the instructional approaches to reading in the introductory lesson for this program). In this unit, students will

▶ Learn about the theme, or message, of a story.
▶ Review the strategy of making predictions and why it is important.
▶ Learn the characteristics of animal tales.
▶ Figure out the difference between a fact and an opinion.
▶ Explore the story structure elements of plot, setting, characters, and problem and solution.
▶ Use context clues to determine the meaning of words.
▶ Make connections with texts.

Unit Plan

[Offline]

45 minutes a day

Lesson 1	Introduce "The Camel and the Pig"
Lesson 2	Explore "The Camel and the Pig"
Lesson 3	Introduce "Heron and the Hummingbird"
Lesson 4	Explore "Heron and the Hummingbird"
Lesson 5	Introduce "The Tortoise and the Hare"
Lesson 6	Explore "The Tortoise and the Hare"
Lesson 7	Introduce "Come to My House"
Lesson 8	Explore "Come to My House"
Lesson 9	Your Choice

Introduce "The Camel and the Pig"

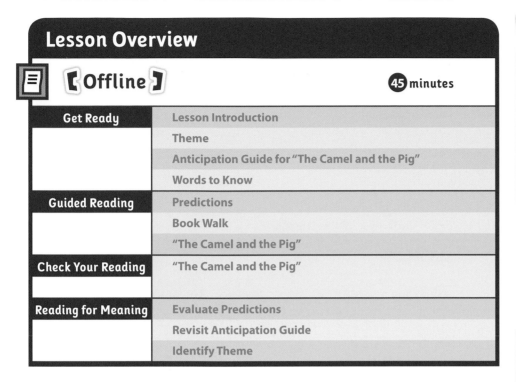

Lesson Overview

[Offline] 45 minutes

Get Ready	Lesson Introduction
	Theme
	Anticipation Guide for "The Camel and the Pig"
	Words to Know
Guided Reading	Predictions
	Book Walk
	"The Camel and the Pig"
Check Your Reading	"The Camel and the Pig"
Reading for Meaning	Evaluate Predictions
	Revisit Anticipation Guide
	Identify Theme

[Materials]

Supplied

- "The Camel and the Pig," *K¹² Classics for Young Readers, Volume A,* pp. 202–205
- *K¹² Language Arts Activity Book,* pp. LC 213–216

Story Synopsis

A tall camel and a short pig learn a big lesson after arguing about who has the better height.

Keywords

prediction – a guess about what might happen that is based on information in a story and what you already know

theme – the author's message or big idea

Advance Preparation

Before beginning the Guided Reading, read "The Camel and the Pig" to locate Words to Know in the text. Preview pages LC 215 and 216 in *K¹² Language Arts Activity Book* to prepare the materials for the Guided Reading. Read the Reading Aid to be aware of stopping points in the story at which students will make predictions.

Big Ideas

▶ Good readers interact with text to make logical predictions before reading; confirm predictions during reading; and revise or make new predictions as they read further.

▶ Readers need to recognize themes so they can identify why an author is writing, or the central message of a piece of literature.

▶ Guided reading provides support to early readers as they practice and apply the reading strategies of proficient readers.

 **Offline** **45** minutes

Work **together** with students to complete Get Ready, Guided Reading, Check Your Reading, and Reading for Meaning activities.

Get Ready

Lesson Introduction

Prepare students for reading and discussing "The Camel and the Pig."

1. Tell students that they are going to read "The Camel and the Pig," a story about two animals of different heights.

2. Explain that before they read the story, you will get ready by

   ▸ Discussing how to identify the theme, or message, of a story
   ▸ Using an anticipation guide to prepare for thinking about the theme of the story
   ▸ Reviewing how we make predictions while reading a story, and why it's important to make them

 Objectives

- Identify theme.
- Activate prior knowledge by previewing text and/or discussing topic.
- Build vocabulary through listening, reading, and discussion.
- Use new vocabulary in written and spoken sentences.

Theme

Introduce the concept that a story can have a theme, or message.

1. Remind students that every story has a plot. The plot is what happens in a story.

2. Tell them that some stories also have a **theme**. The theme is what the story teaches readers. It is the big idea, or message, that the author wants readers to think about. Some common themes are "Money can't buy happiness," "Don't judge others based on what they look like," and "Helping others is a good thing to do." Point out that the theme is not a single word, but a sentence.

3. Explain that the author usually does not directly state the theme, or lesson, of a story. Readers have to think about things the characters in the story say and do, and what the characters learn from those experiences, to infer the theme.

4. Tell students that to figure out the theme of a story, they can ask themselves, "What lesson did the characters learn? What lesson did I learn from reading this story? What message does the author want me to think about?"

5. Model how to identify the theme of a story. Have students think about "Goldilocks and the Three Bears."

   Say: In "Goldilocks and the Three Bears," Goldilocks goes into the bears' house without permission and ends up eating their food, breaking a chair, and sleeping in their beds. When the bears come home, they get angry and scare Goldilocks away. I think the theme of "Goldilocks and the Three Bears" is "You shouldn't use other people's things if you don't have permission," because that is the lesson that Goldilocks learned.

6. Have students think about "Little Red Riding Hood." Remind them that Little Red Riding Hood promised her mother that she would stay on the path through the woods. Instead, she wandered off the path to pick flowers after talking to the wolf, and the wolf almost ate her up.

   ▶ What do you think is the theme, or big idea, of "Little Red Riding Hood"? What lesson do we learn from reading this story? Answers may vary; possible themes are "Do what you promise to do," "Following the rules keeps you safe," or "You should listen to your parents." If students have trouble answering, tell them to think about what lesson Little Red Riding Hood learned in the story.

TIP If students have not read "Little Red Riding Hood," have them think of another story that they're familiar with, such as *The Legend of the Bluebonnet*, in which the theme is "It's good to help others."

Anticipation Guide for "The Camel and the Pig"

Introduce students to a prereading activity to help them think about the theme of the story before reading. Turn to page LC 213 in *K¹² Language Arts Activity Book*.

1. Show students the Activity Book page.
   Say: This activity will help us get ready to read by having us think about the ideas we'll find in "The Camel and the Pig."

2. Point to the first column in the guide.
   Say: Here's a list of statements that you may or may not agree with. I'll read each statement, and then you'll say whether you agree or not.

3. Point to the "Before reading" column.
   Say: We'll put an X under Yes or No depending on whether you agree with the statement or not.

4. Point to the "After reading" column.
   Say: After you read the story, we'll revisit the statements to see if you've changed what you think.

5. Help students to read each statement in the first column of the guide. Have students record what they agree with by placing an X in the Yes or No box in the "Before reading" column.

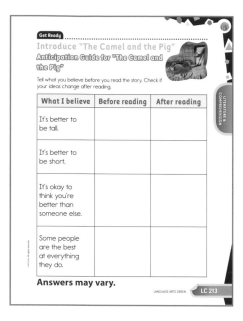

Words to Know

Before reading "The Camel and the Pig," go over Words to Know with students.

1. Read aloud each word and have students repeat it.

2. Ask students if they know what each word means.

   ▸ If students know a word's meaning, have them define it and use it in a sentence.
   ▸ If students don't know a word's meaning, read them the definition and discuss the word with them.

proud – feeling pleased with yourself; having a high opinion of yourself
ripe – ready to be picked and eaten
snout – the part of an animal's head that sticks out, including the nose and mouth

Guided Reading

Predictions
Explore how and why readers make predictions when they read.

1. Remind students that

   ▸ **Predictions** are guesses about what will happen in a story.
   ▸ We use clues in the story and what we know from our personal experience to make predictions.
   ▸ Making predictions makes us want to keep reading a story to see if what we predict happens or not.

2. Have students practice making a prediction.
   Say: Rhonda went to the movies last night. It was very late when she went to bed, and she forgot to set her alarm clock.

   ▸ What do you think will happen in the morning? Possible answers: Rhonda will get up late; Rhonda will be tired.
   ▸ What clues did you use from the story and your personal experience to make that prediction? It was very late when Rhonda went to bed, and she forgot to set her alarm clock. Students may say that when they go to bed late, it's hard to wake up the next day and they feel tired when they get up.

TIP Predictions are neither right nor wrong. We make the best prediction we can, based on the available information. Do not describe a prediction as "wrong," because this may discourage students from making predictions.

Book Walk
Prepare students for reading by taking them on a Book Walk of "The Camel and the Pig." Scan the beginning of the story together and ask students to make predictions about the story. Answers to questions may vary.

1. Turn to the **table of contents** in *K¹² Classics for Young Readers, Volume A*. Help students find the selection and turn to that page.

2. Point to and read aloud the **title of the story**.

   ▸ What do you think the story might be about?

3. Have students look at the **picture next to the first page** of the story.

   ▸ Who do you think are the characters in the story?
   ▸ What do you think might happen in the story?

Objectives
- Make predictions based on text, illustrations, and/or prior knowledge.
- Activate prior knowledge by previewing text and/or discussing topic.
- Read and respond to texts representing a variety of cultures, time periods, and traditions.
- Read aloud grade-level text with appropriate expression, accuracy, and rate.
- Make predictions before and during reading.

"The Camel and the Pig"

It's time to guide students through a preview of the story to prepare them for reading on their own. Gather the Reading Aid on pages LC 215 and 216 in *K¹² Language Arts Activity Book*.

1. Have students sit next to you so that they can see the pictures and words while you introduce and discuss the story.

2. Tell students that each character in this story believes that his height is better, but both of them will soon learn an important lesson.

3. Ask the following questions to help students activate their prior knowledge related to the story. Answers to questions may vary.

   ▸ Are you happy with how tall you are? Why or why not?
   ▸ Is there anything special you can do because of your height?

4. Tell students that you will preview the story to prepare them to read aloud the story to you.

5. Refer to the Reading Aid.

Reading Aid Tear out the Reading Aid for this reading selection. Follow the instructions for folding the page, and then use the page as a guide as you preview the selection with students.

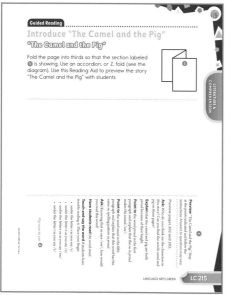
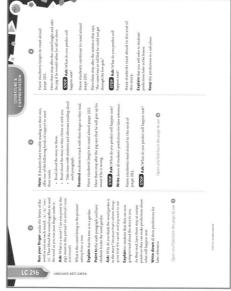

Check Your Reading

"The Camel and the Pig"

Check students' comprehension of "The Camel and the Pig."

1. Have students retell "The Camel and the Pig" in their own words to develop grammar, vocabulary, comprehension, and fluency skills.

2. Ask students the following questions to check their comprehension.

   ▸ Who are the characters in the story? a camel; a pig
   ▸ What do the camel and the pig argue about? which animal has the better height; whether it's better to be tall or short
   ▸ What does the camel say he will give up if he's not right? his hump
   ▸ What does the pig say he will give up if he's not right? his snout
   ▸ Where does the camel see ripe fruit growing? over a garden wall

 TIP If students have trouble responding to a question, help them locate the answer in the text or pictures.

Objectives
- Retell or dramatize a story.
- Answer questions requiring literal recall of details.

Reading for Meaning

Evaluate Predictions

Revisit the predictions that students made when they read the text.

1. Remind students that good readers make predictions by using clues in the words and pictures of a story, along with knowledge from personal experiences. Good readers can explain what clues they used to make a prediction.

2. Ask students the following questions to review and discuss the predictions they made when they read "The Camel and the Pig." **Refer, as necessary, to students' predictions that you wrote down.** Answers to questions may vary.

   ▸ What did you predict would happen after the pig says he will give up his snout if he is wrong? What really happened?
   ▸ What did you predict would happen after the camel eats all he wants? Did you use the picture to help make your prediction?
   ▸ What did you predict would happen after the camel laughs and asks if the pig would rather be tall or short?
   ▸ What did you predict would happen after the story says that the camel was so tall that he could not get through the low gate? What clues from the story or your own experiences did you use to make your prediction?

Objectives
- Evaluate predictions.
- Identify theme.

3. Remind students that it's okay if our predictions don't happen. Tell students to keep the following things in mind.

- ▸ Good readers make predictions that make sense based on the story up to that point.
- ▸ Good readers change their predictions as they read further and get more information.
- ▸ Even if our predictions don't happen, making predictions is important because it helps us be active readers.

Revisit Anticipation Guide

Check students' beliefs after reading the story. Gather the partially completed page LC 213 in *K¹² Language Arts Activity Book* to revisit the statements and students' responses in the Anticipation Guide.

1. Have students read aloud each statement again, and record what they agree with by placing an X in the Yes or No box in the "After reading" column.

2. Compare the responses in the "Before reading" and "After reading" columns.

- ▸ Did you change any of your ideas after reading "The Camel and the Pig"? Answers will vary.
- ▸ If you changed your mind, why did you do that? What did you read in the story that caused you to change your mind? Answers will vary; be sure students give examples from the story.

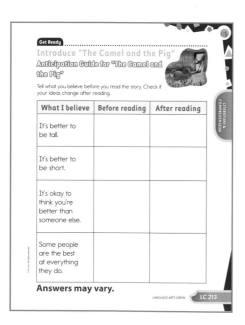

Identify Theme

Check students' ability to identify theme.

1. Remind students that the theme is the big idea, or message, of a story. Readers have to think about what happened in a story to figure out the theme for themselves, because the author usually doesn't directly state the theme.

2. Ask the following questions.

   ▸ What do you think the camel learns? that sometimes it's good to be short
   ▸ What do you think the pig learns? that sometimes it's good to be tall
   ▸ Do you think that it's always better to be tall? Why or why not? Answers will vary.
   ▸ What is the theme of "The Camel and the Pig"? What do you think is the big idea or message that the author wants readers to think about? Students may indicate that the theme is stated in the story as "It is sometimes better to be tall, and sometimes better to be small." You may also guide them to the theme "You should accept others as they are."

TIP If students give a summary of the story, remind them that a summary tells the plot, not the theme. Have them think about what the characters in the story learned from the things that they said and their actions.

Explore "The Camel and the Pig"

Lesson Overview

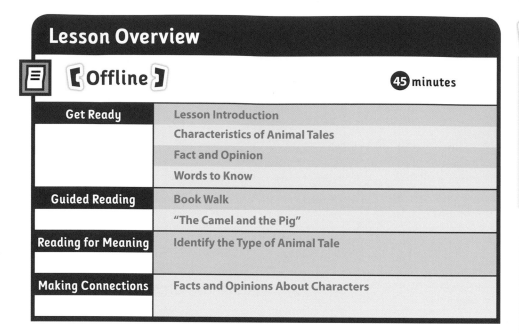

Offline   45 minutes

Get Ready	Lesson Introduction
	Characteristics of Animal Tales
	Fact and Opinion
	Words to Know
Guided Reading	Book Walk
	"The Camel and the Pig"
Reading for Meaning	Identify the Type of Animal Tale
Making Connections	Facts and Opinions About Characters

Materials

Supplied

- "The Camel and the Pig," *K¹² Classics for Young Readers, Volume A,* pp. 202–205
- *K¹² Language Arts Activity Book,* p. LC 217

Keywords

fable – a story that teaches a lesson and may contain animal characters

fact – something that can be proven true

genre – a category for classifying literary works

opinion – something that a person thinks or believes, but which cannot be proven to be true

Big Ideas

▸ Exposing readers to a wide variety of genres provides them with a wide range of background knowledge and increases their vocabulary.

▸ Readers must focus on the specific language of a text to aid in interpretation.

▸ Repeated rereading leads to increased fluency.

 **45** minutes

Work **together** with students to complete Get Ready, Guided Reading, Reading for Meaning, and Making Connections activities.

Get Ready

Lesson Introduction
Prepare students for reading and discussing "The Camel and the Pig."

1. Tell students that they are going to reread "The Camel and the Pig."

2. Explain that before they read the story, you will get ready by discussing

   ▸ A kind of story called an animal tale
   ▸ How to tell a fact from an opinion

Objectives
- Identify genre.
- Identify characteristics of different genres.
- Identify the moral or lesson of a text.
- Identify opinions.
- Identify facts.
- Distinguish fact from opinion.
- Build vocabulary through listening, reading, and discussion.
- Use new vocabulary in written and spoken sentences.

Characteristics of Animal Tales
Introduce students to characteristics of animal tales.

1. Explain that although all animal tales have animal characters that act like people, there are different kinds of animal tales.

   ▸ Fables teach a lesson.
   ▸ "Why" tales explain why animals have a certain features, such as why the giraffe has a long neck.
   ▸ Trickster tales have a main character that tries to outsmart other characters. Br'er Rabbit, Anansi the spider, and Coyote are all tricksters.

2. Remind students that the story "The Camel and the Pig" has animal characters and it teaches a lesson. That means "The Camel and the Pig" is the kind of animal tale that is called a **fable**.

3. Have students practice classifying an animal tale and identifying the **moral**, or lesson, of a fable.
   Say: A crow, suffering from thirst, found a water pitcher. But when he tried to drink, he found he could not reach his beak far enough into the pitcher to get the water. He tried and tried, and then gave up in frustration. Suddenly, he had an idea. He dropped pebble after pebble after pebble into the pitcher. Finally, the water rose to the top and the crow was able to drink.

   ▸ What kind of animal tale is the story about the crow and the pitcher? a fable
   ▸ What is the moral of the story? What lesson does it teach? Guide students to recognize one of the following possible lessons: We can get big things done if we do a little bit at a time; if you really want something, you can figure out a way to get it.
   ▸ What characteristics tell you that it's a fable? It has an animal character that acts like a human, and it teaches a lesson.

Fact and Opinion

Reinforce how to tell the difference between facts and opinions.

1. Remind students that a **fact** is something that is true and can be proven. An **opinion** is something that a person feels or believes.

2. **Read aloud** the following sentences.

   ▸ A watermelon is a fruit. This is a fact.
   ▸ A watermelon is the best-tasting fruit. This is an opinion.

3. Explain that saying that watermelon is the best-tasting fruit is an opinion because you can't prove it's true. It's what someone believes about watermelons. Other people might believe that apples are the best-tasting fruit—that's their opinion.

4. Tell students that readers can usually find both facts and opinions in fiction stories. It's important to know the difference between a fact and an opinion so that we can identify what is true and what is something a person feels or believes.

5. Ask students if each of the following statements is a fact or an opinion.

   ▸ Dogs walk on four legs. fact
   ▸ Dogs make the best pets. opinion
   ▸ Pandas are fun to watch when they play. opinion
   ▸ Pandas have black and white fur. fact

Words to Know

Before reading "The Camel and the Pig," go over Words to Know with students.

1. Read aloud each word and have students repeat it.

2. Ask students if they know what each word means.

   ▸ If students know a word's meaning, have them define it and use it in a sentence.
   ▸ If students don't know a word's meaning, read them the definition and discuss the word with them.

proud – feeling pleased with yourself; having a high opinion of yourself
ripe – ready to be picked and eaten
snout – the part of an animal's head that sticks out, including the nose and mouth

Guided Reading ·

Book Walk

Prepare students for reading by taking them on a Book Walk of "The Camel and the Pig." Scan the story together to revisit the characters and events.

1. Turn to the selection in *K¹² Classics for Young Readers, Volume A.*

2. Have students read aloud the **title of the story**.

3. Have students review the **pictures of the story**. Answers to questions may vary.

   ▸ What facts do you know about real camels?
   ▸ How do you feel about camels? Do you think they are funny looking? Is that a fact or an opinion?
   ▸ What facts do you know about real pigs?
   ▸ What do you believe about pigs? Do you think they have cute tails? Do you think they are dirty? Is that a fact or an opinion?

Objectives

- Activate prior knowledge by previewing text and/or discussing topic.
- Read and respond to texts representing a variety of cultures, time periods, and traditions.
- Read aloud grade-level text with appropriate expression, accuracy, and rate.

"The Camel and the Pig"

It's time for students to reread the story.

1. Tell students that "The Camel and the Pig" should now be familiar to them because they have read it before.

2. Explain that they will reread the story aloud to you, and you are there to give them help if they need it.

3. If students have trouble reading on their own, offer one of the following levels of support to meet their needs.

   ▸ Read aloud the story to them.
   ▸ Read aloud the story as they chime in with you.
   ▸ Take turns with students and alternate reading aloud each paragraph.

4. Remind students to track with their finger as they read.

5. Tell students that as they read, they should think about characteristics of animal tales and look for facts and opinions.

Reading for Meaning

Identify the Type of Animal Tale

Check students' understanding of animal tales and their ability to identify a fable and the lesson it teaches.

1. Have students retell "The Camel and the Pig" in their own words to develop grammar, vocabulary, comprehension, and fluency skills.

2. Remind students that there are different types of animal tales. They all have animals that act like humans, but some teach a lesson; some explain why an animal is the way it is; and others have characters that are tricksters.

3. Ask students the following questions.

   ▸ Does "The Camel and the Pig" explain why an animal is the way it is or does it teach a lesson? teaches a lesson
   ▸ What kind of animal tale is "The Camel and the Pig"? a fable
   ▸ What things in "The Camel and the Pig" tell you it's a fable? It has animals that act like humans, and it teaches a lesson.
   ▸ What lesson does "The Camel and the Pig" teach us? Possible answers: Sometimes it's good to be tall, and other times it's good to be short. It's not better to be tall or short; it's best to be yourself.

Objectives
- Retell or dramatize a story.
- Identify genre.
- Identify characteristics of different genres.
- Identify the moral or lesson of a text.

Making Connections

 Facts and Opinions About Characters

Check students' ability to distinguish facts from opinions. Turn to page LC 217 in *K¹² Language Arts Activity Book*.

1. Remind students that it's important to know the difference between a fact and an opinion so that we can identify what is true and what is something a person feels or believes.

2. Tell students that they will practice identifying facts and opinions about the characters in "The Camel and the Pig."

3. Look at the table with students and explain that they will think of a fact or opinion for each category listed in the first column. They will write the fact or opinion in the table.

4. Point to and help students read aloud the first-row heading, "Character's opinion."

5. Tell students that the characters' opinions are things that the characters in the story think or believe. Have students tell you an opinion that the camel states in the story and then an opinion that the pig states in the story. the camel: It is better to be tall; the pig: It is better to be short.

Objectives
- Identify opinions.
- Identify facts.
- Distinguish fact from opinion.
- Demonstrate understanding through graphic organizers.

6. Help students write the opinions in the first row in the column for each character.

   ▸ If students can't recall opinions stated by each character, refer back to the story and help students find them.

7. Point to and help students read aloud the second-row heading, "Fact about the character."

8. Remind students that facts about the characters are things that we know are true. Have students tell you a fact about the character of the camel that we know from the events of the story and then a fact about the character of the pig. Possible answers: The camel is taller than the pig; the pig is shorter than the camel; the camel reaches over a wall to get fruit; the pig cannot reach over the wall; the camel cannot go through the low gate; the pig can go through the low gate to eat fruit.

9. Help students write a fact in the second row in the column for each character.

   ▸ If students can't recall facts about the characters, refer back to the story and help students find them.

10. Point to and help students read aloud the third-row heading, "My opinion of the character."

11. Have students tell you their opinion, or what they think, about the camel in the story and then their opinion about the pig in the story. Answers will vary.

12. Help students write their opinions in the third row in the column for each character.

    ▸ If students can't think of a personal opinion about each character, refer back to the story and have students look at the pictures of the characters to think of a way to describe them, such as "funny looking" or "cute."

13. Point to and help students read aloud the fourth-row heading, "Fact about this type of animal."

14. Have students tell you a fact, or something that is true, about real camels, and then a fact about real pigs. Possible answers: A camel has a hump on its back; a camel has long legs; a camel lives in the desert; people can ride on a camel; a pig has a curly tail; a pig lives on a farm.

15. Have students test their fact by thinking about whether or not they can prove it is true.

16. Help students write the fact in the fourth row in the column for each character.

   ▸ If students can't recall a fact about each type of animal, ask questions such as "What does this kind of animal look like?" or "Where does this kind of animal live?"

17. Ask the following questions.

   ▸ What is the difference between a fact and an opinion? We can prove that a fact is true; an opinion is what somebody thinks or believes, but we cannot prove that it's true.
   ▸ What are some things that help us recognize opinions? Possible answers: words such as *think*, *believe*, and *feel*; statements such as *it's better* and *it's best*

Making Connections

Explore "The Camel and the Pig"
Facts and Opinions About Characters

Write facts and opinions to complete the table.

Possible answers are shown.	Camel	Pig
Character's opinion	It is better to be tall.	It is better to be short.
Fact about the character	The camel is taller than the pig.	The pig is shorter than the camel.
My opinion of the character	The camel looks funny.	The pig has a cute tail.
Fact about this type of animal	A camel has a hump on its back. A camel lives in the desert.	A pig has a curly tail. A pig lives on a farm.

LANGUAGE ARTS GREEN · LC 217

Introduce "Heron and the Hummingbird"

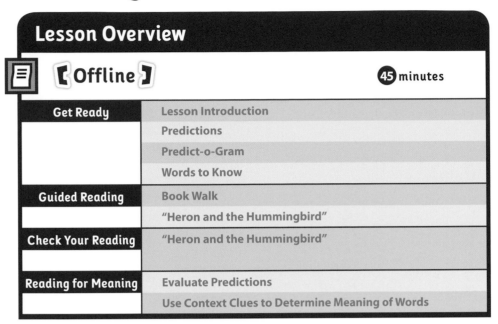

Lesson Overview

Offline　　45 minutes

Get Ready	Lesson Introduction
	Predictions
	Predict-o-Gram
	Words to Know
Guided Reading	Book Walk
	"Heron and the Hummingbird"
Check Your Reading	"Heron and the Hummingbird"
Reading for Meaning	Evaluate Predictions
	Use Context Clues to Determine Meaning of Words

Advance Preparation

Before beginning the Guided Reading, read "Heron and the Hummingbird" to locate Words to Know in the text. Preview pages LC 221 and 222 in *K¹² Language Arts Activity Book* to prepare the materials for the Guided Reading.

Big Ideas

- ▶ Good readers interact with text to make logical predictions before reading; confirm predictions during reading; and revise or make new predictions as they read further.
- ▶ An awareness of story structure elements (setting, characters, plot) provides readers a foundation for constructing meaning when reading new stories and writing their own stories.
- ▶ Guided reading provides support to early readers as they practice and apply the reading strategies of proficient readers.
- ▶ Early learners acquire vocabulary through active exposure (by talking and listening, being read to, and receiving explicit instruction).
- ▶ Verbalizing your thoughts while modeling a reading strategy allows students to see what goes on inside the head of an effective reader; it makes visible the normally hidden process of comprehending text.

Materials

Supplied

- "Heron and the Hummingbird," *K¹² Classics for Young Readers*, Volume A, pp. 206–211
- *K¹² Language Arts Activity Book*, pp. LC 219–222

Story Synopsis

This animal tale explains how a particular bird came to own all the fish in the rivers and lakes of the world.

Keywords

context – the parts of a sentence or passage surrounding a word

prediction – a guess about what might happen that is based on information in a story and what you already know

story structure elements – components of a story; they include character, setting, plot, problem, and solution

 **Offline** **45** minutes

Work **together** with students to complete Get Ready, Guided Reading, Check Your Reading, and Reading for Meaning activities.

Get Ready

Lesson Introduction

Prepare students for reading and discussing "Heron and the Hummingbird," a Hitchiti tale retold by S.E. Schlosser.

1. Tell students that they are going to read "Heron and the Hummingbird," a Hitchiti Indian tale about two birds who like to eat fish.

2. Explain that before they read the story, you will get ready by

   ▸ Reviewing how we make predictions while reading a story, and why it's important to make them
   ▸ Using a Predict-o-Gram to make predictions before reading the story

 Objectives
- Make predictions based on text, illustrations, and/or prior knowledge.
- Demonstrate understanding through graphic organizers.
- Build vocabulary through listening, reading, and discussion.
- Use new vocabulary in written and spoken sentences.

Predictions

Explore how and why readers make predictions when they read.

1. Remind students that

   ▸ **Predictions** are guesses about what will happen in a story.
   ▸ We use clues in the story and what we know from our personal experience to make predictions.
   ▸ Making predictions makes us want to keep reading a story to see if what we predict happens or not.

2. Tell students that predictions are neither right nor wrong. We make the best prediction we can, based on the available information.

✏ Predict-o-Gram

Introduce students to a prereading activity to help them make predictions about the story. Turn to page LC 219 in *K¹² Language Arts Activity Book*.

1. Show students the Activity Book page.
   Say: This Predict-o-Gram will help us get ready to read by using our prior knowledge of the parts of a story to make predictions about "Heron and the Hummingbird."

2. Point to the word bank of story words and phrases.
   Say: Here are words and phrases from the story.

3. Point to each box: "Characters," "Setting," "Problem," "Characters' actions," "Solution."

   Say: Before we read the story, we'll predict which story element each word and phrase from the story tells about and write it in that box. After we read the story, we'll revisit our original predictions to see if we need to move any of the words or phrases to a different box.

4. Help students read each word and phrase. After students decide which box the word or phrase belongs in, help them write it in that box.

5. If students have trouble placing any of the words or phrases, guide them with the following questions.

   ▸ Could any of the words name a character?
   ▸ Does the word name a place? If the word names a place, do you think the word could be related to the setting of the story?
   ▸ Could any of the words or phrases be used to describe a problem? Could any of the words or phrases describe the solution to a problem?
   ▸ Which of the words or phrases could be related to something that characters could do, or their actions?

TIP Students should not be expected to correctly place the words and phrases until *after* reading.

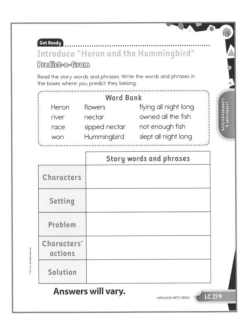

Words to Know

Before reading "Heron and the Hummingbird," go over Words to Know with students.

1. Read aloud each word and have students repeat it.

2. Ask students if they know what each word means.

   ▶ If students know a word's meaning, have them define it and use it in a sentence.

   ▶ If students don't know a word's meaning, read them the definition and discuss the word with them.

awkward – clumsy; not graceful
distract – to draw away someone's attention
nectar – the sweet liquid of a plant that attracts insects and birds
scenery – the way the land looks in a particular place
sleek – smooth and shiny
steady – having a continuous and regular movement
stoically – showing little or no emotion toward pain or pleasure

Guided Reading

Book Walk

Prepare students for reading by taking them on a Book Walk of "Heron and the Hummingbird." Scan the story together and ask students to make predictions about the story. Answers to questions may vary.

1. Turn to the **table of contents** in *K¹² Classics for Young Readers, Volume A*. Help students find the selection and turn to that page.

2. Have students read aloud the **title of the story**.

   ▶ What do you think the story might be about?

3. Have students look at the **pictures of the story**.

   ▶ Based on what you put in the Predict-o-Gram, where do you think the story takes place?

   ▶ Based on what you put in the Predict-o-Gram, what do you think might happen in the story?

Objectives

- Make predictions based on text, illustrations, and/or prior knowledge.
- Activate prior knowledge by previewing text and/or discussing topic.
- Read and respond to texts representing a variety of cultures, time periods, and traditions.
- Read aloud grade-level text with appropriate expression, accuracy, and rate.

"Heron and the Hummingbird"

It's time to guide students through a preview of the story to prepare them for reading on their own. Gather the Reading Aid on pages LC 221 and 222 in *K^{12} Language Arts Activity Book*.

1. Have students sit next to you so that they can see the pictures and words while you introduce and discuss the story.

2. Tell students that you will preview the story to prepare them to read aloud the story to you.

3. Refer to the Reading Aid.

Reading Aid Tear out the Reading Aid for this reading selection. Follow the instructions for folding the page, and then use the page as a guide as you preview the selection with students.

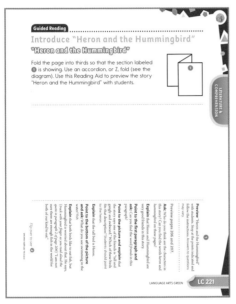
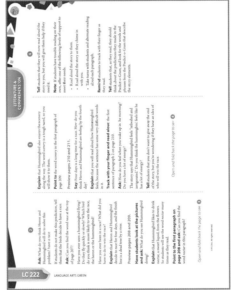

Check Your Reading

"Heron and the Hummingbird"

Check students' comprehension of "Heron and the Hummingbird."

- ▶ Who are the characters in the story? Heron; Hummingbird
- ▶ What do Heron and Hummingbird both like to eat? fish
- ▶ What does Hummingbird also like to eat? nectar
- ▶ What is Hummingbird worried about at the beginning of the story? He's not sure there's enough fish in the world for both of their kind to eat.
- ▶ What do Heron and Hummingbird do to see who gets to own all the fish? They have a race.
- ▶ How long is the race? four days
- ▶ What is the finish line for the race? an old dead tree next to a river

TIP If students have trouble responding to a question, help them locate the answer in the text.

> **Objectives**
> - Identify character(s).
> - Identify important details and/or events of a story.
> - Answer questions requiring literal recall of details.

Reading for Meaning

✏ **Evaluate Predictions**

Revisit the predictions students made using the partially completed Predict-o-Gram on page LC 219 in *K¹² Language Arts Activity Book*. Have students use the Predict-o-Gram as a tool for retelling the story.

1. Remind students that they used their prior knowledge of story elements to make predictions using the Predict-o-Gram. Reinforce that it's okay if their predictions didn't happen.

2. Helps students review what they wrote in each box of the Predict-o-Gram. Have them cross out and change any words or phrases that belong in a different box.

3. Ask students the following questions. Answers to questions may vary.

   ▸ Which words did you predict belonged in the "Characters" box? Why did you decide to put those words there?

   ▸ What did you predict should go in the "Setting" box before you read? Does that word name a place? Did you have to change what you put in the box after you read?

   ▸ Which of the words or phrases did you predict told about the problem? Did you have to change anything in that box after you read?

   ▸ Which of the words or phrases did you predict told about the characters' actions? Did you have to change anything in that box after you read?

   ▸ Which of the words or phrases did you predict told about the solution? Did you have to change anything in that box after you read?

4. Tell students that they have now organized the words and phrases about the story elements in the correct boxes. So the Predict-o-Gram is ready to be used as a tool for retelling the story.

5. Have students retell the story, using the words and phrases from the Predict-o-Gram as a guide.

Objectives

- Evaluate predictions.
- Retell a story naming plot, setting, character(s), problem, and solution.
- Use context and sentence structure to determine meaning of words, phrases, and/or sentences.
- Use illustrations to aid understanding of text.
- Demonstrate understanding by thinking aloud.

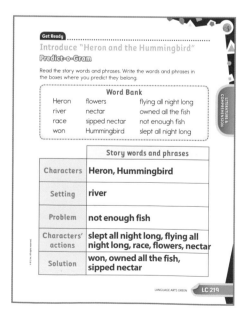

Use Context Clues to Determine Meaning of Words

Check students' ability to use context clues in the words and pictures to determine the meaning of unknown words in the story.

1. Remind students that readers can sometimes figure out what unfamiliar words mean by looking at the words that surround them, as well as the pictures in the story.

2. **Read aloud** the following sentence on page 206 while students study the picture on pages 206 and 207.

   Heron and Hummingbird were very good friends, even though one was tall and gangly and awkward and one was small and sleek and fast.

3. Model how to determine the meaning of the word *gangly* by using picture clues.
   Say: I wonder what *gangly* means. One bird in the picture is tall and thin, and has long, skinny legs. I can say, "One bird was tall and thin, with long, skinny legs, and was awkward." That makes sense, so I think that *gangly* means "tall and thin, with long, skinny legs."

4. **Read aloud** the following sentence on page 206.

   Hummingbird preferred small fish like minnows, and Heron liked the large ones.

5. Model how to determine the meaning of the word *prefer* by using word clues.
   Say: I wonder what *prefer* means. The story says that Heron liked large fish, and Hummingbird preferred small fish. I think what they story says about Heron is a clue about what *prefer* means.

6. Tell students that when they answer the following question, they should think aloud like you did.

   ▶ What do you think *prefer* means? like; As students think aloud, they should mention that the story says Heron likes large fish, so *prefer* must mean "like."

7. **Read aloud** the first sentence on page 208. Tell students to think aloud when they answer the following question.

   ▶ What do you think *zip along* means? fly fast; As students think aloud, they should mention that the story says Hummingbird flies around and around Heron, and the picture shows his wings moving quickly, so *zip along* must mean "fly fast."

8. **Read aloud** the following sentences on page 208.

When Hummingbird noticed that Heron was ahead of him, he hurried to catch up with him, zooming ahead as fast as he could . . . . Hummingbird was tired from all his flitting.

> ▸ What do you think *flitting* means? flying fast or quickly   What words help you figure this out? The story says that Hummingbird hurries and zooms as fast as he can, so he must be flying quickly.

9. **Read aloud** the following sentence on page 208 while students study the picture at the bottom of the page.

When it got dark, he decided to rest. He found a nice spot to perch and slept all night long.

> ▸ What do you think *perch* means? sit   How does the picture help you figure this out? It shows Hummingbird sitting on a branch.

10. **Read aloud** the following sentence on page 210.

Heron stoically kept up a steady flap-flapping of his giant wings, propelling himself forward through the air all day and all night.

> ▸ What do you think *propelling* means? moving   What words help you figure this out? The story says that Heron keeps flapping his wings and that he goes forward through the air, so he must be moving.

Explore "Heron and the Hummingbird"

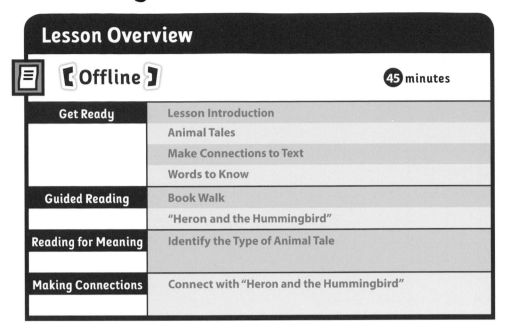

Lesson Overview

Offline

45 minutes

Get Ready	Lesson Introduction
	Animal Tales
	Make Connections to Text
	Words to Know
Guided Reading	Book Walk
	"Heron and the Hummingbird"
Reading for Meaning	Identify the Type of Animal Tale
Making Connections	Connect with "Heron and the Hummingbird"

Big Ideas

▸ Exposing readers to a wide variety of genres provides them with a wide range of background knowledge and increases their vocabulary.
▸ Comprehension is facilitated when readers connect new information to information previously learned.
▸ Repeated rereading leads to increased fluency.

Materials

Supplied
- "Heron and the Hummingbird," *K¹² Classics for Young Readers, Volume A*, pp. 206–211
- *K¹² My Journal*, pp. 2–53

Also Needed
- crayons

Keywords

connection – a link readers make between themselves, information in text, and the world around them

genre – a category for classifying literary works

[Offline] 45 minutes

Work **together** with students to complete Get Ready, Guided Reading, Reading for Meaning, and Making Connections activities.

Get Ready

Lesson Introduction

Prepare students for reading and discussing "Heron and the Hummingbird."

1. Tell students that they are going to reread "Heron and the Hummingbird."

2. Explain that before they read the story, you will get ready by

   ▸ Reviewing characteristics of animal tales
   ▸ Discussing the kinds of connections we can make to the characters and events of a story

> ⭐ **Objectives**
> - Identify genre.
> - Identify characteristics of different genres.
> - Make connections with text: text-to-text, text-to-self, text-to-world.
> - Build vocabulary through listening, reading, and discussion.
> - Use new vocabulary in written and spoken sentences.

Animal Tales

Reinforce characteristics of animal tales.

1. Remind students that there are different kinds of animal tales.

   ▸ Fables teach a lesson
   ▸ "Why" tales explain why animals have certain features, such as why the leopard has spots
   ▸ Trickster tales have a main character that tries to outsmart other characters.

2. Remind students that all animal tales are fiction, or made-up, stories.

3. Have students practice recognizing a "why" tale.
   Say: Long ago, Beaver had a long, bushy tail. One day, there was a contest to see which animal could cut down the biggest tree. Beaver said, "I'm going to win this contest!" and he went to look for the biggest, tallest tree in the woods. When the contest started, Beaver chewed and chewed on the big tree he had found. Soon, the big tree started to fall over. But Beaver wasn't watching, and the big tree fell down on his tail with a BANG! Beaver won the contest, but ever since that day, Beaver has had a flat tail.

   ▸ What do we call a story that has animal characters that act like humans? an animal tale
   ▸ What kind of animal tale is the story about Beaver? a "why" tale
   ▸ What does this "why" tale explain? why Beaver has a flat tail

Make Connections to Text

Explore making connections to text with students.

1. Remind students that good readers think about what a story reminds them of as they're reading. This is called **making a connection**. As they read, good readers make connections to things they have learned before, their prior knowledge, and their personal experiences.

2. Explain that readers who make connections to a story while they read are better able to understand and remember what they read. This is because these readers make reading a more active experience.

   ▸ When readers think, "This story reminds me of a time when I . . ." or "This character is like me because . . . ," they are connecting the text to themselves and their personal experiences.
   ▸ When readers think, "This story reminds me of another story I've read," they are connecting the text to another text.
   ▸ When readers think, "This story reminds me of something I heard about" or "This story reminds me of something that I saw," they are connecting the text to the world around them.

3. Have students practice connecting to text. **Read aloud** the following short story.

   Every Saturday night, Kadeem's family has Game Night. Kadeem and his sister take turns picking out a board game to play. Kadeem's mother makes a big bowl of popcorn, and then the whole family sits at the kitchen table and plays the game together. Game Night is Kadeem's favorite thing to do all week.

4. Ask the following questions. Answers to questions may vary.

   ▸ What does this story remind you of?
   ▸ Is Kadeem anything like you?
   ▸ Does Kadeem's family remind you of your family? How are they alike?
   ▸ Does any part of the story remind you of something that has happened in your own life?
   ▸ What does this story remind you of in the real world?

Words to Know

Before reading "Heron and the Hummingbird," go over Words to Know with students.

1. Read aloud each word and have students repeat it.

2. Ask students if they know what each word means.

   ▸ If students know a word's meaning, have them define it and use it in a sentence.
   ▸ If students don't know a word's meaning, read them the definition and discuss the word with them.

awkward – clumsy; not graceful
distract – to draw away someone's attention
nectar – the sweet liquid of a plant that attracts insects and birds
scenery – the way the land looks in a particular place
sleek – smooth and shiny
steady – having a continuous and regular movement
stoically – showing little or no emotion toward pain or pleasure

Guided Reading

Book Walk

Prepare students for reading by taking them on a Book Walk of "Heron and the Hummingbird." Scan the story together to revisit the characters and events.

1. Turn to the **table of contents** in *K¹² Classics for Young Readers, Volume A*. Help students find the selection and turn to that page.

2. Have students read aloud the **title of the story**.

3. Have students look at the **pictures of the story**.

   ▸ Why do Heron and Hummingbird have a race? to see who gets to own all the fish in the lakes and rivers
   ▸ How long do they race each other? four days
   ▸ Who wins the race? Heron   Why does Heron win? because Hummingbird stops and sleeps at night, but Heron flies all night long

"Heron and the Hummingbird"

It's time for students to reread the story.

1. Tell students that "Heron and the Hummingbird" should now be familiar to them because they have read it before.

2. Explain that they will reread the story aloud to you, and you are there to help if they need it.

3. If students have trouble reading on their own, offer one of the following levels of support to meet their needs.

   ▸ Read aloud the story to them.
   ▸ Read aloud the story as they chime in with you.
   ▸ Take turns with students and alternate reading aloud each paragraph.

4. Remind students to track with their finger as they read.

5. Tell students that as they read, they should think about what kind of animal tale the story is, and they should focus on making connections by thinking about what the story reminds them of.

> **Objectives**
> - Activate prior knowledge by previewing text and/or discussing topic.
> - Read and respond to texts representing a variety of cultures, time periods, and traditions.
> - Read aloud grade-level text with appropriate expression, accuracy, and rate.

Reading for Meaning

Identify the Type of Animal Tale

Check students' understanding of animal tales and their ability to identify a "why" tale.

1. Have students retell "Heron and the Hummingbird" in their own words to develop grammar, vocabulary, comprehension, and fluency skills.

2. Ask students the following questions.

   ▸ What kind of story is "Heron and the Hummingbird"? Possible answers: an animal tale; a "why" tale
   ▸ What things in "Heron and the Hummingbird" tell you it's an animal tale? It has animal characters that act like humans, and it explains why an animal is the way it is.
   ▸ Are animal tales real or made-up? made-up
   ▸ What do we call an animal tale that explains why an animal is the way it is? a "why" tale
   ▸ What does "Heron and the Hummingbird" explain? why herons eat fish and why hummingbirds eat nectar

Objectives

- Retell or dramatize a story.
- Identify genre.
- Identify characteristics of different genres.

Making Connections

 Connect with "Heron and the Hummingbird"

Check students' ability to make a connection to the story. Gather *K¹² My Journal* and have students turn to the next available page for **drawing and writing** in Thoughts and Experiences.

1. Remind students that making connections to the text helps readers better understand and remember a story.

2. Help students think about connections to the characters and events in "Heron and the Hummingbird" by asking the following questions. Answers to questions may vary.

   ▸ Does anything in "Heron and the Hummingbird" remind you of anything in your own life?
   ▸ Heron and Hummingbird have a race. Does this remind you of anything you've ever done with your friends?
   ▸ Did you ever run in a race? Whom did you race against? Who won? What did the winner get?
   ▸ Does the story "Heron and the Hummingbird" remind you of any other stories that you know?

Objectives

- Make connections with text: text-to-text, text-to-self, text-to-world.
- Demonstrate understanding through drawing, discussion, drama, and/or writing.

3. Have students draw a picture in their journal to show a connection they made while reading the story.

   ▸ If students prefer, they can use pictures cut from magazines to show their connection.

4. Help students write one or more sentences that explain the drawing and the connection.

   ▸ Example text-to-text connection: remembering a similar story, such as "The Tortoise and the Hare"
   ▸ Example text-to-self connection: being in a race with friends
   ▸ Example text-to-world connection: watching a sporting event such as a track meet, a swimming race, or the Olympics

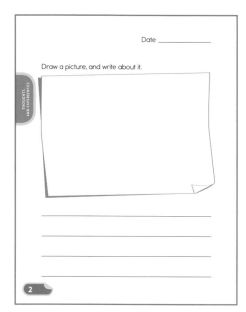

Introduce "The Tortoise and the Hare"

Lesson Overview

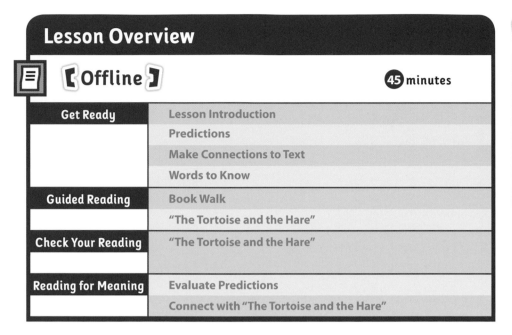

[Offline] **45** minutes

Get Ready	Lesson Introduction
	Predictions
	Make Connections to Text
	Words to Know
Guided Reading	Book Walk
	"The Tortoise and the Hare"
Check Your Reading	"The Tortoise and the Hare"
Reading for Meaning	Evaluate Predictions
	Connect with "The Tortoise and the Hare"

Advance Preparation

Before beginning the Guided Reading, read "The Tortoise and the Hare" to locate Words to Know in the text. Preview pages LC 223 and 224 in *K¹² Language Arts Activity Book* to prepare the materials for the Guided Reading. Read the Guided Reading directions to be aware of stopping points in the story at which students will make predictions.

Big Ideas

▶ Good readers interact with text to make logical predictions before reading; confirm predictions during reading; and revise or make new predictions as they read further.

▶ Comprehension is facilitated when readers connect new information to information previously learned.

▶ Guided reading provides support to early readers as they practice and apply the reading strategies of proficient readers.

[Materials]

Supplied

- "The Tortoise and the Hare," *K¹² Classics for Young Readers, Volume A,* pp. 212–215
- *K¹² Language Arts Activity Book,* pp. LC 223–224

Story Synopsis

Students are introduced to the classic tale of a slow but sure tortoise racing against a quick but overconfident hare.

Keywords

connection – a link readers make between themselves, information in text, and the world around them

fable – a story that teaches a lesson and may contain animal characters

prediction – a guess about what might happen that is based on information in a story and what you already know

 **45 minutes**

Work **together** with students to complete Get Ready, Guided Reading, Check Your Reading, and Reading for Meaning activities.

Get Ready

Lesson Introduction

Prepare students for reading and discussing "The Tortoise and the Hare."

1. Tell students that they are going to read "The Tortoise and the Hare," a story about two animals who race each other.

2. Explain that before they read the story, you will get ready by

   ▸ Reviewing how we make predictions while reading a story, and why it's important to make them
   ▸ Discussing how being familiar with one story can help us make predictions about and understand another story

 Objectives

- Make predictions based on text, illustrations, and/or prior knowledge.
- Make connections with text: text-to-text, text-to-self, text-to-world.
- Build vocabulary through listening, reading, and discussion.
- Use new vocabulary in written and spoken sentences.

Predictions

Review making predictions with students.

1. Remind students that good readers make **predictions** before they read a story and then make more predictions as they read the story and get more information.

2. Remind students that making predictions makes us want to keep reading a story to see if what we predict happens or not.

3. Tell students that the story they are going to read is the kind of animal tale called a **fable**. They can use their knowledge about fables to make predictions about the story.

   ▸ What kind of characters do you predict the story will have? Will they be animals or humans? animals
   ▸ Do you predict the animal characters will act like animals or people? people
   ▸ Do you predict the animal characters will talk? Yes
   ▸ Do you predict the fable will teach us a lesson? Yes

Make Connections to Text

Explore making connections to text with students.

1. Remind students that good readers think about what a story reminds them of as they're reading. This is called **making a connection**. As they read, good readers make connections to things they have learned before, their prior knowledge, and their personal experiences.

2. Explain that readers who make connections to a story while they read are better able to understand and remember what they read. This is because these readers make reading a more active experience.

3. Tell students that sometimes a story may remind them of a story that they've read before. This is making a connection to another text. This can help them understand the new story because they already have an idea of what the characters will be like and what the characters might do.

4. Help students better understand how we make a text-to-text connection. **Say:** In the story of "The Little Rabbit Who Wanted Red Wings," a rabbit wishes it had red wings. This might make some readers think of another story, "The Pine Tree and Its Needles," because that story is about tree that wishes it had different kinds of leaves.

   ▶ What kind of connection can we make between these stories? How are the stories alike? In both stories, the characters wish to change how they look.
   ▶ What do the characters learn at the end of both stories? They learn that changing how they look doesn't make them happy and that they're happier being how they were before.

5. Tell students that as they read "The Tortoise and the Hare," they should see if it reminds them of another story.

Words to Know

Before reading "The Tortoise and the Hare," go over Words to Know with students.

1. Read aloud each word and have students repeat it.

2. Ask students if they know what each word means.

   ▶ If students know a word's meaning, have them define it and use it in a sentence.
   ▶ If students don't know a word's meaning, read them the definition and discuss the word with them.

creep – to crawl; to move slowly
sure – steady; reliable

Guided Reading

Book Walk

Prepare students for reading by taking them on a Book Walk of "The Tortoise and the Hare." Scan the beginning of the story together and ask students to make predictions about the story. Answers to questions may vary.

1. Turn to the **table of contents** in *K¹² Classics for Young Readers, Volume A*. Help students find the selection and turn to that page.

2. Have students read aloud the **title of the story**.

   ▶ What do you think the story might be about?

3. Have students look at the **picture next to the first page** of the story.

4. Ask students the following questions.

   ▶ Where do you think the story takes place?
   ▶ What do you think might happen in the story?

"The Tortoise and the Hare"

It's time to guide students through a preview of the story to prepare them for reading on their own. Gather the Reading Aid on pages LC 223 and 224 in *K¹² Language Arts Activity Book*.

1. Have students sit next to you so that they can see the pictures and words while you introduce and discuss the story.

2. Tell students that you will preview the story to prepare them to read the story aloud to you.

3. Refer to the Reading Aid.

   Reading Aid Tear out the Reading Aid for this reading selection. Follow the instructions for folding the page, and then use the page as a guide as you preview the selection with students.

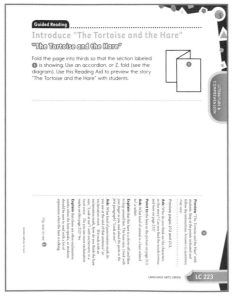
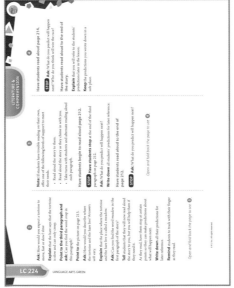

Check Your Reading

"The Tortoise and the Hare"
Check students' comprehension of "The Tortoise and the Hare."

1. Have students retell "The Tortoise and the Hare" in their own words to develop grammar, vocabulary, comprehension, and fluency skills.

2. Ask students the following questions.

   ▶ Who are the characters in the story? a tortoise; a hare
   ▶ Which character is slow and sure? the tortoise
   ▶ What does the hare say he can do faster than any other animal? hop
   ▶ What does the hare do when he is nearly at the river during the race? takes a nap; falls asleep
   ▶ Does the tortoise stop to eat or sleep? No
   ▶ Who wins the race? the tortoise   Why does the tortoise win the race? He never stops creeping along, but the hare stops to eat and sleep.

TIP If students have trouble responding to a question, help them locate the answer in the text or pictures.

Objectives
- Retell or dramatize a story.
- Answer questions requiring literal recall of details.

Reading for Meaning

Evaluate Predictions
Revisit the predictions that students made when they read the text.

1. Remind students that good readers make predictions by using clues in the words and pictures of a story, along with knowledge from personal experiences. Good readers can explain what clues they used to make a prediction.

2. Ask students the following questions to review and discuss the predictions they made when they read "The Tortoise and the Hare." **Refer, as necessary, to students' predictions that you wrote down.** Answers to questions may vary.

   ▶ What did you predict would happen after the hare says the tortoise is slow and gives a great hop? What really happened?
   ▶ What did you predict would happen after the hare tells the tortoise he will get to the river before him? What clues from the story or your own experiences did you use to make your prediction?
   ▶ What did you predict would happen after the hare stops to sleep and says he will get to the river long before the tortoise? Did you use your knowledge of another story to help make your prediction?

Objectives
- Evaluate predictions.
- Make connections with text: text-to-text, text-to-self, text-to-world.

3. Remind students that it's okay if our predictions don't happen. Tell students to keep the following things in mind.

   ▸ Good readers make predictions that make sense based on the story up to that point.
   ▸ Good readers change their predictions as they read further and get more information.
   ▸ Even if our predictions don't happen, making predictions is important because it helps us be active readers.

Connect with "The Tortoise and the Hare"

Check students' ability to make connections to the story.

1. Remind students that making connections to the text helps readers better understand and remember a story.

2. Ask the following questions. Answers to questions may vary.

   ▸ Does anything in "The Tortoise and the Hare" remind you of anything in your own life?
   ▸ The tortoise and the hare have a race. Does this remind you of anything you've done with your friends?
   ▸ Does the tortoise remind you of anybody you know? If so, how are the tortoise and this person alike?
   ▸ The hare brags about how fast he is. Does this remind you of anybody you know?
   ▸ Does the story remind you of another story you know? What happens in that story?

Explore "The Tortoise and the Hare"

Lesson Overview

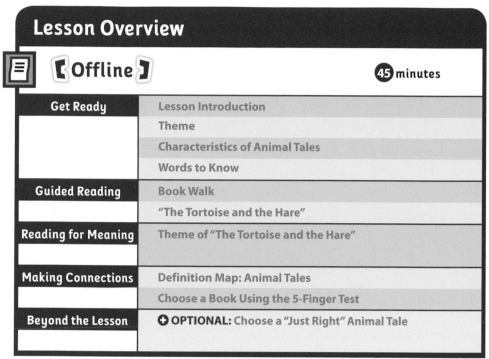

[Offline]   **45** minutes

Get Ready	Lesson Introduction
	Theme
	Characteristics of Animal Tales
	Words to Know
Guided Reading	Book Walk
	"The Tortoise and the Hare"
Reading for Meaning	Theme of "The Tortoise and the Hare"
Making Connections	Definition Map: Animal Tales
	Choose a Book Using the 5-Finger Test
Beyond the Lesson	✚ OPTIONAL: Choose a "Just Right" Animal Tale

Materials

Supplied

- "The Tortoise and the Hare," *K¹² Classics for Young Readers, Volume A,* pp. 212–215
- *Ready . . . Set . . . Read! The Beginning Reader's Treasury,* pp. 92–93
- *K¹² Language Arts Activity Book,* pp. LC 225–227
- Literature & Comprehension Support Materials

Keywords

genre – a category for classifying literary works
theme – the author's message or big idea

Big Ideas

▸ Readers need to recognize themes so they can identify why an author is writing, or the central message of a piece of literature.
▸ Exposing readers to a wide variety of genres provides them with a wide range of background knowledge and increases their vocabulary.
▸ Repeated rereading leads to increased fluency.
▸ Reading a book of their own choosing helps motivate students to read.
▸ Reading for pleasure helps students develop fluency and a lifelong love of reading.

〔 Offline 〕 ⏱ 45 minutes

Work **together** with students to complete Get Ready, Guided Reading, Reading for Meaning, Making Connections, and Beyond the Lesson activities.

Get Ready

Lesson Introduction

Prepare students for reading and discussing "The Tortoise and the Hare."

1. Tell students that they are going to reread "The Tortoise and the Hare."

2. Explain that before they read the story, you will get ready by reviewing

   ▶ How to identify the theme of a story
   ▶ Characteristics of animal tales

Objectives

- Identify theme.
- Identify genre.
- Identify characteristics of different genres.
- Build vocabulary through listening, reading, and discussion.
- Use new vocabulary in written and spoken sentences.

Theme

Explore theme with students.

1. Remind students that some stories have a **theme**. The theme is what the story teaches readers; it is the big idea, or message, that the author wants readers to think about. Some common themes are "It pays to work hard" and "Love is more important than money." Remind students to think of the theme as a sentence, not a single word such as "happiness."

2. Explain that the author usually does not directly state the theme, or message, of a story. To figure out the theme of a story, good readers ask themselves, "What lesson did I learn from reading this story? What big idea did the author want me to think about?"

3. Have students practice identifying the theme of a story.
   Say: In "The Little Red Hen," a hen needs to plant, cut, and grind up wheat to make flour. None of her animal friends will help her, so the little red hen does all the work herself. At the end of the story, only the little red hen has bread to eat.

   ▶ What do you think is the theme of "The Little Red Hen"? What is the big idea that the author wants you to think about? What lesson can be learned from reading this story? Answers to questions may vary; guide students to recognize that the theme is "It pays to work hard" or "Those who do the work get the rewards." If students have trouble answering, tell them to think about the lesson that the animals who didn't help with the work learned.

Characteristics of Animal Tales

Review characteristics of animal tales.

1. Ask students to name three different kinds of animal tales.

   ▸ If students can't recall all three, remind them that there are fables, "why" tales, and trickster tales.

2. Ask the following questions.

   ▸ What do we call a story that has animal characters that act like humans? an animal tale
   ▸ What kind of animal tale teaches a lesson? a fable

3. Remind students that all animal tales are fiction, or made-up, stories.

Words to Know

Before rereading "The Tortoise and the Hare," go over Words to Know with students.

1. Read aloud each word and have students repeat it.

2. Ask students if they know what each word means.

   ▸ If students know a word's meaning, have them define it and use it in a sentence.
   ▸ If students don't know a word's meaning, read them the definition and discuss the word with them.

creep – to crawl; to move slowly
sure – steady; reliable

Guided Reading

Book Walk

Prepare students for reading by taking them on a Book Walk of "The Tortoise and the Hare." Scan the story together to revisit the characters and events.

1. Turn to the selection in *K¹² Classics for Young Readers, Volume A.*

2. Have students read aloud the **title of the story**.

3. Have students review the **pictures of the story**.

   ▸ What are some things from this story that tell you it's an animal tale? Possible answers: The animals act like people; it's a made-up story; it teaches a lesson.
   ▸ Who are the characters in the story? the tortoise and the hare
   ▸ The hare brags about how fast he is. How does the tortoise respond to this? He challenges the hare to a race.

Objectives

- Activate prior knowledge by previewing text and/or discussing topic.
- Read and respond to texts representing a variety of cultures, time periods, and traditions.
- Read aloud grade-level text with appropriate expression, accuracy, and rate.

"The Tortoise and the Hare"

It's time for students to reread the story.

1. Tell students that "The Tortoise and the Hare" should now be familiar to them because they have read it before.

2. Explain that they will reread the story aloud to you, and you are there to help if they need it.

3. If students have trouble reading on their own, offer one of the following levels of support to meet their needs.

   ▸ Read aloud the story to them.
   ▸ Read aloud the story as they chime in with you.
   ▸ Take turns with students and alternate reading aloud each paragraph.

4. Remind students to track with their finger as they read.

5. Tell students that as they read, they should think about the theme, or big idea, of the story.

Reading for Meaning

Theme of "The Tortoise and the Hare"

Check students' ability to identify theme.

1. Have students retell "The Tortoise and the Hare" in their own words to develop grammar, vocabulary, comprehension, and fluency skills.

2. Remind students that the theme is the big lesson, or big idea, of a story. Readers have to think about what happened in a story to figure out the theme, because the author usually doesn't directly state the theme.

3. Ask students the following questions.

   ▸ What do you think the hare learns? You shouldn't waste time if you want to win.
   ▸ What do you think the tortoise learns? If you try hard, you will succeed.
   ▸ Do you think the hare would have won the race if, like the tortoise, he didn't stop to eat or sleep? Why or why not? Answers will vary.
   ▸ What is the theme of "The Tortoise and the Hare"? What is the big idea that the author wants readers to think about? Answers will vary. Students may state something similar to one of the following possible themes: "Do your best if you want to win"; "If you try hard, you will reach your goal"; "If you don't focus on what you're doing, you won't reach your goal."
   ▸ If students give a summary of the story, remind them that a summary of a story tells the plot, not the theme. Have them think about what the characters in the story learned from the events of the story.

Objectives
• Retell or dramatize a story.
• Identify theme.

Making Connections

 Definition Map: Animal Tales

Check students' understanding of the characteristics of animal tales. Turn to page LC 225 in *K¹² Language Arts Activity Book*.

1. Remind students that there are different types of animal tales.

2. Look at the definition map with students. Explain that they will think of an answer for each question in the map to define what an animal tale is. They will write their answers in the boxes.

3. Point to and help students read aloud the heading, "What is it?"

4. Have students tell you their answer and help them write it in the box.

5. Point to and help students read aloud the heading, "What's it like?"

6. Have students tell you at least three characteristics of animal tales and help them write the characteristics in the box.

7. Point to and help students read aloud the heading, "What are some examples?"

8. Have students tell you their answers and help them write them in the boxes.

9. Ask the following questions. Answers to questions may vary.

   ▶ Which is your favorite animal tale from this unit? Why is that your favorite?
   ▶ Do you have another favorite animal tale that was not in this unit? If so, what kind of animal tale is it: a fable, a "why" tale, or a trickster tale?

Objectives

- Identify genre.
- Identify characteristics of different genres.
- Demonstrate understanding through graphic organizers.
- Follow criteria to choose "just right" independent reading materials.

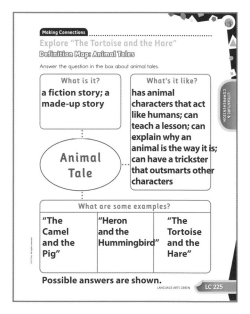

Choose a Book Using the 5-Finger Test

Help students learn how to select a "just right" book to read on their own. Turn to page LC 227 in *K¹² Language Arts Activity Book* and gather *Ready . . . Set . . . Read!*

1. Tell students that you're going to show them how to check whether a book is a "just right" book. This means that the book is a good level for them to read on their own.

2. Explain to students that when they read a "just right" book, they may need to work out some of the words, but this kind of problem-solving is what will push them to increase their reading level.

3. Point to the hand on the Activity Book page.
   Say: You can use your fingers to help figure out if a book is a good level for you to read.

4. Point to each finger on the hand and read aloud the text associated with it, beginning with the thumb.

5. Have students try the 5-Finger Test to find out whether a story is "just right" for them to read.

6. Turn to the table of contents in *Ready . . . Set . . . Read!* Help students find "I Wouldn't" and turn to that page.

7. Have students read aloud page 92 of the story.

8. Every time students come to a word that they don't know, have them hold up one finger, starting with the thumb.

9. Count the number of fingers they are holding up after they have read all of page 92.

   ▸ No fingers means the book is too easy for them to read.
   ▸ One finger means the book is easy. (This would be a good book for practicing reading fluently.)
   ▸ Two fingers means the book is just right.
   ▸ Three fingers means the book is a little hard, and they may need some help to read it.
   ▸ Four fingers means the book is difficult, and students will probably need help to read it.
   ▸ Five fingers means the book is probably too hard, and they should choose a different book.

10. If students have four or more fingers up, tell them that they shouldn't be discouraged. Remind them that the more they read, the more words they will learn. If they keep reading, someday they will be able to read any book they pick.

11. Have students use the bookmark in their Literature & Comprehension Support Materials to keep a log of book and article titles they choose to read.

12. Put the 5-Finger Test page where students can easily see it when they are choosing books for independent reading.

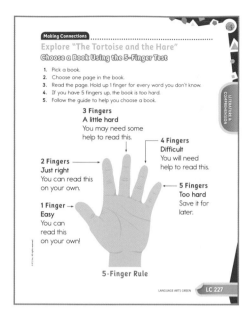

Beyond the Lesson

⊕ OPTIONAL: Choose a "Just Right" Animal Tale

This activity is OPTIONAL. It is intended for students who have extra time, would benefit from practicing the 5-Finger Test to choose a "just right" book, and would enjoy reading more animal tales. Feel free to skip this activity. Gather the 5-Finger Test page (page LC 227 in *K¹² Language Arts Activity Book*).

Objectives

• Follow criteria to choose "just right" independent reading materials.

1. Go to a library to look for the following animal tales. They are listed in order, from easier to more difficult.

   ▸ *The Cat Barked?* by Lydia Monks
   ▸ *Two Cool Coyotes* by Jillian Lund
   ▸ *Anansi's Narrow Waist* by Len Cabral and David Diaz
   ▸ *The Fox and the Stork* by Gerald McDermott
   ▸ *Coyote: A Trickster Tale from the American Southwest* by Gerald McDermott

2. Have students refer to the Activity Book page for the steps and guidelines of the 5-Finger Test.

3. Help students choose one of the books and follow the steps to determine if the book is a "just right" book.

   ▸ If the book is too easy, have them try a book that is further down on the list.
   ▸ If the book is too difficult, have them try a book that is further up on the list.
   ▸ If all of the books are too easy, look for more trickster tales by Gerald McDermott. McDermott has retold many trickster tales from all around the world at varying levels of difficulty.

4. Once students have found a "just right" book, have them read it on their own.

TIP Reading "just right" books will help students increase their reading level, and should be an enjoyable experience that helps children develop a lifelong love of reading.

Introduce "Come to My House"

Lesson Overview

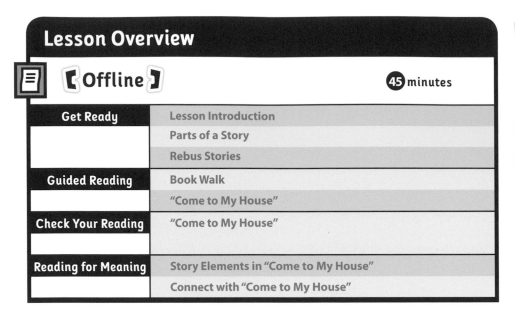

[Offline] **45** minutes

Get Ready	Lesson Introduction
	Parts of a Story
	Rebus Stories
Guided Reading	Book Walk
	"Come to My House"
Check Your Reading	"Come to My House"
Reading for Meaning	Story Elements in "Come to My House"
	Connect with "Come to My House"

Supplied

- *Ready . . . Set . . . Read! The Beginning Reader's Treasury,* pp. 138–141
- *K¹² Language Arts Activity Book,* pp. LC 229–230

Story Synopsis

In this story, which is told in both pictures and words, two friends can't agree about anything and almost miss the chance for a fun play day.

Keywords

connection – a link readers make between themselves, information in text, and the world around them

story structure elements – components of a story; they include character, setting, plot, problem, and solution

Advance Preparation

Preview pages LC 229 and 230 in *K¹² Language Arts Activity Book* to prepare the materials for the Guided Reading.

Big Ideas

▶ An awareness of story structure elements (setting, characters, plot) provides readers a foundation for constructing meaning when reading new stories and writing their own stories.

▶ Comprehension is facilitated when readers connect new information to information previously learned.

▶ Guided reading provides support to early readers as they practice and apply the reading strategies of proficient readers.

[Offline] 45 minutes

Work **together** with students to complete Get Ready, Guided Reading, Check Your Reading, and Reading for Meaning activities.

Get Ready

Lesson Introduction

Prepare students for reading and discussing "Come to My House."

1. Tell students that they are going to read "Come to My House," a story about two friends who want to play together.

2. Explain that before you read the story, you will get ready by

   ▸ Reviewing the parts of a story—plot, setting, characters, problem, and solution
   ▸ Discussing a kind of story called a rebus story, which uses pictures to stand for words

Objectives

- Identify story structure elements—plot, setting, character(s).
- Describe story structure elements—problem and solution.
- Use illustrations to aid understanding of text.

Parts of a Story

Review story structure elements.

1. Remind students that every story has certain parts, or elements. These parts include the characters, setting, problem, solution, and plot.

   ▸ The **characters** are the people or animals in a story.
   ▸ The **setting** is where and when a story takes place.
   ▸ The **problem** is the issue a character must solve in a story.
   ▸ The **solution** is what the character does to solve the problem.
   ▸ The **plot** is what happens in a story.

2. Help students practice naming the characters, setting, problem, and solution of a familiar story.
   Say: Think of "King Midas." This is the plot for "King Midas":

   Once, there was a very rich king named King Midas. He loves gold more than anything in the world. One day, King Midas sees a stranger in his palace. The stranger asks Midas what would make him happy. Midas says he wishes that everything he touched would turn to gold. The stranger grants the king his wish.

   When Midas wakes up the next morning, he has the Golden Touch and everything he touches turns to gold. But Midas can't eat or drink, because the food and water turn to gold, and then he turns his daughter, Marygold, to gold.

Midas is very upset when the stranger reappears and asks what is wrong. The king says he would give up all his riches if he could just have his daughter back. The stranger tells the king to sprinkle water from the river on everything he touched to change it back.

King Midas does what he is told and is happy once again because he has his daughter back.

▶ Who are the characters? King Midas; the stranger; Marygold
▶ What is the setting? the king's palace
▶ What is the king's problem in the story? He turns his daughter into gold.
▶ How is the king's problem solved? He sprinkles water on his daughter and changes her back.

Rebus Stories

Introduce students to rebus stories.

1. Tell students that they are going to read a kind of story called a **rebus story**. A rebus is a picture. A rebus story has words on the pages, but it also has pictures or symbols that stand for words.

   ▶ A rebus story about a dog could use a picture of a dog instead of having the word *dog* written out.
   ▶ A rebus story could have a picture of the sun plus the word *day* after it to stand for the word *Sunday*.

2. The pictures in a rebus story help readers make a connection between the word and the object.

3. Turn to pages 134 and 135 in *Ready . . . Set . . . Read!* Have students look at the words and pictures of the story "A Whale Tale" and name the things that they see.

4. Read aloud the first sentence of "A Whale Tale" to show students how the pictures are read as words. Remember to track with your finger, pausing at the pictures so students can make the connection between the picture and the word it represents.

5. Point to the picture of the man's head in the sentence.

   ▶ What does this picture stand for in this sentence? man

6. Point to the picture of the fish in the sentence.

   ▶ What does this picture stand for in this sentence? fish
   ▶ What word does this picture stand for when you add the –ing that comes after it? fishing

7. Have students read aloud the second sentence in the story, helping as necessary.

   ▶ How did you know to say the word *fish* in this sentence when the word isn't there? because there's a picture of a fish

8. Take turns reading more of the story until you feel that students understand how to read the pictures in a rebus story.

Guided Reading

Book Walk

Prepare students for reading by taking them on a Book Walk of "Come to My House." Scan the story together and ask students to make predictions about the story. Answers to questions may vary.

1. Turn to the **table of contents** in *Ready . . . Set . . . Read!* Help students find the selection and turn to that page.

2. Have students read aloud the **title of the story**.

   ▸ What do you think the story might be about?

3. Have students look at the **pictures of the story**.

   ▸ Who do you think are the characters in the story?

   ▸ What do you think might happen in the story?

Objectives

- Make predictions based on text, illustrations, and/or prior knowledge.
- Activate prior knowledge by previewing text and/or discussing topic.
- Read and listen to a variety of texts for information and pleasure independently or as part of a group.
- Read aloud grade-level text with appropriate expression, accuracy, and rate.

"Come to My House"

It's time to guide students through a preview of the story to prepare them for reading on their own. Gather the Reading Aid on pages LC 229 and 230 in *K¹² Language Arts Activity Book*.

1. Have students sit next to you so that they can see the pictures and words while you introduce and discuss the story.

2. Tell students that you will preview the story to prepare them to read the story aloud to you.

3. Refer to the Reading Aid.

Reading Aid Tear out the Reading Aid for this reading selection. Follow the instructions for folding the page, and then use the page as a guide as you preview the selection with students.

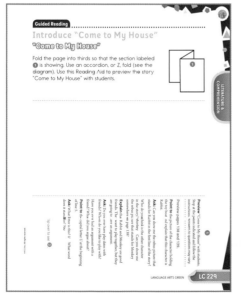
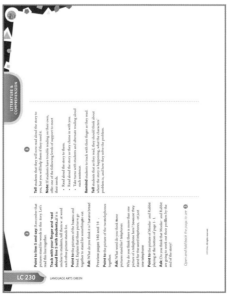

Check Your Reading

"Come to My House"

Check students' comprehension of "Come to My House."

1. Have students retell "Come to My House" in their own words to develop grammar, vocabulary, comprehension, and fluency skills.

2. Ask students the following questions to check their understanding of the rebus pictures.

   ▶ How do Rabbit and Monkey speak to each other at the beginning of the story? Monkey calls Rabbit on the phone.   How do you know that they speak on the telephone? the picture of a phone
   ▶ What does Monkey want Rabbit to come over and play with? his truck

3. Point to page 138.

   ▶ Which picture on this page stands for the word *house*? Verify that students point to one of the pictures of the house.

4. Point to page 139.

   ▶ Which picture on this page stands for the word *book*? Verify that students point to one of the pictures of the book.

5. Point to and have students read aloud the sentence at the top of page 140.

   ▶ What picture does the author use for the word *I* in this sentence? an eye
   ▶ Why does the author use a picture of an eye? because *eye* that you see with sounds the same as the word *I*
   ▶ Why does the author use a picture of a knot in a rope in this sentence? because *knot* in a rope sounds the same as the word *not*

TIP If students have trouble responding to a question, help them locate the answer in the text or pictures.

Reading for Meaning

Story Elements in "Come to My House"

Check students' ability to identify and describe story structure elements.

1. Remind students that a story has certain parts, or elements. These parts include the characters, setting, problem, solution, and plot.

Objectives
- Retell or dramatize a story.
- Answer questions requiring literal recall of details.
- Use illustrations to aid understanding of text.

Objectives
- Identify story structure elements—plot, setting, character(s).
- Describe story structure elements—problem and solution.
- Make connections with text: text-to-text, text-to-self, text-to-world.

2. Ask the following questions.

- ► Who are the characters in "Come to My House"? Rabbit; Monkey
- ► Where does this story take place? Possible answers: Rabbit's house; Monkey's house; halfway between Rabbit's and Monkey's houses
- ► Rabbit and Monkey can't agree where to play. How do they solve their problem? They both pack a bag with their toys, food, and books and start to walk to each other's house. They play with each other halfway between their houses.
- ► What is the plot of the story? Rabbit and Monkey want to play with each other, but each wants to play at his own house. Since they can't agree where to play, they hang up the phones, and they both feel sad. Rabbit fills a bag with his toy, food, and book and starts to walk to Monkey's house. Monkey does the same thing and starts to walk to Rabbit's house. They see each other on the way and have a good time playing right there.

Connect with "Come to My House"

Check students' ability to make connections to the story.

1. Remind students that readers who make connections to a story while they read are better able to understand and remember what they read. This is because these readers make reading a more active experience.

   - ► When readers think, "This story reminds me of something that happened to me," they are connecting the text to themselves.
   - ► When readers think, "This story reminds me of another story I've read," they are connecting the text to another text.
   - ► When readers think, "This story reminds me of something I've heard about" or "This story reminds me of something I saw," they are connecting the text to the real world.

2. Help students connect with the characters and events in "Come to My House" by asking the following questions. Answers to questions may vary.

   - ► Does anything in "Come to My House" remind you of anything in your own life?
   - ► Do you ever make plans to play with a friend? Where do you play? How do you decide where to play?
   - ► Rabbit and Monkey are friends, but they have an argument. Has this ever happened with you and a friend of yours? What did you argue about?
   - ► Does Rabbit or Monkey remind you of anybody you know? If so, how are Rabbit or Monkey and this person alike?
   - ► Does "Come to My House" remind you of another story? Which one? Why does it remind you of this story?
   - ► Does "Come to My House" remind you of something that happened in the real world? What was it? Why did the story make you think of this?

Explore "Come to My House"

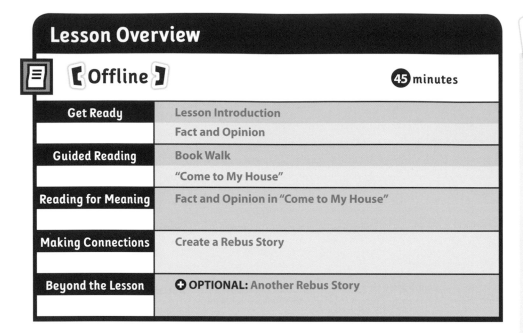

Lesson Overview

[Offline]   45 minutes

Get Ready	Lesson Introduction
	Fact and Opinion
Guided Reading	Book Walk
	"Come to My House"
Reading for Meaning	Fact and Opinion in "Come to My House"
Making Connections	Create a Rebus Story
Beyond the Lesson	⊕ OPTIONAL: Another Rebus Story

Materials

Supplied

- *Ready . . . Set . . . Read! The Beginning Reader's Treasury*, pp. 138–141
- *K¹² Language Arts Activity Book*, pp. LC 231–233
- *K¹² World: Earth and Sky* (optional)
- *K¹² World: People and Places of the Past* (optional)
- *K¹² World: The Science of Inventing* (optional)
- *K¹² World: Critter and Creature Stories* (optional)

Also Needed

- glue stick
- scissors, round-end safety

Keywords

fact – something that can be proven true

opinion – something that a person thinks or believes, but which cannot be proven to be true

Big Ideas

▶ Readers must focus on the specific language of a text to aid in interpretation.
▶ Repeated rereading leads to increased fluency.

 **Offline** 🕙 **45** minutes

Work **together** with students to complete Get Ready, Guided Reading, Reading for Meaning, Making Connections, and Beyond the Lesson activities.

Get Ready

Lesson Introduction

Prepare students for reading and discussing "Come to My House."

1. Tell students that they are going to reread "Come to My House."

2. Explain that before they read the story, you will get ready by reviewing the difference between a fact and an opinion.

Objectives
- Identify facts.
- Identify opinions.
- Distinguish fact from opinion.

Fact and Opinion

Review how to distinguish a fact from an opinion.

1. Ask students to explain the difference between a fact and an opinion.
   - ▸ If students need help, remind them that a **fact** is something that is true and can be proven, and an **opinion** is something that a person feels or believes.

2. **Read aloud** the following statements and ask students which is a fact and which is an opinion.
   - ▸ Most cats have fur. fact
   - ▸ My cat has softer fur than any other cat. opinion

3. Ask the following questions.
   - ▸ Why is the statement "most cats have fur" a fact? because it's true; we can prove it
   - ▸ Why is the statement "my cat has softer fur than any other cat" an opinion? Possible answers: because it's what somebody believes; because somebody else may think that his or her cat has softer fur

4. Remind students that it's important to know the difference between a fact and an opinion so that we can identify what is true and what is something a person feels or believes.

Guided Reading

Book Walk

Prepare students for reading by taking them on a Book Walk of "Come to My House." Scan the story together to revisit the characters and events.

1. Turn to the selection.

2. Have students read aloud the **title of the story** in *Ready . . . Set . . . Read!*

3. Have students review the **words and pictures of the story**.

   ▸ Who are the characters in the story? Rabbit and Monkey
   ▸ Rabbit and Monkey are friends but they have problem. What is it? They want to play together, but each wants to play at his own house.

Objectives

- Activate prior knowledge by previewing text and/or discussing topic.
- Read and listen to a variety of texts for information and pleasure independently or as part of a group.
- Read aloud grade-level text with appropriate expression, accuracy, and rate.

"Come to My House"

It's time for students to reread the story.

1. Tell students that "Come to My House" should now be familiar to them because they have read it before.

2. Explain that they will reread the story aloud to you, and you are there to help if they need it.

3. If students have trouble reading on their own, offer one of the following levels of support to meet their needs.

   ▸ Read aloud the story to them.
   ▸ Read aloud the story as they chime in with you.
   ▸ Take turns with students and alternate reading aloud each sentence.

4. Remind students to track with their finger as they read.

5. Tell students that as they read, they should look for facts and opinions.

Reading for Meaning

Fact and Opinion in "Come to My House"
Check students' ability to distinguish facts from opinions.

1. Have students retell "Come to My House" in their own words to develop grammar, vocabulary, comprehension, and fluency skills.

2. Ask the following questions.

   ▸ The phone rings at Rabbit's house at the beginning of "Come to My House." Is this a fact or an opinion? a fact How do you know? We can prove it's true.

   ▸ Rabbit wants Monkey to come play at his house. Monkey says, "It is better at my house." Is this a fact or an opinion? an opinion How do you know? It's something he thinks or believes; we can't prove it's true. What word helped you figure out that what Monkey says about his house is an opinion? *better*

   ▸ Monkey says he has a new book about dinosaurs. Is this a fact or an opinion? a fact How do you know? We can prove it's true.

   ▸ Rabbit says he has a new book about sharks. Is this a fact or an opinion? a fact How do you know? We can prove it's true.

   ▸ Monkey says his new book is better. Is this a fact or an opinion? an opinion How do you know? It's something he thinks or believes; we can't prove it's true. What word helped you figure out that what Monkey says is an opinion? *better*

Objectives
- Retell or dramatize a story.
- Identify facts.
- Identify opinions.
- Distinguish fact from opinion.

Making Connections

Create a Rebus Story
Have students demonstrate their understanding of rebus stories by creating their own. Turn to pages LC 231–233 in *K¹² Language Arts Activity Book* and gather the glue stick and scissors.

1. Remind students that rebus stories use both words and pictures that stand for words.

2. Tell students that they will cut out and glue pictures to create their own rebus story.

3. Point to the pictures of the cat, dog, panda, and horse on page LC 231. Have students choose **two** of the four characters for their story. Have them cut out the pictures only for those two characters.

4. Have students cut out the remaining rebus pictures on the page.

5. Have them glue one picture of each character in the first two boxes on page LC 233.

Objectives
- Respond to text through art, writing, and/or drama.
- Use illustrations to aid understanding of text.
- Compare and contrast two texts on the same topic.

6. Have students think about which picture would make the most sense in the next box and have them glue that picture.

   ▶ If they are having trouble, guide students to recognize that the house makes the most sense.

7. Have students glue the picture of one of the characters in the next box.

8. For the next boxes, have students think about which two pictures could go together to name a type of sandwich that many children like to eat and have them glue that picture.

   ▶ If they are having trouble, guide students to recognize that the pictures of the peanut and the butter make the most sense.

9. Have students glue two more character pictures in the next two boxes.

10. Ask students what they think belongs in the next box and have them glue that picture.

    ▶ If students have trouble, ask them which picture shows a place where they can go to play.

11. Have students choose **one** of the three playground items: slide, swings, or merry-go-round. Have them glue that picture in the last box.

12. Have students read aloud their rebus story, helping them with printed words as necessary.

13. Ask the following questions. Answers to questions may vary.

    ▶ How is your story the same as "Come to My House"?
    ▶ How is your story different from "Come to My House"?

Reward: Add a sticker for this unit on the My Accomplishments chart to mark successful completion of the unit.

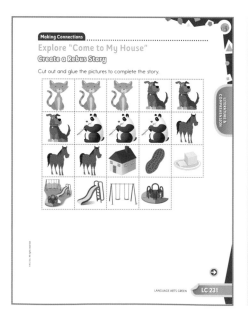

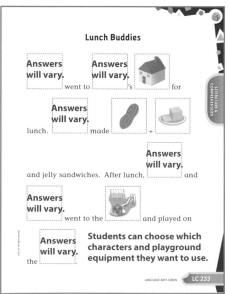

Beyond the Lesson

⊕ OPTIONAL: Another Rebus Story

This activity is OPTIONAL. It is intended for students who have extra time and show interest in reading another rebus story. Feel free to skip this activity.

1. Go to a library to look for a copy of *The Rebus Bears* by Seymour Reit or any other rebus story.

2. Lead a Book Walk, having the students carefully review the rebus pictures.

3. Have students read aloud the story. Remind them that
   - ► They should track with their finger as they read.
   - ► You are there to offer help if they need it.

4. Ask students to think about the story elements such as character, setting, problem, and solution in both stories, and then ask the following questions. Answers to questions may vary.
   - ► Is there anything that's the same about "Come to My House" and *The Rebus Bears*?
   - ► What is different about the two stories?
   - ► Does the book *The Rebus Bears* remind you of another story that you know?
   - ► Which story do you like better, "Come to My House" or *The Rebus Bears*? Why?

TIP Students may also be interested in solving a rebus puzzle on the back of one of the *K¹² World* nonfiction magazines. Be aware that the rebus puzzles include "subtracting" sounds from some of the pictures in order to figure out the target word. Students may need additional help to do this.

Objectives
- Use illustrations to aid understanding of text.
- Compare and contrast story structure elements across texts.
- Make connections with text: text-to-text, text-to-self, text-to-world.

 # Mid-Semester Checkpoint

Unit Focus

In this unit, students will listen to a piece of fiction, a poem, and a nonfiction article. They will demonstrate mastery of content in each genre by listening to a variety of texts, making and checking predictions, identifying story elements and structures of each text, using new vocabulary, comparing and contrasting elements of each text, and retelling.

Unit Plan		**〖Offline〗**	**〖Online〗**
Lesson 1	Mid-Semester Checkpoint	**45** minutes	varies

Mid-Semester Checkpoint

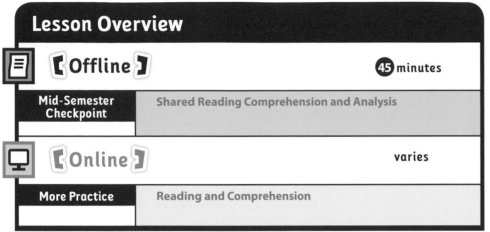

Lesson Overview

📄 **Offline**		45 minutes
Mid-Semester Checkpoint	Shared Reading Comprehension and Analysis	

🖥 **Online**		varies
More Practice	Reading and Comprehension	

Materials

Supplied
- *K¹² Language Arts Assessments*, pp. LC 67–106

Also Needed
- scissors, adult
- crayons
- household objects – stopwatch

Advance Preparation

Read each selection in the Mid-Semester Checkpoint before administering the assessment to locate Words to Know in the text. Cut out the word cards on page LC 83 and the blank story cards on page LC 89.

Offline **45** minutes

Work **together** with students to complete the Mid-Semester Checkpoint.

Mid-Semester Checkpoint ....

Objectives

- Complete a Mid-Semester Checkpoint on the elements of poetry, nonfiction, and fiction.

Shared Reading Comprehension and Analysis

Explain that students are going to show what they have learned so far this semester.

- ▸ Give students pages LC 73–LC 106 of the Mid-Semester Checkpoint.
- ▸ Read the directions on the students' pages together. Use the Learning Coach instructions on pages LC 67–LC 72 to administer the Checkpoint.
- ▸ Use the Checkpoint pages to record student behaviors and responses.
- ▸ When you have finished, use the Answer Key to score the Checkpoint and then enter the results online.
- ▸ Review each exercise with students. Work with students to correct any exercise that they missed.

Part 1. Fiction: "A Trip to the Magic Sea" Activate Prior Knowledge

Ask students the following questions to activate prior knowledge. Note their responses on the Checkpoint pages.

1. Have you ever been bored?

2. What did you do for fun when you were bored?

Before reading "A Trip to the Magic Sea," go over Words to Know with students. Read aloud each word or phrase and have students repeat it. Ask students if they know what each word or phrase means.

- ▸ If students know a word's or phrase's meaning, have them define it and use it in a sentence.

- ▸ If students don't know a word's or phrase's meaning, read them the definition and discuss the word or phrase with them.

bored – weary or restless; dull
paper airplane – a piece of paper folded to look like a toy airplane

Part 2. Fiction: "A Trip to the Magic Sea" Book Walk

Gather the Checkpoint pages with "A Trip to the Magic Sea." Note that there are two versions of the story: One is the full story for the students, and one is a copy for you to follow and mark as the students read aloud. Have students sit next to you so that they can see the story while you do a Book Walk. Read aloud the title and author of the text. Show students the illustration. Ask students the following questions and note their responses on the Checkpoint pages.

3. What do you think the story will be about?

4. What does an author do?

5. What does an illustrator do?

6. Was this story written to teach us, or was it written to entertain us?

7. Is this story going to be fiction or nonfiction?

Part 3. Fiction: "A Trip to the Magic Sea" Shared Reading and Fluency Check

Follow the instructions in the Mid-Semester Checkpoint for assessing students' fluency.

Part 4. Fiction: "A Trip to the Magic Sea" Evaluate Predictions

Read the predictions students wrote in Part 2. Tell students that predictions are neither right nor wrong; they are just the best guess you can make with the information you have. Ask students the following questions and note their responses on the Checkpoint pages.

18. What helped you make your prediction?

19. What else could help a reader make a prediction?

20. Was your prediction accurate?

Part 5. Fiction: "A Trip to the Magic Sea" Draw Conclusions

Explain to students that after reading the story, they have enough information to draw conclusions about what happens next in the story, even though the author did not write any more. Note their response on the Checkpoint pages.

21. What do you think Claire did with her paper airplanes?

Part 6. Fiction: "A Trip to the Magic Sea" Reading Comprehension

Read the questions on the Checkpoint pages to students. Students should write the answers themselves. If necessary, allow them to dictate their responses to you.

Part 7. Fiction: "A Trip to the Magic Sea" Show You Know

Give students crayons and the blank story cards that you cut out from page LC 89. Have students draw pictures of the main events of the story.

32. Draw pictures of the main events of the story.

When they have finished the drawings, students should give you the cards. Put the cards in the order in which the events happened in the story. If necessary, ask students to describe the events depicted in the drawings. Have students retell the story and check whether you have put the cards in the right order.

33. Retell the story using the story cards.

34. Are the cards in the right order?

Part 8. Nonfiction: "The Wright Brothers" Preview the Article

Show students "The Wright Brothers." Point to and read aloud the title of the article. Preview the article with students. Have students find the time line.

35. Point to the time line.

Point to the heading **Two Brothers with One Dream**. Explain that the bold print is used to call attention to the text. This is a heading, and it gives us clues about the next paragraph. Have students read the heading and make a prediction. Note their response on the Checkpoint pages.

36. Read the heading.

37. What do you think this article will be about?

Have students locate other headings in the text. As students point to a heading, read aloud that heading. Note students' responses on the Checkpoint pages.

38. Point to the headings.

39. Why are the headings in bold print?

40. What is the topic of this article?

Before reading "The Wright Brothers," go over Words to Know with students. Read aloud each word and have students repeat it. Ask students if they know what each word means.

  ▶ If students know a word's meaning, have them define it and use it in a sentence.
  ▶ If students don't know a word's meaning, read them the definition and discuss the word with them.

machine – a combination of parts that use force, motion, and energy to do work

Part 9. Nonfiction: "The Wright Brothers" Read Aloud – Main Idea and Supporting Details

Gather the graphic organizer on pages LC 98 and 99.

41. Write each heading from the article in one of the empty boxes. As you listen, write the main idea and one supporting detail in each empty box.

Begin to read aloud "The Wright Brothers." Have students sit next to you so that they can see the words while you read aloud the text. Emphasize the word *machine* when you come to it.

Pause after reading each section. Have students write the main idea and a supporting detail for each section. If necessary, allow them to dictate their responses to you.

Part 10. Nonfiction: "The Wright Brothers" Reading Comprehension

Read the questions and answer choices to students and note their responses on the Checkpoint pages. You may allow students to circle the answers.

Part 11. Poetry: "So High" Activate Prior Knowledge

Explain to students that they will read a poem with you. Ask students the following questions to activate prior knowledge. Note their responses on the Checkpoint pages.

46. What do you know about poems?

47. I've read a story and an article to you. What was their topic?

48. What do you think this poem will be about?

Part 12. Poetry: "So High" Shared Reading and Fluency Check

Follow the instructions in the Mid-Semester Checkpoint for assessing students' fluency.

Part 13. Poetry: "So High" Summarizing

Have students summarize the poem.

53. What is the poem about?

Part 14. Poetry: "So High" Evaluate Predictions

Read the predictions students made in Part 11. Ask students the following questions and note their responses on the Checkpoint pages.

54. What helped you make your prediction?

55. Was your prediction accurate?

Part 15. Poetry: "So High" Reading Comprehension

Read the questions on the Checkpoint pages to students. Students should write the answers themselves. If necessary, allow them to dictate their responses to you.

Part 16. Poetry: "So High" Draw Conclusions

Ask students the following question and note their response on the Checkpoint pages.

61. What is the author writing about when she writes "you do not have feathers and no beak to open wide"?

Part 17. Poetry: "So High" Illustration

Give students crayons. Discuss with students the author's use of imagery, such as "Your wings are long / And shine in the light and You do not have feathers / And no beak to open wide." If necessary, read the poem aloud and tell students to close their eyes and try to picture the airplane as they listen.

62. Draw a picture to go with the poem.

 Reward: Add a sticker for this unit on the My Accomplishments chart to mark successful completion of the unit.

Name _____ Date _____

Mid-Semester Checkpoint
Learning Coach Instructions
Shared Reading Comprehension
and Analysis

Explain that students are going to show what they have learned so far this semester.

- Give students pages LC 73–LC 106 of the Mid-Semester Checkpoint.
- Read the directions on the students' pages together. Use the Learning Coach instructions on pages LC 67–LC 72 to administer the Checkpoint.
- Use the Checkpoint pages to record student behaviors and responses.
- When you have finished, use the Answer Key to score the Checkpoint and then enter the results online.
- Review each exercise with students. Work with students to correct any exercise that they missed.

Part 1. Fiction: "A Trip to the Magic Sea" Activate Prior Knowledge

Ask students the following questions to activate prior knowledge. Note their responses on the Checkpoint pages.

1. Have you ever been bored?
2. What did you do for fun when you were bored?

Before reading "A Trip to the Magic Sea," go over Words to Know with students. Read aloud each word or phrase and have students repeat it. Ask students if they know what each word or phrase means.

- If students know a word's or phrase's meaning, have them define it and use it in a sentence.
- If students don't know a word's or phrase's meaning, read them the definition and discuss the word or phrase with them.

bored – weary or restless; dull
paper airplane – a piece of paper folded to look like a toy airplane

Part 2. Fiction: "A Trip to the Magic Sea" Book Walk

Gather the Checkpoint pages with "A Trip to the Magic Sea." Note that there are two versions of the story: One is the full story for the students, and one is a copy for you to follow and mark as the students read aloud. Have students sit next to you so that they can see the story while you do a Book Walk. Read aloud the title and author of the text. Show students the illustration. Ask students the following questions and note their responses on the Checkpoint pages.

LANGUAGE ARTS GREEN | MID-SEMESTER CHECKPOINT — LC 67

Name _____ Date _____

3. What do you think the story will be about?
4. What does an author do?
5. What does an illustrator do?
6. Was this story written to teach us, or was it written to entertain us?
7. Is this story going to be fiction or nonfiction?

Part 3. Fiction: "A Trip to the Magic Sea" Shared Reading and Fluency Check

Gather the word cards that you cut out from page LC 83. Show them to students. Read the words aloud, pointing to each word as you read it.

Say: You will read aloud Part I and I will read aloud Part II. Then, you will read aloud Part III. These words will be in Parts I and II. Let's review the words together.

Reread the words, again pointing to each word as you read it aloud. Have students repeat each word several times.

Show the cards to students one at a time and ask students to read them.

- Circle any words that students read incorrectly.
- If students have trouble with a word, say, "This is the word [word]. Say [word]."

8. bored
9. Claire
10. story
11. paper airplane
12. finished
13. replied

You will use your copy of "A Trip to the Magic Sea" to note the kinds of errors that students make as they read. As you listen, you may choose to mark up your copy of the story where students have difficulty reading. Make a mark or a note for the following types of errors:

Listen for these types of errors	How many times?	Examples
Reads word incorrectly, does not self-correct.		
Skips a word, does not self-correct.		
Rereads before reading correctly.		
Guesses before reading correctly.		

LC 68 — LANGUAGE ARTS GREEN | MID-SEMESTER CHECKPOINT

Name _____ Date _____

Have students read aloud Part I. Students should read independently. As they read, mark on your copy any words they miss.

Read aloud Part II to students.

Have students read aloud Part III. Students should read independently. As they read, mark on your copy any words they miss.

Circle Yes or No for each question.

14. Did students read with a pace that sounds natural? Yes / No
15. Did students read with appropriate volume? Yes / No
16. Did students pause for periods? Yes / No
17. Did students read with expression? Yes / No

Part 4. Fiction: "A Trip to the Magic Sea" Evaluate Predictions

Read the predictions students wrote in Part 2. Tell students that predictions are neither right nor wrong; they are just the best guess you can make with the information you have. Ask students the following questions and note their responses on the Checkpoint pages.

18. What helped you make your prediction?
19. What else could help a reader make a prediction?
20. Was your prediction accurate?

Part 5. Fiction: "A Trip to the Magic Sea" Draw Conclusions

Explain to students that after reading the story, they have enough information to draw conclusions about what happens next in the story, even though the author did not write any more. Note their response on the Checkpoint pages.

21. What do you think Claire did with her paper airplanes?

Part 6. Fiction: "A Trip to the Magic Sea" Reading Comprehension

Read the questions on the Checkpoint pages to students. Students should write the answers themselves. If necessary, allow them to dictate their responses to you.

Part 7. Fiction: "A Trip to the Magic Sea" Show You Know

Give students crayons and the blank story cards that you cut out from page LC 89. Have students draw pictures of the main events of the story.

32. Draw pictures of the main events of the story.

When they have finished the drawings, students should give you the cards. Put the cards in the order in which the events happened in the story. If necessary, ask students to describe the events depicted in the drawings. Have students retell the story and check whether you have put the cards in the right order.

LANGUAGE ARTS GREEN | MID-SEMESTER CHECKPOINT — LC 69

Name _____ Date _____

33. Retell the story using the story cards.
34. Are the cards in the right order?

Part 8. Nonfiction: "The Wright Brothers" Preview the Article

Show students "The Wright Brothers." Point to and read aloud the title of the article. Preview the article with students.

35. Point to the time line.

Point to the heading **Two Brothers with One Dream**. Explain that the bold print is used to call attention to the text. This is a heading, and it gives us clues about the next paragraph. Have students read the heading and make a prediction. Note their response on the Checkpoint pages.

36. Read the heading.
37. What do you think this article will be about?

Have students locate other headings in the text. As students point to a heading, read aloud the heading. Note students' responses on the Checkpoint pages.

38. Point to the headings.
39. Why are the headings in bold print?
40. What is the topic of this article?

Before reading "The Wright Brothers," go over Words to Know with students. Read aloud each word and have students repeat it. Ask students if they know what each word means.

- If students know a word's meaning, have them define it and use it in a sentence.
- If students don't know a word's meaning, read them the definition and discuss the word with them.

machine – a combination of parts that use force, motion, and energy to do work

Part 9. Nonfiction: "The Wright Brothers" Read Aloud – Main Idea and Supporting Details

Gather the graphic organizer on pages LC 98 and 99.

41. Write each heading from the article in one of the empty boxes. As you listen, write the main idea and one supporting detail in each empty box.

Begin to read aloud "The Wright Brothers." Have students sit next to you so that they can see the words while you read aloud the text. Emphasize the word *machine* when you come to it.

LC 70 — LANGUAGE ARTS GREEN | MID-SEMESTER CHECKPOINT

Name _____ Date _____

Pause after reading each section. Have students write the main idea and a supporting detail for each section. If necessary, allow them to dictate their responses to you.

Part 10. Nonfiction: "The Wright Brothers" Reading Comprehension

Read the questions and answer choices to students and note their responses on the Checkpoint pages. You may allow students to circle the answers.

Part 11. Poetry: "So High" Activate Prior Knowledge

Explain to students that they will read a poem with you. Ask students the following questions to activate prior knowledge. Note their responses on the Checkpoint pages.

46. What do you know about poems?
47. I've read a story and an article to you. What was their topic?
48. What do you think this poem will be about?

Part 12. Poetry: "So High" Shared Reading and Fluency Check

Gather the Checkpoint page with "So High." Cut out the two copies of the poem and give one to students. Read aloud the title of the poem, pointing to each word as you read. Then, have students read aloud the title of the poem, pointing to each word as they read aloud.

Explain to students that a lot of the words in the poem repeat and that they should listen carefully and follow along as you read.

You will use your copy of "So High" to note the kinds of errors that students make as they read.

As you listen, you may choose to mark up your copy of the poem where students have difficulty reading. Make a mark or a note for the following types of errors:

Listen for these types of errors	How many times?	Examples
Reads word incorrectly, does not self-correct.		
Skips a word, does not self-correct.		
Rereads before reading correctly.		
Guesses before reading correctly.		

LANGUAGE ARTS GREEN | MID-SEMESTER CHECKPOINT — LC 71

Name _____ Date _____

Read aloud the first stanza.

Have students read aloud the second stanza. As students read, mark on your copy any words they miss.

Read aloud the third stanza.

Have students read aloud the fourth stanza. As students read, mark on your copy any words they miss.

Circle Yes or No for each question.

49. Did students read with a pace that sounds natural? Yes / No
50. Did students read with appropriate volume? Yes / No
51. Did students pause for periods? Yes / No
52. Did students read with expression? Yes / No

Part 13. Poetry: "So High" Summarizing

Have students summarize the poem.

53. What is the poem about?

Part 14. Poetry: "So High" Evaluate Predictions

Read the predictions students made in Part 13. Ask students the following questions and note their responses on the Checkpoint pages.

54. What helped you make your prediction?
55. Was your prediction accurate?

Part 15. Poetry: "So High" Reading Comprehension

Read the questions on the Checkpoint pages to students. Students should write the answers themselves. If necessary, allow them to dictate their responses to you.

Part 16. Poetry: "So High" Draw Conclusions

Ask students the following question and note their response on the Checkpoint pages.

61. What is the author writing about when she writes "you do not have feathers and no beak to open wide"?

Part 17. Poetry: "So High" Illustrations

Give students crayons. Discuss with students the author's use of imagery, such as "Your wings are long / And shine in the light and You do not have feathers / And no beak to open wide." If necessary, read the poem aloud and tell students to close their eyes and try to picture the airplane as they listen.

62. Draw a picture to go with the poem.

LC 72 — LANGUAGE ARTS GREEN | MID-SEMESTER CHECKPOINT

Name _____ Date _____

Mid-Semester Checkpoint Answer Key
Shared Reading Comprehension
and Analysis

Learning Coach Copy
A Trip to the Magic Sea
by Missy Gimble

I.

Claire was bored. She had read books and made pictures. She had played outside. Now, she was sitting at the kitchen table. She put her head down on her arms and watched her dad make lunch.

"I'm bored, Dad," Claire said.

"Don't worry. We will go on a trip to the beach in a few days. You will have lots to do then," her dad said.

"But, our trip is still three days away," Claire said. "What can I do to have fun until then?" she asked.

Her dad put lunch on the table and sat down. Claire raised her head and started to eat. "Did I ever tell you about Shawn?" her dad asked.

"No," Claire replied.

"He was my best friend when I was a kid. Shawn was never bored. Let me tell you why," said her dad. He took a bite of his lunch and began his story.

LANGUAGE ARTS GREEN | MID-SEMESTER CHECKPOINT — LC 73

Name _____ Date _____

II.

Shawn loved making paper airplanes. He made big planes and small ones. He made them out of all kinds of paper. He knew how to fold their wings in different ways. He did that to make them fly faster or slower. The best thing about Shawn's planes was that they really flew. They didn't just fly across a room. They flew to far-off places.

"Finished!" Shawn said as he folded his piece of paper one last time. He held up his paper airplane and smiled. "Where do I want to go today? I know. I want to go to the Magic Sea!" Shawn closed his eyes. He held on tightly to his paper plane. Then, he started to turn in a circle. Shawn turned around and around until his feet

LC 74 — LANGUAGE ARTS GREEN | MID-SEMESTER CHECKPOINT

Name _____ Date _____

lifted off the ground. When they touched back down, he wasn't standing on a hard floor. He was standing on sand. Shawn opened his eyes and looked around. He was on the beach of the Magic Sea!

Shawn put his plane on the sand and ran to the water. "I wonder if they'll be here today," he thought. Just then, he saw sea animals swimming toward him. A small green whale splashed its tail. A red shark smiled. Pink and green fish swam up to his feet.

"Hi, Shawn!" a striped starfish said. "We're glad you came back. What would you like to do today?"

"Let's go for a ride!" Shawn said. Then, he dove into the water and swam to the shark. Shawn grabbed the shark's tail and held on. The shark swam through waves. He jumped high out of the water. He dove low through sea grass. Then, he took Shawn back to the beach.

Next, Shawn swam with seals. He played with turtles. He raced crabs. But, the sun was starting to set. It was getting late. "I've had a lot of fun, but it's time for me to go home," Shawn said.

"We're glad you came to play. See you next time!" the animals said. They all smiled and waved at Shawn.

LANGUAGE ARTS GREEN | MID-SEMESTER CHECKPOINT — LC 75

LC 76

Shawn picked up his paper plane. He closed his eyes and held on to it tightly. Then, he started to turn in a circle. Shawn turned around and around until his feet lifted off the ground. When they touched back down, he wasn't standing on sand. He was standing on a hard floor. Shawn opened his eyes and looked around. He was back in his room.

"That was another great trip!" Shawn said. He put his paper plane on a shelf full of other planes. He brushed the sand off his feet and went downstairs for dinner.

III.

Claire's dad finished his story. He saw that Claire had finished all her lunch. She had pushed her chair back from the table. She wanted to leave the room. "Claire," he asked, "did my story bore you even more?"

"No, Dad," Claire said. "I want to leave the table, but not because I'm bored. I want to leave so I can go make paper airplanes!"

LC 77

A Trip to the Magic Sea
by Missy Gimble

I.

Claire was bored. She had read books and made pictures. She had played outside. Now, she was sitting at the kitchen table. She put her head down on her arms and watched her dad make lunch.

"I'm bored, Dad," Claire said.

"Don't worry. We will go on a trip to the beach in a few days. You will have lots to do then," her dad said.

"But, our trip is still three days away," Claire said. "What can I do to have fun until then?" she asked.

Her dad put lunch on the table and sat down. Claire raised her head and started to eat. "Did I ever tell you about Shawn?" her dad asked.

"No," Claire replied.

"He was my best friend when I was a kid. Shawn was never bored. Let me tell you why," said her dad. He took a bite of his lunch and began his story.

LC 78

II.

Shawn loved making paper airplanes. He made big planes and small ones. He made them out of all kinds of paper. He knew how to fold their wings in different ways. He did that to make them fly faster or slower. The best thing about Shawn's planes was that they really flew. They didn't just fly across a room. They flew to far-off places.

"Finished!" Shawn said as he folded his piece of paper one last time. He held up his paper airplane and smiled. "Where do I want to go today? I know. I want to go to the Magic Sea!" Shawn closed his eyes. He held on tightly to his paper plane. Then, he started to turn in a circle. Shawn turned around and around until his feet

---

LC 79

lifted off the ground. When they touched back down, he wasn't standing on a hard floor. He was standing on sand. Shawn opened his eyes and looked around. He was on the beach of the Magic Sea!

Shawn put his plane on the sand and ran to the water. "I wonder if they'll be here today," he thought. Just then, he saw sea animals swimming toward him. A small green whale splashed its tail. A red shark smiled. Pink and green fish swam up to his feet.

"Hi, Shawn!" a striped starfish said. "We're glad you came back. What would you like to do today?"

"Let's go for a ride!" Shawn said. Then, he dove into the water and swam to the shark. Shawn grabbed the shark's tail and held on. The shark swam through waves. He jumped high out of the water. He dove low through sea grass. Then, he took Shawn back to the beach.

Next, Shawn swam with seals. He played with turtles. He raced crabs. But, the sun was starting to set. It was getting late. "I've had a lot of fun, but it's time for me to go home," Shawn said.

"We're glad you came to play. See you next time!" the animals said. They all smiled and waved at Shawn.

LC 80

Shawn picked up his paper plane. He closed his eyes and held on to it tightly. Then, he started to turn in a circle. Shawn turned around and around until his feet lifted off the ground. When they touched back down, he wasn't standing on sand. He was standing on a hard floor. Shawn opened his eyes and looked around. He was back in his room.

"That was another great trip!" Shawn said. He put his paper plane on a shelf full of other planes. He brushed the sand off his feet and went downstairs for dinner.

III.

Claire's dad finished his story. He saw that Claire had finished all her lunch. She had pushed her chair back from the table. She wanted to leave the room. "Claire," he asked, "did my story bore you even more?"

"No, Dad," Claire said. "I want to leave the table, but not because I'm bored. I want to leave so I can go make paper airplanes!"

LC 81

Part 1. Fiction: "A Trip to the Magic Sea"
Activate Prior Knowledge
Get ready to read. Listen to the question, and say your answer.

1. **Answers will vary.**

2. **Answers will vary.**

Part 2. Fiction: "A Trip to the Magic Sea"
Book Walk
Do a Book Walk. Listen to the question, and say your answer.

3. **Answers will vary.**

4. **An author writes a story.**

5. **An illustrator draws the pictures.**

6. **to entertain us**

7. **fiction**

LC 83

Part 3. Fiction: "A Trip to the Magic Sea"
Shared Reading and Fluency Check
Cut out the word cards. Read aloud each word.

bored	Claire	replied
story	finished	paper airplane

LC 85

8. **bored**

9. **Claire**

10. **story**

11. **paper airplane**

12. **finished**

13. **replied**

14.–17.

LC 86

Part 4. Fiction: "A Trip to the Magic Sea"
Evaluate Predictions
Listen to the question, and say your answer.

18. **Possible answers: title; illustrations; vocabulary words**
19. **Possible answers: title; illustrations; vocabulary words**
20. **Answers will vary.**

Part 5. Fiction: "A Trip to the Magic Sea"
Draw Conclusions
Listen to the question, and say your answer.

21. **Answers will vary. Students may come to the conclusion that Claire will try to use her paper plane to go to the Magic Sea.**

Literature & Comprehension   **LC 679**

Name _____ Date _____

Part 6. Fiction: "A Trip to the Magic Sea"
Reading Comprehension
Listen to the question, and write the answer.

22. Who are the characters in the story?

Dad, Claire, Shawn

23. What is the setting for Dad and Claire's part of the story?

the kitchen

24. What is the setting for Shawn's part of the story?

his room; the Magic Sea

25. Did Shawn really go to the Magic Sea?

Yes

Name _____ Date _____

26. How can readers tell whether Shawn really went to the Magic Sea?

He shook sand off his pants when he got back.

27. Is this story fiction or nonfiction?

fiction

28. Is this story realistic or fantasy?

fantasy

29. What was Claire's problem?

She was bored.

30. How did Dad help Claire solve her problem?

He told her a story.

31. Read the sentence from the story. How do we know what Claire said?
"I'm bored, Dad," Claire said.

because it has quotation marks

Name _____ Date _____

Part 7. Fiction: "A Trip to the Magic Sea"
Show You Know
Cut out the cards. Draw pictures of the main events on them.
Retell the story.

32.

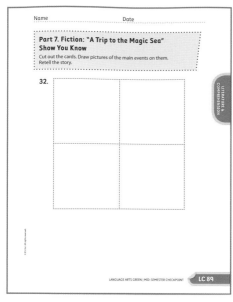

Name _____ Date _____

33. **Students should use the pictures to retell the story correctly.**

34. **Answers will vary.**

Name _____ Date _____

The Wright Brothers
By C.S. Rey

What do you see when you look up at the sky? You might see the sun and clouds if it's daytime. You might see the moon and stars if it's nighttime. Some days, you might see birds and butterflies. People have always seen these things in the sky. But, when you look up at the sky, you might see something else. You might see something that people long ago never saw. You might see airplanes.

Two Brothers with One Dream
Wilbur Wright had a dream. He dreamed of building the first airplane. His brother Orville shared the same dream. Wilbur was born on April 16, 1867. Orville was born on August 19, 1871. When they were young boys, their father gave them a special toy. It was a toy helicopter.

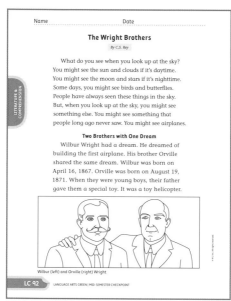

Wilbur (left) and Orville (right) Wright

Name _____ Date _____

The boys loved their toy. They played with it all the time. They learned how it worked. Then, they built their own. From then on, they wanted to learn as much as they could about flying. As they grew older, they didn't just want to *learn* about flying. They wanted to fly. But, how could they fly when no one had built an airplane yet? Wilbur and Orville had a plan to solve their problem. They planned to build the first airplane. They knew it would be hard work. But, they didn't let that stop them.

Learning from Others
The Wright brothers were not the first people to try to build an airplane. Other people had tried, too. Wilbur and Orville learned from those people. They read all about the machines those people had built. They looked at pictures of the machines. They learned why those machines didn't work. The Wright brothers learned a lot. They used what they learned to help build their plane.

Learning from Birds
The Wright brothers knew they had to be able to steer their airplane. They had to be able to steer it on the ground and once it was in the air. But, they didn't know how to make their plane turn from side to side. None of the machines

---

Name _____ Date _____

they had studied could turn safely. The brothers knew how to solve their problem. They looked for help somewhere else. This time, they didn't learn from other people. They didn't learn from machines. They learned from birds.

Wilbur and Orville watched birds as they flew. They saw the birds use their wings to turn. They learned that birds raise and lower parts of their wings to turn from side to side. The Wright brothers used what they learned from birds to help build their plane.

Up, Up, and Away!
Wilbur and Orville spent years learning from other people and from birds. They learned from their own machines, too. They built their first flying machine in 1899. Their machine didn't look the way planes look today. It was small. It was just 5 feet wide. That's about how wide a small car is today. Their first machine didn't have a motor. No one sat on the machine to fly it. The brothers flew it like a kite. They stood on the ground and held ropes that moved the wings.

The Wright brothers spent the next four years building new machines. They tested each one. They learned what worked on each machine. They learned what didn't work, too. They used what they learned to make each machine better.

Name _____ Date _____

They built their machines bigger and bigger. They flew the first ones from the ground like kites. Then, they started riding in the machines to fly them. But none of their machines had motors. They all needed wind to fly.

In 1903, the Wright brothers built a new machine. They called it the *Wright Flyer I*. This machine was not like their others. It was their first one with a motor. On December 17, 1903, the brothers were ready to test their airplane. Orville flew their plane the first time. He flew it for 12 seconds. Then, the brothers took turns flying their plane. They flew it three more times that day. None of their flights lasted a long time. They were all less than a minute. But, their four short flights were all it took. The Wright brothers proved people could fly!

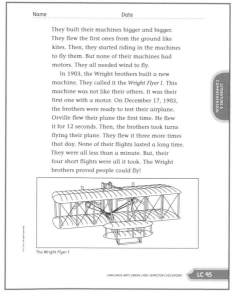

The Wright Flyer I

Name _____ Date _____

The World's First Pilots			
April 16, 1867 Wilbur Wright is born.	**August 19, 1871** Orville Wright is born.	**1899** Wilbur and Orville Wright build their first flying machine. **1903** Wilbur and Orville Wright build the *Wright Flyer I*.	**December 17, 1903** Orville Wright becomes the first person to fly an airplane.

Name _____ Date _____

Part 8. Nonfiction: "The Wright Brothers"
Preview the Article
Listen to the question, and say your answer.

35. **Students should point to the time line.**

36. **Two Brothers with One Dream**

37. **Answers will vary.**

38. **Students should point to the rest of the headings in the article.**

39. **to call them out; to make them stand out to the reader**

40. **the Wright brothers' invention of the airplane**

Name _____ Date _____

Part 9. Nonfiction: "The Wright Brothers"
Read Aloud – Main Idea and Supporting Details
Write each heading. Listen to the article, and write the main idea and one supporting detail for each section.

41.

	First section	Second section
Heading	**Two Brothers with One Dream**	**Learning from Others**
Main idea	**The Wright brothers dreamed of building the first airplane.**	**The Wright brothers learned from other people who tried to build airplanes.**
Supporting detail	**Answers will vary.**	**Answers will vary.**

Name _____ Date _____

	Third section	Fourth section
Heading	**Learning from Birds**	**Up, Up, and Away!**
Main idea	**The Wright brothers studied birds to learn how to steer an airplane.**	**The Wright brothers built many machines before they proved that people could fly.**
Supporting detail	**Answers will vary.**	**Answers will vary.**

Name _____ Date _____

Part 10. Nonfiction: "The Wright Brothers"
Reading Comprehension
Listen to the question, and choose the answer.

42. What did the Wright brothers build?
   A. a toy submarine
   B. an airplane
   C. model birds

43. What did the Wright brothers learn from birds?
   A. how to land
   B. how to take off
   C. how to steer

44. When did the Wright brothers build their first flying machine?
   A. 1899   B. 1903   C. 1939

45. How long did the Wright brothers' first flight last?
   A. 12 hours
   B. 12 minutes
   C. 12 seconds

Student Copy

So High

I stand on the ground
And look up to the sky
I watch you fly
So high, so high

Your wings are long
And shine in the light
I watch you fly
So high, so high

You do not have feathers
And no beak to open wide
I watch you fly
So high, so high

I stand on the ground
And look up to the sky
I watch the airplane fly
So high, so high

Learning Coach Copy

So High

I stand on the ground
And look up to the sky
I watch you fly
So high, so high

Your wings are long
And shine in the light
I watch you fly
So high, so high

You do not have feathers
And no beak to open wide
I watch you fly
So high, so high

I stand on the ground
And look up to the sky
I watch the airplane fly
So high, so high

Name _____ Date _____

Part 11. Poetry: "So High" Activate Prior Knowledge
Get ready to read. Listen to the question, and say your answer.

46. **Possible answers: They have rhyming words; they're short; they have descriptive language; they have patterns.**

47. **airplanes**

48. **Answers may vary, but students should understand that the poem will be about airplanes as well.**

Part 12. Poetry: "So High" Shared Reading and Fluency Check
Read aloud the poem.

49.–52.

Name _____ Date _____

Part 13. Poetry: "So High" Summarizing
Listen to the question, and say your answer.

53. **The author sees an airplane flying in the sky.**

Part 14. Poetry: "So High" Evaluate Predictions
Listen to the question, and say your answer.

54. **Possible answers: title; previous readings**

55. **Answers will vary.**

Name _____ Date _____

Part 15. Poetry: "So High" Reading Comprehension
Listen to the question, and write the answer.

56. What is the topic of "So High"?
   an airplane

57. What do the words *so high, so high* make you feel like?
   Answers will vary.

58. Which words repeat throughout the poem?
   so high, so high

59. Why does the author repeat those words?
   to show how high the airplane flies; it makes the poem sound more interesting

---

Name _____ Date _____

60. Which words rhyme in the poem?
   sky, fly, high

Part 16. Poetry: "So High" Draw Conclusions
Listen to the question, and say your answer.

61. **an airplane**

Part 17. Poetry: "So High" Illustration
Draw a picture to go with the poem.

62. **Student should draw a picture that represents the poem.**

Literature & Comprehension   LC 681

 **varies**

If necessary, work with students to complete the More Practice activity.

More Practice

Objectives
- Evaluate Checkpoint results and choose activities to review.

Reading and Comprehension

If students scored less than 80 percent on the Mid-Semester Checkpoint, they may benefit from completing another Reader's Choice unit. You can find this list online. Additionally, continue to work with students on skills such as making and evaluating predictions and identifying elements of a given story (title, author, illustrator, characters, setting, problem, solution).

American Inventors

Unit Focus

In this unit, students will learn about creative American inventors and how their inventions have affected people's lives. This unit follows the guided-reading instructional approach (see the instructional approaches to reading in the introductory lesson for this program). In this unit, students will

- ▶ Review the strategy of making predictions and why it is important.
- ▶ Learn the characteristics of a biography.
- ▶ Identify the topic of a nonfiction article.
- ▶ Learn ways that information in a nonfiction article can be organized, including by problem and solution, by cause and effect, and in chronological order.
- ▶ Identify the main idea or message of a nonfiction article.
- ▶ Identify facts and opinions in a nonfiction article.
- ▶ Identify the sequence of events in a nonfiction article.

Unit Plan   〔Offline〕

Lesson 1	Introduce "Ben Franklin, American Inventor"	**45** minutes a day
Lesson 2	Explore "Ben Franklin, American Inventor"	
Lesson 3	Introduce "Inventors in the Kitchen"	
Lesson 4	Explore "Inventors in the Kitchen"	
Lesson 5	Introduce "Robert's Rockets"	
Lesson 6	Explore "Robert's Rockets"	
Lesson 7	Introduce "Stephanie Kwolek's Amazing Invention"	
Lesson 8	Explore "Stephanie Kwolek's Amazing Invention"	
Lesson 9	Your Choice	

Introduce "Ben Franklin, American Inventor"

Lesson Overview

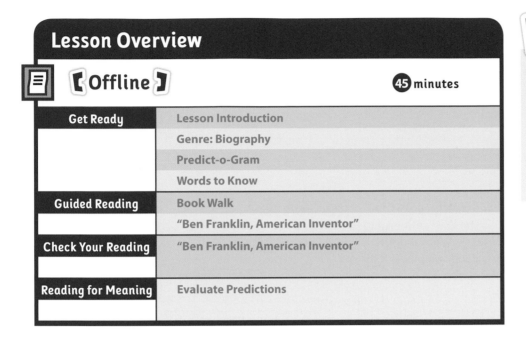

Get Ready	Lesson Introduction	
	Genre: Biography	
	Predict-o-Gram	
	Words to Know	
Guided Reading	Book Walk	
	"Ben Franklin, American Inventor"	
Check Your Reading	"Ben Franklin, American Inventor"	
Reading for Meaning	Evaluate Predictions	

[Offline] — **45** minutes

Advance Preparation

Before beginning the Guided Reading, read "Ben Franklin, American Inventor" to locate Words to Know in the text. Preview pages LC 237 and 238 in *K¹² Language Arts Activity Book* to prepare the materials for the Guided Reading.

Big Ideas

- ▶ Exposing readers to a wide variety of genres provides them with a wide range of background knowledge and increases their vocabulary.
- ▶ Good readers interact with text to make logical predictions before reading; confirm predictions during reading; and revise or make new predictions as they read further.
- ▶ Guided reading provides support to early readers as they practice and apply the reading strategies of proficient readers.

Materials

Supplied

- "Ben Franklin, American Inventor," *K¹² World: The Science of Inventing,* pp. 2–13
- *K¹² Language Arts Activity Book,* pp. LC 235–238

Article Synopsis

Although he spent only a few years in school, Ben Franklin became a successful businessman, invented many things that we still use today, signed the Declaration of Independence, and helped make laws for the young United States.

Keywords

biography – the story of someone's life written by another person

prediction – a guess about what might happen that is based on information in a story and what you already know

topic – the subject of a text

Offline **45 minutes**

Work **together** with students to complete Get Ready, Guided Reading, Check Your Reading, and Reading for Meaning activities.

Get Ready

Lesson Introduction

Prepare students for reading and discussing "Ben Franklin, American Inventor."

1. Tell students that they are going to read "Ben Franklin, American Inventor," an article about a famous American.

2. Explain that before they read the article, you will get ready by discussing

   ▸ A kind of nonfiction writing called biography
   ▸ Predictions we can make about the kind of information we'll find in a nonfiction article

---

Genre: Biography

Introduce students to the kind of writing called biography.

1. Tell students that there is a kind of nonfiction writing called **biography**. A biography tells facts about a person's life. A biography is always written by someone else, not the person the biography is about.

2. Explain that most biographies tell certain things about a person, such as

   ▸ When and where the person was born
   ▸ Places the person lived
   ▸ Facts about the person's family
   ▸ Important things the person did
   ▸ When the person died

   Recognizing these things while we read helps us realize a nonfiction text is a biography.

3. Tell students that biographies tell us important facts about people, and they can bring history to life. When we find out why people from the past did things, it helps us better understand them. Sometimes when we read about famous people from the past, it helps us see that they were a lot like we are.

> **Objectives**
> - Identify genre.
> - Make predictions based on text, illustrations, and/or prior knowledge.
> - Demonstrate understanding through graphic organizers.
> - Build vocabulary through listening, reading, and discussion.
> - Use new vocabulary in written and spoken sentences.
> - Increase concept and content vocabulary.

4. Have students practice identifying a biography.
Say: I'm going to read a paragraph about a famous person that might sound familiar to you.

George Washington was born in the colony of Virginia in America in 1732. He had many brothers and sisters. His older brother, Lawrence, helped him get his first job as a surveyor. Later on, George joined the army and helped fight for American independence. After the war, he became the first president of the United States. George Washington died in 1799.

   ▶ What does this paragraph tell us? facts about George Washington; things about George Washington's life
   ▶ What do we call a nonfiction text that tells facts about someone's life? a biography

---

✏️ **Predict-o-Gram**

Explore making predictions about the content of a biography. Turn to page LC 235 in *K¹² Language Arts Activity Book.*

1. Remind students that **predictions** are guesses about what will happen in a story or information we'll find in an article. We use clues in the story or article and what we know from our personal experience to make predictions.

2. Tell students that they can also make predictions about the kind of information they will find in a fictional story or nonfiction text. This is because they have prior knowledge about the story elements they would find in a fictional story and the kind of information they would find in a nonfiction article.

   ▶ In a fictional story called "The Bear and the Moose," who would you predict are the characters? a bear and a moose
   ▶ In a nonfiction article called "Let's Build a Tree House," what kind of information do you predict you'd find? instructions on how to build a tree house

3. Show students the Activity Book page.
Say: This Predict-o-Gram will help us get ready to read "Ben Franklin, American Inventor." We're going to use our prior knowledge of the kind of information we would find in a biography to make predictions about the article.

4. Point to the word bank of article words and phrases.
Say: Here's a list of words and phrases from the article that tell about Ben Franklin.

5. Point to and read aloud the headings of the category boxes.
Say: Before we read the article, we'll predict which category each word and phrase from the article tells about and write it in that box. After we read the article, we'll revisit our original predictions to see if we need to move any of the words or phrases to a different box.

6. Help students read each word and phrase. After students decide which box the word or phrase belongs in, help them write it in that box.

7. If students have trouble placing any of the words or phrases, guide them with the following questions.

  ▶ Does that word name a place?
  ▶ Does that word name or describe a job a person can do?
  ▶ Does that word name a thing that somebody might have invented?
  ▶ Does that word tell how a person acts, or could that word describe a person?

TIP Do not expect students to place all the words and phrases in the correct boxes until *after* they have read the article.

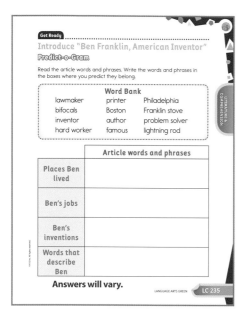

Words to Know

Before reading "Ben Franklin, American Inventor," go over Words to Know with students.

1. Read aloud each word or phrase and have students repeat it.

2. Ask students if they know what each word or phrase means.

  ▶ If students know a word's or phrase's meaning, have them define it and use it in a sentence.
  ▶ If students don't know a word's or phrase's meaning, read them the definition and discuss the word or phrase with them.

almanac – a book published each year, often with a calendar, weather predictions, clever sayings, and other information

Declaration of Independence – a document that declared the American colonies' independence, or freedom, from England

electricity – a form of energy used for heat and light, and for making machines work

experiment – a carefully planned test used to discover something unknown

invention – a machine, tool, or process that did not exist before

lens – a curved piece of glass; when you look through an eyeglass lens, things are clearer

rod – a long, thin piece of metal, wood, or other material

spark – a very small bit of burning material

Guided Reading

Book Walk

Prepare students for reading by taking them on a Book Walk of "Ben Franklin, American Inventor." Scan the article together and ask students to make predictions about the article. Answers to questions may vary.

1. Turn to the **table of contents** in *K¹² World: The Science of Inventing.* Help students find the selection and turn to that page.

2. Point to and read aloud the **title of the article**.

   ▸ What do you think the article might be about?

3. Have students look at the **pictures of the article**.

4. Point to and read aloud any headers, captions, or other features that stand out.

   ▸ What kind of information do you think the article might tell us about Ben Franklin?

   ▸ Have you ever heard of Ben Franklin? What do you already know about him?

Objectives

- Make predictions based on text, illustrations, and/or prior knowledge.

- Activate prior knowledge by previewing text and/or discussing topic.

- Read and listen to a variety of texts for information and pleasure independently or as part of a group.

- Read aloud grade-level text with appropriate expression, accuracy, and rate.

"Ben Franklin, American Inventor"

It's time to guide students through a preview of the article to prepare them for reading on their own. Gather the Reading Aid on pages LC 237 and 238 in *K¹² Language Arts Activity Book.*

1. Have students sit next to you so that they can see the pictures and words while you introduce and discuss the article.

2. Tell students that you will preview the article to prepare them to read the article aloud to you.

3. Refer to the Reading Aid.

Reading Aid Tear out the Reading Aid for this reading selection. Follow the instructions for folding the page, and then use the page as a guide as you preview the selection with students.

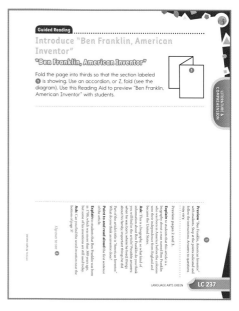

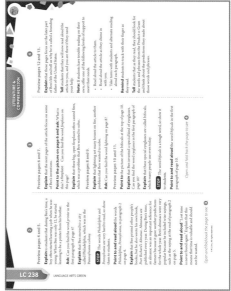

Check Your Reading

"Ben Franklin, American Inventor"

Check students' comprehension of "Ben Franklin, American Inventor."

1. Have students retell "Ben Franklin, American Inventor" in their own words to develop grammar, vocabulary, comprehension, and fluency skills.

2. Ask students the following questions.

   ▸ Where was Ben Franklin born? Boston

   ▸ What was Ben's first job? printer   Whom did he work for? his brother James

   ▸ What happened after Ben wrote a book called *Poor Richard's Almanac*? Possible answers: Many people bought it; he made a lot of money; he didn't have to work so hard as a printer; he had more time for his ideas.

   ▸ Why does a lightning rod need to be taller than the house it's attached to? so the lightning will hit the lightning rod instead of the house; because lightning hits the tallest thing in an area

   ▸ Ben didn't get any money for his inventions. What did he get, instead? prizes; fame

   ▸ Who is the article about? What is the topic? Ben Franklin

 TIP If students have trouble responding to a question, help them locate the answer in the text or pictures.

★ **Objectives**
- Answer questions requiring literal recall of details.
- Identify the topic.

Reading for Meaning

 Evaluate Predictions

Revisit the predictions students made using the Predict-o-Gram on page LC 235 in *K¹² Language Arts Activity Book*. Have students use the Predict-o-Gram as a tool for retelling the article.

1. Remind students that they used their prior knowledge of the kind of information they find in nonfiction articles to make predictions with the Predict-o-Gram. Reinforce that it's okay if their predictions didn't happen.

2. Help students review what they wrote in each box of the Predict-o-Gram. Have them cross out and change any words or phrases that belong in a different box.

3. Have students add any other words or phrases from the article that they think should go into the boxes.

   ▸ Did the article talk about any other inventions that are not already listed in the "Ben's inventions" box? swim fins

   ▸ Are there any other words or phrases in the article that would fit in the "Words that describe Ben" box? Possible answers: smart; leader; founding father. Note that students may decide to place *leader* in the "Ben's jobs" box. Either placement would be correct.

★ **Objectives**
- Evaluate predictions.
- Retell or dramatize a story.
- Identify important details in informational text.
- Use illustrations to aid understanding of text.

4. Ask students the following questions. Answers to questions may vary.

   ▸ Which words did you predict belonged in the "Places Ben lived" box? Do those words name places?

   ▸ What did you predict should go into the "Ben's jobs" box before you read? Why did you decide to put those words there? Did you have to change what you put into that box after you read the article?

   ▸ Which of the words or phrases did you predict named inventions? Did you have to change anything in that box after you read?

   ▸ Which of the words or phrases did you predict belonged in the "Words that describe Ben" box? Did you have to change anything in that box after you read?

5. Tell students that now they have organized the words and phrases that tell about Ben Franklin into the correct boxes. So the Predict-o-Gram can now be used as a tool for retelling the article.

6. Have students retell the article, using the words and phrases from the Predict-o-Gram to retell the key details. Have students refer to the pictures in the article as additional cues for retelling.

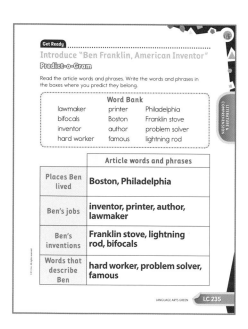

Explore "Ben Franklin, American Inventor"

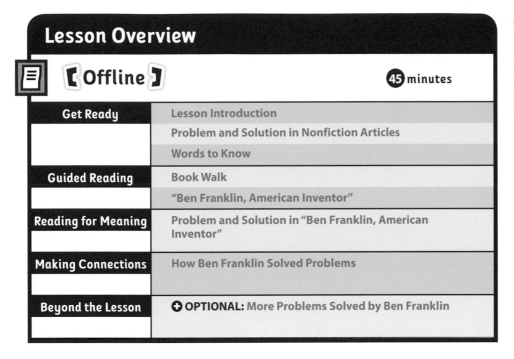

Lesson Overview

[Offline]   **45** minutes

Get Ready	Lesson Introduction
	Problem and Solution in Nonfiction Articles
	Words to Know
Guided Reading	Book Walk
	"Ben Franklin, American Inventor"
Reading for Meaning	Problem and Solution in "Ben Franklin, American Inventor"
Making Connections	How Ben Franklin Solved Problems
Beyond the Lesson	⊕ OPTIONAL: More Problems Solved by Ben Franklin

[Materials]

Supplied

- "Ben Franklin, American Inventor," *K¹² World: The Science of Inventing*, pp. 2–13
- *K¹² Language Arts Activity Book*, p. LC 239
- *K¹² My Journal* (optional)

Keywords

text structure – the organizational pattern of a text, such as cause and effect, compare and contrast, and chronological order

Big Ideas

- ► Comprehension entails an understanding of the organizational patterns of text.
- ► Repeated rereading leads to increased fluency.

[Offline] 45 minutes

Work **together** with students to complete Get Ready, Guided Reading, Reading for Meaning, Making Connections, and Beyond the Lesson activities.

Get Ready

Lesson Introduction

Prepare students for reading and discussing "Ben Franklin, American Inventor."

1. Tell students that they are going to reread "Ben Franklin, American Inventor."

2. Explain that before they read the article, you will get ready by discussing how authors can organize information in a nonfiction article by problem and solution.

> **Objectives**
> - Identify examples of problem and solution.
> - Identify organizational structures of text.
> - Build vocabulary through listening, reading, and discussion.
> - Use new vocabulary in written and spoken sentences.
> - Increase concept and content vocabulary.

Problem and Solution in Nonfiction Articles

Introduce text that is organized to show problem and solution.

1. Tell students that authors can organize information in an article in different ways.

   ► The author might organize information according to the order in which events happen. Texts like this are written **in sequence**.
   ► The author might describe how things are alike and different. We say that texts like these are written to **compare and contrast**.

2. Explain that most of "Ben Franklin, American Inventor" points out problems and then talks about what Ben invented to solve those problems. We say that texts like this are organized by **problem and solution**.

3. Have students practice identifying a problem and solution in a paragraph organized this way.
   Say: I'm going to read a paragraph about an inventor. Listen for how the paragraph is organized.

   Earle Dickson noticed that his wife often cut her fingers while she made dinner. She would cover a cut with a piece of gauze and then tape the gauze to her finger. But the gauze and tape would always come loose and fall off. Earle took a small square of gauze and put it in the center of a piece of tape. He then covered the tape with some fabric to keep it clean and to keep it from sticking to itself. The Band-Aid® was born!

4. Ask the following questions.

   ▶ How is the information in this paragraph organized? by problem and solution

   ▶ What problem did Earle Dickson notice? When his wife covered a cut with gauze and tape, they would fall off.

   ▶ What did Earle invent to solve the problem? the Band-Aid

5. Tell students that they should look for descriptions of problems when they read a nonfiction article. If the article talks about how somebody tried to solve the problems, there's a good chance that the article is organized by problem and solution.

Words to Know

Before reading "Ben Franklin, American Inventor," go over Words to Know with students.

1. Read aloud each word or phrase and have students repeat it.

2. Ask students if they know what each word or phrase means.

   ▶ If students know a word's or phrase's meaning, have them define it and use it in a sentence.

   ▶ If students don't know a word's or phrase's meaning, read them the definition and discuss the word or phrase with them.

almanac – a book published each year, often with a calendar, weather predictions, clever sayings, and other information

Declaration of Independence – a document that declared the American colonies' independence, or freedom, from England

electricity – a form of energy used for heat and light, and for making machines work

experiment – a carefully planned test used to discover something unknown

invention – a machine, tool, or process that did not exist before

lens – a curved piece of glass; when you look through an eyeglass lens, things are clearer

rod – a long, thin piece of metal, wood, or other material

spark – a very small bit of burning material

Guided Reading

Book Walk

Prepare students for reading by taking them on a Book Walk of "Ben Franklin, American Inventor." Scan the article together to revisit the text.

1. Turn to the selection in *K¹² World: The Science of Inventing*.

2. Have students read aloud the **title of the article**.

3. Have students look at the **pictures of the article**.

4. Ask the following questions to help students think about what they already know about Ben Franklin.

   ▸ Where was Ben Franklin born? Boston
   ▸ Why did Ben move to Philadelphia? He didn't like working for his brother.
   ▸ What is *Poor Richard's Almanac* filled with? wise sayings   How did writing this book help Ben? Possible answers: He made money; he didn't have to work so hard as a printer; he had more time to spend on his ideas.

Objectives
- Activate prior knowledge by previewing text and/or discussing topic.
- Read and listen to a variety of texts for information and pleasure independently or as part of a group.
- Read aloud grade-level text with appropriate expression, accuracy, and rate.

"Ben Franklin, American Inventor"

It's time for students to reread the article.

1. Tell students that "Ben Franklin, American Inventor" should now be familiar to them because they have read it before.

2. Explain that they will reread the article aloud to you, and you are there if they need your help.

3. If students have trouble reading on their own, offer one of the following levels of support to meet their needs.

   ▸ Read aloud the article to them.
   ▸ Read aloud the article as they chime in with you.
   ▸ Take turns with students and alternate reading aloud each paragraph or page.

4. Remind students to track with their finger as they read.

5. Tell students that as they read, they should look for examples of how Ben Franklin solved problems.

Reading for Meaning

Problem and Solution in "Ben Franklin, American Inventor"
Check students' ability to identify a problem and how it is solved.

1. Have students retell "Ben Franklin, American Inventor" in their own words to develop grammar, vocabulary, comprehension, and fluency skills. Be sure students retell key details of the nonfiction article.

2. Ask students the following questions.

   ▸ Why did Ben invent swim fins? He wanted to swim faster.
   ▸ What problem did Ben notice about fireplaces in homes? Sparks could get out and set houses on fire.   What did Ben invent to solve this problem? the Franklin stove   How did the Franklin stove solve this problem? It was closed, so sparks couldn't get out of it.
   ▸ In Ben's time, what problem did lightning cause? It set houses on fire.   Why did this happen? because lightning strikes the tallest object in an area   What did Ben invent to solve this problem? the lighting rod
   ▸ Why did Ben invent bifocals? so people could see things nearby and faraway with one pair of glasses
   ▸ How is the information in "Ben Franklin, American Inventor" organized? by problem and solution

Objectives
- Retell or dramatize a story.
- Identify examples of problem and solution.
- Identify organizational structures of text.
- Identify important details in informational text.

Making Connections

How Ben Franklin Solved Problems
Check students' ability to identify how Ben Franklin solved problems. Turn to page LC 239 in *K¹² Language Arts Activity Book.*

1. Remind students that Ben Franklin liked to invent things to make people's lives safer and better.

2. Help students read aloud the column headings, "Problem" and "Solution." Explain that they will draw a line to connect each problem with its solution.

3. Have students look at the first picture at the top of the "Problem" column and read aloud the words in the thought bubble above Ben's head.

   ▸ Help students read the text, as needed.

4. Tell students to look at the pictures in the "Solution" column to find the one that solves the problem. Have students draw a line to connect the two pictures.

Objectives
- Identify examples of problem and solution.

5. Repeat Steps 3 and 4 until all problems and their solutions are connected with lines.

6. Ask students the following questions. Answers to questions may vary.

   ▶ What you think is the most interesting thing that Ben invented? Why?
   ▶ Which of Ben's inventions do you think helped people the most? Why?

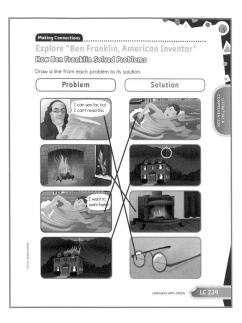

Beyond the Lesson

⊕ **OPTIONAL: More Problems Solved by Ben Franklin**

This activity is OPTIONAL. It is intended for students who have extra time and would like to learn more about Ben Franklin's inventions and ideas. Feel free to skip this activity.

1. Tell students that Ben Franklin invented many more things than the ones mentioned in the article "Ben Franklin, American Inventor." Not only did he invent objects to solve problems, but he also came up with ideas for public services to improve his community.

2. Explain that if students have ever checked out a book from a public library, they have Ben Franklin to thank. Ben helped set up the first lending library in the American colonies and laid the groundwork for our public library system.

Objectives
- Identify relevant sources of information.
- Locate information using features of text and electronic media.
- Identify examples of problem and solution.

3. Ask students where they think they might find information about Ben's other inventions and ideas. If students have trouble naming resources, suggest the following.

> ▸ encyclopedias
> ▸ library books
> ▸ the Internet

4. Help students look for information using one of the listed resources.

5. Ask students the following questions. Answers to questions may vary.

> ▸ What were some other problems that Ben wanted to solve? How did he solve them?
> ▸ Which of Ben's inventions or ideas do you think is the best? Why?
> ▸ Have you ever seen one of Ben's inventions? Which one? Where did you see it?
> ▸ Do you use any of Ben's inventions? Which one(s)?
> ▸ Have you ever used any of the public services that Ben helped to set up?

TIP If they choose to, students can use *K¹² My Journal* to record the information that they find.

Introduce "Inventors in the Kitchen"

Materials

Supplied

- "Inventors in the Kitchen," *K¹² World: The Science of Inventing*, pp. 14–27
- *K¹² Language Arts Activity Book*, pp. LC 241–244

Lesson Overview

[Offline]

45 minutes

Get Ready	Lesson Introduction
	Main Idea of a Nonfiction Article
	Anticipation Guide for "Inventors in the Kitchen"
	Words to Know
Guided Reading	Book Walk
	"Inventors in the Kitchen"
Check Your Reading	"Inventors in the Kitchen"
Reading for Meaning	Genre: Biography
	Revisit Anticipation Guide
	Identify Main Idea

Article Synopsis

Learn the history of several clever inventions and about the people behind them.

Keywords

biography – the story of someone's life written by another person

main idea – the most important idea in a paragraph or text

topic – the subject of a text

Advance Preparation

Before beginning the Guided Reading, read "Inventors in the Kitchen" to locate Words to Know in the text. Preview pages LC 243 and 244 in *K¹² Language Arts Activity Book* to prepare the materials for the Guided Reading.

Big Ideas

- Exposing readers to a wide variety of genres provides them with a wide range of background knowledge and increases their vocabulary.
- Guided reading provides support to early readers as they practice and apply the reading strategies of proficient readers.

 **45** minutes

Work **together** with students to complete Get Ready, Guided Reading, Check Your Reading, and Reading for Meaning activities.

Get Ready ···

Lesson Introduction

Prepare students for reading and discussing "Inventors in the Kitchen."

1. Tell students that they are going to read "Inventors in the Kitchen," a biography about several inventors who have changed how people do things in the kitchen.

2. Explain that before they read the article, you will get ready by

   ▸ Discussing the main idea or message of an article
   ▸ Using an anticipation guide to start thinking about the main idea of the article

Main Idea of a Nonfiction Article

Introduce the idea that a nonfiction article can have a main idea.

1. Remind students that every nonfiction article has a **topic**. The topic is what an article is mostly about.

2. Remind students that a paragraph in a nonfiction article can have a **main idea**. If students don't remember what the main idea of a paragraph is, explain that it is the most important idea of the paragraph.

3. Tell students that there can also be an overall main idea of a nonfiction article. The main idea of an article is what the article teaches readers. It is the message, or most important idea, that the author wants readers to think about. The main idea of an article about someone who grew up in a poor family but studied a lot and became successful might be "Your dreams can come true if you work hard."

4. Explain that the author usually does not directly state the main idea, or message, of an article. Sometimes there is a clue in the title. Thinking about the topic and facts in an article can help readers figure out the main idea. Readers have to think about what they learn from reading the article to infer the main idea.

Objectives

- Identify the main idea.
- Make predictions based on text, illustrations, and/or prior knowledge.
- Build vocabulary through listening, reading, and discussion.
- Use new vocabulary in written and spoken sentences.
- Increase concept and content vocabulary.

5. Tell students that to figure out the main of an article, they can ask themselves, "What lesson did I learn from reading this article? What message does the author want me to think about?" Topics and facts that are repeated in an article can help us figure out the main idea, too.

6. Explain that they shouldn't confuse the topic of an article with the main idea. The topic of an article might be whales, but the main idea might be "The ocean is filled with wonderful things."

7. Model how to identify the main idea of an article. Have students think about the article "Telling Stories Around the World."
Say: In "Telling Stories Around the World," the author gives many facts about the kinds of stories people tell in different parts of the world. I think the main idea of "Telling Stories Around the World" is "Telling stories is important in many cultures," because that is the lesson I learned from reading the article.

8. Have students think about the article "The *Eagle* on the Moon." Remind them that the article was about the space race and how astronauts had to train long and hard before they were ready to try to land on the moon.

   ▸ What do you think is the main idea or message of "The *Eagle* on the Moon"? What lesson did you learn from reading this article? Answers may vary; possible main ideas are "If you work hard, you can do great things" or "Sometimes it takes a team to reach a goal." If students have trouble answering, tell them to think about the title of the article, what the article is mostly about, and what big idea they learned from reading the facts.

TIP If students have not read "The *Eagle* on the Moon," have them think of another article that they're familiar with, such as "Marvelous Mount Rushmore," in which the main idea is "When people work together, they can accomplish big things."

Anticipation Guide for "Inventors in the Kitchen"

Introduce students to a prereading activity to help them think about the main idea of the article. Turn to page LC 241 and 242 in *K¹² Language Arts Activity Book.*

1. Show students the Activity Book pages.
Say: This activity will help us get ready to read by introducing us to some of the ideas we'll find in "Inventors in the Kitchen."

2. Point to the first column in the guide.
Say: Here's a list of statements that you may or may not agree with. I'll read each statement, and then you'll say whether you agree or not.

3. Point to the "Before reading" column.
   Say: We'll write *Yes* or *No*, depending on whether you agree with the statement or not.

4. Point to the "After reading" column.
   Say: After you read the article, we'll revisit the statements to see whether you've changed what you think.

5. Help students read each statement in the first column of the guide. Have students record what they agree with by writing *Yes* or *No* in the "Before reading" column.

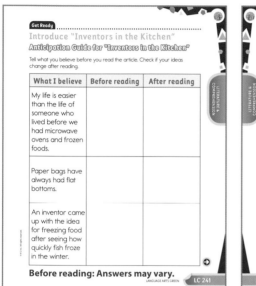
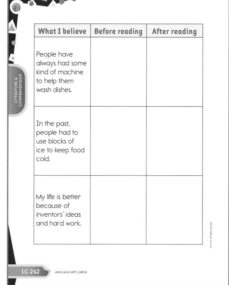

Words to Know

Before reading "Inventors in the Kitchen," go over Words to Know with students.

1. Read aloud each word or phrase and have students repeat it.

2. Ask students if they know what each word or phrase means.

   ► If students know a word's or phrase's meaning, have them define it and use it in a sentence.
   ► If students don't know a word's or phrase's meaning, read them the definition and discuss the word or phrase with them.

invention – a machine, tool, or process that did not exist before

inventor – a person who thinks of and makes new machines or tools, or develops new processes

motor – a machine that uses energy from electricity, gasoline, or another source to make something move or work

power tube – a device that looks like a long, thin light bulb; when electricity is passed through it, it creates short waves of energy called microwaves

rack – a frame or shelf that is used to hold, hang, or show things

World's Fair – a large public display in which many countries show their inventions, arts, crafts, foods, and other products

Guided Reading

Book Walk

Prepare students for reading by taking them on a Book Walk of "Inventors in the Kitchen." Scan the article together and ask students to make predictions about the article. Answers to questions may vary.

1. Turn to the **table of contents** in *K¹² World: The Science of Inventing*. Help students find the selection and turn to that page.

2. Have students read aloud the **title of the article**.

   ▸ What do you think the article might be about?

3. Have students look at the **pictures of the article**.

4. Point to and read aloud any headers, captions, or other features that stand out.

   ▸ What do you think the article might tell us about inventors or inventions?

   ▸ Can you name some things in the kitchen that probably did not exist 100 years ago?

Objectives

- Make predictions based on text, illustrations, and/or prior knowledge.
- Activate prior knowledge by previewing text and/or discussing topic.
- Read and listen to a variety of texts for information and pleasure independently or as part of a group.
- Read aloud grade-level text with appropriate expression, accuracy, and rate.

"Inventors in the Kitchen"

It's time to guide students through a preview of the article to prepare them for reading on their own. Gather the Reading Aid on pages LC 243 and 244 in *K¹² Language Arts Activity Book*.

1. Have students sit next to you so that they can see the pictures and words while you introduce and discuss the article.

2. Tell students that you will preview the article to prepare them to read the article aloud to you.

3. Refer to the Reading Aid.

Reading Aid Tear out the Reading Aid for this reading selection. Follow the instructions for folding the page, and then use the page as a guide as you preview the selection with students.

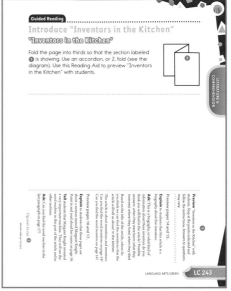
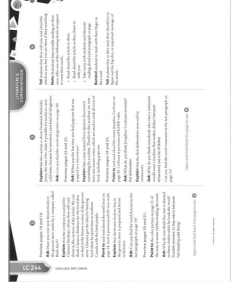

Check Your Reading

"Inventors in the Kitchen"

Check students' comprehension of "Inventors in the Kitchen."

1. Remind students that the topic of an article is what it's mostly about.

2. Ask students the following questions.

   ▸ How were paper bags shaped when Margaret Knight was young? like the letter *V*   Why are bags with flat bottoms better than bags shaped like a *V*? because they can hold more and are easier to set down on the floor or on a table

   ▸ Who came up with the idea for flash freezing? Clarence Birdseye

   ▸ When Frederick McKinley Jones was young, how did people keep food cold when they traveled? They packed it in ice.

   ▸ What happened when Percy Spencer brought a chocolate bar to work and then stood next to a power tube? the chocolate melted   What did Percy discover about power tubes because the chocolate melted? that power tubes could cook food

   ▸ How did people wash dishes when Josephine Cochrane was young? by hand   What would happen to the dishes when they bumped into each other? They broke.

   ▸ What is the topic of the article? inventors and their inventions that we use in the kitchen

TIP If students have trouble responding to a question, help them locate the answer in the text or pictures.

Objectives

- Answer questions requiring literal recall of details.
- Identify the topic.

Reading for Meaning

Genre: Biography

Check students' understanding of the characteristics of a biography.

Objectives
- Identify genre.
- Identify characteristics of different genres.
- Identify important details in informational text.
- Identify the main idea.

- ▸ What kind of article is "Inventors in the Kitchen?" a biography
- ▸ What kind of facts does a biography tell? facts about a person's life; facts about a person and the important things the person did
- ▸ What kind of things did the people in "Inventors in the Kitchen" do? What do they have in common? They all invented something that has to do with food or the kitchen; they all invented something that makes life easier.
- ▸ Why was it so expensive to make paper bags with flat bottoms before Margaret Knight invented her machine? because all the work had to be done by hand   What did Margaret's invention do that changed paper bags? It made bags with flat bottoms.
- ▸ When was Clarence Birdseye born? 1886   How did Clarence come up with the idea for flash freezing? He saw how the Inuit people in northern Canada froze their food.
- ▸ What important thing did Frederick McKinley Jones invent in the 1930s? a new kind of refrigerator   Why was Frederick able to attach his new kind of refrigerator to a truck? because it didn't have to be plugged in
- ▸ What machine did Percy Spencer invent that used power tubes? the microwave oven
- ▸ What important machine did Josephine Cochrane invent? the dishwasher   How did Josephine's invention keep dishes from breaking? The dishes went on racks, so they couldn't bump into each other.

Revisit Anticipation Guide

Check students' beliefs after reading the article. Gather the partially completed pages LC 241 and 242 in *K¹² Language Arts Activity Book* to revisit the statements and students' responses in the Anticipation Guide.

1. Have students read aloud each statement again and record what they agree with by writing *Yes* or *No* in the "After reading" column.

2. Compare the responses in the "Before reading" and "After reading" columns.

   - ▸ Did you change any of your ideas after reading "Inventors in the Kitchen"? Answers will vary.
   - ▸ If you changed your mind, why did you do that? What did you read in the article that caused you to change your mind? Answers will vary; be sure students give examples from the article.

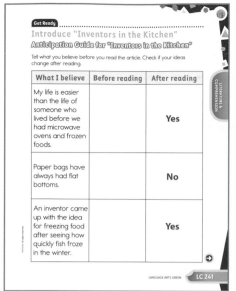
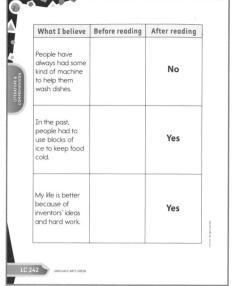

Identify Main Idea

Check students' ability to identify the main idea of a nonfiction article.

1. Remind students that the main idea is the most important idea, or message, of an article. The author of an article usually doesn't directly state the main idea. Readers have to think about the title, topic, and facts of an article to figure out the main idea on their own.

2. Ask the following questions.

   ▸ What does the title of the article "Inventors in the Kitchen" tell you? that it's about people who invented things for the kitchen

   ▸ What kinds of facts are in the article? facts about how inventors made things for the kitchen that make our lives easier

   ▸ What is the main idea of "Inventors in the Kitchen"? What do you think is the most important idea, or message, that the author wants readers to think about? Guide students to recognize that the main idea is "Inventors and their inventions that we use in the kitchen have made life easier and better for everyone."

TIP If students name the topic of the article, remind them that the topic is what the article is mostly about, not the main idea. If they give a list of facts, remind them that thinking about the facts can help them figure out the main idea.

Explore "Inventors in the Kitchen"

Lesson Overview

Offline   45 minutes

Get Ready	Lesson Introduction
	Organization of Nonfiction Articles
	Words to Know
Guided Reading	Book Walk
	"Inventors in the Kitchen"
Reading for Meaning	Text Organization in "Inventors in the Kitchen"
Making Connections	What Would You Invent?

Supplied

- "Inventors in the Kitchen," *K¹² World: The Science of Inventing*, pp. 14–27
- *K¹² Language Arts Activity Book*, p. LC 245

Also Needed

- crayons

Keywords

cause – the reason something happens

effect – the result of a cause

text structure – the organizational pattern of a text, such as cause and effect, compare and contrast, and chronological order

Big Ideas

▸ Comprehension entails an understanding of the organizational patterns of text.

▸ Repeated rereading leads to increased fluency.

 **45 minutes**

Work **together** with students to complete Get Ready, Guided Reading, Reading for Meaning, and Making Connections activities.

Get Ready

Lesson Introduction

Prepare students for reading and discussing "Inventors in the Kitchen."

1. Tell students that they are going to reread "Inventors in the Kitchen."

2. Explain that before they read the article, you will get ready by discussing the different ways that an author can organize information in a nonfiction article.

Organization of Nonfiction Articles

Reinforce how text can be organized to show problem and solution and cause and effect.

1. Remind students that authors can organize information in an article in different ways.

   ► The author might organize information according to the order in which events happen. Texts like this are written **in sequence**.
   ► The author might point out problems and then talk about the ways that people are trying to solve those problems. We say that texts like this are organized by **problem and solution**.
   ► The author might point out how one thing made another thing happen. We say that texts like this are written to show **cause and effect**.

2. Explain that an author might organize information in an article in more than one way. For example, some parts of an article might be organized to point out problems and how they are solved, while other parts of the article might be organized to show sequence of events.

3. Have students practice identifying how information is organized in a nonfiction paragraph.
   Say: One day in the winter of 1903, Mary Anderson was riding a trolley in New York City. She noticed that the operator of the trolley car was driving with the front window wide open, even though it was very cold outside. The trolley operator did this because it was raining hard, and he couldn't see out the window. This experience led Mary to invent a windshield wiper that used a rubber blade to keep windows clear of rain, sleet, and snow.

   ► What problem did the trolley operator have? He couldn't see out the trolley window when it was raining.
   ► How did Mary solve the problem? She invented a windshield wiper that kept windows clear.
   ► How is the information in this paragraph organized? by problem and solution

4. Have students practice identifying a paragraph organized by cause and effect. **Say:** One day in 1948, Georges de Mestral (duh MEHS-trahl) took his dog for a walk in the woods. When Georges got home, he noticed that his pants and his dog's fur were covered with burrs. A burr is a little part of a plant that sticks to things and is hard to remove. Georges got out his microscope to look at one of the burrs. He saw that the burr was made up of tiny hooks, which was why the burr could stick to his pants. Georges got the idea to make a two-sided fastener—one side with little hooks like the burrs, and the other side with soft, tiny loops like the ones in the fabric of his pants. The two sides would stick to each other until you pulled them apart. He thought his invention would be easier to use than a zipper or buttons. Georges called his invention Velcro®.

- ▶ What did Georges notice when he got back from walking in the woods with his dog? Burrs were all over his pants and his dog's fur.
- ▶ What did Georges do with one of the burrs? He looked at it under his microscope.   What did Georges find when he looked at the burr with a microscope? It was made up of tiny hooks.
- ▶ When Georges saw that the burr was made up of tiny hooks, what did it cause him to do? invent a fastener with hooks on one side and loops on the other; invent Velcro
- ▶ How is the information in this paragraph organized? by cause and effect

---

Words to Know

Before reading "Inventors in the Kitchen," go over Words to Know with students.

1. Read aloud each word or phrase and have students repeat it.

2. Ask students if they know what each word or phrase means.

- ▶ If students know a word's or phrase's meaning, have them define it and use it in a sentence.
- ▶ If students don't know a word's or phrase's meaning, read them the definition and discuss the word or phrase with them.

invention – a machine, tool, or process that did not exist before
inventor – a person who thinks of and makes new machines or tools, or develops new processes
motor – a machine that uses energy from electricity, gasoline, or another source to make something move or work
power tube – a device that looks like a long, thin light bulb; when electricity is passed through it, it creates short waves of energy called microwaves
rack – a frame or shelf that is used to hold, hang, or show things
World's Fair – a large public display in which many countries show their inventions, arts, crafts, foods, and other products

Guided Reading

Book Walk

Prepare students for reading by taking them on a Book Walk of "Inventors in the Kitchen." Scan the article together to revisit the text.

1. Turn to the selection in *K¹² World: The Science of Inventing*.

2. Have students read aloud the **title of the article**.

3. Have students look at the **pictures of the article**.

4. Ask the following questions to help students think about what they already know about the article. Answers to questions may vary.

   ▸ Which invention in the article do you find most interesting? Why?

   ▸ Which invention in the article do you think would be the hardest to live without? Why?

Objectives

- Activate prior knowledge by previewing text and/or discussing topic.

- Read and listen to a variety of texts for information and pleasure independently or as part of a group.

- Read aloud grade-level text with appropriate expression, accuracy, and rate.

"Inventors in the Kitchen"

It's time for students to reread the article.

1. Tell students that "Inventors in the Kitchen" should now be familiar to them because they have read it before.

2. Explain that they will reread the article aloud to you, and you are there if they need help.

3. If students have trouble reading on their own, offer one of the following levels of support to meet their needs.

   ▸ Read aloud the article to them.

   ▸ Read aloud the article as they chime in with you.

   ▸ Take turns with students and alternate reading aloud each paragraph or page.

4. Remind students to track with their finger as they read.

5. Tell students that as they read, they should look for ways inventors solved problems and what caused them to come up with their inventions.

Reading for Meaning

Text Organization in "Inventors in the Kitchen"
Check students' understanding of the problem–solution and cause–effect relationships in the article.

Objectives
- Identify examples of problem and solution.
- Describe cause-and-effect relationships in text.

1. Remind students that an author can organize the information in an article in different ways. Some sections of "Inventors in the Kitchen" are organized by problem and solution, and other sections are organized by cause and effect.

2. Ask students the following questions to check their understanding of problem and solution in nonfiction text.

   ▸ Why were flat-bottomed paper bags expensive at one time? because they had to be made by hand
   ▸ What did Margaret Knight do to solve this problem? She invented a machine that did all the work to make a paper bag with a flat bottom.
   ▸ When Frederick McKinley Jones was young, what did people have to do when they wanted to travel with cold food? They had to pack it in ice. What would happen if the ice melted? The food would go bad.
   ▸ What did Frederick invent to solve this problem? a new kind of refrigerator that didn't have to be plugged in
   ▸ What did Frederick attach his new refrigerator to? trucks   How did this solve the problem of moving cold food? People could move cold food in refrigerator trucks and not have to worry about ice melting and the food going bad.
   ▸ When Josephine Cochrane was young, people had to wash dishes by hand. What was the problem with washing dishes by hand? The dishes would bump into each other and break.   How did Josephine solve this problem? She invented a dishwasher that held dishes on racks.

3. Ask students the following questions to check their understanding of cause and effect in nonfiction text.

   ▸ Clarence Birdseye spent time in northern Canada when he was young. What caused the fish there to stay good for a long time? The fish froze quickly because it was so cold.   What did this cause Clarence to do? He figured out a way to freeze food quickly.
   ▸ One day, Percy Spencer brought a chocolate bar to work and then stood next to a power tube. What was the effect when he stood there? His chocolate bar melted.
   ▸ What was the effect when Percy put popcorn kernels next to the power tube? They began to pop.
   ▸ What did Percy do with the power tubes? He used them to invent the first microwave oven.

Making Connections

 What Would You Invent?

Encourage students to solve a problem by thinking of an invention. Turn to page LC 245 in *K¹² Language Arts Activity Book* and gather the crayons.

1. Tell students that everything around them was invented by someone, and most inventions solved some problem.

2. Have them think about a problem they think needs to be solved. Read aloud the following examples to spark their imagination.

   Problem: Sometimes, there's no place to sit.
   Invention that solves the problem: chair pants—pants that turn into a chair when you need to sit down

   Problem: You don't have time to walk the dog.
   Invention that solves the problem: a self-walking dog leash

   Problem: It's dark and raining outside, and you need to walk home.
   Invention that solves the problem: an umbrella with a built-in flashlight

3. Have students write what problem they want to solve on the Activity Book page. If students have trouble thinking of a problem, suggest the following.

   ▸ It's hard to tie your shoes.
   ▸ You don't like to make your bed every morning.
   ▸ It's hard to reach books or games that are up on a high shelf.

4. Tell them to draw a picture of their invention.

5. Have students think of a name for their invention and then have them write it on the line below their picture.

6. Have students explain the problem and how their invention solves it.

 Objectives

- Demonstrate understanding through drawing, discussion, drama, and/or writing.
- Make connections with text: text-to-text, text-to-self, text-to-world.
- Identify examples of problem and solution.

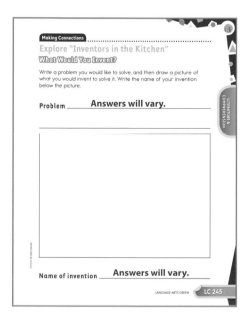

Introduce "Robert's Rockets"

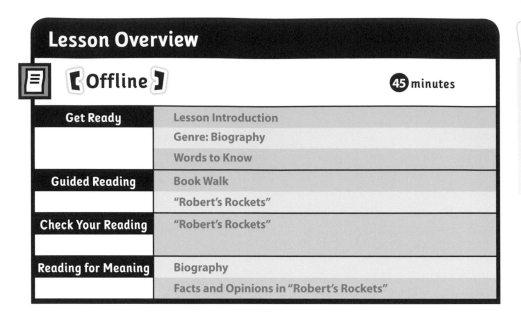

Lesson Overview

[Offline] **45** minutes

Get Ready	Lesson Introduction
	Genre: Biography
	Words to Know
Guided Reading	Book Walk
	"Robert's Rockets"
Check Your Reading	"Robert's Rockets"
Reading for Meaning	Biography
	Facts and Opinions in "Robert's Rockets"

Advance Preparation

Before beginning the Guided Reading, read "Robert's Rockets" to locate Words to Know in the text. Preview pages LC 247 and 248 in *K¹² Language Arts Activity Book* to prepare the materials for the Guided Reading.

Big Ideas

▸ Exposing readers to a wide variety of genres provides them with a wide range of background knowledge and increases their vocabulary.
▸ Guided reading provides support to early readers as they practice and apply the reading strategies of proficient readers.

Materials

Supplied

- "Robert's Rockets," *K¹² World: The Science of Inventing*, pp. 28–37
- *K¹² Language Arts Activity Book*, pp. LC 247–248

Article Synopsis

Robert H. Goddard believed he could build a rocket that could fly into space. Although many critics thought his ideas were impossible to achieve, he worked hard to make his dream come true—which is why he is now known as the "father of rocket science."

Keywords

biography – the story of someone's life written by another person

fact – something that can be proven true

opinion – something that a person thinks or believes, but which cannot be proven to be true

topic – the subject of a text

⟦ Offline ⟧ 45 minutes

Work **together** with students to complete Get Ready, Guided Reading, Check Your Reading, and Reading for Meaning activities.

Get Ready ....

Lesson Introduction
Prepare students for reading and discussing "Robert's Rockets."

1. Tell students that they are going to read "Robert's Rockets," an article about a scientist with a big dream.

2. Explain that before they read the article, you will get ready by reviewing the characteristics of biographies.

Genre: Biography
Explore the characteristics of a biography.

1. Remind students that there is a kind of nonfiction writing called **biography**. A biography tells facts about a person's life. A biography is always written by someone else, not the person the biography is about.

2. Explain that a biography might include some or all of the following information about the person who is the subject of the text.

   ▸ When and where the person was born and lived
   ▸ Facts about the person's family
   ▸ Important things the person did
   ▸ When the person died

3. Tell students that biographies tell us important facts about people, and they can bring history to life. When we find out why people from the past did things, it helps us better understand those people. Sometimes when we read about famous people from the past, it helps us see that they were a lot like we are.

> **Objectives**
> - Identify genre.
> - Identify characteristics of different genres.
> - Build vocabulary through listening, reading, and discussion.
> - Use new vocabulary in written and spoken sentences.
> - Increase concept and content vocabulary.

4. Have students practice identifying a biography.
   Say: I'm going to read a paragraph about a famous person.

   Christopher Columbus was born in 1451 in Genoa, Italy. At that time, most people believed the earth was flat—but Columbus didn't agree. He thought that it was round. Because of his belief, Columbus said that he could get to Asia—and the riches there—more quickly by sailing west instead of by traveling east. In those days, people thought that the only way to reach Asia was to travel over land toward the east. Columbus sailed west to try out his idea, and on the way, he bumped into an unknown land. He was the first white European to arrive in America! When Columbus returned from his trip, people were amazed by his stories and wanted to see the new land for themselves. Columbus sailed to America many more times before he died in 1506.

   ► What does this paragraph tell us? facts about Christopher Columbus; things Christopher Columbus did
   ► What do we call a nonfiction text that tells facts about someone's life? a biography

---

Words to Know
Before reading "Robert's Rockets," go over Words to Know with students.

1. Read aloud each word and have students repeat it.

2. Ask students if they know what each word means.

   ► If students know a word's meaning, have them define it and use it in a sentence.
   ► If students don't know a word's meaning, read them the definition and discuss the word with them.

engine – a machine that uses energy from electricity or a fuel such as gasoline to do work
fuel – something that is burned to supply heat or power; examples include gasoline, coal, and oil
gunpowder – a black powder used in firing guns and making fireworks; it explodes when fire touches it
invent – to think of and make or develop a machine, tool, or process that did not exist before
invention – a machine, tool, or process that did not exist before
launch – to set in motion; to send off
NASA – a U.S. government organization that studies space travel; *NASA* stands for National Aeronautics and Space Administration
oxygen – a gas that is part of the air; a chemical element

Guided Reading

Book Walk

Prepare students for reading by taking them on a Book Walk of "Robert's Rockets." Scan the article together and ask students to make predictions about the article. Answers to questions may vary.

1. Turn to the **table of contents** in *K¹² World: The Science of Inventing*. Help students find the selection and turn to that page.

2. Have students read aloud the **title of the article**.

   ▸ What do you think the article might be about?

3. Have students look at the **pictures of the article**.

4. Point to and read aloud any headers, captions, or other features that stand out.

   ▸ What do you think the article might tell us about Robert H. Goddard?

   ▸ Have you ever seen a rocket take off in a movie or on TV? What was it like?

Objectives

- Make predictions based on text, illustrations, and/or prior knowledge.

- Activate prior knowledge by previewing text and/or discussing topic.

- Read and listen to a variety of texts for information and pleasure independently or as part of a group.

- Read aloud grade-level text with appropriate expression, accuracy, and rate.

"Robert's Rockets"

It's time to guide students through a preview of the article to prepare them for reading on their own. Gather the Reading Aid on pages LC 247 and 248 in *K¹² Language Arts Activity Book*.

1. Have students sit next to you so that they can see the pictures and words while you introduce and discuss the article.

2. Tell students that you will preview the article to prepare them to read the article aloud to you.

3. Refer to the Reading Aid.

   Reading Aid Tear out the Reading Aid for this reading selection. Follow the instructions for folding the page, and then use the page as a guide as you preview the selection with students.

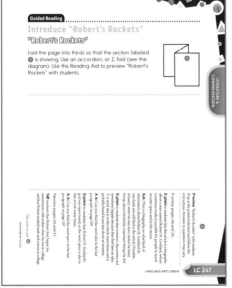

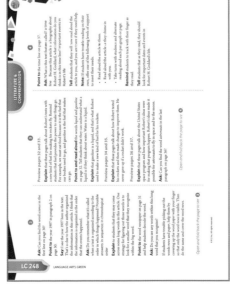

Check Your Reading

"Robert's Rockets"

Check students' comprehension of "Robert's Rockets."

1. Have students retell "Robert's Rockets" in their own words to develop grammar, vocabulary, comprehension, and fluency skills. Be sure students retell key details of the nonfiction article. Have students refer to the pictures in the article as an aid for retelling.

2. Ask students the following questions.

   ▶ What did Robert think about when he sat high up in a cherry tree when he was 17 years old? a machine that could go into space
   ▶ What did Robert study in college? math and science
   ▶ Where did Robert set off his first rocket? in a basement
   ▶ Why did Robert build and test so many rockets? because he wanted to make them better and more powerful; because he wanted to build one that could fly into space
   ▶ What did NASA name after Robert? a flight center
   ▶ Whom is the article about? Robert H. Goddard   What is the topic? Robert's invention of the rocket

 TIP If students have trouble responding to a question, help them locate the answer in the text or pictures.

★ **Objectives**
- Retell or dramatize a story.
- Answer questions requiring literal recall of details.
- Identify the topic.
- Identify important details in informational text.
- Use illustrations to aid understanding of text.

Reading for Meaning

Biography

Ask students the following questions to check their understanding of the characteristics of a biography.

   ▶ What kind of facts does a biography tell? facts about a person's life; facts about a person and the things that person did
   ▶ What kind of information might you find about the person who is the subject of a biography? Possible answers: when the person was born and died; where the person lived; family facts; important things the person did
   ▶ What person is "Robert's Rockets" about? Robert H. Goddard
   ▶ Where did Robert grow up? Worcester and Boston; Massachusetts
   ▶ What was Robert's dream? to build a rocket that could fly into space
   ▶ Did all of Robert's rockets work? No   Did Robert give up when one of his rockets didn't work? No
   ▶ What did Robert do when one of his rockets didn't work? He found out why it didn't work so he could make the next one better.
   ▶ When did Robert become ill and die? 1945

★ **Objectives**
- Identify genre.
- Identify characteristics of different genres.
- Identify facts in informational text.
- Identify opinions.
- Distinguish fact from opinion.

Facts and Opinions in "Robert's Rockets"

Check students' understanding of facts and opinions.

1. Remind students that a **fact** is something that you can prove is true, and an **opinion** is something that a person believes or feels.

2. Ask students the following questions.

   ▸ Robert wrote reports about his ideas. Is this a fact or an opinion? a fact How do you know? You can prove he wrote the reports.

   ▸ People said Robert's ideas were impossible. Is what they said about Roberts's ideas a fact or an opinion? an opinion How do you know? It's something they believed about Robert's ideas.

   ▸ One newspaper wrote that Robert did not understand science. Is what the newspaper article said a fact or an opinion? an opinion How do you know? The person who wrote the newspaper article believed that about Robert, but somebody else may have believed that Robert's inventions showed that he did understand science.

   ▸ Robert used a fuel that was made out of gasoline and oxygen. Is this a fact or an opinion? a fact How do you know? You can prove that Robert used this kind of fuel.

Explore "Robert's Rockets"

Lesson Overview

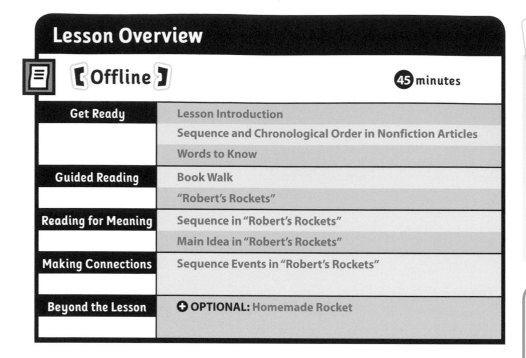

[Offline]   **45** minutes

Get Ready	Lesson Introduction
	Sequence and Chronological Order in Nonfiction Articles
	Words to Know
Guided Reading	Book Walk
	"Robert's Rockets"
Reading for Meaning	Sequence in "Robert's Rockets"
	Main Idea in "Robert's Rockets"
Making Connections	Sequence Events in "Robert's Rockets"
Beyond the Lesson	➕ OPTIONAL: Homemade Rocket

Big Ideas

▸ Comprehension entails an understanding of the organizational patterns of text.

▸ Repeated rereading leads to increased fluency.

Materials

Supplied

- "Robert's Rockets," *K¹² World: The Science of Inventing*, pp. 28–37
- *K¹² Language Arts Activity Book*, pp. LC 249–251

Also Needed

- glue stick
- scissors, round-end safety

Keywords

main idea – the most important idea in a paragraph or text

sequence – order

text structure – the organizational pattern of a text, such as cause and effect, compare and contrast, and chronological order

[Offline] **45** minutes

Work **together** with students to complete Get Ready, Guided Reading, Reading for Meaning, Making Connections, and Beyond the Lesson activities.

Get Ready

Lesson Introduction

Prepare students for reading and discussing "Robert's Rockets."

1. Tell students that they are going to reread "Robert's Rockets."

2. Explain that before they read the article, you will get ready by discussing how authors of nonfiction can organize articles in the order in which events happened.

Sequence and Chronological Order in Nonfiction Articles

Explore how authors can organize information in nonfiction texts.

1. Remind students that authors can organize information in an article in different ways. A nonfiction text can be written **in sequence**, to **compare and contrast**, or to show **problem and solution** or **cause and effect**. For example, we can say that the article "Ben Franklin, American Inventor" is organized by problem and solution, because the article talks about the ideas and inventions that Ben Franklin came up with to solve problems.

2. Explain that a **biography**, which is a nonfiction text that tells facts about a person's life, is often written in sequence. This means that it tells about events in the person's life in the order that the events happened. A signal, or clue, that a biography is organized in sequence is when the author includes dates or mentions years in the text.

3. Tell students that when an article tells the years of important events, we can say that it's written **in sequence**. We can also say that it's written in **chronological order**, or time order.
   Say: I'm going to read a paragraph about a famous person.

   Thomas Edison was born in 1847. In 1868, Thomas got a patent for his first invention—an electric vote-recording machine. In 1879, he invented the modern light bulb, which changed the world. He invented the first movie camera in 1904. Altogether, Thomas got patents for more than 1,000 inventions. He died in 1931.

   ► What does this paragraph tell us? facts about Thomas Edison; facts about the things Thomas Edison invented
   ► How is the text of the Thomas Edison biography organized? in sequence; in chronological order; in time order
   ► In what year was Thomas Edison born? 1847
   ► Did Edison invent the light bulb before or after he invented the first movie camera? before

Words to Know

Before reading "Robert's Rockets," go over Words to Know with students.

1. Read aloud each word and have students repeat it.

2. Ask students if they know what each word means.

    ▸ If students know a word's meaning, have them define it and use it in a sentence.

    ▸ If students don't know a word's meaning, read them the definition and discuss the word with them.

engine – a machine that uses energy from electricity or a fuel such as gasoline to do work

fuel – something that is burned to supply heat or power; examples include gasoline, coal, and oil

gunpowder – a black powder used in firing guns and making fireworks; it explodes when fire touches it

invent – to think of and make or develop a machine, tool, or process that did not exist before

invention – a machine, tool, or process that did not exist before

launch – to set in motion; to send off

NASA – a U.S. government organization that studies space travel; *NASA* stands for National Aeronautics and Space Administration

oxygen – a gas that is part of the air; a chemical element

Guided Reading

Book Walk

Prepare students for reading by taking them on a Book Walk of "Robert's Rockets." Scan the article together to revisit the text.

1. Turn to the selection in *K¹² World: The Science of Inventing*.

2. Have students read aloud the **title of the article**.

3. Have students look at the **pictures of the article**.

4. Ask the following question to help students think about what they already know about the article. Answers to questions may vary.

    ▸ Why do you think Robert wanted to make a rocket that could go into space?

    ▸ What were some of the things Robert did to make his dream of space travel come true?

Objectives

-   Activate prior knowledge by previewing text and/or discussing topic.
-   Read and listen to a variety of texts for information and pleasure independently or as part of a group.
-   Read aloud grade-level text with appropriate expression, accuracy, and rate.

"Robert's Rockets"

It's time for students to reread the article.

1. Tell students that "Robert's Rockets" should now be familiar to them because they have read it before.

2. Explain that they will reread the article aloud to you, and you are there if they need help.

3. If students have trouble reading on their own, offer one of the following levels of support to meet their needs.

   ▸ Read aloud the article to them.
   ▸ Read aloud the article as they chime in with you.
   ▸ Take turns with students and alternate reading aloud each paragraph or page.

4. Remind students to track with their finger as they read.

5. Tell students that as they read, they should look for dates that signal the order of the events in the article.

Reading for Meaning

Sequence in "Robert's Rockets"

Check students' understanding of sequence and chronological order.

▸ When an article has dates or years in it, how is the information probably organized? Possible answers: in sequence, or chronological order; in time order

▸ When Robert was 17 years old, he climbed a cherry tree and got an idea about rockets. Did this happen before or after he studied math and science in college? before   How do you know? The article is written in sequence, or chronological order, and climbing the cherry tree comes first.

▸ Did Robert launch a rocket with a new kind of fuel before or after he set off a rocket in a basement? after   How do you know? Robert set off the rocket in the basement in 1907, and he launched the rocket that used the new kind of fuel in 1926. So launching the rocket with the new fuel happened after.

▸ Did NASA name a new space flight center for Robert before or after he died? after   How do you know? Robert died in 1945, and the new space flight center was named for him in 1959.

▸ What happened in 1969? Astronauts flew to the moon.

Objectives
- Identify organizational structures of text.
- Identify sequence of events in informational text.
- Identify chronological order.
- Identify the main idea.

Main Idea in "Robert's Rockets"
Check students' understanding of main idea in nonfiction articles.

1. Remind students that a nonfiction article can have a main idea, which is the most important idea, or message, in the text. The author of an article usually doesn't directly state the main idea. Readers have to think about the title, topic, and facts of an article to figure out the main idea.

2. Ask students the following questions.

   ▸ How do you think Robert felt when his rockets didn't work the way he hoped? Answers will vary.
   ▸ Why do you think Robert didn't give up? Guide students to understand that Robert believed in his dream, so he did everything he could to make it come true.
   ▸ Do you think it was easy for Robert to improve his rockets? Guide students to recognize that Robert worked hard and spent a lot of time working to improve his rockets.
   ▸ What is the main idea of "Robert's Rockets"? Possible answers: If you work hard, your dreams can come true; if you believe in yourself, you can make great things happen.

Making Connections

Sequence Events in "Robert's Rockets"
Check students' understanding of the sequence of events in "Robert's Rockets." Turn to pages LC 249–251 in *K¹² Language Arts Activity Book* and gather the glue stick and scissors.

1. Remind students that a biography can be organized in sequence. One way that readers can check whether they understand what they read is by telling the sequence of events.

2. Remind students that if an article includes the dates or years when important events happened, we can say that the events are in chronological order.

3. Explain that students will use facts with pictures to show the sequence, or chronological order, of events in "Robert's Rockets." They will also practice reading and following simple directions.

Objectives
- Read text to perform a specific task.
- Identify sequence of events in informational text.
- Identify chronological order.
- Demonstrate understanding through graphic organizers.

4. Have students complete the Activity Book pages, helping them with the instructions as needed.

5. Have students retell the sequence of events using the pictures as a guide.

TIP Refer back to "Robert's Rockets" if students have trouble recalling the order of events in the article.

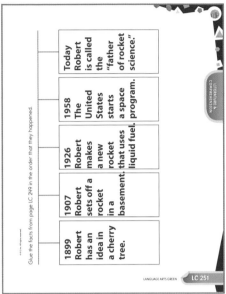

Beyond the Lesson

● OPTIONAL: Homemade Rocket

This activity is OPTIONAL. It is intended for students who have extra time and would enjoy making a small rocket of their own. Feel free to skip this activity. **Note:** Students should complete this activity **only** with adult supervision.

1. Tell students that they can get an idea of how Robert Goddard's rockets powered with liquid fuel worked by making their own rocket.

2. Go to the NASA website http://spaceplace.nasa.gov/pop-rocket/.

Objectives
- Make connections with text: text-to-text, text-to-self, text-to-world.

3. Help students gather materials and follow the directions for making a bubble-powered rocket.

4. Find a clear open space and then follow the website directions for launching the bubble-powered rocket. **Be sure** that all participants wear **appropriate eye protection**.

5. Ask the following questions.

   ▸ Robert H. Goddard's first liquid fuel rocket went up 41 feet. Do you think your rocket went lower or higher than Robert's rocket? Answers will vary. You may want to give students a general idea of how much 41 feet is by taking 41 steps of approximately one foot each and marking your starting and ending points.

   ▸ What caused your rocket to go up? The gas bubbles rushed down, which pushed the rocket up.   Do you think this is similar to how the liquid fuel in Robert's rockets worked? Yes

   ▸ How did you feel when your rocket took off? Answers will vary.

   ▸ How do you think Robert felt the first time he launched a liquid fuel rocket? Answers will vary.

Introduce "Stephanie Kwolek's Amazing Invention"

Lesson Overview

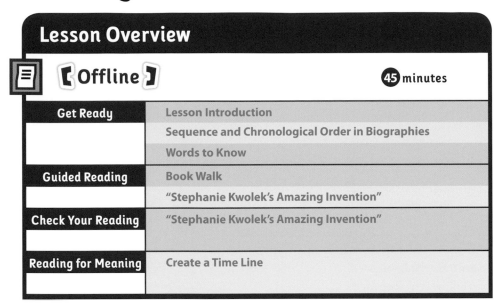

[Offline] ⏱ **45** minutes

Get Ready	Lesson Introduction
	Sequence and Chronological Order in Biographies
	Words to Know
Guided Reading	Book Walk
	"Stephanie Kwolek's Amazing Invention"
Check Your Reading	"Stephanie Kwolek's Amazing Invention"
Reading for Meaning	Create a Time Line

Advance Preparation

Before beginning the Guided Reading, read "Stephanie Kwolek's Amazing Invention" to locate Words to Know in the text. Preview pages LC 253 and 254 in *K¹² Language Arts Activity Book* to prepare the materials for the Guided Reading.

Big Ideas

▸ Exposing readers to a wide variety of genres provides them with a wide range of background knowledge and increases their vocabulary.
▸ Comprehension entails an understanding of the organizational patterns of text.
▸ Guided reading provides support to early readers as they practice and apply the reading strategies of proficient readers.

[Materials]

Supplied
- "Stephanie Kwolek's Amazing Invention," *K¹² World: The Science of Inventing*, pp. 38–49
- *K¹² Language Arts Activity Book*, pp. LC 253–257

Also Needed
- whiteboard (optional)
- glue stick
- scissors, round-end safety

Article Synopsis

If Stephanie Kwolek had had the money to go to medical school, she might never have invented Kevlar and saved thousands of lives.

Keywords

biography – a the story of someone's life written by another person

chronological order – a way to organize that puts details in time order

sequence – order

text structure – the organizational pattern of a text, such as cause and effect, compare and contrast, and chronological order

time line – a line showing dates and events in the order that they happened

[Offline] **45** minutes

Work **together** with students to complete Get Ready, Guided Reading, Check Your Reading, and Reading for Meaning activities.

Get Ready

Lesson Introduction

Prepare students for reading and discussing "Stephanie Kwolek's Amazing Invention."

1. Tell students that they are going to read "Stephanie Kwolek's Amazing Invention," a nonfiction article about the woman who invented Kevlar®.

2. Explain that before they read the article, you will get ready by reviewing the characteristics of texts written in sequence, or chronological order.

Objectives
- Identify sequence of events in informational text.
- Identify chronological order.
- Build vocabulary through listening, reading, and discussion.
- Use new vocabulary in written and spoken sentences.
- Increase concept and content vocabulary.

Sequence and Chronological Order in Biographies

Review how authors can organize nonfiction texts in sequence.

1. Remind students that authors can organize information in an article in different ways. Most biographies are written **in sequence**. This means that the author describes the important events in a person's life in the order in which the events happened.

2. Explain that a signal, or clue, that a biography is organized in sequence is when the author includes dates or mentions years in the text. When an article tells the years of important events, we can also say that it's written in **chronological order**, or time order.

3. On a whiteboard or sheet of paper, write down three important events in your life and the years of those events, such as the year and location of your birth and the year you graduated from high school or college. Use simple statements, such as "Mary Diaz was born in 1975 in Portland, Oregon."

4. Have students use the information you wrote to practice stating biographical information in sequence. Students should give a brief oral biography about you, referring to the information you wrote.

5. Ask the following questions. Answers to questions may vary.
   ▸ Did you tell when and where I was born?
   ▸ Did you tell dates and years?
   ▸ Did you tell the important events in my life in sequence, or chronological order?

Words to Know
Before reading "Stephanie Kwolek's Amazing Invention," go over Words to Know with students.

1. Read aloud each word and have students repeat it.

2. Ask students if they know what each word means.

   ▸ If students know a word's meaning, have them define it and use it in a sentence.

   ▸ If students don't know a word's meaning, read them the definition and discuss the word with them.

armor – a special metal covering that is worn to protect a person in battle
bulletproof – very hard or impossible for bullets to pierce
chemical – one of the many substances that make up the world's materials
chemistry – the study of the substances that make up the world's materials
fiber – a small thread of a cloth or clothlike material
laboratory – a place for doing scientific experiments
natural – found in nature; not made by humans
nylon – a very strong man-made material
spin – to twist and pull a material so that it becomes long and thin
steel – a hard, strong metal made mostly of iron that is used to make cars, tools, building materials, and many other things

Guided Reading

Book Walk
Prepare students for reading by taking them on a Book Walk of "Stephanie Kwolek's Amazing Invention." Scan the article together and ask students to make predictions about the article. Answers to questions may vary.

1. Turn to the **table of contents** in *K¹² World: The Science of Inventing*. Help students find the selection and turn to that page.

2. Have students read aloud the **title of the article**.

   ▸ What do you think the article might be about?

3. Have students look at the **pictures of the article**.

4. Point to and read aloud any headers, captions, or other features that stand out.

   ▸ Do you think your clothes are made out of natural fibers, such as cotton, or man-made fibers, such as nylon or polyester?

   ▸ Have you ever heard of a bulletproof vest? What do you think would make a bulletproof vest strong enough to stop a bullet?

Objectives

- Make predictions based on text, illustrations, and/or prior knowledge.

- Activate prior knowledge by previewing text and/or discussing topic.

- Read and listen to a variety of texts for information and pleasure independently or as part of a group.

- Read aloud grade-level text with appropriate expression, accuracy, and rate.

"Stephanie Kwolek's Amazing Invention"

It's time to guide students through a preview of the article to prepare them for reading on their own. Gather the Reading Aid on pages LC 253 and 254 in *K¹² Language Arts Activity Book.*

1. Have students sit next to you so that they can see the pictures and words while you introduce and discuss the article.

2. Tell students that the article explains how a scientist named Stephanie Kwolek invented a strong, new fiber called Kevlar that has saved many lives.

3. Tell students that you will preview the article to prepare them to read the article aloud to you.

4. Refer to the Reading Aid.

Reading Aid Tear out the Reading Aid for this reading selection. Follow the instructions for folding the page, and then use the page as a guide as you preview the selection with students.

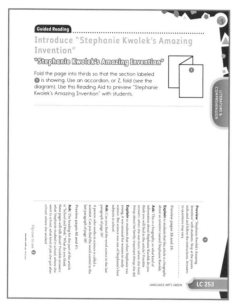
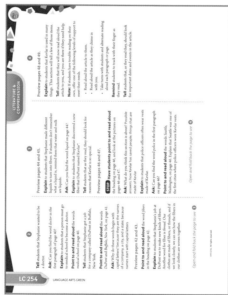

Check Your Reading

"Stephanie Kwolek's Amazing Invention"

Check students' comprehension of "Stephanie Kwolek's Amazing Invention."

1. Have students retell "Stephanie Kwolek's Amazing Invention" in their own words to develop grammar, vocabulary, comprehension, and fluency skills. Be sure students retell key details of the nonfiction article. Have students refer to the pictures in the article as an aid for retelling.

2. Ask students the following questions.

   ▸ Why did Stephanie Kwolek's teachers think she should be a scientist? because she was so good at science in school
   ▸ What did Stephanie study in college? science; chemistry
   ▸ What did she want to be? a doctor
   ▸ Why did Stephanie go to work for DuPont? so she could save money for medical school
   ▸ What was Stephanie's job at DuPont? finding ways to make new kinds of fibers
   ▸ What was special about the fiber Stephanie discovered while she was working on a fiber to improve car tires? Possible answers: It was very light; it was very strong; it was stronger than steel.
   ▸ What is the topic of the article? Whom is it about? Stephanie Kwolek

TIP If students have trouble responding to a question, help them locate the answer in the text or pictures.

Objectives

- Retell or dramatize a story.
- Answer questions requiring literal recall of details.
- Identify the topic.
- Identify important details in informational text.
- Use illustrations to aid understanding of text.

Reading for Meaning

Create a Time Line

Check students' ability to arrange a sequence of events in chronological order. Turn to pages LC 255–257 in *K¹² Language Arts Activity Book* and gather the glue stick and scissors.

1. Remind students that the events in a biography are usually written in sequence, or chronological order.

2. Tell students that they will create a **time line** to show the order in which events in Stephanie Kwolek's life happened.

3. Point to and read aloud the year and information found in each fact box on page LC 255.

Objectives

- Identify chronological order.
- Identify sequence of events in informational text.
- Create and/or interpret a time line.

4. Have students cut out the fact boxes and then have them put the boxes in the order in which the events happened.

5. Help students glue the fact boxes in chronological order to the time line on page LC 257.

6. Have students read aloud the year and the information in each box on the Stephanie Kwolek time line.

7. Ask the following questions.

▸ What is the first event in the time line of Stephanie Kwolek's life? 1923: She was born in New Kensington, Pennsylvania.

▸ If Stephanie was born in 1923, how old was she when she started working for DuPont? 23 years old; If students aren't ready to do the math for this question, show them how you subtract 1923 from 1946 to get the answer.

▸ When was Stephanie trying to make a new fiber to improve car tires? 1965   What did she accidentally discover when she was working on a new fiber for car tires? Kevlar

▸ What is the last event in the time line? 1975: Police officers in Seattle, Washington, start to use Kevlar vests.

TIP Refer back to the article if students have trouble recalling the order in which things happened.

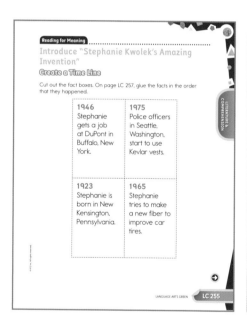

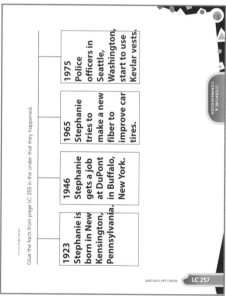

Explore "Stephanie Kwolek's Amazing Invention"

Lesson Overview

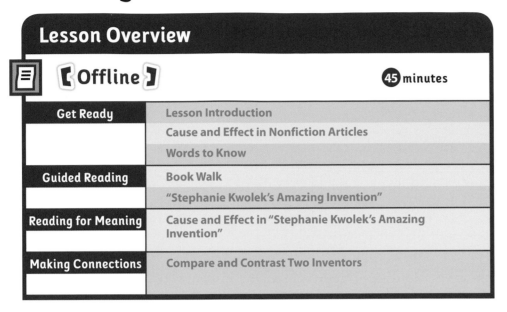

[Offline]	**45** minutes

Get Ready	Lesson Introduction
	Cause and Effect in Nonfiction Articles
	Words to Know
Guided Reading	Book Walk
	"Stephanie Kwolek's Amazing Invention"
Reading for Meaning	Cause and Effect in "Stephanie Kwolek's Amazing Invention"
Making Connections	Compare and Contrast Two Inventors

Big Ideas

▶ Comprehension entails an understanding of the organizational patterns of text.
▶ Repeated rereading leads to increased fluency.

[Materials]

Supplied

- "Stephanie Kwolek's Amazing Invention," *K¹² World: The Science of Inventing*, pp. 38–49
- "Robert's Rockets," *K¹² World: The Science of Inventing*, pp. 28–37
- *K¹² Language Arts Activity Book*, p. LC 259

Keywords

cause – the reason something happens
compare – to explain how two or more things are alike
contrast – to explain how two or more things are different
effect – the result of a cause

 **45 minutes**

Work **together** with students to complete Get Ready, Guided Reading, Reading for Meaning, and Making Connections activities.

Get Ready

Lesson Introduction

Prepare students for reading and discussing "Stephanie Kwolek's Amazing Invention."

1. Tell students that they are going to reread "Stephanie Kwolek's Amazing Invention."

2. Explain that before they read the article, you will get ready by discussing cause and effect in nonfiction articles.

 Objectives

- Describe cause-and-effect relationships in text.
- Build vocabulary through listening, reading, and discussion.
- Use new vocabulary in written and spoken sentences.
- Increase concept and content vocabulary.

Cause and Effect in Nonfiction Articles

Explore how nonfiction articles can have examples of cause and effect.

1. Remind students that a **biography** describes the important events in a person's life. We often find examples of **cause and effect** in a biography, especially biographies about inventors. This is because inventors often notice things that cause them to come up with ideas for new inventions.

2. Share the following examples of cause and effect in inventors' lives with students.

    Cause: Clarence Birdseye saw how quickly fish froze in northern Canada.
    Effect: Clarence developed flash freezing to freeze food quickly.

    Cause: Percy Spencer put popcorn kernels next to a power tube.
    Effect: The popcorn popped.

3. Have students practice recognizing cause and effect in nonfiction text.
    Say: When Richard James was in the navy, he worked with a special kind of spring, which is a metal coil. He was trying to figure out a way to use these special springs to hang up sensitive equipment on ships. One day, Richard was working when one of the springs came loose and fell on the floor. He saw that the spring kept "walking" forward after it hit the ground. This gave Richard an idea and led him to invent a toy called the Slinky®.

4. Ask the following questions.

    ▶ What caused Richard to notice that a spring could walk? A spring fell while he was working, and it walked forward on the floor.
    ▶ What was the effect of Richard's watching the spring walk? It gave him an idea for a new toy; he invented the Slinky.
    ▶ Do you think Richard would have invented the Slinky if he hadn't been working with a special kind of spring? Why or why not? Answers will vary.

Words to Know

Before reading "Stephanie Kwolek's Amazing Invention," go over Words to Know with students.

1. Read aloud each word and have students repeat it.

2. Ask students if they know what each word means.

   ▶ If students know a word's meaning, have them define it and use it in a sentence.

   ▶ If students don't know a word's meaning, read them the definition and discuss the word with them.

armor – a special metal covering that is worn to protect a person in battle
bulletproof – very hard or impossible for bullets to pierce
chemical – one of the many substances that make up the world's materials
chemistry – the study of the substances that make up the world's materials
fiber – a small thread of a cloth or clothlike material
laboratory – a place for doing scientific experiments
natural – found in nature; not made by humans
nylon – a very strong man-made material
spin – to twist and pull a material so that it becomes long and thin
steel – a hard, strong metal made mostly of iron that is used to make cars, tools, building materials, and many other things

Guided Reading

Book Walk

Prepare students for reading by taking them on a Book Walk of "Stephanie Kwolek's Amazing Invention." Scan the article together to revisit the text.

1. Turn to the selection in *K¹² World: The Science of Inventing*.

2. Have students read aloud the **title of the article**.

3. Have students look at the **pictures of the article**.

4. Ask the following question to help students think about what they already know about the article.

   ▶ What were some of the important events in Stephanie Kwolek's life? Possible answers: going to college; getting a job with DuPont; inventing Kevlar

   ▶ What do you think would have happened if Stephanie had had the money to pay for medical school? Possible answers: She might not have worked for DuPont; she might not have discovered Kevlar.

Objectives

- Activate prior knowledge by previewing text and/or discussing topic.
- Read and listen to a variety of texts for information and pleasure independently or as part of a group.
- Read aloud grade-level text with appropriate expression, accuracy, and rate.

"Stephanie Kwolek's Amazing Invention"
It's time for students to reread the article.

1. Tell students that "Stephanie Kwolek's Amazing Invention" should now be familiar to them because they have read it before.

2. Explain that they will reread the article aloud to you, and you are there if they need help.

3. If students have trouble reading on their own, offer one of the following levels of support to meet their needs.

   ▶ Read aloud the article to them.
   ▶ Read aloud the article as they chime in with you.
   ▶ Take turns with students and alternate reading aloud each paragraph or page.

4. Remind students to track with their finger as they read.

5. Tell students that as they read, they should look for examples of cause and effect in Stephanie's life.

Reading for Meaning

Cause and Effect in "Stephanie Kwolek's Amazing Invention"
Check students' understanding of cause-and-effect relationships.

> **Objectives**
> • Describe cause-and-effect relationships in text.

   ▶ Stephanie was good at math and science. What did this cause her teachers to tell her? that she would make a good scientist
   ▶ What was the effect of Stephanie's going to college and studying science? She became an expert in chemistry.
   ▶ What caused Stephanie to take a job at DuPont? She didn't have enough money for medical school; she needed to save money for medical school.
   ▶ Why caused Stephanie to change her mind about becoming a doctor? She liked her job at DuPont and wanted to stay there.
   ▶ What happened when Stephanie was working on a fiber to improve car tires? She discovered Kevlar.
   ▶ What is the effect of using Kevlar to make bulletproof vests and armor? It saves lives; it helps keep police officers and soldiers safe.
   ▶ Why is Kevlar used to make firefighters' clothes? It blocks heat and fire.
   ▶ Why has Stephanie won many prizes? because she is a great inventor

Making Connections

 Compare and Contrast Two Inventors
Check students' ability to compare and contrast information about two scientists. Turn to page LC 259 in *K¹² Language Arts Activity Book*.

> **Objectives**
> • Compare and contrast elements across informational texts.
> • Demonstrate understanding through graphic organizers.

1. Tell students that they will compare and contrast two scientists: Stephanie Kwolek and Robert H. Goddard.

   ▶ Students may need to refer back to the article "Robert's Rockets" on pages 28–37 in *K¹² World: The Science of Inventing*.

2. Show students the Activity Book page. Read aloud the column headings.

3. Have students read aloud the first biography fact in the center column.

4. Help students write their answers in the boxes for Robert H. Goddard and then Stephanie Kwolek.

5. Repeat Steps 3 and 4 until the table is filled out.

6. Ask the following questions.

   ▶ Which of the inventors was born first? Robert

   ▶ Were Robert and Stephanie ever alive during the same time? Yes

   ▶ What subject did both Robert and Stephanie study in college? science   What was different about what each inventor did in college? Possible answers: Robert studied math and built rockets; Stephanie became an expert in chemistry.

   ▶ Did either article mention whether people criticized or said negative things about the inventors? People said that Robert's ideas were impossible and that he didn't understand science.

   ▶ What was so important about Robert's and Stephanie's ideas and inventions? Robert's work led to the United States starting a space program and sending astronauts into space; because of Stephanie's work, we have Kevlar, which is very light but very strong; Kevlar is used in vests and armor that help protect police officers and soldiers; Kevlar has saved many lives.

Reward: Add a sticker for this unit on the My Accomplishments chart to mark successful completion of the unit.

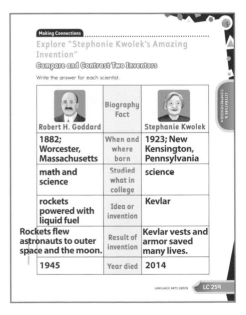

Making Connections

Explore "Stephanie Kwolek's Amazing Invention"

Compare and Contrast Two Inventors

Write the answer for each scientist.

Robert H. Goddard	Biography Fact	Stephanie Kwolek
1882; Worcester, Massachusetts	When and where born	1923; New Kensington, Pennsylvania
math and science	Studied what in college	science
rockets powered with liquid fuel	Idea or invention	Kevlar
Rockets flew astronauts to outer space and the moon.	Result of invention	Kevlar vests and armor saved many lives.
1945	Year died	2014

LANGUAGE ARTS GREEN   LC 259

A Friend Indeed

Unit Focus

Students will read texts centered on friendship. This unit follows the guided-reading instructional approach (see the instructional approaches to reading in the introductory lesson for this program). In this unit, students will

- ▶ Explore the use of imagery, descriptive language, and personification in poetry.
- ▶ Identify the narrator of a text.
- ▶ Review why we call up prior knowledge related to a story before reading.
- ▶ Make, support, and evaluate predictions.
- ▶ Make connections to text.
- ▶ Review the story structure elements of plot, setting, characters, and problem and solution.
- ▶ Practice choosing a "just right" book for independent reading.
- ▶ Identify fantasy elements in a story.
- ▶ Self-monitor comprehension by summarizing a story.
- ▶ Think like a story character to determine the qualities of a good friend.

Unit Plan

[Offline]

		45 minutes a day
Lesson 1	Explore "My Shadow"	
Lesson 2	Introduce *Who Will Be My Friends?*	
Lesson 3	Explore *Who Will Be My Friends?*	
Lesson 4	Explore *Frog and Toad Are Friends* (A)	
Lesson 5	Explore *Frog and Toad Are Friends* (B)	
Lesson 6	Explore *Frog and Toad Are Friends* (C)	
Lesson 7	Explore *Danny and the Dinosaur* (A)	
Lesson 8	Explore *Danny and the Dinosaur* (B)	
Lesson 9	Your Choice	

Explore "My Shadow"

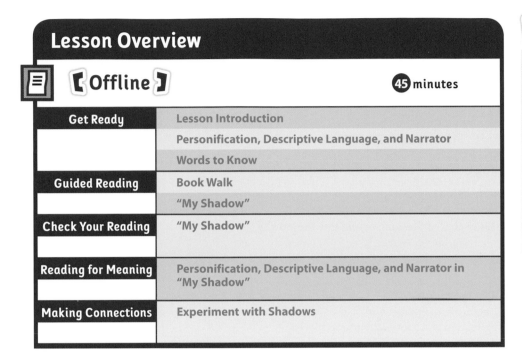

Lesson Overview

Offline   **45** minutes

Get Ready	Lesson Introduction
	Personification, Descriptive Language, and Narrator
	Words to Know
Guided Reading	Book Walk
	"My Shadow"
Check Your Reading	"My Shadow"
Reading for Meaning	Personification, Descriptive Language, and Narrator in "My Shadow"
Making Connections	Experiment with Shadows

Advance Preparation

Before beginning the Guided Reading, read "My Shadow" to locate Words to Know in the text. Preview pages LC 261 and 262 in *K¹² Language Arts Activity Book* to prepare the materials for the Guided Reading.

Big Ideas

- ▶ Interpreting text requires close attention to content and literary elements.
- ▶ Good readers use prior knowledge and text clues to infer or draw conclusions about what is implied but not directly stated in text.
- ▶ The use of imagery and sensory language creates detailed pictures in the reader's mind, so the reader can understand and appreciate the ideas and feelings the writer conveys.
- ▶ Readers must focus on the specific language of a text to aid in interpretation.
- ▶ Guided reading provides support to early readers as they practice and apply the reading strategies of proficient readers.

Materials

Supplied

- *Listen, My Children: Poems for First Graders,* pp. 22–23
- *K¹² Language Arts Activity Book,* pp. LC 261–262

Also Needed

- household objects – flashlight

Poetry Synopsis

A young boy describes a friend who almost never leaves his side.

Keywords

first-person point of view – the telling of a story by a character in that story, using words such as *I, me,* and *my*

imagery – language that helps readers imagine how something looks, sounds, smells, feels, or tastes

infer – to use clues and what you already know to make a guess

inference – a guess you make using the clues in a text and what you already know

narrator – the teller of a story

personification – giving human qualities to something that is not human; for example, "The thunder shouted from the clouds."

[Offline] 45 minutes

Work **together** with students to complete Get Ready, Guided Reading, Check Your Reading, Reading for Meaning, and Making Connections activities.

Get Ready

Lesson Introduction

Prepare students for reading and discussing "My Shadow."

1. Tell students that they are going to read "My Shadow," a poem about a boy and his shadow.

2. Explain that before they read the poem, you will get ready by discussing how

   ▸ A poet uses words that help you see images when you read a poem.
   ▸ A poet sometimes makes things that aren't human sound like they are.
   ▸ A character in a story or poem can be the narrator.

Objectives

- Identify author's use of imagery and descriptive language.
- Identify literary devices: personification and/or simile.
- Identify the narrator of a text.
- Identify first-person point of view.
- Build vocabulary through listening, reading, and discussion.
- Use new vocabulary in written and spoken sentences.

Personification, Descriptive Language, and Narrator

Explore personification, descriptive language, and narration in poems.

1. Remind students that poets carefully choose the words in their poems. They often use descriptive words and phrases that help readers imagine pictures in their head. For example, "Grace gulped down a big glass of freezing-cold milk" is more descriptive than "Grace drank a glass of milk," because it helps paint a picture in readers' head.

2. Explain that descriptive language makes a poem more interesting and helps readers visualize what the poet wants you to imagine. When readers visualize, they're more likely to understand and remember what they read.

3. Remind students that poets sometimes make animals or objects sound like they're human. For example, a poet might say, "The rock laughed as it rolled down the hill." We know that a rock isn't human and can't really laugh. But poets do this to help us imagine an interesting picture and think about certain feelings, such as happiness or sadness.

4. Tell students that when they hear the words such as *I*, *me*, and *my*, it means that a character in the story is the **narrator** and is telling the story. It's the same for a poem.

5. Tell students that you're going to play a guessing game with riddles, and they will have to figure out who is speaking. This will help them to review how poets make objects sound as if they're human and how the narrator can be a character in the poem or story.

Say: I am sitting in the kitchen sink with a dirty face. I don't have any hands. I wish someone would wash my face!

   ▸ Who is sitting in the kitchen sink with a dirty face? a dish
   ▸ Who is the narrator, or the teller, of the riddle? the dish
   ▸ What makes the dish sound as if it's a human? Possible answers: It's speaking; it has a face.
   ▸ What words tell you that the dish is talking? *I* and *my*

6. Remind students that poets also use descriptive language to help readers visualize a picture. **Read aloud** another riddle.

   I have long, skinny legs and arms, but I'm so, so sad because I can't stroll or dance. I get warm when people sit on me.

   ▸ Who is speaking? a chair   What words tell you that the chair is speaking? *I* and *me*
   ▸ Who is the narrator of the riddle? the chair
   ▸ What parts of the riddle make the chair sound as if it's a person? Possible answers: It has arms and legs; it feels sad.
   ▸ What words help you imagine what the chair looks like? *long*, *skinny*, and *legs and arms*

7. If students wish to come up with their own riddle, have them describe an object and then you guess what it is. Tell students how you could guess what they described by the words they used.

8. Take turns playing the game, as time allows.

Words to Know

Before reading "My Shadow," go over Words to Know with students.

1. Read aloud each word and have students repeat it.

2. Ask students if they know what each word means.

   ▸ If students know a word's meaning, have them define it and use it in a sentence.
   ▸ If students don't know a word's meaning, read them the definition and discuss the word with them.

arrant – complete; total
notion – a thought or idea
nursie – another way of saying *nurse*, usually a woman who is paid to look after a child or several children
proper – good

Guided Reading

Book Walk

Prepare students by taking them on a Book Walk of "My Shadow." Scan the poem together and ask students to make predictions about the poem.

1. Turn to the **table of contents** in *Listen, My Children*. Help students find "My Shadow" and turn to that page.

2. Point to and read aloud the **title of the poem** and the **name of the poet**.

3. Have students look at the **picture**. Answers to questions may vary.

   ▸ What do you think the poem might be about?
   ▸ Can you always see your shadow?

4. If students are interested, take them outside so that they can find their shadows and notice the different sizes of their shadows. Use a flashlight indoors, if it is not a sunny day.

Objectives
- Make predictions based on text, illustrations, and/or prior knowledge.
- Activate prior knowledge by previewing text and/or discussing topic.
- Read and discuss poetry.
- Read aloud grade-level text with appropriate expression, accuracy, and rate.

"My Shadow"

It's time to guide students through a preview of the poem to prepare them for reading on their own. Gather the Reading Aid on pages LC 261 and 262 in *K¹² Language Arts Activity Book*.

1. Have students sit next to you so that they can see the picture and words while you introduce and discuss the poem.

2. Tell students that you will preview the poem to prepare them to read it aloud to you.

3. Refer to the Reading Aid.

Reading Aid Tear out the Reading Aid for this reading selection. Follow the instructions for folding the page and then use the page as a guide as you preview the selection with students.

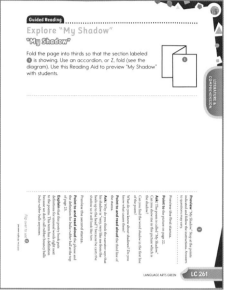
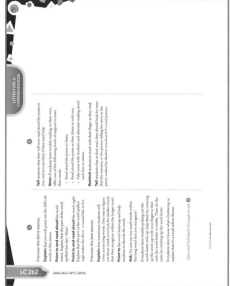

Check Your Reading

"My Shadow"

Check students' comprehension of "My Shadow."

1. Have students retell "My Shadow" in their own words to develop grammar, vocabulary, comprehension, and fluency skills.

2. Ask students the following questions.

   ▶ What is the poem about? what a boy thinks about his shadow
   ▶ What does the boy in the poem say happens when he jumps into bed? His shadow jumps in before he does.
   ▶ What does the boy say is the funniest thing about his shadow? how he likes to grow
   ▶ Why does the boy say his shadow is a coward? because his shadow always stays close beside him
   ▶ Why does the boy say his shadow is lazy? because his shadow stayed at home fast asleep in bed

TIP If students have trouble responding to a question, help them locate the answer in the text or pictures.

Objectives
- Retell or dramatize a story.
- Answer questions requiring literal recall of details.

Reading for Meaning

Personification, Descriptive Language, and Narrator in "My Shadow"
Check students' ability to identify personification, descriptive language, and the narrator.

1. Remind students that poets make poems interesting by making things sound as if they're human.

   ▸ Why does the poet use the words *he* and *him* when the boy in the poem is talking about his shadow? to make it sound as if the shadow is alive or human

   ▸ What are some things the boy says his shadow does that make it sound as if it is human? Possible answers: goes in and out; jumps; shoots up; doesn't know how to play; is a coward; sleeps

2. Check students' ability to recognize descriptive language in "My Shadow."

   ▸ In "My Shadow," the poet writes that sometimes the shadow "shoots up taller like an India-rubber ball" and other times the shadow "gets so little that there's none of him at all." What do you imagine when you hear these descriptions? Answers will vary.   Why do you think the poet describes the shadow this way? Possible answers: to help us imagine how the shadow grows and shrinks; to paint a picture in the reader's head

   ▸ The boy in the poem says that his shadow "sticks" to him. What do you think the poet wants you to imagine when you hear that word? The shadow is so close to the boy that it's as if it's glued to him.

   ▸ At the end of the poem, the poet writes, "I rose and found the shining dew on every buttercup." What do you see in your head when you hear these words? Possible answers: sparkling flowers; little diamonds on flowers   Which words helped you imagine the flowers sparkling? *shining dew*

3. Ask the following question to check students' ability to recognize **first-person point of view**.

   ▸ Who is telling the story in this poem? Who is the narrator? the boy with the shadow

   ▸ Which words in the poem let us know that the boy in the poem is telling the story? the words *my*, *I*, and *me*

TIP Although an objective for this lesson is to identify first-person point of view, there is no need to introduce the term at this time.

Making Connections

· ·

Experiment with Shadows

Check students' understanding of shadows. Gather the flashlight.

1. Close the drapes, blinds, and doors to increase the shadow effect.

2. Tell students to imagine that the flashlight is the sun.

3. Use the flashlight to experiment with making shadows. Remind students to **never** point a flashlight beam directly into someone's eyes.

4. Have students observe what their shadow looks like when you shine the flashlight so that their shadow shows on a wall.

5. Use an object and the flashlight to show how a shadow changes as you point the flashlight beam at an object from different directions.

   ▸ Down below it
   ▸ High above it
   ▸ Directly across from it
   ▸ Close up to it
   ▸ Far away from it

6. Ask the following questions based on the outcome of the experiment and prior knowledge of "My Shadow."

   ▸ Where do you think the sun is when the shadow "shoots up taller like an India-rubber ball"? Is it down low or up high in the sky? down low
   ▸ Where is the sun when the shadow "gets so little"? Is it down low or high above in the sky? high above
   ▸ Why isn't the narrator's shadow with him in final stanza of the poem? Where is the sun? The sun isn't up yet, so there's no shadow to see.
   ▸ Why is the shadow very much like the narrator of the poem? The shape of the boy makes the shadow.
   ▸ How do the picture on page 22 and experimenting with the flashlight help you better understand why the shadow and the boy act alike? Possible answers: The picture shows how the shadow does exactly what the boy does; using the flashlight helps us understand how shining light on someone makes a shadow of the person that does exactly what the person does.

Objectives

- Make inferences based on text and/or prior knowledge.
- Make connections with text: text-to-text, text-to-self, text-to-world.

Introduce *Who Will Be My Friends?*

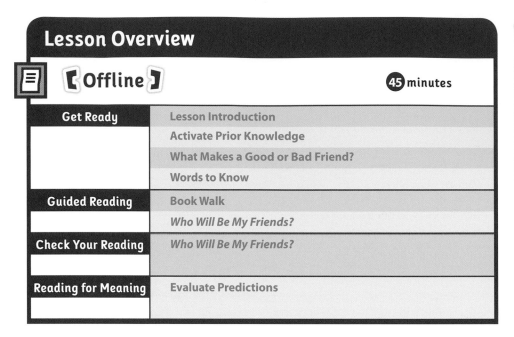

Lesson Overview

Offline — 45 minutes

Get Ready	Lesson Introduction
	Activate Prior Knowledge
	What Makes a Good or Bad Friend?
	Words to Know
Guided Reading	Book Walk
	Who Will Be My Friends?
Check Your Reading	*Who Will Be My Friends?*
Reading for Meaning	Evaluate Predictions

Materials

Supplied

- *Who Will Be My Friends?* by Syd Hoff
- *K¹² Language Arts Activity Book*, pp. LC 263–266

Story Synopsis

Freddy has moved into a new house. He has a new room and lives on a new street. Now all he needs is new friends.

Keywords

prediction – a guess about what might happen that is based on information in a story and what you already know

prior knowledge – things you already know from experience

Advance Preparation

Before beginning the Guided Reading, read *Who Will Be My Friends?* to locate Words to Know in the text. Preview pages LC 265 and 266 in *K¹² Language Arts Activity Book* to prepare the materials for the Guided Reading. Read the Reading Aid to be aware of stopping points in the story at which students will make predictions.

Big Ideas

- Good readers interact with text to make logical predictions before reading; confirm predictions during reading; and revise or make new predictions as they read further.
- Activating prior knowledge provides a framework for a reader to organize and connect new information to information previously learned; readers who activate prior knowledge before reading are more likely to understand and recall what they read.
- Guided reading provides support to early readers as they practice and apply the reading strategies of proficient readers.

【 Offline 】 **45** minutes

Work **together** with students to complete Get Ready, Guided Reading, Check Your Reading, and Reading for Meaning activities.

Get Ready

Lesson Introduction

Prepare students for reading and discussing *Who Will Be My Friends?*

1. Tell students that they will read *Who Will Be My Friends?*, a book about a boy who moves to a new neighborhood.

2. Explain that before they read, you will get ready by

   ▸ Discussing how we use prior knowledge to better understand what we read
   ▸ Calling up prior knowledge about friends and friendship

> **Objectives**
> - Activate prior knowledge by previewing text and/or discussing topic.
> - Build vocabulary through listening, reading, and discussion.
> - Use new vocabulary in written and spoken sentences.

Activate Prior Knowledge

Explore how activating prior knowledge helps readers better understand and remember what they read.

1. Remind students that everything we already know is called our **prior knowledge**. One of the reasons we preview a story before reading is to call up our prior knowledge related to the story. This helps us get our brain ready to read.

2. Remind students that our brain works like a file cabinet. When we preview text, we open the drawers in our brain that are filled with information, or prior knowledge, related to what we will be reading.

3. Explain that when we read, our brain connects the new information we learn to the prior knowledge that we have already filed away. This makes it easier for us to understand and remember what we read.

4. Tell students that the book they will read is about friends and friendship, so thinking about what they already know about friends and friendship will help them better understand and connect with the story.

✏️ What Makes a Good or Bad Friend?

Have students share their ideas about the qualities of a good friend and a bad friend.
Turn to page LC 263 in *K¹² Language Arts Activity Book.*

1. Tell students they are going to activate their prior knowledge related to the book by thinking about what makes a good friend and what makes a bad friend.

2. Show students the Activity Book page. Help them read aloud the headings.

3. Explain that they will list what they feel are the differences between a good and a bad friend.

4. Have students think about what makes a good friend, such as someone who likes to play with them.

5. Help students write their ideas about what makes a good friend in the smiley face. An example is provided.

   ▸ Students are not expected to fill the entire chart with characteristics at this time; they may add to the chart later in this unit, as they read more stories about friendship.

6. If students have trouble coming up with ideas, have them think about a person whom they consider a good friend and then ask the following questions.

   ▸ What do you like about this person?
   ▸ What do you enjoy doing with this person?
   ▸ Why do you think this person is a good friend?
   ▸ Could any of the ideas we just discussed be listed in the smiley face?

7. Explain to students that sometimes we don't like the things that our friends do or the way they act. Sometimes our friends might do things that make us feel like they're being a bad friend.

8. Help students write their ideas about what makes us feel like a friend is being a bad friend in the frowny face. An example is provided.

TIP Keep the chart in a safe place for use throughout this unit.

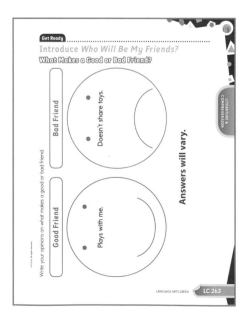

Words to Know

Before reading *Who Will Be My Friends?*, go over Words to Know with students.

1. Read aloud each word and have students repeat it.

2. Ask students if they know what each word means.

   ▸ If students know a word's meaning, have them define it and use it in a sentence.

   ▸ If students don't know a word's meaning, read them the definition and discuss the word with them.

beat – a regular path that a police officer walks through a neighborhood
shake – to take someone's hand and move it up and down, as in greeting, congratulating, or making a promise

Guided Reading

Book Walk

Prepare students by taking them on a Book Walk of *Who Will Be My Friends?* Scan the beginning of the book together and ask students to make predictions about the story. Answers to questions may vary.

1. Have students look at the **picture** on the cover.

2. Have students read the **title of the book** and the **name of the author**.

   ▸ What do you think the book might be about?

3. Have students look at the **pictures up to page 9** of the book.

   ▸ Did you ever have to make new friends? Who became your friend? Where did you meet your new friend?

Who Will Be My Friends?

It's time to guide students through a preview of the story to prepare them for reading on their own. Gather the Reading Aid on pages LC 265 and 266 in *K¹² Language Arts Activity Book*.

1. Have students sit next to you so that they can see the pictures and words while you introduce and discuss the story.

2. Tell students that you will preview the story to prepare them to read aloud the story to you.

3. Refer to the Reading Aid.

Objectives

- Make predictions based on text, illustrations, and/or prior knowledge.
- Activate prior knowledge by previewing text and/or discussing topic.
- Read and listen to a variety of texts for information and pleasure independently or as part of a group.
- Read aloud grade-level text with appropriate expression, accuracy, and rate.
- Make predictions before and during reading.

Reading Aid Tear out the Reading Aid for this reading selection. Follow the instructions for folding the page and then use the page as a guide as you preview the selection with students.

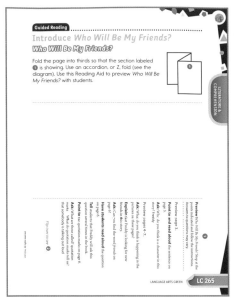
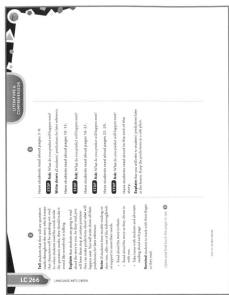

Check Your Reading

Who Will Be My Friends?

Check students' comprehension of *Who Will Be My Friends?*

1. Have students retell *Who Will Be My Friends?* in their own words to develop grammar, vocabulary, comprehension, and fluency skills.

2. Ask students the following questions.

   ▶ Who are the characters in the story? Freddy; dog; cat; police officer; mailman; street cleaner; boys playing ball

   ▶ What is Freddy looking for in the story? new friends

   ▶ Whom does Freddy try to make friends with first? a dog

   ▶ Why can't the street cleaner play with Freddy? He has to clean the street; he has to do his job.

   ▶ Why don't the boys playing ball make friends with Freddy at first? Answers will vary.

   ▶ Why do the boys want to play with Freddy at the end of the story? They need someone who is good at throwing and catching a ball.

TIP If students have trouble responding to a question, help them locate the answer in the text or pictures.

Objectives
- Retell or dramatize a story.
- Identify character(s).
- Answer questions requiring literal recall of details.

Reading for Meaning

Evaluate Predictions

Revisit the predictions students made while reading *Who Will Be My Friends?*

1. Ask the following questions to review and discuss the predictions students made while reading. **Refer, as necessary, to students' predictions that you wrote down.** Answers to questions may vary.

   ▸ What did you predict would happen after the dog and cat didn't roll the ball back to Freddy? Did your prediction happen, or did something else happen?

   ▸ What did you predict would happen after the police officer said he couldn't play with Freddy? What really happens?

   ▸ Were you surprised when the boys went on playing after Freddy asked them who would be his friend? What did you predict was going to happen? What did you use to make that prediction—information from the words and pictures of the story or your prior knowledge?

   ▸ What did you predict would happen after the boys watched Freddy throw his ball high in the air and catch it? Did you use your prior knowledge to make your prediction?

2. Remind students that it's okay if our predictions don't happen. Tell students to keep the following things in mind.

   ▸ Good readers make predictions that make sense based on the story up to that point.

   ▸ Good readers change their predictions as they read further and get more information.

   ▸ Even if our predictions don't happen, making predictions is important because it helps us be active readers.

Objectives
- Evaluate predictions.
- Support predictions with evidence from text and/or prior knowledge.

Explore *Who Will Be My Friends?*

Lesson Overview

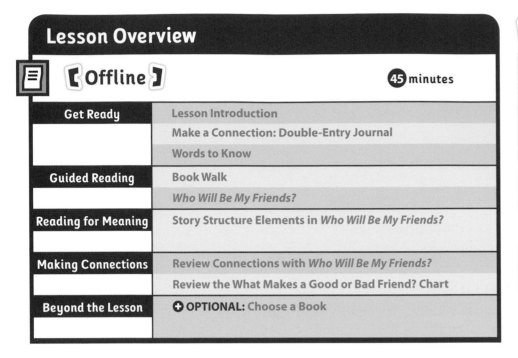

[Offline] 45 minutes

Get Ready	Lesson Introduction
	Make a Connection: Double-Entry Journal
	Words to Know
Guided Reading	Book Walk
	Who Will Be My Friends?
Reading for Meaning	Story Structure Elements in *Who Will Be My Friends?*
Making Connections	Review Connections with *Who Will Be My Friends?*
	Review the What Makes a Good or Bad Friend? Chart
Beyond the Lesson	⊕ OPTIONAL: Choose a Book

[Materials]

Supplied

- *Who Will Be My Friends?* by Syd Hoff
- *K¹² Language Arts Activity Book*, pp. LC 227 (optional), 263
- *K¹² My Journal*, pp. 2–53

Keywords

connection – a link readers make between themselves, information in text, and the world around them

story structure elements – components of a story; they include character, setting, plot, problem, and solution

Advance Preparation

Gather the partially completed chart on page LC 263 (What Makes a Good or Bad Friend?) in *K¹² Language Arts Activity Book* for Making Connections. If you plan to do the Beyond the Lesson, gather page LC 227 (Choose a Book Using the 5-Finger Test).

Big Ideas

- Comprehension is facilitated when readers connect new information to information previously learned.
- An awareness of story structure elements (setting, characters, plot) provides readers a foundation for constructing meaning when reading new stories and writing their own stories.
- Repeated rereading leads to increased fluency.
- Reading a book of their own choosing helps motivate students to read.
- Reading for pleasure helps students develop fluency and a lifelong love of reading.

[Offline] 45 minutes

Work **together** with students to complete Get Ready, Guided Reading, Reading for Meaning, Making Connections, and Beyond the Lesson activities.

Get Ready

Lesson Introduction
Prepare students for reading and discussing *Who Will Be My Friends?*

1. Tell students that they are going to reread *Who Will Be My Friends?*

2. Explain that that before they reread the story, you will get ready by reviewing how we can make connections to characters and events in a story.

> **Objectives**
> - Make connections with text: text-to-text, text-to-self, text-to-world.
> - Build vocabulary through listening, reading, and discussion.
> - Use new vocabulary in written and spoken sentences.

Make a Connection: Double-Entry Journal
Explore making connections to text with students. Gather *K¹² My Journal* and have students turn to the next available page for **writing** in Thoughts and Experiences.

1. Remind students that good readers think about what a story reminds them of as they're reading. This is called **making a connection**. As they read, good readers make connections to things they have learned before, their prior knowledge, and their personal experiences.

2. Readers who make connections while they read are better able to understand and remember what they read. This is because these readers make reading a more active experience.

   ▸ When readers think, "This story reminds me of a time when I . . . " or "This character reminds me of . . . ," they are connecting the text to themselves and their personal experiences.
   ▸ When readers think, "This story reminds me of another story I've read," they are connecting the text to another text.
   ▸ When readers think, "This story reminds me of something I heard about," they are connecting the text to the world around them.

3. Have students practice making connections to text. **Read aloud** the following short story:

   Nestor was excited. Today was his playdate with Jeremy. Nestor was excited about the playdate because Jeremy had a new box of building blocks.

   When Nestor got to Jeremy's house, the boys got busy building a castle. When they were done, Nestor stood up to admire their work. He especially liked the giant round tower they built.

   When it was time to go home, Nestor thanked Jeremy for letting him play with his building blocks, and then they made plans for a playdate at Nestor's house next week. Nestor said that he couldn't wait to show Jeremy his new football!

4. Ask the following questions. Answers to questions may vary.

- What does this story remind you of?
- Is the character Nestor anything like you?
- Do you think Nestor is a good friend? Why or why not?
- Does the story make you think of a friend of yours? How is your friend like Nestor or Jeremy?
- Does the story remind you of any other stories you've read?
- What parts in the story remind you of something that has happened in your own life?
- Does this story remind you of anything in the real world?

5. Tell students they are going to draw a T-chart in their journal. A T-chart looks like the capital letter T. They will use the T-chart as a double-entry journal to record their connections as they reread *Who Will Be My Friends?*

6. Have students draw a line down the center of the page and then a crossbar near the top, leaving room for column headings.

7. Help them write "Things from the story" at the top of the left column and "My connections" at the top of the right column.

8. Tell students they will use the double-entry journal to keep track of connections they make to the book *Who Will Be My Friends?* For example, if students make a connection to baseball while reading, they might write "kids playing baseball" in the left column and "baseball is my favorite game" across from it in the right column.

- If students are not ready to write on their own, allow them to dictate their statements as you record them in the double-entry journal.

9. Explain that they will review the connections they make to the story after reading.

Date _____

Use this page to write.

THOUGHTS AND EXPERIENCES

_____

_____

_____

_____

_____

_____

_____

_____

_____

_____

28

Words to Know

Before reading *Who Will Be My Friends?*, go over Words to Know with students.

1. Read aloud each word and have students repeat it.

2. Ask students if they know what each word means.

   ▸ If students know a word's meaning, have them define it and use it in a sentence.
   ▸ If students don't know a word's meaning, read them the definition and discuss the word with them.

beat – a regular path that a police officer walks through a neighborhood
shake – to take someone's hand and move it up and down, as in greeting, congratulating, or making a promise

Guided Reading

Book Walk

Prepare students by taking them on a Book Walk of *Who Will Be My Friends?* Scan the story together to revisit the characters and events.

1. Have students read aloud the **title of the book** and the **name of the author**.

2. Have students review the **pictures in the book**.

   ▸ Who are some of the characters Freddy asks to be his friend? police officer; mail carrier; street cleaner; boys playing ball

 Who Will Be My Friends?

It's time for students to reread the story. Gather *K¹² My Journal*.

1. Tell students that *Who Will Be My Friends?* should now be familiar to them because they have read it before.

2. Explain that they will reread the story aloud to you, and you are there if they need help.

3. If students have trouble reading on their own, offer one of the following levels of support to meet their needs.

   ▸ Read aloud the story to them.
   ▸ Read aloud the story as they chime in with you.
   ▸ Take turns with students and alternate reading aloud each page.

4. Remind students to track with their finger as they read.

5. Tell students that as they read, they should think about the elements that make up the story.

6. Remind students that they will pause to write in their double-entry journal whenever they make a connection to the story.

Objectives

- Activate prior knowledge by previewing text and/or discussing topic.
- Read and listen to a variety of texts for information and pleasure independently or as part of a group.
- Read aloud grade-level text with appropriate expression, accuracy, and rate.

Reading for Meaning

Story Structure Elements in *Who Will Be My Friends?*
Check students' ability to identify story structure elements.

Objectives
- Identify the main character(s).
- Identify story structure elements—plot, setting, character(s).
- Describe story structure elements—problem and solution.
- Retell or dramatize a story.

1. Remind students that every story has certain parts, or elements, such as characters.

2. Ask students to name the elements of a story. If students have trouble recalling all of the parts, remind them that

   - The **characters** are the people or animals in a story.
   - The **setting** is where and when a story takes place.
   - The **problem** is the issue a character must solve in a story.
   - The **solution** is how the character solves the problem.

3. Ask the following questions.

   - What is the setting of *Who Will Be My Friends?* Freddy's new neighborhood
   - Who is the main, or most important, character in *Who Will Be My Friends?* Freddy
   - What is Freddy's problem? He needs to make new friends.
   - How does Freddy first try to solve his problem? He rolls a ball to a dog. Does the dog want to be Freddy's friend? No   How do you know? Possible answers: He doesn't play with the ball; he doesn't roll the ball back to Freddy.
   - The police officer, mail carrier, and street cleaner all tell Freddy that they are his friend. Why don't they play ball with him? They have to do their jobs.
   - How does Freddy finally solve his problem and make new friends? He shows some boys how well he can throw and catch a ball.

4. Remind students that the plot is what happens in a story. When you tell the plot, you mention only the most important characters and things that happen in a story.

   - What is the plot of *Who Will Be My Friends?* Possible answer: Freddy moves into a new neighborhood. He likes his new room and street, but he doesn't have any friends. Freddy walks all over his new neighborhood asking, "Who will be my friends?" When Freddy asks some boys playing ball if they will be his friends, they just keep playing ball. So Freddy throws his ball high in the air over and over, and he catches it each time. The boys see that Freddy is a good ballplayer, so they say they will be his friends.

Making Connections

Review Connections with *Who Will Be My Friends?*

Review the connections students made to the story in their double-entry journal. Gather *K¹² My Journal*.

1. Have students read aloud each item in the "Things from the story" column and their associated connection in the "My connections" column.

2. Ask the following questions. Answers to questions may vary.

   ▸ Does anything in the story remind you of something in your own life?
   ▸ Do the characters remind you of anybody you know?
   ▸ Does anything in the story remind you of another story that you know?
   ▸ Does anything in the story remind you of something in the real world?

Objectives

- Make connections with text: text-to-text, text-to-self, text-to-world.
- Demonstrate understanding through drawing, discussion, drama, and/or writing.

Review the What Makes a Good or Bad Friend? Chart

Review what students wrote in their What Makes a Good or Bad Friend? chart. Gather page LC 263 in *K¹² Language Arts Activity Book*.

1. Have students read aloud the "Good Friend" heading and then each statement they wrote in the smiley face. Repeat for the "Bad Friend" heading and frowny face.

2. Ask the following questions. Answers to questions may vary.

   ▸ After reading *Who Will Be My Friends?*, do you have more ideas about what makes a good or bad friend?
   ▸ What do you think Freddy would say is important when looking for a good friend?
   ▸ The police officer, mail carrier, and street cleaner all tell Freddy that they are his friend, but they can't play ball with him because they have to do their jobs. What does this tell you about what it means to be a friend?
   ▸ Do you think the boys at the end of the story will be good friends to Freddy? Why or why not?

3. Have students add any new ideas they have about good or bad friends to the chart.

TIP Keep the chart in a safe place for use throughout this unit.

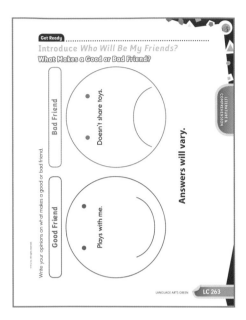

Beyond the Lesson

✚ OPTIONAL: Choose a Book

This activity is OPTIONAL. It is intended for students who have extra time and would enjoy choosing and independently reading a book with a theme similar to the theme of *Who Will Be My Friends?* or a book by the same author. Feel free to skip this activity. Gather page LC 227 (Choose a Book Using the 5-Finger Test) in *K¹² Language Arts Activity Book*.

Objectives
- Follow criteria to choose "just right" independent reading materials.

1. Review with students how to select a book that is "just right" to read.

2. Go to a library and look for the following suggested books. Some of these books are related to themes in *Who Will Be My Friends?* Others are by the same author, Syd Hoff. They are listed in order from easier to more difficult.

   ▸ *Sammy the Seal* by Syd Hoff
   ▸ *We Are Best Friends* by Aliki
   ▸ *My Best Friend Moved Away* by Nancy Carlson
   ▸ *Captain Cat* by Syd Hoff
   ▸ *Double-Header* by Gail Herman
   ▸ *Mrs. Brice's Mice* by Syd Hoff
   ▸ *Chester* by Syd Hoff
   ▸ *Here Comes the Strikeout!* by Leonard Kessler

3. Have students refer to the Activity Book page for the steps and guidelines of the 5-Finger Test as they check if a book is "just right" for them.

4. Once students have found a "just right" book, have them read it on their own.

TIP Students do not have to limit themselves to the listed books. If students would prefer different books, help them use the 5-Finger Test with books of their own choice.

Explore *Frog and Toad Are Friends* (A)

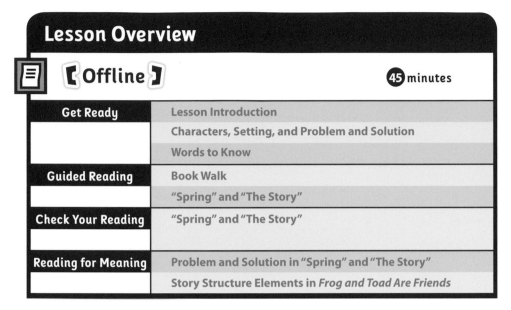

Lesson Overview

[Offline] 45 minutes

Get Ready	Lesson Introduction
	Characters, Setting, and Problem and Solution
	Words to Know
Guided Reading	Book Walk
	"Spring" and "The Story"
Check Your Reading	"Spring" and "The Story"
Reading for Meaning	Problem and Solution in "Spring" and "The Story"
	Story Structure Elements in *Frog and Toad Are Friends*

Advance Preparation

Before beginning the Guided Reading, read "Spring" and "The Story" to locate Words to Know in the text. Preview pages LC 267 and 268 in *K¹² Language Arts Activity Book* to prepare the materials for the Guided Reading.

Big Ideas

- ► Comprehension requires an understanding of story structure.
- ► An awareness of story structure elements (setting, characters, plot) provides readers a foundation for constructing meaning when reading new stories and writing their own stories.
- ► Guided reading provides support to early readers as they practice and apply the reading strategies of proficient readers.

Materials

Supplied

- *Frog and Toad Are Friends* by Arnold Lobel
- *K¹² Language Arts Activity Book*, pp. LC 267–270

Story Synopses

In "Spring," the first story in *Frog and Toad Are Friends*, Frog faces a big challenge when he tries to get Toad out of bed to play outside with him. In "The Story," Toad has trouble thinking of a story to tell his ailing friend. But he has some unusual methods to help himself think of one.

Keywords

character – a person or animal in a story

problem – an issue a character must solve in a story

setting – when and where a story takes place

solution – how a character solves a problem in a story

story structure elements – components of a story; they include character, setting, plot, problem, and solution

 **Offline** **45** minutes

Work **together** with students to complete offline Get Ready, Guided Reading, Check Your Reading, and Reading for Meaning activities.

Get Ready

Lesson Introduction

Prepare students for reading and discussing "Spring" and "The Story" in *Frog and Toad Are Friends*.

1. Tell students that they are going to read the first two stories in *Frog and Toad Are Friends*, a book about two friends named Frog and Toad.

2. Explain that before they read, you will help them get ready by reviewing the elements, or things, that make up stories.

Objectives
- Activate prior knowledge by previewing text and/or discussing topic.
- Build vocabulary through listening, reading, and discussion.
- Use new words in written and spoken sentences.

Characters, Setting, and Problem and Solution

Review the story structure elements of characters, setting, and problem and solution.

1. Tell students that, as they read stories about Frog and Toad, they will be looking for **story structure elements**, or the parts that make up stories. These parts are the characters, setting, and problem and solution.

2. Remind students that the people or animals in a story are called **characters**. The most important characters are the **main characters**.

3. Remind students that the **setting is where a story takes place**. The setting also includes **when a story takes place**. This could be a time of day or a certain time of year, such as summer or fall.

4. Remind students that a story often has a **problem** that the characters try to solve.

Words to Know
Before reading "Spring" and "The Story" in *Frog and Toad Are Friends*, go over Words to Know with students.

1. Read aloud each word and have students repeat it.

2. Ask students if they know what each word means.

   ▸ If students know a word's meaning, have them define it and use it in a sentence.

   ▸ If students don't know a word's meaning, read them the definition and discuss the word with them.

porch – a structure or covered space attached to a house
shutters – wooden or metal covers that close over a window and keep out the light

Guided Reading

Book Walk
Prepare students by taking them on a Book Walk of *Frog and Toad Are Friends*. Scan "Spring" and "The Story" together and ask students to make predictions. Answers to questions may vary.

1. Have students look at the **picture** on the cover.

2. Point to and read aloud the **book title**.

   ▸ What do you think the stories in this book might be about?

3. Point to and read aloud the **name of the author**.

4. Read aloud the story titles on the **contents** page. Explain to students that in this lesson, they will read "Spring" and "The Story."

5. Have students **look at the pictures in "Spring" and "The Story."**

   ▸ Who do you think are the characters?

   ▸ What do you think might happen in these two stories?

Objectives

- Make predictions based on text, illustrations, and/or prior knowledge.
- Activate prior knowledge by previewing text and/or discussing topic.
- Read and listen to a variety of texts for information and pleasure independently or as part of a group.
- Read aloud grade-level text with appropriate expression, accuracy, and rate.

"Spring" and "The Story"
It's time to guide students through a preview of the stories to prepare them for reading on their own. Gather the Reading Aid on pages LC 267 and 268 in *K¹² Language Arts Activity Book*.

1. Have students sit next to you so that they can see the pictures and words while you introduce and discuss the stories.

2. Tell students that Frog and Toad are best friends who do many things together. Stories about Frog and Toad are often funny because the characters do silly things.

3. Ask the following questions. Answers to questions may vary.

  ▶ Do you have a best friend?
  ▶ What do you like to do with your best friend?

4. Tell students that you will preview the stories to prepare them to read aloud the stories to you.

5. Refer to the Reading Aid.

Reading Aid Tear out the Reading Aid for this reading selection. Follow the instructions for folding the page, and then use the page as a guide as you preview the selection with students.

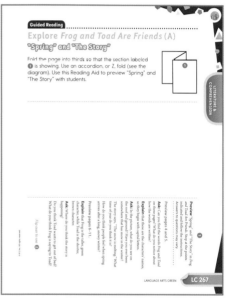
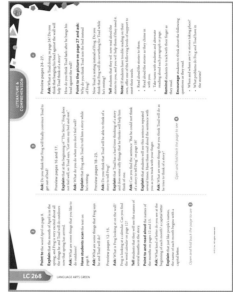

Check Your Reading

"Spring" and "The Story"

Check students' comprehension of "Spring" and "The Story."

1. Have students retell "Spring" in their own words to develop grammar, vocabulary, comprehension, and fluency skills.

2. Ask the following questions.

  ▶ Who are the main, or most important, characters in "Spring"? Frog; Toad
  ▶ Where does "Spring" take place? at Toad's house
  ▶ What time of year is it? spring
  ▶ How long has Toad been asleep? since November
  ▶ Why does Frog want Toad to get out of bed? so they can play together outside
  ▶ What is something Frog wants to do outside with Toad? Possible answers: skip through meadows; run through the woods; swim in the river

Objectives
- Retell or dramatize a story.
- Identify the main character(s).
- Identify setting.
- Answer questions requiring literal recall of details.

3. Have students retell "The Story" in their own words to develop grammar, vocabulary, comprehension, and fluency skills.

4. Ask the following questions.

   ▸ Who are the main characters in "The Story"? Frog; Toad
   ▸ Where does "The Story" take place? at Toad's house
   ▸ What time of year is it? summer
   ▸ Why does Frog get into bed? He isn't feeling well.
   ▸ What does Frog ask Toad to do while he's resting in bed? tell him a story

Reading for Meaning

Problem and Solution in "Spring" and "The Story"
Check students' understanding of problem and solution.

   ▸ What is the problem in "Spring"? Frog wants to play outside with Toad, but Toad won't get out of bed.
   ▸ What are some things that Frog does to try to solve his problem? Possible answers: He pushes Toad out of bed and takes him onto the porch to see what a beautiful day it is; he tells Toad all the fun things they can do outside together; he tells Toad he will miss all the fun.
   ▸ How does Frog finally solve the problem? He tricks Toad into thinking it's the month of May by tearing the pages off the calendar.
   ▸ What is the problem at the beginning of "The Story"? Toad wants to tell Frog a story, but he can't think of one.
   ▸ What are some things that Toad does to try to solve the problem? walks up and down the front porch; stands on his head; pours water on his head; bangs his head against the wall Do any of these things help Toad solve the problem? No
   ▸ How is the problem finally solved? Frog says he doesn't need to hear a story anymore, and then Frog tells Toad a story instead.

 Story Structure Elements in *Frog and Toad Are Friends*
Check students' ability to identify the story structure elements of setting, and problem and solution. Turn to pages LC 269 and 270 in *K¹² Language Arts Activity Book*.

1. Tells students they will use a chart to record the setting and the problem and solution for each story in *Frog and Toad Are Friends*.

2. Help students locate the "Setting" column. Then help them locate the row for recording information for "Spring."

Objectives
- Describe story structure elements—problem and solution.
- Identify setting.
- Compare and contrast story structure elements within a text.
- Demonstrate understanding through graphic organizers.

3. Help students write the setting for "Spring" in the correct box.

 ▸ If students are not ready to write on their own, allow them to dictate answers to you.

4. Repeat Steps 2 and 3 for the "Problem" and "Solution" columns.

 ▸ If students have trouble recalling the problem and solution for a story, read aloud any portions of the story that will help them recall the answers.

5. Repeat Steps 2–4 for "The Story."

TIP Keep the Activity Book pages in a safe place so that students can record the setting and the problem and solution as they read each story in *Frog and Toad Are Friends*.

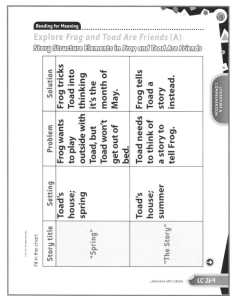

Reading for Meaning

Explore *Frog and Toad Are Friends* (A)

Story Structure Elements in *Frog and Toad Are Friends*

Fill in the chart.

Story title	Setting	Problem	Solution
"Spring"	Toad's house; spring	Frog wants to play outside with Toad, but Toad won't get out of bed.	Frog tricks Toad into thinking it's the month of May.
"The Story"	Toad's house; summer	Toad needs to think of a story to tell Frog.	Frog tells Toad a story instead.

Story title	Setting	Problem	Solution
"A Lost Button"			
"A Swim"			
"The Letter"			

Explore *Frog and Toad Are Friends* (B)

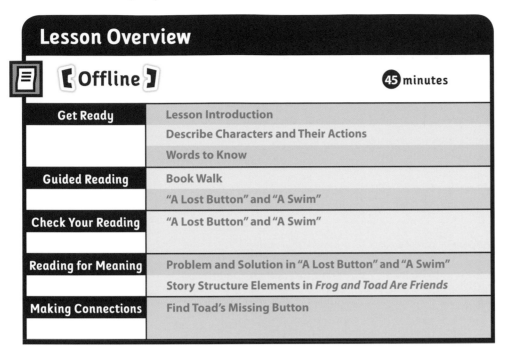

Lesson Overview

[Offline]   45 minutes

Get Ready	Lesson Introduction
	Describe Characters and Their Actions
	Words to Know
Guided Reading	Book Walk
	"A Lost Button" and "A Swim"
Check Your Reading	"A Lost Button" and "A Swim"
Reading for Meaning	Problem and Solution in "A Lost Button" and "A Swim"
	Story Structure Elements in *Frog and Toad Are Friends*
Making Connections	Find Toad's Missing Button

Advance Preparation

Before beginning the Guided Reading, read "A Lost Button" and "A Swim" to locate Words to Know in the text. Preview pages LC 271 and 272 in *K¹² Language Arts Activity Book* to prepare the materials for the Guided Reading and gather the partially completed chart on pages LC 269 and 270 (Story Structure Elements in *Frog and Toad Are Friends*).

Big Ideas

- ► Comprehension requires an understanding of story structure.
- ► An awareness of story structure elements (setting, characters, plot) provides readers a foundation for constructing meaning when reading new stories and writing their own stories.
- ► To understand and interpret a story, readers need to understand and describe characters and what they do.
- ► Guided reading provides support to early readers as they practice and apply the reading strategies of proficient readers.

[Materials]

Supplied

- *Frog and Toad Are Friends* by Arnold Lobel
- *K¹² Language Arts Activity Book*, pp. LC 269–273

Also Needed

- crayons

Story Synopses

In "A Lost Button," the third story in *Frog and Toad Are Friends*, Toad searches high and low for a button that has fallen off his jacket. In "A Swim," Toad goes to great lengths to keep his friends from seeing him in his bathing suit to avoid embarrassment.

Keywords

character – a person or animal in a story

problem – an issue a character must solve in a story

setting – when and where a story takes place

solution – how a character solves a problem in a story

story structure elements – components of a story; they include character, setting, plot, problem, and solution

 **Offline** ⏱ **45** minutes

Work **together** with students to complete offline Get Ready, Guided Reading, Check Your Reading, Reading for Meaning, and Making Connections activities.

Get Ready

Lesson Introduction

Prepare students for reading and discussing two stories in *Frog and Toad Are Friends*.

1. Tell students that they are going to read two stories in *Frog and Toad Are Friends*, "A Lost Button" and "A Swim."

2. Explain that before they read the stories, you will help them get ready by talking about characters—describing them and discussing their actions and feelings.

Objectives
- Describe character(s).
- Identify details that explain characters' actions and feelings.
- Build vocabulary through listening, reading, and discussion.
- Use new vocabulary in written and spoken sentences.

Describe Characters and Their Actions

Explore the story structure element of characters.

1. Remind students that there is more than one way to describe **characters**. We can describe how they look, act, and feel.

2. **Read aloud** the following short story and questions to practice describing characters and the way they act and feel.

Betty is a rabbit. She has pink eyes and white fur. Betty loves to eat carrots. Every morning, she goes out in her garden to pick a bunch of fresh carrots to eat for lunch. Eating carrots makes Betty happy.

> ▶ What does Betty look like? rabbit; pink eyes; white fur
> ▶ What does Betty love to do? eat carrots
> ▶ Why does Betty pick carrots every morning? so she can eat them for lunch
> ▶ How does Betty feel when she eats carrots? happy

Words to Know

Before reading "A Lost Button" and "A Swim" in *Frog and Toad Are Friends,* go over Words to Know with students.

1. Read aloud each word and have students repeat it.

2. Ask students if they know what each word means.

   ▸ If students know a word's meaning, have them define it and use it in a sentence.

   ▸ If students don't know a word's meaning, read them the definition and discuss the word with them.

dragonfly – a brightly colored insect that lives near water and has a long, thin body and four wings

riverbank – the ground at the edge of a river

shiver – to shake because of cold or fear

sparrow – a small songbird with brown or gray feathers

Guided Reading

Book Walk

Prepare students by taking them on a Book Walk of *Frog and Toad Are Friends.* Scan "A Lost Button" and "A Swim" together and ask students to make predictions.

1. Have students point to and read aloud the **book title**.

2. Have students point to and read aloud the **name of the author**.

3. Read aloud the story titles on the **contents** page. Explain to students that they're going to read "A Lost Button" and "A Swim."

4. Have students look at the **pictures from page 28 to page 52**. Discuss the following questions to prepare for reading. Answers to questions may vary.

   ▸ Where do you think "A Lost Button" takes place? What do you think might happen in this story?

   ▸ Where do you think "A Swim" takes place? What do you think might happen in this story?

Objectives

• Make predictions based on text, illustrations, and/or prior knowledge.

• Activate prior knowledge by previewing text and/or discussing topic.

• Read and listen to a variety of texts for information and pleasure independently or as part of a group.

• Read aloud grade-level text with appropriate expression, accuracy, and rate.

"A Lost Button" and "A Swim"

It's time to guide students through a preview of the stories to prepare them for reading on their own. Gather the Reading Aid on pages LC 271 and 272 in *K¹² Language Arts Activity Book.*

1. Have students sit next to you so that they can see the pictures and words while you introduce and discuss the stories.

2. Tell students that you will preview the stories together to prepare them to read aloud the stories to you.

3. Refer to the Reading Aid.

Reading Aid Tear out the Reading Aid for this reading selection. Follow the instructions for folding the page and then use the page as a guide as you preview the selection with students.

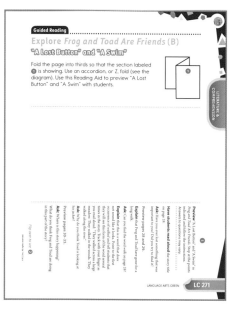
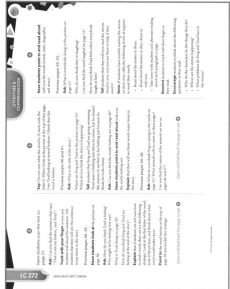

Check Your Reading

"A Lost Button" and "A Swim"

Check students' comprehension of "A Lost Button" and "A Swim."

1. Have students retell "A Lost Button" in their own words to develop grammar, vocabulary, comprehension, and fluency skills.

2. Ask the following questions.

   ▸ What does Frog look like? Possible answers: green; long legs; big eyes; long feet

   ▸ What does Toad look like? Possible answers: brown; big eyes; big mouth; long feet

   ▸ Why do Frog and Toad go back to all the places where they walked? to look for Toad's lost button

Objectives
- Retell or dramatize a story.
- Describe character(s).
- Identify details that explain characters' actions and feelings.
- Answer questions requiring literal recall of details.

▸ What does Toad say every time somebody finds a button and gives it to him? "That is not my button."

▸ Why does Toad run home and slam the door after Frog finds a thin button? because he's angry that none of the buttons anyone has found are his button

▸ How do you think Toad feels when he finds his button on the floor of his house? Possible answers: happy; embarrassed   Why do you think he feels this way? Answers will vary.

▸ What does Frog do when Toad gives him his jacket? He jumps for joy. Why does Frog do this? He thinks the jacket is beautiful.

3. Have students retell "A Swim" in their own words to develop grammar, vocabulary, comprehension, and fluency skills.

4. Ask the following questions.

▸ Why does Toad tell Frog not to look when he puts on his bathing suit? because Toad thinks he looks funny in his bathing suit

▸ Why do the animals stay even though Toad wants them to go away? They want to see Toad in his bathing suit.

▸ What do the animals do when Toad comes out of the water? laugh at him   Why do they laugh? because they think Toad looks funny in his bathing suit

▸ How do you think Toad feels when the animals laugh at him? Possible answers: embarrassed; unhappy   Why do you think he feels this way? Answers will vary.

TIP If students have trouble describing Frog and Toad, have them look at the pictures. If students have trouble answering other questions, ask them to think about each question as you read aloud the part of the story with the answer.

Reading for Meaning

Problem and Solution in "A Lost Button" and "A Swim"
Check students' understanding of problem and solution.

▸ What is the problem in "A Lost Button"? Frog and Toad cannot find Toad's lost button.

▸ How do Frog and Toad try to solve the problem? They go back to every place they walked to look for it.   Does this solve the problem? No

▸ How does the problem get solved? Toad finds the button on the floor of his house.

▸ What is Toad's problem at the beginning of "A Swim"? Toad doesn't want anyone to see him in his bathing suit.

▸ What does Toad do to solve his problem? He stays in the water.

▸ Toad stays in the water, but this leads to another problem. What is the other problem? Toad gets colder and colder.

Objectives

- Describe story structure elements—problem and solution.
- Identify setting.
- Compare and contrast story structure elements within a text.
- Demonstrate understanding through graphic organizers.

Story Structure Elements in *Frog and Toad Are Friends*

Check students' ability to identify the story structure elements of setting, and problem and solution. Gather partially completed pages LC 269 and 270 in *K¹² Language Arts Activity Book*.

1. Tell students that they will continue to record the setting and the problem and solution for each story in *Frog and Toad Are Friends*. If students have trouble recalling the setting or the problem and solution, reread that part of the story.

2. Point to the "Setting" column heading for the "A Lost Button" row in the graphic organizer.

3. Help students write the setting in the correct box.

4. Repeat Steps 2 and 3 for the "Problem" and "Solution" columns.

5. Repeat Steps 2–4 for "A Swim."

TIP Keep the Activity Book pages in a safe place so that students can continue to record each story's setting and problem and solution as they read.

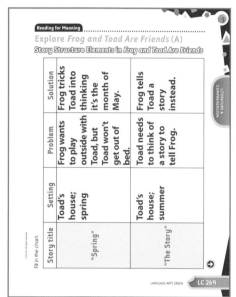

Reading for Meaning

Explore *Frog and Toad Are Friends* (A)

Story Structure Elements in *Frog and Toad Are Friends*

Fill in the chart.

Story title	Setting	Problem	Solution
"Spring"	Toad's house; spring	Frog wants to play outside with Toad, but Toad won't get out of bed.	Frog tricks Toad into thinking it's the month of May.
"The Story"	Toad's house; summer	Toad needs to think of a story to tell Frog.	Frog tells Toad a story instead.

LANGUAGE ARTS GREEN **LC 269**

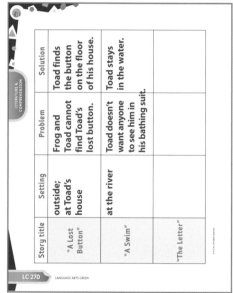

LC 270 LANGUAGE ARTS GREEN

Story title	Setting	Problem	Solution
"A Lost Button"	outside; at Toad's house	Frog and Toad cannot find Toad's lost button.	Toad finds the button on the floor of his house.
"A Swim"	at the river	Toad doesn't want anyone to see him in his bathing suit.	Toad stays in the water.
"The Letter"			

Making Connections

• •

Find Toad's Missing Button

Help students use clues to determine which button is Toad's. Turn to page LC 273 in *K¹² Language Arts Activity Book*.

1. Tell students that they can figure out which button is Toad's by knowing what it is not. For example, Toad says his button is not thin. That means his button must be thick. Toad says his button is not small. That means it must be big.

2. Read aloud the list of things that do not describe Toad's button, pausing after each item so students have time to look at each button on the page.

3. As you read the list, have students eliminate the buttons that are not Toad's by crossing them out.

4. Ask students to point to the correct button after reading the complete list. The button is big, thick, round, and white with four holes.

5. Read aloud the sentence starter located at the bottom of the page and ask students how they would complete the sentence. Be sure the attributes they mention are correct. big; thick; round; white; four holes

6. Help students write their answer on the blank line.

7. Have students read aloud the completed sentence **with** you as you track the words with your finger.

Objectives

- Draw conclusions using text, illustrations, and/or prior knowledge.
- Demonstrate understanding through drawing, discussion, drama, and/or writing.

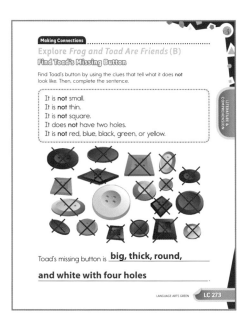

Explore *Frog and Toad Are Friends* (C)

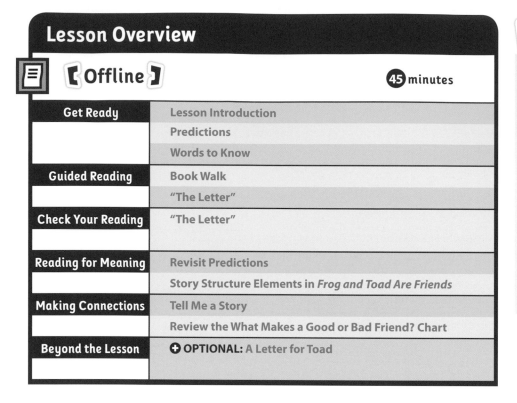

Lesson Overview

Offline — **45** minutes

Get Ready	Lesson Introduction
	Predictions
	Words to Know
Guided Reading	Book Walk
	"The Letter"
Check Your Reading	"The Letter"
Reading for Meaning	Revisit Predictions
	Story Structure Elements in *Frog and Toad Are Friends*
Making Connections	Tell Me a Story
	Review the What Makes a Good or Bad Friend? Chart
Beyond the Lesson	➕ OPTIONAL: A Letter for Toad

Materials

Supplied

- *Frog and Toad Are Friends* by Arnold Lobel
- *K¹² Language Arts Activity Book*, pp. LC 263, 269–270, 275–277
- *K¹² My Journal*, pp. 2–53 (optional)

Also Needed

- craft sticks
- glue stick
- scissors, round-end safety

Story Synopsis

In "The Letter," the fifth and final story in *Frog and Toad Are Friends*, Toad is sad because he never gets any mail. His best friend, Frog, has a plan to remedy the situation.

Keywords

prediction – a guess about what might happen that is based on information in a story and what you already know

problem – an issue a character must solve in a story

setting – when and where a story takes place

solution – how a character solves a problem in a story

story structure elements – components of a story; they include character, setting, plot, problem, and solution

Advance Preparation

Before beginning the Guided Reading, read "The Letter" to locate Words to Know in the text. Preview pages LC 275 and 276 in *K¹² Language Arts Activity Book* to prepare the materials for the Guided Reading. Gather the partially completed charts on pages LC 269 and 270 (Story Structure Elements in *Frog and Toad Are Friends*) for Reading for Meaning and LC 263 (What Makes a Good or Bad Friend?) for Making Connections.

Big Ideas

- Good readers interact with text to make logical predictions before reading; confirm predictions during reading; and revise or make new predictions as they read further.
- Comprehension requires an understanding of story structure.
- An awareness of story structure elements (setting, characters, plot) provides readers a foundation for constructing meaning when reading new stories and writing their own stories.
- Guided reading provides support to early readers as they practice and apply the reading strategies of proficient readers.
- Readers should be able to retell the story (or information) in their own words, not repeat what was written.

 **45** minutes

Work **together** with students to complete offline Get Ready, Guided Reading, Check Your Reading, Reading for Meaning, Making Connections, and Beyond the Lesson activities.

Get Ready

Lesson Introduction

Prepare students for reading and discussing "The Letter," the final story in *Frog and Toad Are Friends*.

1. Tell students that they are going to read the final story in *Frog and Toad Are Friends*, "The Letter."

2. Explain that before they read the story, you will help them get ready by discussing how prior knowledge from other stories can help us make predictions about a new story.

 Objectives
- Make predictions based on text, illustrations, and/or prior knowledge.
- Build vocabulary through listening, reading, and discussion.
- Use new vocabulary in written and spoken sentences.

Predictions

Review making predictions with students.

1. Remind students that **a prediction is a guess** about what might happen in a story.

   ▸ What information do we use to make predictions? information in a story and our prior knowledge

2. Explain to students that information we've learned from reading stories that are similar to a new story can also help us make predictions. For example, we know a lot about the characters Frog and Toad because we've read stories about them.

   ▸ Based on what you know about Frog and Toad, do you predict that they will be nice to each other or mean to each other in a new Frog and Toad story? nice to each other

TIP Predictions are neither right nor wrong. We make the best predictions we can, based on the information we have. Do not describe a prediction as "wrong," because this may discourage students from making predictions.

Words to Know

Before reading "The Letter" in *Frog and Toad Are Friends*, go over Words to Know with students.

1. Read aloud the word and have students repeat it.

2. Ask students if they know what the word means.

   ▶ If students know the word's meaning, have them define it and use it in a sentence.

   ▶ If students don't know the word's meaning, read them the definition and discuss the word with them.

envelope – a folded paper covering in which you mail a letter or other papers

Guided Reading

Book Walk

Prepare students by taking them on a Book Walk of *Frog and Toad Are Friends*. Scan the beginning of "The Letter" and ask students to make predictions.

1. Have students point to and read aloud the **book title**.

2. Have students read aloud the **name of the author**.

3. Explain to students that they're going to read the story "The Letter." Have them locate the story title on the **contents** page and then turn to the first page of the story.

4. Have students look at the **pictures on pages 53–55**. Answers to questions may vary.

   ▶ Where do you think "The Letter" takes place?

   ▶ What do you think might happen in the story?

Objectives

- Make predictions based on text, illustrations, and/or prior knowledge.

- Activate prior knowledge by previewing text and/or discussing topic.

- Make predictions before and during reading.

- Read and listen to a variety of texts for information and pleasure independently or as part of a group.

- Read aloud grade-level text with appropriate expression, accuracy, and rate.

"The Letter"

It's time to guide students through a preview of the story to prepare them for reading on their own. Gather the Reading Aid on pages LC 275 and 276 in *K¹² Language Arts Activity Book*.

1. Have students sit next to you so that they can see the pictures and words while you introduce and discuss the story.

2. Tell students that you will preview the story to prepare them to read aloud to you.

3. Refer to the Reading Aid.

Reading Aid Tear out the Reading Aid for this reading selection. Follow the instructions for folding the page, and then use the page as a guide as you preview the selection with students.

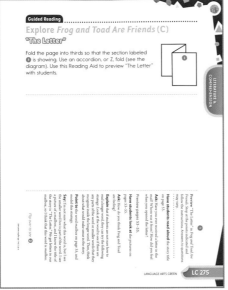
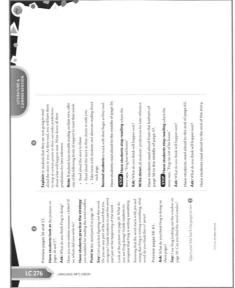

Check Your Reading

"The Letter"

Check students' comprehension of "The Letter."

1. Have students retell "The Letter" in their own words to develop grammar, vocabulary, comprehension, and fluency skills.

2. Ask students the following questions.

   ▸ Why is waiting for the mail a sad time for Toad? because he never gets any mail

   ▸ What does Frog do once he gets home? writes a letter to Toad

   ▸ Whom does Frog ask to deliver the letter to Toad? a snail

   ▸ Frog runs back to Toad's house and then tells Toad that he should do something. What does Frog want Toad to do? wait for the mail some more

   ▸ How long does it take for the snail to deliver the letter? four days

> **Objectives**
> - Retell or dramatize a story.
> - Answer questions requiring literal recall of details.

Reading for Meaning

Objectives

- Evaluate predictions.
- Support predictions with evidence from text and/or prior knowledge.
- Identify setting.
- Describe story structure elements—problem and solution.
- Compare and contrast story structure elements within a text.
- Demonstrate understanding through graphic organizers.

Revisit Predictions

Revisit the predictions students made while reading "The Letter." **Refer, as necessary, to the predictions you wrote down.**

▶ What did you predict would happen after Frog hurried home? Answers will vary.   Were they any clues in the story or anything you learned about Frog and Toad in other stories that helped you make this prediction? Answers will vary; guide students to recognize that Frog and Toad do nice things for each other in the previous stories, so it's reasonable to predict that Frog would do something nice for Toad again.

▶ What did you predict would happen after Frog puts the letter in an envelope and runs out of his house? Answers will vary.   Have you had any personal experience that helped you make this prediction? Answers will vary; guide students to recognize that if they have ever mailed a letter, that experience probably helped them make the prediction.

▶ What did you predict would happen after Frog and Toad sit on the porch to wait for the mail? Answers will vary.   Did your prediction happen? If your prediction did not happen, what happened instead? Answers will vary.

▶ If you predicted it would take a long time for the letter to arrive, what personal knowledge about snails helped you make your prediction? Answers will vary.

Story Structure Elements in *Frog and Toad Are Friends*

Check students' understanding of the story structure elements of setting and problem and solution. Gather partially completed pages LC 269 and 270 in *K¹² Language Arts Activity Book.*

1. Point to the "Setting" column heading for the "The Letter" row in the graphic organizer.

2. Help students write the settings in the correct box.

   ▶ Was there more than one setting in "The Letter"? Yes

3. Repeat Steps 1 and 2 for the "Problem" and "Solution" columns.

4. Have students review their answers in the graphic organizer for all the stories in *Frog and Toad Are Friends* and then ask the following questions.

▸ Where do most of the stories take place? at Toad's house

▸ Which problems does Frog solve? Possible answers: the problem of Toad not wanting to get out of bed in "Spring"; the problem of Toad not being able to think of a story to tell in "The Story"; the problem of Toad never getting any mail in "The Letter"

▸ Which problems does Toad solve? Possible answers: finding his lost button in "The Lost Button"; not wanting to get out of the water in "A Swim"

▸ Do you think Frog or Toad is better at solving problems? Why do you think that? Answers will vary.

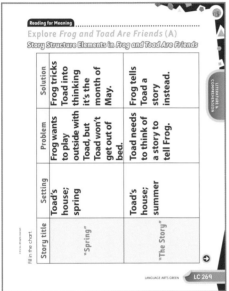

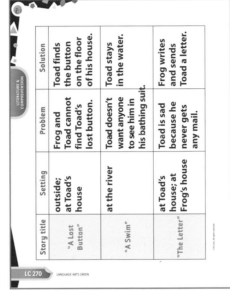

Reading for Meaning

Explore *Frog and Toad Are Friends* (A)

Story Structure Elements in *Frog and Toad Are Friends*

Fill in the chart.

Story title	Setting	Problem	Solution
"Spring"	Toad's house; spring	Frog wants to play outside with Toad, but Toad won't get out of bed.	Frog tricks Toad into thinking it's the month of May.
"The Story"	Toad's house; summer	Toad needs to think of a story to tell Frog.	Frog tells Toad a story instead.

LC 269   LANGUAGE ARTS GREEN

Story title	Setting	Problem	Solution
"A Lost Button"	outside; at Toad's house	Frog and Toad cannot find Toad's lost button.	Toad finds the button on the floor of his house.
"A Swim"	at the river	Toad doesn't want anyone to see him in his bathing suit.	Toad stays in the water.
"The Letter"	at Toad's house; at Frog's house	Toad is sad because he never gets any mail.	Frog writes and sends Toad a letter.

LC 270   LANGUAGE ARTS GREEN

Making Connections

Tell Me a Story

Check students' ability to retell a story, including all the story structure elements of characters, setting, plot, and problem and solution. Turn to page LC 277 in *K¹² Language Arts Activity Book* and gather the scissors, craft sticks, and glue stick.

1. Have students choose their favorite story from *Frog and Toad Are Friends* to retell using stick puppets.

   ▶ Ask students to explain why they picked that particular story.

2. Help students cut out the pictures of Frog and Toad on the Activity Book page and glue them to the craft sticks.

3. Have students retell their favorite Frog and Toad story using the puppets.

4. Remind students that when they retell a story they should

   ▶ Name the main characters.
   ▶ Describe the setting.
   ▶ Identify the problem and solution.
   ▶ Include the most important things that happen in the story in the order that they happen.

> ### Objectives
> - Retell a story using various media.
> - Retell a story naming plot, setting, character(s), problem, and solution.
> - Demonstrate understanding through drawing, discussion, drama, and/or writing.

Review the What Makes a Good or Bad Friend? Chart

Have students review and add new ideas to their What Makes a Good or Bad Friend? chart. Gather page LC 263 in *K¹² Language Arts Activity Book*.

1. Have students read aloud the "Good Friend" heading and each statement they wrote in the smiley face. Repeat for the "Bad Friend" heading and frowny face.

2. Ask the following questions. Answers to questions may vary.

   ▸ After reading *Frog and Toad Are Friends*, do you have more ideas about what makes a good or bad friend?
   ▸ What do you think Frog would say is important when looking for a good friend?
   ▸ What do you think Toad would say is important when looking for a good friend?
   ▸ Do you think Frog and Toad are good friends to each other? Why or why not?

3. Have students add any new ideas they have about good or bad friends to the chart.

TIP Keep the chart in a safe place for use throughout this unit.

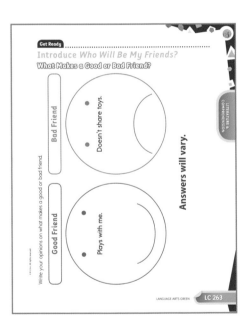

Beyond the Lesson

 OPTIONAL: A Letter for Toad

This activity is OPTIONAL. It is intended for students who have extra time and would benefit from practicing their writing skills. Feel free to skip this activity. Gather *K¹² My Journal* and have students turn to the next available page for **writing** in Thoughts and Experiences.

1. Remind students that Frog writes a letter to Toad in the story "The Letter."

2. Tell students they are going to write Toad a letter, too.

3. Have students think about what to include in their letter.

   ‣ Suggest they write the letter as though Toad were a good friend of theirs.

4. Help students compose and write their letter in their journal.

5. When they finish, have students read aloud what they wrote.

6. Ask students how Toad might feel when he gets their letter in the mail.

Objectives

- Make connections with text: text-to-text, text-to-self, text-to-world.
- Demonstrate understanding through drawing, discussion, drama, and/or writing.

Explore *Danny and the Dinosaur* (A)

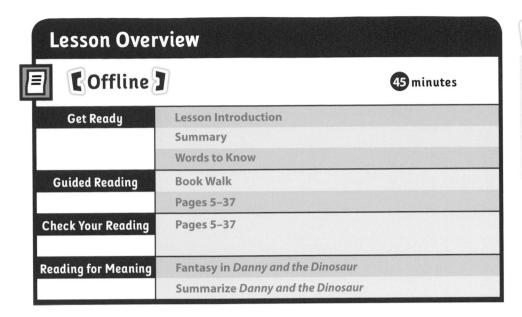

Lesson Overview

[Offline]   45 minutes

Get Ready	Lesson Introduction
	Summary
	Words to Know
Guided Reading	Book Walk
	Pages 5–37
Check Your Reading	Pages 5–37
Reading for Meaning	Fantasy in *Danny and the Dinosaur*
	Summarize *Danny and the Dinosaur*

Advance Preparation

Before beginning the Guided Reading, read pages 5–37 of *Danny and the Dinosaur* to locate Words to Know in the text. Preview pages LC 279 and 280 in *K¹² Language Arts Activity Book* to prepare the materials for the Guided Reading.

Big Ideas

- ▶ Guided reading provides support to early readers as they practice and apply the reading strategies of proficient readers.
- ▶ Comprehension requires the reader to self-monitor understanding.

[Materials]

Supplied

- *Danny and the Dinosaur* by Syd Hoff
- *K¹² Language Arts Activity Book*, pp. LC 279–280

Story Synopsis

In the first half of the book, Danny makes friends with a friendly dinosaur he meets at a museum. Danny has fun riding on the dinosaur as they explore the town and visit the zoo.

Keywords

fantasy – a story with characters, settings, or other elements that could not really exist

self-monitor – to notice if you do or do not understand what you are reading

summarize – to tell in order the most important ideas or events of a text

summary – a short retelling that includes only the most important ideas or events of a text

 **45 minutes**

Work **together** with students to complete Get Ready, Guided Reading, Check Your Reading, and Reading for Meaning activities.

Get Ready

Lesson Introduction

Prepare students for reading and discussing *Danny and the Dinosaur*.

1. Tell students that they are going to read pages 5 to 37 of *Danny and the Dinosaur*, a story about a boy who makes friends with an unusual animal.

2. Explain that before they read the first half of the story, you will get ready by reviewing how to give a summary.

> **Objectives**
> - Summarize a story.
> - Build vocabulary through listening, reading, and discussion.
> - Use new vocabulary in written and spoken sentences.

Summary

Reinforce how to give a summary.

1. Remind students that good readers can check their understanding of what they read by doing a summary. **A summary is a very short retelling that includes only the most important ideas or events of a text.** Giving a summary is not the same as a full retelling of a story, because a summary **doesn't include very many details**.

2. Tell students that a good way to do a summary is to ask the question, "Who did what?" A good reader tries to answer this question after reading parts or all of a story.
   Say: If we read a story about a man who lives a cabin in the woods and becomes friends with a bear, a good summary might be, "A man makes friends with a bear."

3. Have students think about the book *Who Will Be My Friends?* and ask the following questions.

   ▸ What is a summary of *Who Will Be My Friends?* Possible answer: A boy tries to make new friends.
   ▸ What question does a summary answer? Who did what?
   ▸ Did your summary answers the question, "Who did what?" for *Who Will Be My Friends?* Answers will vary.

Words to Know

Before reading *Danny and the Dinosaur*, go over Words to Know with students.

1. Read aloud each word and have students repeat it.

2. Ask students if they know what each word means.

   ▸ If students know a word's meaning, have them define it and use it in a sentence.
   ▸ If students don't know a word's meaning, read them the definition and discuss the word with them.

bundle – a package
museum – a building where interesting and important objects of art, history, or science are put on display

Guided Reading

Book Walk

Prepare students by taking them on a Book Walk of *Danny and the Dinosaur*. Scan the beginning of the book together and ask students to make predictions about the story. Answers to questions may vary.

1. Have students look at the **picture** on the cover.

2. Have students read aloud the **title of the book** and the **name of the author**.

   ▸ What do you think the book might be about?

3. Have students look at the **pictures on the first few pages** of the story.

   ▸ Have you ever been to a museum? What did you see there?
   ▸ What would you do if you could spend the day with a dinosaur? Where would you go? What games would you play?

Objectives

- Make predictions based on text, illustrations, and/or prior knowledge.
- Activate prior knowledge by previewing text and/or discussing topic.
- Read and listen to a variety of texts for information and pleasure independently or as part of a group.
- Read aloud grade-level text with appropriate expression, accuracy, and rate.

Pages 5–37

It's time to guide students through a preview of the story to prepare them for reading on their own. Gather the Reading Aid on pages LC 279 and 280 in *K¹² Language Arts Activity Book*.

1. Have students sit next to you so that they can see the pictures and words while you introduce and discuss the story.

2. Tell students that you will preview the story in order to prepare them to read aloud pages 5–37 of the book to you.

3. Refer to the Reading Aid.

Reading Aid   Tear out the Reading Aid for this reading selection. Follow the instructions for folding the page, and then use the page as a guide as you preview the selection with students.

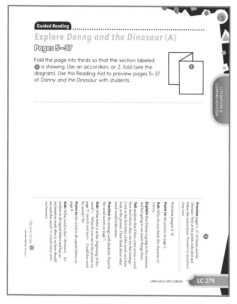

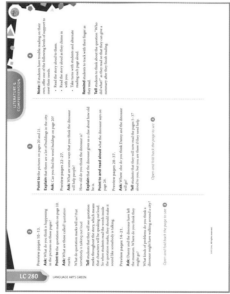

Check Your Reading

Pages 5–37
Check students' comprehension of *Danny and the Dinosaur*.

1. Have students retell pages 5–37 of *Danny and the Dinosaur* in their own words to develop grammar, vocabulary, comprehension, and fluency skills.

2. Ask the following questions.

   ▶ Where does the beginning of the story take place? What is the setting? at a museum
   ▶ What are some of the settings of the middle of the story? in a town or city; a ball game; a zoo
   ▶ Who are the characters in the story? Danny; dinosaur; policeman; people waiting for a bus; people at a ball game; people and animals at a zoo
   ▶ Why does Danny go to the museum? to see what's inside
   ▶ What does the dinosaur do for Danny? takes him for a ride
   ▶ What happens when Danny and the dinosaur go to a zoo? Everybody runs to see the dinosaur.

 TIP If students have trouble responding to a question, help them locate the answer in the text or pictures.

 Objectives
- Retell or dramatize a story.
- Identify setting.
- Identify character(s).
- Answer questions requiring literal recall of details.

Reading for Meaning

Fantasy in *Danny and the Dinosaur*
Check students' ability to distinguish fantasy from reality in *Danny and the Dinosaur*.

1. Remind students that sometimes parts of stories are **fantasy**, which means they are make-believe and could never happen in the real world. Some parts of *Danny and the Dinosaur* could happen in the real world, while other parts are fantasy.

2. Ask students the following questions.

   ▶ Can a boy really visit a museum? Yes
   ▶ Can a boy really see a model of a dinosaur in a museum? Yes
   ▶ Can a dinosaur in a museum really come to life? No   How do you know? This can't happen in the real world.
   ▶ Danny gets on the dinosaur's neck to go for a ride. Could this really happen, or is it fantasy? fantasy   How do you know? There aren't any dinosaurs alive today.
   ▶ People in the story ride the dinosaur's tail instead of taking the bus. Is this realistic or fantasy? fantasy
   ▶ Can a boy really go to a ball game? Yes
   ▶ Can a dinosaur really talk? No

 Objectives
- Distinguish fantasy from realistic text.
- Summarize a story.
- Self-monitor comprehension of text.

Summarize *Danny and the Dinosaur*

Check students' ability to summarize a story.

1. Remind students that a summary is a very short retelling of the most important ideas or events of a text. A summary should answer the question, "Who did what?"

2. Have students practice summarizing.

   ► Who did what in the beginning of the story? Tell what happens in one or two sentences. Possible answer: Danny goes to the museum and meets a dinosaur.
   ► Who did what after Danny meets the dinosaur? Tell what happens in one or two sentences. Possible answer: The dinosaur takes Danny for a ride through the city, and they see many things and go to many places.
   ► Summarize what's happened so far in the story in one or two sentences that answer the question, "Who did what?" Possible answer: Danny meets a dinosaur at a museum. The dinosaur takes Danny for a ride, and they visit many places together.

3. Ask the following questions to check students' comprehension of summarizing.

   ► What is a summary? a short retelling that includes only the most important ideas or events of a text
   ► What question does a summary answer? Who did what?
   ► Were you able to answer the question, "Who did what?" for this half of the book? Answers will vary.
   ► Do you think that you understand the part of the book that you've read so far? Answers will vary.

TIP If students don't think they understand the story, reread the story aloud, pausing to let students ask questions as you read.

Explore *Danny and the Dinosaur* (B)

Lesson Overview

[Offline]　　　　　　　　　　　　　　　45 minutes

Get Ready	Lesson Introduction
	Words to Know
Guided Reading	Book Walk
	Pages 38–64
Check Your Reading	Pages 38–64
Reading for Meaning	Summarize *Danny and the Dinosaur*
Making Connections	What Makes a Good or Bad Friend?
	A Good Friend

Advance Preparation

Before beginning the Guided Reading, read pages 38–64 of *Danny and the Dinosaur* to locate Words to Know in the text. Preview pages LC 281 and 282 in *K¹² Language Arts Activity Book* to prepare the materials for the Guided Reading and gather the partially completed chart on page LC 263 (What Makes a Good or Bad Friend?) for Making Connections.

Big Ideas

▸ Guided reading provides support to early readers as they practice and apply the reading strategies of proficient readers.
▸ Comprehension requires the reader to self-monitor understanding.

[Materials]

Supplied

● *Danny and the Dinosaur* by Syd Hoff
● *K¹² Language Arts Activity Book*, pp. LC 263, 281–284

Story Synopsis

In the second half of the book, Danny and the dinosaur go looking for Danny's friends. They all spend the afternoon playing, and then it's time to say good-bye.

Keywords

summarize – to tell in order the most important ideas or events of a text
summary – a short retelling that includes only the most important ideas or events of a text

[Offline] 45 minutes

Work **together** with students to complete Get Ready, Guided Reading, Check Your Reading, Reading for Meaning, and Making Connections activities.

Get Ready

Lesson Introduction

Prepare students for reading and discussing *Danny and the Dinosaur*.

1. Tell students that they are going to read the second half of *Danny and the Dinosaur*.

2. Explain that before they read the second half of the story, you will get ready by reviewing what happened in the first half.

Objectives
- Build vocabulary through listening, reading, and discussion.
- Use new vocabulary in written and spoken sentences.

Words to Know

Before reading *Danny and the Dinosaur*, go over Words to Know with students.

1. Read aloud each word and have students repeat it.

2. Ask students if they know what each word means.

   ▸ If students know a word's meaning, have them define it and use it in a sentence.
   ▸ If students don't know a word's meaning, read them the definition and discuss the word or with them.

delighted – happy; pleased
merry-go-round – a carousel; a round platform that turns and has seats in the form of animals that go up and down on poles

Guided Reading

Book Walk

Prepare students by taking them on a Book Walk of *Danny and the Dinosaur*. Scan pages 38–64 of the book together and ask students to make predictions.

1. Have students read aloud the **title of the book** and the **name of the author**.

2. Have students review the events of the story so far by giving a **summary** of the first half of the book.

   ▸ If students need help recalling characters and events, have them look at the pictures on pages 5–37 to refresh their memory.

Objectives
- Summarize a story.
- Make predictions based on text, illustrations, and/or prior knowledge.
- Activate prior knowledge by previewing text and/or discussing topic.
- Read and listen to a variety of texts for information and pleasure independently or as part of a group.
- Read aloud grade-level text with appropriate expression, accuracy, and rate.

3. Have students look at the **pictures on pages 38–64** of the story. Answers to questions may vary.

  ▸ What do you think this part of the book might be about?
  ▸ What do you think your friends would do if they saw you riding on a dinosaur?
  ▸ Do you think it would be fun to play hide-and-seek with a dinosaur? Who do you think would win? Why?

Pages 38–64

It's time to guide students through a preview of the second half of the story to prepare them for reading on their own. Gather the Reading Aid on pages LC 281 and 282 in *K¹² Language Arts Activity Book*.

1. Have students sit next to you so that they can see the pictures and words while you introduce and discuss the story.

2. Tell students that you will preview pages 38–64 the story to prepare them to read aloud the second half of the book to you.

3. Refer to the Reading Aid.

Reading Aid Tear out the Reading Aid for this reading selection. Follow the instructions for folding the page and then use the page as a guide as you preview the selection with students.

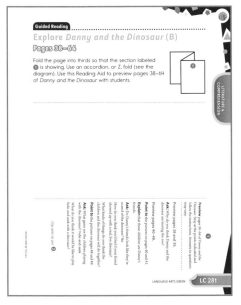
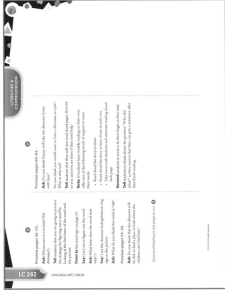

Check Your Reading

Pages 38–64

Check students' comprehension of the second half of *Danny and the Dinosaur*.

1. Have students retell pages 38–64 of *Danny and the Dinosaur* in their own words to develop grammar, vocabulary, comprehension, and fluency skills.

2. Ask the following questions.

   ▶ Where does this part of the story take place? What is the setting? in a neighborhood
   ▶ Who are new characters we meet in this part of the story? Danny's friends
   ▶ What is the first thing Danny's friends want to do with the dinosaur? go for a ride
   ▶ Why does the dinosaur get out of breath? He runs around and around the block, going faster and faster.
   ▶ What happens when Danny's friends hide from the dinosaur when they play hide-and-seek? He can't find them and gives up.
   ▶ Why do the children pretend they can't find the dinosaur when it's his turn to hide? because he's too big to hide and the children want him to win

TIP If students have trouble responding to a question, help them locate the answer in the text or pictures.

> **Objectives**
> • Identify setting.
> • Identify character(s).
> • Answer questions requiring literal recall of details.

Reading for Meaning

Summarize *Danny and the Dinosaur*

Check students' ability to summarize a story.

1. Remind students that a summary is a very short retelling of the most important ideas or events of a text. A summary should answer the question, "Who did what?"

2. Have students practice summarizing.

   ▶ Who does what in the beginning of this part of the story? Tell what happens in one or two sentences. Possible answer: Danny and the dinosaur find Danny's friends, and the dinosaur takes them for a ride.
   ▶ Give a summary of what happens after the dinosaur takes the children for a ride. Possible answer: Danny teaches the dinosaur to do some tricks, and then the children and the dinosaur play hide-and-seek.
   ▶ Who does what at the end of the story? Tell what happens in one or two sentences. Possible answer: Danny and the dinosaur say good-bye because the dinosaur has to go back to the museum.
   ▶ Summarize what happens in the second half of the book in one or two sentences that answer the question, "Who did what?" Possible answer: Danny and the dinosaur play with Danny's friends, and then they all go home and the dinosaur goes back to the museum.

> **Objectives**
> • Summarize a story.
> • Self-monitor comprehension of text.

3. Ask the following questions to check students' comprehension of summarizing.

  ▶ What is a summary? a short retelling that includes only the most important ideas or events of a text
  ▶ What question does a summary answer? Who did what?
  ▶ Were you able to answer the question, "Who did what?" for this half of the book? Answers will vary.
  ▶ Do you think that you understand the story? Answers will vary.

TIP If students don't think they understand the story, reread the story aloud, pausing to let students ask questions as you read.

Making Connections

What Makes a Good or Bad Friend?

Have students review and add new ideas to their What Makes a Good or Bad Friend? chart. Gather page LC 263 in *K¹² Language Arts Activity Book*.

1. Have students read aloud the "Good Friend" heading and each statement they wrote in the smiley face. Repeat for the "Bad Friend" heading and frowny face.

2. Ask the following questions. Answers to questions may vary.

  ▶ After reading *Danny and the Dinosaur*, do you have more ideas about what makes a good or bad friend?
  ▶ What do you think Danny would say is important when looking for a good friend?
  ▶ Danny and the dinosaur do many fun things together. Do you think doing fun things together is part of being a good friend?
  ▶ What does the dinosaur do that makes you think he is a good friend?

3. Have students add any new ideas they have about good or bad friends to the chart.

Objectives
- Make connections with text: text-to-text, text-to-self, text-to-world.
- Demonstrate understanding through drawing, discussion, drama, and/or writing.
- Demonstrate understanding through graphic organizers.
- Make inferences based on text and/or prior knowledge.

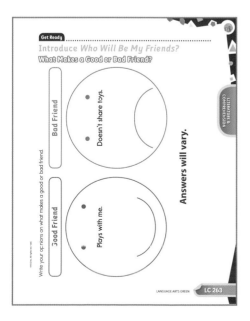

A Good Friend

Check students' understanding of the characters in this unit's stories and the characteristics of good friends. Turn to pages LC 283 and 284 in *K¹² Language Arts Activity Book*.

1. Have students think about how all of the stories they read in this unit were about friends and friendship.

2. Tell students that they are going to complete a sentence that describes what each main character from *Who Will Be My Friends?*, *Frog and Toad Are Friends*, and *Danny and the Dinosaur* would say about the qualities of a good friend.

3. Help students read aloud the starter sentence and the characters' names on the Activity Book pages.

4. Tell students to think about each character's actions in the books and then write what they think that character would say about what makes a good friend. They should complete the sentence "A good friend is someone who . . ." for each character.

5. Have students read aloud each completed sentence.

6. Ask the following questions. Answers to questions may vary.

   ▸ Do you agree with what the characters would say makes a good friend?
   ▸ Which character would you like to be friends with? Why?

Reward: Add a sticker for this unit on the My Accomplishments chart to mark successful completion of the unit.

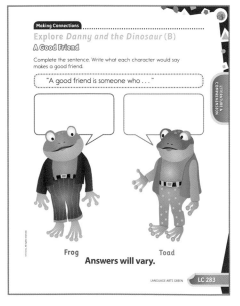

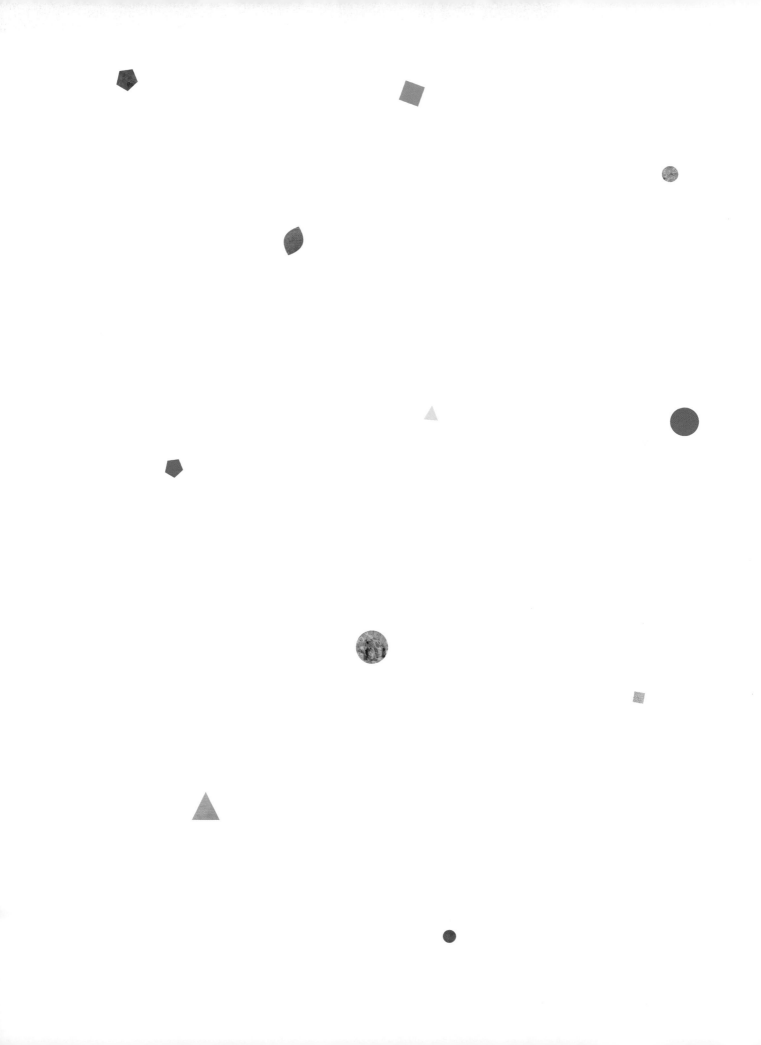

Creative Characters

Unit Focus

Students will read texts whose characters are imaginative problem solvers. This unit follows the guided-reading instructional approach (see the instructional approaches to reading in the introductory lesson for this program). In this unit, students will

▶ Make inferences about characters based on what they say and do.
▶ Explore the story structure element of problem and solution.
▶ Review what happens in the beginning, middle, and end of a story.
▶ Explore how illustrations provide additional information that can help them better understand a story.
▶ Check that they understand what they've read by retelling.
▶ Practice identifying story structure elements—characters, setting, and plot.
▶ Identify the narrator of a poem.
▶ Explore how poets use personification to make nonhuman things sound like they are human.

Unit Plan

Offline

Lesson 1	Introduce *A Picture for Harold's Room*	**45** minutes a day
Lesson 2	Explore *A Picture for Harold's Room*	
Lesson 3	Introduce *And I Mean It, Stanley*	
Lesson 4	Explore *And I Mean It, Stanley*	
Lesson 5	Explore *Harry and the Lady Next Door* (A)	
Lesson 6	Explore *Harry and the Lady Next Door* (B)	
Lesson 7	Explore *Harry and the Lady Next Door* (C)	
Lesson 8	Explore Poems About Creative Characters	
Lesson 9	Your Choice	

Introduce *A Picture for Harold's Room*

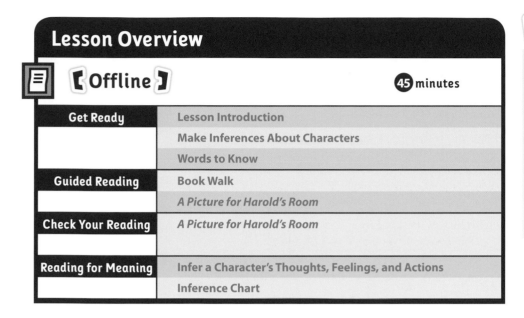

Lesson Overview

[Offline]   ⏱ 45 minutes

Get Ready	Lesson Introduction
	Make Inferences About Characters
	Words to Know
Guided Reading	Book Walk
	A Picture for Harold's Room
Check Your Reading	*A Picture for Harold's Room*
Reading for Meaning	Infer a Character's Thoughts, Feelings, and Actions
	Inference Chart

Advance Preparation

Before beginning the Guided Reading, read *A Picture for Harold's Room* to locate Words to Know in the text. Preview pages LC 285 and 286 in *K¹² Language Arts Activity Book* to prepare the materials for the Guided Reading.

Big Ideas

- ▸ To understand and interpret a story, readers need to understand and describe characters and what they do.
- ▸ Good readers use prior knowledge and text clues to infer or draw conclusions about what is implied but not directly stated in text.
- ▸ Guided reading provides support to early readers as they practice and apply the reading strategies of proficient readers.

[Materials]

Supplied

- *A Picture for Harold's Room* by Crockett Johnson
- *K¹² Language Arts Activity Book*, pp. LC 285–287

Also Needed

- crayons

Story Synopsis

Harold wants to hang a picture on the wall in his room. He draws picture after picture and ends up as small as a mouse inside the fantasy world that he creates. How will this little artist get back to his room?

Keywords

character – a person or animal in a story

infer – to use clues and what you already know to make a guess

inference – a guess you make using the clues in a text and what you already know

Work **together** with students to complete Get Ready, Guided Reading, Check Your Reading, and Reading for Meaning activities.

Get Ready

Lesson Introduction
Prepare students for reading and discussing *A Picture for Harold's Room*.

1. Tell students that they will read *A Picture for Harold's Room*, a story about a boy who likes to draw pictures.

2. Explain that before they read the story, you will help them get ready by discussing how we can make inferences about characters based on their actions.

Objectives
- Make inferences based on text and/or prior knowledge.
- Build vocabulary through listening, reading, and discussion.
- Use new vocabulary in written and spoken sentences.

Make Inferences About Characters
Explore making inferences about characters.

1. Remind students that we can **infer**, or figure out, things about characters by what they do and say.

2. Have students explain what kind of clues they use to make an inference. If they have trouble answering, remind them that to make an **inference**, we use
   ▶ Hints or clues in the words and pictures of a story
   ▶ Our own prior knowledge from past experiences

3. Model how to make an inference.
   Say: Toby spent an hour at the pet shop looking for the perfect toy for his cat, Snowball. I can infer that Toby really loves Snowball. I made this inference because Toby spent an hour looking for the toy, and I know from my past experience that people would do that only if they really cared about their pet.

4. Have students practice making inferences about characters.
   Say: Amanda Pig stared at the egg on her plate with a frown on her face. What can you infer about Amanda? Possible answers: She doesn't want to eat her egg; she doesn't like eggs.
   Say: Janette started to jump up and down when her mother said she could go to the zoo with her friends. What can you infer about Janette? Possible answers: She is excited; she really wants to go to the zoo.

Words to Know

Before reading *A Picture for Harold's Room*, go over Words to Know with students.

1. Read aloud each word or phrase and have students repeat it.

2. Ask students if they know what each word or phrase means.

   ▸ If students know a word's or phrase's meaning, have them define it and use it in a sentence.
   ▸ If students don't know a word's or phrase's meaning, read them the definition and discuss the word or phrase with them.

lighthouse – a tower with a flashing light that shows ships the way or warns them of danger
ocean liner – a very large ship that takes people from one place to another
steep – having a sharp slope
usual – normal
wade – to walk through water

Guided Reading

Book Walk

Prepare students for reading by taking them on a Book Walk of *A Picture for Harold's Room*. Scan the book together and ask students to make predictions about the story. Answers to questions may vary.

1. Have students look at the **picture** on the cover.

2. Have students read aloud the **book title** and the **name of the author**.

   ▸ What do you think the book might be about?

3. Have students look at the **pictures in the book**.

   ▸ What do you think might happen in the story?
   ▸ Do you like to draw pictures? What do you draw pictures of?
   ▸ What do you use to draw your pictures?

Objectives

- Make predictions based on text, illustrations, and/or prior knowledge.
- Activate prior knowledge by previewing text and/or discussing topic.
- Read and listen to a variety of texts for information and pleasure independently or as part of a group.
- Read aloud grade-level text with appropriate expression, accuracy, and rate.

A Picture for Harold's Room

Guide students through a preview of the story to prepare them for reading on their own. Gather the Reading Aid on pages LC 285 and 286 in *K¹² Language Arts Activity Book*.

1. Have students sit next to you so that they can see the pictures and words while you introduce and discuss the story.

2. Tell students that you will preview the story to prepare them to read aloud the story to you.

3. Refer to the Reading Aid.

Reading Aid Tear out the Reading Aid for this reading selection. Follow the instructions for folding the page, and then use the page as a guide as you preview the selection with students.

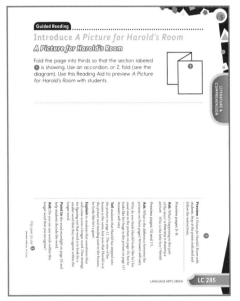
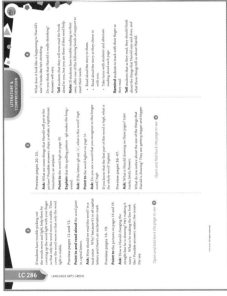

Check Your Reading

A Picture for Harold's Room

Check students' comprehension of *A Picture for Harold's Room*.

1. Have students retell *A Picture for Harold's Room* in their own words to develop grammar, vocabulary, comprehension, and fluency skills.

2. Ask students the following questions.

   ▶ Who is the main character in the story? Harold
   ▶ Why does Harold start drawing? He wants a picture to put on his wall.
   ▶ What size is Harold when he draws the moon? giant
   ▶ How does he get so big? He steps into the picture.
   ▶ What size is Harold when he sits on a pebble to think? very small; as small as a mouse
   ▶ Does Harold's size really change when he is as small as a mouse? No Why does he look so small? He drew the things in his pictures so that they were bigger than he is.

TIP If students have trouble responding to a question, help them locate the answer in the text or pictures.

Objectives
- Retell or dramatize a story.
- Identify the main character(s).
- Answer questions requiring literal recall of details.

Reading for Meaning

Infer a Character's Thoughts, Feelings, and Actions

Check students' ability to make inferences.

▶ Why is Harold glad the people in the town he draws don't wake up and see him? because he would look like a giant, and it would scare them What does this tell you about Harold? Possible answers: He's kind; he cares about other people.

▶ Why does Harold draw a lighthouse? Possible answers: because the ship was too near the rocks; so the ship wouldn't crash into the rocks; to show the sailors where the rocks are What does this tell you about Harold? Possible answers: He's kind; he cares about other people.

▶ What does Harold draw near the train tracks? birds and flowers Why do you think he does this? Possible answers: He likes birds and flowers; he thinks birds and flowers look nice next to the tracks.

▶ What does Harold say to the mouse? "Excuse me." Why do you think Harold says this? He's polite.

▶ What does Harold do to check what size he is at the end of the story? He draws a mirror. How does this show what kind of boy Harold is? It shows he's clever; it shows he has good ideas.

▶ Harold draws another picture on the wall just before he goes to bed. Why do you think he doesn't step into this picture? Possible answers: He doesn't want to change his size again; he's tired and wants to go to bed instead.

Objectives
- Identify details that explain characters' actions and feelings.
- Describe character(s).
- Make inferences based on text and/or prior knowledge.
- Describe people, places, things, locations, actions, events, and/or feelings.
- Demonstrate understanding through graphic organizers.

✏ Inference Chart

Check students' ability to make inferences about a character. Gather the crayons and turn to page LC 287 in *K¹² Language Arts Activity Book*.

1. Tell students they made many inferences about Harold while reading the story.

2. Explain that they will fill out a chart to record the things they learned and inferred.

3. Have students read aloud the instructions on the Activity Book page.

4. Have them read aloud the "Facts About Harold" heading and then write at least one fact about Harold in the space.

5. Have them read aloud the "What Harold Says" heading and then write at least one thing Harold says in the story.

6. Have them read aloud the "What Harold Does" heading and then write at least one thing Harold does in the story.

7. Have them read aloud the "What Harold Thinks or Feels" heading and then write at least one thing Harold thinks or feels in the story.

8. Have students read aloud all the things they've written in the chart. Tell them to think about what they can infer about Harold based on what they've written, and then have students write a sentence on the lines at the bottom of the page.

9. Have students draw a picture of Harold in the center box of the chart.

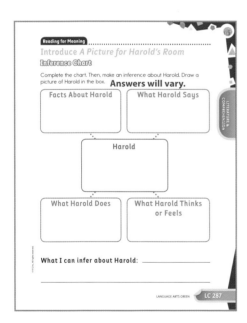

Explore *A Picture for Harold's Room*

Lesson Overview

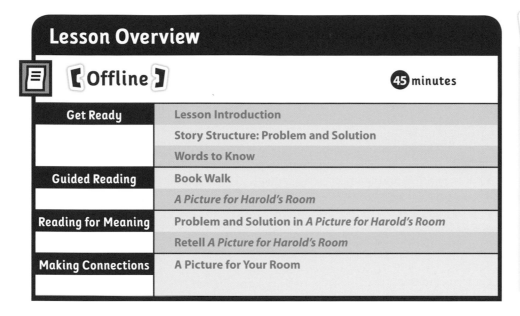

[Offline]   **45** minutes

Get Ready	Lesson Introduction
	Story Structure: Problem and Solution
	Words to Know
Guided Reading	Book Walk
	A Picture for Harold's Room
Reading for Meaning	Problem and Solution in *A Picture for Harold's Room*
	Retell *A Picture for Harold's Room*
Making Connections	A Picture for Your Room

[Materials]

Supplied
- *A Picture for Harold's Room* by Crockett Johnson

Also Needed
- crayon – purple
- glue stick
- household objects – photographs of students
- paper, poster (white)
- scissors, round-end safety

Keywords

problem – an issue a character must solve in a story

retelling – using your own words to tell a story that you have listened to or read

self-monitor – to notice if you do or do not understand what you are reading

solution – how a character solves a problem in a story

story structure elements – components of a story; they include character, setting, plot, problem, and solution

Advance Preparation

Before beginning Making Connections, gather or print photographs of students.

Big Ideas

- Comprehension requires an understanding of story structure.
- An awareness of story structure elements (setting, characters, plot) provides readers a foundation for constructing meaning when reading new stories and writing their own stories.
- Repeated rereading leads to increased fluency.
- Comprehension requires the reader to self-monitor understanding.

[Offline] **45** minutes

Work **together** with students to complete Get Ready, Guided Reading, Reading for Meaning, and Making Connections activities.

Get Ready

Lesson Introduction

Prepare students for reading and discussing *A Picture for Harold's Room*.

1. Tell students that they will reread *A Picture for Harold's Room*.

2. Explain that they before they reread the story, you will help them get ready by discussing the story structure element of problem and solution, and in which parts of a story we find out the problem and solution.

> **Objectives**
> - Build vocabulary through listening, reading, and discussion.
> - Use new vocabulary in written and spoken sentences.

Story Structure: Problem and Solution

Explore the story structure element of problem and solution.

1. Remind students that a **problem** is something that happens that we need to fix. The **solution** is how we fix a problem. Sometimes we have to try more than one thing to solve, or fix, a problem.

2. Explain that characters in stories usually have a problem to solve. The events in the story tell how characters try to solve their problem.

3. Remind students that a story has a beginning, middle, and end. Explain that we usually learn about the characters' problem and how they solve it in certain parts of a story.

   ▸ At the **beginning** of a story, we usually meet characters and learn their problem.
   ▸ In the **middle** of a story, characters usually try to solve their problem. Sometimes characters must try more than one way to solve their problem.
   ▸ At the **end** of a story, characters usually solve their problem.

4. Explain to students that if they know where the problem and solution fit into the order of a story, they will know what to expect as they read. This will help them better understand and remember a story.

Words to Know

Before reading *A Picture for Harold's Room*, go over Words to Know with students.

1. Read aloud each word or phrase and have students repeat it.

2. Ask students if they know what each word or phrase means.

   ▸ If students know a word's or phrase's meaning, have them define it and use it in a sentence.
   ▸ If students don't know a word's or phrase's meaning, read them the definition and discuss the word or phrase with them.

lighthouse – a tower with a flashing light that shows ships the way or warns them of danger
ocean liner – a very large ship that takes people from one place to another
steep – having a sharp slope
usual – normal
wade – to walk through water

Guided Reading

Book Walk

Prepare students for reading by taking them on a Book Walk of *A Picture for Harold's Room*. Scan the book together to revisit the characters and events.

1. Have students read aloud the **book title** and the **name of the author**.

2. Look through the book. Have students review the **pictures**. Answers to questions may vary.

   ▸ Harold draws many things in the story. Which picture do you like best? What do you like about it?
   ▸ What kind of picture would you draw for your room?

Objectives

- Activate prior knowledge by previewing text and/or discussing topic.
- Read and listen to a variety of texts for information and pleasure independently or as part of a group.
- Read aloud grade-level text with appropriate expression, accuracy, and rate.

A Picture for Harold's Room

It's time for students to reread the story aloud.

1. Tell students that *A Picture for Harold's Room* should now be familiar to them because they have read it before.

2. Explain that they will reread the story aloud to you, but you are there if they need help.

3. If students have trouble reading on their own, offer one of the following levels of support to meet their needs.

   ▸ Read aloud the story to them.
   ▸ Read aloud the story as they chime in with you.
   ▸ Take turns with students and alternate reading aloud each page.

4. Remind students to track with their finger as they read.

5. Tell students that as they read, they should notice if Harold has any problems and what he does to solve those problems.

Reading for Meaning

Problem and Solution in *A Picture for Harold's Room*

Check students' ability to recognize and describe how characters solve problems.

Objectives
- Describe story structure elements—problem and solution.
- Retell the beginning, middle, and end of a story.
- Self-monitor comprehension of text.

► What problem does Harold have at the beginning of the story? He needs a picture for the wall in his room.   What does he do to solve this problem? He starts to draw a picture.

► Why does Harold draw rocks at the edge of the sea? so he can step out of the water   What new problem does this cause? The ship is too close to the rocks.   What does Harold do to fix this problem? He draws a lighthouse so the sailors can see where the rocks are.

► What problem does Harold have when he draws an airplane? A jet comes close to him.   What does Harold do to fix this problem? He ducks so the airplane doesn't hit him.

► What is Harold's problem when he sees that he's smaller than a bird? He doesn't know how to get home.   What does Harold do to solve this problem? He crosses out the picture.

► Harold wants to make sure he's his usual size. What does he do to solve this problem? He draws a mirror so he can check his size.

► How does Harold solve his first problem of not having a picture for his room? He draws a new picture on the wall.

► Harold isn't tall enough to draw a picture up high on the wall. How does he fix this problem? He draws a picture of a chair so he can stand on it.

Retell *A Picture for Harold's Room*

Check students' ability to self-monitor their understanding of a story by retelling.

1. Remind students that

   ► One way readers can check their understanding of a story is by retelling it.
   ► **Retelling** means using your own words to tell what happens in a story that you have listened to or read.
   ► A good retelling includes the most important things that happen in the beginning, middle, and end of the story in the order that they happen.
   ► A good retelling includes the characters and the problems they solve.

2. Have students retell the story, reminding them to mention how Harold solves problems during each part. If necessary, have students refer to the pictures in the book to help them with retelling.

   ► Retell the beginning of the story, the part in which Harold wants a picture for his wall. Possible answer: Harold wants to put a picture on his wall, so he takes a purple crayon and draws a little town at the end of a long road. After he steps into the town to draw the moon, Harold is glad that the people in the town didn't see him, because it would have scared them to see a giant.

▸ Retell the middle of the story, the part in which Harold draws the sea, mountains, and railroad tracks. Possible answer: Harold comes to the end of the land, so he draws the sea and a ship. After he draws rocks to step out of the water, Harold sees that the ship might run into them, so he draws a lighthouse to show the sailors where they are. When Harold thinks about how he is taller than everything, he sees that a plane might hit him and he ducks just in time. Then, he draws railroad tracks, birds, and flowers.

▸ Retell the end of the story, the part in which Harold realizes he's smaller than a bird and flower. Possible answer: Harold sees that he is now smaller than a flower or a bird. After he falls into a mouse hole, he sits on a pebble to figure out how to get home. He figures out that he's just in a picture he drew, so he crosses out the picture with his crayon. Harold draws a door with a mirror on the back of it to make sure he's his usual size. Harold still doesn't have a picture for his room, so he draws one on the wall before he goes to bed.

3. Guide students to think about their retelling. Answers to questions may vary.

▸ Did your retelling include the important characters?
▸ Did it include most of the important things that happened, and in the right order?
▸ Did your retelling include Harold's problems and how he solves them?
▸ Do you think that you understand the story?

TIP If students don't think they understand the story, reread the story aloud, pausing to let students ask questions as you read.

Making Connections

A Picture for Your Room

Have students respond to the story by putting themselves in a picture like Harold did. Gather the photographs of the students, purple crayon, glue stick, poster paper, and scissors.

1. Remind students that in some pictures in *A Picture for Harold's Room*, Harold looks like he is a giant, while in others he looks like he's tiny. It all depends on the size of the things he draws around himself.

2. Tell students they need to decide if they want to be a giant or a tiny person in their picture.

▸ If they want to be a giant, the things they draw need to be very small.
▸ If they want to be tiny, the things they draw need to be very big.

3. Have students cut out a picture of themselves from a photograph and glue it to the poster paper.

4. Tell them to draw a scene like Harold does, using a purple crayon. Remind students to draw things either much bigger or smaller than their image from the photograph.

5. Have students describe their drawings when they are done.

6. Have them explain why they chose to be either a giant or a tiny person, and what they would see in the picture if they were really that big or small.

7. Find a good place to display students' drawings.

Objectives
- Respond to text through art, writing, and/or drama.
- Demonstrate understanding through drawing, discussion, drama, and/or writing.

Introduce *And I Mean It, Stanley*

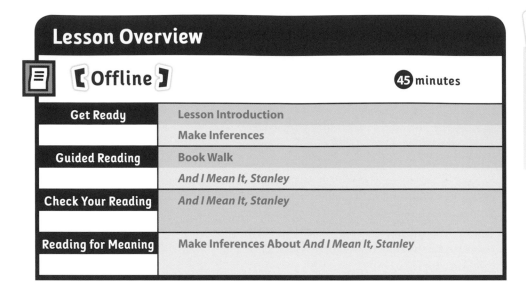

Lesson Overview

[Offline]		**45** minutes
Get Ready	Lesson Introduction	
	Make Inferences	
Guided Reading	Book Walk	
	And I Mean It, Stanley	
Check Your Reading	*And I Mean It, Stanley*	
Reading for Meaning	Make Inferences About *And I Mean It, Stanley*	

Advance Preparation

Preview pages LC 289 and 290 in *K¹² Language Arts Activity Book* to prepare the materials for the Guided Reading.

Big Ideas

▸ Good readers use prior knowledge and text clues to infer or draw conclusions about what is implied but not directly stated in text.

▸ To understand and interpret a story, readers need to understand and describe characters and what they do.

▸ Guided reading provides support to early readers as they practice and apply the reading strategies of proficient readers.

Materials

Supplied

● *And I Mean It, Stanley* by Crosby Bonsall

● *K¹² Language Arts Activity Book*, pp. LC 289–290

Story Synopsis

A girl makes a "truly great thing" in an attempt to coax Stanley out from behind a fence.

Keywords

character – a person or animal in a story

infer – to use clues and what you already know to make a guess

inference – a guess you make using the clues in a text and what you already know

problem – an issue a character must solve in a story

solution – how a character solves a problem in a story

 **45** minutes

Work **together** with students to complete Get Ready, Guided Reading, Check Your Reading, and Reading for Meaning activities.

Get Ready ....

Lesson Introduction

Prepare students for reading and discussing *And I Mean It, Stanley*.

1. Tell students that they will read *And I Mean It, Stanley*, a story about a character who makes a "truly great thing."

2. Explain that before they read the story, you will help them get ready by discussing how we make inferences to understand characters, their actions, and the problems they solve.

Objectives
- Make inferences based on text and/or prior knowledge.
- Support inferences with evidence from text and/or prior knowledge.

Make Inferences

Reinforce how we make inferences.

1. Remind students that good readers are able to **infer**, or figure out, things in a story that the author does not say directly. Readers must think about clues in the story and pictures, along with their own prior knowledge, to make inferences.

2. Have students think about the book *A Picture for Harold's Room*.

   ▸ In one part of the story, Harold draws a daisy and a bird. Then, he falls into a mouse hole. What can we infer about the mouse hole? How did it get there? Harold drew it.   What clue in the story helped you figure that out? Students might say that Harold draws everything else in the story, so they figured out that he drew the mouse hole, too.

   ▸ Harold falls into the mouse hole, and then in the next picture he is standing next to the mouse hole. How do you think Harold got out of the mouse hole? He climbed out.   How did you make that inference? How did you use your prior knowledge? Students might say that one way to get out of a hole is to climb out of it, so that's what Harold must have done.

   ▸ Harold creates a whole world with his purple crayon. What can we infer about Harold based on this? What is Harold like? Possible answers: He's creative; he's imaginative; he loves to draw.

3. Tell students that they will be able to make many inferences about the main character in *And I Mean It, Stanley*.

Guided Reading

Book Walk

Prepare students for reading by taking them on a Book Walk of *And I Mean It, Stanley*. Scan the beginning of the book together and ask students to make predictions about the story. Answers to questions may vary.

1. Have students look at the **picture on the cover**.

2. Have students read aloud the **book title** and the **name of the author**.

   ▸ What do you think the book might be about?

3. Have students look at the **pictures up to page 14** of the book.

   ▸ Do you have a close friend whom you like to play with? What do you do when that friend doesn't want to play when you want to play?

   ▸ Have you ever built something big, such as a fort made out of boxes? What did you make? What did you use to make it?

And I Mean It, Stanley

Guide students through a preview of the story to prepare them for reading on their own. Gather the Reading Aid on pages LC 289 and 290 in *K¹² Language Arts Activity Book*.

1. Have students sit next to you so that they can see the pictures and words while you introduce and discuss the story.

2. Tell students that you will preview the story to prepare them to read aloud the story to you.

3. Refer to the Reading Aid.

Reading Aid Tear out the Reading Aid for this reading selection. Follow the instructions for folding the page and then use the page as a guide as you preview the selection with students.

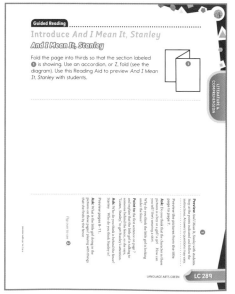
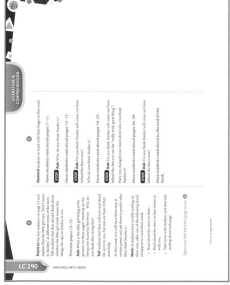

Check Your Reading

And I Mean It, Stanley

Check students' comprehension of *And I Mean It, Stanley*.

1. Have students retell *And I Mean It, Stanley* in their own words to develop grammar, vocabulary, comprehension, and fluency skills.

2. Ask students the following questions.

   ▶ Who is the main character in the story? the girl
   ▶ Where is Stanley? behind the fence
   ▶ Who is Stanley? a dog
   ▶ Why does the girl tell Stanley she can play by herself? because Stanley is behind the fence and won't come out to play with her
   ▶ How does the girl play by herself? She starts to make a great thing.
   ▶ What does the girl use to make the great thing? things that have been thrown out; things she finds next to the fence

 TIP If students have trouble responding to a question, help them locate the answer in the text or pictures.

Objectives

- Retell or dramatize a story.
- Identify the main character(s).
- Answer questions requiring literal recall of details.

Reading for Meaning

Make Inferences About *And I Mean It, Stanley*

Check students' ability to make inferences.

▶ What is the girl's problem in the story? Stanley is behind the fence and won't come out to play.

▶ What does she do to try to solve her problem? She starts to make something that she says is truly great.

▶ The girl says over and over that she doesn't want Stanley to look at what she is making. Do you think she really means it? No   Why do you think she says it if she doesn't mean it? Guide students to recognize that she's trying to get Stanley interested in what she's doing so he'll come out and play with her.

▶ What is the great thing that the girl makes? What does it look like to you? Answers will vary.   Do you like it? Do you think it's great? Answers will vary.

▶ When do we find out who Stanley is? at the end of the story   How do we find out that Stanley is a dog, from the words of the story or from the picture? from the picture

▶ Who did you think Stanley might be while you were reading the story? Answers will vary.   Were you surprised to find out that Stanley is a dog? Answers will vary.

Objectives

- Identify details that explain characters' actions and feelings.
- Describe character(s).
- Make inferences based on text and/or prior knowledge.
- Describe story structure elements—problem and solution.

Explore *And I Mean It, Stanley*

Lesson Overview

Offline — 45 minutes

Get Ready	Lesson Introduction
	Use Pictures to Understand a Story
Guided Reading	Book Walk
	And I Mean It, Stanley
Reading for Meaning	Use Pictures to Understand *And I Mean It, Stanley*
Making Connections	Retell *And I Mean It, Stanley*

Big Ideas

▸ An awareness of story structure elements (setting, characters, plot) provides readers a foundation for constructing meaning when reading new stories and writing their own stories.

▸ Repeated rereading leads to increased fluency.

▸ Comprehension requires the reader to self-monitor understanding.

Materials

Supplied

- *And I Mean It, Stanley* by Crosby Bonsall
- Story Card G

Also Needed

- crayons
- paper, construction
- scissors, round-end safety

Keywords

retelling – using your own words to tell a story that you have listened to or read

self-monitor – to notice if you do or do not understand what you are reading

 **45 minutes**

Work **together** with students to complete Get Ready, Guided Reading, Reading for Meaning, and Making Connections activities.

Get Ready

Lesson Introduction

Prepare students for reading and discussing *And I Mean It, Stanley*.

1. Tell students that they will reread *And I Mean It, Stanley*.

2. Explain that before they reread the story, you will help them get ready by discussing how pictures can give additional information about a story and help readers better understand a story.

Objectives
- Use illustrations to aid understanding of text.
- Identify setting.
- Describe people, places, things, locations, actions, events, and/or feelings.

Use Pictures to Understand a Story

Reinforce how pictures can help readers better understand a story. Gather Story Card G.

1. Remind students that good readers use the pictures to better understand and figure out additional information about a story.

2. Have students study the picture on the story card.

   ▸ Where are the people? What is the setting? in a house; in a living room How can you tell? What clues are in the picture? Possible answers: couches and chairs; bookcase; coffee and dining tables; potted plant; pets; painting on the wall

   ▸ What do you think is happening in this picture? What are the people doing? Possible answers: They're at a party; they're celebrating a holiday.

   ▸ How can you tell it's a party or a celebration? What clues are in the picture? Possible answers: balloons; presents; cupcakes and cookies

   ▸ Who do you think the people are? a family and friends   What personal experience helped you figure this out? Students might say they know that when people have a party at their house, they usually invite their family members and friends.

   ▸ How do you think the people feel? happy   What clues in the picture make you think this? the people are laughing and smiling

Guided Reading

Book Walk

Prepare students for reading by taking them on a Book Walk of *And I Mean It, Stanley*. Scan the book together to revisit the characters and events.

1. Have students read aloud the **book title** and the **name of the author**.

2. Look through the book. Have students review the **pictures**.

   ▸ Who is Stanley? a dog
   ▸ What do you think Stanley is doing behind the fence? Answers will vary.
   ▸ Why does the little girl want Stanley to come out from behind the fence? to play with her

Objectives

- Activate prior knowledge by previewing text and/or discussing topic.
- Read and listen to a variety of texts for information and pleasure independently or as part of a group.
- Read aloud grade-level text with appropriate expression, accuracy, and rate.

And I Mean It, Stanley

It's time to reread the story aloud.

1. Tell students that *And I Mean It, Stanley* should now be familiar to them because they have read it before.

2. Explain that they will reread the story aloud to you, but you are there if they need help.

3. If students have trouble reading on their own, offer one of the following levels of support to meet their needs.

   ▸ Read aloud the story to them.
   ▸ Read aloud the story as they chime in with you.
   ▸ Take turns with students and alternate reading aloud each page.

4. Remind students to track with their finger as they read.

5. Tell students that as they read, they should look at the pictures to help them figure out additional information about the story.

Reading for Meaning

Use Pictures to Understand *And I Mean It, Stanley*

Check students' ability to interpret pictures to better understand a story.

▸ Where does the story take place? outside, next to a fence   Does the story say that, or did you figure it out from the pictures? figured it out from the pictures
▸ What is the weather like? Is it warm or cool outside? It's cool.   What clues in the pictures help you figure this out? The girl is wearing a sweater, tights, boots, and a cap.
▸ The author never mentions the main character by name. How do the pictures help you figure out that the main character is a girl? She's wearing a dress under the sweater.
▸ Point to the picture on page 12. The girl tells Stanley that she is having fun. Does it look like she is having fun? No   What clues in the picture help you figure this out? Possible answers: The girl isn't smiling; the girl doesn't look like she's happy.

Objectives

- Use illustrations to aid understanding of text.
- Identify setting.
- Describe people, places, things, locations, actions, events, and/or feelings.

- Point to the picture on page 27. What items does the girl use to make the "great thing"? Possible answers: a hat; gloves; hangers; boxes; shoes; a fan; boards; a pail; a tub; a sock   Are these things old or new? How can you tell? They're old, because they have holes and cracks in them and she got them out of trash sitting by the fence.

- Point to the picture on pages 30 and 31. How does the girl feel when Stanley comes through the fence? surprised   What clue in the picture helps you figure this out? Possible answers: The look on the girl's face shows that she didn't know Stanley was about to come through the fence; Stanley knocks over the thing she made, which surprises her.

- How does the girl feel at the end of the story? happy   What clue in the picture helps you figure this out? She's smiling while Stanley licks her face.

Making Connections

Retell *And I Mean It, Stanley*

Check students' ability to self-monitor their understanding by retelling the story. Gather the construction paper, scissors, and crayons.

1. Remind students that **retelling** is a way to check that they understand a story they have read. When we retell a story, we use our own words to describe the characters and events in a story.

2. Have students fold the construction paper in half, lengthwise.

3. Have students position the paper so that the fold is along the top. Have them draw a simple wooden fence on the paper.

   - Have students look at the picture on page 7 if they need a visual reference to draw the fence.

4. Help them make two cuts in the fence near the bottom-center of the paper up to the fold, approximately four inches apart, forming a "gate" in the fence that opens by swinging up.

5. Have students draw Stanley "behind the fence," that is, on the half of the paper that is underneath the fence, just under the gate. Tell them to close the gate after they finish drawing the dog.

6. Ask students to retell the story, having them swing up the gate to show Stanley at the end. Possible retelling: A girl is talking to Stanley, who is behind a fence. She tells him she doesn't want to play with him and can play by herself. Then, she tells Stanley that she is making a great thing and that he can't look at it. When she's done building it, Stanley runs out from under the fence, knocks over the great thing, and licks the girl's face.

7. Ask the following questions. Answers to questions may vary.
   - Did your retelling include the characters?
   - Did you retell the events in the order that they happened?
   - Do you think you understand the story?
   - Was it easier to retell the story with or without the fence art?

TIP If students don't think they understand the story, reread the story aloud, pausing to let them ask questions as you read.

Objectives
- Respond to text through art, writing, and/or drama.
- Retell a story using various media.
- Self-monitor comprehension of text.

Explore *Harry and the Lady Next Door* (A)

Lesson Overview

 **[Offline]** 🕐 **45** minutes

Get Ready	Lesson Introduction
	Problem and Solution
	Words to Know
Guided Reading	Book Walk
	"The Party" and "Harry's First Try"
Check Your Reading	"The Party" and "Harry's First Try"
Reading for Meaning	Story Structure Elements in "The Party" and "Harry's First Try"
	Harry's Problem and Solution Chart

Advance Preparation

Before beginning the Guided Reading, read "The Party" and "Harry's First Try" to locate Words to Know in the text. Preview pages LC 291 and 292 in *K¹² Language Arts Activity Book* to prepare the materials for the Guided Reading.

Big Ideas

▶ Good readers use prior knowledge and text clues to infer or draw conclusions about what is implied but not directly stated in text.

▶ To understand and interpret a story, readers need to understand and describe characters and what they do.

▶ An awareness of story structure elements (setting, characters, plot) provides readers a foundation for constructing meaning when reading new stories and writing their own stories.

▶ Guided reading provides support to early readers as they practice and apply the reading strategies of proficient readers.

[Materials]

Supplied

- *Harry and the Lady Next Door* by Gene Zion
- *K¹² Language Arts Activity Book*, pp. LC 291–293

Story Synopses

Harry has a big problem in "The Party." The lady next door sings so high and loud that it makes his ears hurt. Harry makes an attempt to solve his problem in "Harry's First Try."

Keywords

infer – to use clues and what you already know to make a guess

inference – a guess you make using the clues in a text and what you already know

problem– an issue a character must solve in a story

solution – how a character solves a problem in a story

story structure elements – components of a story; they include character, setting, plot, problem, and solution

Offline **45** minutes

Work **together** with students to complete Get Ready, Guided Reading, Check Your Reading, and Reading for Meaning activities.

Get Ready

Lesson Introduction

Prepare students for reading and discussing *Harry and the Lady Next Door*, a book about a dog with a troublesome neighbor.

1. Tell students that they will read the chapters "The Party" and "Harry's First Try" in *Harry and the Lady Next Door*.

2. Explain that before they read the chapters, you will get ready by discussing how characters solve problems.

Objectives

- Describe story structure elements—problem and solution.
- Build vocabulary through listening, reading, and discussion.
- Use new vocabulary in written and spoken sentences.

Problem and Solution

Reinforce how characters in stories solve problems.

1. Remind students that a **character** is a person or animal in a story and that characters often have problems to solve. Sometimes, characters have to try more than one thing to solve their problem.

2. Have students think about the story *A Picture for Harold's Room*.

   ▸ What is Harold's problem at the beginning of the story? He wants a picture for his room.
   ▸ What does Harold do to solve his problem? He draws a picture with a purple crayon.
   ▸ Near the end of *A Picture for Harold's Room*, Harold isn't sure how to get back home. How does he solve this problem? He crosses out the picture.

3. Tell students that the main character in *Harry and the Lady Next Door* has a big problem. As they read the chapters, they will learn all the ways that Harry tries to solve his big problem.

Words to Know

Before reading "The Party" and "Harry's First Try," go over Words to Know with students.

1. Read aloud each word or phrase and have students repeat it.

2. Ask students if they know what each word or phrase means.

   ▸ If students know a word's or phrase's meaning, have them define it and use it in a sentence.
   ▸ If students don't know a word's or phrase's meaning, read them the definition and discuss the word or phrase with them.

howl – to make a long, loud, sad sound, like a dog or wolf
round up – to bring together

Guided Reading

Book Walk

Prepare students for reading by taking them on a Book Walk of *Harry and the Lady Next Door*. Scan the chapters "The Party" and "Harry's First Try" together and ask students to make predictions. Answers to questions may vary.

1. Have students look at the picture on the cover. Point to and read aloud the **book title**.

   ▸ What do you think the book might be about?

2. Read aloud the **names of the author and the illustrator**.

3. Read aloud the chapter titles on the **Contents** page. Explain to students that in this lesson, they will read "The Party" and "Harry's First Try."

4. Have students look at the **pictures in "The Party" and "Harry's First Try."**

   ▸ What is a neighbor? someone who lives next door to you or in your neighborhood
   ▸ Do you have a favorite neighbor? Why do you like this neighbor?
   ▸ Do you like to listen to people sing?
   ▸ What kind of singing do you like?

Objectives

- Make predictions based on text, illustrations, and/or prior knowledge.
- Activate prior knowledge by previewing text and/or discussing topic.
- Read and listen to a variety of texts for information and pleasure independently or as part of a group.
- Read aloud grade-level text with appropriate expression, accuracy, and rate.

"The Party" and "Harry's First Try"

Guide students through a preview of the chapters to prepare them for reading on their own. Gather the Reading Aid on pages LC 291 and 292 in *K¹² Language Arts Activity Book*.

1. Have students sit next to you so that they can see the pictures and words while you introduce and discuss the chapters.

2. Tell students that you will preview the chapters to prepare them to read aloud the chapters to you.

3. Refer to the Reading Aid.

Reading Aid Tear out the Reading Aid for this reading selection. Follow the instructions for folding the page and then use the page as a guide as you preview the selection with students.

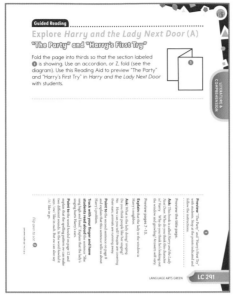

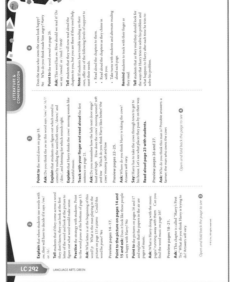

Check Your Reading

"The Party" and "Harry's First Try"

Check students' comprehension of "The Party" and "Harry's First Try."

1. Have students retell "The Party" in their own words to develop grammar, vocabulary, comprehension, and fluency skills.

2. Ask students the following questions about "The Party."

   ▶ What does Harry look like? a white dog with black spots
   ▶ How does Harry feel about all but one of his neighbors? He loves them.
   ▶ Why doesn't Harry love the lady next door? Her singing makes his ears hurt.
   ▶ What do the peanut man and the firemen do when they hear the lady next door sing? They put their hands over their ears.
   ▶ What does the lady next door do when Harry and his friends howl under her window? She keeps on singing; she sings higher and louder than ever.
   ▶ What does the lady next door do when she comes to the party at Harry's house? She starts to sing.

3. Have students retell "Harry's First Try" in their own words to develop grammar, vocabulary, comprehension, and fluency skills.

Objectives

- Retell or dramatize a story.
- Describe character(s).
- Identify details that explain characters' actions and feelings.
- Answer questions requiring literal recall of details.

4. Ask students the following questions about "Harry's First Try."

 ▶ Where is Harry at the beginning of "Harry's First Try"? a quiet spot; outside

 ▶ What sound wakes up Harry? cows mooing

 ▶ What does Harry think about the cows mooing? Possible answers: He thinks it is beautiful music; he thinks it is soft and low.

 ▶ Why does Harry round up the cows? to take them to his family's house

 ▶ How do the cows get back home to their farm? Their owner comes to get them.

TIP If students have trouble responding to a question, help them locate the answer in the text or pictures.

Reading for Meaning

Story Structure Elements in "The Party" and "Harry's First Try"
Check students' understanding of story structure elements in *Harry and the Lady Next Door*.

1. Ask the following questions about "The Party."

 ▶ Where does "The Party" take place? What is the setting? outside the house of the lady next door; inside Harry's family's house

 ▶ What does Harry want to do when the lady next door starts to sing at the party? bite her leg   Why does he want to bite her leg? to get her to stop singing; because she makes his ears hurt   What does he do instead? He bites the leg of the piano.

 ▶ Why do some people whisper "The lucky dog!" when Harry gets sent out of the room? They don't want to hear the lady next door sing either.

 ▶ What happens when Harry pushes the door open to leave the room? The wind blows in and blows the music pages off the piano.

 ▶ What does Harry do with the pages of music that he catches? He runs away with them.   Why do you think he runs away with them? Guide students to understand Harry probably thinks that will stop the lady next door from singing.

2. Ask the following questions about "Harry's First Try."

 ▶ Where does "Harry's First Try" take place? What is the setting? outside at a quiet spot by cows

 ▶ What does Harry wish when he hears the cows mooing? that the lady next door would sing like the cows

 ▶ What idea does Harry get? to take the cows back home so the lady next door can hear them moo   How does Harry get the cows to move? He rounds them up by barking at them.

 ▶ Do the mooing cows solve Harry's problem? No   Why not? The lady next door sings higher and louder than ever.

 ▶ How does the farmer look at the end of the chapter? mad; angry

 ▶ Why is the farmer mad? Harry moved his cows, and now he has to drive them back home.

 ▶ Why do you think Harry has to sleep in the doghouse at the end of "Harry's First Try"? Possible answers: He's being punished for moving the cows; his family isn't happy with him; the owner of the cows is mad at him.

Objectives
- Identify setting.
- Identify details that explain characters' actions and feelings.
- Make inferences based on text and/or prior knowledge.
- Describe story structure elements—problem and solution.
- Use illustrations to aid understanding of text.
- Demonstrate understanding through graphic organizers.

Harry's Problem and Solution Chart

Check students' understanding of how Harry tries to solve the problem of the lady next door. Turn to page LC 293 in *K¹² Language Arts Activity Book*.

1. Explain to students that they will keep track of what happens in the book *Harry and the Lady Next Door* by using the chart on the Activity Book page.

2. Tell students to write Harry's problem on the lines provided. Possible answers: The lady next door sings too high and loud; the lady next door makes Harry's ears hurt when she sings.

3. Help students read aloud the "How does Harry try to solve the problem?" heading in the first column of the chart.

4. Tell students to draw or help them write what Harry does to solve the problem in "Harry's First Try." Harry has cows moo outside the window.

5. Have students write *Yes* or *No* in the "Does it work?" column to tell whether Harry's idea works. No

6. Tell students to draw or help them write what happens to Harry at the end of "Harry's First Try" in the "What happens to Harry?" column. Harry has to sleep in the doghouse.

   ▶ Why does Harry have to sleep in the doghouse at the end of "Harry's First Try"? Possible answers: He's being punished; he's in trouble; his family is angry because he brought the cows.   Do you think Harry deserves to be put in the doghouse? Why or why not? Answers will vary.

TIP Keep the Activity Book page in a safe place so that students can add to the chart after each chapter.

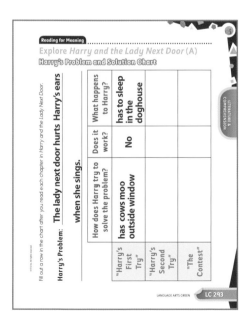

Explore *Harry and the Lady Next Door* (B)

Lesson Overview

[Offline]   **45** minutes

Get Ready	Lesson Introduction
	Plot Structure and Problem and Solution
	Words to Know
Guided Reading	Book Walk
	"Harry's Second Try"
Check Your Reading	"Harry's Second Try"
Reading for Meaning	Story Structure Elements in "Harry's Second Try"
	Harry's Problem and Solution Chart

Advance Preparation

Before beginning the Guided Reading, read "Harry's Second Try" to locate Words to Know in the text. Preview pages LC 295 and 296 in *K¹² Language Arts Activity Book* to prepare the materials for the Guided Reading. Gather the partially completed chart on page LC 293 (Harry's Problem and Solution Chart) for Reading for Meaning.

Big Ideas

- ▶ Good readers use prior knowledge and text clues to infer or draw conclusions about what is implied but not directly stated in text.
- ▶ To understand and interpret a story, readers need to understand and describe characters and what they do.
- ▶ An awareness of story structure elements (setting, characters, plot) provides readers a foundation for constructing meaning when reading new stories and writing their own stories.
- ▶ Guided reading provides support to early readers as they practice and apply the reading strategies of proficient readers.

[Materials]

Supplied

- *Harry and the Lady Next Door* by Gene Zion
- *K¹² Language Arts Activity Book*, pp. LC 293, 295–296

Story Synopsis

In "Harry's Second Try," Harry sees another opportunity to quiet his noisy neighbor. Will it solve his problem or land him in the doghouse . . . *again*?

Keywords

infer – to use clues and what you already know to make a guess

inference – a guess you make using the clues in a text and what you already know

plot – what happens in a story

problem – an issue a character must solve in a story

solution – how a character solves a problem in a story

story structure elements – components of a story; they include character, setting, plot, problem, and solution

 **45 minutes**

Work **together** with students to complete Get Ready, Guided Reading, Check Your Reading, and Reading for Meaning activities.

Get Ready ....

Lesson Introduction

Prepare students for reading and discussing "Harry's Second Try" in *Harry and the Lady Next Door*.

1. Tell students that they will read "Harry's Second Try" in *Harry and the Lady Next Door*.

2. Explain that before they read the chapter, you will get ready by discussing how problem and solution fit into the plot of a story.

Objectives

- Describe story structure elements—problem and solution.
- Build vocabulary through listening, reading, and discussion.
- Use new vocabulary in written and spoken sentences.

Plot Structure and Problem and Solution

Explore where problem and solution fit into the plot of a story.

1. Remind students that every story has a **plot**, the important things that happen in a story. The plot of a story has a beginning, middle, and end.

2. Explain that at the **beginning** of a story, we usually meet the characters and learn their problem. For example, we meet the character Harry in "The Party," which is the first chapter of *Harry and the Lady Next Door* and the beginning of the story. After we meet Harry, we learn about his problem.

   ▶ What is Harry's problem with the lady next door? Her singing hurts his ears.

3. Tell students that in the **middle** of a story, characters usually try to solve their problem. For example, Harry tries to solve his problem with the lady next door by running away with the music pages at the end of "The Party."

   ▶ How does Harry try to solve his problem in the chapter "Harry's First Try?" He rounds up mooing cows and brings them to his house.

4. Explain that characters often must try more than one thing to solve their problem, which is what happens to Harry. The mooing cows don't solve his problem, so he'll have to try something else if he wants to fix it.

5. Tell students that the middle of a story is usually the longest part of a story and can be told over many chapters of a book.

6. Explain that at the **end** of a story, we usually learn how characters solve their problem.

7. Remind students that if they know how the **problem and solution** fit into the order of a story, they will know what to expect as they read. This will help them better understand and remember a story.

Words to Know

Before reading "Harry's Second Try," go over Words to Know with students.

1. Read aloud the word and have students repeat it.

2. Ask students if they know what the word means.

   ▸ If students know the word's meaning, have them define it and use it in a sentence.
   ▸ If students don't know the word's meaning, read them the definition and discuss the word with them.

horn – a musical instrument made of metal that you blow air through, such as a trumpet or tuba

Guided Reading

Book Walk

Prepare students for reading by taking them on a Book Walk of *Harry and the Lady Next Door*. Scan the chapter "Harry's Second Try" together and ask students to make predictions.

1. Have students read aloud the **book title**.

2. Read aloud the **names of the author and the illustrator**.

3. Have students read aloud the chapter titles on the **Contents** page. Explain to students that in this lesson, they will read "Harry's Second Try."

4. Have students look at the **pictures in "Harry's Second Try."** Answers to questions may vary.

   ▸ What do you think might happen in this chapter?
   ▸ Have you ever heard someone play a horn, such as a trumpet or tuba?
   ▸ What did it sound like? Was it loud? Did you like the sound?

> **Objectives**
> - Make predictions based on text, illustrations, and/or prior knowledge.
> - Activate prior knowledge by previewing text and/or discussing topic.
> - Read and listen to a variety of texts for information and pleasure independently or as part of a group.
> - Read aloud grade-level text with appropriate expression, accuracy, and rate.

"Harry's Second Try"

Guide students through a preview of the chapter to prepare them for reading on their own. Gather the Reading Aid on pages LC 295 and 296 in *K¹² Language Arts Activity Book*.

1. Have students sit next to you so that they can see the pictures and words while you introduce and discuss the chapter.

2. Tell students that you will preview the chapter to prepare them to read aloud to you.

3. Refer to the Reading Aid.

Reading Aid Tear out the Reading Aid for this reading selection. Follow the instructions for folding the page and then use the page as a guide as you preview the selection with students.

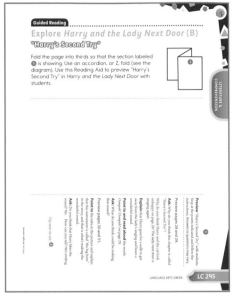
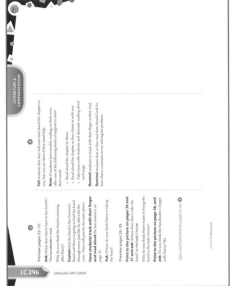

Check Your Reading

"Harry's Second Try"

Check students' comprehension of "Harry's Second Try."

1. Have students retell "Harry's Second Try" in their own words to develop grammar, vocabulary, comprehension, and fluency skills.

2. Ask students the following questions.

   ▶ When does "Harry's Second Try" take place? the next day; the day after Harry brings cows to the house

   ▶ Why does Harry go for a long walk at the beginning of "Harry's Second Try"? The lady next door is singing again.

   ▶ What makes the soft and low sound that Harry hears while he's taking a walk? the big horn in the Firemen's Band

   ▶ What does Harry wish when he hears the big horn playing? that the lady next door would sing like the big horn

   ▶ What does the bandleader throw into the air while he leads the band? a stick

   ▶ What does the band do when Harry runs away with the bandleader's stick? They run after him.

TIP If students have trouble responding to a question, help them locate the answer in the text or pictures.

Objectives
- Retell or dramatize a story.
- Answer questions requiring literal recall of details.

Reading for Meaning

Story Structure Elements in "Harry's Second Try"
Check students' ability to identify story structure elements.

- ▶ Who are the characters in "Harry's Second Try?" Harry; the Firemen's Band and bandleader; the lady next door; Harry's family
- ▶ Why does Harry catch the bandleader's stick and run away with it? He wants the band to follow him.
- ▶ How does the bandleader try to solve his problem of Harry's taking his stick? He runs after Harry.
- ▶ Why does Harry run to the lady's house while the band is running after him? so the lady can hear the band play the soft and low music; so the lady will sing soft and low like the horn
- ▶ Look at the picture of the bandleader at the end of the chapter. How do you think he feels? mad; angry
- ▶ Why is the bandleader mad at the end of the chapter? Possible answers: because Harry took his stick; because Harry took his band to the lady's house; because he had to run after Harry
- ▶ Why does Harry have to spend the night in the doghouse again? Possible answers: because he shouldn't have taken the bandleader's stick and led the band to the lady's house; because he's in trouble; because he's being punished
- ▶ Look at the last picture in the chapter. How do you think Harry feels when he's in the doghouse? sad; not happy   Why do you think Harry feels that way? Possible answers: He doesn't want to sleep in the doghouse; the lady next door is still making his ears hurt.

Objectives
- Identify character(s).
- Describe character(s).
- Identify details that explain characters' actions and feelings.
- Make inferences based on text and/or prior knowledge.
- Use illustrations to aid understanding of text.
- Identify important details and/or events of a story.
- Describe story structure elements—problem and solution.

Harry's Problem and Solution Chart
Check students' understanding of how Harry tries to solve the problem of the lady next door. Gather page LC 293 in *K¹² Language Arts Activity Book*.

1. Remind students that they will keep track of what happens in the book *Harry and the Lady Next Door* by using the chart on the Activity Book page.

2. Have students review Harry's problem, the column headings, and the answers they added to the chart for "Harry's First Try."

3. Have them add answers for "Harry's Second Try."

4. Help students read aloud the "How does Harry try to solve the problem?" heading in the first column of the chart.

5. Tell students to draw or help them write what Harry does to solve the problem in "Harry's Second Try." Harry leads band to the lady's house.

6. Have students write *Yes* or *No* in the "Does it work?" column to tell whether Harry's idea works. No

7. Tell students to draw or help them write what happens to Harry at the end of "Harry's Second Try" in the "What happens to Harry?" column. Harry has to sleep in the doghouse.

   ▸ Why does Harry have to sleep in the doghouse at the end of "Harry's Second Try"? Possible answers: Harry shouldn't have led the band to the house of the lady next door; it was wrong to take the bandleader's stick away from him; Harry's in trouble; Harry's being punished.
   Do you think Harry deserves to be put in the doghouse? Why or why not? Answers will vary.

TIP Keep the Activity Book page in a safe place so that students can add to the chart after each chapter.

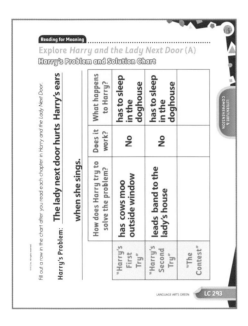

Explore *Harry and the Lady Next Door* (C)

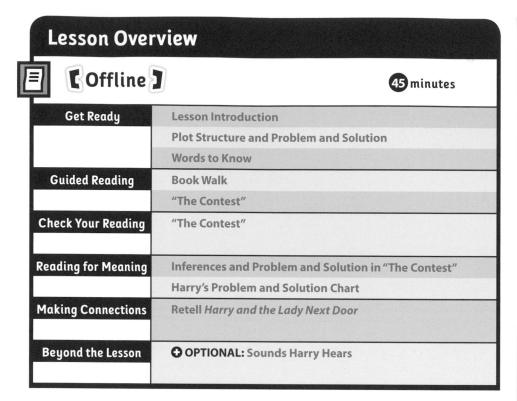

Lesson Overview

[Offline] — **45** minutes

Get Ready	Lesson Introduction
	Plot Structure and Problem and Solution
	Words to Know
Guided Reading	Book Walk
	"The Contest"
Check Your Reading	"The Contest"
Reading for Meaning	Inferences and Problem and Solution in "The Contest"
	Harry's Problem and Solution Chart
Making Connections	Retell *Harry and the Lady Next Door*
Beyond the Lesson	⊕ OPTIONAL: Sounds Harry Hears

Advance Preparation

Before beginning the Guided Reading, read "The Contest" to locate Words to Know in the text. Preview pages LC 297 and 298 in *K¹² Language Arts Activity Book* to prepare the materials for the Guided Reading. Gather the partially completed chart on page LC 293 (Harry's Problem and Solution Chart) for Reading for Meaning.

Big Ideas

- ▶ Good readers use prior knowledge and text clues to infer or draw conclusions about what is implied but not directly stated in text.
- ▶ To understand and interpret a story, readers need to understand and describe characters and what they do.
- ▶ Comprehension requires an understanding of story structure.
- ▶ Guided reading provides support to early readers as they practice and apply the reading strategies of proficient readers.
- ▶ Comprehension requires the reader to self-monitor understanding.

[Materials]

Supplied
- *Harry and the Lady Next Door* by Gene Zion
- *K¹² Language Arts Activity Book*, pp. LC 293, 297–298

Story Synopsis

In "The Contest," Harry comes up with another scheme to rid himself of his loud neighbor. Will it work, or will Harry end up in the doghouse yet again?

Keywords

infer – to use clues and what you already know to make a guess

inference – a guess you make using the clues in a text and what you already know

problem – an issue a character must solve in a story

self-monitor – to notice if you do or do not understand what you are reading

solution – how a character solves a problem in a story

 **Offline** **45** minutes

Work **together** with students to complete Get Ready, Guided Reading, Check Your Reading, Reading for Meaning, Making Connections, and Beyond the Lesson activities.

Get Ready

Lesson Introduction
Prepare students for reading and discussing the chapter "The Contest" in *Harry and the Lady Next Door*.

1. Tell students that they will read "The Contest" in *Harry and the Lady Next Door*.

2. Explain that before they read the chapter, you will get ready by reviewing how problem and solution fit into the plot of a story.

Plot Structure and Problem and Solution
Reinforce how a story has a beginning, middle, and end.

1. Remind students that every story has a beginning, middle, and end. We should expect certain things to happen in each part of the story.

   ‣ In which part of the story do we meet the characters and learn about their problem—the beginning, middle, or end? the beginning
   ‣ In which part of the story do the characters try to solve their problem? the middle

2. Remind students that sometimes characters need to try more than one thing to solve their problem. This is what happens to Harry. When the mooing cows don't solve his problem, he tries something else.

   ‣ How does Harry try to solve his problem after the mooing cows don't work? He leads the Firemen's Band to the lady's house so she can hear the low sound of the horn.

3. Tell students that the middle of a story is usually the longest part of a story and can be told over more than one chapter of a book.

   ‣ In which part of the story do characters usually solve their problem—the beginning, middle, or end? the end

4. Remind students that if they know how the **problem and solution** fit into the order of a story, they will know what to expect as they read. Because "The Contest" is the last chapter of *Harry and the Lady Next Door*, we should expect that Harry will solve his problem in this chapter.

Objectives
- Identify organizational structures of text.
- Describe story structure elements—problem and solution.
- Build vocabulary through listening, reading, and discussion.
- Use new vocabulary in written and spoken sentences.

Words to Know

Before reading "The Contest," go over Words to Know with students.

1. Read aloud each word and have students repeat it.

2. Ask students if they know what each word means.

   ▸ If students know a word's meaning, have them define it and use it in a sentence.
   ▸ If students don't know a word's meaning, read them the definition and discuss the word with them.

bandstand – an outdoor stage
contest – a sport or game that people try to win to get a prize
fuss – noisy confusion
note – a single sound in music
shriek – to scream

Guided Reading

Book Walk

Prepare students for reading by taking them on a Book Walk of *Harry and the Lady Next Door*. Scan the chapter "The Contest" together and ask students to make predictions.

1. Have students read aloud the **book title** and the **names of the author and the illustrator**.

2. Have students read aloud the chapter titles on the **Contents** page. Explain to students that in this lesson, they will read "The Contest."

3. Have students look at the **pictures in "The Contest."** Answers to questions may vary.

   ▸ What do you think might happen in this chapter?
   ▸ Have you ever been to a concert at a park or some other place?
   ▸ What kind of music did you hear? Did you like it?

Objectives

- Make predictions based on text, illustrations, and/or prior knowledge.
- Activate prior knowledge by previewing text and/or discussing topic.
- Read and listen to a variety of texts for information and pleasure independently or as part of a group.
- Read aloud grade-level text with appropriate expression, accuracy, and rate.

"The Contest"

Guide students through a preview of the chapter to prepare them for reading on their own. Gather the Reading Aid on pages LC 297 and 298 in *K¹² Language Arts Activity Book*.

1. Have students sit next to you so that they can see the pictures and words while you introduce and discuss the chapter.

2. Tell students that you will preview the chapter to prepare them to read aloud the story to you.

3. Refer to the Reading Aid.

Reading Aid Tear out the Reading Aid for this reading selection. Follow the instructions for folding the page and then use the page as a guide as you preview the selection with students.

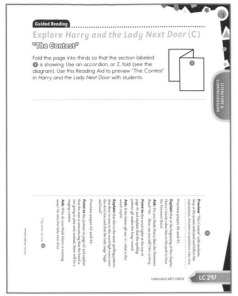

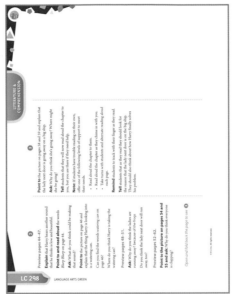

Check Your Reading

"The Contest"

Check students' comprehension of "The Contest."

1. Have students retell "The Contest" in their own words to develop grammar, vocabulary, comprehension, and fluency skills.

2. Ask students the following questions.

   ▶ When does the beginning of "The Contest" take place? at night; a few nights after Harry led the band to the house of the lady next door

   ▶ Where does the beginning of "The Contest" take place? at the park

   ▶ Why does Harry's family go to the park? to hear the Firemen's Band

   ▶ Why doesn't the Firemen's Band play music? The big horn player is out of breath.

   ▶ What happens instead of the band playing? a singing contest

TIP If students have trouble responding to a question, help them locate the answer in the text or pictures.

> **Objectives**
> - Retell or dramatize a story.
> - Identify setting.
> - Answer questions requiring literal recall of details.

Reading for Meaning

Inferences and Problem and Solution in "The Contest"

Check students' ability to make inferences and identify problem and solution.

▸ The Firemen's Band doesn't play music, because the big horn player is out of breath. Why is he out of breath? because he ran after Harry when Harry took the bandleader's stick

▸ Why does Harry run away from the park at the beginning of "The Contest"? The lady next door is going to sing in a contest.

▸ Harry hears a "blurp" sound coming from a watering can. What is making the "blurp" sound? frogs

▸ What does Harry think about the "blurp" sound? It's low and beautiful.

▸ Where does Harry put the watering can? on the stage; on the floor behind the lady next door

▸ Do you think Harry knows what will happen when he puts the watering can on the stage? Why or why not? Answers will vary.

▸ Why does the lady next door win First Prize at the singing contest? Possible answers: because she didn't run off the stage when the frogs jumped out of the watering can; because she was brave; because she was the only one left in the contest once the other ladies ran away

▸ How does the singing contest solve Harry's problem? The lady next door leaves to study music for a long time in a faraway country because she won the contest.

▸ How do you think Harry feels when the lady next door leaves on the ship? happy   Why do you think he wags his tail when the family says "good-bye" to the lady next door? because he won't have to listen to her sing anymore; because his ears won't hurt anymore

▸ Where does Harry sleep at the end of the story? in his family's house

---

Harry's Problem and Solution Chart

Check students' understanding of how Harry tries to solve the problem of the lady next door. Gather page LC 293 in *K¹² Language Arts Activity Book*.

1. Remind students that they have been keeping track of what happens in the book *Harry and the Lady Next Door* by using the chart on the Activity Book page. In this lesson, they will finish filling out the chart and review all their answers.

2. Have students review Harry's problem, the column headings, and the answers they added to the chart for "Harry's First Try" and "Harry's Second Try."

3. Have them add answers for "The Contest."

4. Help students read aloud the "How does Harry try to solve the problem?" heading in the first column of the chart.

5. Tell students to draw or help them write what Harry does to solve the problem in "The Contest." Harry puts a watering can with frogs in it on the stage.

6. Have students write *Yes* or *No* in the "Does it work?" column to tell whether Harry's idea works. Yes   Why does it work? What happens when Harry puts the watering can on the stage? Frogs jump out, and the other ladies run away. So the lady next door wins the singing contest and moves away.

7. Tell students to draw or help them write what happens to Harry at the end of "The Contest" in the "What happens to Harry?" column. Possible answers: Harry gets to go see the lady leave on the ship; he gets to sleep in his family's house.

   ▸ Why does Harry get to sleep on a pillow in his family's house at the end of "The Contest"? Possible answers: He got the lady next door to move away; he's not getting in trouble anymore, because the lady moved away.

8. Point to the picture of Harry in the doghouse at the end of "Harry's Second Try" and the picture of Harry on the last page of the book.

   ▸ Do you think Harry likes sleeping in his family's house better than sleeping in the doghouse? Yes   How do you know? What clues are in the pictures? Harry looks happy when he's sleeping on the pillow, and he looks sad when he's in the doghouse.

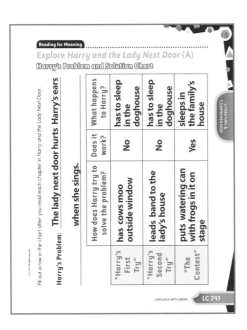

Making Connections

Retell *Harry and the Lady Next Door*

Check students' ability to self-monitor their understanding by retelling the story. Gather page LC 293 in *K¹² Language Arts Activity Book.*

1. Have students use Harry's Problem and Solution Chart to help them retell the story and how Harry solves his problem.

2. Retell the beginning of the story, the part in which we meet Harry and find out about his problem. Possible answer: Harry is a dog who has a neighbor who sings high and loud. Her singing makes Harry's ears hurt. One day, Harry's family has a party, and the lady next door comes and starts to sing. Harry wants to bite her leg, but he bites the leg of the piano instead. Harry has to leave the party, and when he opens the door, the music papers start to fly away. Harry runs away with some of the music.

3. Retell the middle of the story, the part in which Harry tries to solve his problem. Remind students that the middle is usually the longest part of a story. Possible answer: Harry hears cows mooing and gets an idea. He rounds up the cows and leads them home, where the lady next door is still singing. But, she sings higher and louder than ever. Harry gets in trouble for taking the cows and has to sleep in the doghouse. The next day, Harry hears a horn making a wonderful "oompah" sound and he gets another idea. He grabs the bandleader's stick and leads the Firemen's Band to the house of the lady next door. But, she sings even higher and louder than ever. Harry gets in trouble for taking the bandleader's stick and has to sleep in the doghouse again.

4. Retell the end of the story, the part in which Harry solves his problem. Possible answer: Harry's family takes him to hear the Firemen's Band, but there is a singing contest instead. Harry runs away when he sees that the lady next door is in the contest. Harry hears "blurp" coming from inside a watering can, and he gets an idea. He takes the watering can to the concert and puts it on the stage. Everyone in the contest except the lady next door runs away when two frogs jump out of the watering can. The lady next door wins the contest and leaves for another country on a big ship. Harry's problem is solved.

Objectives
- Retell the beginning, middle, and end of a story.
- Describe story structure elements—problem and solution.
- Self-monitor comprehension of text.

5. Ask the following questions. Answers to questions may vary.

   ▸ Did your retelling include the characters?
   ▸ Did you retell the events in the order that they happened?
   ▸ Did your retelling include all the ways Harry tried to solve his problem?
   ▸ Did Harry's Problem and Solution Chart help with your retelling?
   ▸ Do you think you understand the story?

TIP If students don't think they understand the story, read aloud any parts of the story that students are unclear about, pausing to let them ask questions as you read.

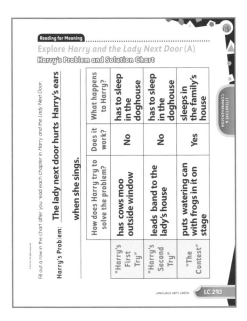

Beyond the Lesson

✚ OPTIONAL: Sounds Harry Hears

This activity is OPTIONAL. It is intended for students who have extra time and would enjoy acting out the sounds that Harry hears. Feel free to skip this activity.

1. Remind students that Harry hears many sounds in *Harry and the Lady Next Door.* Tell them that they will identify what kind of sounds they are and then act them out.

2. Help students scan the book for sounds.

3. Have them stop to act out a sound each time they find one. Sounds in book-order are

   ▸ lady singing
   ▸ peanut whistle
   ▸ fire engine siren
   ▸ cats singing
   ▸ dogs howling
   ▸ cows mooing
   ▸ big horn "oompah"
   ▸ frogs "blurping"
   ▸ Harry barking
   ▸ ship's foghorn

Objectives
- Demonstrate understanding through drawing, discussion, drama, and/or writing.

Explore Poems About Creative Characters

Lesson Overview

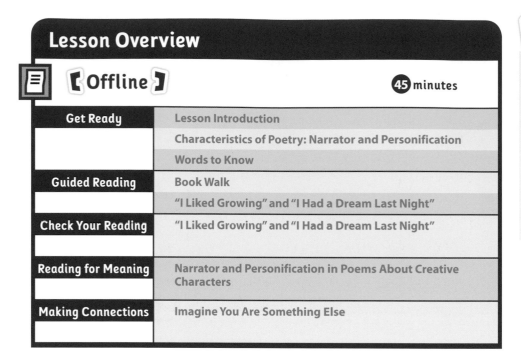

	Offline	**45** minutes
Get Ready	Lesson Introduction	
	Characteristics of Poetry: Narrator and Personification	
	Words to Know	
Guided Reading	Book Walk	
	"I Liked Growing" and "I Had a Dream Last Night"	
Check Your Reading	"I Liked Growing" and "I Had a Dream Last Night"	
Reading for Meaning	Narrator and Personification in Poems About Creative Characters	
Making Connections	Imagine You Are Something Else	

Advance Preparation

Before beginning the Guided Reading, read "I Liked Growing" and "I Had a Dream Last Night" to locate Words to Know in the text. Preview pages LC 299 and 300 in *K¹² Language Arts Activity Book* to prepare the materials for the Guided Reading.

Big Ideas

▸ Good readers use prior knowledge and text clues to infer or draw conclusions about what is implied but not directly stated in text.
▸ Guided reading provides support to early readers as they practice and apply the reading strategies of proficient readers.

Materials

Supplied

● *Ready . . . Set . . . Read!: The Beginning Reader's Treasury*, pp. 96, 102–103
● *K¹² Language Arts Activity Book*, pp. LC 299–301

Also Needed

● crayons (optional)

Poetry Synopses

In "I Liked Growing," a fruit describes its life. In "I Had a Dream Last Night," a character must make a perplexing and possibly difficult decision.

Keywords

first-person point of view – the telling of a story by a character in that story, using pronouns such as *I*, *me*, and *we*

infer – to use clues and what you already know to make a guess

inference – a guess you make using the clues in a text and what you already know

narrator – the teller of a story

personification – giving human qualities to something that is not human; for example: "The thunder shouted from the clouds."

[Offline] 45 minutes

Work **together** with students to complete Get Ready, Guided Reading, Check Your Reading, Reading for Meaning, and Making Connections activities.

Get Ready ....

Lesson Introduction
Prepare students for reading and discussing "I Liked Growing" and "I Had a Dream Last Night."

1. Tell students that they are going to read "I Liked Growing," a poem about an unnamed character, and "I Had a Dream Last Night," a poem about a character that has an unusual dream.

2. Explain that before they read the poems, you will get ready by discussing

   ▸ The narrator of a poem and how we sometimes must infer who the narrator is
   ▸ How a poet can make nonhuman things sound like they are human

---

Characteristics of Poetry: Narrator and Personification
Explore the narrator and personification in poetry.

1. Explain to students that the person speaking in a poem is called the **narrator**. When we hear words such as I, *my*, and *me* in a poem, we know that the narrator is a character in the poem.

2. Tell students that when a character in a poem is the narrator, we get to hear his or her thoughts and see the world through his or her eyes.

3. Explain that sometimes the narrator doesn't say who he or she is directly, so the reader has to **infer** it.

4. Tell students to listen carefully to what you are about to say so they can figure out, or infer, who is speaking.
   Say: Sarah sat down in the special chair. I told her to open her mouth wide, and then I looked inside. I didn't find one cavity!

   ▸ Who is speaking? a dentist
   ▸ What word tells you a dentist is talking? I

5. Remind students that sometimes a poet makes animals or objects sound like they are human. Poets do this to help readers imagine an interesting picture.

Objectives
- Identify the narrator of a text.
- Identify first-person point of view.
- Make inferences based on text and/or prior knowledge.
- Build vocabulary through listening, reading, and discussion.
- Use new vocabulary in written and spoken sentences.

6. Have students practice identifying the narrator and how a poet can make something sound like it is human. **Read aloud** the following poem:

I spent the morning collecting pollen, buzzing from flower to flower.
Then, I flew home to make some honey, sweating hour after hour.
Finally, I finished and got to wash off all that sticky stuff in the shower.

   ▸ Who is the narrator? Who is speaking? a bee   Can a bee really speak? No
   ▸ What word tells you a bee is speaking? I
   ▸ How does the rhyme make the bee sound like it is human? Possible answers: The bee speaks; the bee sweats and takes a shower.

7. Remind students that when they read poetry, they should think about who the narrator of the poem is.

Words to Know
Before reading "I Liked Growing" and "I Had a Dream Last Night," go over Words to Know with students.

1. Read aloud each word and have students repeat it.

2. Ask students if they know what each word means.

   ▸ If students know a word's meaning, have them define it and use it in a sentence.
   ▸ If students don't know a word's meaning, read them the definition and discuss the word with them.

sprang – the past tense of the verb *spring*, which means "to jump up quickly"
stout – having a thick body

Guided Reading

Book Walk
Prepare students by taking them on a Book Walk of "I Liked Growing" and "I Had a Dream Last Night." Scan the poems together and ask students to make predictions. Answers to questions may vary.

1. Turn to the **table of contents** in *Ready . . . Set . . . Read!* Help students find "I Liked Growing" and turn to that page.

2. Point to and read aloud the **poem title** and the **name of the poet**.

3. Have students look at the **pictures**.

   ▸ What do you think the poem might be about?
   ▸ What do you think it would be like to be a plant growing in a garden? What do you think you would see and feel?

Objectives
- Make predictions based on text, illustrations, and/or prior knowledge.
- Activate prior knowledge by previewing text and/or discussing topic.
- Read and discuss poetry.
- Read aloud grade-level text with appropriate expression, accuracy, and rate.

4. Return to the **table of contents**. Help students find "I Had a Dream Last Night" and turn to that page.

5. Point to and read aloud the **poem title** and the **name of the poet**.

6. Have students look at the **pictures**.

   ▸ What do you think the poem might be about?
   ▸ Have you ever had a strange or funny dream?
   ▸ What happened in your dream? What made it strange or funny?

"I Liked Growing" and "I Had a Dream Last Night"

Guide students through a preview of the poems to prepare them for reading on their own. Gather the Reading Aid on pages LC 299 and 300 in *K¹² Language Arts Activity Book*.

1. Have students sit next to you so that they can see the pictures and words while you introduce and discuss the poems.

2. Tell students that you will preview the poems to prepare them to read aloud to you.

3. Refer to the Reading Aid.

Reading Aid Tear out the Reading Aid for this reading selection. Follow the instructions for folding the page and then use the page as a guide as you preview the selection with students.

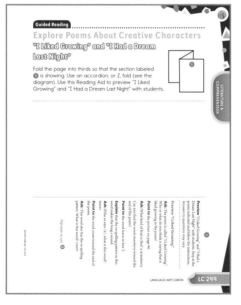

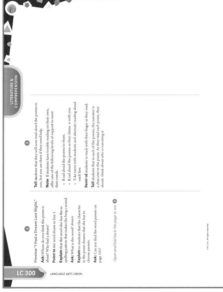

Check Your Reading

"I Liked Growing" and "I Had a Dream Last Night."
Check students' comprehension of "I Liked Growing" and "I Had a Dream Last Night."

1. Have students retell "I Liked Growing" in their own words to develop grammar, vocabulary, comprehension, and fluency skills.

2. Ask students the following questions about "I Liked Growing."

   ▶ Where is the narrator at the beginning of the poem? in a garden; outside
   ▶ What does the narrator look like? warm, red, round
   ▶ Where is the narrator at the end of the poem? in ice cream

3. Have students retell "I Had a Dream Last Night" in their own words to develop grammar, vocabulary, comprehension, and fluency skills.

4. Ask students the following questions about "I Had a Dream Last Night."

   ▶ Where does "I Had a Dream Last Night" take place? Where is the narrator? in bed
   ▶ What does the narrator of the poem have to do in her dream? pick a mother and father
   ▶ What do the people in the dream look like? short and tall, thin and stout

 TIP If students have trouble responding to a question, help them locate the answer in the text or pictures.

> **Objectives**
> • Retell or dramatize a story.
> • Answer questions requiring literal recall of details.

Reading for Meaning

Narrator and Personification in Poems About Creative Characters
Check students' ability to identify personification and make inferences about a poem's narrator.

1. Ask the following questions about "I Liked Growing."

   ▶ Who or what is the character in "I Liked Growing"? a strawberry
   How do you know? What words in the poem help you infer that the character is a strawberry? The character in the poem says it's round and red, and it gets put in ice cream. The pictures show strawberries, too.
   ▶ Who or what is speaking in "I Liked Growing"? the strawberry
   How do you know? What words in the poem help you figure out that the strawberry is speaking? The strawberry uses the words *I* and *me*.
   ▶ How does the poet make the strawberry sound like it's a person? Possible answers: The strawberry is speaking; the strawberry says that it's freezing.
   ▶ How does the strawberry feel at the beginning of the poem? happy
   What does the strawberry say that tells you it's happy? It says it likes growing; it says growing is nice; it feels warm.
   ▶ What does the strawberry mean when it says "Then someone dropped me in a pot"? Someone picked the strawberry and put it in a pot.
   ▶ How do you think the freezing strawberry feels? Do you think the strawberry is happy to be in ice cream? Why or why not? Answers will vary.

> **Objectives**
> • Make inferences based on text and/or prior knowledge.
> • Identify the narrator of a text.
> • Identify first-person point of view.
> • Identify literary devices: personification and/or simile.
> • Identify details that explain characters' actions and feelings.
> • Use illustrations to aid understanding of text.

2. Ask the following questions about "I Had a Dream Last Night."

   ▸ Who is the narrator? Who is speaking in the poem? the person in the poem who has the dream   How do you know? What does the narrator say that helps you figure out who is speaking in the poem? The narrator uses words such as *I* and *me*.

   ▸ Is the narrator a girl or boy? a girl   How do you know? The pictures show the person in bed having the dream is a girl.

   ▸ Point to the picture on page 102. Who are all the people in the bubble above the girl's head? the people she can choose to be her parents How does the picture help you better understand what the narrator sees in her dream? It shows the people she could choose to be her mother and father, and what kind of jobs they have.

   ▸ How does the narrator feel during her dream? confused; She doesn't know what to do.

   ▸ How is the narrator's problem solved? She wakes up.

   ▸ Why do you think the girl says she would choose the parents she already has? Answers may vary; guide students to understand that the girl is happy with the parents she has and wouldn't trade them, even if she could.

   ▸ Point to the picture on page 103. How does this picture help you better understand how the narrator feels? The picture shows how happy her parents are to see her when she wakes up, and she is smiling.

   ▸ How does the narrator feel at the end of the poem? Possible answers: surprised; glad; happy

Making Connections

✏️ **Imagine You Are Something Else**

Help students make a connection to text. Turn page LC 301 in *K¹² Language Arts Activity Book*.

1. Remind students that the poem "I Liked Growing" describes what it's like to be a strawberry.

2. Tell students that they are going to imagine what it's like to be something that is not human and then write a description about it.

   ▸ If students need a prompt, suggest they imagine what it's like to be one of the following objects: a flower, a tree, the sun, a squirrel, a rock, the ocean, or the wind.

   ▸ Note that students do not need to attempt to make their descriptions rhyme.

3. **Read aloud** the following example if students need additional prompting to help them imagine what it would be like if they were something else.

   I Am a Bird
   by A. Student

   I live in a big tree.
   I have two red wings.
   I like to fly in the sky.
   I am glad that I am a bird!

⭐ **Objectives**

- Make connections with text: text-to-text, text-to-self, text-to-world.
- Demonstrate understanding through drawing, discussion, drama, and/or writing.

4. Have students write the title, their name, and their descriptions on the lines.

   ▶ If students are not ready to write on their own, allow them to dictate their answers to you.

5. Have students read aloud their descriptions.

6. Ask the following questions. Answers to questions may vary.

   ▶ Why did you imagine that you were this thing?
   ▶ What kinds of things do you think you would see if you were this thing?
   ▶ How do you think you would feel if you were this thing?
   ▶ What kinds of sounds do you think you'd hear around you?
   ▶ If you were this thing, how do you think your life would be different from the way it is now?

7. If time allows, have students draw a picture of what they described.

Reward: Add a sticker for this unit on the My Accomplishments chart to mark successful completion of the unit.

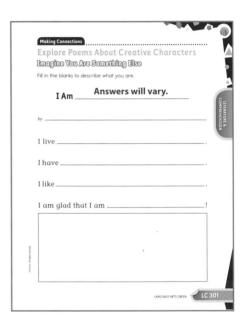

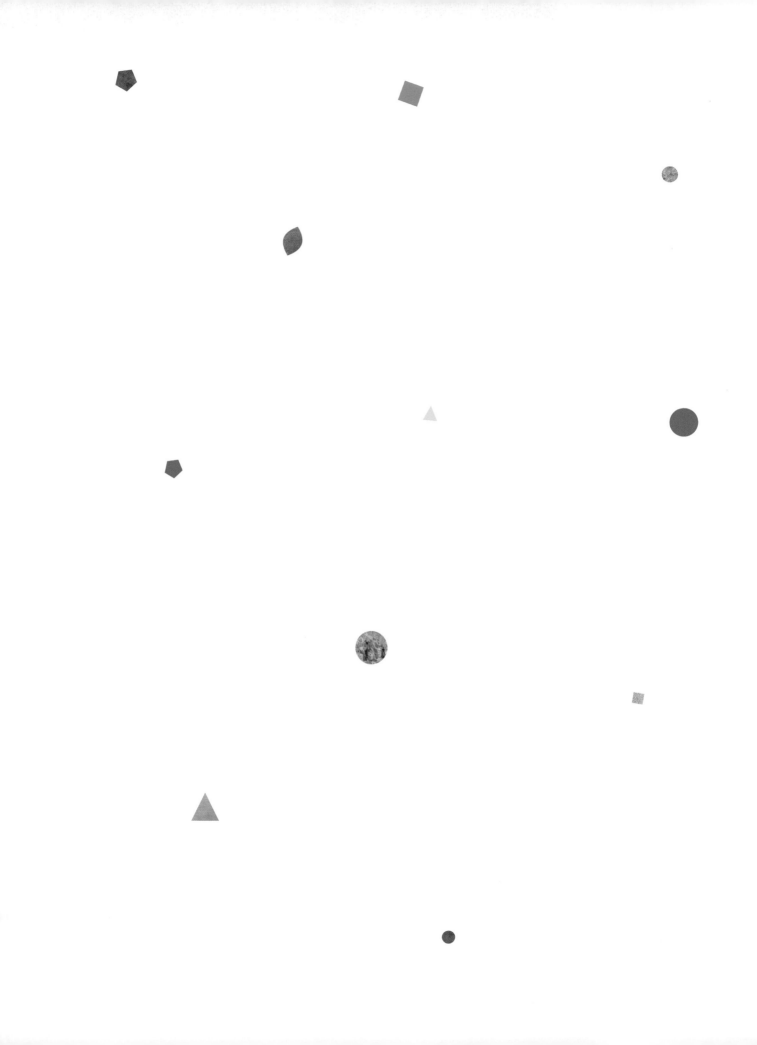

Animals: Fact and Fiction

Unit Focus

Students will read and explore the differences between fiction and nonfiction texts about animals. This unit follows the guided-reading instructional approach (see the instructional approaches to reading in the introductory lesson for this program). In this unit, students will:

▸ Explore rhyme, rhythm, repetition, and patterns in poetry.
▸ Explore story structure elements—characters, setting, plot, and problem and solution.
▸ Explore how writers make nonhuman things sound like they are human.
▸ Check that they understand what they've read by retelling.
▸ Identify sequence in fiction and nonfiction texts.
▸ Review what happens in the beginning, middle, and end of a story.
▸ Draw and support conclusions.
▸ Identify the content and features of informational text.

Unit Plan   〔Offline〕

		🕘 45 minutes a day
Lesson 1	Explore "Over in the Meadow"	
Lesson 2	Explore *Little Bear* (A)	
Lesson 3	Explore *Little Bear* (B)	
Lesson 4	Explore *Little Bear* (C)	
Lesson 5	Introduce "Little Bears"	
Lesson 6	Explore "Little Bears"	
Lesson 7	Explore *Owl at Home* (A)	
Lesson 8	Explore *Owl at Home* (B)	
Lesson 9	Explore *Owl at Home* (C)	
Lesson 10	Introduce "Hunters of the Night"	
Lesson 11	Explore "Hunters of the Night"	
Lesson 12	Your Choice	

"Over in the Meadow"

Lesson Overview

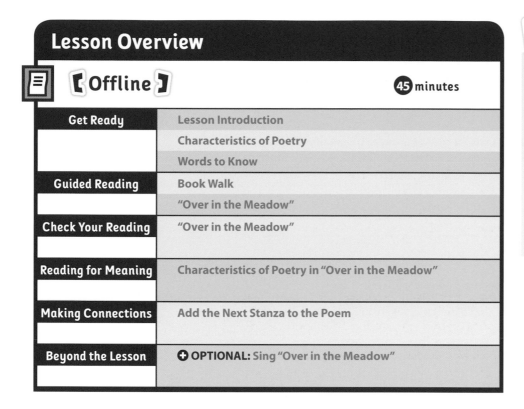

[Offline]   **45** minutes

Get Ready	Lesson Introduction
	Characteristics of Poetry
	Words to Know
Guided Reading	Book Walk
	"Over in the Meadow"
Check Your Reading	"Over in the Meadow"
Reading for Meaning	Characteristics of Poetry in "Over in the Meadow"
Making Connections	Add the Next Stanza to the Poem
Beyond the Lesson	⊕ OPTIONAL: Sing "Over in the Meadow"

Advance Preparation

Before beginning the Guided Reading, read "Over in the Meadow" to locate Words to Know in the text. Preview pages LC 303 and 304 in *K¹² Language Arts Activity Book* to prepare the materials for the Guided Reading.

Big Ideas

- ► Exposing readers to a wide variety of genres provides them with a wide range of background knowledge and increases their vocabulary.
- ► Poems are different from prose in structure and content. They are generally organized in lines and often contain rhymes.
- ► Guided reading provides support to early readers as they practice and apply the reading strategies of proficient readers.

[Materials]

Supplied

- "Over in the Meadow," *K¹² Classics for Young Readers, Volume A,* pp. 216–219
- *K¹² Language Arts Activity Book,* pp. LC 303–306

Also Needed

- crayons (optional)

Poetry Synopsis

"Over in the Meadow" is an upbeat counting poem about mother animals who tell their babies to do various activities, such as "Sing!" or "Swim!" As the poem progresses, the number of baby animals increases by one in each stanza.

Keywords

genre – a category for classifying literary works

[Offline] **45** minutes

Work **together** with students to complete Get Ready, Guided Reading, Check Your Reading, Reading for Meaning, Making Connections, and Beyond the Lesson activities.

Get Ready

Lesson Introduction

Prepare students for reading and discussing "Over in the Meadow."

1. Tell students that they will read "Over in the Meadow," a poem about baby animals and their mothers.

2. Explain that before they read the poem, you will get ready by reviewing characteristics of poetry.

Objectives
- Identify characteristics of different genres.
- Identify structure of poems and poetic elements: rhyme, rhythm, repetition, and/or alliteration.

Characteristics of Poetry

Review characteristics of poetry and discuss patterns in poems.

1. Remind students that poetry is a kind of writing. There are certain things that tell us that we are reading a poem.

2. Have students name things that would tell them they are reading a poem.

3. Ask the following questions if students need prompting.

   ▸ Is a poem written in paragraphs or stanzas? stanzas
   ▸ Do some poems have words that rhyme? Yes
   ▸ Do some poems have rhythm, or a beat, that you can clap to? Yes
   ▸ What do the words of a poem help you see in your head? pictures
   ▸ Do poets sometimes repeat words or lines in poems? Yes

4. Tell students that some poems follow a pattern. A poem has a pattern when parts of the poem follow a particular arrangement of words. Read the following poem aloud as an example of a poem with a pattern.

   One, two, buckle my shoe;
   Three, four, shut the door;
   Five, six, pick up sticks;
   Seven, eight, lay them straight.

   Say: There are three things that make up the pattern in this poem.

   ▸ Each line begins with two numbers.
   ▸ The words after the numbers describe something you do.
   ▸ The second number in each line rhymes with the last word in the line.

5. Tell students to listen for the pattern as you reread the poem.

   ▸ Did you notice the numbers go from one to eight, in order?
     Answers will vary.

6. Tell students that a poem that has numbers in order is called a counting poem. These kinds of poems can help young readers practice counting numbers. The poem they are going to read is a counting poem.

Words to Know

Before reading "Over in the Meadow," go over Words to Know with students.

1. Read aloud each word and have students repeat it.

2. Ask students if they know what each word means.

   ▸ If students know a word's meaning, have them define it and use it in a sentence.
   ▸ If students don't know a word's meaning, read them the definition and discuss the word with them.

burrow – to dig
muskrat – a small animal with brown fur, webbed feet, and a long, hairless tail; muskrats live in and around water
reed – a kind of tall grass
snug – cozy; tight

Guided Reading

Book Walk

Prepare students by taking them on a Book Walk of "Over in the Meadow." Scan the poem together and ask students to make predictions about the poem.

1. Turn to the **table of contents** in *K¹² Classics for Young Readers, Volume A*. Help students find "Over in the Meadow" and turn to that page.

2. Point to and read aloud the **poem title**. Answers to questions may vary.

   ▸ What do you think the poem might be about?
   ▸ Have you ever walked in a meadow? What kinds of animals did you see? What were the animals doing? What sounds did the animals make?

Objectives

- Make predictions based on text, illustrations, and/or prior knowledge.
- Activate prior knowledge by previewing text and/or discussing topic.
- Build vocabulary through listening, reading, and discussion.
- Use new vocabulary in written and spoken sentences.
- Read and discuss poetry.
- Read aloud grade-level text with appropriate expression, accuracy, and rate.

"Over in the Meadow"

Guide students through a preview of the poem to prepare them for reading on their own. Gather the Reading Aid on pages LC 303 and 304 in *K¹² Language Arts Activity Book*.

1. Have students sit next to you, so they can see the picture and words while you introduce and discuss the poem.

2. Tell students that you will preview the poem to prepare them to read aloud the poem to you.

3. Refer to the Reading Aid.

Reading Aid Tear out the Reading Aid for this reading selection. Follow the instructions for folding the page, and then use the page as a guide as you preview the selection with students.

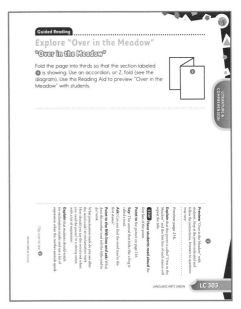
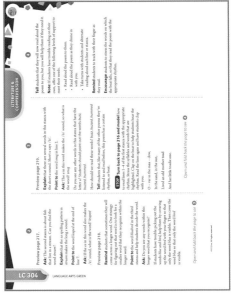

Check Your Reading

"Over in the Meadow"

Check students' comprehension of "Over in the Meadow."

1. Have students retell "Over in the Meadow" **while acting out the physical motions of each animal in each stanza**.

2. Ask students the following questions.

   ▸ Where does the poem take place? in a meadow
   ▸ How many babies does the mother fish have? two
   ▸ Where do the mother bluebird and her little bluebirds live? in a hole in a tree
   ▸ What does the mother honeybee tell her little honeybees to do? buzz

TIP If students have trouble responding to a question, help them locate the answer in the text or pictures.

Objectives
- Retell or dramatize a story.
- Identify setting.
- Answer questions requiring literal recall of details.

Reading for Meaning

Characteristics of Poetry in "Over in the Meadow"
Check students' ability to recognize rhyme, repetition, and pattern in "Over in the Meadow."

▸ What line is repeated at the beginning of each stanza? *Over in the meadow*

▸ Read aloud the first four lines of the poem. What word rhymes with *sun*? *one*

▸ Read aloud the first four lines in the third stanza of the poem. What two words rhyme? *tree* and *three*

▸ Read aloud the first four lines in the fifth stanza of the poem. What two words rhyme? *beehive* and *five*

▸ The first stanza in the poem is about a mother toad and her one baby toad. Who is the mother in the second stanza? a fish   How many babies does the mother fish have? two

▸ The third stanza in the poem is about a mother bluebird and her three baby bluebirds. Who is the mother in the fourth stanza? a muskrat   How many babies does the mother muskrat have? four

▸ Who is the mother in the fifth stanza? a honeybee   How many babies does the mother honeybee have? five

▸ What is the pattern in the poem? What do you notice about the number of babies a mother has in each stanza? Each stanza has one more baby than the stanza before it.

▸ How many babies do you think there would be if there were another stanza in the poem? six   Why would you expect six babies in the next stanza? because the number six comes after the number five, and there is always one more baby in the next stanza

Objectives
- Identify structure of poems and poetic elements: rhyme, rhythm, repetition, and/or alliteration.

Making Connections

 Add the Next Stanza to the Poem
Check students' understanding of the pattern in "Over in the Meadow." Turn to pages LC 305 and 306 in *K¹² Language Arts Activity Book.*

1. Tell students they are going to write the next stanza in "Over in the Meadow."

2. Open *K¹² Classics for Young Readers, Volume A,* to page 216, so students can refer back to the poem.

3. Point to the pictures for each family grouping. Have students name the animal and count the babies in each picture, beginning with the toads.

   ▸ If we add a new stanza, how many babies should there be in that stanza? six

4. Read aloud each line in the stanza on the Activity Book page, one at a time. Say the word *blank* each time there is an answer blank.

5. Have students write a word in each answer blank, following the same pattern as the other stanzas. For example, students should write an action word in the blank in line 5.

Objectives
- Respond to text through art, writing, and/or drama.
- Identify and replicate the pattern of a poem.

6. When you come to the fourth line, remind students that the stanza they're writing comes directly after the one with the mother honeybee and her five babies.

  ▸ What number should you write in the answer blank? six   Why? because there should be one more baby in the next stanza

7. Have students read aloud the poem when all answer blanks have been filled in.

8. Ask students the following questions.

  ▸ What animal did you choose to write about? Answers should match what students wrote on the Activity Book page.
  ▸ How many babies does this animal have? six
  ▸ What do you notice about the words *sticks* and *six*? They rhyme.
  ▸ In your stanza, where do the mother and her babies live? Answers should match what students wrote on the Activity Book page.
  ▸ What does the mother have her babies do? Answers should be an action word and should match what students wrote on the Activity Book page.
  ▸ How many babies would there be if you wrote the next stanza in the poem? seven   Why? because the number seven comes after the number six, and there is always one more baby in the next stanza

9. If time allows, have students draw a picture that shows the animals their stanza describes.

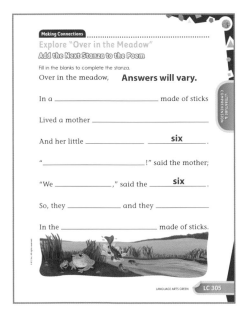

Beyond the Lesson •••

⊕ **OPTIONAL: Sing "Over in the Meadow"**

This activity is OPTIONAL. It is intended for students who have extra time and would enjoy learning how to sing the poem. Feel free to skip this activity.

1. Explain to students that the poem "Over in the Meadow" can be sung as a song.

2. Search the Internet for "Over in the Meadow song" to find an audio or video clip of the tune.

   ▸ A video of the song with the subtitled words and a "bouncing ball" can be found at www.barefootbooks.com/story/childrens-crafts-activities/over_in_the_meadow_video/.

3. Help students hear the rhythm of the song by clapping on the beat.

4. Ask the following questions. Answers to questions may vary.

   ▸ How is the song the same as the poem?
   ▸ How is the song different from the poem?
   ▸ Do you prefer singing or reading "Over in the Meadow"? Why?

Objectives

- Respond to poetic devices of rhyme, rhythm, and/or alliteration.
- Locate information using features of text and electronic media.
- Compare and contrast two texts on the same topic.

Explore *Little Bear* (A)

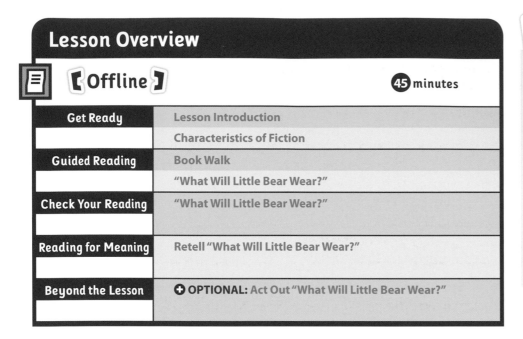

Lesson Overview

[Offline] **45** minutes

Get Ready	Lesson Introduction
	Characteristics of Fiction
Guided Reading	Book Walk
	"What Will Little Bear Wear?"
Check Your Reading	"What Will Little Bear Wear?"
Reading for Meaning	Retell "What Will Little Bear Wear?"
Beyond the Lesson	⊕ OPTIONAL: Act Out "What Will Little Bear Wear?"

Advance Preparation

Preview pages LC 307 and 308 in *K¹² Language Arts Activity Book* to prepare the
materials for the Guided Reading.

Big Ideas

- ▶ Exposing readers to a wide variety of genres provides them with a wide range
  of background knowledge and increases their vocabulary.
- ▶ An awareness of story structure elements (setting, characters, plot) provides
  readers a foundation for constructing meaning when reading new stories and
  writing their own stories.
- ▶ Comprehension requires the reader to self-monitor understanding.
- ▶ Guided reading provides support to early readers as they practice and apply the
  reading strategies of proficient readers.

[Materials]

Supplied

- *Little Bear* by Else
  Holmelund Minarik
- *K¹² Language Arts Activity
  Book*, pp. LC 307–311

Also Needed

- scissors, round-end safety
- household objects –
  children's winter clothing
  (hat, coat, warm pants)
  (optional)

Story Synopsis

Little Bear is cold, so Mother
Bear gives him a hat, then a
coat, and then a pair of snow
pants to put on. But Little
Bear is still cold. What else can
Mother Bear offer him?

Keywords

fiction – make-believe stories

genre – a category for
classifying literary works

retelling – using your own
words to tell a story that you
have listened to or read

self-monitor – to notice if
you do or do not understand
what you are reading

story structure elements –
components of a story; they
include character, setting,
plot, problem, and solution

[Offline] 45 minutes

Work **together** with students to complete Get Ready, Guided Reading, Check Your Reading, Reading for Meaning, and Beyond the Lesson activities.

Get Ready ·

Lesson Introduction
Prepare students for reading and discussing "What Will Little Bear Wear?"

1. Tell students that they will read "What Will Little Bear Wear?" in *Little Bear*.

2. Explain that before they read the story, you will get ready by reviewing characteristics of fiction.

Objectives
- Identify characteristics of different genres.

Characteristics of Fiction
Reinforce characteristics of fiction writing.

1. Remind students that **fiction** stories are made-up stories. All fiction stories have certain things in common—they all have story structure elements, such as characters and setting.

2. Ask students to name and explain story structure elements that make up a fiction story.

3. If students are unable to explain any **story structure elements**, review the following list with them.

   ▸ **Characters** – the people or animals in a story
   ▸ **Setting** – when and where a story takes place
   ▸ **Problem** – something that needs to be fixed by a character
   ▸ **Solution** – how a character fixes a problem
   ▸ **Plot** – the important events that happen in a story

4. Explain to students that, in addition to story structure elements, fiction books and stories might include any of the following text features.

   ▸ **Title** – the name of the book, story, or chapter
   ▸ **Author** – the person who wrote the book or story
   ▸ **Illustrator** – the person who drew the pictures
   ▸ **Table of contents** – a list of chapters in a book
   ▸ **Pictures** – the images on the pages
   ▸ **Bold and italic words** – words that have special emphasis

Guided Reading

Book Walk

Prepare students for reading by taking them on a Book Walk of *Little Bear*. Scan the story "What Will Little Bear Wear?" together and ask students to make predictions.

1. Have students read aloud the **book title**.

2. Read aloud the **names of the author and the illustrator**.

3. Have students read aloud the story titles on the **Contents** page. Explain to students that in this lesson, they will read "What Will Little Bear Wear?"

4. Have students look at the **pictures in "What Will Little Bear Wear?"** Answers to questions may vary.

   ▶ What do you think might happen in this story?
   ▶ Does it snow where you live?
   ▶ What do you wear when it's cold outside?

Objectives

- Make predictions based on text, illustrations, and/or prior knowledge.
- Activate prior knowledge by previewing text and/or discussing topic.
- Read and listen to a variety of texts for information and pleasure independently or as part of a group.
- Read aloud grade-level text with appropriate expression, accuracy, and rate.

"What Will Little Bear Wear?"

Guide students through a preview of the story to prepare them for reading on their own. Gather the Reading Aid on pages LC 307 and 308 in *K¹² Language Arts Activity Book*.

1. Have students sit next to you so that they can see the pictures and words while you introduce and discuss the story.

2. Tell students that you will preview the story to prepare them to read aloud to you.

3. Refer to the Reading Aid.

Reading Aid Tear out the Reading Aid for this reading selection. Follow the instructions for folding the page, and then use the page as a guide as you preview the selection with students.

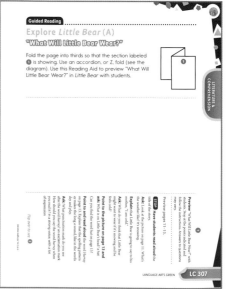

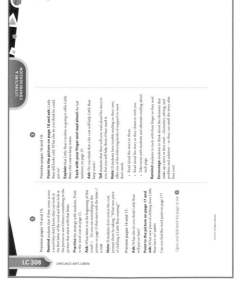

Check Your Reading

"What Will Little Bear Wear?"

Check students' comprehension of "What Will Little Bear Wear?"

1. Have students retell "What Will Little Bear Wear?" in their own words to develop grammar, vocabulary, comprehension, and fluency skills.

2. Ask students the following questions.

   ▸ Who are the characters in "What Will Little Bear Wear?" Little Bear; Mother Bear

   ▸ Where does the story take place? at Little Bear's house

   ▸ What is Little Bear's problem? He's cold.

   ▸ How does Mother Bear try to help Little Bear solve his problem? She gives him a hat, coat, and snow pants to put on.

   ▸ What does Little Bear tell his mother after he puts on the hat, coat, and snow pants? He's still cold.

   ▸ What does Mother Bear do when Little Bear says he'd like a fur coat? She takes off his hat, coat, and snow pants.

   ▸ Does this solve Little Bear's problem? Yes   How do you know? Little Bear isn't cold anymore.

TIP If students have trouble responding to a question, help them locate the answer in the text or pictures.

Objectives
- Retell or dramatize a story.
- Identify character(s).
- Identify setting.
- Describe story structure elements—problem and solution.
- Answer questions requiring literal recall of details.

Reading for Meaning

Retell "What Will Little Bear Wear?"

Check students' understanding of the order of events in "What Will Little Bear Wear?" Turn to pages LC 309–311 in *K¹² Language Arts Activity Book* and gather the scissors.

1. Remind students that Mother Bear gives Little Bear items of clothing in a particular order, or sequence, in the story.

2. Tell students they are going to retell the story using character cutouts.

3. Help students cut out the paper characters and clothes, and then bend the tabs back on the clothes.

4. Have them use the paper character cutouts and clothes to retell the story.

5. Tell students to

   ▸ Retell the story in sequence.

   ▸ Use time-order words, such as *first*, *next*, and *then*.

   ▸ Use the tabs to fasten the paper clothes to Little Bear.

Objectives
- Retell a story using various media.
- Retell a story naming plot, setting, character(s), problem, and solution.
- Use time-order words.
- Self-monitor comprehension of text.

6. Ask the following questions to have students self-monitor their comprehension of the story. Answers to questions may vary.

   ▸ Did your retelling include the characters?
   ▸ Did you put clothes on Little Bear in the same order as in the story?
   ▸ Did you use time order words, such as *first*, *next*, and *then*?
   ▸ Do you think you understand the story?
   ▸ Was it easier to retell the story with or without the paper cutouts?

(TIP) If students don't think they understand the story, reread the story aloud, pausing to let students ask questions as you read.

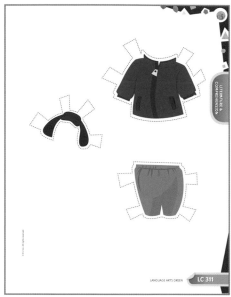

Beyond the Lesson

✚ OPTIONAL: Act Out "What Will Little Bear Wear?"

This activity is OPTIONAL. It is intended for students who have extra time and would enjoy acting out the story by putting on winter clothes. Feel free to skip this activity. Gather the children's winter clothes.

1. Tell students they are going to act out "What Will Little Bear Wear?"

2. Have two students volunteer to play Little Bear and Mother Bear.

   ▸ If there is only one student, you should play Mother Bear.

3. Have students act out the story with Mother Bear handing Little Bear the items of clothing in the same order as in the story, and then removing them when Little Bear says he's still cold after putting on the snow pants.

   ▸ In the story, Little Bear is wearing a fur coat after he takes off the hat, coat, and snow pants. Do you have a fur coat under your clothes? No
   ▸ In the story, Little Bear isn't cold when he realizes that he has a fur coat. Are you warmer or colder when you take off your winter clothes? colder

Objectives
• Respond to text through art, writing, and/or drama.

Explore *Little Bear* (B)

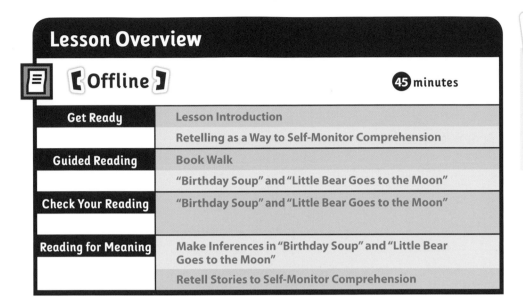

Lesson Overview

[Offline] ⏱ 45 minutes

Get Ready	Lesson Introduction
	Retelling as a Way to Self-Monitor Comprehension
Guided Reading	Book Walk
	"Birthday Soup" and "Little Bear Goes to the Moon"
Check Your Reading	"Birthday Soup" and "Little Bear Goes to the Moon"
Reading for Meaning	Make Inferences in "Birthday Soup" and "Little Bear Goes to the Moon"
	Retell Stories to Self-Monitor Comprehension

Advance Preparation

Preview pages LC 313 and 314 in *K¹² Language Arts Activity Book* to prepare the materials for the Guided Reading.

Big Ideas

▸ Exposing readers to a wide variety of genres provides them with a wide range of background knowledge and increases their vocabulary.

▸ An awareness of story structure elements (setting, characters, plot) provides readers a foundation for constructing meaning when reading new stories and writing their own stories.

▸ Good readers use prior knowledge and text clues to infer or draw conclusions about what is implied but not directly stated in text.

▸ Comprehension requires the reader to self-monitor understanding.

▸ Guided reading provides support to early readers as they practice and apply the reading strategies of proficient readers.

[Materials]

Supplied

- *Little Bear* by Else Holmelund Minarik
- *K¹² Language Arts Activity Book*, pp. LC 313–314

Story Synopses

In "Birthday Soup," it's Little Bear's birthday, but he can't find Mother Bear or his birthday cake. So he makes a pot of birthday soup for his friends to enjoy. In "Little Bear Goes to the Moon," Little Bear has a fun adventure by pretending to fly to the moon while wearing his new space helmet.

Keywords

fiction – make-believe stories

genre – a category for classifying literary works

infer – to use clues and what you already know to make a guess

inference – a guess you make using the clues in a text and what you already know

retelling – using your own words to tell a story that you have listened to or read

self-monitor – to notice if you do or do not understand what you are reading

story structure elements – components of a story; they include character, setting, plot, problem, and solution

[Offline] 45 minutes

Work **together** with students to complete Get Ready, Guided Reading, Check Your Reading, and Reading for Meaning activities.

Get Ready

Lesson Introduction

Prepare students for reading and discussing "Birthday Soup" and "Little Bear Goes to the Moon."

1. Tell students that they will read "Birthday Soup" and "Little Bear Goes to the Moon," the next two stories in the book *Little Bear*.

2. Explain that before they read the stories, you will get ready by reviewing how and why we retell stories.

> **Objectives**
> - Describe story structure elements—problem and solution.
> - Self-monitor comprehension of text.

Retelling as a Way to Self-Monitor Comprehension

Review how retelling a story is a way to self-monitor comprehension.

1. Remind students that **retelling means using your own words to tell a story** that you have listened to or read. Retelling a story is a good way to check that you understand what you have read.

2. Explain that when we retell a story, it is important to mention the characters, the setting, how characters solve problems, and important events that happen in the story.

3. Remind students that a story has a beginning, middle, and end, and that readers can expect to learn certain things in each part.

4. Explain that at the **beginning** of a story, we usually meet the characters and learn their **problem**. For example, in the book *Harry and the Lady Next Door*, we meet the character Harry in the first chapter "The Party," which is the beginning of the story. After we meet Harry, we learn about his problem. If necessary, have students refer back to the pictures in *Harry and the Lady Next Door* to refresh their memory.

   ▸ What is Harry's problem with the lady next door? Her singing hurts his ears.

5. Tell students that in the **middle** of a story, characters usually try to solve their problem. For example, Harry first tries to solve his problem with the lady next door by running away with her music pages.

   ▸ How does Harry try to solve his problem in "Harry's First Try"? He rounds up mooing cows and brings them to his house.

6. Explain that characters often must try more than one thing to solve their problem, which is what happens to Harry. The mooing cows don't solve his problem, so he has to try something else to fix it.

   ▶ What does Harry try next to solve his problem in "Harry's Second Try"? He leads the Fireman's Band to the house of the lady next door. Does this solve his problem? No

7. Explain that at the **end** of a story, we usually learn how characters solve their problem.

   ▶ How does Harry finally solve his problem in the last chapter of the book, "The Contest"? He puts a watering can with frogs inside of it on the stage, which ends up causing the lady next door to win a singing contest and move far away.

8. Remind students that if they know how the **problem and solution** fit into the order of a story, they will know what to expect as they read. This will help them better understand and remember a story.

   ▶ Do you think that you understand the story of *Harry and the Lady Next Door*? Answers will vary.

TIP If students have not read *Harry and the Lady Next Door*, choose another story or book that students are familiar with as an example of how problem and solution fit into the beginning, middle, and end of a story.

Guided Reading •••

Book Walk
Prepare students for reading by taking them on a Book Walk of *Little Bear*. Scan the stories "Birthday Soup" and "Little Bear Goes to the Moon" together and ask students to make predictions.

1. Have students read aloud the **book title**.

2. Read aloud the **names of the author and the illustrator**.

3. Have students read aloud the story titles on the **Contents** page. Explain to students that in this lesson, they will read "Birthday Soup" and "Little Bear Goes to the Moon."

4. Have students look at the **pictures in "Birthday Soup" and "Little Bear Goes to the Moon."** Answers to questions may vary.

   ▶ What do you think might happen in these stories?
   ▶ How do you think you make birthday soup? What do you think is in it?
   ▶ Do you ever pretend to go somewhere far away to see new things? Where do you pretend to go? What do you see?

Objectives

- Make predictions based on text, illustrations, and/or prior knowledge.
- Activate prior knowledge by previewing text and/or discussing topic.
- Read and listen to a variety of texts for information and pleasure independently or as part of a group.
- Read aloud grade-level text with appropriate expression, accuracy, and rate.

"Birthday Soup" and "Little Bear Goes to the Moon"

Guide students through a preview of the stories to prepare them for reading on their own. Gather the Reading Aid on pages LC 313 and 314 in *K¹² Language Arts Activity Book*.

1. Have students sit next to you so that they can see the pictures and words while you introduce and discuss the stories.

2. Tell students that you will preview the stories to prepare them to read aloud to you.

3. Refer to the Reading Aid.

Reading Aid Tear out the Reading Aid for this reading selection. Follow the instructions for folding the page, and then use the page as a guide as you preview the selection with students.

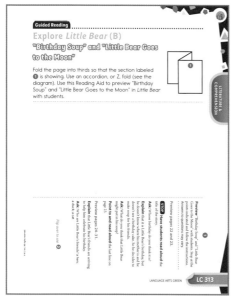
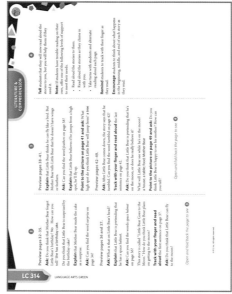

Check Your Reading

"Birthday Soup" and "Little Bear Goes to the Moon"
Check students' comprehension of "Birthday Soup" and "Little Bear Goes to the Moon."

1. Ask students the following questions about "Birthday Soup."

   ▶ Where does "Birthday Soup" take place? at Little Bear's house
   ▶ Whose birthday is it? Little Bear's
   ▶ Why does Little Bear make a pot of birthday soup? Possible answers: because he doesn't have a birthday cake; because he wants to feed his friends when they come to visit; all his friends like soup
   ▶ What does Little Bear put in the soup? carrots, potatoes, peas, and tomatoes

2. Ask students the following questions about "Little Bear Goes to the Moon."

   ▶ How does Little Bear plan to get to the moon fly
   ▶ What does Little Bear think the moon looks like after he jumps out of the tree? just like earth
   ▶ Who does Little Bear find inside the house on the moon? Mother Bear

TIP If students have trouble responding to a question, help them locate the answer in the text or pictures.

Objectives
- Identify setting.
- Answer questions requiring literal recall of details.

Reading for Meaning

Make Inferences in "Birthday Soup" and "Little Bear Goes to the Moon"
Check students' ability to make inferences using text and pictures in *Little Bear*.

1. Remind students that sometimes the author doesn't say things directly. Good readers use text and picture clues to figure out things about a story on their own.

2. Ask the following questions about "Birthday Soup."

   ▶ Little Bear's mother doesn't come when he calls her name at the beginning of the story. Why doesn't Little Bear go look for her? because his friends are coming over and he needs to make them something to eat
   ▶ What does Little Bear do with the presents his friends bring him? He puts them on the dinner table.   How did you figure this out? from looking at the pictures in the story
   ▶ Why does Cat tell Little Bear to close his eyes and count to three just before Little Bear eats a spoonful of soup? so Little Bear will be surprised when Mother Bear gives him his birthday cake
   ▶ Did Mother Bear really forget Little Bear's birthday? No   How do you know? She gives Little Bear a birthday cake at the end of the story.
   ▶ Why is Little Bear hugging his mother in the picture at the end of the story? He's happy she made him a birthday cake; he's glad she didn't forget his birthday.   How do you know? What do you know from your own experience that tells you this? Students might say they like to hug people when they do something nice for them.

Objectives
- Make inferences based on text and/or prior knowledge.
- Support inferences with evidence from text and/or prior knowledge.
- Use illustrations to aid understanding of text.
- Retell the beginning, middle, and end of a story.
- Identify story sequence.
- Self-monitor comprehension of text.

3. Ask the following questions about "Little Bear Goes to the Moon."

   ▸ What does Little Bear use for a space helmet? a box   How do you know this? The pictures in the story show a box on his head.
   ▸ Why does Little Bear climb to the top of a little tree at the top of a little hill? He thinks he needs to jump from a high spot to get up into the sky.
   ▸ Does Little Bear really go to the moon or is he pretending? pretending   How do you know this? Possible answers: The pictures in the story show he's walking in the woods; he sees things like trees and birds and walks back to his house; bears can't really fly to the moon.
   ▸ Why do you think Mother Bear says she's on the moon and her little bear flew to earth? because she wants to pretend, too; because she thinks it's funny   Why do you think this? What prior knowledge did you use? Students might say it's fun to play along with a friend in a game of pretend.

Retell Stories to Self-Monitor Comprehension

Check students' ability to recall the sequence of story events and self-monitor their understanding by retelling a story.

1. Tell students they will retell both stories. Have them look at the pictures in the stories as a reference for retelling.

2. Have students retell the beginning of "Birthday Soup," the part in which we learn about Little Bear's problem. Possible answer: It's Little Bear's birthday, but he can't find his mother or his birthday cake. He needs to make something for his friends to eat when they come to visit.

3. Retell the middle of the story, the part in which Little Bear tries to solve his problem and his friends come to visit, one by one. Remind students to tell the story in sequence, or the order in which things happen. Possible answer: Little Bear decides to make birthday soup. His friends come to visit while he is making the soup. Hen comes first, then Duck, and then Cat. Little Bear brings his friends bowls of soup when it's done.

4. Retell the end of the story, the part in which Mother Bear surprises Little Bear. Possible answer: Cat tells Little Bear to shut his eyes and count to three. When he opens his eyes again, Little Bear sees Mother Bear and a big birthday cake. Little Bear is happy that his mother didn't forget his birthday and that she made him a cake after all.

5. Have students retell the beginning of "Little Bear Goes to the Moon," the part where Little Bear tells his mother he's going to fly to the moon. Possible answer: Little Bear has a new space helmet, so he tells his mother he's going to fly to the moon. She tells him he can't fly, but he says he's going to the moon anyway.

6. Retell the middle of the story, the part in which Little Bear flies to the moon. Possible answer: Little Bear climbs a tree, closes his eyes, and jumps. He sees trees and birds and thinks the moon looks just like the earth. He walks until he comes to a house that looks just like his house. Inside, he finds lunch on a table and a bear that looks just like his mother. She tells him that her little bear put on his space helmet and flew to earth, and that he can eat the lunch since her little bear is gone.

7. Retell the end of the story, the part in which Little Bear tells Mother Bear to stop fooling. Possible answer: Little Bear tells Mother Bear to stop fooling, and that they are on the earth. Mother Bear tells him he can have a nap after he eats lunch, and that she knows he is her little bear.

8. Ask the following questions. Answers to questions may vary.

   ▸ Did your retellings include the characters?
   ▸ Did you retell the events in the order that they happened?
   ▸ Did you retell the order in which Little Bear's friends came to his house in "Birthday Soup"?
   ▸ Did your retelling include the most important things that Little Bear does and says in "Little Bear Goes to the Moon"?
   ▸ Did looking at the pictures in the stories help with your retellings?
   ▸ Do you think you understand the stories?

TIP If students don't think they understand a story, read aloud any parts of the story students are unclear about, pausing to let students ask questions as you read.

Explore *Little Bear* (C)

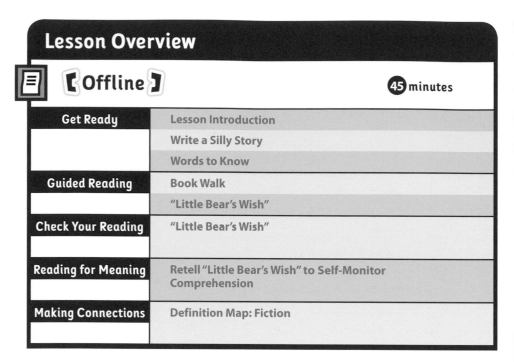

Lesson Overview

[Offline] 45 minutes

Get Ready	Lesson Introduction
	Write a Silly Story
	Words to Know
Guided Reading	Book Walk
	"Little Bear's Wish"
Check Your Reading	"Little Bear's Wish"
Reading for Meaning	Retell "Little Bear's Wish" to Self-Monitor Comprehension
Making Connections	Definition Map: Fiction

Advance Preparation

Before beginning the Guided Reading, read "Little Bear's Wish" to locate Words to Know in the text. Preview pages LC 317 and 318 in *K¹² Language Arts Activity Book* to prepare the materials for the Guided Reading.

Big Ideas

▸ Exposing readers to a wide variety of genres provides them with a wide range of background knowledge and increases their vocabulary.

▸ An awareness of story structure elements (setting, characters, plot) provides readers a foundation for constructing meaning when reading new stories and writing their own stories.

▸ Comprehension requires the reader to self-monitor understanding.

▸ Guided reading provides support to early readers as they practice and apply the reading strategies of proficient readers.

[Materials]

Supplied

- *Little Bear* by Else Holmelund Minarik
- *K¹² Language Arts Activity Book*, pp. LC 315–319

Story Synopsis

In "Little Bear's Wish," Little Bear can't sleep because he keeps thinking about the big wishes in his head. So Mother Bear tells him a story about . . . *Little Bear*!

Keywords

fiction – make-believe stories

genre – a category for classifying literary works

retelling – using your own words to tell a story that you have listened to or read

self-monitor – to notice if you do or do not understand what you are reading

story structure elements – components of a story; they include character, setting, plot, problem, and solution

 Offline **45** minutes

Work **together** with students to complete Get Ready, Guided Reading, Check Your Reading, Reading for Meaning, and Making Connections activities.

Get Ready ....

Lesson Introduction

Prepare students for reading and discussing "Little Bear's Wish."

1. Tell students that they will be reading "Little Bear's Wish," the last story in the book *Little Bear*.

2. Explain that before they read, you will get ready by thinking of words to complete a story and reviewing characteristics of fiction.

Write a Silly Story

Review characteristics of fiction stories. Turn to page LC 315 in *K¹² Language Arts Activity Book*.

1. Remind students that **fiction** stories are made-up. Most fiction stories have the **story structure elements** of characters, setting, problem and solution, and plot.

2. Tell students they are going to review the elements of a story by helping you write a silly fiction story. You will ask them to call out words to fill in the blanks on the Activity Book page. Then, they will read aloud the completed story.

3. Look below each blank line to see the type of word needed to fill the blank. Read aloud the type of word needed and have students call out an answer. Print their answers in the blanks.

4. Have students read aloud the story once all the answer blanks are filled.

Objectives

- Identify story structure elements—plot, setting, character(s).
- Describe story structure elements—problem and solution.
- Build vocabulary through listening, reading, and discussion.
- Use new vocabulary in written and spoken sentences.

5. Ask the following questions. Answers should match students' story.

  ▸ Who are the characters in the story?
  ▸ What kind of thing is the main character?
  ▸ What is the setting?
  ▸ What problem does the main character have to solve?
  ▸ How does she solve it?
  ▸ What is the plot, or the most important events, of the story?

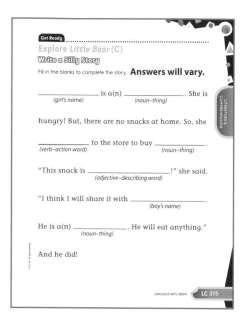

Words to Know

Before reading "Little Bear's Wish," go over Words to Know with students.

1. Read aloud each word and have students repeat it.

2. Ask students if they know what each word means.

  ▸ If students know a word's meaning, have them define it and use it in a sentence.
  ▸ If students don't know a word's meaning, read them the definition and discuss the word with them.

chopsticks – thin sticks that are used for eating food
tunnel – a long hole dug through the ground
Vikings – Vikings were men who sailed from areas of northern Europe and attacked villages over a thousand years ago

Guided Reading

Book Walk

Prepare students for reading by taking them on a Book Walk of *Little Bear*. Scan the story "Little Bear's Wish" together and ask students to make predictions.

1. Have students read aloud the **book title**.

2. Read aloud the **names of the author and the illustrator**.

3. Have students read aloud the story titles on the **Contents** page. Explain to students that in this lesson, they will read "Little Bear's Wish."

4. Have students look at the **pictures in "Little Bear's Wish."** Answers to questions may vary.

   ▸ What do you think might happen in this story?
   ▸ Did you ever have trouble falling asleep because you couldn't stop thinking about something? What was it?
   ▸ Have you ever wished you could visit a faraway place? Where would you like to go?

Objectives

- Make predictions based on text, illustrations, and/or prior knowledge.
- Activate prior knowledge by previewing text and/or discussing topic.
- Read and listen to a variety of texts for information and pleasure independently or as part of a group.
- Read aloud grade-level text with appropriate expression, accuracy, and rate.

"Little Bear's Wish"

Guide students through a preview of the story to prepare them for reading on their own. Gather the Reading Aid on pages LC 317 and 318 in *K¹² Language Arts Activity Book*.

1. Have students sit next to you so that they can see the pictures and words while you introduce and discuss the story.

2. Tell students that you will preview the story to prepare them to read aloud to you.

3. Refer to the Reading Aid.

Reading Aid Tear out the Reading Aid for this reading selection. Follow the instructions for folding the page, and then use the page as a guide as you preview the selection with students.

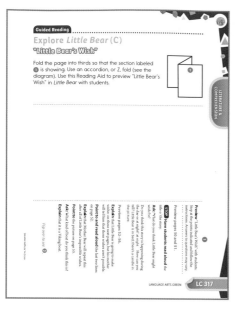
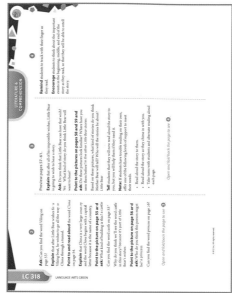

Check Your Reading

"Little Bear's Wish"

Check students' comprehension of "Little Bear's Wish."

▶ Why can't Little Bear fall asleep? He can't stop thinking about his wishes.

▶ What is Little Bear's first wish? that he could sit on a cloud and fly all around

▶ Where does Little Bear say he would go in a big red car? a big castle

▶ What would the princess in the castle give Little Bear? cake

▶ What does Mother Bear say to Little Bear after each of his wishes? "You can't have that wish, my Little Bear."

▶ What does Mother Bear do to help Little Bear fall asleep? tells a story

Objectives
- Answer questions requiring literal recall of details.

Reading for Meaning

Retell "Little Bear's Wish" to Self-Monitor Comprehension

Check students' ability to recall the order of story events and self-monitor their understanding by retelling a story.

1. Tell students they will retell "Little Bear's Wish." Have them look at the pictures in the story as a reference for retelling.

2. Have students retell the beginning of "Little Bear's Wish," the part in which we learn about Little Bear's problem. Possible answer: Little Bear is in bed in his bedroom. He can't fall asleep because he is wishing.

Objectives
- Use illustrations to aid understanding of text.
- Retell the beginning, middle, and end of a story.
- Retell a story naming plot, setting, character(s), problem, and solution.
- Identify story sequence.
- Self-monitor comprehension of text.

3. Retell the middle of the story, the part in which Little Bear tells Mother Bear about all his wishes. Possible answer: Little Bear tells his mother about all the things he wishes. He wishes he could fly around on a cloud, find a Viking boat, go through a tunnel all the way to China, and drive a big red car to a castle where a princess gives him cake. Mother Bear says he can't have those wishes. So Little Bear wishes Mother Bear would tell him a story. Mother Bear says he can have that wish.

4. Retell the end of the story, the part in which Mother Bear tells Little Bear a story to solve Little Bear's problem. Possible answer: Mother Bears tells a story about Little Bear: how he put on clothes to play in the snow, how he put on a space helmet and pretended to go to the moon, and how he made birthday soup. Little Bear says now he can go to sleep.

5. Ask the following questions. Answers to questions may vary.

   ▸ Did your retelling include the characters and setting?
   ▸ Did you retell the order in which Little Bear makes his wishes?
   ▸ Did you retell the order in which Mother Bear tells the story about the things Little Bear does?
   ▸ Did looking at the pictures in the chapter help with your retelling?
   ▸ Do you think you understand the story?

TIP If students don't think they understand a story, read aloud any parts of the story students are unclear about, pausing to let students ask questions as you read.

Making Connections

●●

Definition Map: Fiction
Check students' understanding of the characteristics of fiction. Turn to page LC 319 in *K¹² Language Arts Activity Book*.

1. Remind students that there are different types of writing.

2. Look at the Activity Book page with students. Explain that they will think of an answer for each question in the map to define the genre of fiction. Then, they will write their answers in the boxes.

3. Point to and help students read aloud the "What is it?" heading.

4. Have students tell you their answer and help them write it in the box.

5. Point to and help students read aloud the "What is it like?" heading.

Objectives
- Identify characteristics of different genres.
- Demonstrate understanding through graphic organizers.

6. Have students tell you at least three characteristics of fiction writing and help them write the characteristics in the box.

7. Point to and help students read aloud the "What are some examples?" heading.

8. Have students tell you names of fiction books or stories that they are familiar with and help them write the titles in the boxes.

9. Ask students the following questions.

   ▸ Which is your favorite story in *Little Bear*? Why is that your favorite? Answers will vary.
   ▸ Based on how you defined fiction in the definition map, is that story fiction or nonfiction? fiction
   ▸ Is your favorite story in *Little Bear* a made-up story? Yes   Does it have characters and a setting? Yes   Who are the characters and what is the setting? Answers will vary.
   ▸ Does your favorite story have a problem and solution? What are they? Answers will vary.

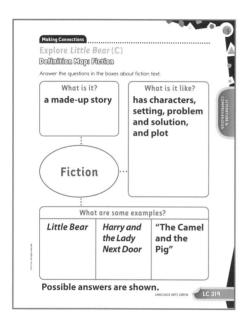

Introduce "Little Bears"

Lesson Overview

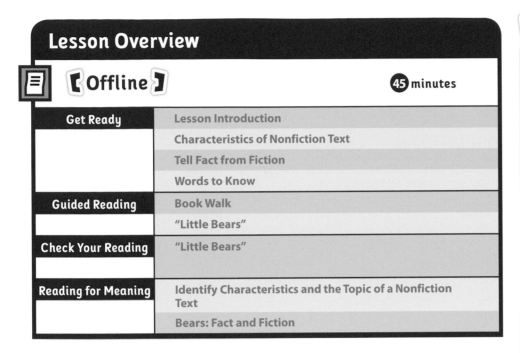

[Offline] **45** minutes

Get Ready	Lesson Introduction
	Characteristics of Nonfiction Text
	Tell Fact from Fiction
	Words to Know
Guided Reading	Book Walk
	"Little Bears"
Check Your Reading	"Little Bears"
Reading for Meaning	Identify Characteristics and the Topic of a Nonfiction Text
	Bears: Fact and Fiction

Advance Preparation

Before beginning the Guided Reading, read "Little Bears" to locate Words to Know in the text. Preview pages LC 321 and 322 in *K¹² Language Arts Activity Book* to prepare the materials for the Guided Reading.

Big Ideas

▶ Exposing readers to a wide variety of genres provides them with a wide range of background knowledge and increases their vocabulary.
▶ Nonfiction texts differ from fiction texts in that they describe real or true things in life, rather than things made up by the author.
▶ Guided reading provides support to early readers as they practice and apply the reading strategies of proficient readers.

[Materials]

Supplied

- "Little Bears," *K¹² World: Critter and Creature Stories*, pp. 16–29
- *K¹² Language Arts Activity Book*, pp. LC 320–323

Article Synopsis

Follow two baby bears through their first year of life in the wild.

Keywords

fact – something that can be proven true

genre – a category for classifying literary works

informational text – text written to explain and give information on a topic

nonfiction – writings about true things

topic – the subject of a text

[Offline] 45 minutes

Work **together** with students to complete Get Ready, Guided Reading, Check Your Reading, and Reading for Meaning activities.

Get Ready

Lesson Introduction
Prepare students for listening to and discussing "Little Bears."

1. Tell students that they are going to read "Little Bears," an article about a year in the life of two real bear cubs and their mother.

2. Explain that before they read the article, you will get ready by

   ▸ Discussing characteristics of nonfiction texts
   ▸ Reading two paragraphs to practice telling the difference between fact and fiction

> **Objectives**
> • Identify characteristics of different genres.
> • Distinguish fact from fiction.
> • Identify the topic.
> • Build vocabulary through listening, reading, and discussion.
> • Use new vocabulary in written and spoken sentences.
> • Increase concept and content vocabulary.

Characteristics of Nonfiction Text
Reinforce the characteristics of nonfiction text.

1. Tell students that authors write texts for different reasons. Sometimes authors write to entertain us. Texts written to entertain are usually fiction stories. They are filled with made-up characters and events. Fiction stories are not about real-life things.

2. Explain that when authors write to inform us, they usually write **informational**, or **nonfiction**, texts. Unlike fiction, nonfiction texts are filled with **facts**. They are texts about real people, animals, and events. Everything in a nonfiction text is true.

3. Kinds of nonfiction texts include

   ▸ newspaper stories
   ▸ magazine articles
   ▸ biographies

4. Tell students that another characteristic of nonfiction text is that it has a **topic**. The topic is the subject of a nonfiction text, or what the text is mostly about. The title of an article often gives a clue about the topic. For example, an article with the title "The Buzz About Bees" is probably filled with facts about bees.

5. Explain that if readers understand why an author wrote a text, they will have a better understanding of the text. If readers know they are going to read a nonfiction text, such as a magazine article, they can expect to read facts about the topic of the article.

Tell Fact from Fiction

Check students' understanding of how to tell if a text is fiction or nonfiction. Turn to page LC 320 in *K¹² Language Arts Activity Book*.

1. Tell students they are going to read aloud two paragraphs about dogs. One paragraph is fiction and the other is nonfiction.

2. Help students read aloud the two paragraphs on the Activity Book page.

   ▶ Which paragraph is a nonfiction text about real things? Paragraph 2
   ▶ How can you tell Paragraph 2 is nonfiction? What characteristics of nonfiction texts does it have? Possible answers: It has facts; it's about real dogs, not made-up ones; it informs readers about dogs; it has a topic.
   ▶ What is the topic of Paragraph 2? Possible answers: dogs; facts about dogs; how a dog uses its nose

3. Remind students that they are going to read a nonfiction article. Because they know what to expect in a nonfiction text, they will be better able to understand it and remember facts in the article.

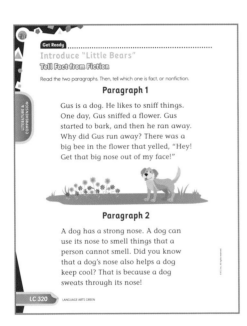

Words to Know

Before reading "Little Bears," go over Words to Know with students.

1. Read aloud each word and have students repeat it.

2. Ask students if they know what each word means.

   ► If students know a word's meaning, have them define it and use it in a sentence.

   ► If students don't know a word's meaning, read them the definition and discuss the word with them.

beehive – a container in which bees live and make and store honey

cub – a young lion, bear, or wolf

den – a cave or resting place for a wild animal such as a bear or wolf

groom – to clean or brush

hibernate – to sleep through the winter

motor – a machine that gives something power to make it work

nurse – to drink milk from a mother's body

yearling – an animal that is between one and two years old

Guided Reading

Book Walk

Prepare students for reading by taking them on a Book Walk of "Little Bears." Scan the magazine article together and ask students to make predictions about the article.

1. Turn to the **table of contents** in *K¹² World: Critter and Creature Stories*. Help students find the selection and turn to that page.

2. Have students read aloud the **article title**.

3. Have students look at the **pictures of the article**. Remind them that pictures help show ideas that are in the text.

   ► Based on the title of the article, the pictures, and your prior knowledge of nonfiction texts, what do you think this article will be about? facts about bears

   ► What do you think the article will tell us about bears? Answers will vary; students may mention information such as where bears live, what they eat, and how they play.

   ► What do you know about baby bears? Have you ever read any books or seen any TV shows with information about bears? Answers will vary.

Objectives

- Make predictions based on text, illustrations, and/or prior knowledge.
- Activate prior knowledge by previewing text and/or discussing topic.
- Read for information.
- Read aloud grade-level text with appropriate expression, accuracy, and rate.

"Little Bears"

Guide students through a preview of the article to prepare them for reading on their own. Gather the Reading Aid on pages LC 321 and 322 in *K¹² Language Arts Activity Book*.

1. Have students sit next to you so that they can see the pictures and words while you introduce and discuss the article.

2. Tell students that you will preview the article to prepare them to read aloud the article to you.

3. Refer to the Reading Aid.

Reading Aid Tear out the Reading Aid for this reading selection. Follow the instructions for folding the page, and then use the page as a guide as you preview the selection with students.

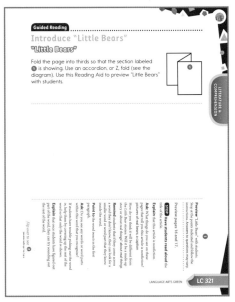
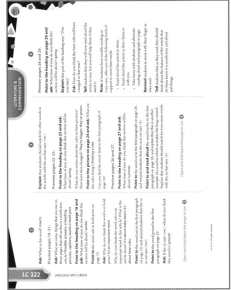

Check Your Reading

"Little Bears"

Check students' comprehension of "Little Bears."

1. Have students retell "Little Bears" in their own words to develop grammar, vocabulary, comprehension, and fluency skills.

Objectives

- Retell or dramatize a story.
- Identify facts in informational text.
- Answer questions requiring literal recall of details.

2. Ask students the following questions.

- ▶ What is a bear's home called? a den
- ▶ What do bears do all winter long? sleep; hibernate
- ▶ What does a mother bear do to keep her cubs warm in the den? cuddles with them; blows on them with her warm breath
- ▶ What time of year do new cubs first go outside the den? in the spring
- ▶ Why does a mother bear leave her cubs near a tree when she looks for food? so they can climb up the tree if a person or strange bear comes by while she's gone

TIP If students have trouble responding to a question, help them locate the answer in the text or pictures.

Reading for Meaning

Identify Characteristics and the Topic of a Nonfiction Text
Explore characteristics of nonfiction texts with students.

- ▶ What kind of writing is "Little Bears"? Possible answers: nonfiction; informational text; a nonfiction magazine article
- ▶ How can you tell the article is a nonfiction text? It tells facts about real bears; it's not a made-up story.
- ▶ Why do authors write articles like "Little Bears"? Possible answers: to inform readers; to teach readers about something; to tell facts
- ▶ What is the topic of "Little Bears"? What is the article mostly about? Possible answers: bears; bear cubs; what bears do the first year they live; how bear cubs are born and grow

> **Objectives**
> - Identify genre.
> - Identify characteristics of different genres.
> - Identify the topic.
> - Distinguish fiction text from nonfiction text.
> - Identify facts in informational text.
> - Compare and contrast two texts on the same topic.
> - Demonstrate understanding through graphic organizers.

✎ **Bears: Fact and Fiction**
Check students' understanding of how the bears are alike and different in "Little Bears" and *Little Bear*. Turn to page LC 323 in *K¹² Language Arts Activity Book*.

1. Remind students that this kind of graphic organizer is called a Venn diagram. It can be used to show how things are alike and how they are different.

2. Explain that they will use it to show how the bear cubs in the article "Little Bears" and the character Little Bear in the book *Little Bear* are alike in some ways and different in other ways.

3. Ask students to name things that describe only the real bear cubs and help them write these attributes in the left circle of the Venn diagram. Possible answers: are real; live in the woods; hibernate in a den; eat ants, honey and fish

4. Ask students to name things that describe only the character Little Bear and help them write these attributes in the right circle of the Venn diagram. Possible answers: is not real; lives in a house; sleeps in a bed; wears clothes; eats soup and cake; can talk

5. Ask students to name things that describe both the real bear cubs and Little Bear. Help them write these attributes in the center of the Venn diagram, where the circles overlap. Possible answers: have a mother; have fur; like to play; can climb trees

6. Ask the following questions to encourage comparison of the bear cubs and discussion. Answers to questions may vary.

   ► How are the real bear cubs and the made-up bear cub alike?
   ► How are the real bear cubs and the made-up bear cub different?
   ► Do you think a real bear cub would like to wear clothes or live in a house? Why or why not?

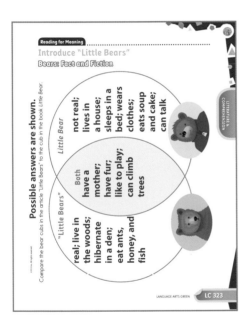

Explore "Little Bears"

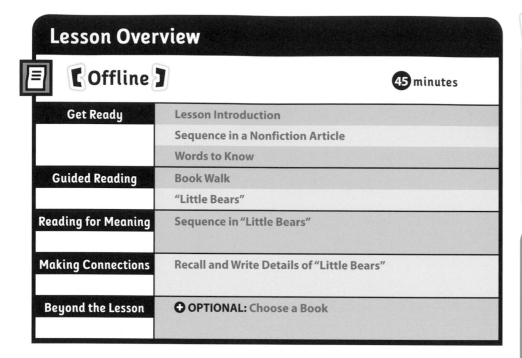

Lesson Overview

[Offline]   **45** minutes

Get Ready	Lesson Introduction
	Sequence in a Nonfiction Article
	Words to Know
Guided Reading	Book Walk
	"Little Bears"
Reading for Meaning	Sequence in "Little Bears"
Making Connections	Recall and Write Details of "Little Bears"
Beyond the Lesson	⊕ OPTIONAL: Choose a Book

[Materials]

Supplied

- "Little Bears," *K¹² World: Critter and Creature Stories*, pp. 16–29
- *K¹² Language Arts Activity Book*, p. LC 227 (optional)
- *K¹² My Journal*, pp. 28–53

Keywords

detail – a piece of information in a text

genre – a category for classifying literary works

informational text – text written to explain and give information on a topic

nonfiction – writings about true things

Advance Preparation

If you plan to do the Beyond the Lesson, gather page LC 227 (Choose a Book Using the 5-Finger Test) in *K¹² Language Arts Activity Book*.

Big Ideas

▸ Exposing readers to a wide variety of genres provides them with a wide range of background knowledge and increases their vocabulary.

▸ Nonfiction texts differ from fiction texts in that they describe real or true things in life, rather than things made up by the author.

▸ Comprehension entails an understanding of the organizational patterns of text.

▸ Repeated rereading leads to increased fluency.

[Offline] 45 minutes

Work **together** with students to complete Get Ready, Guided Reading, Reading for Meaning, Making Connections, and Beyond the Lessons activities.

Get Ready ··

Lesson Introduction
Prepare students for reading and discussing "Little Bears."

1. Tell students that they are going to reread "Little Bears."

2. Explain that before they reread the article, you will get ready by reviewing different ways that the information in nonfiction texts can be organized.

Sequence in a Nonfiction Article
Review the how authors can organize nonfiction texts in sequence.

1. Remind students that authors can organize information in an article in different ways.

   ▸ The author might point out problems and then talk about the ways that people are trying to solve those problems. We say that texts like this are organized by **problem and solution**. The article "Ben Franklin, American Inventor" is an example of this.
   ▸ The author might point out how things are alike and different. We say that these texts are written to **compare and contrast**. The article "Colonial Kids" is an example of this.
   ▸ The author might organize information according to the order in which events happen. Texts like this are written **in sequence**. This is how the information in "Little Bears" is organized.

2. Tell students that an article that mentions time periods such as days, months, or seasons is probably organized in sequence.

3. Check students' understanding of sequence based on time periods.

   ▸ Imagine you are reading an article about the different holidays in each month of a year. If the article is written in sequence, what month would you expect to read about after the month of January? February
   ▸ Imagine you are reading an article about the weather during the four seasons of a year. If the article is written in sequence, what season would you expect to read about after the season of fall? winter

> **Objectives**
> - Identify organizational structures of text.
> - Identify sequence of events in informational text.
> - Build vocabulary through listening, reading, and discussion.
> - Use new vocabulary in written and spoken sentences.
> - Increase concept and content vocabulary.

4. Have students practice identifying the order of events in a paragraph organized in sequence.

Read aloud: Farmer Joan planted a corn crop last spring. After lots of rain, the corn grew tall during the summer. Farmer Joan used a hoe to keep weeds away from her crop. In the fall, the corn was done growing, and she cut it down. Then, she took the corn to the market to sell. In the winter, the ground where the corn grew was covered with snow. The next spring, the snow melted, and Farmer Joan planted a new crop of corn.

> ▶ How is the information in the paragraph organized? Possible answers: in sequence; in the order in which things happen; in time order
> ▶ Farmer Joan uses a hoe to keep weeds away from her corn crop. In what season does this happen? summer   Does Farmer Joan use the hoe before or after she plants the crop? after   How do you know? The article says Farmer Joan plants the corn in the spring, and summer comes after spring.
> ▶ When does Farmer Joan sell the corn? in the fall   How do you know? The article says Farmer Joan takes the corn to the market after she cuts it down, and she cuts it down in the fall.

5. Tell students that if they recognize that an article is written in sequence, they will know what to expect when they're reading. This will help them better understand and remember the information in the article.

Words to Know

Before reading "Little Bears," go over Words to Know with students.

1. Read aloud each word and have students repeat it.

2. Ask students if they know what each word means.

> ▶ If students know a word's meaning, have them define it and use it in a sentence.
> ▶ If students don't know a word's meaning, read them the definition and discuss the word with them.

beehive – a container in which bees live and make and store honey
cub – a young lion, bear, or wolf
den – a cave or resting place for a wild animal such as a bear or wolf
groom – to clean or brush
hibernate – to sleep through the winter
motor – a machine that gives something power to make it work
nurse – to drink milk from a mother's body
yearling – an animal that is between one and two years old

Guided Reading

Book Walk

Prepare students for reading by taking them on a Book Walk of "Little Bears." Scan the article together to revisit the text.

1. Turn to the selection.

2. Have students read aloud the **article title**.

3. Have students look at the **pictures of the article**.

4. Ask the following questions to help students think about what they already know about the article. Answers to questions may vary.

   ▸ What is your favorite picture in the article?
   ▸ Why do you like this picture?
   ▸ What did you learn about bears from looking at this picture and reading the caption?

Objectives

- Activate prior knowledge by previewing text and/or discussing topic.
- Read for information.
- Read aloud grade-level text with appropriate expression, accuracy, and rate.

"Little Bears"

It's time for students to reread the article aloud.

1. Tell students that "Little Bears" should now be familiar to them because they have read it before.

2. Explain that they will reread the article aloud to you, but you are there if they need help.

3. If students have trouble reading on their own, offer one of the following levels of support to meet their needs.

   ▸ Read aloud the article to them.
   ▸ Read aloud the article as they chime in with you.
   ▸ Take turns with students and alternate reading aloud each paragraph or page.

4. Remind students to track with their finger as they read.

5. Tell students to think about how the information in the article is organized while they read.

Reading for Meaning

Sequence in "Little Bears"

Check students' understanding of sequence in "Little Bears."

Objectives
- Identify organizational structures of text.
- Identify sequence of events in informational text.
- Identify facts in informational text.

1. Remind students that the four seasons have an order, or sequence. The sequence is winter, spring, summer, and fall.

2. Ask students the following questions.

   ▸ When an article has seasons in it, how is the information probably organized? Possible answers: in sequence; in time order; in the order of the seasons; in the order that the seasons happen; winter, spring, summer, fall

   ▸ A fat bear is alone and looking for a place to make a den. Does this happen before or after she has babies? before   How do you know? The article is written in sequence, and the bear looks for a den first.

   ▸ The bear cubs are pink and have no fur. What season is it? winter How do you know? Bear cubs are born in January, and January is a winter month.

   ▸ The bear cubs leave the den for the first time. In what season does this happen? spring

   ▸ The bears stay cool in the summer by sitting in the shade of a tree. Does this happen before or after the snow melts? after   How do you know? The article says the snow melts in the spring, and summer comes after spring.

   ▸ A mother bear and her cubs eat lots of food to grow fat. Does this happen before or after the mother bear makes a new den? before   How do you know? The article says the bears eat lots of food in the summer, and the mother looks for a new den in the fall. Summer comes before fall.

   ▸ The cubs are yearlings and ready to live on their own. When does this happen? Possible answers: the next spring; after they hibernate for another winter; after they are a year old

TIP Refer back to the article if students have trouble recalling the order in which things happened.

Making Connections

 Recall and Write Details of "Little Bears"

Check students' ability to recall details from the article by having them write an acrostic poem. Gather *K¹² My Journal* and have students turn to the next available page for **writing** in Thoughts and Experiences.

Objectives
- Respond to text through art, writing, and/or drama.
- Identify important details in informational text.

1. Tell students that they will write a type of poem called an acrostic poem using details from the article "Little Bears." Remind students that a detail is a piece of information in a text.

2. Explain that in an acrostic poem, the first letter of each line of the poem spells a word. That word is the subject of the poem.

3. Have students print "BEARS" down the left side of the page, with a capital letter on each line.

4. Point to the letters in BEARS one by one and help students think of a detail from the article that begins with that letter. Then, help them write the detail on the associated line. If students have trouble thinking of a detail that begins with a particular letter, suggest one of the first words given in the examples below. Then have students think of a sentence that begins with that word. Examples of details:

- **B**orn without fur. / **B**aby bears are tiny.
- **E**at honey when they get older. / **E**yes are closed when born.
- **A**re as small as kittens / **A**re pink when they are born.
- **R**un and jump as they play. / **R**eady for winter after eating in summer and fall.
- **S**niff to find food. / **S**leep in the winter.

5. Have students verify the details that they write are accurate by having them locate the information in the article.

6. If students enjoy the activity and time allows, have them write another acrostic poem in their journal. Have them choose from the words CUBS, DEN, or HIBERNATE or any other word related to the topic of the article.

TIP Acrostic poems don't have to rhyme.

Date _____

Use this page to write.

_____
_____
_____
_____
_____
_____
_____
_____
_____
_____

28

Beyond the Lesson

⊕ OPTIONAL: Choose a Book

This activity is OPTIONAL. It is intended for students who have extra time and would enjoy choosing and independently reading a book with a topic similar to the topic of "Little Bears." Feel free to skip this activity. Gather page LC 227 in *K¹² Language Arts Activity Book.*

1. Review with students how to select a book that is "just right" to read.

2. Go to a library and look for the following suggested books. These books are related to the topic of "Little Bears." They are listed in order from easier to more difficult.

   ‣ *A Bear for You* by Kirsten Hall
   ‣ *A Bear Cub Grows Up* by Pam Zollman
   ‣ *Bears Are Curious* by Joyce Milton
   ‣ *Bears and Their Cubs* by Linda Tagliaferro
   ‣ *Bear Cub* by Pam Pollack
   ‣ *Black Bear Cub* by Alan Lind
   ‣ *Bears* by Bobbie Kalman

3. Have students refer to the Activity Book page for the steps and guidelines of the 5-Finger Test as they check if a book is "just right" for them.

4. Once students have found a "just right" book, have them read it on their own.

TIP Students do not have to limit themselves to the listed books. If students would prefer different books, help them use the 5-Finger Test with books of their own choice.

Objectives
• Follow criteria to choose "just right" independent reading materials.

Explore *Owl at Home* (A)

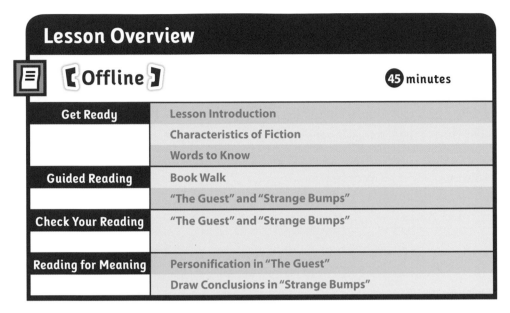

Lesson Overview

[Offline]   **45** minutes

Get Ready	Lesson Introduction
	Characteristics of Fiction
	Words to Know
Guided Reading	Book Walk
	"The Guest" and "Strange Bumps"
Check Your Reading	"The Guest" and "Strange Bumps"
Reading for Meaning	Personification in "The Guest"
	Draw Conclusions in "Strange Bumps"

Advance Preparation

Before beginning the Guided Reading, read "The Guest" and "Strange Bumps" to locate Words to Know in the text. Preview pages LC 325 and 326 in *K¹² Language Arts Activity Book* to prepare the materials for the Guided Reading.

Big Ideas

▸ Exposing readers to a wide variety of genres provides them with a wide range of background knowledge and increases their vocabulary.

▸ An awareness of story structure elements (setting, characters, plot) provides readers a foundation for constructing meaning when reading new stories and writing their own stories.

▸ Good readers use prior knowledge and text clues to infer or draw conclusions about what is implied but not directly stated in text.

▸ Guided reading provides support to early readers as they practice and apply the reading strategies of proficient readers.

Materials

Supplied

● *Owl at Home* by Arnold Lobel

● *K¹² Language Arts Activity Book*, pp. LC 325–326

Story Synopses

In "The Guest," Owl entertains a most unusual visitor. In "Strange Bumps," Owl can't get to sleep due to a pair of mysterious and annoying lumpy bumps in his bed.

Keywords

fiction – make-believe stories

genre – a category for classifying literary works

personification – giving human qualities to something that is not human; for example: "The thunder shouted from the clouds."

problem – an issue a character must solve in a story

solution – how a character solves a problem in a story

story structure elements – components of a story; they include character, setting, plot, problem, and solution

[Offline] ⏱ 45 minutes

Work **together** with students to complete Get Ready, Guided Reading, Check Your Reading, and Reading for Meaning activities.

Get Ready ··

Lesson Introduction

Prepare students for reading and discussing "The Guest" and "Strange Bumps."

1. Tell students that they will read "The Guest" and "Strange Bumps" in *Owl at Home*.

2. Explain that before they read the stories, you will get ready by reviewing the characteristics of fiction.

Objectives
- Identify genre.
- Identify characteristics of different genres.
- Identify character(s).
- Identify setting.
- Describe story structure elements—problem and solution.
- Retell or dramatize a story.
- Build vocabulary through listening, reading, and discussion.
- Use new vocabulary in written and spoken sentences.

Characteristics of Fiction

Review characteristics of fiction writing.

1. Remind students that some stories are true, and some are made-up.

   ▸ What do we call stories that are made-up? fiction

2. Remind them that most fiction stories have the same story structure elements.

   ▸ What are the story structure elements? characters, setting, plot, problem and solution

3. Tell students to think about the story structure elements in the story "What Will Little Bear Wear?" in the book *Little Bear*.

   ▸ Who are the characters in "What Will Little Bear Wear?" Little Bear and Mother Bear
   ▸ What is the setting of the story? Little Bear's house
   ▸ What is Little Bear's problem? He's cold.
   ▸ How does Mother Bear try to help Little Bear solve his problem? She gives him a hat, coat, and snow pants to wear.
   ▸ Does this solve Little Bear's problem? No
   ▸ How does Little Bear finally solve his problem? Mother Bear tells him he has a fur coat underneath all his clothes, so he takes off the hat, coat, and pants and isn't cold anymore.
   ▸ What is the plot of "What Will Little Bear Wear"? Little Bear is cold, so Mother Bear gives him a hat, then a coat, and then a pair of snow pants to wear. When Little Bear says he's still cold, Mother Bear tells him he has a fur coat on under all his clothes. So Mother Bear helps Little Bear take off the hat, coat, and pants to find his fur coat. Then, he isn't cold anymore.
   ▸ Are Little Bear and Mother Bear real or made-up bears? made-up
   ▸ What do we call stories that have made-up characters and events? fiction

Words to Know

Before reading "The Guest" and "Strange Bumps," go over Words to Know with students.

1. Read aloud each word or phrase and have students repeat it.

2. Ask students if they know what each word or phrase means.

   ▸ If students know a word's or phrase's meaning, have them define it and use it in a sentence.
   ▸ If students don't know a word's or phrase's meaning, read them the definition and discuss the word or phrase with them.

guest – a visitor
window shade – a blind for a window, made of heavy cloth or paper, that can be pulled up and down

Guided Reading

Book Walk

Prepare students for reading by taking them on a Book Walk of *Owl at Home*. Scan the stories "The Guest" and "Strange Bumps" together and ask students to make predictions.

1. Have students read aloud the **book title**.

2. Read aloud the name of the **author**.

3. Have students read aloud the story titles on the **Contents** page. Explain to students that in this lesson, they will read "The Guest" and "Strange Bumps."

4. Have students look at the **pictures in "The Guest" and "Strange Bumps."** Answers to questions may vary.

   ▸ What do you think might happen in these stories?
   ▸ Have you ever had a guest at your house who caused problems? What happened?
   ▸ What do you think the strange bumps might be?
   ▸ Have you ever felt nervous about something when you were trying to fall asleep? What was making you nervous?

Objectives

- Make predictions based on text, illustrations, and/or prior knowledge.
- Activate prior knowledge by previewing text and/or discussing topic.
- Read and listen to a variety of texts for information and pleasure independently or as part of a group.
- Read aloud grade-level text with appropriate expression, accuracy, and rate.

"The Guest" and "Strange Bumps"

Guide students through a preview of the stories to prepare them for reading on their own. Gather the Reading Aid on pages LC 325 and 326 in *K¹² Language Arts Activity Book*.

1. Have students sit next to you, so they can see the pictures and words while you introduce and discuss the stories.

2. Tell students that you will preview the stories to prepare them to read aloud to you.

3. Refer to the Reading Aid.

Reading Aid Tear out the Reading Aid for this reading selection. Follow the instructions for folding the page, and then use the page as a guide as you preview the selection with students.

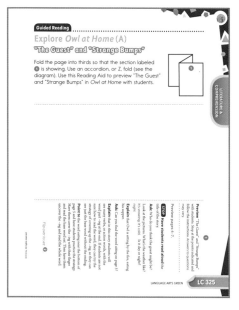

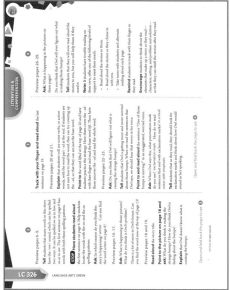

Check Your Reading

"The Guest" and "Strange Bumps"

Check students' comprehension of "The Guest" and "Strange Bumps."

1. Have students retell "The Guest" in their own words to develop grammar, vocabulary, comprehension, and fluency skills.

2. Ask students the following questions to check their comprehension of "The Guest."

   ▸ Who are the characters in "The Guest"? Owl; Winter
   ▸ Where does the story take place? at Owl's house
   ▸ What time of day is it? nighttime
   ▸ Why does Owl stop eating his supper to open the front door? He hears a loud sound at his front door.
   ▸ What is Owl's problem? Winter is blowing around Owl's house and making a mess.
   ▸ How does Owl solve his problem? Owl tells Winter to go away.

3. Have students retell "Strange Bumps" in their own words to develop grammar, vocabulary, comprehension, and fluency skills.

4. Ask students the following questions to check their comprehension of "Strange Bumps."

   ▸ Where does the story take place? at Owl's house; in Owl's bedroom
   ▸ What is Owl's problem? He sees two strange bumps under his blanket at the bottom of his bed.
   ▸ What does Owl worry the bumps might do while his is asleep? grow bigger and bigger
   ▸ What happens when Owl moves his feet up and down? The bumps move up and down, too.
   ▸ How does Owl solve his problem? He lets the bumps stay on his bed and he sleeps in a chair downstairs.

TIP If students have trouble responding to a question, help them locate the answer in the text or pictures.

Objectives
- Retell or dramatize a story.
- Identify character(s).
- Identify setting.
- Describe story structure elements—problem and solution.
- Answer questions requiring literal recall of details.

Reading for Meaning

Personification in "The Guest"

Check students' understanding of personification.

1. Remind students that authors sometimes make things that aren't human sound like they are. For example, an author might write, "The tree cried when her bird friends flew away." We know that a tree isn't human and can't really cry. But authors do this to help us imagine an interesting picture and think about certain feelings, such as happiness or sadness.

2. The story title is "The Guest."

   ▶ Who is the guest in the story? Winter   Can Winter really be somebody's guest? No   Why not? because winter isn't human

3. The story says Owl hears Winter "banging and pounding" on his front door.

   ▶ Can Winter really do this? No   Why not? because winter isn't human

4. Read aloud the text on page 11.

   ▶ What phrases in the story make it sound like Winter is a person? "ran around the room" and "blew out the fire"   Why do you think the author used these words? to help us imagine an interesting picture of Winter

5. The story says Owl yells at Winter, but Winter doesn't listen to him.

   ▶ What do you need in order to listen to someone? ears   Does Winter have ears? No   What picture do you see in your head when you think about Winter not listening to Owl? Answers will vary.

6. Have students look at the picture at the end of the story on page 17.

   ▶ Can you think of a sentence that makes it sound like the fire in the fireplace is human? Answers will vary; if students need help, give them an example sentence, such as "The fire licked the snow on the floor."

Objectives
- Identify literary devices: personification and/or simile.
- Draw conclusions using text, illustrations, and/or prior knowledge.
- Support conclusions with evidence from text and/or prior knowledge.

Draw Conclusions in "Strange Bumps"

Check students' ability to draw and support conclusions.

1. Remind students that good readers are able to use clues in the words and pictures in a story to help them figure out things that the author doesn't say directly. They also use their personal experience and prior knowledge to draw conclusions.

2. At the beginning of the story, Owl yawns.

   ▸ How do you think Owl feels? tired; ready to fall asleep   How did you figure that out, or draw that conclusion? Answers will vary; students might say they know from personal experience that people yawn when they're tired and ready to go to sleep.

3. Owl can't sleep after he sees the bumps in his bed, even though he is tired.

   ▸ How do you think Owl feels? Why can't he sleep? He's scared. He's worried because he doesn't know what the bumps are.   Does the author say directly that Owl is scared or worried? No   How did you draw that conclusion? What clues from the story and your prior knowledge helped you figure that out? Answers will vary; students might say that Owl's eyes are very big in this pictures, which means he's scared. They might say that they might know from personal experience that it's hard to fall asleep when they're feeling scared.

4. Owl jumps up and down on top of his bed until it falls down.

   ▸ Why did the bed fall down? Owl jumps on it too hard or too many times.   How did you draw that conclusion? Did anything like that ever happen to you? Answers may vary; students might tell of a time when they or someone they know broke a toy or piece of furniture this way.

   ▸ Why does Owl jump up and down on top of his bed? How does he feel? upset; mad; angry   How did you draw that conclusion? What clues in the story helped you figure that out? Owl shouts and cries out loud, which shows he's mad about the bumps.

5. Point to the picture at the end of the story on page 29.

   ▸ How do you think Owl feels when he's downstairs in front of the fire? happy; relaxed; relieved   How did you draw that conclusion? What clues in the story and the picture helped you figure that out? Owl says it's safe in front of the fire, and his eyes are closed in the picture; Owl must be asleep, which means he doesn't feel upset anymore.

Explore *Owl at Home* (B)

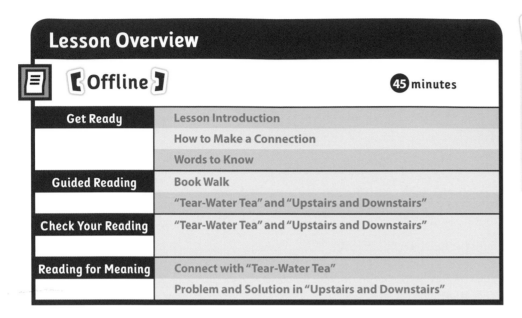

Lesson Overview

[Offline] 45 minutes

Get Ready	Lesson Introduction
	How to Make a Connection
	Words to Know
Guided Reading	Book Walk
	"Tear-Water Tea" and "Upstairs and Downstairs"
Check Your Reading	"Tear-Water Tea" and "Upstairs and Downstairs"
Reading for Meaning	Connect with "Tear-Water Tea"
	Problem and Solution in "Upstairs and Downstairs"

Advance Preparation

Before beginning the Guided Reading, read "Tear-Water Tea" and "Upstairs and Downstairs" to locate Words to Know in the text. Preview pages LC 327 and 328 in *K¹² Language Arts Activity Book* to prepare the materials for the Guided Reading.

Big Ideas

▶ An awareness of story structure elements (setting, characters, plot) provides readers a foundation for constructing meaning when reading new stories and writing their own stories.

▶ Comprehension is facilitated when readers connect new information to information previously learned.

▶ To understand and interpret a story, readers need to understand and describe characters and what they do.

▶ Guided reading provides support to early readers as they practice and apply the reading strategies of proficient readers.

Materials

Supplied

- *Owl at Home* by Arnold Lobel
- *K¹² Language Arts Activity Book*, pp. LC 327–328
- Story Card G

Story Synopses

In "Tear-Water Tea," Owl makes a pot of tea with a most unusual source of water. In "Upstairs and Downstairs," Owl is convinced that he can be two places at once if he just runs fast enough.

Keywords

character – a person or animal in a story

connection – a link readers make between themselves, information in text, and the world around them

problem – an issue a character must solve in a story

solution – how a character solves a problem in a story

 **45** minutes

Work **together** with students to complete Get Ready, Guided Reading, Check Your Reading, and Reading for Meaning activities.

Get Ready

Lesson Introduction

Prepare students for reading and discussing "Tear-Water Tea" and "Upstairs and Downstairs."

1. Tell students that they will read "Tear-Water Tea" and "Upstairs and Downstairs" in *Owl at Home*.

2. Explain that before they read the stories, you will get ready by reviewing how and why readers make connections with a text.

 Objectives
- Make connections with text: text-to-text, text-to-self, text-to-world.
- Build vocabulary through listening, reading, and discussion.
- Use new vocabulary in written and spoken sentences.

How to Make a Connection

Review how to make connections with a text. Gather Story Card G.

1. Remind students that readers who make connections to a story while they read are better able to understand and remember what they read. This is because these readers make reading a more active experience.

2. Explain that readers can connect to a text three different ways. One way is when a text makes readers think about something that happened in their own life. We call this connecting a text to self.

   ▶ What are two other ways readers can connect to a text? **when a story makes you think about another story you've read (text to text); when a story makes you think about something that happens in the real world (text to world)**

3. Read aloud the following two ways readers can make a connection to a text if students have trouble recalling them.

   ▶ When readers think, "This story reminds me of another story I've read," they are connecting the text to another text.
   ▶ When readers think, "This story reminds me of something I've heard about" or "This story reminds me of something I saw," they are connecting the text to the real world.

4. Have students look the picture on the story card while you **read aloud** the following story.

   Once a year, the whole Ramirez family gets together. Grandma, Grandpa, Mom, Dad, aunts, uncles, and all the kids spend the whole day eating homemade food, talking, playing, and sharing presents. Everyone has a good time.

5. Ask students the following questions. Answers will vary; if students have trouble making a connection, offer one of your own as an example.

▶ Do the picture and story remind you of anything? What do they make you think about?

▶ Does this story make you think about another story you've read? What is the story? How are the stories alike?

▶ Does this story make you think about something that happens in the real world? What is it? Why does it make you think about this?

Words to Know

Before reading "Tear-Water Tea" and "Upstairs and Downstairs," go over Words to Know with students.

1. Read aloud each word and have students repeat it.

2. Ask students if they know what each word means.

▶ If students know a word's meaning, have them define it and use it in a sentence.

▶ If students don't know a word's meaning, read them the definition and discuss the word with them.

boil – to heat a liquid until it starts to bubble and give off steam; to cook certain foods, you must boil them until they are very hot and bubbly

kettle – a container with a spout used for heating liquids such as water

Guided Reading

Book Walk

Prepare students for reading by taking them on a Book Walk of *Owl at Home*. Scan the stories "Tear-Water Tea" and "Upstairs and Downstairs" together and ask students to make predictions.

1. Have students read aloud the **book title**.

2. Read aloud the **name of the author**.

3. Have students read aloud the story titles on the **Contents** page. Explain to students that in this lesson, they will read "Tear-Water Tea" and "Upstairs and Downstairs."

4. Have students look at the **pictures in "Tear-Water Tea" and "Upstairs and Downstairs."** Answers to questions may vary.

▶ What do you think might happen in these stories?

▶ Have you ever drunk tea? What was it like?

▶ What do you think a person would use to make tear-water tea?

▶ Have you ever wanted to be two places at the same time? What were the two places and why did you want to be in both those places?

Objectives

- Make predictions based on text, illustrations, and/or prior knowledge.
- Activate prior knowledge by previewing text and/or discussing topic.
- Read and listen to a variety of texts for information and pleasure independently or as part of a group.
- Read aloud grade-level text with appropriate expression, accuracy, and rate.

"Tear-Water Tea" and "Upstairs and Downstairs"

Guide students through a preview of the stories to prepare them for reading on their own. Gather the Reading Aid on page LC 327 and 328 in *K¹² Language Arts Activity Book*.

1. Have students sit next to you so that they can see the pictures and words while you introduce and discuss the stories.

2. Tell students that you will preview the stories to prepare them to read aloud to you.

3. Refer to the Reading Aid.

Reading Aid Tear out the Reading Aid for this reading selection. Follow the instructions for folding the page, and then use the page as a guide as you preview the selection with students.

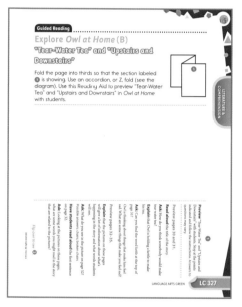
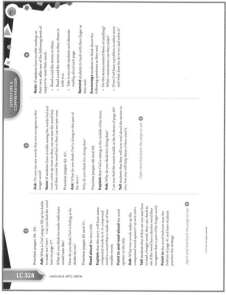

Check Your Reading

"Tear-Water Tea" and "Upstairs and Downstairs"

Check students' comprehension of "Tear-Water Tea" and "Upstairs and Downstairs."

1. Have students retell "Tear-Water Tea" in their own words to develop grammar, vocabulary, comprehension, and fluency skills.

2. Ask students the following questions to check their comprehension of "Tear-Water Tea."

   ▸ Where does "Tear-Water Tea" take place? at Owl's house
   ▸ What does Owl decide to make at the beginning of the story? tear-water tea
   ▸ How does Owl get the water for the tea? from his tears
   ▸ How does Owl make himself cry? He thinks of sad things.
   ▸ What is something that makes Owl cry? Answers will vary; accept any of the things mentioned in the story.
   ▸ How does Owl feel when he's making himself cry? sad How does Owl feel when he is drinking his tea at the end of the story? happy Why does Owl feel happy? He has his tear-water tea, which is always very good.

3. Have students retell "Upstairs and Downstairs" in their own words to develop grammar, vocabulary, comprehension, and fluency skills.

4. Ask students the following questions to check their comprehension of the "Upstairs and Downstairs."

   ▸ Where does "Upstairs and Downstairs" take place? at Owl's house
   ▸ What does Owl wonder when he is downstairs? how his upstairs is
   ▸ What does Owl wonder when he is upstairs? how his downstairs is
   ▸ What does Owl think he can do if he runs very, very fast? be upstairs and downstairs at the same time
   ▸ How long does Owl run up and down the stairs? all evening

TIP If students have trouble responding to a question, help them locate the answer in the text or pictures.

Objectives
- Retell or dramatize a story.
- Identify setting.
- Answer questions requiring literal recall of details.

Reading for Meaning

Connect with "Tear-Water Tea"

Help students make a connection with "Tear-Water Tea."

Objectives

- Make connections with text: text-to-text, text-to-self, text-to-world.
- Describe character(s).
- Describe story structure elements—problem and solution.

1. Remind students that readers who make connections to a story while they read are better able to understand and remember what they read.

2. Help students make connections with the character and events in "Tear-Water Tea" by asking the following questions. Answers to questions may vary.

   ▸ Does anything in "Tear-Water Tea" remind you of something in your own life?

   ▸ Do you ever think about things that make you feel sad? What are they? Why does thinking about these things make you feel sad?

   ▸ Owl is happy when he drinks the tea because it is always very good. Is there something that you drink or eat that always makes you feel happy? What is it? Why do you think it makes you feel happy?

   ▸ Does Owl remind you of anybody you know? If so, how is Owl like that person?

   ▸ Does "Tear-Water Tea" remind you of another story? Which one? Why does it remind you of this story?

   ▸ Does "Tear-Water Tea" remind you of something that has happened in the real world? What was it? Why does the story make you think of this?

Problem and Solution in "Upstairs and Downstairs"

Check students' ability to identify problem and solution in "Upstairs and Downstairs."

▸ What is Owl's problem in "Upstairs and Downstairs"? He wants to be upstairs and downstairs at the same time.

▸ How does Owl think he can solve this problem? by running up and down the stairs fast

▸ What does Owl do when running up and down the stairs fast doesn't work? He runs faster and faster.

▸ What happens when Owl runs up and down the stairs faster and faster? He gets very tired.   Is he ever in both places at the same time? No   Does he ever solve his problem? No

▸ Where does Owl end up? sitting on the tenth step of the stairs   Why do you think Owl decides to sit there? Possible answers: because it's right in the middle of upstairs and downstairs; because he needs to rest

▸ How do you think Owl feels when he realizes he can't solve his problem by running up and down the stairs very, very fast? Do you think Owl will try something else to solve his problem? Why or why not? Answers will vary.

Explore *Owl at Home* (C)

Lesson Overview

	[Offline]	**45** minutes
Get Ready	Lesson Introduction	
	Retelling to Self-Monitor Understanding	
Guided Reading	Book Walk	
	"Owl and the Moon"	
Check Your Reading	"Owl and the Moon"	
Reading for Meaning	Personification in "Owl and the Moon"	
	Retell "Owl and the Moon"	
Making Connections	Create a Features of Fiction Poster	

Materials

Supplied
- *Owl at Home* by Arnold Lobel
- *K¹² Language Arts Activity Book*, pp. LC 329–332

Also Needed
- glue stick
- household objects –old children's books and fiction magazines
- index cards
- paper, poster – white
- scissors, round-end safety

Story Synopsis

Owl strikes up an unusual friendship in "Owl and the Moon," which is the final story in *Owl at Home*.

Advance Preparation

Preview pages LC 329 and 330 in *K¹² Language Arts Activity Book* to prepare the materials for the Guided Reading.

Big Ideas

▶ Exposing readers to a wide variety of genres provides them with a wide range of background knowledge and increases their vocabulary.

▶ An awareness of story structure elements (setting, characters, plot) provides readers a foundation for constructing meaning when reading new stories and writing their own stories.

▶ Comprehension requires the reader to self-monitor understanding.

▶ Verbalizing your thoughts while modeling a reading strategy allows students to see what goes on inside the head of an effective reader; it makes visible the normally hidden process of comprehending text.

▶ Guided reading provides support to early readers as they practice and apply the reading strategies of proficient readers.

Keywords

fiction – make-believe stories

genre – a category for classifying literary works

retelling – using your own words to tell a story that you have listened to or read

self-monitor – to notice if you do or do not understand what you are reading

story structure elements – components of a story; they include character, setting, plot, problem, and solution

 **45** minutes

Work **together** with students to complete Get Ready, Guided Reading, Check Your Reading, Reading for Meaning, and Making Connections activities.

Get Ready

Lesson Introduction
Prepare students for reading and discussing "Owl and the Moon."

1. Tell students that they will read "Owl and the Moon" in *Owl at Home*.

2. Explain that before they read the story, you will get ready by reviewing how retelling a story is a way to check that you understand what you've read.

Objectives
- Retell a story naming plot, setting, character(s), problem, and solution.
- Self-monitor comprehension of text.

Retelling to Self-Monitor Understanding
Reinforce that retelling a story is a way to self-monitor comprehension of a story.

1. Remind students that one way readers can check their understanding of a story is by retelling it.

2. Explain that **retelling** means using your own words to tell what happens in a story that you have listened to or read.

   ► A good retelling includes the characters, the setting, the problem, and how the characters solve the problem.
   ► A good retelling describes the plot of a story. The plot is the important things that happen in the beginning, middle, and end of the story in the order that they happen.

3. Have students practice by having them retell "Upstairs and Downstairs." Possible retelling: Owl's house has an upstairs and a downstairs. When Owl is upstairs, he wonders how his downstairs is. When he is downstairs, he wonders how his upstairs is. Owl wants to be upstairs and downstairs at the same time. He decides he could do this if if he runs up and down the stairs very, very fast. Owl runs up and down the stairs over and over, and faster and faster, but he is never in both places at the same time. Owl gets tired from all the running, so he sits on the middle step of the stairs to rest.

4. Guide students to think about their retelling. Answers to questions may vary.

   ► Did your retelling include the name of the character?
   ► Did it include most of the important things that happened, and in the right order?
   ► Did your retelling include Owl's problem and how he tries to solve it?
   ► Did your retelling explain that Owl doesn't solve his problem?
   ► Do you think that you understand the story?

TIP If students don't think they understand the story, reread the story aloud, pausing to let students ask questions as you read.

Guided Reading

Book Walk

Prepare students for reading by taking them on a Book Walk of *Owl at Home*. Scan the story "Owl and the Moon" together and ask students to make predictions.

1. Have students read aloud the **book title**.

2. Read aloud the **name of the author**.

3. Have students read aloud the story titles on the **Contents** page. Explain to students that in this lesson, they will read "Owl and the Moon."

4. Have students look at the **pictures in "Owl and the Moon."** Answers to questions may vary.

   ▸ What do you think might happen in this story?
   ▸ Have you ever seen the moon at night? What did it look like?
   ▸ Have you ever noticed that it gets darker outside when the moon goes behind clouds? Why do you think this happens?

Objectives

- Make predictions based on text, illustrations, and/or prior knowledge.
- Activate prior knowledge by previewing text and/or discussing topic.
- Read and listen to a variety of texts for information and pleasure independently or as part of a group.
- Read aloud grade-level text with appropriate expression, accuracy, and rate.

"Owl and the Moon"

Guide students through a preview of the story to prepare them for reading on their own. Gather the Reading Aid on pages LC 329 and 330 in *K¹² Language Arts Activity Book*.

1. Have students sit next to you so that they can see the pictures and words while you introduce and discuss the story.

2. Tell students that you will preview the story in order to prepare them to read it aloud to you.

3. Refer to the Reading Aid.

Reading Aid Tear out the Reading Aid for this reading selection. Follow the instructions for folding the page, and then use the page as a guide as you preview the selection with students.

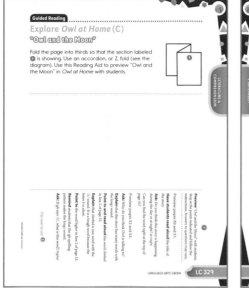
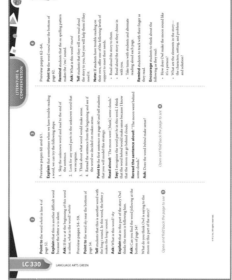

Check Your Reading

"Owl and the Moon"

Check students' comprehension of "Owl and the Moon."

- ▶ Where does the beginning of "Owl and the Moon" take place? by the seashore
- ▶ Where is Owl sitting? on a rock
- ▶ Why does Owl think the moon must be his friend? because they are looking at each other
- ▶ What does Owl notice about the moon while he walks home? It keeps following him.
- ▶ Why does Owl tell the moon that it can't come home with him? His house is small and the moon wouldn't fit through the door, and he doesn't have anything to give him for supper.
- ▶ Why does Owl think the moon is finally gone? It goes behind some clouds.

TIP If students have trouble responding to a question, help them locate the answer in the text or pictures.

Objectives
- Identify setting.
- Answer questions requiring literal recall of details.

Reading for Meaning

Personification in "Owl and the Moon"

Check students' understanding of personification.

1. Remind students that authors sometimes make animals or things sound like they're human. For example, an author might write, "The wind howled all night long." We know that the wind can't really howl. But, authors do this to help us imagine an interesting picture or better imagine a sound, and to think about certain feelings, such as loneliness or joy.

2. Read aloud the text on page 53.

   ▸ What does Owl say that makes it sound like the moon is a person? "You must be looking back at me" and "we must be very good friends." Why do you think the author used these words? to help us imagine how Owl feels about the moon; to help us imagine how Owl thinks the moon is alive and his friend

3. The story says that the moon keeps following Owl home.

   ▸ Can the moon really follow someone home? No   Why not? because the moon isn't human

4. Read aloud what Owl says to the moon in the middle of page 58.

   ▸ What does Owl say that makes it sound like the moon is a person? He says that he doesn't think the moon can hear him.   Why does Owl think that the moon can't hear him? because the moon keeps following him even though Owl has asked the moon to stop following him

5. Have students look at the picture at the end of the story on page 64.

   ▸ Can you think of a sentence that makes it sound like the moon is human? Answers will vary; if students need help, give them an example sentence, such as "The moon smiled at Owl."

Retell "Owl and the Moon"

Check students' ability to retell "Owl and the Moon." Turn to page LC 331 in *K¹² Language Arts Activity Book.*

1. Tell students they are going to retell "Owl and the Moon" using a Retelling Hand to remind them of what should be included in a retelling.

2. Point to the Retelling Hand and explain what each symbol on the fingers stands for.

   ▸ Thumb: The butterfly and little boy stand for the characters.
   ▸ Index finger: The house stands for the setting.
   ▸ Middle finger: The stair steps with the numbers on each step stand for the plot, because we tell the events of a story in the order they happen.
   ▸ Ring finger: The number sentence stands for the problem a character needs to solve, because 1 + 1 is a problem.
   ▸ Little finger: The number 2 is the answer, or solution, to 1 + 1, so this stands for the solution to the problem in the story.
   ▸ Palm: The heart stands for how you feel about the story and how you connect with it.

3. Have students retell the story, referring to the Retelling Hand.
   Possible retelling: Owl is the character in the story. The story takes place by the seashore, on the path to Owl's house, and in Owl's house.

   At the beginning of the story, Owl is sitting on a rock by the seashore and watches the moon rise. He thinks that they are looking at each other and that they must be friends. When Owl goes home, he thinks the moon is following him. He keeps telling the moon not to follow him. The moon finally goes behind some clouds, and Owl thinks it's gone. When Owl gets home and goes to bed, he feels a little sad. Suddenly, the room fills with silver light. Owl sees the moon outside his window. Owl tells the moon he thinks he's a good, round friend.

   The problem in the story is that the moon keeps following Owl. Owl's problem is solved when the moon goes behind a cloud. Students may also say why they like or do not like the story.

4. Guide students to think about their retelling. Answers to questions may vary.

   ▸ Did your retelling include the important characters?
   ▸ Did your retelling explain where the story happens?
   ▸ Did your retelling include most of the important things that happened and in the right order?
   ▸ Did your retelling include Owl's problem and how he solves it?
   ▸ Do you like the story? Why or why not?
   ▸ Do you think that you understand the story?
   ▸ Was it easier to retell the story with or without the Retelling Hand?

TIP If students don't think they understand the story, reread the story aloud, pausing to let students ask questions as you read.

Making Connections

 Create a Features of Fiction Poster

Reinforce students' knowledge of the characteristics of fiction writing by having students create a Features of Fiction poster. Turn to page LC 332 in *K¹² Language Arts Activity Book* and gather the materials needed to make the poster.

1. Remind students that all fiction stories have story structure elements, such as characters and a setting. Fiction books and stories also include text features, such as a title and the author's name.

2. Tell students to think about the all things they can expect to find in a fiction story.

3. Help students read aloud the directions on the Activity Book page, and then have them begin to make their poster.

   ▶ Explain any of the directions that students find unclear.
   ▶ Monitor students' progress to make sure they are following the directions as written.
   ▶ Have students arrange the index cards on the poster board **before** gluing them down, so they can be sure there is enough room for all the cards and any pictures that students may want to include.

Objectives
- Read text to perform a specific task.
- Identify characteristics of different genres.
- Distinguish fiction text from nonfiction text.
- Respond to text through art, writing, and/or drama.

4. If students need prompting, share the following list of story structure elements and suggested pictures or drawings to represent those elements.

Story Structure Elements

- ▸ **Characters** – faces of people or animals
- ▸ **Setting** – a house or a room
- ▸ **Plot** – three stair steps with the numbers 1, 2, 3 written on the steps
- ▸ **Problem** – an unsolved number sentence $(1 + 1)$
- ▸ **Solution** – the answer to the number sentence (2)

5. Share the following list of text features that might be found in a fiction book or story if students need prompting. Note that students do not need to include all of these features on their poster. If students choose to cut out pictures to represent these features, provide them with old children's books or fiction magazines for the cutouts.

Text Features

- ▸ **Title** – a cutout of the title of a book or story
- ▸ **Author** – a cutout of an author's name
- ▸ **Illustrator** – a cutout of an illustrator's name
- ▸ **Table of contents** – a cutout of a table of contents
- ▸ **Pictures** – cutouts of illustrations
- ▸ **Bold and italic words** – large, hand-printed words

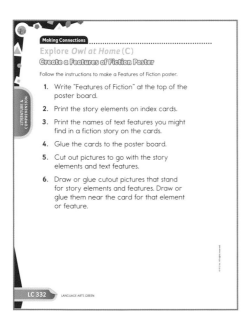

Introduce "Hunters of the Night"

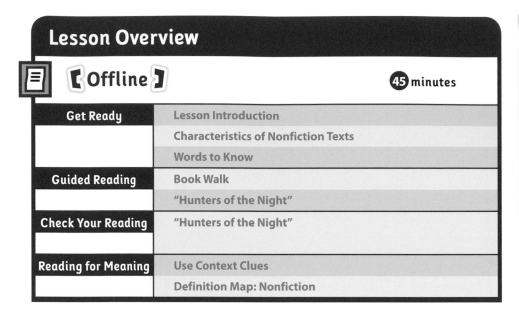

Lesson Overview

[Offline]   **45** minutes

Get Ready	Lesson Introduction
	Characteristics of Nonfiction Texts
	Words to Know
Guided Reading	Book Walk
	"Hunters of the Night"
Check Your Reading	"Hunters of the Night"
Reading for Meaning	Use Context Clues
	Definition Map: Nonfiction

Materials

Supplied

- "Hunters of the Night," *K¹² World: Critter and Creature Stories,* pp. 30–41
- *K¹² Language Arts Activity Book,* pp. LC 333–335
- Story Card H

Article Synopsis

Did you know there are more than 150 types of owls? Learn this and other amazing facts about these fascinating flying creatures.

Keywords

fact – something that can be proven true

genre – a category for classifying literary works

informational text – text written to explain and give information on a topic

nonfiction – writings about true things

topic – the subject of a text

Advance Preparation

Before beginning the Guided Reading, read "Hunters of the Night" to locate Words to Know in the text. Preview pages LC 333 and 334 in *K¹² Language Arts Activity Book* to prepare the materials for the Guided Reading.

Big Ideas

▸ Exposing readers to a wide variety of genres provides them with a wide range of background knowledge and increases their vocabulary.

▸ Nonfiction texts differ from fiction texts in that they describe real or true things in life, rather than things made up by the author.

▸ Guided reading provides support to early readers as they practice and apply the reading strategies of proficient readers.

 **45** minutes

Work **together** with students to complete Get Ready, Guided Reading, Check Your Reading, and Reading for Meaning activities.

Get Ready

Lesson Introduction

Prepare students for reading and discussing "Hunters of the Night."

1. Tell students that they will read "Hunters of the Night," a nonfiction article about owls.

2. Explain that before they read the article, you will get ready by reviewing the characteristics of nonfiction text.

Characteristics of Nonfiction Texts

Review the characteristics of nonfiction text. Gather Story Card H.

1. Remind students that authors write texts for different reasons. When authors write to inform us, they usually write **informational**, or **nonfiction**, texts.

2. Explain that nonfiction texts are filled with **facts** about real people, animals, or events. The information in a nonfiction text is true.

3. Ask students to name kinds of nonfiction texts. Read aloud the following list if they need help.

   ▶ newspaper stories
   ▶ magazine articles
   ▶ biographies

4. Remind students that a nonfiction text has a **topic**. The title of an article often gives a clue about the topic.

5. Remind students that if they know they are going to read a nonfiction text, they can expect to read facts about a particular topic. The topic will be about something real, such as a person, animal, or event.

6. Have students study the picture on the story card.

Objectives

- Identify features of informational text.
- Identify the topic.
- Identify genre.
- Build vocabulary through listening, reading, and discussion.
- Use new vocabulary in written and spoken sentences.
- Increase concept and content vocabulary.

7. Tell students to imagine that the picture is from a nonfiction article about a family going on vacation to Hawaii.

   ▸ If the article is nonfiction, are the people in the article real or made-up characters? real   How do you know that? Nonfiction articles have facts in them; nonfiction articles are about real people or things.
   ▸ What is the topic of the article with this picture? a vacation to Hawaii
   ▸ Based on what you know about nonfiction texts and the topic, what kind of facts do you think you might find in the article? Answers will vary; if students have trouble answering, suggest that they might expect to read about when the family takes their vacation, how they get to Hawaii, where they stay, and what they do while they are there.
   ▸ What do we call something that can be proven to be true? a fact
   ▸ What do we call texts that are about real things and are filled with facts? nonfiction; informational texts
   ▸ What is a topic? the subject of a nonfiction text; what a nonfiction text is mostly about

---

Words to Know

Before reading "Hunters of the Night," go over Words to Know with students.

1. Read aloud each word and have students repeat it.

2. Ask students if they know what each word means.

   ▸ If students know a word's meaning, have them define it and use it in a sentence.
   ▸ If students don't know a word's meaning, read them the definition and discuss the word with them.

burrow – a tunnel or hole in the ground dug by an animal
cactus – a desert plant that has thick stems and sharp points called spines; the plural of *cactus* is *cacti*
chick – a young bird
down – soft, fluffy bird feathers
keen – having sharp hearing, sight, or thinking
owlet – a baby owl
prey – an animal that is hunted and eaten by another animal
talon – a sharp claw on a bird's foot
tuft – a bunch of feathers or hair growing together or joined at one end and loose at the other end

Guided Reading ....

Book Walk

Prepare students for reading by taking them on a Book Walk of "Hunters of the Night." Scan the magazine article together and ask students to make predictions about the article.

1. Turn to the **table of contents** in *K¹² World: Critter and Creature Stories*. Help students find the selection and turn to that page.

2. Have students read aloud the **article title**.

3. Have students look at the **pictures of the article**. Remind them that pictures help show ideas that are in the text.

   ▸ Based on the title of the article, the pictures, and your prior knowledge of nonfiction texts, what do you think this article is mostly about? What do you think the topic might be? facts about owls

   ▸ What do you already know about owls? Answers will vary; students may mention information such as owls are awake at night, owls can see well in the dark, or owls hoot.

   ▸ Have you ever seen an owl in real life? Where did you see it? What was it doing? What did it look like? Answers will vary.

"Hunters of the Night"

Guide students through a preview of the article to prepare them for reading on their own. Gather the Reading Aid on pages LC 333 and 334 in *K¹² Language Arts Activity Book*.

1. Have students sit next to you so that they can see the pictures and words while you introduce and discuss the article.

2. Tell students that you will preview the article to prepare them to read aloud the article to you.

3. Refer to the Reading Aid.

Objectives

- Make predictions based on text, illustrations, and/or prior knowledge.
- Activate prior knowledge by previewing text and/or discussing topic.
- Read for information.
- Read aloud grade-level text with appropriate expression, accuracy, and rate.
- Use context and sentence structure to determine meaning of words, phrases, and/or sentences.

Reading Aid Tear out the Reading Aid for this reading selection. Follow the instructions for folding the page, and then use the page as a guide as you preview the selection with students.

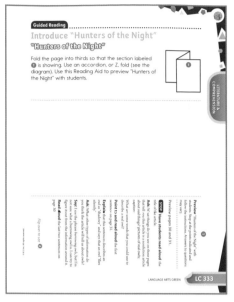
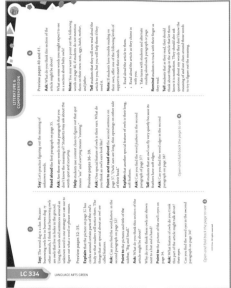

Check Your Reading

"Hunters of the Night"

Check students' comprehension of "Hunters of the Night."

1. Have students retell "Hunters of the Night" in their own words to develop grammar, vocabulary, comprehension, and fluency skills.

2. Ask students the following questions.

   ▸ What is the topic of "Hunters of the Night"? What is the article mostly about? Possible answers: owls; how owls hunt for food
   ▸ How does the title "Hunters of the Night" give a clue about the topic of the article? Owls hunt at night, and the article is about owls.
   ▸ When do most owls hunt their prey? at night
   ▸ Owls can't move their eyes the way people can. What do they have to do to see what's beside or behind them? twist their heads around
   ▸ What are the long, thin openings on either side of an owl's head? ears
   ▸ When do owls build nests and lay eggs? in the winter

TIP If students have trouble responding to a question, help them locate the answer in the text or pictures.

> ### Objectives
> - Retell or dramatize a story.
> - Identify the topic.
> - Identify facts in informational text.
> - Answer questions requiring literal recall of details.

Reading for Meaning

Use Context Clues

Check students' ability to use context clues to determine the meaning of unknown words and phrases.

1. Remind students that they can use the words, sentences, and even picture clues around an unknown word to figure out the meaning.

2. **Read aloud** the second paragraph on page 32.

   ▸ Are there any words in this paragraph that you don't know the meaning of? Answers will vary.
   ▸ What do you think the word *pests* means? If students can't tell you that a pest is something that causes problems or destroys things, point out the context clue "such as rats and mice" to help them figure it out.

3. **Read aloud** the caption at the top of page 38.

   ▸ Are there any words in this caption that you don't know the meaning of? Answers will vary.
   ▸ What do you think the phrase *swoop down on their prey* means? If students can't tell you that it means that owls fly down quickly to catch an animal, help them use page 38's context clues about hunting and the picture clue that shows an owl flying to figure it out.

Definition Map: Nonfiction

Explore characteristics of nonfiction texts with students. Turn to page LC 335 in *K¹² Language Arts Activity Book*.

1. Remind students that a nonfiction text has certain characteristics, such as a topic and facts.

   ▸ What kind of writing is "Hunters of the Night"? Possible answers: nonfiction; informational text; a nonfiction magazine article
   ▸ How can you tell the article is a nonfiction text? Possible answers: It tells facts about real owls; it has a topic; it has photographs.
   ▸ Are the owls in the article made-up characters or real? real

2. Look at the definition map on the Activity Book page with students. Explain that they will think of an answer for each question in the map to define nonfiction, or informational text. Then, they will write their answers in the boxes.

3. Point to and help students read aloud the "What is it?" heading.

4. Have students tell you their answer and help them write it in the box.

5. Point to and help students read aloud the "What is it like?" heading.

6. Have students tell you at least three characteristics of nonfiction and help them write the characteristics in the box.

7. Point to and help students read aloud the "What are some examples?" heading.

8. Have students tell you their answers and help them write them in the boxes. Note that students may give titles of nonfiction articles they have read. Or, they may answer in more general terms, such as "a newspaper article" or "a magazine article." Either type of response would be correct.

9. Ask the following questions. Answers to questions may vary.

   ▸ Based on how you defined nonfiction in the definition map, is "Hunters of the Night" fiction or nonfiction? nonfiction

   ▸ What is your favorite fact in "Hunters of the Night"? Why is that your favorite?

   ▸ What do you think about owls? Did reading the article change how you feel about them?

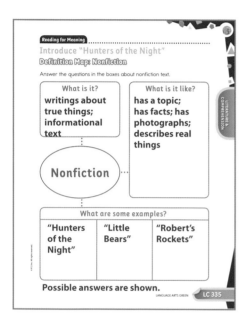

Explore "Hunters of the Night"

Lesson Overview

Get Ready	Lesson Introduction
	Text Features in Nonfiction Texts
	Words to Know
Guided Reading	Book Walk
	"Hunters of the Night"
Reading for Meaning	Text Features in "Hunters of the Night"
Making Connections	Create a Features of Nonfiction Poster

Big Ideas

- ▸ Exposing readers to a wide variety of genres provides them with a wide range of background knowledge and increases their vocabulary.
- ▸ Nonfiction texts differ from fiction texts in that they describe real or true things in life, rather than things made up by the author.
- ▸ Comprehension is facilitated by an understanding of physical presentation (for example: headings, subheads, graphics, and other features).
- ▸ Repeated rereading leads to increased fluency.

[Materials]

Supplied

- "Hunters of the Night" *K¹² World: Critter and Creature Stories*, pp. 30–41
- *K¹² Language Arts Activity Book*, p. LC 336

Also Needed

- glue stick
- household objects – old children's nonfiction magazines
- index cards
- paper, poster – white
- scissors, round-end safety

Keywords

fact – something that can be proven true

genre – a category for classifying literary works

informational text – text written to explain and give information on a topic

nonfiction – writings about true things

text feature – part of a text that helps a reader locate information and determine what is most important; some examples are the title, table of contents, headings, pictures, and glossary

visual text support – a graphic feature that helps a reader better understand text, such as a picture, chart, or map

[Offline] 45 minutes

Work **together** with students to complete Get Ready, Guided Reading, Reading for Meaning, and Making Connections activities.

Get Ready

Lesson Introduction

Prepare students for reading and discussing "Hunters of the Night."

1. Tell students that they are going to reread "Hunters of the Night."

2. Explain that before they reread the article, you will get ready by reviewing features in nonfiction texts.

Objectives

- Identify features of informational text.
- Identify purpose of and information provided by informational text features.
- Build vocabulary through listening, reading, and discussion.
- Use new vocabulary in written and spoken sentences.
- Increase concept and content vocabulary.

Text Features in Nonfiction Texts

Review organizational and visual text features that can be found in nonfiction text.

1. Remind students that magazines and the articles in them have text features that help readers better understand and find information.

2. Gather *K¹² World: Critter and Creature Stories* and have students locate and explain the following organizational **text features** in the magazine.

   ▸ table of contents a list of the titles of the articles in a magazine
   ▸ glossary an alphabetical list of important words and their meanings
   ▸ index an alphabetical list that shows where to find important words or subjects in a magazine

3. Turn to page 30 in *K¹² World: Critter and Creature Stories* and have students locate an example of each of the following **visual text supports** in the article and explain its function.

   ▸ picture Students may indicate any picture or photo in the article. A picture shows what something looks like.
   ▸ caption Students may indicate any caption in the article. A caption explains what's in the picture or photograph near it.
   ▸ label Students may indicate the photograph of the owl with the beak and talons labeled. A label names parts of a picture.
   ▸ a chart or diagram Students may indicate the diagram on page 33 that explains the size of some types of owls. A chart or diagram explains something or shows how it works.
   ▸ bold words Students may indicate any word in bold print in the article. Bold print indicates important words.

4. Have students turn to page 30 and locate the title of the article.

   ▸ What is the title of the article? "Hunters of the Night"
   ▸ What does the title tell about? the topic of the article

Words to Know

Before reading "Hunters of the Night," go over Words to Know with students.

1. Read aloud each word and have students repeat it.

2. Ask students if they know what each word means.

   ▸ If students know a word's meaning, have them define it and use it in a sentence.

   ▸ If students don't know a word's meaning, read them the definition and discuss the word with them.

burrow – a tunnel or hole in the ground dug by an animal

cactus – a desert plant that has thick stems and sharp points called spines; the plural of *cactus* is *cacti*

chick – a young bird

down – soft, fluffy bird feathers

keen – having sharp hearing, sight, or thinking

owlet – a baby owl

prey – an animal that is hunted and eaten by another animal

talon – a sharp claw on a bird's foot

tuft – a bunch of feathers or hair growing together or joined at one end and loose at the other end

Guided Reading

Book Walk

Prepare students for reading by taking them on a Book Walk of "Hunters of the Night." Scan the article together to revisit the text.

1. Turn to the selection.

2. Have students read aloud the **article title**.

3. Have students look at the **pictures of the article**.

4. Ask the following questions to help students think about what they already know about the article. Answers to questions may vary.

   ▸ What is something you have learned about owls?
   ▸ Why kind of owl in the article is your favorite? Why?

Objectives

- Activate prior knowledge by previewing text and/or discussing topic.
- Read for information.
- Read aloud grade-level text with appropriate expression, accuracy, and rate.

"Hunters of the Night"

It's time for students to reread the article aloud.

1. Tell students that "Hunters of the Night" should now be familiar to them because they have read it before.

2. Explain that they will reread the article aloud to you, but you are there if they need help.

3. If students have trouble reading on their own, offer one of the following levels of support to meet their needs.

   ▸ Read aloud the article to them.
   ▸ Read aloud the article as they chime in with you.
   ▸ Take turns with students and alternate reading aloud each paragraph or page.

4. Remind students to track with their finger as they read.

5. Tell students to be aware of text features in the article as they read.

Reading for Meaning

Text Features in "Hunters of the Night"

Check students' understanding of text features in "Hunters of the Night."

1. Remind students that good readers use text features, such as pictures, captions, and labels, to better understand the information in a magazine article.

2. Turn to pages 30 and 31. Have students study the pages.

   ▸ How do the title and pictures help a reader figure out the topic of the article? Possible answer: The pictures show owls and the title mentions hunters, so the topic must be about owls that hunt.

3. Turn to page 32 and read aloud the first paragraph. Then, point to the label that reads *beak*.

   ▸ What is this word? *beak*
   ▸ Why is there a line drawn from this word to a circle on the picture of the owl? to show what a beak is; to show where a beak is on an owl
   ▸ What do we call this kind of text feature? a label; a diagram

4. Turn to page 33 and point to the diagram of the two owls.

   ▸ Why is there a baseball bat next to the taller owl? to show how big the owl is in real life
   ▸ How does the diagram help the reader understand the size of the smaller owl? It shows that the smaller owl is about the size of your hand.

5. Point to the word *prey* on page 34.

   ▸ Why is this word darker than the other words? It's an important word in the article.   Where can we find out what this word means? in the back of the magazine; in the glossary

Objectives

- Identify characteristics of different genres.
- Identify purpose of and information provided by informational text features.
- Identify genre.
- Distinguish fiction text from nonfiction text.

6. Turn to the glossary on page 44 and have students locate the word *prey*.

   ▶ What is the meaning of the word *prey*? an animal that is hunted and eaten by another animal

7. Turn to the index on page 45 and have students locate the word *prey*.

   ▶ According the index, on what pages can I find the word *prey*? pages 34 and 38

8. Turn to page 36 and read aloud the text. Then, point to the picture on page 37.

   ▶ How does this picture help the reader better understand the information in the article? Possible answers: It shows how an owl can hear a mouse make a noise; it shows how an owl can tell where a mouse is when the mouse makes a sound.

9. Point to the circled pictures on page 41 and read aloud the captions next to them.

   ▶ How do these pictures help the reader better understand the information in the article? It shows how baby owls look while they grow up.
   ▶ What do we call the text near a picture? a caption

10. Ask the following questions to check students' ability to identify characteristics of nonfiction texts.

    ▶ What do we call magazine articles that are about real things and are filled with facts? Possible answers: nonfiction texts; informational texts; nonfiction magazine articles
    ▶ Are we more likely to find facts in fiction stories or in nonfiction texts? nonfiction texts

Making Connections

✏️ **Create a Features of Nonfiction Poster**

Reinforce students' knowledge of characteristics of nonfiction text by having students create a Features of Nonfiction poster. Gather materials needed for making the poster and turn to page LC 336 in *K¹² Language Arts Activity Book*.

1. Remind students that nonfiction texts are filled with facts about real things. Nonfiction texts such as magazines and the articles in magazines have text features that help readers better understand and locate information in the text.

   ▶ Features such as a table of contents, index, and headings in the articles help readers locate information.
   ▶ Features such as the glossary help readers better understand words in a nonfiction article.
   ▶ Visual supports, such as maps, diagrams, and pictures with captions, help readers better understand the information in an article.

2. Tell students they are going to make a Features of Nonfiction poster. Have them think about all the text features they would expect to find in a nonfiction magazine and the articles in the magazine.

> **Objectives**
> - Respond to text through art, writing, and/or drama.
> - Read text to perform a specific task.
> - Identify characteristics of different genres.
> - Identify features of informational text.
> - Distinguish fiction text from nonfiction text.

3. Help students read aloud the directions on the Activity Book page, and then have them begin to make their poster.

   ▸ Explain any of the directions that students find unclear.
   ▸ Monitor students' progress to make sure they are following the directions as written.
   ▸ Have students arrange the index cards on the poster board **before** gluing them down so they can be sure there is enough room for all the cards.
   ▸ Tell students to cut out examples of each item named on the cards from old nonfiction magazines. **Do not allow** students to cut out features from any K^{12} magazines.

4. Share the following list of organizational text features and visual text supports with students if they need prompting.

Organizational Text Features

   ▸ Table of contents
   ▸ Titles
   ▸ Headings
   ▸ Glossary
   ▸ Index

Visual Text Supports

   ▸ Pictures
   ▸ Captions
   ▸ Labels
   ▸ Maps
   ▸ Diagrams or charts
   ▸ Bold and italic words

Reward: Add a sticker for this unit on the My Accomplishments chart to mark successful completion of the unit.

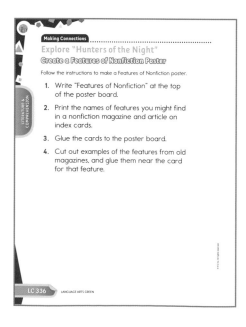

Let's Put on a Show

Unit Focus

In this unit, students will explore plays. This unit follows the guided-reading instructional approach (see the instructional approaches to reading in the introductory lesson for this program). Students will

► Read and explore plays.
► Explore the characteristics that are unique to plays—script, dialogue, audience, stage directions, and scenes.
► Review story structure elements—characters, setting, plot, and problem and solution.
► Check that they understand what they've read by retelling.
► Review the characteristics of fables.
► Identify the moral or lesson of a fable presented as a play.
► Read with fluency and expression as they act out a play.

Unit Plan		**[Offline]**
Lesson 1	Introduce "The Hummingbird and the Butterfly"	**45** minutes a day
Lesson 2	Explore "The Hummingbird and the Butterfly"	
Lesson 3	Introduce "The Lion and the Mouse"	
Lesson 4	Explore "The Lion and the Mouse"	

Introduce "The Hummingbird and the Butterfly"

Lesson Overview

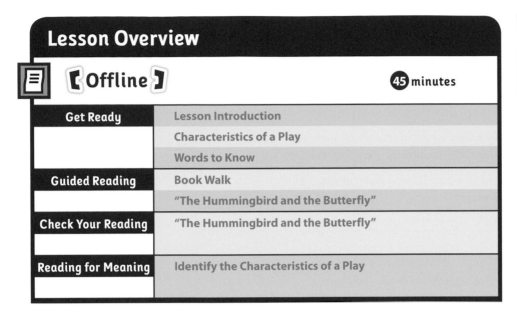

[Offline]		**45** minutes
Get Ready	Lesson Introduction	
	Characteristics of a Play	
	Words to Know	
Guided Reading	Book Walk	
	"The Hummingbird and the Butterfly"	
Check Your Reading	"The Hummingbird and the Butterfly"	
Reading for Meaning	Identify the Characteristics of a Play	

Advance Preparation

Before beginning the Guided Reading, read "The Hummingbird and the Butterfly" to locate Words to Know in the text. Preview pages LC 337 and 338 in *K¹² Language Arts Activity Book* to prepare the materials for the Guided Reading.

Big Ideas

▸ Exposing readers to a wide variety of genres provides them with a wide range of background knowledge and increases their vocabulary.
▸ Comprehension is facilitated by an understanding of physical presentation (headings, subheads, graphics and other features).
▸ Guided reading provides support to early readers as they practice and apply the reading strategies of proficient readers.

[Materials]

Supplied

● "The Hummingbird and the Butterfly," *K¹² Classics for Young Readers, Volume A,* pp. 220–223
● *K¹² Language Arts Activity Book,* pp. LC 337–338

Play Synopsis

A hummingbird wants to make friends with a beautiful, new creature, only to be turned down because of a past offense. What big lesson will the hummingbird learn?

Keywords

dialogue – the words that characters say in a written work
genre – a category for classifying literary works

[Offline] 45 minutes

Work **together** with students to complete Get Ready, Guided Reading, Check Your Reading, and Reading for Meaning activities.

Get Ready

Lesson Introduction

Prepare students for reading and discussing "The Hummingbird and the Butterfly."

1. Tell students that they will read "The Hummingbird and the Butterfly," a play about an animal that learns a lesson about kindness.

2. Explain that before they read the play, you will help them get ready by discussing the characteristics of a play.

Characteristics of a Play

Introduce the characteristics of a play. Answers to questions may vary.

1. Tell students that sometimes a story is told as a play.

   ▸ Do you know what a play is?

2. If students do not know what a play is, explain that it is different from a story that you read to yourself. A play is a story that is written so that it can be acted out by actors.

3. Ask students if they've ever seen a play.

   ▸ What was the play about? What story did it tell?
   ▸ What was the play like?
   ▸ What did you like about the play?

4. If students have not seen a play, explain that it is like watching a movie or TV show. The difference is that the actors perform the play live on a stage in front of people. Movies and TV shows are filmed and watched later in a movie theater or at home.

5. Tell students that a play has the same story structure elements as a story you might read in a book. It has characters and a setting. The characters have problems to solve, and what happens in a play is the plot. A play may also have a theme or moral.

6. Explain that most of the words we read in a play are meant to be spoken. The words the actors say out loud are called the **dialogue**. The dialogue is written on pages called a script. The play that students will be reading is written as a script that actors could use to perform.

Objectives
- Identify characteristics of different genres.
- Build vocabulary through listening, reading, and discussion.
- Use new vocabulary in written and spoken sentences.
- Increase concept and content vocabulary.

Words to Know

Before reading "The Hummingbird and the Butterfly," go over Words to Know with students.

1. Read aloud each word and have students repeat it.

2. Ask students if they know what each word means.

   ▸ If students know a word's meaning, have them define it and use it in a sentence.

   ▸ If students don't know a word's meaning, read them the definition and discuss the word with them.

caterpillar – an insect that is round and long like a worm, but has legs; it might be brightly colored

creature – a living person or animal

Guided Reading

Book Walk

Prepare students for reading by taking them on a Book Walk of "The Hummingbird and the Butterfly." Scan the play together and ask students to make predictions. Answers to questions may vary.

1. Turn to the **table of contents** in *K¹² Classics for Young Readers, Volume A*. Help students find "The Hummingbird and the Butterfly" and turn to that page.

2. Point to and read aloud the **play title**.

   ▸ What do you think this play might be about?

3. Have students look at the **pictures of the play**.

   ▸ Where do you think the story being told in the play takes place?
   ▸ Have you ever seen a real hummingbird, butterfly, or caterpillar? What do you know about these creatures? Do you think they are nice to look at?

4. Explain that when plays are written on a page, they look different from poems, fiction stories, and nonfiction articles and books.

5. Tell students that as they read plays, they should notice how they are different from the stories and articles they have read.

Objectives

- Make predictions based on text, illustrations, and/or prior knowledge.
- Activate prior knowledge by previewing text and/or discussing topic.
- Read and listen to a variety of texts for information and pleasure independently or as part of a group.
- Read aloud grade-level text with appropriate expression, accuracy, and rate.

"The Hummingbird and the Butterfly"

Guide students through a preview of the play to prepare them for reading on their own. Gather the Reading Aid on pages LC 337 and 338 in *K¹² Language Arts Activity Book*.

1. Have students sit next to you, so they can see the pictures and words while you introduce and discuss the play.

2. Tell students that you will preview the play to prepare them to read aloud the play to you.

3. Refer to the Reading Aid.

Reading Aid   Tear out the Reading Aid for this reading selection. Follow the instructions for folding the page and then use the page as a guide as you preview the selection with students.

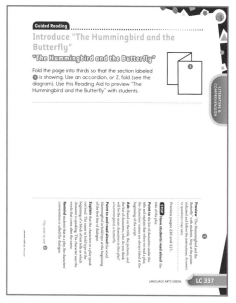

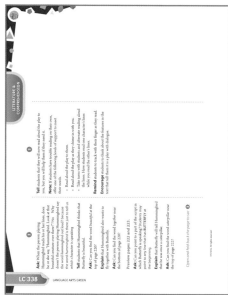

Check Your Reading

"The Hummingbird and the Butterfly"

Check students' comprehension of "The Hummingbird and the Butterfly."

1. Have students retell "The Hummingbird and the Butterfly" in their own words to develop grammar, vocabulary, comprehension, and fluency skills.

2. Ask students the following questions.

   ▶ Who are the characters in the play? Hummingbird; Butterfly
   ▶ Where does the story being told in the play take place? outside; by some flowers
   ▶ Why does Hummingbird want to be friends with Butterfly at the beginning of the play? because Butterfly has pretty wings, just like Hummingbird
   ▶ What did Butterfly used to be? a caterpillar
   ▶ What did Hummingbird do when Butterfly was a caterpillar? Possible answers: made fun of the caterpillar; said the caterpillar was ugly; said the caterpillar looked like an ugly, furry worm

Objectives
- Retell or dramatize a story.
- Identify the main character(s).
- Answer questions requiring literal recall of details.

TIP If students have trouble responding to a question, help them locate the answer in the text or pictures.

Reading for Meaning

Identify the Characteristics of a Play

Explore the characteristics of a play.

1. Ask the following questions.

   ▶ What kind of writing is "The Hummingbird and the Butterfly"? a play
   ▶ How can you tell "The Hummingbird and the Butterfly" is a play? Possible answers: All the words are spoken; the words are written as a script.
   ▶ What do we call the words that the characters say to each other in a play? the dialogue

2. Turn to page 221 and point to the name **BUTTERFLY** at the top of the page.

   ▶ Why is this name in bold text? because it's the name of a character
   ▶ Are the words after a character's name meant to be read silently or said out loud? said out loud
   ▶ Which character speaks the words that are written after this name? Butterfly
   ▶ Why does Butterfly say these words? Possible answers: because the word *Butterfly* at the beginning of the line tell us that the Butterfly character says these words; because it's a play; because the characters say the words in a play; because it's part of the dialogue

Objectives
- Identify genre.
- Identify characteristics of different genres.

Explore "The Hummingbird and the Butterfly"

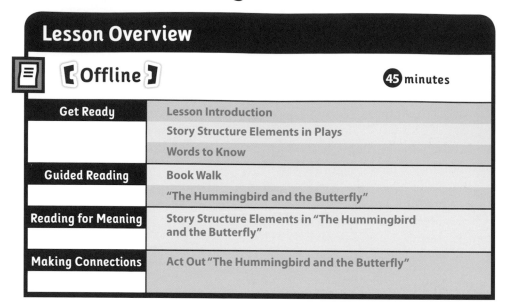

Lesson Overview

[Offline] **45** minutes

Get Ready	Lesson Introduction
	Story Structure Elements in Plays
	Words to Know
Guided Reading	Book Walk
	"The Hummingbird and the Butterfly"
Reading for Meaning	Story Structure Elements in "The Hummingbird and the Butterfly"
Making Connections	Act Out "The Hummingbird and the Butterfly"

[Materials]

Supplied

- "The Hummingbird and the Butterfly," *K¹² Classics for Young Readers, Volume A*, pp. 220–223
- *K¹² Language Arts Activity Book*, p. LC 339
- "The Hummingbird and the Butterfly" (printout)

Also Needed

- crayons
- craft sticks (2)
- glue stick
- scissors, round-end safety

Keywords

story structure elements – components of a story; they include character, setting, plot, problem, and solution

Advance Preparation

Before beginning Making Connections, print two copies of "The Hummingbird and the Butterfly" from the online lesson.

Big Ideas

- ▶ Comprehension requires an understanding of story structure.
- ▶ An awareness of story structure elements (setting, characters, plot) provides readers a foundation for constructing meaning when reading new stories and writing their own stories.
- ▶ To understand and interpret a story, readers need to understand and describe characters and what they do.
- ▶ Repeated rereading leads to increased fluency.

[Offline] 45 minutes

Work **together** with students to complete Get Ready, Guided Reading, Reading for Meaning, and Making Connections activities.

Get Ready

Lesson Introduction

Prepare students for reading and discussing "The Hummingbird and the Butterfly."

1. Tell students that they will reread the play "The Hummingbird and the Butterfly."

2. Explain that before they reread the play, you will get ready by discussing how a play has story structure elements.

> **Objectives**
> - Identify story structure elements—plot, setting, character(s).
> - Describe story structure elements—problem and solution.
> - Build vocabulary through listening, reading, and discussion.
> - Use new vocabulary in written and spoken sentences.
> - Increase concept and content vocabulary.

Story Structure Elements in Plays

Explore story structure elements in plays.

1. Remind students that a play tells a story, which means it has the same story structure elements as a story you might read in a book.

2. Review **story structure elements** with students.

   ▸ What do we call the people or animals in a story or a play? characters
   ▸ What is the setting of a story or play? where and when a story or play takes place
   ▸ What do characters have to solve in a story or play? problems
   ▸ Does a play have a plot? Yes   Why? because a play tells a story, and what happens in a story is the plot

Words to Know

Before reading "The Hummingbird and the Butterfly," go over Words to Know with students.

1. Read aloud each word and have students repeat it.

2. Ask students if they know what each word means.

   ▸ If students know a word's meaning, have them define it and use it in a sentence.
   ▸ If students don't know a word's meaning, read them the definition and discuss the word with them.

caterpillar – an insect that is round and long like a worm, but has legs; it might be brightly colored
creature – a living person or animal

Guided Reading

Objectives
- Activate prior knowledge by previewing text and/or discussing topic.
- Read and respond to texts representing a variety of cultures, time periods, and traditions.
- Read aloud grade-level text with appropriate expression, accuracy, and rate.

Book Walk

Prepare students for reading by taking them on a Book Walk of "The Hummingbird and the Butterfly." Scan the play together to revisit the characters and events.

1. Turn to the selection in *K¹² Classics for Young Readers, Volume A*.

2. Have students read aloud the **play title**.

3. Have students review the **pictures of the play**. Answers to questions may vary.

   ▸ Do you think Hummingbird would be a good friend to have? Why or why not?

   ▸ Do you think Butterfly would be a good friend to have? Why or why not?

"The Hummingbird and the Butterfly"

It's time for students to reread the play aloud.

1. Tell students that "The Hummingbird and the Butterfly" should now be familiar to them because they have read it before.

2. Explain that they will reread the play aloud to you, but you are there to help them if they need it.

3. If students have trouble reading on their own, offer one of the following levels of support to meet their needs.

   ▸ Read aloud the play to them.
   ▸ Read aloud the play aloud as they chime in with you.
   ▸ Take turns with students and alternate reading aloud each line of dialogue.

4. Remind students to track with their finger as they read.

5. Tell students to think about how the play tells a story as they read.

Reading for Meaning

Story Structure Elements in "The Hummingbird and the Butterfly"
Check students' understanding of story structure elements in a play.

- ▶ Who are the characters in the play? Hummingbird; Butterfly
- ▶ What is the setting? outside; near some flowers
- ▶ What is Hummingbird's problem? Butterfly doesn't want to be friends with Hummingbird.
- ▶ Why doesn't Butterfly want to be friends with Hummingbird? Hummingbird made fun of Butterfly when Butterfly was a caterpillar.
- ▶ Why did Hummingbird make fun of Butterfly when Butterfly was a caterpillar? because Hummingbird thought the caterpillar looked like an ugly worm
- ▶ How does Hummingbird solve the problem? Hummingbird apologizes to Butterfly.
- ▶ What lesson does Hummingbird learn? It's important to be kind to others, no matter what they look like.
- ▶ What is the plot of the play "The Hummingbird and the Butterfly"? Possible answer: Hummingbird sees a creature with beautiful wings and wants to be friends. But Butterfly doesn't want to be friends with Hummingbird because Hummingbird made fun of Butterfly when Butterfly was a caterpillar. Hummingbird apologizes for being mean to Butterfly. Butterfly is glad that Hummingbird has learned that it is important to be kind to everyone, no matter what they look like. Butterfly says that they can be friends.

Objectives

- Identify character(s).
- Identify setting.
- Identify details that explain characters' actions and feelings.
- Identify story structure elements—plot, setting, character(s).
- Describe story structure elements—problem and solution.
- Identify the moral or lesson of a text.

Making Connections

Act Out "The Hummingbird and the Butterfly"
Have students practice their reading fluency and demonstrate their understanding by acting out the play with stick puppets. Turn to page LC 339 in *K¹² Language Arts Activity Book* and gather the copies of the script, crayons, craft sticks, glue sticks, and scissors.

1. Tell students that they are going to act out the play using stick puppets.

2. Explain that acting out a play can help readers improve their expression and fluency when they read.

3. Have students color the characters on the Activity Book page.

4. Help students cut out and then glue the hummingbird and butterfly to craft sticks.

Objectives

- Respond to text through art, writing, and/or drama.
- Retell or dramatize a story.
- Demonstrate understanding through drawing, discussion, drama, and/or writing.
- Speak audibly and clearly to express thoughts, feelings, and ideas.
- Read text to perform a specific task.

5. If there is only one student, have the student pick which character he or she would like to play, with you playing the other character.

   ▶ If there is more than one student, have each read one character.

6. Remind students that when they read their character's dialogue, they should not read the bold name of the character in the script. They should only read the words that the character actually says out loud.

7. Have students practice reading their character's dialogue aloud at least once before performing with others or you.

8. Have students act out the play with the stick puppets.

9. Ask the following questions when students are done acting out the play. Answers to questions may vary.

   ▶ Did you like playing a character in the play?
   ▶ Did you learn anything new about your character by saying the character's dialogue?
   ▶ How does your character feel at the beginning of the play?
   ▶ How does your character feel at the end of the play?

Introduce "The Lion and the Mouse"

Lesson Overview

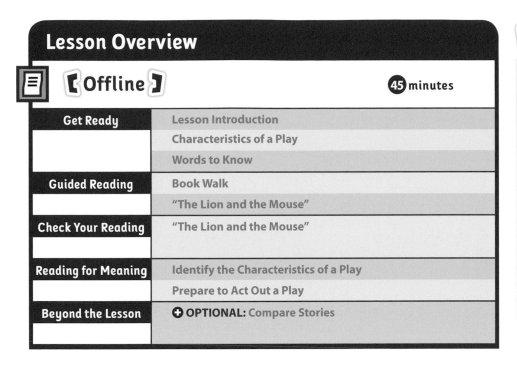

Offline — 45 minutes

Get Ready	Lesson Introduction
	Characteristics of a Play
	Words to Know
Guided Reading	Book Walk
	"The Lion and the Mouse"
Check Your Reading	"The Lion and the Mouse"
Reading for Meaning	Identify the Characteristics of a Play
	Prepare to Act Out a Play
Beyond the Lesson	⊕ OPTIONAL: Compare Stories

Advance Preparation

Before beginning the Guided Reading, read "The Lion and the Mouse" to locate Words to Know in the text. Preview pages LC 341 and 342 in *K¹² Language Arts Activity Book* to prepare the materials for the Guided Reading.

Big Ideas

▸ Exposing readers to a wide variety of genres provides them with a wide range of background knowledge and increases their vocabulary.

▸ Comprehension is facilitated by an understanding of physical presentation (headings, subheads, graphics and other features).

▸ Guided reading provides support to early readers as they practice and apply the reading strategies of proficient readers.

Materials

Supplied

● "The Lion and the Mouse," *K¹² Classics for Young Readers, Volume A,* pp. 224–233
● *K¹² Language Arts Activity Book,* pp. LC 341–345

Also Needed

● glue
● household objects – string
● yarn, yellow or gold
● scissors, round-end safety

Play Synopsis

The classic fable of a noble lion being helped by a lowly mouse comes to life as a play.

Keywords

dialogue – the words that characters say in a written work

genre – a category for classifying literary works

[Offline] **45** minutes

Work **together** with students to complete Get Ready, Guided Reading, Check Your Reading, Reading for Meaning, and Beyond the Lesson activities.

Get Ready

Lesson Introduction
Prepare students for reading and discussing "The Lion and the Mouse."

1. Tell students that they will read "The Lion and the Mouse," a play that teaches a lesson about helping others.

2. Explain that before they read the play, you will help them get ready by

   ▸ Reviewing characteristics of plays
   ▸ Learning about scenes and stage directions in plays

Objectives
- Identify genre.
- Identify characteristics of different genres.
- Build vocabulary through listening, reading, and discussion.
- Use new vocabulary in written and spoken sentences.
- Increase concept and content vocabulary.

Characteristics of a Play
Reinforce the characteristics of a play.

1. Remind students that a story can be written on pages and acted out on a stage.

   ▸ What do we call a story that is acted out on a stage? a play
   ▸ What do we call the pages that have the words that the actors say? a script
   ▸ What do we call the words that the actors say to each other while they act out the play? the dialogue

2. Remind them that a play has the same story structure elements as a story you might read in a book. That means a play has characters, a setting, problem and solution, and a plot. A play may also have a theme or moral.

3. Explain that sometimes a play is broken into sections called scenes.

   ▸ Sometimes there is more than one scene in a play to show the passing of time, or the order of events. For example, Scene I might be about what happens in the morning, and Scene II might be about what happens later that day.
   ▸ Scenes can also be used to show a different setting in the play. For example, Scene I might take place in the woods, and Scene II might take place inside a house.

4. Tell students that sometimes a script has words that tell the actors what to do on stage. These words are called stage directions. For example, a stage direction might tell an actor to shake her head or put her hands over her eyes and pretend she's crying. Stage directions help the actors make the play seem more real.

5. Tell students that the play they will be reading has two scenes and several stage directions.

Words to Know

Before reading "The Lion and the Mouse," go over Words to Know with students.

1. Read aloud each word and have students repeat it.

2. Ask students if they know what each word means.

   ▸ If students know a word's meaning, have them define it and use it in a sentence.
   ▸ If students don't know a word's meaning, read them the definition and discuss the word with them.

gnaw – to chew again and again
hammock – a swinging bed made of netting that is hung between two trees or poles
mercy – kind treatment by a person who has some power over another person
racket – a loud noise
rude – not polite; having bad manners
scamper – to run quickly or playfully
valley – an area of low land between mountains or hills

Guided Reading

Book Walk

Prepare students for reading by taking them on a Book Walk of "The Lion and the Mouse." Scan the play together and ask students to make predictions. Answers to questions may vary.

1. Turn to the **table of contents** in *K¹² Classics for Young Readers, Volume A*. Help students find "The Lion and the Mouse" and turn to that page.

2. Point to and help students read aloud the **play title**.

   ▸ What do you think this play might be about?

3. Have students look at the **pictures of the play**.

   ▸ Where do you think the story being told in the play takes place?
   ▸ Have you ever heard the story of the lion and the mouse? If you have, what do you remember about the story?

4. Remind them that plays written on the page look different from poems, fiction stories, and nonfiction articles and books.

Objectives

- Make predictions based on text, illustrations, and/or prior knowledge.
- Activate prior knowledge by previewing text and/or discussing topic.
- Read and listen to a variety of texts for information and pleasure independently or as part of a group.
- Read aloud grade-level text with appropriate expression, accuracy, and rate.

"The Lion and the Mouse"

Guide students through a preview of the play to prepare them for reading on their own. Gather the Reading Aid on pages LC 341 and 342 in *K¹² Language Arts Activity Book*.

1. Have students sit next to you so that they can see the pictures and words while you introduce and discuss the play.

2. Tell students that you will preview the play to prepare them to read aloud the play to you.

3. Refer to the Reading Aid.

Reading Aid Tear out the Reading Aid for this reading selection. Follow the instructions for folding the page and then use the page as a guide as you preview the selection with students.

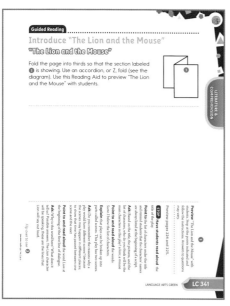
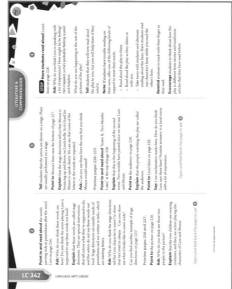

Check Your Reading

"The Lion and the Mouse"

Check students' comprehension of "The Lion and the Mouse."

1. Have students retell "The Lion and the Mouse" in their own words to develop grammar, vocabulary, comprehension, and fluency skills.

Objectives

- Retell or dramatize a story.
- Identify the main character(s).
- Answer questions requiring literal recall of details.

2. Ask students the following questions.

    ▶ Who are the characters in the play? Lion; Mouse

    ▶ Where does the story being told in the play take place? outside; in a place that has hills and valleys

    ▶ Why is Lion tired at the beginning of the play? He just ate a big meal.

    ▶ Why does Mouse climb up on Lion at the beginning of the play? He thinks Lion is a hill.

    ▶ Why does Lion let Mouse go? Possible answers: Mouse is so small he won't fill Lion's stomach; eating mice gives Lion the hiccups.

    ▶ What is Lion doing the next time Mouse sees him? He's trapped in a net and yelling for help.

TIP If students have trouble responding to a question, help them locate the answer in the text or pictures.

Reading for Meaning

Identify the Characteristics of a Play

Explore the characteristics of a play.

1. Ask students the following questions.

    ▶ What kind of writing is "The Lion and the Mouse"? a play

    ▶ How can you tell "The Lion and the Mouse" is a play? Possible answer: The words are spoken out loud; the words are written as a script; it's broken up into two scenes; the pictures show actors on a stage.

    ▶ What do we call the words that the characters say to each other in a play? the dialogue

2. Turn to page 227 and point to the name **MOUSE** at the top of the page.

    ▶ Why is this name in bold text? Possible answers: because it's the name of a character; because these are the lines that Mouse will say out loud

    ▶ Do you say the name of a character at the beginning of a line out loud when you're acting out the play? No

3. Point to the stage directions that follow **MOUSE**.

    ▶ What are these words? stage directions

    ▶ What are stage directions? They tell the actors what to do on the stage.

    ▶ Do you read the stage directions out loud when you're acting out the play? No

4. Point to and read aloud **Scene II** at the top of page 228.

    ▶ Why do plays have scenes? to show the passing of time; to show a new setting

5. Point to the audience on page 231.

    ▶ What do we call the people who sit in seats and watch a play? the audience

Objectives

- Identify genre.
- Identify characteristics of different genres.
- Respond to text through art, writing, and/or drama.

Prepare to Act Out a Play

Help students make costumes to wear while acting out the play. Turn to pages LC 343–345 in *K¹² Language Arts Activity Book* and gather the glue, string, yarn, and scissors.

1. Tell students they will act out "The Lion and the Mouse" later on.

2. Explain that they are going to make costumes for the two characters.

3. Help students cut out the masks on the Activity Book pages.

4. Help them cut and glue lengths of yarn (for the mane) to the lion mask and string (for whiskers) to both masks.

5. Have students brainstorm ideas for adding to their costumes. For example,

   ▸ A short rope for the lion's tail (attached with a safety pin)
   ▸ A brown or yellow sweatshirt for the body of the lion
   ▸ Brown or yellow mittens for the lion's paws
   ▸ A long, thin string for the mouse's tail (attached with a safety pin)
   ▸ A gray sweatshirt for the body of the mouse
   ▸ Gray mittens for the mouse's paws

TIP Keep the masks in a safe place for later use.

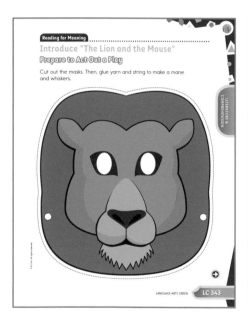

Beyond the Lesson

⊕ OPTIONAL: Compare Stories

This activity is OPTIONAL. It is intended for students who have extra time and would enjoy reading "The Lion and the Mouse" in the form of a story. Feel free to skip this activity.

1. Remind students that a play is a story that is acted out on stage. Tell them that many plays are based on stories in books.

2. Go to a library and look for a copy of *The Lion and the Mouse*. The story may also be found in a collection of *Aesop's Fables*.

   ▸ Have students use the 5-Finger Test to see if the book is a good choice.

3. Lead a Book Walk and then have students read aloud the story.

4. If students have trouble reading on their own, offer one of the following levels of support to meet their needs.

   ▸ Read aloud the story to them.
   ▸ Read aloud the story as they chime in with you.
   ▸ Take turns with students and alternate reading aloud each paragraph or page.

5. Review story structure elements as presented in the book (characters, setting, problem and solution, and plot).

6. Have students tell how the book and the play are alike and different.

7. Have students explain which they like better, the story or the play, and why.

Objectives

- Compare and contrast two texts on the same topic.
- Compare and contrast story structure elements across texts.
- Identify characteristics of different genres.

Explore "The Lion and the Mouse"

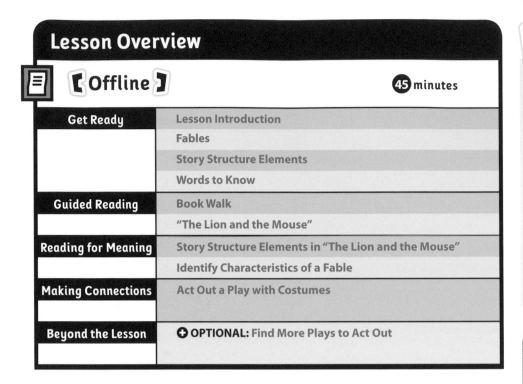

Lesson Overview

Offline   45 minutes

Get Ready	Lesson Introduction
	Fables
	Story Structure Elements
	Words to Know
Guided Reading	Book Walk
	"The Lion and the Mouse"
Reading for Meaning	Story Structure Elements in "The Lion and the Mouse"
	Identify Characteristics of a Fable
Making Connections	Act Out a Play with Costumes
Beyond the Lesson	⊕ OPTIONAL: Find More Plays to Act Out

Materials

Supplied

- "The Lion and the Mouse," *K¹² Classics for Young Readers, Volume A,* pp. 224–233
- "The Lion and the Mouse" (printout)

Also Needed

- prepared lion and mouse masks from the Introduce "The Lion and the Mouse" lesson and costumes

Keywords

fable – a story that teaches a lesson and may contain animal characters

genre – a category for classifying literary works

moral – the lesson of a story, particularly a fable

story structure elements – components of a story; they include character, setting, plot, problem, and solution

Advance Preparation

Before beginning Making Connections, print two copies of "The Lion and the Mouse" from the online lesson.

Big Ideas

- ▸ Exposing readers to a wide variety of genres provides them with a wide range of background knowledge and increases their vocabulary.
- ▸ Comprehension requires an understanding of story structure.
- ▸ An awareness of story structure elements (setting, characters, plot) provides readers a foundation for constructing meaning when reading new stories and writing their own stories.
- ▸ To understand and interpret a story, readers need to understand and describe characters and what they do.
- ▸ Repeated rereading leads to increased fluency.

⸢ Offline ⸥ ⏱ 45 minutes

Work **together** with students to complete Get Ready, Guided Reading, Reading for Meaning, Making Connections, and Beyond the Lesson activities.

Get Ready ....

Lesson Introduction

Prepare students for reading and discussing "The Lion and the Mouse."

1. Tell students that they will reread "The Lion and the Mouse."

2. Explain that before they reread the play, you will get ready by reviewing fables and story structure elements.

Fables

Reinforce the characteristics of fables.

1. Remind students of the characteristics of a **fable**. A fable

   ▸ Is a kind of animal tale.
   ▸ Has animal characters that act like people.
   ▸ Teaches a lesson, which is called a **moral**.

2. Have students think about "The Hummingbird and the Butterfly."

   ▸ Who are the characters in the play "The Hummingbird and the Butterfly"? Hummingbird; Butterfly
   ▸ Do these animal characters act like humans? Yes
   ▸ Does one of the characters in the play learn a lesson? Yes   Which one? Hummingbird
   ▸ What do we call a lesson that is learned? a moral
   ▸ Do you think the story being told in "The Hummingbird and the Butterfly" is a fable? Yes   Why is the story being told in "The Hummingbird and the Butterfly" a fable? because it has animal characters that act like humans and it teaches a lesson
   ▸ What lesson does Hummingbird learn? What is the moral of the story? It's important to be kind to others, no matter what they look like.

⭐ **Objectives**

- Identify characteristics of different genres.
- Identify the moral or lesson of a text.
- Identify story structure elements—plot, setting, character(s).
- Describe story structure elements—problem and solution.
- Build vocabulary through listening, reading, and discussion.
- Use new vocabulary in written and spoken sentences.
- Increase concept and content vocabulary.

Story Structure Elements

1. Remind students that a play tells a story. Plays like "The Lion and the Mouse" are fiction, which means they are made-up. All fiction stories and plays have certain things in common.

2. Ask students to name and explain story structure elements that make up a fiction story or play.

3. If students are unable to explain any **story structure elements**, review the following list with them.

   - **Characters** – the people or animals in a story or play
   - **Setting** – when and where a story or play takes place
   - **Plot** – the important events that happen in a story or play
   - **Problem** – something that needs to be fixed by a character
   - **Solution** – how a character fixes a problem

Words to Know

Before reading "The Lion and the Mouse," go over Words to Know with students.

1. Read aloud each word and have students repeat it.

2. Ask students if they know what each word means.

   - If students know a word's meaning, have them define it and use it in a sentence.
   - If students don't know a word's meaning, read them the definition and discuss the word with them.

gnaw – to chew again and again
hammock – a swinging bed made of netting that is hung between two trees or poles
mercy – kind treatment by a person who has some power over another person
racket – a loud noise
rude – not polite; having bad manners
scamper – to run quickly or playfully
valley – an area of low land between mountains or hills

Guided Reading ....

Book Walk

Prepare students for reading by taking them on a Book Walk of "The Lion and the Mouse." Scan the play together to revisit the characters and events.

1. Turn to the selection in *K¹² Classics for Young Readers, Volume A*.

2. Have students read aloud the **play title**.

3. Point to and read aloud the **text just below the title**. Explain that this play is based on a fable written a long time ago by a man named Aesop.

   ▸ Since the play is based on a fable, what would you expect to find in the story? Possible answers: animals that act like people; a moral

4. Have students review the **pictures of the play**.

5. Point to and read aloud **Scene I** on page 224.

   ▸ Why are some plays broken into scenes? to show a new setting; to show the passing of time

6. Point to the picture of the stage on page 224.

   ▸ What is this called? a stage

7. Point to the audience on page 224.

   ▸ What do we call the people who watch a play? the audience

8. Point to the first stage direction on page 225.

   ▸ What is this text called? a stage direction
   ▸ What does a stage direction tell an actor? how to act; what to do on the stage
   ▸ Does an actor say the stage direction aloud? Is it part of the dialogue? No

---

"The Lion and the Mouse"

It's time for students to reread the play aloud.

1. Tell students that "The Lion and the Mouse" should now be familiar to them because they have read it before.

2. Explain that they will reread the play aloud to you, but you are there to help them if they need it.

3. If students have trouble reading on their own, offer one of the following levels of support to meet their needs.

   ▸ Read aloud the play to them.
   ▸ Read aloud the play as they chime in with you.
   ▸ Take turns with students and alternate reading aloud each line of dialogue.

4. Remind students to track with their finger as they read.

5. Tell students to listen for the moral of the story being told in the play.

> **Objectives**
> - Activate prior knowledge by previewing text and/or discussing topic.
> - Identify characteristics of different genres.
> - Read and respond to texts representing a variety of cultures, time periods, and traditions.
> - Read aloud grade-level text with appropriate expression, accuracy, and rate.

Reading for Meaning

Story Structure Elements in "The Lion and the Mouse"
Check students' understanding of story structure elements in a play.

- ▶ Who are the characters in the play? Lion; Mouse
- ▶ What is the setting of Scene I? outside; in a place that has hills and valleys
- ▶ What is Mouse's problem in Scene I? He's caught by Lion and might get eaten.
- ▶ How does Mouse's feel when he is caught? scared
- ▶ How does Mouse solve his problem? Possible answers: He begs Lion to let him go; he tells Lion that he wouldn't fill Lion's stomach; he says one day he might be able to grant Lion a favor in return.
- ▶ What does Lion do when Mouse says he might be able to grant him a favor in return someday? He laughs.   Why does Lion laugh? Why does he think this is funny? Possible answer: He thinks Mouse is too small to help him.
- ▶ What is the setting of Scene II? in the same place as Scene I
- ▶ When does Scene II take place? two months after Scene I
- ▶ What is Lion's problem in Scene II? He's trapped in the hunters' net.
- ▶ How does Lion feel about being trapped? Possible answers: scared; mad; upset
- ▶ How does Lion try to solve his problem? He yells for someone to help him.
- ▶ How does Mouse help Lion solve his problem? He chews all the ropes in the net and sets Lion free.
- ▶ How does Lion feel when he is set free? Possible answers: happy; grateful
- ▶ What is the plot of "The Lion and the Mouse"? Possible answer: Lion captures and almost eats Mouse. But, Mouse begs Lion to let him go. Lion lets Mouse go after all, and Mouse says that maybe one day he will be able to return the favor. Lion laughs at this idea. Two months later, Lion is trapped in a net by hunters. Lion begs Mouse to help him get free. Mouse gnaws at the ropes in the net and sets Lion free. Lion thanks Mouse and apologizes for laughing at him when Mouse said he might be able to help Lion one day.
- ▶ Do you think Lion and Mouse will stay friends? Why or why not? Answers will vary.
- ▶ Do you think Lion and Mouse will be able to help each other again? If so, how? Answers will vary.

Objectives
- Identify character(s).
- Identify story structure elements—plot, setting, character(s).
- Identify details that explain characters' actions and feelings.
- Describe story structure elements—problem and solution.
- Identify genre.
- Identify characteristics of different genres.

Identify Characteristics of a Fable
Check students' ability to recognize the characteristics of a fable.

- ▶ Are there animal characters in "The Lion and the Mouse" that act like humans? Yes
- ▶ What do we call a lesson that is learned? the moral
- ▶ What kind of story is being told in "The Lion and the Mouse"? a fable   How do you know? Possible answers: It has animal characters that act like humans, and one of the characters learns a lesson; it has a moral.
- ▶ Who learns a lesson in the play? Lion
- ▶ What lesson does Lion learn? What is the moral of the play? Even the smallest friends are important and helpful.

Making Connections

Act Out a Play with Costumes

Have students practice reading with fluency and expression by acting out "The Lion and the Mouse." Gather the copies of the script and costumes.

1. Tell students that they are going to act out the play wearing costumes.

   ▸ Remind them that we act out a play to better understand the characters.

2. If there is more than one student, have each choose a character to act out. If there is only one student, you can read the other role.

3. Help students put on their costumes and give them a script.

4. Remind students that when they read their character's dialogue, they should not read the bold name of the character or the stage directions that are in italic. They should only read the words that the character actually says.

5. Have students practice reading their character's dialogue aloud at least once before performing the play.

6. Ask the following questions when students are done acting out the play. Answers to questions may vary.

   ▸ Did you like playing a character in the play?
   ▸ Did you learn anything new about your character by saying the character's dialogue?
   ▸ How does your character feel at the beginning of Scene I?
   ▸ How does your character feel at the end of Scene I?
   ▸ How does your character feel at the beginning of Scene II?
   ▸ How does your character feel at the end of the play?

Objectives

- Respond to text through art, writing, and/or drama.
- Retell or dramatize a story.
- Demonstrate understanding through drawing, discussion, drama, and/or writing.
- Read aloud grade-level text with appropriate expression, accuracy, and rate.
- Speak audibly and clearly express thoughts, feelings, and ideas.
- Read text to perform a specific task.

Reward: Add a sticker for this unit on the My Accomplishments chart to mark successful completion of the unit.

Beyond the Lesson

⊕ OPTIONAL: Find More Plays to Act Out

This activity is OPTIONAL. It is intended for students who have extra time and would enjoy acting out another play. Feel free to skip this activity.

1. Help students search the Internet for scripts of plays to perform.

   ▸ Suggested keywords for search: kids' plays, reader's theater, play scripts for kids

2. Make as many copies of the script for the selected play as necessary or have students read their parts directly from the computer screen.

3. Have students practice reading aloud their lines.

4. Ask the following questions after students have acted out the play. Answers should reflect the story structure elements and possible moral of the selected play.

   ▸ Who are the characters in the play?
   ▸ What is the setting?
   ▸ Does the play have a problem that needs to be solved? If so, what is the problem? How is the problem solved?
   ▸ What is the plot of the play?
   ▸ Does the play have a moral? If so, what is it?

(TIP) If the selected play has more roles than there are students, the play can be performed by students using different voices for the various characters.

Objectives

- Locate information using features of text and electronic media.
- Respond to text through art, writing, and/or drama.
- Retell or dramatize a story.
- Demonstrate understanding through drawing, discussion, drama, and/or writing.
- Speak audibly and clearly express thoughts, feelings, and ideas.
- Read text to perform a specific task.
- Identify story structure elements—plot, setting, character(s).
- Describe story structure elements—problem and solution.
- Identify the moral or lesson of a text.

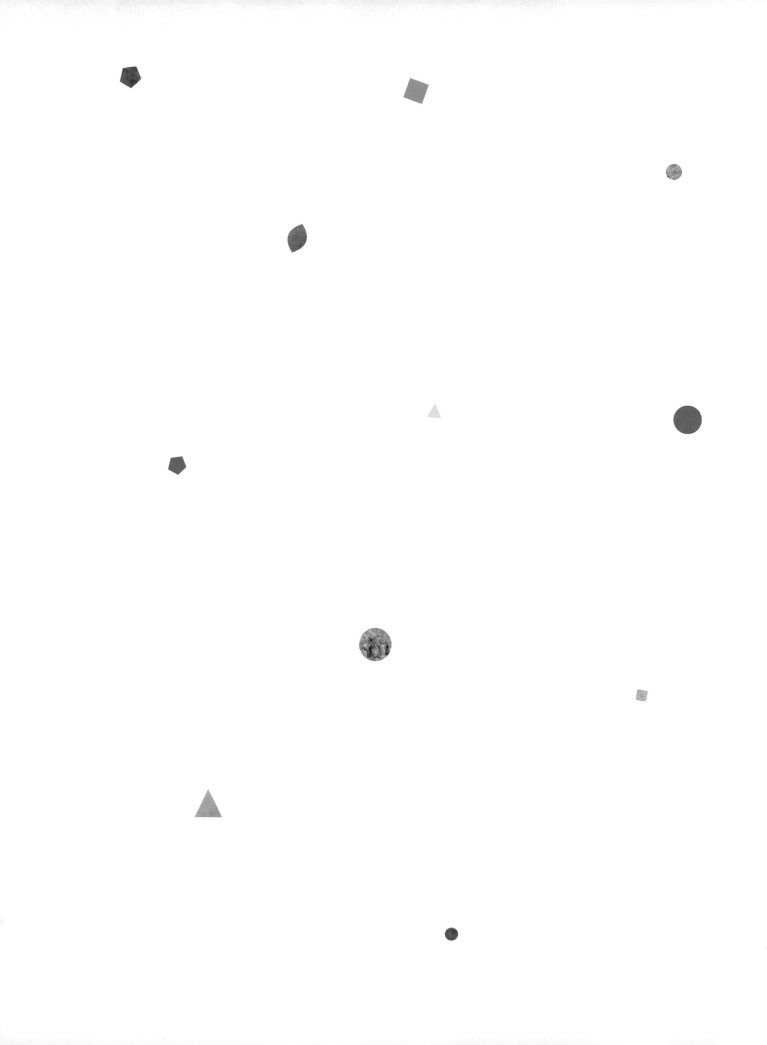

Semester Review and Checkpoint

Unit Focus

In this unit, students will review elements of poetry, nonfiction, and fiction.
Students will read aloud a piece of fiction, a nonfiction article, and a poem. They will demonstrate mastery of content and characteristics of each genre.

Unit Plan		[Offline]	[Online]
Lesson 1	Semester Review	**45** minutes	
Lesson 2	Semester Checkpoint	**45** minutes	varies

Semester Review

Lesson Overview

[Offline]   **45** minutes

Semester Review	Lesson Introduction
	Poetry Review
	Nonfiction Review
	Fiction Review

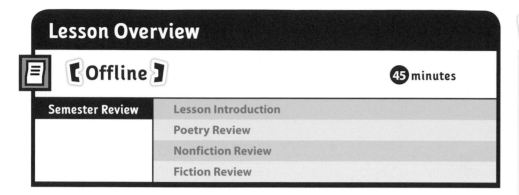

[Materials]

Supplied

- *Listen, My Children: Poems for First Graders*, pp. 19–20
- "Marvelous Mount Rushmore," *K¹² World: People and Places of the Past*, pp. 28–39
- *Frog and Toad Are Friends*, pp. 53–64

[Offline] 45 minutes

Work **together** with students to complete the Semester Review.

Semester Review ···

Lesson Introduction

Prepare students for reviewing what they have learned about poems, nonfiction articles, and fiction stories.

1. Tell students that they will reread the poem "Thanksgiving Day" and review characteristics of poetry, such as rhyme, repetition, descriptive language, and narrator.

2. Tell them that they will reread the article "Marvelous Mount Rushmore," and review characteristics of nonfiction text and how to check that they understand what they've read by giving a summary.

3. Tell them that they will reread the story "The Letter" in *Frog and Toad Are Friends*, and review the story structure elements of fiction stories and how to check that they understand what they've read by retelling a story.

Objectives
- Complete a Semester Review on the elements of poetry, nonfiction, and fiction.

Poetry Review

Help students review characteristics of poetry in "Thanksgiving Day" by Lydia Maria Child.

1. Have students call up their prior knowledge related to the poem "Thanksgiving Day" and the genre of poetry. Answers to questions may vary.

   ▸ Do you celebrate Thanksgiving? If not, is there another holiday that is important to you and your family?
   ▸ What kinds of things do people do on Thanksgiving?
   ▸ What kind of writing is "Thanksgiving Day?" a poem; poetry
   ▸ What are some features you would expect to find in this poem? Possible answers: stanzas; rhyming words; short lines; repeated words

2. **Have students read aloud the entire poem.** Remind students to track with their finger.

3. Remind students that poets often repeat words or lines, and that poems often rhyme. Then have students reread the first stanza.

   ▸ In the first stanza, what word rhymes with *go*? *snow*   What word rhymes with *way*? *sleigh*
   ▸ What line is repeated throughout this poem? *Over the river and through the wood*

4. Tell students that the author uses a lot of descriptive language that helps readers imagine what something looks, sounds, or feels like.

   ► What are some phrases that help you see and hear the things described in the poem? Possible answers: *white and drifted snow*; *Hear the bells ring, "Ting-a-ling-ding!"*; *Grandmother's cap I spy!*
   ► What phrases help you imagine how cold the wind feels? *stings the toes* and *bites the nose*
   ► What lines help you imagine the excitement that the person in the poem feels? *We seem to go / Extremely slow— / It is so hard to wait!*

5. Remind students that sometimes a story or poem is narrated by a character that is in the story or poem. This is the case if the story or poem has words such as *we, me, my,* or *I.*

   ► Is this poem being narrated by somebody in the poem? Yes   How can you tell? It has the words *we, my,* and *I.*

6. Remind students that sometimes we can draw conclusions, or figure things out that a poet or author does not say directly.

   ► If the narrator is going to "grandfather's house," who do you think the narrator might be? Possible answers: a boy; a girl; a boy or girl riding in the sleigh; the grandchild of the grandfather
   ► What conclusions can we draw about who might be riding in the sleigh with the narrator? Students may say that members of the narrator's family might be in the sleigh.
   ► In what season do you think the poem is taking place? Students may say either fall or winter.   How did you draw that conclusion? Students may say that it's fall because Thanksgiving happens in the fall. Or, they may say that it's winter because it's snowing, which happens in the winter.

7. Remind students that poets often make things sound like they are alive even though those things could not be alive.

   ► What does the poet describe in the second stanza? the wind
   ► What does the poet say about the wind that makes it sound like it's alive? *It stings the toes / And bites the nose*   Could the wind really sting or bite? No   Why not? It's not alive.

8. Remind students that making connections to text helps readers better understand and remember what they read. Answers to questions may vary.

   ► Does this poem remind you of anything in your life?
   ► Does this poem remind you of another poem or story that you've read?

Nonfiction Review

Help students review characteristics of nonfiction text in "Marvelous Mount Rushmore" in *K¹² World: People and Places of the Past.*

1. Have students call up their prior knowledge related to the article "Marvelous Mount Rushmore" and the characteristics of nonfiction text.

   ▸ What do you remember about Mount Rushmore? Answers will vary.
   ▸ This article is nonfiction. What is the difference between fiction stories and nonfiction texts? Fiction stories are made-up stories; nonfiction texts are about real things and have facts in them.
   ▸ What are some things you would expect to find in a nonfiction article? Possible answers: maps; headings; photographs; captions; diagrams; words in bold type; facts

2. **Have students read aloud the entire article.** Remind students to track with their finger.

   ▸ What is the topic of this article? What is it mostly about? Mount Rushmore
   ▸ Why do you think the author wrote this article? to teach us about how Mount Rushmore was made

3. Ask the following questions about text features for organizing and locating information.

   ▸ On page 28, why is the word *carve* in bold type? It's an important word in the article.   Where can I find the meaning of the word *carve*? in the back of the magazine; in the glossary
   ▸ What do we call these words in bigger type at the top of page 34? a heading   What does a heading tell us? what that section of the article will be about
   ▸ If I want to find information in the article about the presidents that are on Mount Rushmore, which heading should I look under? Four Important Presidents

4. Ask the following questions about visual text features.

   ▸ On page 29, why are the photographs at the bottom of the page? to show us people who were important to making Mount Rushmore
   ▸ What do we call the text next to the photos at the bottom of page 29? a caption   What information does this caption tell us? the names of the men in the photos
   ▸ Why is there a map on page 29? to show us where Mount Rushmore is located
   ▸ Look at the diagram on page 38. What does this diagram explain? the size of the faces on Mount Rushmore   What does each drawing of a little yellow person stand for? 1 child

5. The article states that George Washington "was the first president of the United States."

   ▸ Is this a fact or an opinion? a fact   How do we know that this is a fact? because we can prove that it's true
   ▸ If the article had said that George Washington was the smartest and the bravest U.S. president, would that be a fact or an opinion? an opinion   How can we tell that this is an opinion? Possible answers: We can't prove that it's true; people could say that a different president was the smartest and bravest U.S. president.

6. Remind students that we can often find examples of cause and effect in nonfiction articles. For example, Theodore Roosevelt cared about nature. The result, or the effect, of this is that he helped protect special places like the Grand Canyon.

   ▸ The text on page 34 says that blasters used dynamite to blast away big pieces of rock. What was the effect on the rock that was left after the blasting? It looked like an enormous egg.
   ▸ The text on page 34 says that "holes made it easier to carve the rock." What caused the holes? Drillers made the holes in the rock.

7. Remind students that readers can check that they understand what they've read by giving a summary. A summary is similar to a retelling, but it is much shorter and has fewer details. A good summary answers the question "Who did what?"

   ▸ Who was involved with making Mount Rushmore? Doane Robinson, Gutzon Borglum, and about 400 workers
   ▸ How would you summarize the article "Marvelous Mount Rushmore?" Answers will vary, but the summary but should be similar to this statement: Doane Robinson, Gutzon Borglum, and about 400 workers made a huge sculpture of four presidents' heads on Mount Rushmore.

Fiction Review

Help students review features of fiction stories in "The Letter" in *Frog and Toad Are Friends*.

1. Have students call up their prior knowledge related to the story "The Letter" and the characters of Frog and Toad. Answers to questions may vary.

   ▸ What do you remember about the characters Frog and Toad?
   ▸ Have you ever received a letter in the mail? How did you feel when you got the letter?
   ▸ Toad is feeling sad in the beginning of the story. What are some things that make you feel sad?

2. **Have students read aloud the entire story.** Remind students to track with their finger.

   ▸ Is this story fiction or nonfiction? fiction   How can you tell that it's fiction? Possible answers: It's a made-up story; frogs and toads can't really talk; the things in the story couldn't happen in real life.

   ▸ Why do you think the author wrote this story? to entertain

   ▸ Did you make any connections to this story? Does it remind you of another story that you know? Does it remind you of anything in your life? Do the characters remind you of anyone you know? Answers will vary.

3. Remind students that fiction stories are made up of certain parts called story structure elements, which include characters, setting, plot, and problem and solution.

   ▸ Who are the characters in "The Letter"? Frog, Toad, a snail

   ▸ What is the setting? Where does most of the story happen? at Toad's house

   ▸ What is the problem in the story? Toad is sad because he never gets any mail.

   ▸ How is Toad's problem solved? Frog writes Toad a letter and sends it to Toad's house.

4. Remind students that we can check that we understand what we've read by retelling the plot of the story. When we retell the plot, we can break it up into the events that happen in the beginning, middle, and end of the story. Explain that when we retell, we should tell not only the most important events of the plot, but we should also name the characters and setting and explain the problem and how the characters solve it.

   ▸ What happens in the beginning of "The Letter"? Example retelling: Toad is sitting outside of his house feeling sad because he never gets any mail.

   ▸ What happens in the middle of the story? Example retelling: Frog goes home and writes Toad a letter. Frog asks a snail to deliver the letter. Frog goes back to Toad's house and tells Toad that he should wait for the mail some more.

   ▸ What happens in the end of the story? Example retelling: Frog tells Toad that he wrote him a letter, which makes both of them feel happy. The snail gets to Toad's house with the letter four days later.

5. Remind students that fiction stories can have examples of cause and effect. For example, things that happen can cause characters to feel a certain way.

   ▸ Toad never gets any mail. What is the effect of this on Toad? He feels sad when he waits for the mail.
   ▸ Toad tells Frog that he's sad because he never gets any mail. What does this cause Frog to do? He goes home and writes Toad a letter.

6. Remind students that we can draw conclusions about things the author does not directly state in a story. We can figure out things about a story's characters and events by thinking about information in the story and things we know from our own experiences.

   ▸ Based on Frog's actions, how would you describe Frog? Possible answers: kind; caring; a good friend
   ▸ Why does it take so long for the letter to arrive at Toad's house? because a snail brings it   What do you know about snails that helped you draw this conclusion? Snails move very slowly.

Semester Checkpoint

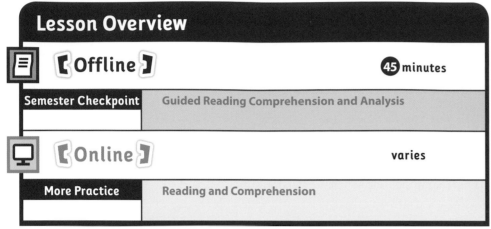

Lesson Overview

Offline   45 minutes

| Semester Checkpoint | Guided Reading Comprehension and Analysis |

Online   varies

| More Practice | Reading and Comprehension |

Materials

Supplied
- *K¹² Language Arts Assessments,* pp. LC 107–160

Also Needed
- scissors, adult
- glue stick
- household objects – stopwatch

Advance Preparation

Read each selection in the Semester Checkpoint before administering the assessment to locate Words to Know in the text. Cut out the word cards on pages LC 125, 143, 145, and 149.

 **45** minutes

Work **together** with students to complete the Semester Checkpoint.

Semester Checkpoint

Guided Reading Comprehension and Analysis

Explain that students are going to show what they have learned this semester.

Objectives
- Complete a Semester Checkpoint on the elements of poetry, nonfiction, and fiction.

▸ Give students pages LC 115–LC 160 of the Semester Checkpoint.

▸ Read the directions on the students' pages together. Use the Learning Coach instructions on pages LC 107–LC 114 to administer the Checkpoint.

▸ Use the Checkpoint pages to record student behaviors and responses.

▸ When you have finished, use the Answer Key to score the Checkpoint and then enter the results online.

▸ Review each exercise with students. Work with students to correct any exercise that they missed.

Part 1. Fiction: "Bad Dog, Chester!" Activate Prior Knowledge

Ask students the following questions to activate prior knowledge. Note their responses on the Checkpoint pages.

1. What do you know about dogs?

2. What are some things pets can do to get in trouble?

Before students read "Bad Dog, Chester!," go over Words to Know with students. Read aloud each word and have students repeat it. Ask students if they know what each word means.

▸ If students know a word's meaning, have them define it and use it in a sentence.

▸ If students don't know a word's meaning, read them the definition and discuss the word with them.

glance – to look at something quickly
perch – a bar or branch on which a bird can sit
ruined – destroyed or spoiled

Part 2. Fiction: "Bad Dog, Chester!" Book Walk

Gather the Checkpoint pages with "Bad Dog, Chester!" Note that there are two versions of the story: One is the full story for the students, and the other is a copy for you to follow and mark as students read aloud. Have students sit next to you so that they can see the story while you do a Book Walk. Read aloud the title and author of the text. Show students the illustration. Ask students the following questions and have them write their responses on the Checkpoint pages. If necessary, allow them to dictate their responses to you.

3. Was this story written to teach us or was it written to entertain us?

4. Is this story going to be fiction or nonfiction?

Part 3. Fiction: "Bad Dog, Chester!" Guided Reading and Fluency Check
Gather the word cards from page LC 125. Show them to students. Read aloud the words, pointing to each word as you read it.

Reread the words, again pointing to each word as you read it aloud. Have students repeat each word several times.

Show the cards to students, one card at a time, and ask students to read them.

- ▸ Circle any words that students read incorrectly.
- ▸ If students have trouble with a word, say, "This is the word [word]. Say [word]."

5. furniture

6. glance

7. ruined

8. perch

9. curtains

Say: You will read aloud the story to me. If you would like to read the story to yourself first, you may.

Use your copy of "Bad Dog, Chester!" to note the kinds of errors that students make as they read. As you listen, you may choose to mark up your copy of the story where students have difficulty reading.

Follow the instructions in the Semester Checkpoint for assessing students' fluency.

Part 4. Fiction: "Bad Dog, Chester!" Evaluate Predictions
Read the prediction students wrote in Part 2. Tell students that predictions are neither right nor wrong; they are just the best guess you can make with the information you have. Ask students the following questions and have students write their responses on the Checkpoint pages. If necessary, allow them to dictate their responses to you.

14. What helped you make your prediction?

15. What else could help a reader make a prediction?

16. Was your prediction accurate?

Part 5. Fiction: "Bad Dog, Chester!" Problem and Solution
Explain to students that during the story, Chester has a problem that needs to be solved. Ask students the following questions and have them write their responses on the Checkpoint pages. If necessary, allow them to dictate their responses to you.

17. What is Chester's problem in this story?

18. What is a solution?

19. How does Chester solve his problem?

Part 6. Fiction: "Bad Dog, Chester!" Reading Comprehension
Read the questions on the Checkpoint pages to students. Students should write their responses. If necessary, allow them to dictate their responses to you.

Part 7. Fiction: "Bad Dog, Chester!" Show You Know

Turn to the graphic organizer on page LC 131. Before students complete the graphic organizer, ask the following questions. Note students' responses on the Checkpoint pages.

25. Who is telling the story in "Bad Dog, Chester!"?

26. What happens first in the story?

27. What happens next?

28. What happens last?

Have students complete the graphic organizer independently. Students should be able to identify the title, characters, setting, problem, and solution. Additionally, they should write a brief plot summary of the story. If necessary, allow them to dictate their responses to you.

29.–34. Complete the graphic organizer. **Note:** In the "Plot summary" cell, the answer is the maximum content acceptable for a summary. Students' summary may be briefer, but it should answer the guiding question: "Who did what in the story?"

Part 8. Nonfiction: "The First Chimp in Space" Preview the Article

Gather the Checkpoint pages with "The First Chimp in Space." Have students sit next to you so that they can see the story while you preview the article. Show students "The First Chimp in Space." Point to and read aloud the title of the article. Preview the article with students.

35. What do you think will be the topic of this article?

Point to the heading **Learning from Animals**. Explain that the bold print is used to call attention to the text. This is a heading, and it gives us clues about the next paragraph. Have students read the heading and make a prediction. Note their response on the Checkpoint pages.

36. Read the first heading.

37. What do you think this section will be about?

Have students locate and read aloud the other headings in the text and make a prediction about each section. Note students' responses on the Checkpoint pages.

38. Read the second heading.

39. What do you think this section will be about?

40. Read the third heading.

41. What do you think this section will be about?

42. Read the fourth heading.

43. What do you think this section will be about?

Part 9. Nonfiction: "The First Chimp in Space" Guided Reading and Fluency Check

Before students read "The First Chimp in Space," go over Words to Know with students. Read aloud each word and have students repeat it. Ask students if they know what each word means.

▶ If students know a word's meaning, have them define it and use it in a sentence.
▶ If students don't know a word's meaning, read them the definition and discuss the word with them.

complete – finish
lever – a bar or handle used to work a machine
international – involving different countries

Gather the word cards from pages LC 143 and 145. Show them to students. Read the words aloud, pointing to each word as you read it.

Reread the words, again pointing to each word as you read it aloud. Have students repeat each word several times.

Show the cards to students, one card at a time, and ask students to read them.

▶ Circle any words that students read incorrectly.
▶ If students have trouble with a word, say, "This is the word [*word*]. Say [*word*]."

44. scientist

45. machine

46. chimpanzee

47. complete

48. lever

49. international

50. mission

Say: You will read aloud the article to me. If you would like to read the article to yourself first, you may.

Use your copy of "The First Chimp in Space" to note the kinds of errors that students make as they read. As you listen, you may choose to mark up your copy of the story where students have difficulty reading.

Follow the instructions in the Semester Checkpoint for assessing students' fluency.

Part 10. Nonfiction: "The First Chimp in Space" Create a Time Line
Gather the time line boxes on page LC 149. Have students fill in the six major events in Ham's life. Then have them cut out the events and paste them on the time line on page LC 151 in the order that they happened.

55.–60. Complete the time line.

Part 11. Nonfiction: "The First Chimp in Space" Reading Comprehension
Have students read and answer the questions on the Checkpoint pages. Students should circle their answers.

Part 12. Poetry: "My Day" Activate Prior Knowledge
Explain to students that they will read a poem with you. Ask students the following questions to activate prior knowledge. Note their responses on the Checkpoint pages.

66. What do you know about poems?

67. You've read a story and an article. What are they mostly about? What kind of characters do they have?

68. What do you think this poem will be about?

Part 13. Poetry: "My Day" Guided Reading and Fluency Check
Gather the Checkpoint page with "My Day." Cut out the two copies of the poem and give one to students. Read aloud the title of the poem, pointing to each word as you read. Then have students read aloud the title of the poem, pointing to each word as they read aloud.
Say: You will read aloud the poem to me. If you would like to read the poem to yourself first, you may.

Use your copy of "My Day" to note the kinds of errors that students make as they read.

Follow the instructions in the Semester Checkpoint for assessing students' fluency.

Part 14. Poetry: "My Day" Draw Conclusions
Have students draw conclusions about the poem. Ask students the following questions and note their responses on the Checkpoint pages.

73. What is the poem about?

74. What lines from the poem helped you figure out what the poem is about?

Part 15. Poetry: "My Day" Reading Comprehension
Read the questions on the Checkpoint pages to students. Students should write the answers themselves. If necessary, allow them to dictate their responses to you.

Part 16. Poetry: "My Day" Write Your Own Poem
Turn to the poetry frame on page LC 160. Have students complete the poem independently. Students should use words from the word bank to complete the poem using the same rhyming pattern as the author used in "My Day." If necessary, allow them to dictate their responses to you.

Reward: Add a sticker for this unit on the My Accomplishments chart to mark successful completion of the unit.

Name .... Date ....

Semester Checkpoint Learning Coach Instructions Guided Reading Comprehension and Analysis

Explain that students are going to show what they have learned this semester.

- Give students pages LC 115–LC 160 of the Semester Checkpoint.
- Read the directions on the students' pages together. Use the Learning Coach instructions on pages LC 107–LC 114 to administer the Checkpoint.
- Use the Checkpoint pages to record student behaviors and responses.
- When you have finished, use the Answer Key to score the Checkpoint and then enter the results online.
- Review each exercise with students. Work with students to correct any exercise that they missed.

Part 1. Fiction: "Bad Dog, Chester!" Activate Prior Knowledge

Ask students the following questions to activate prior knowledge. Note their responses on the Checkpoint pages.

1. What do you know about dogs?
2. What are some things pets can do to get in trouble?

Before students read "Bad Dog, Chester!," go over Words to Know with students. Read aloud each word and have students repeat it. Ask students if they know what each word means.

- If students know a word's meaning, have them define it and use it in a sentence.
- If students don't know a word's meaning, read them the definition and discuss the word with them.

glance – to look at something quickly
perch – a bar or branch on which a bird can sit
ruined – destroyed or spoiled

Part 2. Fiction: "Bad Dog, Chester!" Book Walk

Gather the Checkpoint pages with "Bad Dog, Chester!" Note that there are two versions of the story: One is the full story for the students, and the other is a copy for you to follow and mark as students read aloud. Have students sit next to you so that they can see the story while you do a Book Walk. Read aloud the title and author of the text. Show students the illustration. Ask students the following questions and have them write their responses on the Checkpoint pages. If necessary, allow them to dictate their responses to you.

Name .... Date ....

3. Was this story written to teach us, or was it written to entertain us?
4. Is this story going to be fiction or nonfiction?

Part 3. Fiction: "Bad Dog, Chester!" Guided Reading and Fluency Check

Gather the word cards from page LC 125. Show them to students. Read aloud the words, pointing to each word as you read it. Reread the words, again pointing to each word as you read it aloud. Have students repeat each word several times. Show the cards to students, one card at a time, and ask students to read them.

- Circle any words that students read incorrectly.
- If students have trouble with a word, say, "This is the word [*word*]. Say [*word*]."

5. furniture
6. glance
7. ruined
8. perch
9. curtains

Say: You will read aloud the story to me. If you would like to read the story to yourself first, you may.

Use your copy of "Bad Dog, Chester!" to note the kinds of errors that students make as they read. As you listen, you may choose to mark up your copy of the story where students have difficulty reading. Make a mark or a note for the following types of errors:

Listen for these types of errors	How many times?	Examples
Reads word incorrectly, does not self-correct.		
Skips a word, does not self-correct.		
Rereads before reading correctly.		
Guesses before reading correctly.		

Name .... Date ....

Have students read aloud the story. Students should read independently. As students read, mark on your copy any words they miss.

Circle *Yes* or *No* for each question.

10. Did students read with a pace that sounds natural? Yes / No
11. Did students read with appropriate volume? Yes / No
12. Did students pause for periods? Yes / No
13. Did students read with expression? Yes / No

Part 4. Fiction: "Bad Dog, Chester!" Evaluate Predictions

Read the prediction students wrote in Part 2. Tell students that predictions are neither right nor wrong; they are just the best guess you can make with the information you have. Ask students the following questions and have students write their responses on the Checkpoint pages. If necessary, allow them to dictate their responses to you.

14. What helped you make your prediction?
15. What else could help a reader make a prediction?
16. Was your prediction accurate?

Part 5. Fiction: "Bad Dog, Chester!" Problem and Solution

Explain to students that during the story, Chester has a problem that needs to be solved. Ask students the following questions and have them write their responses on the Checkpoint pages. If necessary, allow them to dictate their responses to you.

17. What is Chester's problem in this story?
18. What is a solution?
19. How does Chester solve his problem?

Part 6. Fiction: "Bad Dog, Chester!" Reading Comprehension

Read the questions on the Checkpoint pages to students. Students should write their responses. If necessary, allow them to dictate their responses to you.

Part 7. Fiction: "Bad Dog, Chester!" Show You Know

Turn to the graphic organizer on page LC 131. Before students complete the graphic organizer, ask the following questions. Note students' responses on the Checkpoint pages.

25. Who is telling the story in "Bad Dog, Chester!"?
26. What happens first in the story?
27. What happens next?
28. What happens last?

Name .... Date ....

Have students complete the graphic organizer independently. Students should be able to identify the title, characters, setting, problem, and solution. Additionally, they should write a brief plot summary of the story. If necessary, allow them to dictate their responses to you.

29.–34. Complete the graphic organizer.

Part 8. Nonfiction: "The First Chimp in Space" Preview the Article

Gather the Checkpoint pages with "The First Chimp in Space." Have students sit next to you so that they can see the story while you preview the article. Show students "The First Chimp in Space." Point to and read aloud the title of the article. Preview the article with students.

35. What do you think will be the topic of this article?

Point to the heading **Learning from Animals**. Explain that the bold print is used to call attention to the text. This is a heading, and it gives us clues about the next paragraph. Have students read the heading and make a prediction. Note their response on the Checkpoint pages.

36. Read the first heading.
37. What do you think this section will be about?

Have students locate and read aloud the other headings in the text and make a prediction about each section. Note students' responses on the Checkpoint pages.

38. Read the second heading.
39. What do you think this section will be about?
40. Read the third heading.
41. What do you think this section will be about?
42. Read the fourth heading.
43. What do you think this section will be about?

Part 9. Nonfiction: "The First Chimp in Space" Guided Reading and Fluency Check

Before students read "The First Chimp in Space," go over Words to Know with students. Read aloud each word and have students repeat it. Ask students if they know what each word means.

- If students know a word's meaning, have them define it and use it in a sentence.
- If students don't know a word's meaning, read them the definition and discuss the word with them.

Name .... Date ....

complete – finish
lever – a bar or handle used to work a machine
international – involving different countries

Gather the word cards from pages LC 143 and 145. Show them to students. Read the words aloud, pointing to each word as you read it. Reread the words, again pointing to each word as you read it aloud. Have students repeat each word several times. Show the cards to students, one card at a time, and ask students to read them.

- Circle any words that students read incorrectly.
- If students have trouble with a word, say, "This is the word [*word*]. Say [*word*]."

44. scientist
45. machine
46. chimpanzee
47. complete
48. lever
49. international
50. mission

Say: You will read aloud the article to me. If you would like to read the article to yourself first, you may.

Use your copy of "The First Chimp in Space" to note the kinds of errors that students make as they read. As you listen, you may choose to mark up your copy of the story where students have difficulty reading. Make a mark or a note for the following types of errors:

Listen for these types of errors	How many times?	Examples
Reads word incorrectly, does not self-correct.		
Skips a word, does not self-correct.		
Rereads before reading correctly.		
Guesses before reading correctly.		

Name .... Date ....

Have students read aloud the article. Students should read independently. As students read, mark on your copy any words they miss.

Circle *Yes* or *No* for each question.

51. Did students read with a pace that sounds natural? Yes / No
52. Did students read with appropriate volume? Yes / No
53. Did students pause for periods? Yes / No
54. Did students read with expression? Yes / No

Part 10. Nonfiction: "The First Chimp in Space" Create a Time Line

Gather the time line boxes on page LC 149. Have students fill in the six major events in Ham's life. Then have them paste the events on the time line on page LC 151 in the order that they happened.

55.–60. Complete the time line.

Part 11. Nonfiction: "The First Chimp in Space" Reading Comprehension

Have students read and answer the questions on the Checkpoint pages. Students should circle their answers.

Part 12. Poetry: "My Day" Activate Prior Knowledge

Explain to students that they will read a poem with you. Ask students the following questions to activate prior knowledge. Note their responses on the Checkpoint pages.

66. What do you know about poems?
67. You've read a story and an article. What are they mostly about? What kind of characters do they have?
68. What do you think this poem will be about?

Part 13. Poetry: "My Day" Guided Reading and Fluency Check

Gather the Checkpoint page with "My Day." Cut out the two copies of the poem and give one to students. Read aloud the title of the poem, pointing to each word as you read. Then, have students read aloud the title of the poem, pointing to each word as they read aloud.

Say: You will read aloud the poem to me. If you would like to read the poem to yourself first, you may.

Use your copy of "My Day" to note the kinds of errors that students make as they read.

Name .... Date ....

As you listen, you may choose to mark up your copy of the poem where students have difficulty reading. Make a mark or a note for the following types of errors:

Listen for these types of errors	How many times?	Examples
Reads word incorrectly, does not self-correct.		
Skips a word, does not self-correct.		
Rereads before reading correctly.		
Guesses before reading correctly.		

Have students read aloud the poem. Students should read independently. As students read, mark on your copy any words they miss.

Circle *Yes* or *No* for each question.

69. Did students read with a pace that sounds natural? Yes / No
70. Did students read with appropriate volume? Yes / No
71. Did students pause for periods? Yes / No
72. Did students read with expression? Yes / No

Part 14. Poetry: "My Day" Draw Conclusions

Have students draw conclusions about the poem. Ask students the following questions and note their responses on the Checkpoint pages.

73. What is the poem about?
74. What lines from the poem helped you figure out what the poem is about?

Part 15. Poetry: "My Day" Reading Comprehension

Read the questions on the Checkpoint pages to students. Students should write the answers themselves. If necessary, allow them to dictate their responses to you.

Name .... Date ....

Part 16. Poetry: "My Day" Write Your Own Poem

Turn to the poetry frame on page LC 160. Have students complete the poem independently. Students should use words from the word bank to complete the poem using the same rhyming pattern as the author used in "My Day." If necessary, allow them to dictate their responses to you.

Name .... Date ....

Semester Checkpoint Answer Key Guided Reading Comprehension and Analysis

Learning Coach Copy

Bad Dog, Chester!

by Missy Tisch

Every day I hear the same thing: "Bad dog, Chester!" Some days I hear it as soon as I wake up. Some days I hear it after lunch. Some days I hear it at bedtime. But, I'm not a bad dog. You might not believe me, but it's true. I know all my commands. I never jump up on people. I don't beg for food. I'm a good dog. I know what you're wondering. If I'm such a good dog, then why do I hear "Bad dog, Chester!" every day? I'll tell you why. Gabby.

Gabby is the bird. Since she moved in, life has never been the same. Gabby has a cage, but the door is always open. She gets to fly all over the house. Most people think she's the perfect bird. But, they don't see the Gabby that I see. Gabby is the one that knocked over the vase of flowers. Gabby is the one that ruined the curtains. Gabby is the one that got the furniture dirty. But, Gabby doesn't hear "Bad bird, Gabby!" Do you know why? Because after Gabby does something bad, she flies into her cage. She sits on her perch,

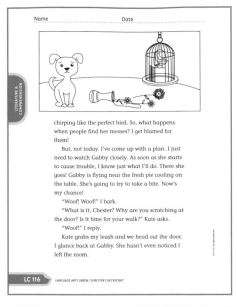

Name _____ Date _____

chirping like the perfect bird. So, what happens when people find her messes? I get blamed for them!

But, not today. I've come up with a plan. I just need to watch Gabby closely. As soon as she starts to cause trouble, I know just what I'll do. There she goes! Gabby is flying near the fresh pie cooling on the table. She's going to try to take a bite. Now's my chance!

"Woof! Woof!" I bark.

"What is it, Chester? Why are you scratching at the door? Is it time for your walk?" Kate asks.

"Woof!" I reply.

Kate grabs my leash and we head out the door. I glance back at Gabby. She hasn't even noticed I left the room.

LC 116   LANGUAGE ARTS GREEN | SEMESTER CHECKPOINT

Name _____ Date _____

When Kate and I get back from our walk, the kitchen is a mess. Pie is everywhere. Pie is on the table. Pie is on the floor. Pie is on the chairs. I look at Kate. She's not happy. She looks at me, and I can see that she knows the truth now.

"Bad bird, Gabby!" Kate says. "Good boy, Chester. I'm sorry I blamed you for everything."

That's all I needed to hear. I give Kate a big lick on the face and help her clean up the kitchen. After all, fresh pie is my favorite!

LANGUAGE ARTS GREEN | SEMESTER CHECKPOINT   LC 117

Name _____ Date _____

Bad Dog, Chester!

by Missy Tisch

Every day I hear the same thing: "Bad dog, Chester!" Some days I hear it as soon as I wake up. Some days I hear it after lunch. Some days I hear it at bedtime. But, I'm not a bad dog. You might not believe me, but it's true. I know all my commands. I never jump up on people. I don't beg for food. I'm a good dog. I know what you're wondering. If I'm such a good dog, then why do I hear "Bad dog, Chester!" every day? I'll tell you why. Gabby.

Gabby is the bird. Since she moved in, life has never been the same. Gabby has a cage, but the door is always open. She gets to fly all over the house. Most people think she's the perfect bird. But, they don't see the Gabby that I see. Gabby is the one that knocked over the vase of flowers. Gabby is the one that ruined the curtains. Gabby is the one that got the furniture dirty. But, Gabby doesn't hear "Bad bird, Gabby!" Do you know why? Because after Gabby does something bad, she flies into her cage. She sits on her perch,

LANGUAGE ARTS GREEN | SEMESTER CHECKPOINT   LC 119

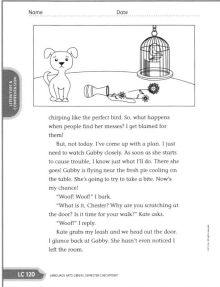

Name _____ Date _____

chirping like the perfect bird. So, what happens when people find her messes? I get blamed for them!

But, not today. I've come up with a plan. I just need to watch Gabby closely. As soon as she starts to cause trouble, I know just what I'll do. There she goes! Gabby is flying near the fresh pie cooling on the table. She's going to try to take a bite. Now's my chance!

"Woof! Woof!" I bark.

"What is it, Chester? Why are you scratching at the door? Is it time for your walk?" Kate asks.

"Woof!" I reply.

Kate grabs my leash and we head out the door. I glance back at Gabby. She hasn't even noticed I left the room.

LC 120   LANGUAGE ARTS GREEN | SEMESTER CHECKPOINT

Name _____ Date _____

When Kate and I get back from our walk, the kitchen is a mess. Pie is everywhere. Pie is on the table. Pie is on the floor. Pie is on the chairs. I look at Kate. She's not happy. She looks at me, and I can see that she knows the truth now.

"Bad bird, Gabby!" Kate says. "Good boy, Chester. I'm sorry I blamed you for everything."

That's all I needed to hear. I give Kate a big lick on the face and help her clean up the kitchen. After all, fresh pie is my favorite!

LANGUAGE ARTS GREEN | SEMESTER CHECKPOINT   LC 121

Name _____ Date _____

Part 1. Fiction: "Bad Dog, Chester!"
Activate Prior Knowledge
Get ready to read. Listen to the question, and say the answer.

1. **Answers will vary.**

2. **Answers will vary.**

Part 2. Fiction: "Bad Dog, Chester!"
Book Walk
Do a Book Walk. Listen to the question, and write the answer.

3. to entertain us

4. fiction

LANGUAGE ARTS GREEN | SEMESTER CHECKPOINT   LC 123

Name _____ Date _____

Part 3. Fiction: "Bad Dog, Chester!"
Guided Reading and Fluency Check
Cut out the word cards. Read aloud each word.

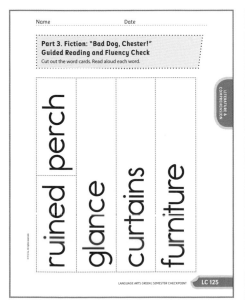

ruined   perch
glance   curtains   furniture

LANGUAGE ARTS GREEN | SEMESTER CHECKPOINT   LC 125

Name _____ Date _____

5. furniture

6. glance

7. ruined

8. perch

9. curtains

10.–13.

LANGUAGE ARTS GREEN | SEMESTER CHECKPOINT   LC 127

Name _____ Date _____

Part 4. Fiction: "Bad Dog, Chester!"
Evaluate Predictions
Listen to the question, and write the answer.

14. **Possible answers: title; illustrations;**
Words to Know

15. **Possible answers: title; illustrations;**
Words to Know

16. **Answers will vary.**

_____

Part 5. "Bad Dog, Chester!" Problem and Solution
Listen to the question, and write the answer.

17. **Chester is always getting in trouble**
for things he didn't do.

LC 128   LANGUAGE ARTS GREEN | SEMESTER CHECKPOINT

Panel 1 (LC 129)

Name _____ Date _____

18. a way to fix a problem

19. Chester gets Kate to take him for a walk when he knows Gabby wants the pie.

Part 6. Fiction: "Bad Dog, Chester!" Reading Comprehension
Listen to the question, and write the answer.

20. Who is narrating the story?

Chester

21. What is the setting?

the kitchen

Panel 2 (LC 130)

Name _____ Date _____

22. What are some examples of cause and effect in this story?

Students should name at least two examples of cause and effect from the story.

23. Is this story realistic fiction or fantasy fiction?

fantasy fiction

24. How do you know?

Chester is telling the story, and dogs can't do that in the real world.

Part 7. Fiction: "Bad Dog, Chester!" Show You Know
Listen to the question, and say the answer. Then, complete the graphic organizer.

25. Chester

26. Chester tells how he's always getting in trouble for things Gabby does.

Panel 3 (LC 131)

Name _____ Date _____

27. Chester comes up with a plan to catch Gabby making a mess.

28. Kate catches Gabby making a mess and apologizes to Chester.

29.–34.

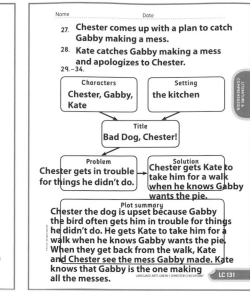

Characters
Chester, Gabby, Kate

Setting
the kitchen

Title
Bad Dog, Chester!

Problem
Chester gets in trouble for things he didn't do.

Solution
Chester gets Kate to take him for a walk when he knows Gabby wants the pie.

Plot summary
Chester the dog is upset because Gabby the bird often gets him in trouble for things he didn't do. He gets Kate to take him for a walk when he knows Gabby wants the pie. When they get back from the walk, Kate and Chester see the mess Gabby made. Kate knows that Gabby is the one making all the messes.

Panel 4 (LC 133)

Name _____ Date _____

Learning Coach Copy

The First Chimp in Space
by Maude Drayber

Chimpanzees are smart animals. They can be trained to do a lot of things. One chimp was trained for a very special job. His name was Ham. Ham's job wasn't on earth. His job was in space!

Learning from Animals

The first rockets to fly to space didn't carry people. They carried animals. Some carried mice. Some carried dogs. Other kinds of animals flew to space, too. Scientists learned from the animals. They learned it was safe to fly to space. But, they wanted to know more. They wanted to know if astronauts would be able to complete tasks in space. They decided to send a chimp to space to find out. They chose Ham.

Training for the Big Day

Ham was born in 1957. In 1959, he began training for his space flight. Ham learned a lot of things. He learned to wear a special suit. He learned how it would feel to ride in a rocket. Ham had to learn a job, too. He learned how to push a lever when he saw a light flash. He was good at his job. Scientists knew Ham could do his job on earth. They hoped he could do it in space, too.

Panel 5 (LC 134)

Name _____ Date _____

3 . . . 2 . . . 1 . . . Blast Off!

January 31, 1961, was Ham's big day. That was the day he flew to space. Scientists got Ham ready for his flight. They fed him. They got him dressed. They hooked him up to machines. The machines let them see how Ham was feeling during his flight. They could see how fast or slow Ham was breathing. They could see how fast or slow his heart was beating. The machines let them know if Ham was safe.

Scientists wanted to know more than how Ham felt during his flight. They wanted to know if he could do his job, too. When it was time, the light in the rocket flashed for Ham. Would Ham push the lever? Scientists didn't have to wait long to find out. Ham pushed the lever almost as fast as he pushed it on earth. The scientists were thrilled! Ham had done more than just ride in a rocket. He had proved it was possible to complete tasks in space.

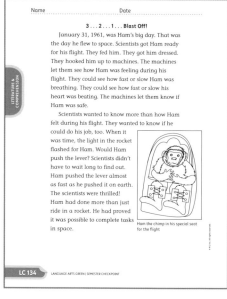

Ham the chimp in his special seat for the flight

Panel 6 (LC 135)

Name _____ Date _____

After the Mission

Ham flew to space just one time. His flight was short. It was less than 17 minutes long. But, his flight was more important than the flights of all the other animals.

In 1963, Ham went to live at the National Zoo. It is a famous zoo in Washington, D.C. He lived there for a long time. In 1980, Ham moved. He went to live at the North Carolina Zoo. It was his home for the rest of his life. He died there in 1983. Ham is buried at a special place. He is buried at the International Space Hall of Fame. The Hall of Fame is in New Mexico. A lot of people go to see Ham's grave each year. They go to learn more about his special flight. And, they go to thank the most important chimp of all time.

Panel 7 (LC 137)

Name _____ Date _____

Student Copy

The First Chimp in Space
by Maude Drayber

Chimpanzees are smart animals. They can be trained to do a lot of things. One chimp was trained for a very special job. His name was Ham. Ham's job wasn't on earth. His job was in space!

Learning from Animals

The first rockets to fly to space didn't carry people. They carried animals. Some carried mice. Some carried dogs. Other kinds of animals flew to space, too. Scientists learned from the animals. They learned it was safe to fly to space. But, they wanted to know more. They wanted to know if astronauts would be able to complete tasks in space. They decided to send a chimp to space to find out. They chose Ham.

Training for the Big Day

Ham was born in 1957. In 1959, he began training for his space flight. Ham learned a lot of things. He learned to wear a special suit. He learned how it would feel to ride in a rocket. Ham had to learn a job, too. He learned how to push a lever when he saw a light flash. He was good at his job. Scientists knew Ham could do his job on earth. They hoped he could do it in space, too.

Panel 8 (LC 138)

Name _____ Date _____

3 . . . 2 . . . 1 . . . Blast Off!

January 31, 1961, was Ham's big day. That was the day he flew to space. Scientists got Ham ready for his flight. They fed him. They got him dressed. They hooked him up to machines. The machines let them see how Ham was feeling during his flight. They could see how fast or slow Ham was breathing. They could see how fast or slow his heart was beating. The machines let them know if Ham was safe.

Scientists wanted to know more than how Ham felt during his flight. They wanted to know if he could do his job, too. When it was time, the light in the rocket flashed for Ham. Would Ham push the lever? Scientists didn't have to wait long to find out. Ham pushed the lever almost as fast as he pushed it on earth. The scientists were thrilled! Ham had done more than just ride in a rocket. He had proved it was possible to complete tasks in space.

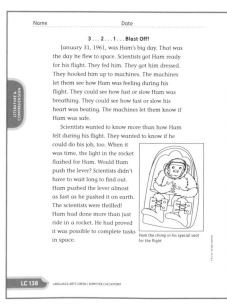

Ham the chimp in his special seat for the flight

Panel 9 (LC 139)

Name _____ Date _____

After the Mission

Ham flew to space just one time. His flight was short. It was less than 17 minutes long. But, his flight was more important than the flights of all the other animals.

In 1963, Ham went to live at the National Zoo. It is a famous zoo in Washington, D.C. He lived there for a long time. In 1980, Ham moved. He went to live at the North Carolina Zoo. It was his home for the rest of his life. He died there in 1983. Ham is buried at a special place. He is buried at the International Space Hall of Fame. The Hall of Fame is in New Mexico. A lot of people go to see Ham's grave each year. They go to learn more about his special flight. And, they go to thank the most important chimp of all time.

Name _____ Date _____

Part 8. Nonfiction: "The First Chimp in Space"
Preview the Article
Listen to the question, and say your answer.

35. chimps traveling in space

36. Learning from Animals

37. how animals can teach us things

38. Training for the Big Day

39. how the chimp was trained to go into space

40. 3 . . . 2 . . . 1 . . . Blast Off!

41. what it was like for the chimp in space

42. After the Mission

43. what the chimp did when he came home

Name _____ Date _____

Part 9. Nonfiction: "The First Chimp in Space"
Guided Reading and Fluency Check
Cut out the word cards. Read aloud each word.

scientist

chimpanzee

machine

complete

Name _____ Date _____

international

mission

lever

Name _____ Date _____

44. scientist

45. machine

46. chimpanzee

47. complete

48. lever

49. international

50. mission

51.–54.

Name _____ Date _____

Part 10. Nonfiction: "The First Chimp in Space"
Create a Time Line
Write the year and the six major events from Ham's life in each box. Then, cut out the events, and paste them on the time line in the order that they happened.

55.–60.

19___	19___	19___

19___	19___	19___

Name _____ Date _____

Glue the facts from page LC 149 in the order they happened.

1957 Ham the chimp is born.	1959 Ham begins training for space flight.	1961 Ham goes to space.	1963 Ham moves to National Zoo.	1980 Ham moves to North Carolina Zoo.	1983 Ham is buried in New Mexico.

Name _____ Date _____

Part 11. Nonfiction: "The First Chimp in Space"
Reading Comprehension
Listen to the question, and choose the answer.

61. What is the topic of the article "The First Chimp in Space"?
   A. chimpanzees moving to different states
   B. chimpanzees traveling to space *(selected)*
   C. chimpanzees working at the zoo

62. Which statement is a fact?
   A. Chimpanzees are cute.
   B. Chimpanzees like space.
   C. Chimpanzees have been to space. *(selected)*

63. Which statement is an opinion?
   A. Ham probably liked going to space. *(selected)*
   B. Scientists could tell how Ham was feeling during his flight.
   C. Ham learned how to push a lever.

Name _____ Date _____

64. What did Ham learn first?
   A. how to ride in a rocket
   B. how to do a job
   C. how to wear a special suit *(selected)*

65. If you wanted to learn more about Ham, what would be a good source of information?
   A. a cartoon about chimps traveling in space
   B. a book of facts about Ham and other animals that have worked in space *(selected)*
   C. a story a friend told you about chimps working and traveling

---

Name _____ Date _____

Student Copy
My Day

Alone in our big house,
I look for a small mouse.
When I don't find my tasty snack,
I purr and nap on my striped back.

Alone in the long and quiet hall,
I watch shadows dance on the white wall.
When they chase me through the big door,
I roll with them on the soft floor.

Alone on your cozy bed,
I stretch and rest my tired head.
When you climb under the cool sheet,
I curl up next to your warm feet.

Learning Coach Copy
My Day

Alone in our big house,
I look for a small mouse.
When I don't find my tasty snack,
I purr and nap on my striped back.

Alone in the long and quiet hall,
I watch shadows dance on the white wall.
When they chase me through the big door,
I roll with them on the soft floor.

Alone on your cozy bed,
I stretch and rest my tired head.
When you climb under the cool sheet,
I curl up next to your warm feet.

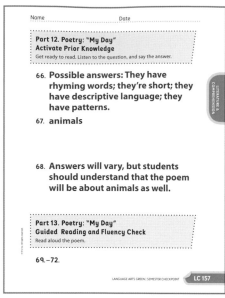

Part 12. Poetry: "My Day"
Activate Prior Knowledge
Get ready to read. Listen to the question, and say the answer.

66. **Possible answers: They have rhyming words; they're short; they have descriptive language; they have patterns.**

67. **animals**

68. **Answers will vary, but students should understand that the poem will be about animals as well.**

Part 13. Poetry: "My Day"
Guided Reading and Fluency Check
Read aloud the poem.

69.–72.

LANGUAGE ARTS GREEN | SEMESTER CHECKPOINT — LC 157

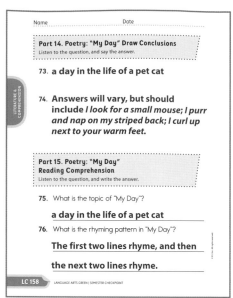

LC 158 — LANGUAGE ARTS GREEN | SEMESTER CHECKPOINT

Part 14. Poetry: "My Day" Draw Conclusions
Listen to the question, and say the answer.

73. **a day in the life of a pet cat**

74. **Answers will vary, but should include *I look for a small mouse; I purr and nap on my striped back; I curl up next to your warm feet.***

Part 15. Poetry: "My Day"
Reading Comprehension
Listen to the question, and write the answer.

75. What is the topic of "My Day"?

a day in the life of a pet cat

76. What is the rhyming pattern in "My Day"?

The first two lines rhyme, and then

the next two lines rhyme.

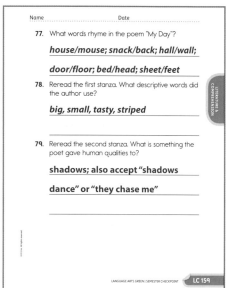

77. What words rhyme in the poem "My Day"?

house/mouse; snack/back; hall/wall;

door/floor; bed/head; sheet/feet

78. Reread the first stanza. What descriptive words did the author use?

big, small, tasty, striped

79. Reread the second stanza. What is something the poet gave human qualities to?

shadows; also accept "shadows

dance" or "they chase me"

LANGUAGE ARTS GREEN | SEMESTER CHECKPOINT — LC 159

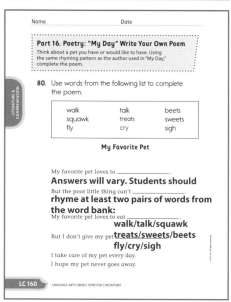

LC 160 — LANGUAGE ARTS GREEN | SEMESTER CHECKPOINT

Part 16. Poetry: "My Day" Write Your Own Poem
Think about a pet you have or would like to have. Using the same rhyming pattern as the author used in "My Day," complete the poem.

80. Use words from the following list to complete the poem.

walk	talk	beets
squawk	treats	sweets
fly	cry	sigh

My Favorite Pet

My favorite pet loves to _____.
Answers will vary. Students should
But the poor little thing can't _____.
rhyme at least two pairs of words from the word bank:
My favorite pet loves to eat _____
walk/talk/squawk
But I don't give my pet **treats/sweets/beets**
fly/cry/sigh
I take care of my pet every day.
I hope my pet never goes away.

 Online varies

If necessary, work with students to complete the More Practice activity.

More Practice

Reading and Comprehension
If students scored less than 80 percent on the Semester Checkpoint, they may benefit from completing another Reader's Choice unit. You can find this list online. Additionally, continue to work with students on skills such as making and evaluating predictions and identifying elements of a given story (title, author, illustrator, characters, setting, problem, solution).

Objectives
- Evaluate Checkpoint results and choose activities to review.

Writing Skills

Complete Sentences

Unit Focus

In this unit, students will begin learning about grammar, usage, and mechanics. Before you begin working with students in this unit, watch the introduction to Writing Skills in Lesson 1 online. This introduction will provide you with important information about the Writing Skills program. You do not have any other work to do for Lesson 1.

Beginning in Lesson 2, you will work with students to learn about complete sentences. Complete sentences are the basis for all written and spoken communication. They are the building blocks of all writing. By learning the rules and parts of complete sentences, students will be laying the foundation for future success as writers.

▸ Sentences are used to communicate complete ideas.
▸ Sentences have two parts: a naming part (the subject) and an action part (the predicate).
▸ Sentences begin with a capital letter and end with an end mark.

Although these lessons teach about the subject and predicate, you should not use these terms with students. Instead, refer to the *naming part* of a sentence and the *action part* of a sentence. At this point, it is more important for students to understand what a subject and predicate do, rather than to know the proper terminology.

A key part in getting students excited about writing is to have fun with these lessons. Lessons involve games and wordplay. When students are writing their own sentences, encourage them to be silly, fanciful, and creative. Even at this early stage, students can learn that writing can be joyous and exciting.

Unit Plan		**Offline**	**Online**
Lesson 1	Introduction to Writing Skills	5 minutes	10 minutes
Lesson 2	The Sentence	15 minutes	
Lesson 3	Sentence Beginnings and Endings	15 minutes	
Lesson 4	Review Complete Sentences	5 minutes	10 minutes
Lesson 5	Unit Checkpoint	15 minutes	varies

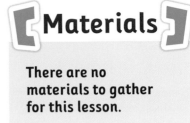

Introduction to Writing Skills

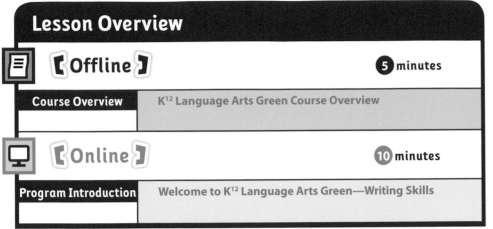

Lesson Overview

	**[Offline]**	**5** minutes
Course Overview	K¹² Language Arts Green Course Overview	

	[Online]	**10** minutes
Program Introduction	Welcome to K¹² Language Arts Green—Writing Skills	

[Offline] **5** minutes

Review the General Course Structure and Overview and the K¹² Language Arts Green Writing Skills Program Overview.

Course Overview ....

K¹² Language Arts Green Course Overview
You will review the information on pages viii–xxii and xxxiv–xxxix in *K¹² Language Arts Lesson Guide* if you have not already done so. Go to page viii to get started.

Objectives
- Understand the general course overview and structure in K¹² Language Arts Green.

[Online] **10** minutes

View the program introduction for K¹² Language Arts Green Writing Skills.

Program Introduction ....

Welcome to K¹² Language Arts Green—Writing Skills
Go online to view the introduction to learn how to navigate through the program and help students successfully complete their learning journey.

Objectives
- Navigate the K¹² Language Arts Green Writing Skills program online.

The Sentence

Lesson Overview

Offline   **15** minutes

Get Ready	Lesson Introduction
	Act Out Sentences
Learn	Sentence Parts
Try It	Make Complete Sentences

Materials

Supplied
- *K¹² Language Arts Activity Book*, pp. WS 1–2

Also Needed
- whiteboard (optional)
- crayons

Keywords
predicate – the verb or verb phrase in a sentence
sentence – a group of words that tells a complete thought
subject – a word or words that tell whom or what the sentence is about

Content Background

▶ A sentence is made up of two parts. The part that tells who or what does something is the subject. The part that tells the action that the subject does is called the predicate. The predicate includes the verb.

▶ In lessons of this unit, you should refer to the subject as the *naming part* of the sentence. You should refer to the predicate as the *action part* of the sentence.

Big Ideas

Complete sentences are the key to all communication.

Offline   **15** minutes

Work **together** with students to complete Get Ready, Learn, and Try It activities.

Get Ready

Lesson Introduction
Prepare students for the lesson.

1. **Say:** If I said "the dog," would you know what I was trying to tell you? Probably not, because I didn't tell you what the dog was doing. That was not a complete sentence.

Objectives
- Share ideas with others.

2. Explain that students will learn about complete sentences, and how we use complete sentences to communicate.

3. Tell students that they will practice recognizing and writing complete sentences.

Act Out Sentences

Help students recognize how the parts of a sentence work together to communicate an idea.

1. **Say:** We're going to work together to share an idea. I will name a person or animal, and you will name what the person or animal does.

2. Give students a subject and have them suggest the action.

   ► The monkey _____. Possible answers: sleeps, plays, eats
   ► My friend _____. Possible answers: runs, rests, laughs
   ► The firefighter _____. Possible answers: helps, sits, climbs

3. Ask students which sentence was their favorite. Act out that sentence together.

4. Write the sentence that was their favorite on a whiteboard or a sheet of paper. **Say:** We made a complete sentence to share an idea. We're going to learn more about how to make complete sentences to share ideas.

Learn

Sentence Parts

Introduce students to the two parts of a sentence: the naming part and the action part. Turn to page WS 1 in *K¹² Language Arts Activity Book*.

1. Write the following sentence on a whiteboard or a sheet of paper, and have students read it with you.

   Willy hops like a frog.

2. Explain that a sentence always has two parts: a **naming part**, which names whom the sentence is about, and an **action part**.

3. Point to the sentence and ask students which is the naming part. Willy

4. Underline the naming part.

5. Point to the sentence and ask students which is the action. hops like a frog

6. Draw two lines under the action part.

7. Help students understand that complete sentences can be very short and simple, such as *I sat*, or long and complicated, such as *I sat on a big log all day long.*

8. Ask students to identify the naming part and the action part in each sentence. The naming part is *I* in both sentences. The action part is *sat* in the first sentence and *sat on a big log all day long* in the second sentence.

Objectives
- Identify subject.
- Identify predicate.

9. Read the rule and the example on the Activity Book page.

10. Have students complete the rest of the Activity Book page. Provide support as necessary.

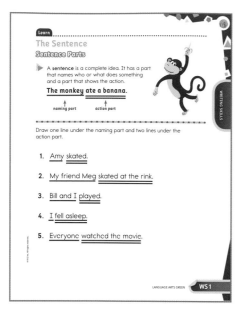

Try It

Make Complete Sentences

Help students practice recognizing and writing complete sentences. Turn to page WS 2 in *K¹² Language Arts Activity Book*.

1. Read the first set of directions to students. Have them make a check (✓) if the sentence is complete. Have them make an X (✘) if the sentence is not complete.

2. Read the second set of directions to students. Help students write a complete sentence with a naming part and an action part.

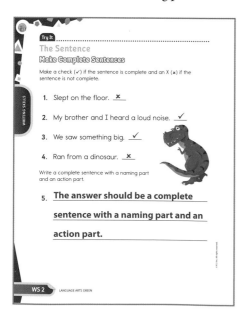

Objectives
- Recognize word groups that are sentences.
- Write complete sentences.

Sentence Beginnings and Endings

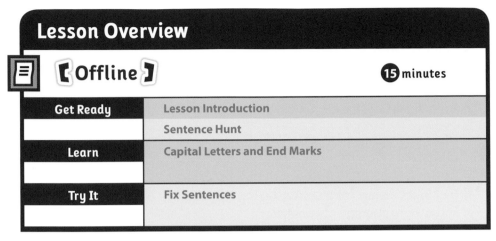

Lesson Overview

[Offline]   15 minutes

Get Ready	Lesson Introduction
	Sentence Hunt
Learn	Capital Letters and End Marks
Try It	Fix Sentences

Materials

Supplied
- *K¹² Language Arts Activity Book*, pp. WS 3–6

Also Needed
- scissors, adult
- whiteboard (optional)

Keywords
sentence – a group of words that tells a complete thought

Advance Preparation

For the Get Ready, cut out the word groups on page WS 3 in *K¹² Language Arts Activity Book*.

Big Ideas

To express ideas in a meaningful way that others can understand, one needs to understand the conventions of standard grammar, usage, and mechanics.

[Offline]  15 minutes

Work **together** with students to complete Get Ready, Learn, and Try It activities.

Get Ready •••

Lesson Introduction
Prepare students for the lesson.

1. Tell students that they will review what makes a complete sentence.

2. Explain that they will learn about how to begin and end a complete sentence.

3. Tell students that they will practice writing complete sentences.

Objectives
- Recall what a sentence is.
- Recognize word groups that are sentences.

Sentence Hunt

Help students recognize the difference between a complete sentence and an incomplete sentence. Gather the word groups that you cut out.

1. Place the word groups face down in a pile.

2. **Say:** Remember that a complete sentence has two parts.

   ▶ What are the two parts of a sentence? a naming part and an action part

3. **Say:** Let's play a game. There are seven strips of paper here. Some have complete sentences on them, and some have incomplete sentences on them. I'm going to hide the strips in this room. Your job is to find them and tell me which ones have complete sentences on them.

4. Have students close their eyes and count to 20. Hide the strips in different places in the room.

5. Tell students to find all the strips. As they find each one, ask if what appears on the card is a complete sentence or not. Have students put the complete sentences in one pile and the incomplete sentences in another.

6. Go through the piles together to see if students have correctly identified the complete sentences. I made a snow fort. We drank hot chocolate. The dog barked.

TIP If students are having trouble telling the difference between complete sentences and incomplete sentences, ask them whether a naming part is on the card. Then ask whether an action part is on the card. Ask students to come up with the missing part to make all sentences complete.

Learn

Capital Letters and End Marks

Introduce capital letters and end marks to students. Help them understand that a complete sentence must begin with a capital letter and end with an end mark. Turn to page WS 5 in *K¹² Language Arts Activity Book.*

Objectives
- Recognize that a sentence begins with a capital letter.
- Recognize that a sentence ends with an end mark.

1. Write the following sentence on a whiteboard or a sheet of paper and have students read it with you.

   Ted sat.

2. **Say:** No sentence can be complete without two very important buddies, a capital letter and an end mark.

3. As you name the capital letter and end mark, point to them in the sentence.

4. **Say:** These buddies always work together. Sometimes they are close together. Sometimes they are far apart.

5. Write the following sentence and have students read it with you.

   Ted sat in the big chair with his cat.

6. Point out the capital letter and end mark.

7. Tell students that whenever they are writing a complete sentence, they need to do a "buddy check" to make sure both buddies (the capital letter and the end mark) are there.

8. Write the following sentence but do not add a period.

   Mary ran home

   ▸ Do a buddy check of this sentence. Are both buddies there? No   What is missing? the end mark

9. Write the following sentence but do not capitalize the *w.*

   who chased Mary?

10. Point to the question mark and explain that it is the end mark for a question. It is also a buddy with the capital letter.

    ▸ Do a buddy check of this sentence. Are both buddies there? No   What is missing? the capital letter

11. Read the rule and the example on the Activity Book page.

12. Have students complete the rest of the Activity Book page. Provide support as necessary.

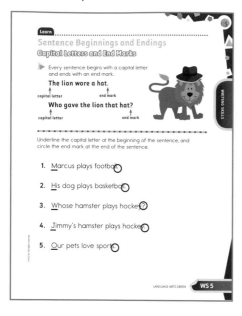

Try It

 Fix Sentences

Help students practice making complete sentences that begin with capital letters and end with end marks. Turn to page WS 6 in *K¹² Language Arts Activity Book*.

1. Read the first set of directions to students.

2. Read each sentence to students. Show them how to put a line through the small letter and write a capital letter above it. Have them add an end mark to the end.

3. Read the second set of directions to students.

4. Help students write a complete sentence that begins and ends correctly.

Objectives
- Capitalize the first word in a sentence.
- Use an end mark to end a sentence.
- Write a sentence that begins and ends correctly.

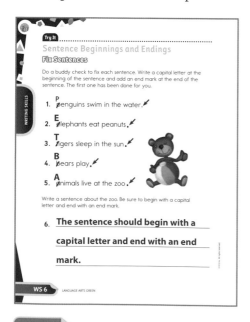

Review Complete Sentences

Lesson Overview

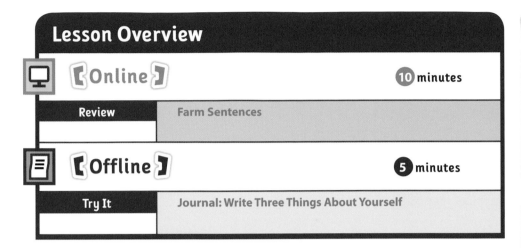

🖥 **[Online]**		**10** minutes
Review	**Farm Sentences**	

📄 **[Offline]**		**5** minutes
Try It	**Journal: Write Three Things About Yourself**	

[Materials]

Supplied
- *K¹² My Journal*, pp. 120–121

Also Needed
- crayons

Keywords

predicate – the verb or verb phrase in a sentence

sentence – a group of words that tells a complete thought

subject – a word or words that tell whom or what the sentence is about

[Online] 🔟 minutes

Students will review what they have learned about complete sentences to prepare for the Unit Checkpoint. Help students locate the online activity and provide support as needed.

Review ···

Farm Sentences

Students will work online to review what they have learned about complete sentences, the naming part and action part, and capital letters and end marks.

Offline Alternative

No computer access? Pick a book that your students are familiar with. Have them identify the naming part and action part in appropriate sentences in the book. Ask them how they know that the sentences they are looking at are complete. Have them do buddy checks to look for capital letters and end marks.

Objectives

- Identify subject.
- Identify predicate.
- Recognize word groups that are sentences.
- Recognize that a sentence begins with a capital letter.
- Recognize that a sentence ends with an end mark.
- Capitalize the first word in a sentence.
- Use an end mark to end a sentence.

[Offline] 5 minutes

Students will write on their own in their journal. Help students locate the offline activity.

Try It

✏️ **Journal: Write Three Things About Yourself**

Students will write in their journal on their own. Gather *K¹² My Journal* and have students turn to pages 120 and 121 in Writing Skills. To help students prepare, ask the following question:

Where is your favorite place to play?

1. Tell students that there are a lot of things they could say to describe where they like to play.

2. Read the prompt with students. Have students respond to the prompt in their journal. As necessary, remind them that there are no correct or incorrect answers.

3. Have students write at least three things to describe themselves. Tell them that they may write whatever they like about themselves, but they must use complete sentences to describe each thing. Students can then use the space provided to draw a picture.

4. If students feel comfortable sharing what they wrote, allow them to share with you or their peers.

TIP The amount of time students need to complete this activity will vary. Allow them to use the rest of the allotted time to complete this activity. If they have more they would like to write, you may let them complete their entry at a later time. If students are having trouble getting started, you might tell them to just list ideas or words. They may even draw a picture and describe it to you. You can transcribe their words for them.

Objectives
- Freewrite about a topic.
- Write in a journal.

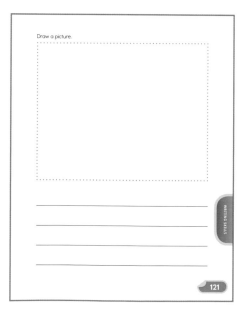

Unit Checkpoint

Lesson Overview

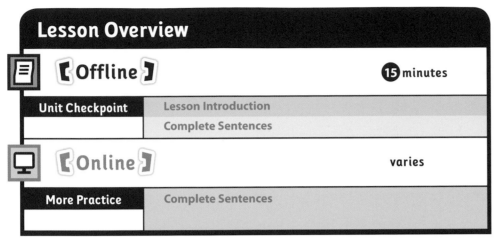

 **[Offline]**		**15** minutes
Unit Checkpoint	Lesson Introduction	
	Complete Sentences	
[Online]		varies
More Practice	Complete Sentences	

[Materials]

Supplied

- *K¹² Language Arts Assessments,* pp. WS 1–4

[Offline] **15** minutes

Work **together** with students to complete the Unit Checkpoint.

Unit Checkpoint

Lesson Introduction

Prepare students for the lesson.

1. Tell students that they are going to complete a Unit Checkpoint to show what they have learned.

2. Explain that if they miss one or more questions, they can continue to practice this grammar skill.

Complete Sentences

Explain that students are going to show what they have learned about recognizing and writing complete sentences with correct capitalization and end marks.

1. Give students the Unit Checkpoint pages.

2. Read the directions together. If needed, read the questions and answer choices to students. Have students complete the Checkpoint on their own.

Objectives

- Identify subject.
- Identify predicate.
- Recognize word groups that are sentences.
- Recognize that a complete sentence begins with a capital letter and has an end mark.
- Use a capital letter to begin a sentence and an end mark to end it.

3. Use the Answer Key to score the Checkpoint and then enter the results online.

4. Review each exercise with students. Work with students to correct any exercise that they missed.

 TIP Students who answered one or more questions incorrectly should continue to practice this grammar skill. Write different incomplete sentences and ask students to identify what is wrong with each. Help them find the missing naming parts, action parts, capital letters, and end marks.

Reward: When students score 80 percent or above on the Unit Checkpoint, add a sticker for this unit on the My Accomplishments chart.

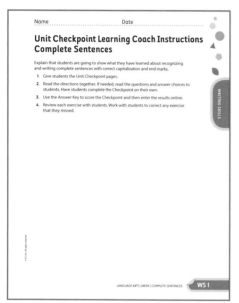

Name _____ Date _____

**Unit Checkpoint Learning Coach Instructions
Complete Sentences**

Explain that students are going to show what they have learned about recognizing and writing complete sentences with correct capitalization and end marks.

1. Give students the Unit Checkpoint pages.
2. Read the directions together. If needed, read the questions and answer choices to students. Have students complete the Checkpoint on their own.
3. Use the Answer Key to score the Checkpoint and then enter the results online.
4. Review each exercise with students. Work with students to correct any exercise that they missed.

WS 1 | LANGUAGE ARTS GREEN | COMPLETE SENTENCES

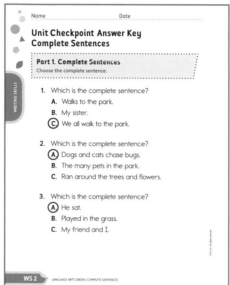

Name _____ Date _____

**Unit Checkpoint Answer Key
Complete Sentences**

Part 1. Complete Sentences
Choose the complete sentence.

1. Which is the complete sentence?
   A. Walks to the park.
   B. My sister.
   C. We all walk to the park.

2. Which is the complete sentence?
   A. Dogs and cats chase bugs.
   B. The many pets in the park.
   C. Ran around the trees and flowers.

3. Which is the complete sentence?
   A. He sat.
   B. Played in the grass.
   C. My friend and I.

WS 2 | LANGUAGE ARTS GREEN | COMPLETE SENTENCES

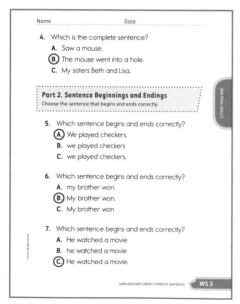

Name _____ Date _____

4. Which is the complete sentence?
   A. Saw a mouse.
   B. The mouse went into a hole.
   C. My sisters Beth and Lisa.

Part 2. Sentence Beginnings and Endings
Choose the sentence that begins and ends correctly.

5. Which sentence begins and ends correctly?
   A. We played checkers.
   B. we played checkers
   C. we played checkers.

6. Which sentence begins and ends correctly?
   A. my brother won.
   B. My brother won.
   C. My brother won

7. Which sentence begins and ends correctly?
   A. He watched a movie
   B. he watched a movie
   C. He watched a movie.

WS 3 | LANGUAGE ARTS GREEN | COMPLETE SENTENCES

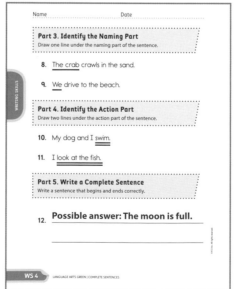

Name _____ Date _____

Part 3. Identify the Naming Part
Draw one line under the naming part of the sentence.

8. The crab crawls in the sand.

9. We drive to the beach.

Part 4. Identify the Action Part
Draw two lines under the action part of the sentence.

10. My dog and I swim.

11. I look at the fish.

Part 5. Write a Complete Sentence
Write a sentence that begins and ends correctly.

12. Possible answer: The moon is full.
    _____

WS 4 | LANGUAGE ARTS GREEN | COMPLETE SENTENCES

 **varies**

If necessary, work with students to complete the More Practice activity.

More Practice

Complete Sentences

If students scored less than 80 percent on the Unit Checkpoint, have them complete the appropriate review activities listed in the table online. Help students locate the activities and provide support as needed.

Objectives

- Evaluate Checkpoint results and choose activities to review.

Write Strong Sentences

Unit Focus

In this unit, students will complete a writing assignment. Start by watching the introduction to Composition in Lesson 1 online. This introduction will tell you how to help your students become better writers. You do not have any other work to do for Lesson 1.

In Lesson 2, you will work with students to review basic sentence structure and end marks. Students will begin to think about the sentence as a complete thought. Sentences may be either basic or complex, but they all are the building blocks of communication. In Lessons 2–4, students will review and learn that

▶ A complete sentence has a naming part and an action part.
▶ A complete sentence begins with a capital letter and ends with an end mark.
▶ Simple sentences can be expanded by adding detail, especially by asking *where*, *when*, and *how* questions.
▶ Two sentences can be combined to create one more-complicated sentence.

In the final lesson of this unit, students will write three to five complete sentences describing a picture. Students will use words such as *and*, *or*, *but*, *on*, *during*, and *by* to give their sentences detail.

Unit Plan		**〖Offline〗**	**〖Online〗**
Lesson 1	How to Evaluate Writing		15 minutes
Lesson 2	Get Started with Sentences	15 minutes	
Lesson 3	Make the Sentence Bigger	15 minutes	
Lesson 4	Make One from Two	15 minutes	
Lesson 5	Write Sentences	15 minutes	varies

How to Evaluate Writing

Lesson Overview

[Online] 🕐 **15** minutes

Program Introduction	Welcome to K¹² Language Arts Green—Writing Skills: How to Evaluate Writing

[Materials]

There are no materials to gather for this lesson.

[Online] 🕐 **15** minutes

View the program introduction for K¹² Language Arts Green Writing Skills: How to Evaluate Writing.

Program Introduction

Welcome to K¹² Language Arts Green—Writing Skills: How to Evaluate Writing

Go online to view the introduction to learn how to evaluate students' writing using rubrics and sample responses.

Objectives

- Evaluate students' writing in the K¹² Language Arts Green Writing Skills program using rubrics and sample responses.

Get Started with Sentences

Lesson Overview

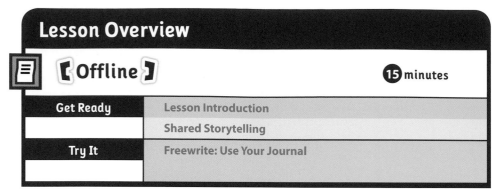

Offline		**15** minutes
Get Ready	Lesson Introduction	
	Shared Storytelling	
Try It	Freewrite: Use Your Journal	

Materials

Supplied
- *K¹² My Journal*, pp. 122–123

Also Needed
- crayons

Keywords

freewriting – a way for a writer to pick a topic and write as much as possible about it within a set time limit

Content Background

In this lesson, students will freewrite in their journal. The purpose of the journal lessons is to get students comfortable with putting ideas down on paper. Freewriting does not need to be grammatically correct. It does not need to be in complete sentences. Journals should not be evaluated and definitely should **not** be marked up with any kind of corrections. Freewriting should help students develop a love of writing. Once that love takes root, students will be motivated to learn more about the rules of writing.

Big Ideas

- ▸ To be complete, a sentence must answer the questions *who* and *what* (naming part and action part).
- ▸ Freewriting can help a person overcome writer's block and apprehension.

 **15 minutes**

Work **together** with students to complete Get Ready and Try It activities.

Get Ready

Lesson Introduction

Prepare students for the lesson.

 Objectives
- Generate ideas for writing.

1. Explain that in this lesson, students will be writing in their journal. Explain that a journal is a place for students to be creative. Students' journal entries will not be judged or graded. The journal is the students' writing playground.

2. Explain that students will freewrite.
   Say: In freewriting, you write whatever comes into your mind. You can write absolutely anything you want, to answer the question you are asked. Don't worry about making your writing perfect.

Shared Storytelling

Use this game to get students creating stories spontaneously.

1. Tell students that you are going to create a story together, word by word. You will take turns adding one word at a time to the story.

2. **Say:** For example, I say, "Once upon a time, a frog . . . ."

   Point to a student to add a word.
   Point to yourself and add the next word.
   Point to a student to add a word.

3. Continue adding words until you finish the sentence.

4. Continue the game until students are comfortably adding words. Keep playing until you have made a crazy, fun story.

TIP The purpose of this game is to get students adding words with ease. You are helping them find and use language spontaneously. If students are hesitating, increase the tempo as part of the game. Clap a steady beat and make it get faster and faster as the story goes along.

Try It

 Freewrite: Use Your Journal

Prepare students to freewrite. Gather *K¹² My Journal* and have students turn to pages 122 and 123 in Writing Skills. Read the prompt at the top of the page to students.

 Objectives
- Freewrite on a topic.
- Write in a journal.

1. Ask students what they like to write about. Answers will vary.

2. Have students freewrite in their journal about their own writing ideas.

   ▶ Explain that they are freewriting, or writing ideas on the page.
   ▶ Tell them to write anything that comes to mind to answer the question.
   ▶ Tell them that they can write whatever they wish to answer the question about writing. They can tell a story, write a list, or just jot down ideas.

3. If students are struggling, help by asking questions. Answers to questions will vary.

   ▶ Do you have any favorite stories? Do you ever make up stories in your head?
   ▶ Do you have a favorite pet, sport, friend, or activity you could write about?
   ▶ Do you like to write about things that have happened to you?
   ▶ Do you like to write about facts you know?

   If questions don't work, remind students of how they created a story during the shared storytelling activity. Encourage them to just start writing and see what happens.

4. Have students draw a picture that shows what kinds of things they like to write about.

5. Have students explain their ideas and picture to you. Do not evaluate students' writing. As long as students have written some ideas on paper, their responses are acceptable.

6. Encourage students to write as many ideas as they can.

TIP The amount of time students need to complete this activity will vary. If students are having trouble getting started, you might tell them to just list ideas or words. They may even draw a picture and describe it to you. You can transcribe their words for them. Students need only work for 15 minutes. If they have more they would like to write, you might want to have them complete their entry at a later time, but it is not required.

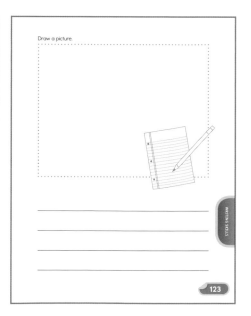

Make the Sentence Bigger

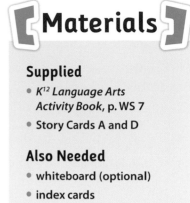

Lesson Overview

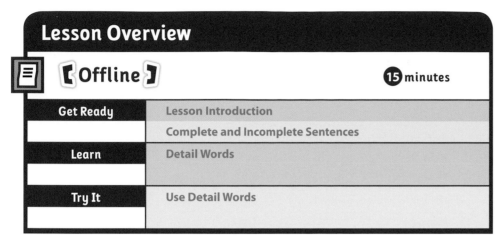

	[Offline]	**15** minutes
Get Ready	Lesson Introduction	
	Complete and Incomplete Sentences	
Learn	Detail Words	
Try It	Use Detail Words	

Materials

Supplied
- *K¹² Language Arts Activity Book*, p. WS 7
- Story Cards A and D

Also Needed
- whiteboard (optional)
- index cards

Keywords

sentence – a group of words that tells a complete thought

Advance Preparation

In this lesson, you will use Story Cards. Each card has a picture that students will use as inspiration for writing or storytelling. Before this lesson, look over the Story Cards so you understand how to use them. Pay particular attention to the two Story Cards used in this lesson—A and D. You will be using only the pictures on the front of the Story Cards and the notes in the Lesson Guide, not the text on the back of the cards.

Content Background

- In this lesson, students will begin working with prepositions. Prepositions are words such as *on, in, into, with, during,* and *while.* Prepositions connect nouns and pronouns to other words in a sentence. Often, prepositions describe location (*near, between, under*), direction (*toward, from*), and time (*until, before*).
- Although students will be using prepositions in this lesson, they do not need to know the word *preposition.* It is important that students understand how to use prepositions to add to their sentences.

Big Ideas

- To be complete, a sentence must answer the questions *who* and *what* (naming part and action part).
- A sentence contains a complete thought.
- We can expand a sentence to include the ideas *why, how,* and *when.*
- A sentence must start with a capital letter and end with an end mark.

 **Offline** **15** minutes

Work **together** with students to complete Get Ready, Learn, and Try It activities.

Get Ready

Lesson Introduction

Prepare students for the lesson.

1. Tell students that they will be learning to add ideas to sentences.

2. Explain to students that they will write their own complete sentences.

3. Remind students that complete sentences always start with a capital letter and end with an end mark.

 Objectives
- Distinguish between complete and incomplete sentences.

Complete and Incomplete Sentences

Use this activity to remind students how to make a complete sentence. Gather Story Card A.

1. Show students the picture on the front of Story Card A. Explain that you are going to say things that describe the card. Sometimes you will use complete sentences, and sometimes you will use incomplete sentences.

2. Tell students that you are going to read them some sentences. Their job is to say whether each sentence is complete or incomplete.

   ‣ The family incomplete
   ‣ eats dinner incomplete
   ‣ The family eats dinner. complete
   ‣ A glass is on the table. complete
   ‣ also has milk incomplete
   ‣ Everyone incomplete
   ‣ Everyone is happy. complete

3. Keep a tally of how many sentences students get right. Each correct answer is worth one point. When students have five points, they win.

4. After the game, have students pick their favorite sentence. Work together to write it on a whiteboard or sheet of paper, pointing out the capital letter and end mark as you write them.

TIP Allow students to make up their own examples of complete and incomplete sentences, using the story card for inspiration.

Learn

Detail Words

Introduce students to the idea that adding details to sentences can make those sentences more interesting. Help them learn prepositions and prepositional phrases by using words such as *during, while, toward, under, over, inside,* and *outside.* Gather Story Card D.

1. Hold up Story Card D. Read the sentence aloud and write it on a whiteboard or sheet of paper.

    The family walks.

2. **Say:** You can add detail to a simple sentence like this by asking questions such as *where, when,* and *how.*

3. Read the sentence aloud again.

    ▸ Where does the family walk? in the woods

    Add to the sentence on the board so it now reads:

    The family walks in the woods.

4. Have students read the new version of the sentence with you.

    ▸ When does the family walk? during the day

    Add to the sentence on the board so it now reads:

    The family walks in the woods during the day.

5. Have students read the new version of the sentence with you. Copy the words *in* and *during* onto index cards. Explain that these are great detail words.

6. Write more simple sentences on the whiteboard or paper. Ask students *where, when,* and *how* questions and have them add details.

    The birds flew.
    The girl ran.
    The rabbit sat.

7. Each time students use a new preposition, write it on a new index card. Explain that the students are going to become "word collectors." In this activity, they are collecting detail words (prepositions).

TIP If you have a room in your learning space, the prepositions you collect can go up on a wall. When they are writing, students will be able to refer to words they have learned. You can even turn the activity of collecting detail words (prepositions) into a game to play when you are reading books or going places.

Objectives
- Add details to sentences.
- Use frequently occurring prepositions (for example, *during, beyond, toward*).
- Understand and use prepositions and prepositional phrases in the context of reading, writing, and speaking.

Try It

✏️ **Use Detail Words**

Help students understand how to add detail to sentences with prepositions. Turn to page WS 7 in *K¹² Language Arts Activity Book*.

1. Read the directions and sentences with students. Help them complete the exercises.

2. Provide support as necessary.

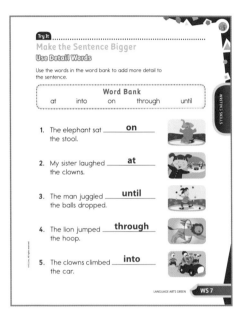

Try It

Make the Sentence Bigger

Use Detail Words

Use the words in the word bank to add more detail to the sentence.

Word Bank

at   into   on   through   until

1. The elephant sat __on__ the stool.

2. My sister laughed __at__ the clowns.

3. The man juggled __until__ the balls dropped.

4. The lion jumped __through__ the hoop.

5. The clowns climbed __into__ the car.

LANGUAGE ARTS GREEN   **WS 7**

Make One from Two

Lesson Overview

[Offline]   15 minutes

Get Ready	Lesson Introduction
	Combine the Sentences
Learn	Use Joining Words
Try It	Combine the Sentences

[Materials]

Supplied
- *K¹² Language Arts Activity Book*, pp. WS 8–9
- Story Card F

Keywords

sentence – a group of words that tells a complete thought

Content Background

▸ Two sentences with similar parts can be joined together into one longer sentence. If two sentences are about the same subject, they can be made into one sentence with a combined subject. If two sentences use the same verb, they can be made into one. Two simple sentences can be combined into one longer sentence. To combine sentences, use conjunctions such as *and*, *but*, *or*, and *so*.

▸ When combining two simple sentences, you use a comma as well as a conjunction. At this time, students do not need to be able to use the comma correctly. The purpose is for students to understand how to use conjunctions to expand their sentences.

Big Ideas

▸ To be complete, a sentence must answer the questions *who* and *what* (naming part and action part).

▸ A sentence contains a complete thought.

▸ We can expand a sentence to include the ideas *why*, *how*, and *when*.

▸ A sentence must start with a capital letter and end with an end mark.

[Offline] ⏱ **15** minutes

Work **together** with students to complete Get Ready, Learn, and Try It activities.

Get Ready ••

Lesson Introduction

Prepare students for the lesson.

1. Tell students that they will be learning about combining, or joining, sentences.

2. Tell students that they will practice writing complete sentences.

3. Remind students that complete sentences always have a naming part and an action part. Remind them that complete sentences always start with a capital letter and end with an end mark.

> ### Objectives
> - Combine sentences that have common elements.
> - Distinguish between complete and incomplete sentences.

Combine the Sentences

Introduce students to the idea that sentences can be combined by using words such as *and* and *but*.

1. Tell students that you are going to play a game in which you make sentences longer.

2. Explain that, to warm up, you are going to say some incomplete sentences, and students have to say what is missing, the naming part or the action part.

   ▸ My sister *the action part*
   ▸ You *the action part*
   ▸ Walked to the store with a dog *the naming part*
   ▸ A crazy squirrel *the action part*

3. **Say:** Now that we have warmed up, we will play a game using the word *and*. I am going to make up a sentence and you will use *and* to help me make the sentence longer.

4. Explain that you will say a simple sentence, and then students will add information to the sentence using the word *and*.

5. Say the sentence "The dog went to the park." Then begin the sentence again, but this time say "The dog and" and encourage students to add another naming part. Once they have added a naming part, finish the sentence. Repeat, allowing students to add many naming parts to the sentence.

   ▸ The dog went to the park.
   ▸ The dog and _____ went to the park.
   ▸ The dog and _____ and _____ and _____ went to the park.

6. Repeat the game using *and* in the action part.

   ▸ The dog played catch.
   ▸ The dog played catch and _____ .
   ▸ The dog played catch and _____ and _____ and _____ and _____ .

Learn

Use Joining Words

Introduce students to the idea that sentences can be combined using words such as *and*, *but*, *for*, *nor*, *or*, *so*, and *yet*. Turn to page WS 8 in *K¹² Language Arts Activity Book*. Gather Story Card F.

1. Point to the conjunctions on the Activity Book page.

2. **Say:** These are joining words. We use these words to combine two sentences into one sentence.

3. Show students Story Card F and read the sentence aloud.

   The girls play.

4. Ask questions and encourage students to make the naming parts of the sentence more complex by using the joining words.

   ▸ What if the boys are playing, too? The girls and boys play.
   ▸ What if only one group is playing, the girls or the boys? The girls play or the boys play.

Objectives
- Combine sentences that have common elements.
- Use frequently occurring conjunctions (for example, *and, but, or, so, because*).

5. Repeat the original simple sentence, *The girls play.* Ask questions and encourage students to make the action parts of the sentence more complex by using joining words.

   ▸ What if the girls laugh, too? The girls play and laugh.
   ▸ What if you didn't know which the girls were doing, playing or laughing? The girls play or laugh.

6. Read the sentences aloud.

   The girls play. The boys laugh.

7. Explain that these two sentences can be joined together with a joining word.

   The girls play, and the boys laugh.

8. Read the directions on the Activity Book page.

9. Have students complete the Activity Book page. Provide support as necessary.

Try It

···

Combine the Sentences

Help students recognize how to combine sentences by using conjunctions such as *and*, *or*, and *but*. Turn to page WS 9 in *K¹² Language Arts Activity Book*.

1. Read the directions to students. Read the sentences together.

2. Have students complete the Activity Book pages. Provide support as necessary.

TIP Remind students that a sentence must begin with a capital letter and end with an end mark.

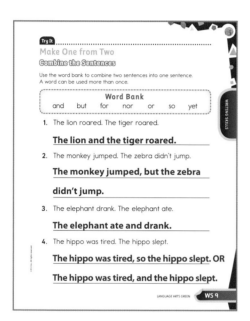

Write Sentences

Lesson Overview

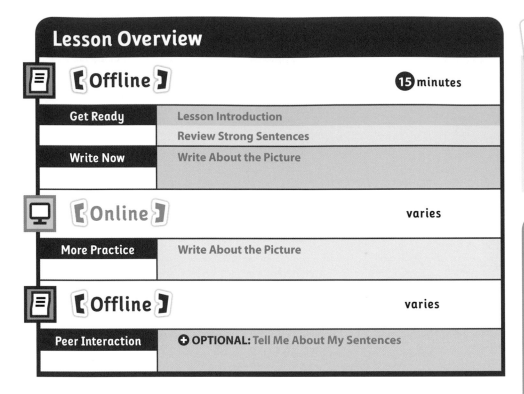

Offline	**15 minutes**

Get Ready	Lesson Introduction
	Review Strong Sentences
Write Now	Write About the Picture

Online	**varies**

More Practice	Write About the Picture

Offline	**varies**

Peer Interaction	**＋ OPTIONAL:** Tell Me About My Sentences

Materials

Supplied

- *K¹² Language Arts Activity Book*, pp. WS 11–13
- Write About the Picture: Rubric and Sample Responses (printout)

Keywords

publishing – the stage or step of the writing process in which the writer makes a clean copy of the piece and shares it

revising – the stage or step of the writing process in which the writer rereads and edits the draft, correcting errors and making changes in content or organization that improve the piece

Big Ideas

- ► To be complete, a sentence must answer the questions *who* and *what* (naming part and action part).
- ► A sentence contains a complete thought.
- ► We can expand a sentence to include the ideas *why*, *how*, and *when*.
- ► A sentence must start with a capital letter and end with a punctuation mark.

[Offline] 15 minutes

Work **together** with students to complete Get Ready and Write Now activities.

Get Ready

Lesson Introduction
Prepare students for the lesson. Tell students that they are going to be writing complete sentences using detail words such as *under* and *during* and joining words such as *and* and *but*.

Review Strong Sentences
Help students prepare for the final writing activity.

1. Tell students that they are going to be writing detailed complete sentences. Explain that they will first practice adding details to a simple sentence.

2. Read the following sentences, encouraging students to add details by using detail words (prepositions) and joining words (conjunctions.)

   ▸ We read. Possible answer: at the park
   ▸ I smiled at her. I thanked her. Possible answer: I smiled and thanked her.
   ▸ The fox hid. The wolf hid. Possible answer: The fox and the wolf hid.

> **Objectives**
> - Use frequently occurring conjunctions (for example, *and, but, or, so, because*).
> - Use frequently occurring prepositions (for example, *during, beyond, toward*).

Write Now

 **Write About the Picture**
Help students write their sentences. Turn to pages WS 11 and 12 in *K¹² Language Arts Activity Book*.

1. Show students the picture on the Activity Book page and tell them that they are going to write sentences about the picture.

2. Have students write three to five complete sentences about the picture. Make sure students write in pencil.

3. Tell students to use at least two detail words and at least two joining words from the word bank.

4. Have students read their sentences aloud. Ask them if their detail words and joining words make sense.

5. Ask students to review their sentences, making sure that each has a naming part and an action part, as well as a capital letter at the beginning and an end mark at the end.

> **Objectives**
> - Spell common, frequently used words correctly.
> - Use a capital letter to begin a sentence and an end mark to end it.
> - Use correct grammar and sentence formation.
> - Use frequently occurring conjunctions (for example, *and, but, or, so, because*).
> - Use frequently occurring prepositions (for example, *during, beyond, toward*).
> - Write a series of related sentences.
> - Write complete sentences.
> - Write sentences with appropriate spacing between words.
> - Write sentences with legible handwriting.

6. Tell students that they are now ready to publish their writing. **Publishing** their writing means putting it into its final form to be shared with others. Have students use an eraser to correct any mistakes and a pencil to add detail to their sentences. If they wish, they may use the next page to rewrite final versions of the sentences.

7. Use the materials and instructions in the online lesson to evaluate students' finished writing. You will be looking at students' writing to evaluate the following:

   ▸ **Purpose and Content:** Most of the sentences are about the picture.
   ▸ **Structure and Organization:** There are at least three sentences. At least one preposition and one conjunction were used.
   ▸ **Grammar and Mechanics:** Most sentences are a complete thought. Most have a naming part and an action part. All sentences have a capital letter at the beginning and an end mark.

8. Enter students' scores for each rubric category online.

9. If students' writing scored a 1 in any criterion, work with students to revise and proofread their work.

TIP The amount of time students need to complete this activity will vary. If students are growing tired or distracted and have not yet finished their published sentences, have them take a break and then return to the assignment.

Reward: When students' writing achieves "meets objectives" in all three categories on the grading rubric, add a sticker for this unit on the My Accomplishments chart.

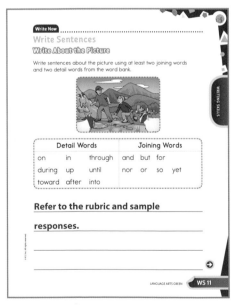

 **varies**

If necessary, work with students to complete the More Practice activity.

More Practice

Write About the Picture

If students' writing scored "doesn't meet objectives" in any category, have them complete the appropriate review activity listed in the table online.

Objectives
- Evaluate writing and choose activities to review and revise.

- Follow the online instructions to help students edit and revise their work.
- Impress upon students that revising makes their work better. Writing is a process, and each time they revise their work, they are making their writing stronger and better.
- When you provide feedback, always begin with something positive. For example, you might point out a detail they wrote (even if it's the only detail) and explain how it helps you picture the scene: "You wrote that the leaves were 'orange and gold.' That detail, the color of the leaves, really helps me picture the forest."
- Place the final written work together with the rubric and the sample papers in the writing portfolio. This information is useful for you to track progress, and it helps students to refer back to their own work. They can see how they improve and review feedback to remember areas that need revising.
- Help students locate the activities and provide support as needed.

 **varies**

If necessary, work with students to complete the Peer Interaction activity.

Peer Interaction

✚ OPTIONAL: Tell Me About My Sentences

This activity is OPTIONAL. It is intended for students who have extra time and would benefit from extra practice. Feel free to skip this activity.

Objectives
- Use guidance from adults and peers to revise writing.
- Collaborate with peers on writing projects.

Students can benefit from exchanging sentences with someone they know or another student. This activity will work best if students exchange their sentences with other students who completed the same activity, but you may copy the Activity Book page and send it to someone else who is willing to give students feedback.

Students should receive feedback on the content of their sentences. To complete this optional activity, turn to page WS 13 in *K¹² Language Arts Activity Book*.

1. Have students exchange sentences with other students.

2. Have students use the Activity Book page to provide others with feedback about their writing.

3. Have students use the feedback provided from other students to revise their own sentences.

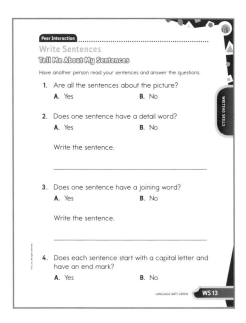

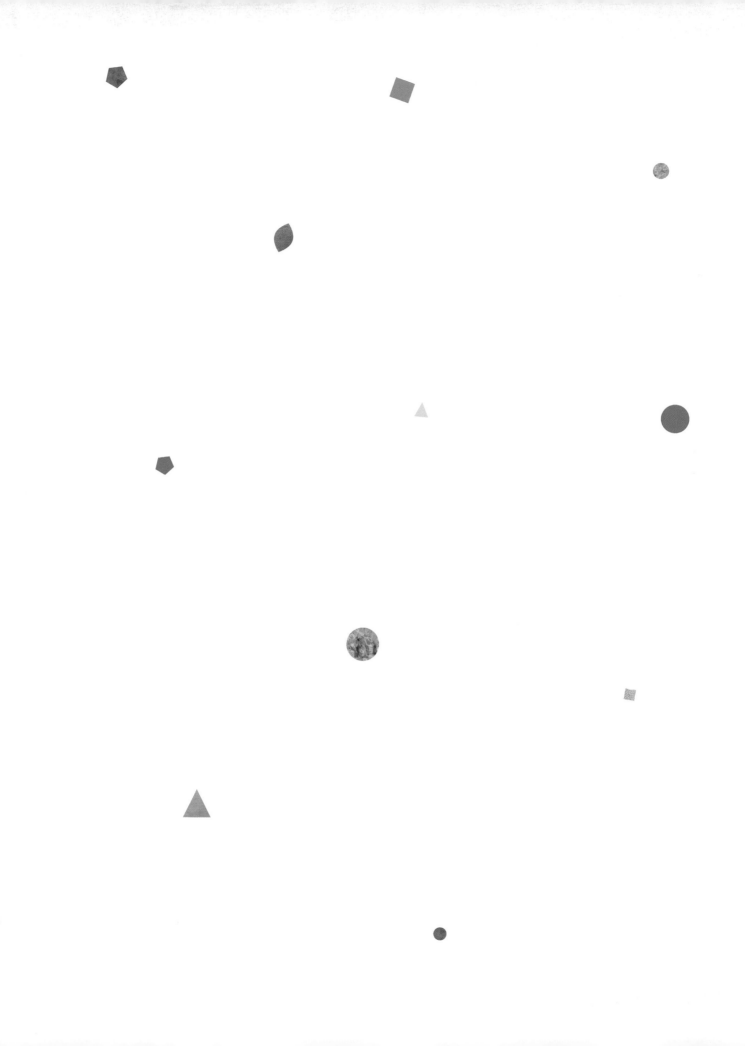

Kinds of Sentences

Unit Focus

In this unit, students will learn that there are four kinds of sentences. They will learn how to identify and write all four kinds. Each kind of sentence begins with a capital letter and ends with a punctuation mark.

▶ A **statement** tells something. It is the most common kind of sentence.

▶ A **question** asks something. Often, questions begin with specific words, such as *who*, *what*, *how*, and *where*.

▶ An **exclamation** expresses strong emotions. Hearing a sentence spoken often makes it easier to identify an exclamation.

▶ A **command** gives an order or makes a request. The word *please* in a sentence indicates a command that is a request.

Unit Plan		[Offline]	[Online]
Lesson 1	Statements and Commands	**15** minutes	
Lesson 2	Questions	**15** minutes	
Lesson 3	Exclamations	**15** minutes	
Lesson 4	Review Kinds of Sentences	**5** minutes	**10** minutes
Lesson 5	Unit Checkpoint	**15** minutes	varies

Statements and Commands

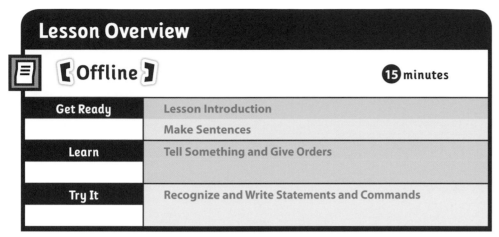

Lesson Overview

Materials

Offline	15 minutes

Get Ready	Lesson Introduction
	Make Sentences
Learn	Tell Something and Give Orders
Try It	Recognize and Write Statements and Commands

Materials

Supplied
- *K¹² Language Arts Activity Book*, pp. WS 15–18

Also Needed
- scissors, adult
- whiteboard (optional)
- crayons

Advance Preparation

For the Get Ready, cut out the cards on page WS 15 in *K¹² Language Arts Activity Book*.

Content Background

- ▶ There are four kinds of sentences. All sentences begin with a capital letter and end with a punctuation mark.
- ▶ A statement, or telling sentence, is also known as a declarative sentence. It usually ends with a period.

  Example: Sandy flew the kite in the open field.

- ▶ A command is also known as an imperative sentence. It usually ends with a period, but it may sometimes end with an exclamation point.

  Example: Stop at the next corner.
  Example: Stop the car!

  Note that the subject of an imperative sentence is always *you*, even though it is not stated:

  Example: (You) Stop at the next corner.

Big Ideas

Using the four kinds of sentences helps writers and speakers to express their ideas and feelings accurately.

Keywords

command – a kind of sentence that gives an order or makes a request
complete sentence – a group of words that tells a complete thought
statement – a kind of sentence that tells something

 **15 minutes**

Work **together** with students to complete Get Ready, Learn, and Try It activities.

Get Ready

Lesson Introduction

Prepare students for the lesson.

1. Tell students that they will review how a sentence begins and ends.

2. Explain that they will learn about two kinds of sentences: statements and commands.

3. Tell students that they will practice recognizing and writing statements and commands.

Objectives

• Recognize that a sentence begins with a capital letter.

• Recognize that a sentence ends with an end mark.

Make Sentences

Use this quick activity to review sentences with students. Gather the cards that you cut out.

1. Display the cards in random order.

2. Read the sentence parts aloud with students.

3. Have students match two parts to make a complete sentence. The sentences may be funny or serious.

4. Have students point to the capital letter at the beginning of the sentence and the period at the end.

5. Have them make more sentences until they have used as many cards as they can.

6. **Say:** What is a sentence? A sentence is a group of words that tells a complete thought. It begins with a capital letter and ends with an end mark.

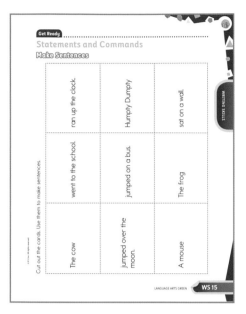

Learn

Tell Something and Give Orders

Introduce students to two kinds of sentences: statements and commands. Turn to page WS 17 in *K¹² Language Arts Activity Book*.

1. Write these two sentences on a whiteboard or a sheet of paper and have students read them with you.

   Sue likes to run.
   Run with Sue.

2. Explain that the first sentence is a **statement**, or telling sentence. Statements tell readers something and usually end with a period.

   ▸ What does this statement tells readers? It tells them that Sue likes to run.

3. Explain that the second sentence is a **command**. Commands order someone to do something and usually end with a period.

   ▸ What does this command order someone to do? It orders someone to run with Sue.

4. Tell students that sometimes an exclamation mark is used to end a command if the command shows excitement. *Example:* Run!

Objectives

- Recognize commands.
- Recognize statements.

5. Read the two rules on the Activity Book page. Explain the examples to students as needed.

6. Have students complete the Activity Book page. Provide support as necessary. If students are unfamiliar with the hokey pokey, tell them that it is a fun dance for children.

TIP Young students sometimes think that all commands show excitement. Many commands do not. Help students distinguish between ordinary commands and those that truly show excitement.

Ordinary command: Open your notebook.
Command that shows excitement: Get your notebook away from the dog!

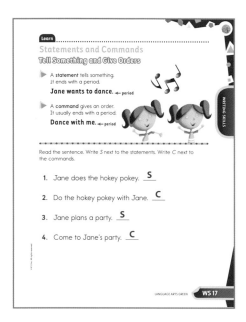

Try It

 Recognize and Write Statements and Commands

Help students practice adding capital letters and punctuation to sentences and writing statements and commands correctly. Turn to page WS 18 in *K¹² Language Arts Activity Book.*

1. Read the first set of directions to students. Read the sentences together. If necessary, help students figure out what letters are missing from the beginning of sentences.

    ▸ Johnny plays with Max.
    ▸ Sit, Max.

2. Have students complete Exercises 1 and 2. Provide support as necessary.

3. Read the second and third sets of directions to students. Have students complete Exercises 3 and 4. Provide support as necessary.

 Objectives

- Use a period to end a command.
- Use a period to end a statement.
- Write statements.
- Write commands.
- Use a capital letter to begin a sentence and an end mark to end it.

Reward: When students complete the activity, allow them to color the picture of Johnny and Max.

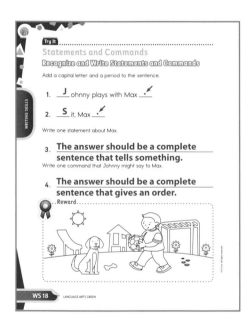

Questions

Lesson Overview

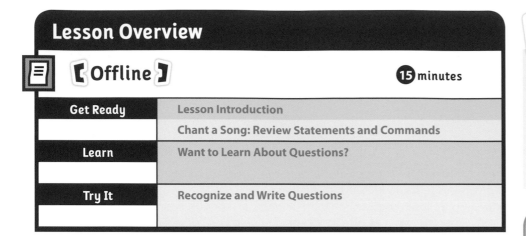

[**Offline**]   **15** minutes

Get Ready	Lesson Introduction
	Chant a Song: Review Statements and Commands
Learn	Want to Learn About Questions?
Try It	Recognize and Write Questions

Materials

Supplied
- *K¹² Language Arts Activity Book*, pp. WS 19–20

Also Needed
- whiteboard (optional)

Keywords

command – a kind of sentence that gives an order or makes a request

question – a kind of sentence that asks something

statement – a kind of sentence that tells something

Content Background

▸ There are four kinds of sentences. All sentences begin with a capital letter and end with a punctuation mark.

▸ A question, or asking sentence, is also known as an interrogative sentence. It ends with a question mark.

Example: Where is the beach?

Big Ideas

Using the four kinds of sentences helps writers and speakers to express their ideas and feelings accurately.

 **15** minutes

Work **together** with students to complete Get Ready, Learn, and Try It activities.

Get Ready

Lesson Introduction
Prepare students for the lesson.

1. Tell students that they will review statements and commands.

2. Explain that they will learn about questions.

3. Tell students that they will practice recognizing and writing questions.

> ★ **Objectives**
> - Recognize statements.
> - Recognize commands.
> - Use a period to end a statement.
> - Use a period to end a command.

Chant a Song: Review Statements and Commands
Use this quick activity to review statements and commands with students.

1. Chant this song together.

   A statement is a telling sentence,
   telling sentence, telling sentence.
   A statement is a telling sentence,
   "Ducks can quack."

2. Write *Ducks can quack* on a whiteboard or a sheet of paper, but do not add the period at the end of the sentence. Ask students to write the end mark that completes the statement.

3. Read the sentence "Quack like a duck" to students. Then write the sentence, but do not add the period.

   ▸ What kind of sentence is this? a command

4. Have students write the end mark that completes the command. Students should add a period to the sentence.

Learn

Want to Learn About Questions?

Introduce students to questions. Turn to page WS 19 in *K¹² Language Arts Activity Book.*

Objectives
* Recognize questions.

1. Write the sentence on a whiteboard or sheet of paper and have students read it with you.

   What is your name?

2. Explain that this sentence is a **question**. A question is a sentence that asks something.

   ▸ What does this question ask? It asks my name.

3. Tell students that questions begin with capital letters, just as other kinds of sentences do. However, questions do not end with periods, but with question marks.

4. Point to the question mark in the sentence you wrote and have students practice writing a question mark.

5. Read the rule and the example on the Activity Book page.

6. Have students complete the Activity Book page. Provide support as necessary.

TIP Children often have difficulty distinguishing between questions and answers. Make a list of common words that are used when asking questions, such as the following:

can	what	who
do	when	why
how	where	will

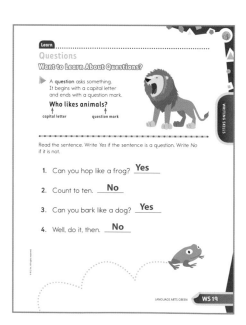

Try It

···

 Recognize and Write Questions

Help students practice recognizing, punctuating, and writing questions. Turn to page WS 20 in *K¹² Language Arts Activity Book.*

1. Read the first set of directions to students. Read the sentences together.

2. Have students complete Exercises 1–3. Provide support as necessary.

3. Read the second set of directions to students. Have students complete Exercise 4. Provide support as necessary.

TIP Some students may have difficulty mastering the shape of the question mark when they try to write it. Model how to write a question mark several times and give students the opportunity to practice as necessary.

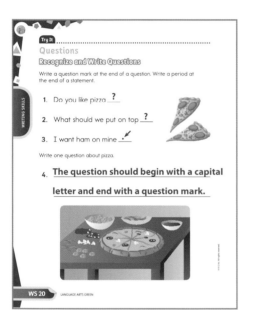

Objectives

- Recognize questions.
- Use a capital letter to begin a sentence.
- Use a question mark to end a question.
- Write questions.

Exclamations

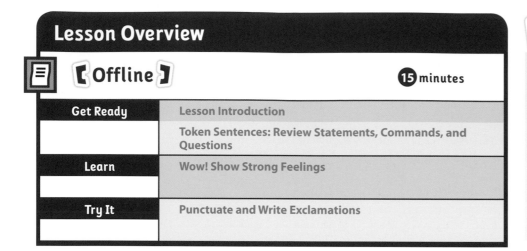

Lesson Overview

Offline		15 minutes
Get Ready	Lesson Introduction	
	Token Sentences: Review Statements, Commands, and Questions	
Learn	Wow! Show Strong Feelings	
Try It	Punctuate and Write Exclamations	

Materials

Supplied
- *K¹² Language Arts Activity Book*, pp. WS 21–22

Also Needed
- household objects – coins, buttons, beads, or other small tokens (8)
- whiteboard (optional)

Keywords

command – a kind of sentence that gives an order or makes a request

exclamation – a kind of sentence that shows strong feeling

question – a kind of sentence that asks something

statement – a kind of sentence that tells something

Advance Preparation

For the Get Ready, gather eight coins, buttons, beads, or other small tokens.

Content Background

▸ There are four kinds of sentences. All sentences begin with a capital letter and end with a punctuation mark.

▸ An exclamation is also known as an exclamatory sentence. It ends with an exclamation point.

Example: We won the contest!

Big Ideas

Using the four kinds of sentences helps writers and speakers express their ideas and feeling accurately.

 **15 minutes**

Work **together** with students to complete Get Ready, Learn, and Try It activities.

Get Ready

Lesson Introduction

Prepare students for the lesson.

⭐ **Objectives**
- Recognize commands.
- Recognize questions.
- Recognize statements.

1. Tell students that they will review statements, commands, and questions.

2. Explain that they will learn about another kind of sentence—exclamations.

3. Tell students that they will practice recognizing and writing exclamations.

Token Sentences: Review Statements, Commands, and Questions

Use this quick activity to review statements, commands, and questions with students. Gather the eight small tokens.

1. On a flat surface, arrange the eight tokens in the shape of a question mark.

2. Remind students there is more than one kind of sentence. Some sentences are questions. Questions ask something, and they end with question marks. Other sentences are statements, which tell readers something. Still other sentences are commands, which order someone to do something.

3. Tell students that you are going to say several sentences. Explain that for every sentence that is a question, students should remove a token from the question mark. If a sentence is not a question—if it is a statement or a command—they should tell which kind of sentence it is but not remove a token.

4. Begin with these sentences and then add others.

   ▸ May I ride my bike? question
   ▸ Where is my helmet? question
   ▸ Ride with me. command
   ▸ My bike is red. statement
   ▸ What color is your bike? question

5. Continue to play until all tokens have been collected.

TIP As a challenge, you may wish to have students provide a question for the last token.

Learn

Wow! Show Strong Feelings

Introduce students to exclamations. Turn to page WS 21 in *K¹² Language Arts Activity Book*.

Objectives
- Recognize exclamations.

1. Have students use facial and hand gestures to show these strong feelings.

   - very happy
   - extremely surprised
   - really sleepy
   - scared

2. After students act out *scared*, write the sentence on a whiteboard or sheet of paper and have students read it with you.

   I'm so scared!

3. Explain that this sentence is an **exclamation**. An exclamation is a sentence that shows strong feeling.

   - What feeling does this exclamation show? strong fear

4. Tell students that exclamations begin with capital letters, just as other kinds of sentences do. However, exclamations do not end with periods or question marks, but with exclamation marks.

5. Point to the exclamation mark in the sentence and have students write an exclamation mark.

6. Read the rule and example on the Activity Book page with students. Explain the example to students as needed.

7. Have students complete the Activity Book page. Provide support as necessary.

TIP Students on the autism spectrum may not understand facial expressions. Have them look in a mirror as they mime the facial expressions that correspond to the phrases that show strong feeling.

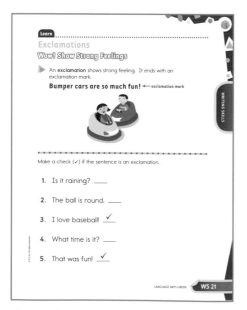

Try It ··

✏️ **Punctuate and Write Exclamations**

Help students practice punctuating and writing exclamations. Turn to page WS 22 in *K¹² Language Arts Activity Book*.

1. Read the first set of directions to students. Read the sentences together.

2. Have students complete Exercises 1–4. Provide support as necessary.

3. Read the second set of directions to students. Have students complete Exercise 5. Provide support as necessary.

Objectives
- Use an exclamation mark to end an exclamation.
- Write exclamations.

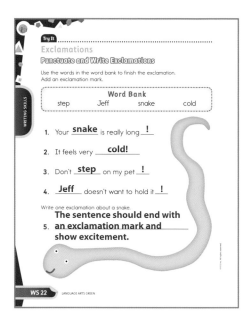

Try It ···

Exclamations

Punctuate and Write Exclamations

Use the words in the word bank to finish the exclamation.
Add an exclamation mark.

Word Bank

| step | Jeff | snake | cold |

1. Your **snake** is really long **!**

2. It feels very **cold!**

3. Don't **step** on my pet **!**

4. **Jeff** doesn't want to hold it **!**

Write one exclamation about a snake.

5. **The sentence should end with an exclamation mark and show excitement.**

WS 22   LANGUAGE ARTS GREEN

Review Kinds of Sentences

Lesson Overview

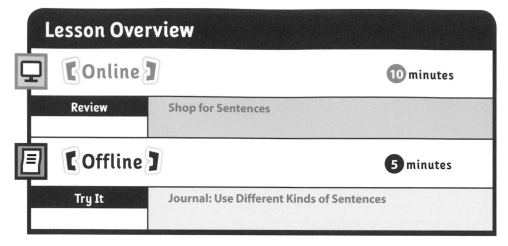

Online — 10 minutes

| Review | Shop for Sentences |

Offline — 5 minutes

| Try It | Journal: Use Different Kinds of Sentences |

Materials

Supplied
- *K¹² My Journal,* pp. 124–125

Also Needed
- crayons

Keywords

command – a kind of sentence that gives an order or makes a request

exclamation – a kind of sentence that shows strong feeling

question – a kind of sentence that asks something

statement – a kind of sentence that tells something

 **Online** **10 minutes**

Students will go over what they have learned about recognizing and writing the four kinds of sentences to review for the Unit Checkpoint. Help students locate the online activity and provide support as needed.

Review

Shop for Sentences

Students will work online to review what they have learned about the four kinds of sentences: statements, questions, exclamations, and commands.

Offline Alternative

No computer access? Choose one of your students' favorite books. Open to any page and have them identify what kinds of sentences they see. Have them explain how they know what kind of sentence each one is.

Objectives
- Recognize statements.
- Recognize commands.
- Recognize questions.
- Recognize exclamations.
- Use a capital letter to begin a sentence and an end mark to end it.
- Use a period to end a statement.
- Use a question mark to end a question.
- Use an exclamation mark to end an exclamation.
- Use a period to end a command.

 **Offline** **5 minutes**

Students will write on their own in their journal. Help students locate the offline activity.

Try It

 Journal: Use Different Kinds of Sentences

Students will write in their journal on their own. Gather *K¹² My Journal* and have students turn to pages 124 and 125 in Writing Skills.

1. To help students prepare, recite "Twinkle, Twinkle, Little Star" with them. Tell students that the rhyme tells about wondering what a star is, but students probably wonder about many other things, too.

Objectives
- Write in a journal.
- Freewrite about a topic.

2. Read the journal prompt with students. Have students respond to the prompt in their journal. As necessary, remind them that there are no correct or incorrect answers.

3. Have students write about at least one thing they wonder about, but tell them that they may write about as many as they would like. Encourage them to use as many different kinds of sentences as they can.

4. If students feel comfortable sharing what they wrote, allow them to share with you or their peers.

TIP The amount of time students need to complete this activity will vary. Allow them to use the rest of the allotted time to complete this activity. If they have more they would like to write, you may let them complete their entry at a later time. If students are having trouble getting started, you might tell them to just list ideas or words. They may even draw a picture and describe it to you. You can transcribe their words for them.

Unit Checkpoint

Lesson Overview

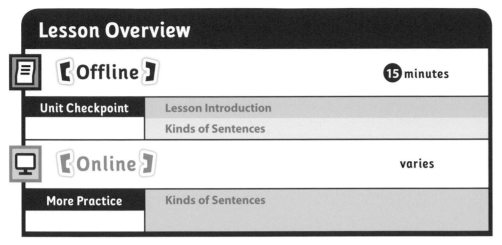

📄 **[Offline]**		**15** minutes
Unit Checkpoint	Lesson Introduction	
	Kinds of Sentences	
🖥 **[Online]**		**varies**
More Practice	Kinds of Sentences	

[Materials]

Supplied

- *K¹² Language Arts Assessments*, pp. WS 5–8

[Offline] **15** minutes

Work **together** with students to complete the Unit Checkpoint.

Unit Checkpoint

Lesson Introduction

Prepare students for the lesson.

1. Tell students that they are going to complete a Unit Checkpoint to show what they have learned.

2. Explain that if they miss one or more questions, they can continue to practice this grammar skill.

Kinds of Sentences

Explain that students are going to show what they have learned about recognizing different kinds of sentences and capitalizing and punctuating them correctly.

1. Give students the Unit Checkpoint pages.

2. Read the directions together. If needed, read the questions and answer choices to students. Have students complete the Checkpoint on their own.

⭐ Objectives

- Recognize commands.
- Recognize exclamations.
- Recognize questions.
- Recognize statements.
- Use a capital letter to begin a sentence.
- Use a period to end a command.
- Use a period to end a statement.
- Use a question mark to end a question.
- Use an exclamation mark to end an exclamation.

3. Use the Answer Key to score the Checkpoint and then enter the results online.

4. Review each exercise with students. Work with students to correct any exercise that they missed.

 TIP Students who answered one or more questions incorrectly should continue to practice this grammar skill. Suggest multiple sentences that students classify by kind, based on the content and the end marks. Also encourage students to write or say different kinds of sentences.

Reward: When students score 80 percent or above on the Unit Checkpoint, add a sticker for this unit on the My Accomplishments chart.

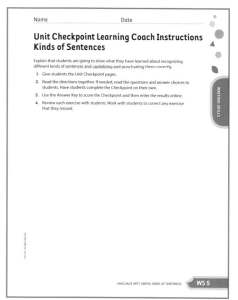

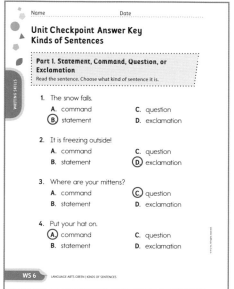

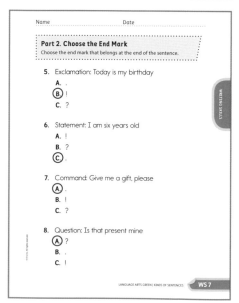

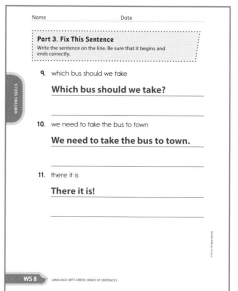

 **varies**

If necessary, work with students to complete the More Practice activity.

More Practice

Kinds of Sentences

If students scored less than 80 percent on the Unit Checkpoint, have them complete the appropriate review activities listed in the table online. Help students locate the activities and provide support as needed.

 Objectives

- Evaluate Checkpoint results and choose activities to review.

Follow and Write a Sequence

Unit Focus

In this unit, students will learn about order and sequencing the written word. They will learn how written instructions must be conveyed in a specific order, and they will learn how to write a coherent, short narrative with a clear beginning, middle, and end. Students will

- Use the word *how* to clearly explain an action or activity.
- Follow instructions in a step-by-step process.
- Give directions for a step-by-step process.
- Learn order words such as *first*, *next*, *then*, and *finally*.
- Use a graphic organizer to prepare to write instructions in a paragraph form with order words.

In the final writing assignment, students will take a set of step-by-step instructions that they have created and transform them into a narrative paragraph.

Learning to create a sequence and following the steps in a process is crucial for young, emerging writers. One of the most important writing skills is learning how to create a cohesive beginning, middle, and end. The coherence of any form of writing—a story, poem, or essay, for example—depends on a clear narrative that uses the appropriate organizational structure. Sequencing in chronological order is the foundation of writing a narrative. Although this lesson does not focus on creating a complex narrative, the skills developed here form the foundation for developing the understanding that writing has a clear structure.

Unit Plan		〔Offline〕	〔Online〕
Lesson 1	Get Started with Directions	15 minutes	
Lesson 2	Follow Directions	15 minutes	
Lesson 3	Put Steps in Order	15 minutes	
Lesson 4	Plan the Steps	15 minutes	
Lesson 5	Write the Steps	15 minutes	varies

Get Started with Directions

Lesson Overview

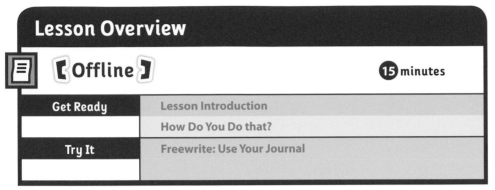

	Offline	**15** minutes
Get Ready	Lesson Introduction	
	How Do You Do that?	
Try It	Freewrite: Use Your Journal	

Materials

Supplied
- *K¹² My Journal,* pp. 126–127

Also Needed
- crayons

Keywords
freewriting – a way for a writer to pick a topic and write as much as possible about it within a set time limit

Content Background

In this lesson, students will freewrite in their journal. The purpose of the journal lessons is to get students comfortable with putting ideas down on paper. Freewriting does not need to be grammatically correct. It does not need to be in complete sentences. Journals should not be evaluated and definitely should **not** be marked up with any kind of corrections. Freewriting should help students develop a love of writing. Once that love takes root, students will be motivated to learn more about the rules of writing.

Big Ideas

- Freewriting can help a person overcome writer's block and apprehension.
- Sequencing ideas is the beginning of writing a personal narrative or experience story.

 **Offline** **15** minutes

Work **together** with students to complete Get Ready and Try It activities.

Get Ready

Lesson Introduction
Prepare students for the lesson.

1. Explain to students that they will be writing in their journal. Remind them that their journal is their place to be creative and explore writing. They will not be judged or graded.

2. Explain that they will freewrite about how to do something.
   Say: In freewriting, you write whatever comes into your mind. You can write absolutely anything you want to answer the question you are asked.

 Objectives
- Identify a process as a series of steps.
- Follow steps in a process.

How Do You Do that?

Tell students that you are going to play a game about giving instructions.

1. Put an object on the floor (such as a cup or a pencil) and tell students that you are going to pick it up, and then you will explain exactly how you picked it up.

2. Pick up the object. When you pick it up, be sure to do the following things:

   ▸ Look at the floor before you pick it up.
   ▸ Bend your knees.
   ▸ Pick it up with your right hand.
   ▸ Hop a little when you stand back up.

3. **Say:** I will tell you exactly how I picked that up. I looked at the floor, I bent my knees, I picked it up with my right hand, and I hopped when I stood up.

4. Have students pick up the object exactly as you did. If they miss any steps, have them try again, making sure they include every step. (If students become frustrated because they keep making mistakes, move on to the next step.)

5. Switch roles. Have students place the object on a shelf or table while you watch. Try to copy their actions exactly and have them give you notes on how to include every step.

TIP This game helps students think about creating steps. To help them think about their own actions, try making deliberate mistakes for students to correct. If students used their left hand to pick up the object, use your right. If they stood on their toes, keep your feet flat on the floor.

Try It

✎ **Freewrite: Use Your Journal**

Help students freewrite to explain how they do a favorite activity. Gather *K¹² My Journal* and have students turn to pages 126 and 127 in Writing Skills.

Objectives
- Generate ideas for writing.
- Freewrite about a topic.
- Write in a journal.

1. Read the prompt at the top of the page to students.

2. Ask students to name a favorite activity.

3. Ask students to think about how they would explain to another person how to do that activity.

4. Have students write their instructions on how to do the activity.

   ▸ Explain that they are freewriting, or writing ideas on the page.
   ▸ Tell them that they can explain how to do the activity in any way they want. They can focus on the main parts of the activity or a specific set of details.

5. If students are struggling, help by asking questions. Answers to questions may vary.

   ▸ When you do this activity, what is the very first thing you do?
   ▸ What is the next thing you do?
   ▸ How do you know that you have finished the activity?

6. If they wish, students can also draw a picture to illustrate how to do their activity.

7. Have students explain their ideas and picture to you. Do not evaluate students' writing. As long as students have written some ideas on paper, their responses are acceptable.

8. Encourage students to write as many ideas as they can.

(TIP) The amount of time students need to complete this activity will vary. If students are having trouble getting started, you might tell them to just list ideas or words. They may even draw a picture and describe it to you. You can transcribe their words for them. Students need only work for 15 minutes. If they have more they would like to write, they may do so later, but it is not required.

My Favorite Activity

Date _____

What do you like to do? Explain how you do it.

_____

_____

_____

_____

_____

_____

_____

126

Draw a picture.

_____

_____

_____

127

Follow Directions

Lesson Overview

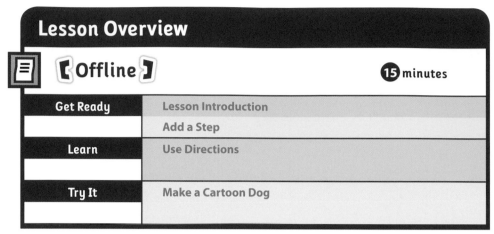

Get Ready	Lesson Introduction
	Add a Step
Learn	Use Directions
Try It	Make a Cartoon Dog

[Offline] **15** minutes

[Materials]

Supplied
- *K¹² Language Arts Activity Book*, pp. WS 23–27

Also Needed
- whiteboard (optional)
- scissors, round-end safety
- paper, drawing

Advance Preparation

Before beginning the Get Ready, look over the list of steps so that you are ready to read them aloud to students.

Content Background

A set of written steps is also known as a how-to piece of writing. It is important for young writers to understand that a process, or a series of steps, or a sequence has a specific order that must be followed. Although it might seem obvious to an adult, it is important for students to explicitly learn that for a process to work, steps need to be in order and complete.

Big Ideas

A sequence follows a logical order.

[Offline] **15** minutes

Work **together** with students to complete Get Ready, Learn, and Try It activities.

Lesson Introduction
Prepare students for the lesson.

1. Explain that students are going to learn about following directions.

2. Tell students that when following directions, they must be sure they complete all the steps and do them in the correct order.

> **Objectives**
> - Identify a process as a series of steps.
> - Follow steps in a process.

Add a Step

Help students think about the correct order of directions by having them play this simple game. Turn to page WS 23 in *K¹² Language Arts Activity Book*.

1. Tell students that they are going to play a game in which they have to remember a list of directions in order and that they will get points for remembering the steps in order. Tell them that you are will read the steps and that they will do what you describe.

2. Show students the Activity Book page—just this once—and point out the numbers on the steps. Don't show them the page again, because the object of the game is for them to remember the directions in order.

3. Read Step 1 from the list on the Activity Book page. Have students do that action. Give students one point.

4. Explain that you will now read Steps 1 and 2 and students have to do those steps in order. Read the steps and have students do the actions.

5. Continue reading the steps, adding a new step each time. Students have to hear all the steps **before** they can begin to do the list of actions, which will make the game a test of memory. Remind them that they only get a point if they can do all the steps you list, in order.

6. As you are moving through the list, if students forget to do a step, tell them they can still get a point if they can name the step they skipped.

7. Go through the steps and see how many points students can earn. You can do the exercises, too, to make the game more competitive.

TIP Order is important in directions. This activity is not only a fun warm-up to get students active and excited for the lesson, but it is also a way to reinforce the idea that directions need to be followed in order.

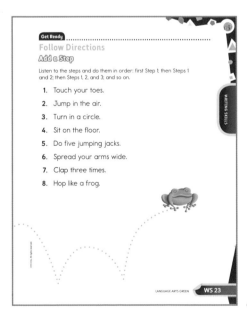

Learn

Use Directions

Introduce students to the idea that we follow the steps in directions to achieve an outcome. Help them learn that steps must be followed in order, and that by numbering steps we understand what order they are supposed to be in. Turn to page WS 25 in *K¹² Language Arts Activity Book* and gather the scissors.

Objectives
- Follow the directions in a process.
- Identify a process as a series of steps.

1. Tell students that we use directions to explain how to do something. Directions are made up of steps.

2. Explain that directions usually have to be done in a specific order.

3. On a whiteboard or sheet of paper, write the numbers 1 to 4. Explain that numbering directions tells us in what order to do them.

4. Tell students that you are going to ask for four directions, in order, for putting on a coat.

5. Have students actually walk through the act of putting on a coat. As they do so, have them explain each step as they do it. Possible answer:
   1 Take the coat off the hanger.
   2 Put your one arm in the coat.
   3 Put your other arm in the coat.
   4 Starting at the top, button the buttons.

6. As students explain their steps, write them in order next to the numbers on the whiteboard or paper.

7. Turn to the Activity Book page. Explain to students that the instructions on the page are not in order. They need cut out the steps, put the steps in order, and add a step that is missing. Read the instructions with students and help them complete the activity.

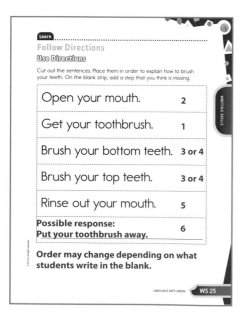

Try It

Make a Cartoon Dog

Help students practice following directions. Turn to page WS 27 in *K¹² Language Arts Activity Book* and gather the drawing paper.

1. Read the directions and steps with students.

2. Have students complete the Activity Book page. Help them if they need it.

Objectives
- Follow the directions in a process.

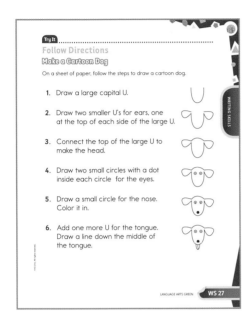

Put Steps in Order

Lesson Overview

[Offline] **15** minutes

Get Ready	Lesson Introduction
	Story Order
Learn	Order Words
Try It	Use Order Words

[Materials]

Supplied
- *K¹² Language Arts Activity Book*, pp. WS 29–33

Also Needed
- scissors, adult
- whiteboard (optional)

Keywords

order words – words that connect ideas or a series of steps, or create a sequence, such as *first*, *next*, *later*, *finally*

Advance Preparation

For the Get Ready, cut out the picture cards on page WS 29 in *K¹² Language Arts Activity Book*.

Content Background

Good writing has a clear beginning, middle, and end. Order words such as *first*, *then*, *next*, and *finally* make the transitions between ideas fluid.

Big Ideas

- Sequencing ideas is the beginning of writing a personal narrative or experience story.
- Good writers use transitions to help create coherence in text.

[Offline] 15 minutes

Work **together** with students to complete Get Ready, Learn, and Try It activities.

Get Ready

Lesson Introduction
Prepare students for the lesson.

1. Tell students that they will continue learning about steps and following directions.

2. Explain that they will learn how stories have a beginning, middle, and end.

3. Tell students that they will learn to use order words to make their steps clear.

Objectives
- Organize ideas through sequencing.

Story Order
Prepare students for the lesson by introducing them to the idea that stories have a beginning, middle, and end, and that those parts have to come in specific order, just like directions go in a specific order. Gather the picture cards that you cut out.

1. Lay out the picture cards face up in a random order.

2. Tell students that stories have a beginning, middle, and end. Ask them to put the cards in the correct order. Once they have done so, ask them to tell you a story to narrate the pictures. Prompt them with the words *first*, *then*, *next*, and *finally* as you encourage them to create the story.

3. If students put the cards in an order different from the expected sequence of events, ask questions to direct them to the suggested order.

    ▸ What order would you put them in if the story ended with the boy finishing the castle?
    ▸ Does the castle get bigger and bigger as the boy builds it?
    ▸ Can you begin the story by having the boy pull the blocks out of the box?

Learn

Order Words

Introduce students to the order words *first, next, then,* and *finally*. Help students understand that you can organize ideas by putting them in order and using words to tell the order. Turn to pages WS 31 and 32 in *K¹² Language Arts Activity Book.*

1. **Say:** When we are telling a story or explaining something, it helps to put our ideas in order. **Order words** help us do that.

2. On a whiteboard or sheet of paper, write *First, Next, Then,* and *Finally.* Point to each word and read it with students.

3. **Say:** *First* is a beginning word. What is the first thing you do when you read a book? Possible answers: pick out the book; open the book

4. **Say:** *Next* and *then* are middle words. They connect the middle parts together. When you are reading your book, what do you do next? Possible answers: read a chapter; read a page; look at a picture

5. **Say:** Then what do you do? Answers will vary.

6. **Say:** *Finally* is an ending word. It tells the last thing we do. You have been reading your book, and finally you . . . . Possible answers: finish the story; close the book; put the book back on the shelf

7. Explain that students are going to practice finding the right order words to connect parts of the story on the Activity Book page.

8. Read the directions and exercises with students. Have them complete the Activity Book page.

Objectives
- Use transitions to signal order.

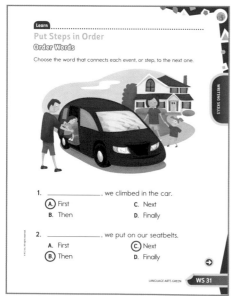

Try It

Use Order Words

Help students practice using words such as *first, next, then,* and *finally*. Turn to page WS 33 in *K¹² Language Arts Activity Book*.

1. Read the directions to students. Read the sentences together.

2. Have students complete the Activity Book page.

> **Objectives**
> • Use transitions to signal order.

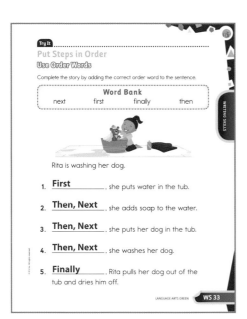

Plan the Steps

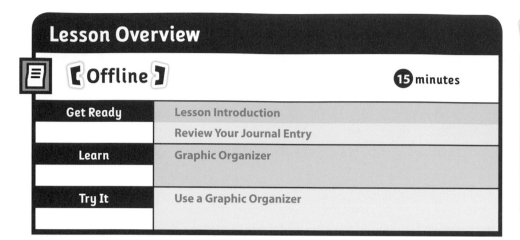

Lesson Overview

[Offline]   **15** minutes

Get Ready	Lesson Introduction
	Review Your Journal Entry
Learn	Graphic Organizer
Try It	Use a Graphic Organizer

[Materials]

Supplied
- *K¹² Language Arts Activity Book*, p. WS 34
- *K¹² My Journal*, pp. 126–127

Also Needed
- whiteboard (optional)

Keywords

graphic organizer – a visual device, such as a diagram or chart, that helps a writer plan a piece of writing

Content Background

Graphic organizers are tools to help organize writing. In this lesson, students will use a graphic organizer for simple steps. Understanding how to use this tool will lay the foundation for future writing in which students can use a graphic organizer to plan and organize their thoughts into a coherent structure.

Big Ideas

- ▶ Following a specific organizational structure is a useful tool for novice writers; however, writers require the freedom and flexibility to follow their ideas to completion.
- ▶ Writers use various methods to plan, and novices should use what works for them: freewriting, listing, graphic organizers, or other methods.
- ▶ Engaging students in prewriting activities improves the quality of writing.

 **15 minutes**

Work **together** with students to complete Get Ready, Learn, and Try It activities.

Get Ready ···

Lesson Introduction
Prepare students for the lesson.

1. Tell students that they will review their journal entry about a favorite activity.

2. Explain that they will learn how to use a graphic organizer to prepare for a piece of writing.

3. Tell students that they will fill in their steps in a graphic organizer.

★ **Objectives**
- Brainstorm and develop possible topics.
- Choose a topic.

Review Your Journal Entry
Help students think about planning a piece of writing using a graphic organizer.
Gather *K¹² My Journal* and turn to pages 126 and 127.

1. Help students read over their journal entry in which they explained how to do a favorite activity.

2. Ask students if they would like to continue writing about this activity or write about a new favorite activity.

3. If students want to write about a new activity, ask them for three possible topics. Write these topics on a whiteboard or sheet of paper. Help them pick one topic to write about.

4. Ask students to quickly explain their activity to you, step by step.
   Say: What do you think are the most important steps in your activity?

My Favorite Activity — Date _____	Draw a picture.
What do you like to do? Explain how you do it.	
126	127

Learn

Graphic Organizer

Introduce the graphic organizer to students. Turn to page WS 34 in *K¹² Language Arts Activity Book*.

1. Show students the **graphic organizer** on the Activity Book page. Explain that it is a tool that writers use to plan a piece of writing. It can help us see how steps or ideas are connected.

2. Explain that one way to organize ideas is to put them in a list.
   Say: This graphic organizer has boxes and arrows. The boxes show the steps. The arrows show how the steps are connected. They show the order that the steps have to be in.

   ▸ One step is written in each box.
   ▸ The steps need to be in the correct order.
   ▸ The first step is written in the first box, the second in the second box, and so on.

3. Ask students to think for a moment about how they will write the steps for their own activity in the graphic organizer. (They will complete the graphic organizer in the Try It activity.)

Objectives
- Organize ideas through sequencing.

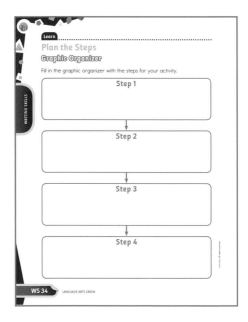

Try It

Use a Graphic Organizer

Help students practice using a graphic organizer. Turn to page WS 34 in *K¹² Language Arts Activity Book*.

1. Read the directions to students. Explain that they are to write the steps for their activity in the graphic organizer.

2. Have students complete the Activity Book page.

3. If students wish to write more than four steps for their activity, print another copy of the graphic organizer as needed.

TIP Keep the graphic organizer in a safe place so students can refer to it later.

Objectives
- Organize ideas through sequencing.
- Write steps in a process.

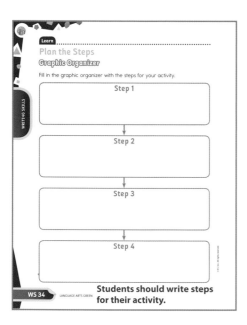

Write the Steps

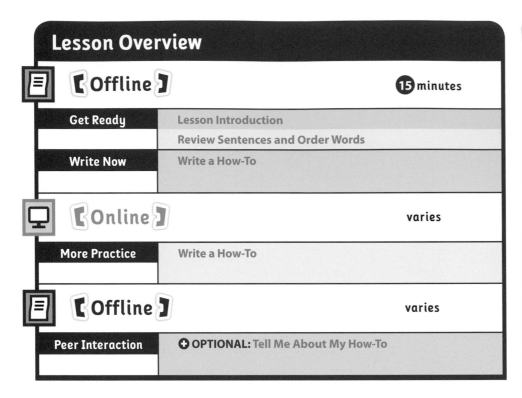

Lesson Overview

Offline		15 minutes
Get Ready	Lesson Introduction	
	Review Sentences and Order Words	
Write Now	Write a How-To	

Online		varies
More Practice	Write a How-To	

Offline		varies
Peer Interaction	⊕ OPTIONAL: Tell Me About My How-To	

Materials

Supplied
- *K¹² Language Arts Activity Book*, pp. WS 34–40
- Write About a Favorite Activity: Rubric and Sample Responses (printout)

Keywords

publishing – the stage or step of the writing process in which the writer makes a clean copy of the piece and shares it

revising – the stage or step of the writing process in which the writer rereads and edits the draft, correcting errors and making changes in content or organization that improve the piece

Advance Preparation

Have students gather completed page WS 34 (Graphic Organizer) in *K¹² Language Arts Activity Book*.

Big Ideas

▸ A sequence follows a logical order.
▸ Sequencing ideas is the beginning of writing a personal narrative or experience story.
▸ Good writers use transitions to help create coherence in text.
▸ Writing requires rewriting or revision.

[Offline] 🕒 **15** minutes

Work **together** with students to complete Get Ready and Write Now activities.

Get Ready

Lesson Introduction
Prepare students for the lesson.

1. Tell students that they will review how to write complete sentences.

2. Explain that they will review how to use order words like *first*, *next*, *then*, and *finally*.

3. Tell students that they will write out their complete instructions for doing their activity.

Review Sentences and Order Words
Prepare students for their writing assignment by quickly reviewing complete sentences and the order words *first*, *next*, *then*, and *finally*. Turn to page WS 35 in *K¹² Language Arts Activity Book*. Ask students to identify what is wrong with each sentence on the page. You may write their answers in the blanks for them. You may also wish to have them correct the sentences.

Write Now

Write a How-To

Help students write their how-to. Turn to pages WS 37 and 38 in *K¹² Language Arts Activity Book* and gather the completed graphic organizer.

1. Have students reread their steps in the graphic organizer. Tell them that they are going to use a pencil to write complete instructions to their steps for their activity.

2. Tell students that they must include all of the steps in order, and they need to use order words such as *first, next, then,* and *finally*. Tell students that they can add steps if they think it will make their instructions more clear.

3. Tell students they must write in pencil; they must write legibly; and there should be an appropriate amount of space between each sentence.

4. Have students read their finished sentences aloud. Ask them if their steps sound like they are in the right order with the order words they used in each step.

5. Ask students to review their sentences, making sure that each has a naming part and an action part, as well as a capital letter at the beginning and an end mark at the end. Tell them to make corrections, if needed.

6. Tell students that they are ready to publish their writing. **Publishing** their writing means putting it into its final form to be shared with others. Have students use an eraser to correct any mistakes or a pencil to add any detail to their sentences. If they wish, they may use the back of the page to rewrite final versions of their sentences.

7. Use the materials and instructions in the online lesson to evaluate students' finished writing. You will be looking at students' writing to evaluate the following:

   ▸ **Purpose and Content:** Most of the steps tell how to do something.
   ▸ **Structure and Organization:** There are four steps in the correct order. The steps are written in paragraph form using the words *first, next, then,* and *finally* to signal order.
   ▸ **Grammar and Usage:** Most sentences are a complete thought. Most have a naming part and an action part. All sentences have a capital letter at the beginning and an end mark.

Objectives

- Spell common, frequently used words correctly.
- Use a capital letter to begin a sentence and an end mark to end it.
- Use an appropriate organizational plan in writing.
- Use correct grammar and sentence formation.
- Use transitions to signal order.
- Write a how-to (directions to complete a task).
- Write complete sentences.
- Write sentences with appropriate spacing between words.
- Write sentences with legible handwriting.
- Write a series of related sentences.

8. Enter students' scores for each rubric category online.

9. If students' writing scored a 1 in any criterion, work with students to proofread and revise their work.

Reward: When students' writing achieves "meets objectives" in all three categories on the grading rubric, add a sticker for this unit on the My Accomplishments chart.

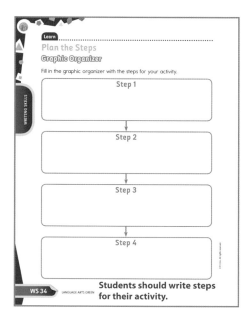

Learn ....

Plan the Steps
Graphic Organizer

Fill in the graphic organizer with the steps for your activity.

Step 1

Step 2

Step 3

Step 4

Students should write steps for their activity.

WS 34   LANGUAGE ARTS GREEN

Write Now ....

Write the Steps
Write a How-To

Write four sentences that tell how to do something. If you have more than four steps, write more sentences. Use the order words *first, next, then,* and *finally.*

Refer to the rubric and sample responses.

LANGUAGE ARTS GREEN   WS 37

Online varies

If necessary, work with students to complete the More Practice activity.

More Practice

Write a How-To

If students' writing scored "doesn't meet objectives" in any category, have them complete the appropriate review activity listed in the table online.

> **Objectives**
> • Evaluate writing and choose activities to review and revise.

- ▸ Follow the online instructions to help students revise and proofread their work.
- ▸ Impress upon students that revising makes their work better. Writing is a process, and each time they revise their work, they are making their writing stronger and better.
- ▸ When you provide feedback, always begin with something positive. For example, you might point out a detail they wrote (even if it's the only detail) and explain how it helps you picture the scene: "You wrote that the leaves were 'orange and gold.' That detail, the color of the leaves, really helps me picture the forest."
- ▸ Place the final written work together with the rubric and the sample papers in the writing portfolio. This information is useful for you to track progress, and it helps students to refer back to their own work. They can see how they improve and review feedback to remember areas that need revising.
- ▸ Help students locate the activities and provide support as needed.

 **Offline** 15 minutes

If necessary, work with students to complete the Peer Interaction activity.

Peer Interaction

⊕ OPTIONAL: Tell Me About My How-To

This activity is OPTIONAL. It is intended for students who have extra time and would benefit from extra practice. Feel free to skip this activity.

> **Objectives**
> • Use guidance from adults and peers to revise writing.
> • Collaborate with peers on writing projects.

    Students can benefit from exchanging writing with someone they know or another student. This activity will work best if students exchange their how-to piece with other students who completed the same activity, but you may copy the Activity Book pages and send them to someone else who is willing to give students feedback. Students should receive feedback on the content of their writing. To complete this optional activity, turn to pages WS 39 and 40 in *K¹² Language Arts Activity Book*.

1. Have students exchange their writing with other students.

2. Have students use the Activity Book pages to provide others with feedback about their writing.

3. Have students use the feedback provided from other students to revise their own how-to piece.

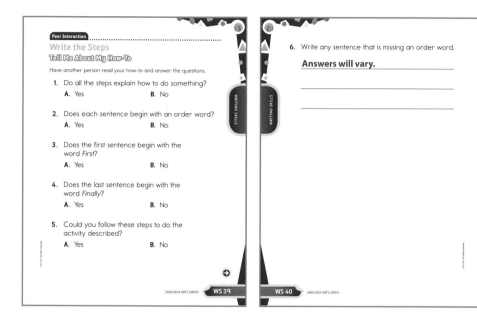

UNIT OVERVIEW Nouns

Unit Focus

In this unit, students will learn to identify and use nouns. Students will learn that

- ▶ Nouns name people, places, and things.
- ▶ Common nouns name any person, place, or thing.
- ▶ Proper nouns name a specific person, place, or thing.
- ▶ Possessive nouns show that a particular person or thing has or owns something.
- ▶ Many possessive nouns are formed by adding an apostrophe and an *s*.

Nouns are one of the basic building blocks of the English language. By being able to recognize nouns and telling the difference between the types of nouns, students will begin to develop a rich vocabulary to use in writing.

Throughout this unit, students will learn about nouns that can be touched, seen, or heard. As you are doing these activities, look for opportunities to identify nouns in the world around you. Understanding that nouns are usually real things will help students identify them more quickly and easily.

Unit Plan		〖 Offline 〗	〖 Online 〗
Lesson 1	Common Nouns	15 minutes	
Lesson 2	Proper Nouns	15 minutes	
Lesson 3	Possessive Nouns	15 minutes	
Lesson 4	Review Nouns	5 minutes	10 minutes
Lesson 5	Unit Checkpoint	15 minutes	varies

Common Nouns

Lesson Overview

[Offline] **15** minutes

Get Ready	Lesson Introduction
	Review Sentences and Introduce Nouns
Learn	Find the Nouns
Try It	Use Nouns

[Materials]

Supplied
- *K¹² Language Arts Activity Book*, pp. WS 41–42

Also Needed
- whiteboard (optional)

Keywords

common noun – a word that names any person, place, or thing
noun – a word that names a person, place, or thing

Content Background

A noun names a person, place, or thing. A common noun names any person, place, or thing. Common nouns are words like *boy*, *girl*, *river*, *dog*, *apple*, and *house*.

Big Ideas

- ▶ A noun is a basic part of speech.
- ▶ Understanding nouns gives students a basic vocabulary for building sentences and understanding how language works.

[Offline] **15** minutes

Work **together** with students to complete Get Ready, Learn, and Try It activities.

Get Ready

Lesson Introduction
Prepare students for the lesson.

1. Tell students that they will first review how to make a complete sentence.

2. Explain that they will be learning about nouns. A noun is a word that names a person, place, or thing.

Objectives
- Recall what a sentence is.
- Identify nouns.

Review Sentences and Introduce Nouns

Review with students that a sentence has two parts. Then introduce nouns to students by showing examples in a sentence.

1. Ask students what two things are needed to make a complete sentence. a naming part and an action part

2. Write the following words on a whiteboard or sheet of paper and read them with students.

    My brother

    ► Are these words a complete sentence? No   What is missing? the action part

3. Write the following words on the whiteboard or paper and read them with students.

    throws a ball at the beach.

    ► Are these words a complete sentence? No   What is missing? the naming part

4. Write both sets of words together to make the following sentence and read it with students.

    My brother throws a ball at the beach.

    ► Is this a complete sentence? Yes

5. **Say:** The sentence I wrote has some naming words. Which word names a person? a place? a thing? *Brother* is a person; *beach* is a place; *ball* is a thing.

6. Explain that each of these words is a noun.

Learn

· ·

Find the Nouns

Introduce common nouns to students. Turn to page WS 41 in *K¹² Language Arts Activity Book*.

1. On a whiteboard or sheet of paper, write the following words in a column and have students read them with you.

    person, place, thing

2. **Say:** A **noun** is a word that names a person, place, or thing. A noun can be found at the beginning, middle, or end of a sentence.

3. Write the following sentence beside the column and have students read it with you.

    The family ate sandwiches at the diner.

4. Tell students that there are three nouns in the sentence you wrote: one that names a person or persons, one that names a place or places, and one that names a thing or things. Ask them to draw lines from each type of noun listed in the column to the correct noun in the sentence. *Person* should connect to *family*; *place* should connect to *diner*; *thing* should connect to *sandwiches*.

5. Read the rule and the example on the Activity Book page.

Objectives

• Identify nouns.

6. Have students complete the Activity Book page. Provide support as necessary.

TIP Some students may think that *we* and *I* are nouns. If students circle these words, explain that these words are special words that take the place of nouns, but they are not nouns. Students will learn about pronouns at another time.

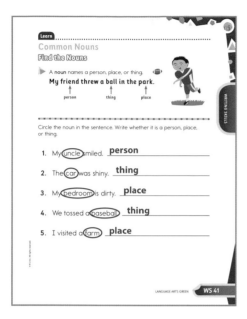

Try It

Use Nouns

Help students practice using common nouns. Turn to page WS 42 in *K¹² Language Arts Activity Book*.

1. Read the directions to students.

2. Read each sentence to students and have them fill in each blank with a noun from the appropriate column in the word bank.

Objectives
- Use nouns.

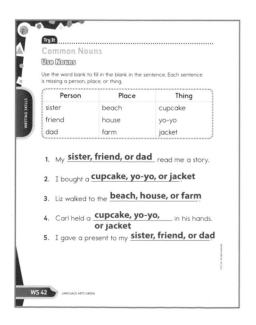

Proper Nouns

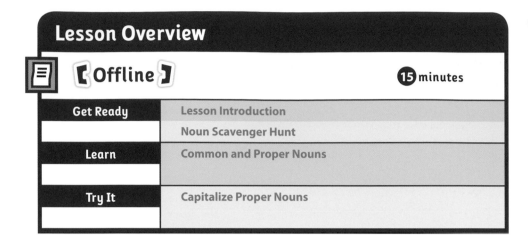

Lesson Overview

Offline		**15** minutes
Get Ready	Lesson Introduction	
	Noun Scavenger Hunt	
Learn	Common and Proper Nouns	
Try It	Capitalize Proper Nouns	

Materials

Supplied
- *K¹² Language Arts Activity Book*, pp. WS 43–45

Also Needed
- whiteboard (optional)

Keywords
common noun – a word that names any person, place, or thing
noun – a word that names a person, place, or thing
proper noun – a word that names a specific person, place, or thing

Content Background

A noun is a word that names a person, place, or thing. A common noun names any person, place, or thing, but a proper noun names a specific person, place, or thing. *Friend* is a common noun, but the name of a specific friend, *Ryan*, is a proper noun. Proper nouns always begin with a capital letter.

Big Ideas

- A noun is a basic part of speech.
- Understanding nouns gives students a basic vocabulary for building sentences and understanding how language works.

 **15** minutes

Work **together** with students to complete Get Ready, Learn, and Try It activities.

Get Ready

Lesson Introduction
Prepare students for the lesson.

1. Remind students that nouns are words that name a person, place, or thing.

2. Explain that they will be learning about proper nouns, which are words that name a specific person, place, or thing.

 Objectives
- Recall what a noun is.
- Identify nouns.

Noun Scavenger Hunt

Reinforce what a noun is by having students go on a scavenger hunt to find some nouns. Turn to page WS 43 in *K¹² Language Arts Activity Book*.

1. **Say:** What do nouns name? a person, place, or thing

2. Explain to students that they are going to go on a noun scavenger hunt to complete the Activity Book page. They should try to find three nouns to put in the Person column, three to put in the Place column, and three to put in the Thing column. If students have difficulty finding nouns that name places, suggest they look outside the room or out a window.

3. Ask students to quickly move around the room looking for nouns. When they correctly find and identify a noun, ask which column it should go in.

4. Write all the nouns they find in the appropriate column.

TIP This scavenger hunt is more than a fun game. Physically moving about the room and finding nouns will help students understand that many nouns are things that can be seen and touched.

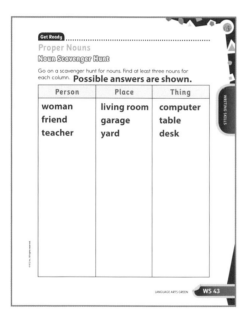

Learn •

Common and Proper Nouns

Introduce proper nouns to students. Help them learn the difference between common and proper nouns. Turn to page WS 44 in *K¹² Language Arts Activity Book*.

1. **Say:** If I were to say the word *student* to you, would you know which student I was talking about? No

   Now, if I were to say [student's name], would you know which student I was talking about? That's right! I'm talking about you.

Objectives

• Identify proper and common nouns.

2. On a whiteboard or sheet of paper, write the word *student* and the student's name beside it.

3. Point to the word *student* and explain that this word is a **common noun**. It is talking about any student. Point to the student's name and explain that this word is a **proper noun**. It is talking about a specific student.

4. **Say:** Proper nouns name specific people, days and months, books and movies, and countries.

5. On the whiteboard or paper, write the words *cat, country,* and *month* in a column going down the left side and the words *America, May,* and *Fluffy* in a column going down the right side.

6. Read the three common nouns in the left column. Explain that they are common nouns. They name something in general. Read the three proper nouns in the right column. Explain that they are proper nouns. They name something specific.

7. Ask students to match the common nouns to the corresponding proper nouns. Help students draw lines between each common noun and its matching proper noun. cat, Fluffy; country, America; month, May

8. Point to the proper nouns and explain that proper nouns always start with a capital letter.

9. Read the rule and the example on the Activity Book page.

10. Have students complete the Activity Book page. Provide support as necessary.

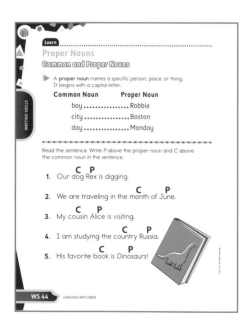

Try It

Capitalize Proper Nouns

Help students practice using proper nouns. Turn to page WS 45 in *K[12] Language Arts Activity Book.*

1. Read the first set of directions to students. Read the sentences together. Point to the example.

2. Show them how to put a line through the lowercase letter and write a capital letter above it.

3. Have students complete Exercises 1–4. Provide support as necessary.

4. Read the second set of directions to students. Read the sentences together.

5. Help students write a proper noun in each blank in Exercises 5 and 6.

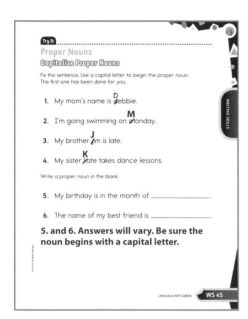

Try It

Proper Nouns

Capitalize Proper Nouns

Fix the sentence. Use a capital letter to begin the proper noun. The first one has been done for you.

1. My mom's name is Debbie.

2. I'm going swimming on Monday.

3. My brother Jim is late.

4. My sister Kate takes dance lessons.

Write a proper noun in the blank.

5. My birthday is in the month of _____.

6. The name of my best friend is _____.

5. and 6. Answers will vary. Be sure the noun begins with a capital letter.

LANGUAGE ARTS GREEN   WS 45

Possessive Nouns

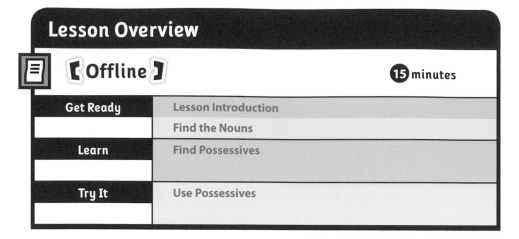

Lesson Overview

[Offline]   **15** minutes

Get Ready	Lesson Introduction
	Find the Nouns
Learn	Find Possessives
Try It	Use Possessives

[Materials]

Supplied
- *K¹² Language Arts Activity Book,* pp. WS 46–47
- Story Card J

Also Needed
- whiteboard (optional)

Keywords

noun – a word that names a person, place, or thing
possessive noun – the form of a noun that shows ownership

Content Background

▸ A possessive noun is used to show ownership. If you want to say that a ball belongs to Ed, you can make the noun *Ed* possessive: *It is Ed's ball.*

▸ Most singular nouns are made possessive by adding an apostrophe and the letter *s* to the end of a word. *Dog* becomes *dog's,* as in *the dog's bone.* Most plural nouns end in *s.* These plural nouns are made possessive by adding an apostrophe **after** the *s. Dogs* becomes *dogs',* as in *all the dogs' bones.* This lesson will focus only on forming the possessive of singular nouns.

Big Ideas

▸ A noun is a basic part of speech.
▸ Understanding nouns gives students a basic vocabulary for building sentences and understanding how language works.

[Offline] **15** minutes

Work **together** with students to complete Get Ready, Learn, and Try It activities.

Get Ready ···

Lesson Introduction
Prepare students for the lesson.

1. Tell students that they will review what nouns are.

2. Explain that they will learn about possessive nouns, which are nouns that show ownership.

Objectives
- Recall what a noun is.
- Identify nouns.

Find the Nouns
Practice identifying nouns.

1. Lay down Story Card J and look at it with students. Gather Story Card J. After a few moments, turn the card over.

2. Ask students how many nouns they think they will be able to find on the card: three? four? five?

3. Turn the card over and help students find nouns. Ask questions to help guide them to the different kinds of nouns.

   ▸ What noun names a place in the picture? beach; ocean
   ▸ What nouns name things in the picture? Answers may include: ball; umbrella; chair; sand castle.
   ▸ What nouns name people in the picture? Answers may include: boys; girls; men; women; mommies; daddies.

Learn

Find Possessives
Introduce possessive nouns to students. Turn to page WS 46 in *K¹² Language Arts Activity Book*.

Objectives
• Identify possessive nouns.

1. On a whiteboard or sheet of paper, write the following words in a column and read them with students.

   the rabbit, Mel, my friend

2. Point to the words *rabbit, Mel,* and *friend*.

   ▸ What kind of words are they? nouns
   ▸ What would we say if the rabbit has a carrot? It is the rabbit's carrot. or if Mel has a book? It is Mel's book.   or if my friend has a robot? It is my friend's robot.

3. On the whiteboard or paper, add an apostrophe and an *s* to each of the nouns.

   the rabbit's, Mel's, my friend's

4. As you point to each possessive noun, say *the rabbit's carrot, Mel's book, my friend's robot*.

5. Explain that these words are called **possessive nouns**. When we add an apostrophe and an *s* to the end of a word, that makes it possessive.

6. **Say:** *Possess* means to have or own. The rabbit possesses the carrot. Mel possesses the book. My friend possesses the robot.

7. Chant the following rhyme with students to help them remember how to make a possessive noun.

   To make it possess,
   Add apostrophe *s*.

8. Read the rule and the example on the Activity Book page.

9. Have students complete the Activity Book page. Provide support as necessary.

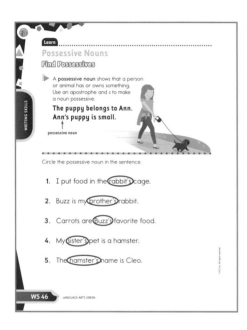

Try It ....

Use Possessives

Help students practice finding and using possessive nouns. Turn to page WS 47 in *K¹² Language Arts Activity Book*.

1. Read the first set of directions to students. Read the sentences together.

2. Have students complete Exercises 1 and 2. Provide support as necessary.

3. Read the second set of directions to students. Have students complete Exercises 3–5. Provide support as necessary.

Objectives
- Identify and use possessive nouns in sentences.

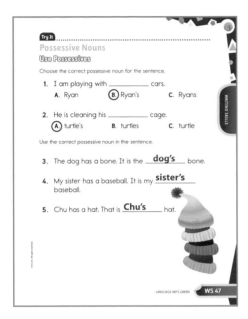

Try It ....
Possessive Nouns
Use Possessives

Choose the correct possessive noun for the sentence.

1. I am playing with _____ cars.
   A. Ryan   (B) Ryan's   C. Ryans

2. He is cleaning his _____ cage.
   (A) turtle's   B. turtles   C. turtle

Use the correct possessive noun in the sentence.

3. The dog has a bone. It is the **dog's** bone.

4. My sister has a baseball. It is my **sister's** baseball.

5. Chu has a hat. That is **Chu's** hat.

LANGUAGE ARTS GREEN   **WS 47**

Review Nouns

Lesson Overview

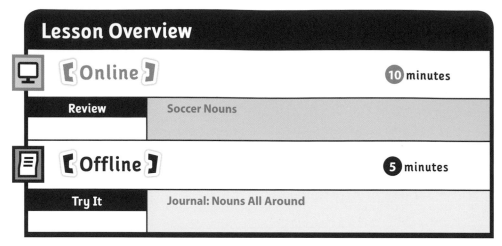

Online — 10 minutes

Review	Soccer Nouns

Offline — 5 minutes

Try It	Journal: Nouns All Around

Materials

Supplied
- *K¹² My Journal*, pp. 128–129

Also Needed
- crayons

Keywords

common noun – a word that names any person, place, or thing

noun – a word that names a person, place, or thing

possessive noun – the form of a noun that shows ownership

proper noun – a word that names a specific person, place, or thing

 **Online** 10 minutes

Students will review what they have learned about nouns to prepare for the Unit Checkpoint. Help students locate the online activity and provide support as needed.

Review

Soccer Nouns

Students will work online to review what they have learned about common nouns, proper nouns, and possessive nouns.

Objectives
- Identify nouns.
- Identify possessive nouns.
- Identify and use proper and common nouns.
- Use a capital letter to begin a proper noun.

Offline Alternative

No computer access? Find a book or magazine and look for three examples of each type of noun: common nouns, proper nouns, and possessive nouns. Once students have found the nouns, have them write three sentences, each using one type of noun.

 **5** minutes

Students will write on their own in their journal. Help students locate the offline activity.

Try It ....

Journal: Nouns All Around

Students will write in their journal on their own. Gather *K¹² My Journal* and have students turn to pages 128 and 129 in Writing Skills.

1. To help students prepare, ask them to look around the room for a minute and see if they can find a person, a place, and a thing. Ask if they can find any proper nouns.

2. Read the prompt with students. Have students respond to the prompt in their journal. As necessary, remind them that there are no correct or incorrect answers.

3. If students feel comfortable sharing what they wrote, allow them to share with you or their peers.

TIP The amount of time students need to complete this activity will vary. Allow them to use the rest of the allotted time to complete this activity. If they have more they would like to write, you may let them complete their entry at a later time. If students are having trouble getting started, you might tell them to draw a picture and describe it to you. You can transcribe their words for them.

Objectives
- Freewrite about a topic.
- Write in a journal.

Things I See   Date _____

List ten nouns in the room you are in.

_____
_____
_____
_____
_____
_____
_____
_____
_____
_____

128

Draw a picture.

_____
_____
_____
_____

129

Unit Checkpoint

Lesson Overview

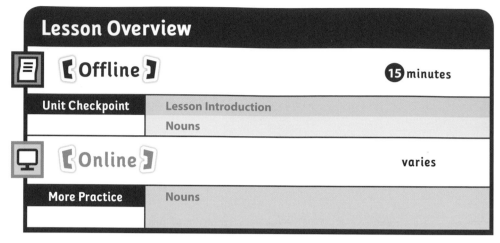

Offline		15 minutes
Unit Checkpoint	Lesson Introduction	
	Nouns	

Online		varies
More Practice	Nouns	

Materials

Supplied

- *K¹² Language Arts Assessments*, pp. WS 9–12

[Offline] 15 minutes

Work **together** with students to complete the Unit Checkpoint.

Unit Checkpoint

Lesson Introduction

Prepare students for the lesson.

1. Tell students that they are going to complete a Unit Checkpoint to show what they have learned.

2. Explain that if they miss one or more questions, they can continue to practice this grammar skill.

Objectives

- Identify and use possessive nouns in sentences.
- Identify possessive nouns.
- Identify proper and common nouns.
- Use a capital letter to begin a proper noun.
- Use nouns.

Nouns

Explain that students are going to show what they have learned about identifying and using common, proper, and possessive nouns.

1. Give students the Unit Checkpoint pages.

2. Read the directions together. If needed, read the questions and answer choices to students. Have students complete the Checkpoint on their own.

3. Use the Answer Key to score the Checkpoint and then enter the results online.

4. Review each exercise with students. Work with students to correct any exercise that they missed.

 TIP Students who answered one or more questions incorrectly should continue to practice this grammar skill. Write several sentences and ask students to identify the nouns in each sentence. Help them find common nouns, proper nouns, and possessive nouns.

Reward: When students score 80 percent or above on the Unit Checkpoint, add a sticker for this unit on the My Accomplishments chart.

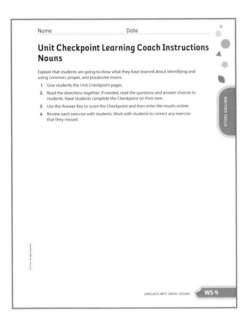

Name _____ Date _____

Unit Checkpoint Learning Coach Instructions
Nouns

Explain that students are going to show what they have learned about identifying and using common, proper, and possessive nouns.

1. Give students the Unit Checkpoint pages.

2. Read the directions together. If needed, read the questions and answer choices to students. Have students complete the Checkpoint on their own.

3. Use the Answer Key to score the Checkpoint and then enter the results online.

4. Review each exercise with students. Work with students to correct any exercise that they missed.

LANGUAGE ARTS GREEN | NOUNS — WS 9

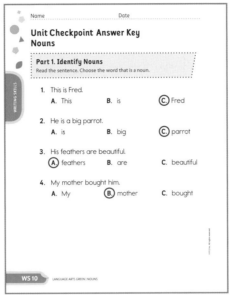

Name _____ Date _____

Unit Checkpoint Answer Key
Nouns

Part 1. Identify Nouns
Read the sentence. Choose the word that is a noun.

1. This is Fred.
   A. This   B. is   C. Fred

2. He is a big parrot.
   A. is   B. big   C. parrot

3. His feathers are beautiful.
   A. feathers   B. are   C. beautiful

4. My mother bought him.
   A. My   B. mother   C. bought

WS 10 — LANGUAGE ARTS GREEN | NOUNS

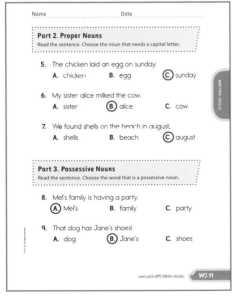

Name _____ Date _____

Part 2. Proper Nouns
Read the sentence. Choose the noun that needs a capital letter.

5. The chicken laid an egg on sunday.
   A. chicken   B. egg   C. sunday

6. My sister alice milked the cow.
   A. sister   B. alice   C. cow

7. We found shells on the beach in august.
   A. shells   B. beach   C. august

Part 3. Possessive Nouns
Read the sentence. Choose the word that is a possessive noun.

8. Mel's family is having a party.
   A. Mel's   B. family   C. party

9. That dog has Jane's shoes!
   A. dog   B. Jane's   C. shoes

LANGUAGE ARTS GREEN | NOUNS — WS 11

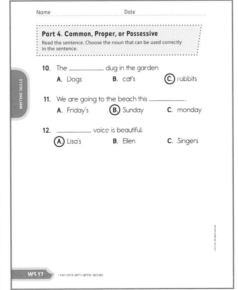

Name _____ Date _____

Part 4. Common, Proper, or Possessive
Read the sentence. Choose the noun that can be used correctly in the sentence.

10. The _____ dug in the garden.
    A. Dogs   B. cat's   C. rabbits

11. We are going to the beach this _____.
    A. Friday's   B. Sunday   C. monday

12. _____ voice is beautiful.
    A. Lisa's   B. Ellen   C. Singers

WS 12 — LANGUAGE ARTS GREEN | NOUNS

 **varies**

If necessary, work with students to complete the More Practice activity.

More Practice

••

Nouns

If students scored less than 80 percent on the Unit Checkpoint, have them complete the appropriate review activities listed in the table online. Help students locate the activities and provide support as needed.

 Objectives

- Evaluate Checkpoint results and choose activities to review.

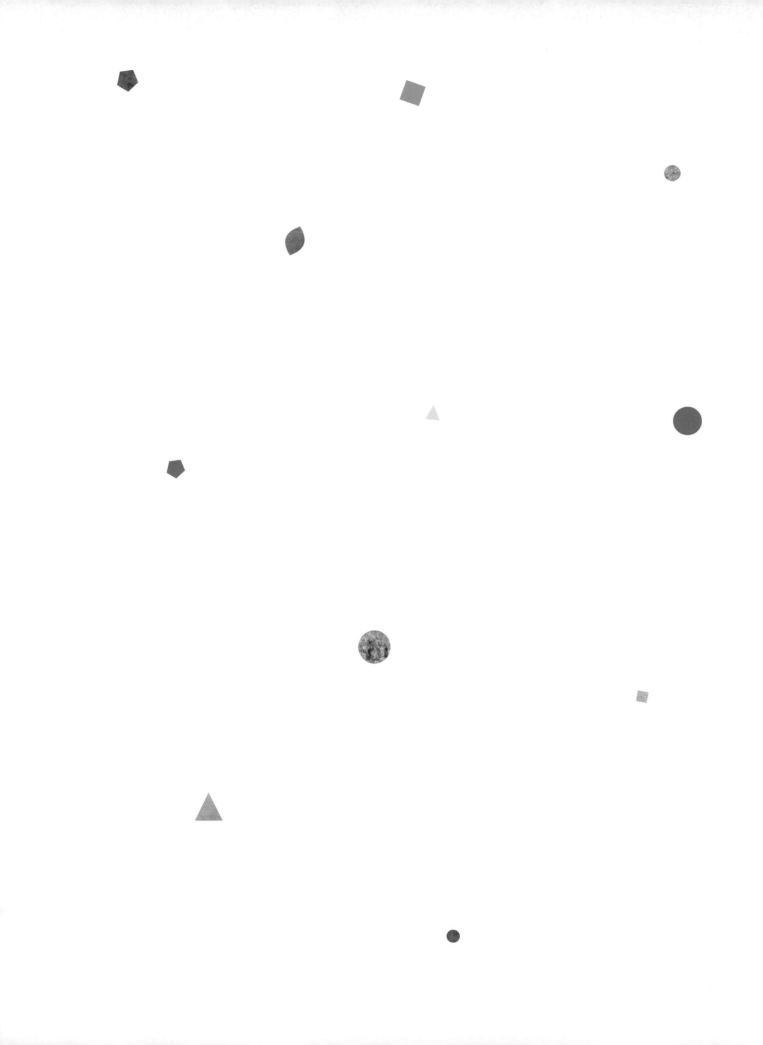

Write to Inform or Explain

Unit Focus

In this unit, students will learn about doing research on a topic to learn facts. They will also learn how to put the facts into their own words. Students will

▶ Review how to tell the difference between facts and opinions.
▶ Learn how to do research to find and confirm facts.
▶ Learn how to put facts and ideas into their own words.
▶ Use a fact cube to organize their research.
▶ Create a presentation to explain their facts to an audience.

In this unit, you will help students differentiate between minor facts and those that are important enough to be in their oral report. You will be doing a lot of reading together, as well as asking questions to aid students' comprehension of what they are reading. This unit requires a balance between letting students follow their interests and directing them toward pertinent information.

At the end of the unit, students will give a final presentation of their work. It would be helpful to assemble an audience of friends, family members, and other students. If other people are unavailable, you might even make an audience of pets or stuffed animals.

Unit Plan		[Offline]	[Online]
Lesson 1	Get Started with Facts	**15** minutes	
Lesson 2	Find Facts	**15** minutes	
Lesson 3	Write in Your Own Words	**15** minutes	
Lesson 4	Create a Fact Cube	**15** minutes	varies
Lesson 5	Share Your Fact Cube	**15** minutes	

Get Started with Facts

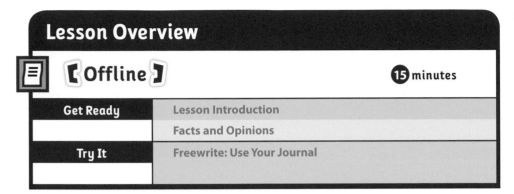

Lesson Overview

Offline		15 minutes
Get Ready	Lesson Introduction	
	Facts and Opinions	
Try It	Freewrite: Use Your Journal	

Content Background

As students learn to do research, they need to understand the difference between facts and opinions. Students need to understand that facts are tested and provable truths, and opinions are what an individual or group thinks about something. Both are useful in research, but in this unit, students will focus on facts. Students must also learn the difference between facts that are very significant and those that are less essential. When choosing only a few facts to report, students need to choose the most relevant facts possible. Students must also learn that using research to write something involves learning facts and then putting those facts into their own words. Simply repeating facts, exactly as they are written elsewhere, is plagiarism.

Big Ideas

Journal writing is a form of freewriting. It is an opportunity to get ideas on paper without concern for correctness of the language or the format of a piece of writing.

Materials

Supplied
- *K¹² My Journal*, pp. 130–131

Keywords

fact – something that can be proven true

freewriting – a way for a writer to pick a topic and write as much as possible about it within a set time limit

 **15** minutes

Work **together** with students to complete Get Ready and Try It activities.

Get Ready

Lesson Introduction
Prepare students for the lesson.

1. Explain that in this lesson, students will be writing in their journal. Remind students that a journal is a place to be creative and explore writing. They will not be judged or graded.

2. Explain that students will freewrite about facts they know about a person they know.
   Say: In freewriting, you write whatever comes into your mind. You can write absolutely anything you want, to answer the question you are asked.

 Objectives
- Distinguish between fact and opinion.

Facts and Opinions
Review the difference between facts and opinions.

1. Remind students that a **fact** is something that can be proven, and an **opinion** is what a person thinks.

2. Hold up your hand and point to it.

   ▸ What is this? a hand
   ▸ Is that a fact or opinion? fact   Why? because it is true

   Say: That's right. We could look up the word *hand* in a dictionary. There would be a definition of what a *hand* is, and there might be a picture that looks like this.

   ▸ My hand has five fingers. Is that a fact or opinion? fact   Why? because it is true; because we can count them

   Say: That's right. We can count them—one, two, three, four, five.

   ▸ This hand is funny looking. Is that a fact or opinion? opinion
      Why? because it is what you think, not the truth

Try It

Freewrite: Use Your Journal

Help students freewrite to name three facts about someone they know. Gather *K¹² My Journal* and have students turn to pages 130 and 131 in Writing Skills. Read the prompt at the top of the page to students. Answers to questions may vary.

1. Ask students to think of a person about whom they can list three facts.

2. Ask them to write those three facts in the journal. Explain that they are freewriting, or writing ideas on the page.

3. Ask them to think about the difference between facts and opinions.

   ► How would you prove each of the facts you are listing about the person you thought of?

4. If students are struggling, help by asking questions.

   ► Is the person a boy or a girl?
   ► Is the person related to you?
   ► Do you know where the person lives?

5. Once students have listed their facts, ask them to write an explanation of how they know that these are facts.

6. Have students explain their facts to you. Do not evaluate students' writing. As long as students have written some ideas on paper, their responses are acceptable.

TIP The amount of time students need to complete this activity will vary. If students are having trouble getting started, you might tell them to just list ideas or words. Students need only work for 15 minutes. If they have more they would like to write, you might want to have them complete their entry at a later time, but it is not required.

Objectives
- Generate ideas for writing.
- Freewrite on a topic.
- Write in a journal.

It's a Fact!   Date _____

Write three facts about someone you know.

1. _____
2. _____
3. _____

How do you know these are facts?

_____
_____
_____
_____

130

131

Find Facts

Lesson Overview

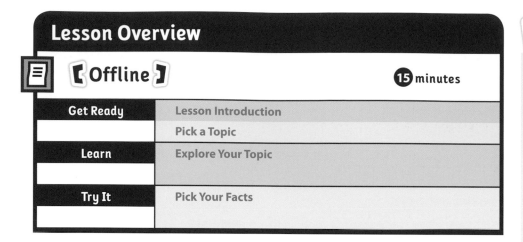

【Offline】 **15** minutes

Get Ready	Lesson Introduction
	Pick a Topic
Learn	Explore Your Topic
Try It	Pick Your Facts

Materials

Supplied

- *K¹² Language Arts Activity Book*, pp. WS 49–52
- *K¹² World: Earth and Sky* (optional)
- *K¹² World: People and Places of the Past* (optional)
- *K¹² World: The Science of Inventing* (optional)
- *K¹² World: Critter and Creature Stories* (optional)

Also Needed

- household objects – additional nonfiction texts that students might enjoy (optional)
- whiteboard (optional)

Keywords

fact – something that can be proven true

Content Background

In this lesson, students will be provided short "mini articles" to use for their research. These mini articles are based on longer nonfiction articles from the magazines *K¹² World: Earth and Sky* and *K¹² World: People and Places of the Past*. If students want to research a different topic, you might refer to the magazines *K¹² World: The Science of Inventing* or *K¹² World: Critter and Creature Stories* as research materials, or students may use a nonfiction text you have handy.

Big Ideas

- ▸ Writing helps build reading skills, and reading more helps improve writing skills.
- ▸ Start with the source that best serves your needs.

 **15** minutes

Work **together** with students to complete Get Ready, Learn, and Try It activities.

Get Ready ....

Lesson Introduction
Prepare students for the lesson.

1. Explain that students are going to learn about doing research, or finding information and facts.

2. Tell students that they will hear about three different topics and decide which topic they want to research.

> **Objectives**
> • Choose a topic.

Pick a Topic
Use this activity to explain to students that they are going to be working on a presentation. Gather the magazines or other nonfiction texts.

1. **Say:** In a presentation, we tell a about a specific topic.

2. Tell students that in this presentation, they will be explaining facts about their topic.

3. **Say:** I am going to tell you something about each topic, and you are going to think of one thing that interests you about each topic.

4. Read the following titles and topic introductions to students.

   ▸ George Washington: Learn about an American hero who went on to become the first president of the United States.
   ▸ Women in Space: For a long time, only men were allowed to become astronauts. Then, these amazing women began to travel to space.

5. Ask students to name one thing they think is interesting about each topic. Tell them it can be anything at all. Answers may include: George Washington was the first President; women weren't always allowed in space.

6. Ask students if they would like to use one of these topics for their presentation.

   ▸ If students are not interested in either topic, you might have them look through *The Science of Inventing* or *Critter and Creature Stories* to find a topic.
   ▸ If you have additional texts for them to explore, give them to students. For example, a favorite book about dinosaurs would make a great choice for the presentation.

7. Once students have picked their topic, write the topic title on a whiteboard or a sheet of paper.

TIP Research materials are provided for the topics George Washington and women in space. If students choose a different topic, you will need to provide research materials.

Learn

Explore Your Topic

Help students understand how to research facts and learn the difference between essential facts, lesser facts, and opinions. Turn to pages WS 49 and 50 in *K¹² Language Arts Activity Book.*

Objectives
• Identify facts.
• Do shared research about a topic.

1. Tell students that they are going to read an article on their topic and look for the most important facts and opinions.

2. Explain that some facts are more important than others. It is important to learn the difference between facts that are worth reporting and facts that may not be worth reporting.

3. **Say:** Here are two facts about an astronaut named Mae Jemison: Mae Jemison liked to dance; Mae Jemison was the first African American female astronaut.

   ▸ Which fact seems more important? Mae Jemison was the first African American female astronaut.

4. Discuss what makes this fact important.

   ▸ Being the first person to do something is usually very important.
   ▸ Enjoying dancing has nothing to do with being an astronaut.

5. Find the article on the chosen topic on the Activity Book pages. Read the article with students. If students are using other texts for research, read those texts with them instead.

6. As students are reading, stop and ask questions to guide their comprehension about what they are reading and direct them toward the most important facts. Here are some examples.

- ▸ George Washington was a surveyor. Do you think that is an important fact? Yes
- ▸ At first, women weren't allowed in space. That's interesting. Is that a fact you want to write about? Answers will vary.
- ▸ George Washington was a general. Is that a fact or an opinion? fact

TIP If students want to learn more about George Washington or women in space, they can read the longer articles located in *K¹² World: People and Places of the Past* or *K¹² World: Earth and Sky*, respectively.

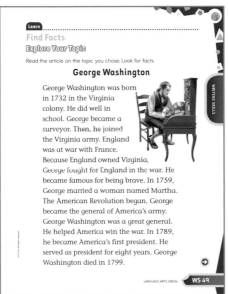

Try It

···

✏️ **Pick Your Facts**

Help students write down the facts they want to use in their report. Turn to pages WS 51 and 52 in *K¹² Language Arts Activity Book.*

1. Read the directions to students.

2. Have students complete the Activity Book pages. Provide support as necessary.

3. Keep the pages in a safe place so students can refer to them later.

TIP If students are struggling with the amount of writing in this activity, you may have them dictate their facts as you do most of the writing. Write their words verbatim at this time. Another option would be to take turns writing facts: You write fact 1, they write fact 2, and so on.

Objectives
- Do shared research about a topic.
- Plan the writing.

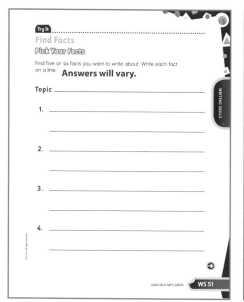

Write in Your Own Words

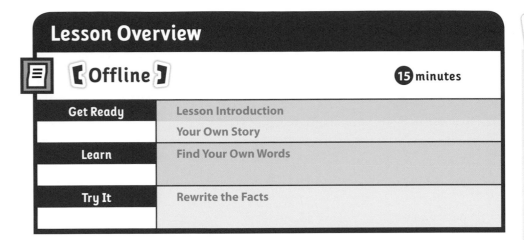

Lesson Overview

[Offline]   **15** minutes

Get Ready	Lesson Introduction
	Your Own Story
Learn	Find Your Own Words
Try It	Rewrite the Facts

Materials

Supplied

- *K¹² Language Arts Activity Book*, pp. WS 51–56
- *K¹² World: Earth and Sky* (optional)
- *K¹² World: People and Places of the Past* (optional)
- *K¹² World: The Science of Inventing* (optional)
- *K¹² World: Critter and Creature Stories* (optional)

Also Needed

- household objects – additional nonfiction texts that students might enjoy (optional)
- whiteboard (optional)

Keywords

fact – something that can be proven true

Advance Preparation

Have students gather their completed pages WS 51 and 52 (Pick Your Facts) in *K¹² Language Arts Activity Book.*

Content Background

It is important for students to learn that writing about what they have researched is different from simply copying facts or information. Students must understand that they need to put information into their own words. If they don't, it is plagiarism. Students do not need to know the word *plagiarism*. It is important that they understand that it is wrong to copy someone else's words and use them as their own.

Big Ideas

Use what you already know to help you understand new information.

〔 Offline 〕 15 minutes

Work **together** with students to complete Get Ready, Learn, and Try It activities.

Get Ready

Lesson Introduction
Prepare students for the lesson.

Objectives
- Recognize the importance of rephrasing information and ideas in one's own words.

1. Explain that students are going to learn about using their own words to report facts that they have read and researched.

2. Tell students that they must never copy someone else's writing word for word and use it as if it were their own.

Your Own Story
Use this storytelling activity to help students understand plagiarism.

1. Ask a student to tell a true story about something funny or interesting that happened to him or her. If students have difficulty coming up with something, ask them how they feel about a pet, a friend, a sibling, or a recent important day.

2. Once the student has finished telling the story, say that you have a story to tell.

3. Repeat the story back to students as if the events happened to you and as if the feelings were yours. Try to make your story exactly like the one you just heard.

   ▸ Was it fair that I told your story as if it had happened to me? No

4. Explain that it isn't fair because it is not your story, but the student's story. It isn't fair for another person to tell that story and pretend it happened to him or her.

5. Tell the story again, but this time, tell it about the student. Use the student's name, change some of the words, and make sure you mention that you first heard the story from the student.

Learn

 Find Your Own Words

Introduce rephrasing to students. Turn to pages WS 53 and 54 in *K¹² Language Arts Activity Book.*

1. Write the following sentence on a whiteboard or sheet of paper and read it with students.

   In 1983, Sally Ride became the first American woman to go into space.

2. **Say:** We're going to find the most important words in this sentence. I think the most important words in this sentence are *Sally Ride.*

3. Circle the words *Sally Ride* and put a 1 above them.

4. Explain that the other important words are *first woman*, *1983*, and *space*.

5. Circle each of those words and phrases. Explain that many new sentences can be made from those key ideas.

6. With students, review Examples 1, 2, and 3 on the Activity Book page. These are three different ways that the information about Sally Ride can be rewritten.

7. Ask students to come up with two more ways to create a sentence using this information.

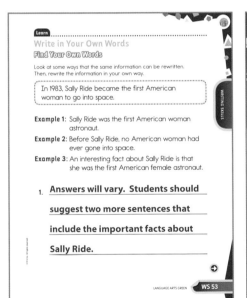

Try It

 Rewrite the Facts

Help students rewrite in their own words the facts they researched. Turn to pages WS 55 and 56 in *K¹² Language Arts Activity Book* and gather the completed Pick Your Facts pages.

1. Have students read over the facts on the Pick Your Facts pages that they are going to put in their presentation.

2. Read the directions on the Rewrite the Facts pages to students.

3. Have students complete the Activity Book pages. Provide support as necessary. Students may refer to their sources when rewriting their facts if they need more information.

TIP Keep the Activity Book pages in a safe place so students can refer to them later.

Objectives
- Plan the writing.
- Spell common, frequently used words correctly.
- Use a capital letter to begin a sentence and an end mark to end it.
- Use facts.
- Write a series of related sentences.
- Write sentences about the topic.
- Write sentences with appropriate spacing between words.
- Write sentences with legible handwriting.

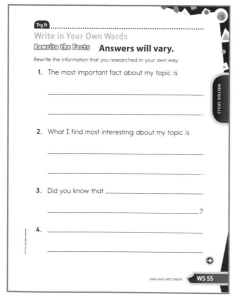

Create a Fact Cube

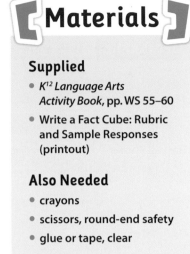

Materials

Supplied

- *K¹² Language Arts Activity Book*, pp. WS 55–60
- Write a Fact Cube: Rubric and Sample Responses (printout)

Also Needed

- crayons
- scissors, round-end safety
- glue or tape, clear

Keywords

fact – something that can be proven true

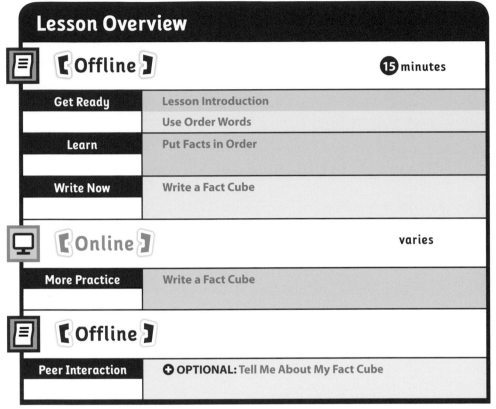

Lesson Overview

Offline — 15 minutes

Get Ready	Lesson Introduction
	Use Order Words
Learn	Put Facts in Order
Write Now	Write a Fact Cube

Online — varies

| More Practice | Write a Fact Cube |

Offline

| Peer Interaction | ⊕ OPTIONAL: Tell Me About My Fact Cube |

Advance Preparation

Have students gather their completed pages WS 55 and 56 (Rewrite the Facts) in *K¹² Language Arts Activity Book*.

Content Background

A fact cube is a graphic organizer; it will help students arrange their facts for their presentation. Students will be able to use their fact cube when they are presenting to an audience.

Big Ideas

Use what you already know to help you understand new information.

[Offline] 15 minutes

Work **together** with students to complete Get Ready, Learn, and Write Now activities.

Get Ready

Lesson Introduction

Prepare students for the lesson.

1. Explain that students are going to put their facts in the right order.

2. Tell students that they are going to use a fact cube to organize their facts for their presentation.

> **Objectives**
> - Organize ideas through sequencing.
> - Use transitions to signal order.

Use Order Words

Play this quick rhyming game to remind students how to use order words.

1. **Say:** I am going to say a rhyme and you have to do exactly as I say.

   First, you touch your nose.
   Next, you touch your toes.
   Then, you close your eyes.
   And finally, you reach ... up ... to ... the ... sky.

2. Repeat the entire chant a few times, getting faster each time.

3. Tell students that it is their turn to make up the actions. You will start the rhyme, and they will fill in the blanks. Answers will vary.

   First, you _____ .
   Next, you _____ .
   Then, you _____ .
   Finally, you _____ .

Learn

Put Facts in Order

Introduce putting facts in order to students. Help them understand that facts need to be put in an order that makes sense. Gather the completed Rewrite the Facts pages.

1. Help students look over their list of facts on the Activity Book pages. Have them revise their writing to include complete sentences, making sure that each sentence begins with a capital letter and ends with a punctuation mark.

2. Tell students that writing to explain something is just like telling a story. Stories have a beginning, middle, and end. Students' presentations should have a beginning, middle, and end as well.

3. Explain that when you are giving information about a person or event, a good way to put things in order is to tell the events that happened earliest first and then report the remaining facts in the order in which they happened.

4. If students did not write about a person's life, have them select another chronological order (such as the stages of a butterfly) or an order that makes logical sense, such as the order of importance of the facts.

5. Tell students to look at their facts.

   ▸ What is the very first thing that happened to the subject of your presentation? Answers will vary.

6. Have students write the number *1* and the word *first* next to that fact.

7. Explain that using words like *first*, *next*, *then*, and *finally* will help the audience understand how the facts connect.

8. Have students continue to number their facts. Next to the middle facts, have them write the words *next* or *then*. Next to the final fact, have them write the word *finally*.

Objectives

- Organize ideas through sequencing.
- Use transitions to signal order.
- Recognize the purpose of revising.
- Revise by adding or deleting text.
- Recognize the importance of using an appropriate organizational pattern in writing.

Write Now

 Write a Fact Cube

Help students copy their facts onto a fact cube. Turn to pages WS 57–59 in *K¹²*
Language Arts Activity Book and gather the crayons, scissors, and tape or glue.

1. Read the directions to students.

2. Help students copy their facts onto the fact cube. Tell students they must write
   in pencil and they must write legibly.

3. Have students draw a picture on the cube that illustrates at least one of their
   facts. Provide support as necessary. If you wish, students may find an image on
   the Internet, then print it and glue it to the cube.

4. Ask students to review their sentences, making sure that each has a naming
   part and an action part, as well as a capital letter at the beginning and an end
   mark at the end.

5. When students have completed the cube, read aloud their facts.

6. Tell students that they are ready to publish their writing. **Publishing** their
   writing means putting it into its final form to be shared with others. Have
   students use an eraser to correct any mistakes and a pencil to add any desired
   details to their facts.

7. Have students cut out their fact cube, fold it, and glue or tape the tabs.

8. Use the materials and instructions in the online lesson to evaluate students'
   finished writing. You will be looking at students' writing to evaluate the
   following:

   ▸ **Purpose and Content:** There are five important facts (main ideas) about
     a topic. There is a picture related to the topic.
   ▸ **Structure and Organization:** The facts are written one per side on the
     cube. The student has decided on an order for the facts.
   ▸ **Grammar and Usage:** Most sentences contain a complete thought. Most
     have a naming part and an action part. All sentences have a capital letter at
     the beginning and an end mark.

Objectives

- Spell common, frequently used words correctly.
- Use a capital letter to begin a sentence and an end mark to end it.
- Use an appropriate organizational plan in writing.
- Use facts.
- Write a series of related sentences.
- Write complete sentences.
- Write sentences about the topic.
- Write sentences with appropriate spacing between words.
- Write sentences with legible handwriting.
- Recognize the purpose of feedback.

9. Enter students' scores for each rubric category online.

10. If students' writing scored a 1 in any criterion, work with students to proofread and revise their work.

Reward: When students' writing achieves "meets objectives" in all three categories on the grading rubric, add a sticker for this unit on the My Accomplishments chart.

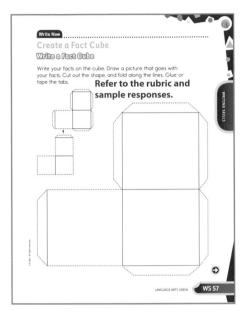

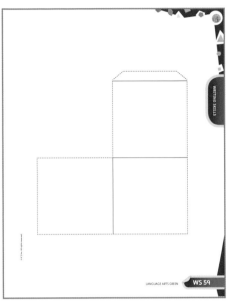

 **varies**

If necessary, work with students to complete the More Practice activity.

More Practice

Objectives
- Evaluate writing and choose activities to review and revise.

Write a Fact Cube

If students' writing scored "doesn't meet objectives" in any category, have them complete the appropriate review activity listed in the table online.

▸ Follow the online instructions to help them edit and revise their work.

▸ Impress upon students that revising makes their work better. Writing is a process, and each time they revise their story, they are making their writing stronger and better.

▸ When you provide feedback, always begin with something positive. For example, you might point out a detail they wrote (even if it's the only detail) and explain how it helps you picture the scene: "You wrote that the leaves were 'orange and gold.' That detail, the color of the leaves, really helps me picture the forest."

▸ Place the final written work together with the rubric and the sample papers in the writing portfolio. This information is useful for you to track progress, and it helps students to refer back to their own work. They can see how they improve and review feedback to remember areas that need revising.

▸ Help students locate the activities and provide support as needed.

 **varies**

If necessary, work with students to complete the Peer Interaction activity.

Peer Interaction ·······································

✚ OPTIONAL: Tell Me About My Fact Cube

This activity is OPTIONAL. It is intended for students who have extra time and would benefit from extra practice. Feel free to skip this activity.

Students can benefit from exchanging fact cubes and presentations with someone they know or another student. This activity will work best if students exchange their fact cubes with other students who completed the same activity, but you may copy the Activity Book page and send it to someone else who is willing to give students feedback. Students should receive feedback on the content of their writing. To complete this optional activity, turn to page WS 61 in *K¹² Language Arts Activity Book*.

1. Have students exchange fact cubes with other students.

2. Have students use the Activity Book page to provide others with feedback about their writing.

3. Have students use the feedback provided to revise their own writing.

Objectives
- Use guidance from adults and peers to revise writing.
- Collaborate with peers on writing projects.

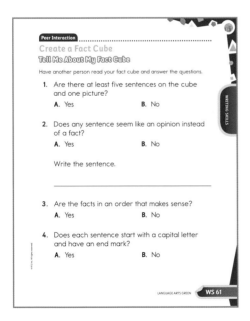

Share Your Fact Cube

Lesson Overview

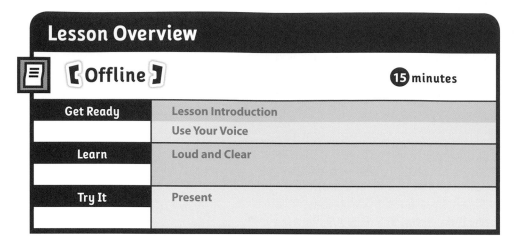

Get Ready	Lesson Introduction
	Use Your Voice
Learn	Loud and Clear
Try It	Present

Offline — 15 minutes

Materials

Supplied
- *K¹² Language Arts Activity Book*, p. WS 57–59

Keywords

audience – a writer's readers
presentation – an oral report, usually with visuals

Advance Preparation

Have students gather their completed fact cube from pages WS 57–59 (Write a Fact Cube) in *K¹² Language Arts Activity Book*. Set up a few chairs facing forward. Invite friends, family members, other students, and even pets to sit in the chairs and listen to students' presentations.

Big Ideas

Good public speakers speak clearly, make eye contact, and use appropriate expression for their subject matter and audience.

Offline — 15 minutes

Work **together** with students to complete Get Ready, Learn, and Try It activities.

Get Ready

Lesson Introduction
Prepare students for the lesson.

1. Explain that students are going to finish their fact cube project.

2. Tell students that they are going to give a final presentation on their topic.

Objectives
- Provide a sense of closure.
- Speak audibly and clearly to express thoughts, feelings, and ideas.

Use Your Voice

Use this exercise to get students speaking in a loud and clear voice.

1. Ask students what their presentation is about. Tell them that they should start with that information when giving a presentation.

2. Ask students to take five steps backward.

3. **Say:** Introduce your presentation again. You have to say it loudly enough for me to hear, but you can't shout.

4. Repeat the activity, having students get farther and farther away. Have them say their introduction in a loud voice, but without shouting.

5. Encourage students to maintain eye contact with you at all times. Encourage them to speak clearly, no matter how loud they are.

6. Once students have found a good, loud speaking voice, ask them to repeat their introduction, this time adding the words *and that's why* at the beginning. Tell them that saying the introduction again in a different way is a good way to end a presentation. It is called a conclusion.

TIP If students are having a hard time finding a loud voice without shouting, have them make a "loud body." Have them spread their arms and legs wide, taking up as much space as possible with their body. Ask them to find a voice to match that body.

Learn

Loud and Clear

Introduce presentation skills to students. Have them practice their presentation with their fact cube before giving their final presentation.

1. Tell students that to be good presenters, they need to keep a few ideas in mind. Say this presentation chant to help them remember.

   Keep your head up and your voice clear.
   Be yourself and speak loudly so others can hear.

2. Tell students that although they have their fact cube, it is important for presenters to really understand the facts for themselves.

3. **Say:** People in the audience might not know anything about your topic. You might need to explain more about your facts.

4. Ask students to read over their fact cube. Ask them to think of one other thing they can say about each fact in case there are questions.

5. Ask students to pick one fact and tell you more about it.

6. Have students practice their entire presentation, including their title, introduction, and closing sentence. Remind them to say the chant before they practice.

Objectives
- Identify audience.
- Provide a sense of closure.
- Speak audibly and clearly to express thoughts, feelings, and ideas.

Try It

Present

Help students present their fact cube. Have friends and family members come to listen to students talk about their topic. Gather the completed fact cube (Write a Fact Cube pages).

1. Remind students that they should begin with their title and introduction, and finish with the closing statement. Remind students to use transition words such as *first*, *next*, *then*, and *finally*.

2. Have students say the presentation chant before they begin.

3. Introduce students to the audience. Tell the audience that you will take one question at the end of each presentation.

4. Have students present their fact cube.

5. After each presentation, ask one member of the audience to ask a question about the topic and have the student presenter answer.

6. Provide feedback to students after they finish presenting their fact cube. Use these questions to guide your review and your discussion with students. Your feedback should include suggestions about any of these elements that were missing from the presentation.

   ▸ Did the student read loudly and clearly during the presentation?
   ▸ Did the student look up and make eye contact with the audience?
   ▸ Did the student tell more about the facts written on the cube?
   ▸ What could the student do to improve the presentation?

Objectives
- Identify audience.
- Provide a sense of closure.
- Speak audibly and clearly to express thoughts, feelings, and ideas.
- Use transitions to signal order.

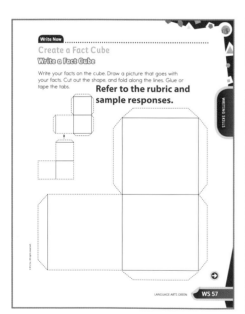

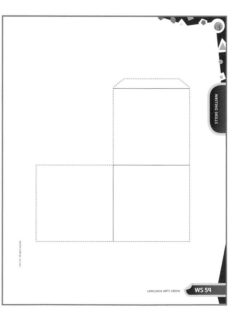

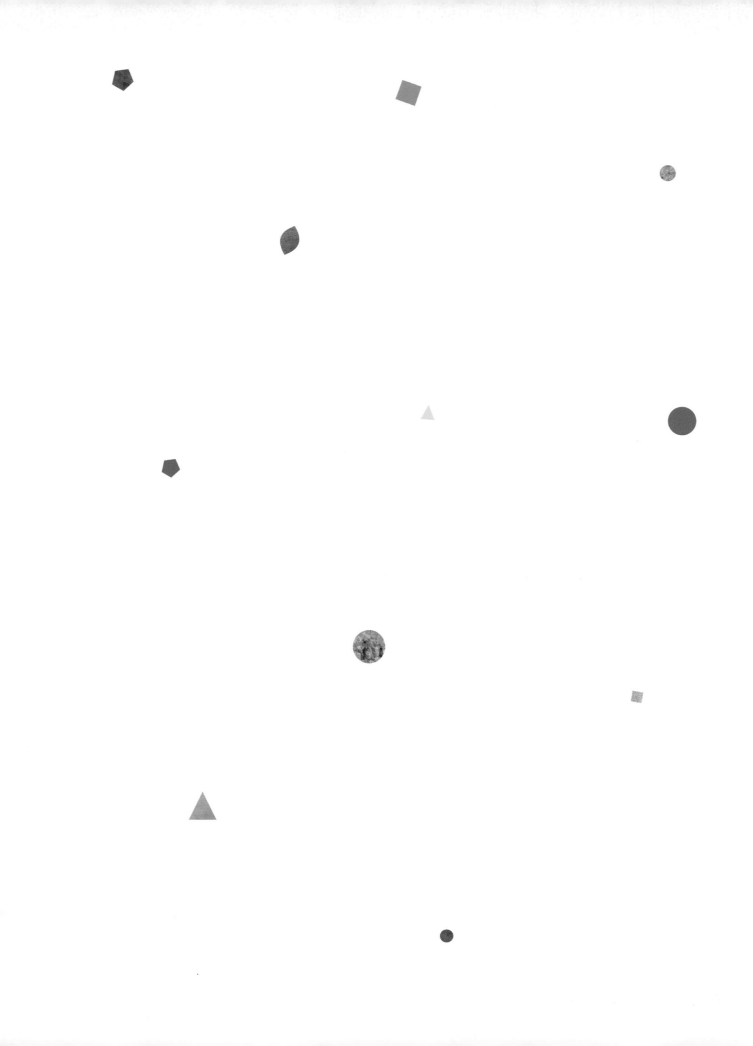

Verbs

Unit Focus

In this unit, students will learn about verbs. Verbs show action, or something that is happening. Verbs can show a physical action or a mental action. In this unit, students will

▶ Learn to identify verbs in a sentence.
▶ Learn how to use an action verb in a sentence.
▶ Learn how to use singular verbs with singular nouns.
▶ Learn how to use plural verbs with plural nouns.

A verb is one of the basic building blocks of the English language. Every complete sentence needs to have a verb. Action verbs can help make students' writing exciting and dynamic. The more comfortable students become with verbs, the more interesting they can make their words on the page.

Unit Plan		[Offline]	[Online]
Lesson 1	Action Verbs	15 minutes	
Lesson 2	Verbs with Nouns	15 minutes	
Lesson 3	More Verbs with Nouns	15 minutes	
Lesson 4	Review Verbs	5 minutes	10 minutes
Lesson 5	Unit Checkpoint	15 minutes	varies

Action Verbs

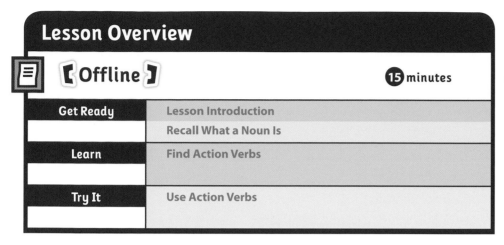

Lesson Overview

[Offline]   15 minutes

Get Ready	Lesson Introduction
	Recall What a Noun Is
Learn	Find Action Verbs
Try It	Use Action Verbs

Materials

Supplied
- *K¹² Language Arts Activity Book,* pp. WS 63–64

Also Needed
- whiteboard (optional)

Keywords

action verb – a word that shows action

Content Background

Verbs are words that show action or being. Action verbs show physical or mental action with words such as *run, jump, sit, dream,* and *sleep.* Being verbs are words such as *am, is, are, was,* and *were.* These verbs usually link the subject to a noun or adjective that follows the verb. In this unit, students will learn only about action verbs.

Big Ideas

Action verbs make writing come alive for readers.

[Offline] 15 minutes

Work **together** with students to complete Get Ready, Learn, and Try It activities.

Get Ready

Lesson Introduction
Prepare students for the lesson.

1. Explain that in this lesson, students will be learning about verbs. Verbs are words that show action.

2. Tell students that to learn about verbs, they must first remember what the two parts of a sentence are and what a noun is.

Objectives
- Recall what a noun is.
- Recall what a sentence is.

Recall What a Noun Is

Help students review nouns.

1. Write the following sentence on a whiteboard or a sheet of paper and read it with students.

   The horse runs.

   ► What are the two things that a sentence must have?
   a naming part and an action part

2. Tell students to draw one line under the naming part of the sentence and two lines under the action part. Students should draw one line under *horse* and two lines under *runs*.

3. Point to the word *horse*.

   ► What kind of word is this? noun
   ► What does a noun name? a person, place, or thing

4. Repeat that a noun is a word that names a person, place, or thing. Tell students that we also have a name for an action word, such as *runs*. An action word is called a verb.

Learn •

Find Action Verbs

Help students learn to identify action verbs. Turn to page WS 63 in *K¹² Language Arts Activity Book*.

> **Objectives**
> • Identify verbs in sentences.

1. **Say:** Let's do some actions! Let's jump up and down.

   Have students jump with you.

   Say: When we do this, we say that we _____ . jump

   Write *jump* on a whiteboard or piece of paper.

2. Run around the room. Have students run with you.
   Say: When we do this, we say that we _____ . run

   Write *run* on the whiteboard or paper.

3. Explain that the next question is tricky. Lie down on the floor and pretend to sleep. Have students pretend to sleep with you.
   Say: When we do this, we say that we _____ . sleep

   Write *sleep* on the whiteboard or paper.

4. Explain that all of these words show actions. They are **verbs**. Each of the verbs shows someone doing something.

5. Write the word *think* on the whiteboard or paper. Read it with students. Explain that even the word *think* is an action verb, because when we think, we are doing something with our brain.

6. Read the rule on the Activity Book page. Explain the example to students as needed.

7. Read the instructions on the Activity Book page. Help students complete the activity.

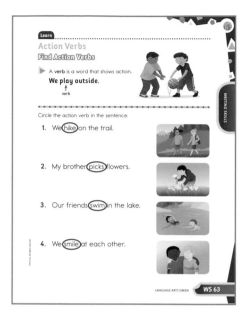

Try It

Use Action Verbs

Help students identify and use action verbs. Turn to page WS 64 in *K¹² Language Arts Activity Book*.

1. Read the first set of instructions to students. Read the sentences together.

2. Have students complete Exercises 1 and 2.

3. Read the second set of instructions to students. Have students complete Exercises 3–5. Provide support as necessary.

Objectives
- Identify verbs in sentences.
- Use action verbs in sentences.

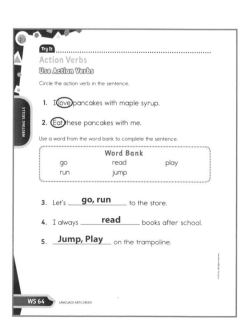

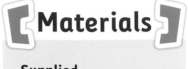

Verbs with Nouns

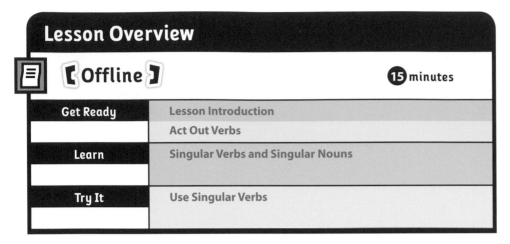

Lesson Overview

Offline 15 minutes

Get Ready	Lesson Introduction
	Act Out Verbs
Learn	Singular Verbs and Singular Nouns
Try It	Use Singular Verbs

Materials

Supplied
- *K¹² Language Arts Activity Book*, pp. WS 65–69

Also Needed
- scissors, adult
- whiteboard (optional)

Keywords

plural – more than one of something

singular – one of something

Advance Preparation

For the Get Ready, cut out the cards on page WS 65 in *K¹² Language Arts Activity Book*.

Content Background

► Subjects and verbs must agree in sentences. *Agreement* means that singular nouns work with singular verbs and plural nouns work with plural verbs.

   Example: My friend laughs at your jokes. (*Friend* is a singular noun, and *laughs* is a singular verb.)

   Example: Our friends laugh at your jokes. (*Friends* is a plural noun, and *laugh* is a plural verb.)

► In this unit, students will work only with regular present tense verbs. Regular present tense verbs show action that is happening now and end in an *s* when they are singular and no *s* when they are plural.

Big Ideas

Action verbs make writing come alive for readers.

 Offline 15 minutes

Work **together** with students to complete Get Ready, Learn, and Try It activities.

Get Ready

Objectives
- Identify verbs in sentences.
- Recall what a verb is.

Lesson Introduction

Prepare students for the lesson.

1. Explain that in this lesson, students will be learning more about verbs. Verbs are words that show action.

2. Explain that they are going to learn how to make nouns and verbs work together in a sentence.

Act Out Verbs

Get students thinking about verbs by using their body. Gather the cards that you cut out.

1. **Say:** What do verbs show? action

2. Show students the three cards. Tell students that they are going to use their body to show which word on each card is a verb.

3. Hold up the first card and read it with students. *I sit on the floor.*

4. **Say:** Use your body to show me what the verb is. Students should sit.
   - What is the verb? *sit*

5. Repeat Step 4 with the other two cards. Have students first act out the verb, then say what the verb is. (Have students make a "thinking face" for the card that uses the verb *think*.)

TIP Encouraging students to use their body to show each verb will reinforce that action verbs are often something that a person does.

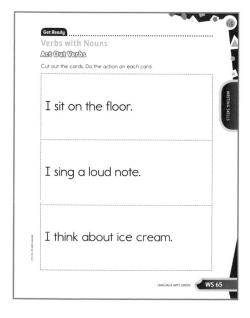

Learn

Singular Verbs and Singular Nouns

Help students learn that nouns and verbs must agree. Turn to pages WS 67 and 68 in *K¹² Language Arts Activity Book*.

Objectives
- Identify verbs that agree with their subjects.
- Define *singular*.
- Define *plural*.

1. Write the following sentences on a whiteboard or a sheet of paper and read them with students.

    The dog howls.
    The dogs howl.

2. Point to the first sentence.

    ▸ Is this sentence about one dog or more than one dog? one dog

    Write the word *singular* next to the sentence.

3. Point to the second sentence.

    ▸ Is this sentence about one dog or more than one dog? more than one dog

    Write the word *plural* next to the sentence.

4. Explain that the word *singular* means one and the word *plural* means more than one.

5. Tell students that to make a sentence work, the noun and the verb have to work together. Both have to be singular, or both have to be plural.

6. **Say:** Nouns and verbs are so great at working together that they will even share a letter. They agree to share an *s*.

    ▸ When both the noun and verb are singular, the verb gets the *s* at the end.
    ▸ When both the noun and verb are plural, the noun gets the *s* at the end.

7. Tell students that they are going to work on sentences where the noun is singular. That means the verb uses the *s*.

8. Read the rule and example on the Activity Book pages with students. Explain the example to students as needed.

9. Have students complete the Activity Book pages. Provide support as necessary.

TIP For some students, agreement between the noun and verb is easier to understand if students hear the sentence. Try reading aloud the sentences on the Activity Book pages while students listen, and see if they can more easily identify which sentence is correct.

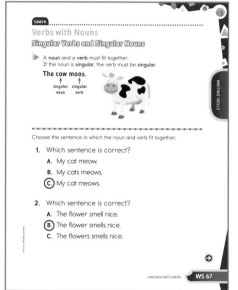

Learn

Verbs with Nouns
Singular Verbs and Singular Nouns

▶ A **noun** and a **verb** must fit together.
If the noun is **singular**, the verb must be **singular**.

The cow moos.

singular   singular
noun   verb

Choose the sentence in which the noun and verb fit together.

1. Which sentence is correct?
   A. My cat meow.
   B. My cats meows.
   C. My cat meows.

2. Which sentence is correct?
   A. The flower smell nice.
   B. The flower smells nice.
   C. The flowers smells nice.

WRITING SKILLS

LANGUAGE ARTS GREEN   **WS 67**

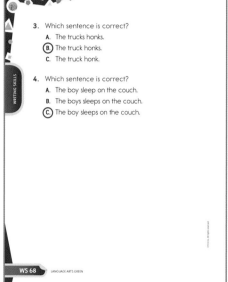

WS 68   LANGUAGE ARTS GREEN

WRITING SKILLS

3. Which sentence is correct?
   A. The trucks honks.
   B. The truck honks.
   C. The truck honk.

4. Which sentence is correct?
   A. The boy sleep on the couch.
   B. The boys sleeps on the couch.
   C. The boy sleeps on the couch.

Try It

Use Singular Verbs

Help students use singular verbs and nouns. Turn to page WS 69 in *K¹² Language Arts Activity Book*.

1. Read the first set of instructions to students. Read the sentences together.

2. Have students complete Exercises 1–3.

3. Read the second set of instructions to students. Have students complete Exercises 4 and 5. Provide support as necessary.

Objectives

- Use a verb that agrees with its subject.

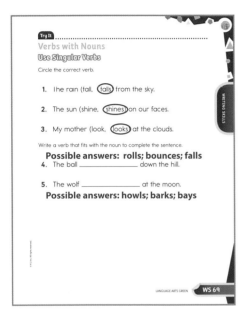

More Verbs with Nouns

Lesson Overview

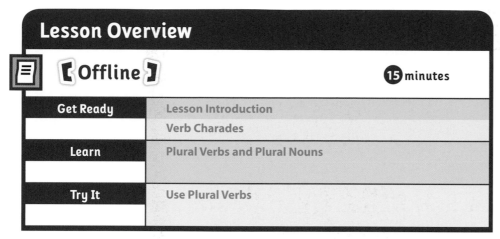

Offline — 15 minutes

Get Ready	Lesson Introduction
	Verb Charades
Learn	Plural Verbs and Plural Nouns
Try It	Use Plural Verbs

Materials

Supplied
- *K¹² Language Arts Activity Book*, pp. WS 70–71

Also Needed
- whiteboard (optional)

Keywords

plural – more than one of something
singular – one of something

Content Background

Singular nouns must use singular verbs and plural nouns must use plural verbs. Usually, plural nouns end with an *s* and plural verbs do not end with an *s*.

Example: The boys swing high in the air. (The plural noun *boys* ends in *s*. The plural verb *swing* does not end in *s*.)

Big Ideas

Action verbs make writing come alive for readers.

Offline 15 minutes

Work **together** with students to complete Get Ready, Learn, and Try It activities.

Get Ready

Lesson Introduction
Prepare students for the lesson. Explain that in this lesson, students will be learning more about how nouns and verbs work together.

Objectives
- Recall what a verb is.

Verb Charades

Help students remember what verbs are.

1. **Say:** What do verbs show? action

2. Explain that you are going to play verb charades. You will take turns showing action verbs. To start, you will act out a verb and students will guess what it is.

3. Make a kicking motion with your leg, over and over.

   ▸ What verb am I acting out? *kick*

4. Tell students it's their turn to show an action verb. Have them act out an action verb. Try to guess the verb.

5. Continue the game for a few more turns.

Learn

Plural Verbs and Plural Nouns

Help students learn more about how nouns and verbs work together. Turn to page WS 70 in *K¹² Language Arts Activity Book*.

1. Write the following sentences on a whiteboard or a sheet of paper and read them with students.

   The girl runs.
   The girls run.

2. Have students point to each sentence and say which has a singular noun and singular verb and which has a plural noun and plural verb. Singular: *The girl runs.* Plural: *The girls run.*

3. **Say:** When both the noun and verb are singular, the verb gets the *s*. When both the noun and verb are plural, the noun gets the *s*.

4. Explain that students are going to work on sentences that have plural nouns and verbs.

Objectives
- Identify verbs that agree with their subjects.

5. Read the rule and example on the Activity Book page with students. Explain the example to students as needed.

6. Have students complete the Activity Book page. Provide support as necessary.

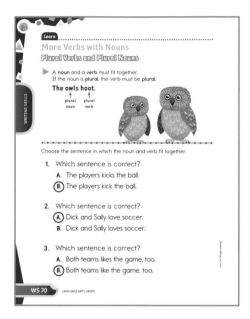

Try It

Use Plural Verbs

Help students use plural verbs and nouns. Turn to page WS 71 in *K¹² Language Arts Activity Book*.

1. Read the first set of directions to students. Read the sentences together.

2. Have students complete Exercises 1–3.

3. Read the second set of directions to students. Have students complete Exercises 4 and 5. Provide support as necessary.

Objectives

- Use a verb that agrees with its subject.

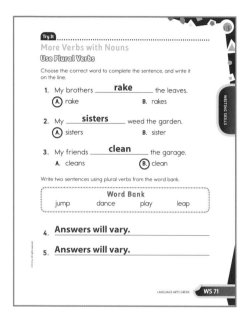

Review Verbs

Lesson Overview

Online — 10 minutes

Review	Track and Field Day

Offline — 5 minutes

Try It	Journal: Verbs You Like and Verbs You Don't Like

Materials

Supplied
- *K¹² My Journal,* pp. 132–133

Also Needed
- crayons

Keywords

action verb – a word that shows action

plural – more than one of something

singular – one of something

Online — 10 minutes

Students will review what they have learned about verbs to prepare for the Unit Checkpoint. Help students locate the online activity and provide support as needed.

Review

Track and Field Day
Students will work online to review what they have learned about verbs.

Offline Alternative

No computer access? Find a magazine or newspaper that tells a story that has action. Have students find as many action verbs as possible. Help them identify singular verbs and plural verbs by looking for the *s*. Have students choose one or more of the verbs and use them in sentences.

Objectives

- Identify verbs in sentences.
- Identify verbs that agree with their subjects.
- Use a verb that agrees with its subject.
- Use action verbs in sentences.

[Offline] 5 minutes

Students will write on their own in their journal. Help students locate the offline activity.

Try It ....

✏️ **Journal: Verbs You Like and Verbs You Don't Like**

Students will go to their journal and write on their own. Gather *K¹² My Journal* and have students turn to pages 132 and 133 in Writing Skills.

1. To help students prepare, ask them to think about one thing they like doing and one thing they do not like doing.

2. Read the prompt with students. Have them respond to the prompt in their journal. As necessary, remind them that there are no correct or incorrect answers.

TIP The amount of time students need to complete this activity will vary. Allow them to use the rest of the allotted time to complete this activity. If they have more they would like to write, you may let them complete their entry at a later time. If students are having trouble getting started, suggest that they draw a picture that has a lot of action and describe it to you. You can transcribe their words for them.

Objectives

- Write in a journal.
- Freewrite about a topic.

Action!   Date _____

Write five verbs you do like to do, **or** five verbs you do not like to do, **or** five verbs you want to learn to do.

_____

_____

_____

_____

_____

_____

_____

132

Draw a picture.

⌐ ⌐

_____

_____

_____

133

Unit Checkpoint

Lesson Overview

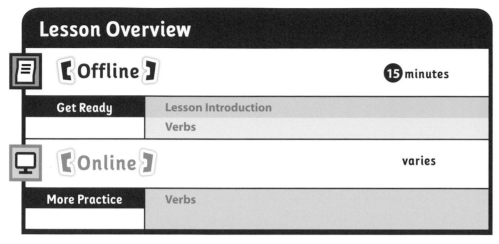

📄 **〔 Offline 〕**		🕐 **15** minutes
Get Ready	Lesson Introduction	
	Verbs	

🖥 **〔 Online 〕**		**varies**
More Practice	Verbs	

〔 Materials 〕

Supplied

- *K¹² Language Arts Assessments*, pp. WS 13–16

〔 Offline 〕 🕐 **15** minutes

Work **together** with students to complete the Unit Checkpoint.

Unit Checkpoint ●

Lesson Introduction

Prepare students for the lesson.

1. Tell students that they are going to complete a Unit Checkpoint to show what they have learned.

2. Explain that if they miss one or more questions, they can continue to practice this grammar skill.

> ⭐ **Objectives**
> - Identify verbs in sentences.
> - Identify verbs that agree with their subjects.
> - Use a verb that agrees with its subject.
> - Use action verbs in sentences.

Verbs

Explain that students are going to show what they have learned about identifying and using action verbs.

1. Give students the Unit Checkpoint pages.

2. Read the directions together. If needed, read the questions and answer choices to students. Have students complete the Checkpoint on their own.

3. Use the Answer Key to score the Checkpoint and then enter the results online.

4. Review each exercise with students. Work with students to correct any exercise that they missed.

 TIP Students who answered one or more questions incorrectly should continue to practice this grammar skill. Write several sentences and ask students to identify the verbs in each sentence. Help them find action verbs and practice making verbs and nouns agree.

Reward: When students score 80 percent or above on the Unit Checkpoint, add a sticker for this unit on the My Accomplishments chart.

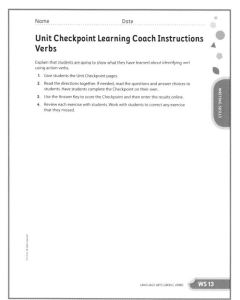

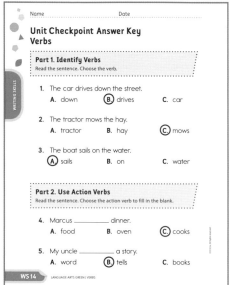

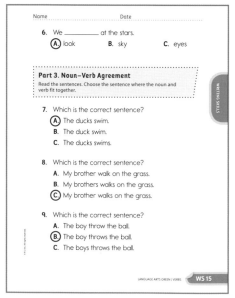

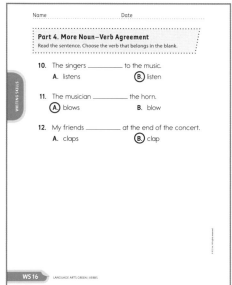

 **varies**

If necessary, work with students to complete the More Practice activity.

More Practice

Verbs

If students scored less than 80 percent on the Unit Checkpoint, have them complete the appropriate review activities listed in the table online. Help students locate the activities and provide support as needed.

 Objectives
- Evaluate Checkpoint results and choose activities to review.

Friendly Letter

Unit Focus

In this unit, students will learn how to write a friendly letter. They will pick someone to whom to tell some news, write in letter format, and mail their letter. Students will

▶ Think about what kind of information should go in a letter.
▶ Think about who the audience for a letter is.
▶ Learn the proper form for a letter.
▶ Learn how to properly address an envelope.

Students will write and revise a letter, adding details and making corrections. Letter writing is a great opportunity for young writers to experience what it means to have a particular audience for their writing. They are writing with a certain person in mind, and the act of mailing the letter means that someone will definitely read what they have written. This unit will help students become more thoughtful and intentional with their writing, and it will provide an exciting opportunity for students to see the results of their work.

Unit Plan		[Offline]	[Online]
Lesson 1	Get Started with Your News	**15** minutes	
Lesson 2	Friendly Letter Form	**15** minutes	
Lesson 3	Draft Your Letter	**15** minutes	
Lesson 4	Address an Envelope	**15** minutes	
Lesson 5	Write and Mail Your Letter	**15** minutes	varies

Get Started with Your News

Lesson Overview

[Offline]   **15** minutes

Get Ready	Lesson Introduction
	What Is News?
Try It	Freewrite: Use Your Journal

[Materials]

Supplied
- *K¹² Language Arts Activity Book*, p. WS 73
- *K¹² My Journal*, pp. 134–135

Also Needed
- scissors, adult
- whiteboard (optional)

Keywords

freewriting – a way for a writer to pick a topic and write as much as possible about it within a set time limit

news – information about, or report of, recent events

Advance Preparation

For the Get Ready, cut out the cards on page WS 73 in *K¹² Language Arts Activity Book*.

Content Background

To begin thinking about how to write a letter, students must first think about how to explain events in their own lives. This activity teaches them the concept of news, or noteworthy events that can be reported to another person.

Big Ideas

Friendly letters are written to share news, information, ideas, or feelings.

 **15 minutes**

Work **together** with students to complete Get Ready and Try It activities.

Get Ready

Lesson Introduction
Prepare students for the lesson.

1. Explain that in this lesson, students will be writing in their journal. Remind students that their journal is a place for them to be creative and explore writing. They will not be judged or graded.

2. Explain that students will freewrite news, or things that have recently happened to them that they would like to share.

 Objectives
- Define *news*.
- Identify newsworthy events.

What Is News?
Help students think of what to write about. Gather the cards from page WS 73 in *K¹² Language Arts Activity Book*.

1. Write the word *news* on a whiteboard or a sheet of paper, and read it with students.

2. Explain to students that we use the word *news* to describe events from our lives that are important or interesting.

3. Tell students that they are going to look at some statements that Alexander made. They have to decide which information is important, and therefore news, and which information is not important.

4. Help students divide the sentence cards into two piles: *news* and *not news*.

Try It

. . . .

✏️ Freewrite: Use Your Journal

Help students freewrite about something fun they have done. Gather *K¹² My Journal* and have students turn to pages 134 and 135 in Writing Skills. Read aloud the prompt at the top of the page to students.

Objectives

- Generate ideas for writing.
- Freewrite about a topic.
- Write in a journal.

1. Ask students to think of something fun they did last weekend.

2. Ask students to think about what they did, and which parts are important enough to be called *news*. Have them write that news in their journal.

   ▸ Explain that they are freewriting, or writing ideas on the page.
   ▸ Tell them that they can tell their news in any way they want. They can focus on the main parts of the activity, or write about a specific set of details.

3. If students are struggling, help by asking questions. Answers to questions may vary.

   ▸ Was this the first time you did this?
   ▸ Were you alone, or were you with someone?
   ▸ Why was this activity fun?

4. Have students explain their news to you. Do not evaluate students' writing. As long as students have written some ideas on paper, their responses are acceptable.

TIP The amount of time students need to complete this activity will vary. Allow them to use the rest of the allotted time to complete this activity. If they have more they would like to write, you may let them complete their entry at a later time. If students are having trouble getting started, you might tell them to just list ideas or words. They may even draw a picture and describe it to you. You can transcribe their words for them.

Last Weekend   Date _____

Write about something fun that you did last weekend.

_____

_____

_____

_____

_____

_____

_____

WRITING SKILLS

134

Draw a picture.

_____

_____

_____

WRITING SKILLS

135

Friendly Letter Form

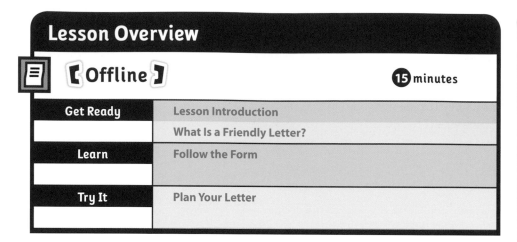

Lesson Overview

Offline · 15 minutes

Get Ready	Lesson Introduction
	What Is a Friendly Letter?
Learn	Follow the Form
Try It	Plan Your Letter

Materials

Supplied
- *K¹² Language Arts Activity Book*, pp. WS 75–78
- *K¹² My Journal*, pp. 134–135

Also Needed
- scissors, adult
- household objects – envelope

Advance Preparation

For the Get Ready, cut out the letter on page WS 75 in *K¹² Language Arts Activity Book*. Put it in an envelope. If possible, put the envelope in a mailbox from which students can retrieve it.

Big Ideas

- When a writer uses the correct letter format, including capitalization and punctuation, the reader can focus on the writer's ideas.
- Writing varies by purpose and audience. The specific reason for writing and the writer's intended readers (audience) determine the correct form and language to use.
- A friendly letter is written to share thoughts and feelings. It follows a specific form.

Keywords

body (of a friendly letter) – the main text of a friendly letter

closing (of a friendly letter) – the part of a friendly letter that follows the body *Example: Your friend* or *Love*

friendly letter – a kind of letter used to share thoughts, feelings, and news

greeting – the part of a letter that begins with the word *Dear* followed by a person's name; also called the salutation

heading – the first part of a letter that has the writer's address and the date

signature – the end of a letter where the writer writes his or her name

[Offline] 15 minutes

Work **together** with students to complete Get Ready, Learn, and Try It activities.

Get Ready ....

Lesson Introduction
Prepare students for the lesson.

1. Introduce students to the friendly letter. Tell them that a friendly letter is used to send someone news.

2. Explain the parts of a letter, and help students organize facts that go into a letter.

> **Objectives**
> - Recognize what a friendly letter is.
> - Identify the audience of a friendly letter.
> - Identify the purpose of a friendly letter.

What Is a Friendly Letter?
Teach students what a friendly letter is by preparing a letter they can find in a mailbox.

1. Tell students that you have something special for them. If you were able to place the letter in a mailbox, take students to the mailbox and let them retrieve it. Otherwise, pull out the friendly letter in its envelope and show it to them.

2. Open the envelope with students and look at the letter. Tell students that this is a friendly letter. Discuss some uses of friendly letters.

   ▶ To share news
   ▶ To invite you to a party or event
   ▶ To give you important information

3. Read the friendly letter with students. Discuss what is in the letter.

   ▶ Who is the letter written to? Cousin Jack
   ▶ Who is the letter from? Alison
   ▶ What is the letter about? Alison is in a play.

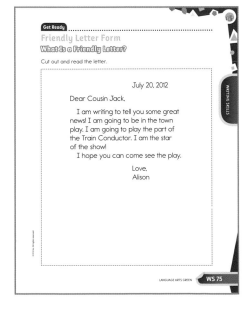

Learn

Follow the Form

Help students understand the parts of a letter. Turn to page WS 77 in *K¹² Language Arts Activity Book*.

Objectives
- Recognize the parts of a friendly letter.

1. Explain to students that a friendly letter is made up of different parts. Each part of the letter gives an important piece of information.

2. Have students touch their head, mouth, body, legs, and feet as you say the following chant:

   The head is the date, the mouth is the greeting,
   Next you have the whole body,
   Then the closing's your legs.
   And the signature is your feet.
   Date, greeting, body, closing, feet.

3. Read the directions on the Activity Book page.

4. **Say:** A letter is like a person. Let's look at it from its head to its feet.

5. Point to the date and explain that this is the date. It is the head of the letter. Touch your head and tell students we start with the date to remember when we thought of our news. Have students write *date* on the appropriate line.

6. Point to the greeting and explain that it is the greeting. It is the mouth of the letter. Touch your mouth and tell students that we use our mouths to say hello. Have students write *greeting* on the appropriate line.

7. Point to the body and explain that it is the body of the letter. Touch the trunk of your body and tell students that the body has all the important parts of the letter, the way our body has important parts like the heart. Have students write *body* on the appropriate line.

8. Point to the closing and explain that this is the closing. It is the legs of the letter. Touch your legs and explain that we say good-bye with the closing and we walk away. Have students write *closing* on the appropriate line.

9. Point out that the signature is where students put their name. *Signature* is a word that means your name. Have students write *name* on the appropriate line.

10. Have students look over the letter again.

    ▸ What parts of the letter are capitalized? *the date, the greeting, new sentences, the closing, and the signature*
      Say: Underline the capital letters in the date and greeting in the letter.

    ▸ What parts of the letter have commas? *the greeting and the closing*
      Say: Circle the commas in the letter.

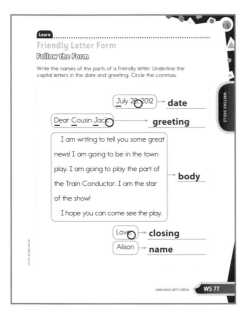

Try It

 Plan Your Letter

Help students fill in the graphic organizer. Turn to page WS 78 in *K¹² Language Arts Activity Book* and pages 134 and 135 in *K¹² My Journal*.

1. Read the instructions on the Activity Book page to students.

2. Have students review their journal entry to decide whether they want to write about the events mentioned there or some other news.

3. Have students fill in each blank on the graphic organizer to prepare them to write a friendly letter. Have them write the date, a greeting, three ideas or pieces of news that they are going to write about, and a closing. Tell them that they will write their signature, their own name, when they are ready to sign their letter.

4. Provide support as necessary.

Objectives
- Identify the audience of a friendly letter.
- Identify the purpose of a friendly letter.
- Recognize the parts of a friendly letter.
- Use a graphic organizer to plan.
- Use established conventions for a friendly letter.

Try It

Friendly Letter Form

Plan Your Letter

Fill in the blanks with information for the letter you plan to write.

Date _____

Greeting _____

Body _____

1. _____

2. _____

3. _____

Closing _____

Name _____

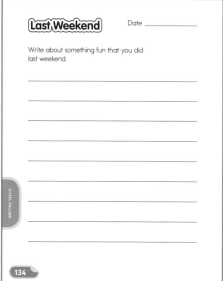

Last Weekend   Date _____

Write about something fun that you did last weekend.

_____
_____
_____
_____
_____
_____
_____
_____

Draw a picture.

_____
_____
_____
_____

Draft Your Letter

Lesson Overview

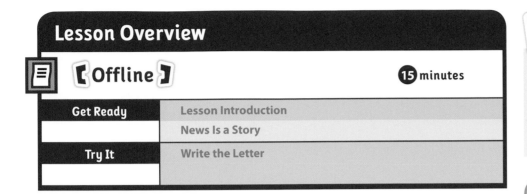

[Offline]　　　　　　　　　**15** minutes

Get Ready	Lesson Introduction
	News Is a Story
Try It	Write the Letter

Advance Preparation

Have students gather completed page WS 78 (Plan Your Letter) in *K¹² Language Arts Activity Book*.

Big Ideas

▸ When a writer uses the correct letter format, including capitalization and punctuation, the reader can focus on the writer's ideas.

▸ Writing varies by purpose and audience. The specific reason for writing and the writer's intended readers (audience) determine the correct form and language to use.

Materials

Supplied

- *K¹² Language Arts Activity Book*, pp. WS 78–79
- Story Card C

Keywords

body (of a friendly letter) – the main text of a friendly letter

closing (of a friendly letter) – the part of a friendly letter that follows the body *Example: Your friend* or *Love*

friendly letter – a kind of letter used to share thoughts, feelings, and news

greeting – the part of a letter that begins with the word *Dear* followed by a person's name; also called the salutation

heading – the first part of a letter that has the writer's address and the date

signature – the end of a letter where the writer writes his or her name

[Offline] 15 minutes

Work **together** with students to complete Get Ready and Try It activities.

Get Ready ....

Lesson Introduction

Prepare students for the lesson.

1. Tell students that they will review how to put parts of a story in order.

2. Tell them that they are going to use a graphic organizer to draft their letter.

News Is a Story

Help students understand how to put the different parts of news in order. Gather Story Card C.

1. Tell students that when you are giving people news, you are telling them a story.

2. Tell students that for people to understand their news, they need to tell the facts, ideas, and opinions in a way that makes sense.

3. Show students Story Card C.

   ▶ What is happening in the picture? People are making a building.

4. Have students make up a news story about the building as if they were reporters on TV or radio. If students have difficulty, start them off by saying, "We are getting a new library in our town!" Prompt them to think of details about the library. Answers to questions may vary.

   ▶ Who is building the library?
   ▶ Who will use it?
   ▶ Why is it being built?
   ▶ Where might it be located?
   ▶ How will it change the community?

5. As students are describing their news, tell them that they need to help the audience understand that things happen in a specific order. Have them use words like *first*, *next*, *then*, and *finally* as they tell their story.

6. Once students have told their news story like a reporter, have them pretend the story is a joke, a fairy tale, or a scary story. Remind them to use transition words each time they say something new.

TIP It can be hard for students to understand that simple facts are a story. By acting out their news dramatically, students start to hear how their facts connect in an interesting way.

> **Objectives**
> - Organize ideas in a logical order.
> - Organize ideas through sequencing.
> - Use transitions to connect ideas.
> - Identify important questions that need to be answered.

Try It

✏️ **Write the Letter**

Help students draft their letter. Turn to page WS 79 in *K¹² Language Arts Activity Book* and gather the completed graphic organizer on page WS 78.

1. Read the instructions on the Activity Book page to students. Have students refer to the graphic organizer as they fill in the form letter. Have them copy the date, greeting, closing, and signature. To write their greeting, they will need to select a person to whom they are writing.

2. Have students write their facts as complete sentences in the body. Encourage them to use transitions words such as *first*, *next*, *then*, and *finally*.

3. Provide support as necessary.

★ **Objectives**

- Use a capital letter to begin a sentence and an end mark to end it.
- Use established conventions for a friendly letter.
- Write a narrative with a beginning, middle, and end.
- Write a series of related sentences.
- Write complete sentences.
- Write sentences with appropriate spacing between words.
- Write sentences with legible handwriting.

Address an Envelope

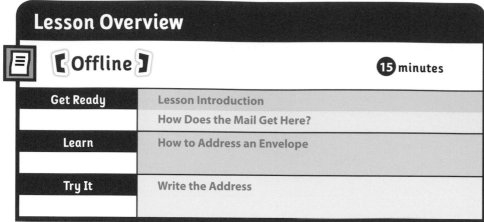

Lesson Overview

Offline 15 minutes

Get Ready	Lesson Introduction
	How Does the Mail Get Here?
Learn	How to Address an Envelope
Try It	Write the Address

Materials

Supplied

- *K¹² Language Arts Activity Book*, pp. WS 81–83

Also Needed

- scissors, adult
- whiteboard (optional)
- household objects – envelope, stamp

Advance Preparation

For the Get Ready, cut out the cards on page WS 81 in *K¹² Language Arts Activity Book*. For the Try It, gather an envelope and a stamp. Find the addresses for the people to whom students want to write and copy the addresses on a sheet of paper.

Big Ideas

Envelopes must be addressed in a precise format for the post office to deliver the mail accurately.

〔 Offline 〕 ⑮ minutes

Work **together** with students to complete Get Ready, Learn, and Try It activities.

Get Ready

Lesson Introduction
Prepare students for the lesson.

Objectives
• Understand how the mail is delivered.

1. Tell students that a letter needs to be addressed in the correct way for the post office to deliver it.

2. Explain that when you send a letter, it has to go through many steps to reach its destination.

How Does the Mail Get Here?
Help students understand how the mail gets from one place to another. Gather the cards from page WS 81 in *K¹² Language Arts Activity Book*.

1. Lay the cards on the floor, spaced about 1 foot apart, and read them with students.

2. Explain that it takes a lot of steps for a letter to get to where it is going.

3. Hold students' hands and hop together from card to card, saying the following chant:

   First, your house,
   Then, your post office,
   Next, your friend's post office,
   Finally, your friend's house.

4. Have students turn around and hop back from card to card to show how a reply could be sent back from a friend's house to their house.

Learn

How to Address an Envelope

Help students understand how to address an envelope. Turn to page WS 83 in
K¹² Language Arts Activity Book.

1. Look at the envelope on the Activity Book page. Explain that the words in the upper left corner are the address of the person sending the letter, and the words in the middle are the address of the person receiving the letter.

2. On a whiteboard or a sheet of paper, draw an upside-down V, narrow at the top and wide at the bottom.

3. Point to the tip of the V, and explain that when you write an address, you start with something small, like just one person.

4. Move your hands from the tip of the V down to the mouth of the V. As you do, explain that in an address, you move from something small to something big. You move from a person to a street to a city to a state.

5. Point to the envelope on the Activity Book page. Tell students that both addresses follow the same small-to-big pattern. Read each address with students. Explain that the two capital letters near the end of each address are a short way of writing the name of a state. The letters *AK* stand for Alaska, and the letters *AZ* stand for Arizona.

6. When you get to the end of each address, point to the zip code and explain that it is a special way for the post office to keep track of addresses.

7. Point out the stamp to students. Tell them that it costs money to mail a letter, and a stamp is proof that you paid.

TIP To help students understand the structure of an address, you might take a walk around the neighborhood. Point out house numbers and street names, and find something that has the name of the town as well. Looking at a map is another good way to connect this concept to everyday life.

Try It

Write the Address

Help students address an envelope. Gather the envelope, the stamp, and the sheet of paper with recipients' addresses.

1. Tell students that they are going to address an envelope.

2. Give students the envelope. Tell them their own address and have them write it in the upper left corner of the envelope.

3. Show students the address of the person they are writing to. Have them copy it onto the center of the envelope.

4. Have students put the stamp on the envelope.

TIP Keep the stamped, addressed envelope in a safe place. Students will need it to mail their completed letter.

Objectives
- Address an envelope.
- Use a capital letter to begin a proper noun.
- Use abbreviations for addresses, units of measurement, days, months, and titles.

Write and Mail Your Letter

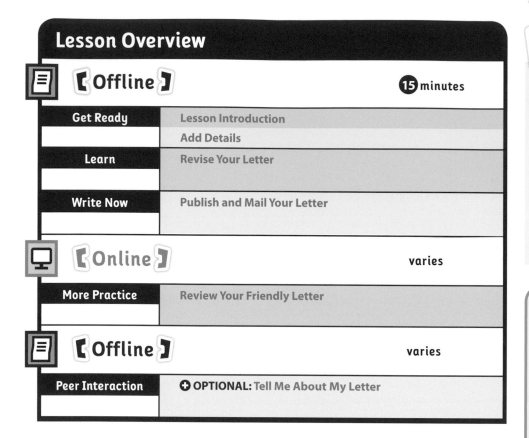

Lesson Overview

Offline — 15 minutes

Get Ready	Lesson Introduction
	Add Details
Learn	Revise Your Letter
Write Now	Publish and Mail Your Letter

Online — varies

More Practice	Review Your Friendly Letter

Offline — varies

Peer Interaction	⊕ OPTIONAL: Tell Me About My Letter

Materials

Supplied
- *K¹² Language Arts Activity Book*, pp. WS 79, 85–87
- Publish and Mail Your Letter: Rubric and Sample Responses (printout)

Also Needed
- household objects – addressed envelope

Keywords

body (of a friendly letter) – the main text of a friendly letter

closing (of a friendly letter) – the part of a friendly letter that follows the body *Example: Your friend or Love*

friendly letter – a kind of letter used to share thoughts, feelings, and news

greeting – the part of a letter that begins with the word *Dear* followed by a person's name; also called the salutation

heading – the first part of a letter that has the writer's address and the date

publishing – the stage or step of the writing process in which the writer makes a clean copy of the piece and shares it

revising – the stage or step of the writing process in which the writer rereads and edits the draft, correcting errors and making changes in content or organization that improve the piece

signature – the end of a letter where the writer writes his or her name

Advance Preparation

Gather students' draft letter on page WS 79 (Write the Letter) in *K¹² Language Arts Activity Book*. Gather the envelope that students addressed.

Big Ideas

► When a writer uses the correct letter format, including capitalization and punctuation, the reader can focus on the writer's ideas.

► Writing varies by purpose and audience. The specific reason for writing and the writer's intended readers (audience) determine the correct form and language to use.

► A friendly letter is written to share thoughts and feelings. It follows a specific form.

 **15** minutes

Work **together** with students to complete Get Ready, Learn, and Write Now activities.

Get Ready ....

Lesson Introduction
Prepare students for the lesson.

1. Explain that students are going to finish their letter.

2. Tell students that they are going to publish their letter by mailing it.

> **Objectives**
> • Add details to sentences.
> • Identify important questions that need to be answered.

Add Details
Gather students' draft letter on page WS 79 in *K¹² Language Arts Activity Book* and have them reread their work. Help students think about how to add details to their news.

1. Tell students that to make their letters more interesting, they need to add details.

2. **Say:** The boy won the race.
   Explain that to make this idea more interesting, we can ask questions.

   ▸ Which boy won? The tall boy won the race.
   ▸ Where did he win? The tall boy won the race at the park.
   ▸ Why did he win? The tall boy won the race at the park because he was fast.

3. Have students ask *which, where, why,* and *how* questions while looking at their letter to see if they can think of details to add.

Learn

Revise Your Letter

Gather students' draft letter on page WS 79 in *K¹² Language Arts Activity Book* and have them reread their work in preparation for revising it. Help students add to their draft and fix parts that need corrections. Students can make notes on their draft to prepare for writing the final version.

1. Help students revise their letter. Read their draft and discuss changes they could make.

2. Encourage students to add more detail by asking questions about their news.

   ▸ At what time did this happen?
   ▸ How did this make you feel?
   ▸ Was anyone else with you when this happened?

3. Help students find incomplete sentences. Make sure that all sentences have a naming part and an action part.

4. Help students find places where they need to add a capital letter or a punctuation mark.

5. Help students put their ideas in order, using order words such as *first*, *then*, *next*, and *finally*.

Objectives

- Add details to sentences.
- Identify important questions that need to be answered.
- Recognize that a complete sentence begins with a capital letter and has an end mark.
- Edit a letter for errors in capitalization and punctuation.
- Organize ideas in a logical order.
- Use transitions to connect ideas.

Write Now

 Publish and Mail Your Letter

Help students complete the final copy of their letter. Turn to page WS 85 in *K¹² Language Arts Activity Book.*

1. Help students rewrite their letter on the form on the Activity Book page.

2. Encourage students to write clearly and legibly.

3. Once students have finished writing their letter, have them put the letter into the envelope but not seal the envelope. After you have reviewed the letter, you and the students can walk to the mailbox to mail it.

4. Use the materials and instructions in the online lesson to evaluate students' finished writing. You will be looking at students' writing to evaluate the following:

   ▶ **Purpose and Content:** The letter is to someone appropriate and communicates information about something fun or newsworthy that the writer did. There are a few details. There is some evidence of revision.

   ▶ **Structure and Organization:** Most of the letter follows correct letter format (date, greeting, body, closing, and name), although there may be one mistake.

   ▶ **Grammar and Mechanics:** The letter has mostly complete sentences and makes good use of verbs and describing words. There is some evidence of proofreading.

5. Enter students' scores for each rubric category online.

6. If students' writing scored a 1 in any criterion, work with students to proofread and revise their work.

TIP The amount of time students need to complete this activity will vary. Students need only work for 15 minutes.

 Reward: When students' writing achieves "meets objectives" in all three categories on the grading rubric, add a sticker for this unit on the My Accomplishments chart.

Objectives

- Organize ideas through sequencing.
- Spell common, frequently used words correctly.
- Use a capital letter to begin a sentence and an end mark to end it.
- Use capital letters in the greeting and closing of a letter.
- Use commas in the greeting and closing of a letter.
- Use correct format for a letter.
- Use established conventions for a friendly letter.
- Write a letter.
- Write a series of related sentences.
- Write complete sentences.
- Write sentences with appropriate spacing between words.
- Write sentences with legible handwriting.

 **varies**

If necessary, work with students to complete the More Practice activity.

More Practice

Review Your Friendly Letter

If students' writing did not meet objectives, have students complete the appropriate review activity listed in the table online.

Objectives
- Evaluate writing and choose activities to review and revise.

► Follow the online instructions to help students edit and revise their work.

► Impress upon students that revising makes their work better. Writing is a process, and each time they revise their work, they are making their writing stronger and better.

► When you provide feedback, always begin with something positive. For example, you might point out a detail students wrote (even if it's the only detail) and explain how it helps you picture the scene: "You wrote that the leaves were 'orange and gold.' That detail, the color of the leaves, really helps me picture the forest."

► Place the final written work together with the rubric and the sample letters in the writing portfolio. This information is useful for you to track progress, and it helps students to refer back to their own work. They can see how they improve and review feedback to remember areas that need revising.

► Help students locate the activities and provide support as needed.

 **15 minutes**

If necessary, work with students to complete the Peer Interaction activity.

Peer Interaction

⊕ OPTIONAL: Tell Me About My Letter

This activity is OPTIONAL. It is intended for students who have extra time and would benefit from extra practice. Feel free to skip this activity.

Objectives
- Use guidance from adults and peers to revise writing.
- Collaborate with peers on writing projects.

Students can benefit from exchanging letters with someone they know or another student. This activity will work best if students exchange their letter with other students who are taking the same class, but you may copy the Activity Book page and send it to someone else who is willing to give students feedback. Students should receive feedback on the content of their letter. To complete this optional activity, turn to page WS 87 in *K¹² Language Arts Activity Book*.

1. Have students exchange letters with other students.

2. Have students use the Activity Book page to provide others with feedback about their writing.

3. Have students use the feedback provided from other students to revise their own letter.

Pronouns

Unit Focus

In this unit, students will learn to recognize and use pronouns, words that take the place of nouns. Students will learn to

- ▶ Recognize and use personal pronouns.
- ▶ Recognize and use possessive pronouns.
- ▶ Recognize and use indefinite pronouns.

When students are able to use pronouns properly, they are able to make their writing more dynamic and interesting. Sentences that use pronouns read more clearly and are easier to understand because pronouns help avoid repetition.

Unit Plan		〔Offline〕	〔Online〕
Lesson 1	Personal Pronouns	**15** minutes	
Lesson 2	Possessive Pronouns	**15** minutes	
Lesson 3	Indefinite Pronouns	**15** minutes	
Lesson 4	Review Pronouns	**10** minutes	**5** minutes
Lesson 5	Unit Checkpoint	**15** minutes	varies

Personal Pronouns

Lesson Overview

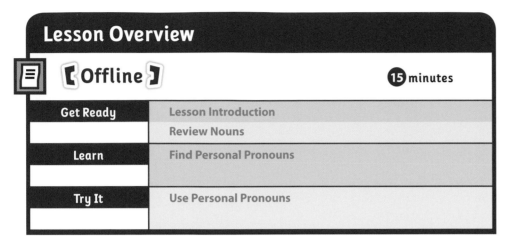

Offline   **15** minutes

Get Ready	Lesson Introduction
	Review Nouns
Learn	Find Personal Pronouns
Try It	Use Personal Pronouns

Materials

Supplied
- *K¹² Language Arts Activity Book*, pp. WS 89–90
- Story Card G

Also Needed
- whiteboard (optional)

Keywords

pronoun – a word that takes the place of one or more nouns

Content Background

▸ Pronouns are words that take the place of nouns. They may be masculine (*he*), feminine (*she*), or neuter (*it*). They may be singular (*I*) or plural (*them*).

▸ Personal pronouns are the most common kind of pronoun. *I, me, you, she, her, he, him, it, we, us, they,* and *them* are the personal pronouns. This lesson focuses on personal pronouns.

Big Ideas

Using pronouns helps writers avoid monotony because they do not have to keep repeating the same nouns.

 **30 minutes**

Work **together** with students to complete Get Ready, Learn, and Try It activities.

Get Ready

Lesson Introduction

Prepare students for the lesson.

1. Tell students that they will review what a noun is.

2. Explain that they will be learning about pronouns. A pronoun is a word that takes the place of a noun.

3. Tell students that they will practice recognizing and using pronouns in sentences.

 Objectives
- Recall what a noun is.

Review Nouns

Help students review nouns. Gather Story Card G.

1. Tell students that they are going to play a finding game.
   Say: I am going to turn over a story card, and I want you to name all the people you see.

2. Turn over Story Card G. Encourage students to use their fingers to keep track of the number of people they find as they call them out.

3. Give students about 10 seconds to search. Then ask them how many people they found.

4. Repeat the game, this time looking for things.

5. Once students have found as many things as possible, talk about what they were looking for.

   ▸ What kind of word names people and things? a noun
   ▸ What else can a noun name? a place

TIP Although a noun names a person, place, or thing, these lessons about pronouns will focus on taking the place of nouns that name people and things. Help students focus more on these kinds of nouns.

Learn

Find Personal Pronouns

Help students learn to identify pronouns. Turn to page WS 89 in *K¹² Language Arts Activity Book.*

1. Write the following sentence on a whiteboard or sheet of paper and have students read it with you:
   Tom jogged, and Tom played, and then Mom fed Tom.

2. **Say:** This sentence doesn't sound very good. The name *Tom* is used too much.

3. Explain that the sentence can be improved by using pronouns. Explain that pronouns take the place of nouns.

4. In the sentence, replace the second *Tom* with *he* and the third *Tom* with *him.* Read the new sentence with students:
   Tom jogged, and he played, and then Mom fed him.

5. Explain that *he* and *him* are pronouns. These pronouns replace nouns that name people.

6. Write the following pairs of sentences on the whiteboard and read them with students:
   Jane ran. She ran.
   The cat yawned. It yawned.
   James talked to his parents. James talked to them.

7. Point to the words *she*, *it*, and *them* and explain that they are all pronouns.

8. Write the word *I* on the whiteboard. Point to it and tell students that *I* is always capitalized, even when it is not the first word in a sentence.

9. Read the rules on the Activity Book page. Explain the examples to students as needed.

10. Read the instructions on the Activity Book page. Help students complete the activity.

Objectives

- Recognize pronouns.

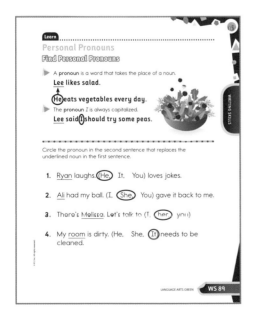

Try It

Use Personal Pronouns

Help students identify and use pronouns. Turn to page WS 90 in *K¹² Language Arts Activity Book*.

1. Read the first set of instructions to students. Have them choose a pronoun from the word bank to fill in the blank in each sentence.

2. Read the second set of instructions to students. Have students find the pronoun *I* in each sentence and correct it. You may want to model putting a slash through the *i* and writing *I* above it.

3. Provide assistance as necessary.

Objectives
- Use singular and plural pronouns.
- Use a capital letter for the pronoun *I*.

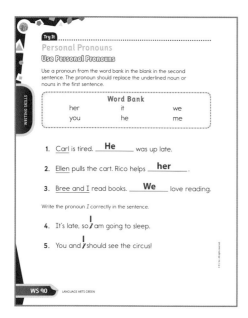

Possessive Pronouns

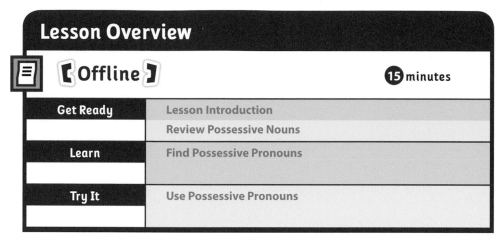

Lesson Overview

[Offline]   15 minutes

Get Ready	Lesson Introduction
	Review Possessive Nouns
Learn	Find Possessive Pronouns
Try It	Use Possessive Pronouns

[Materials]

Supplied
- *K¹² Language Arts Activity Book*, pp. WS 91–94

Also Needed
- scissors, adult
- whiteboard (optional)

Keywords

possessive pronoun – the form of a pronoun that shows ownership
pronoun – a word that takes the place of one or more nouns

Advance Preparation

For the Get Ready, cut out the cards on page WS 91 in *K¹² Language Arts Activity Book*.

Content Background

▸ Possessive pronouns are words used to show ownership. They replace possessive nouns. The possessive noun *Bella's* can be replaced by *her*, and the possessive noun *dog's* can be replaced by *its*. Notice that the possessive pronoun *its* does not have an apostrophe. Unlike possessive nouns, possessive pronouns do not use apostrophes. When written as *it's*, the word is a contraction for *it is*, not a possessive pronoun.

▸ Note that the possessive pronouns *my*, *your*, *her*, *his*, *its*, *our*, and *their* are called possessive adjectives in some grammar programs. However, this program refers to them as possessive pronouns.

Big Ideas

Using pronouns helps writers avoid monotony because they do not have to keep repeating the same nouns.

 **15** minutes

Work **together** with students to complete Get Ready, Learn, and Try It activities.

Get Ready

Lesson Introduction
Prepare students for the lesson.

1. Tell students that they will first review what a possessive noun is.

2. Explain that they will be learning about possessive pronouns. A possessive pronoun is a word that takes the place of a possessive noun.

3. Tell students that they will practice recognizing and using possessive pronouns in sentences.

 Objectives
- Recall what a possessive noun is.

Review Possessive Nouns
Use this exercise to help students recall how to recognize and use possessive nouns. Gather the cards from page WS 91 in *K¹² Language Arts Activity Book*.

1. Lay the cards face up on a flat surface.

2. Show students the *'s* card. Explain that they can use this card to make a possessive noun.

3. Demonstrate how to do it by making your own phrase. Lay out the cards *the*, *dog*, and *hat*. Slide the *'s* card after the word *dog*.

   ▸ What does the phrase say? *the dog's hat*
   ▸ Who does the hat belong to? the dog

4. Have students use the cards to make phrases. Tell them that they can make any silly combination they want, just as long as the phrase starts with *the* and they add the *'s* after the first noun.

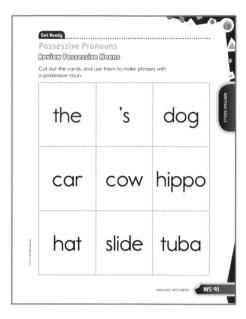

Learn

Find Possessive Pronouns

Help students learn to identify possessive pronouns. Turn to page WS 93 in *K¹² Language Arts Activity Book*.

1. Write the following sentences on a whiteboard or sheet of paper and have students read them with you:
   Maria has a ball. It is Maria's ball.

2. Underline the word *Maria's* and tell students that it is a possessive noun.

   ▶ What word could we replace *Maria's* with? *her*

3. Replace the word *Maria's* with the word *her*. Read the new sentence with students:
   It is her ball.

4. Explain that *her* is a possessive pronoun. Tell students that possessive pronouns replace possessive nouns.

 Objectives
- Identify possessive pronouns.

5. Write the following pairs of sentences on the whiteboard, underline *the boy's* in the first sentence, and read the sentences with students:
   That is <u>the boy's</u> bat. That is his bat.

   ▶ Have students point to the possessive pronoun in the second sentence. *his*

6. Write the following pairs of sentences on the whiteboard, underline *my family's* in the first sentence, and read the sentences with students:
   That is <u>my family's</u> house. That is our house.

   ▶ Have students point to the possessive pronoun in the second sentence. *our*

7. Read the rule and the example on the Activity Book page. Explain the example to students as needed.

8. Read the instructions on the Activity Book page. Help students complete the activity.

TIP It is a common mistake to add an apostrophe to the possessive pronoun *its* and write it as *it's*, which is the contraction for *it is*. You may want to tell students that possessive pronouns do not use apostrophes and draw attention to this particular pronoun, so students don't make this mistake.

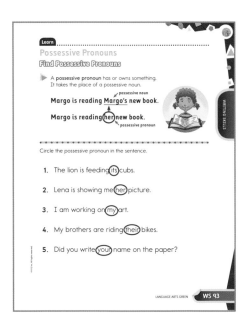

Try It

Use Possessive Pronouns

Help students identify and use possessive pronouns. Turn to page WS 94 in *K¹² Language Arts Activity Book*.

1. Read the first set of instructions to students. Have them circle the possessive pronoun in each sentence.

2. Read the second set of instructions to students. Have them choose a possessive pronoun from the word bank to complete each sentence.

3. Provide assistance as necessary.

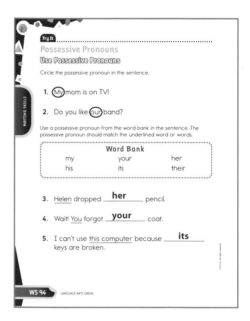

Indefinite Pronouns

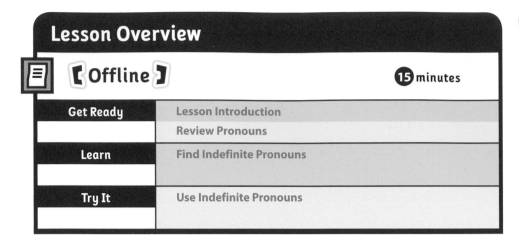

Lesson Overview

Offline		**15** minutes
Get Ready	Lesson Introduction	
	Review Pronouns	
Learn	Find Indefinite Pronouns	
Try It	Use Indefinite Pronouns	

Materials

Supplied
- *K¹² Language Arts Activity Book*, pp. WS 95–98

Also Needed
- scissors, adult
- whiteboard (optional)

Keywords

indefinite pronoun – the form of a pronoun that refers to an unnamed person or group

pronoun – a word that takes the place of one or more nouns

Advance Preparation

For the Get Ready, cut out the cards on page WS 95 in *K¹² Language Arts Activity Book*.

Content Background

▶ Unlike pronouns such as *he, she, it,* and *them,* some pronouns do not take the place of a specific noun. Instead, they refer to an unnamed person or thing or to an unnamed group. Examples of these pronouns are *someone, anybody, most, all,* and *everyone.* These pronouns are called indefinite pronouns.

▶ Although students will be learning about indefinite pronouns, you should not use this term with them. The emphasis should be on students' ability to use indefinite pronouns in speaking and writing.

Big Ideas

Using pronouns helps writers avoid monotony because they do not have to keep repeating the same nouns.

 **15 minutes**

Work **together** with students to complete Get Ready, Learn, and Try It activities.

Get Ready

Lesson Introduction
Prepare students for the lesson.

1. Tell students that they will review what pronouns are.

2. Explain that they will be learning about another kind of pronoun, the kind that does not take the place of a specific noun.

3. Tell students that they will practice recognizing and using the pronouns in sentences.

Objectives
- Recall what a pronoun is.

Review Pronouns
Help students review pronouns by playing a matching game. Gather the cards from page WS 95 in *K¹² Language Arts Activity Book*.

1. Lay the cards face up on a flat surface. Make sure they are mixed up.

2. Tell students that there are four pairs of cards. Each pair has a noun and a pronoun that could replace that noun.

3. Have students match the nouns with their pronouns.

4. Remind students that these kinds of pronouns replace specific nouns in a sentence.

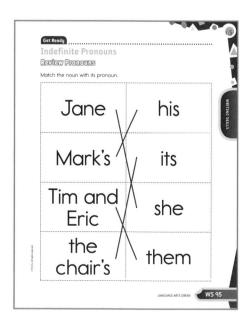

Learn

Find Indefinite Pronouns

Introduce indefinite pronouns to students. Turn to page WS 97 in *K¹² Language Arts Activity Book*.

Objectives

- Recognize indefinite pronouns.

1. Write the following words on a whiteboard or sheet of paper and read them with students:
   somebody, anyone, most

   ▸ Can you tell what nouns these words have replaced? No

2. Explain that some pronouns replace words that haven't been named. They can refer to a group or a single unnamed person or thing.

3. Tell students that there are a lot of pronouns like the three you just wrote. More examples are *someone, more, nobody,* and *neither.* They are all pronouns that replace words that haven't been named.

4. Read the rule on the Activity Book page. Explain the example to students as needed.

5. Read the instructions on the Activity Book page. Help students complete the activity.

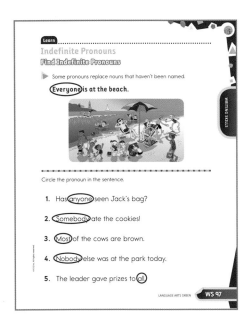

Try It

Use Indefinite Pronouns

Help students identify and use indefinite pronouns. Turn to page WS 98 in *K¹² Language Arts Activity Book*.

Objectives
* Use indefinite pronouns.

1. Read the first set of instructions to students. Have them use the pronouns in the word bank to fill in the blanks so that the sentences describe the pictures.

2. Read the second set of instructions to students. Have them write a sentence using the pronoun *anyone*.

3. Provide assistance as necessary.

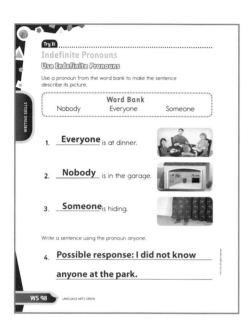

Review Pronouns

Lesson Overview

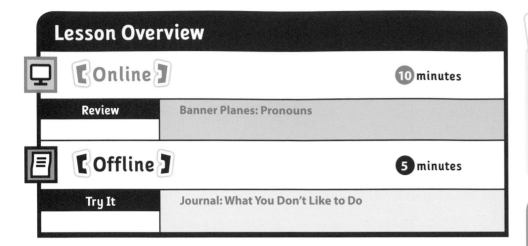

	Online	10 minutes
Review	Banner Planes: Pronouns	

	Offline	5 minutes
Try It	Journal: What You Don't Like to Do	

 **Online** 10 minutes

Students will review what they have learned about pronouns to prepare for the Unit Checkpoint. Help students locate the online activity and provide support as needed.

Review

Banner Planes: Pronouns
Students will work online to review what they have learned about personal pronouns, possessive pronouns, and indefinite pronouns.

Offline Alternative

No computer access? Many early readers use simple sentences. Read through some books and help students make a list of all the different pronouns they find. Have them identify which nouns are being replaced by pronouns, when possible.

Materials

Supplied
- *K¹² My Journal*, pp. 136–137

Also Needed
- crayons

Keywords

indefinite pronoun – the form of a pronoun that refers to an unnamed person or group
possessive pronoun – the form of a pronoun that shows ownership
pronoun – a word that takes the place of one or more nouns

Objectives
- Identify possessive pronouns.
- Recognize indefinite pronouns.
- Recognize pronouns.
- Use a capital letter for the pronoun *I*.
- Use indefinite pronouns.
- Use possessive pronouns.
- Use singular and plural pronouns.

[Offline] 5 minutes

Students will write on their own in their journal. Help students locate the offline activity.

Try It

. . . .

Journal: What You Don't Like to Do

Students will write in their journal on their own. Gather *K¹² My Journal* and have students turn to pages 136 and 137 in Writing Skills.

1. To help students prepare, ask them to think of one thing they dislike doing. Tell them to close their eyes for a moment and pretend that they are doing that thing.

2. Read the prompt with students. Have students respond to the prompt in their journal. As necessary, remind them that there are no correct or incorrect answers.

TIP The amount of time students need to complete this activity will vary. Allow them to use the rest of the allotted time to complete this activity. If they have more they would like to write, you may let them complete their entry at a later time. If students are having trouble getting started, you might tell them to just list ideas or words. They may even draw a picture and describe it to you. You can transcribe their words for them.

Objectives
- Write in a journal.
- Freewrite about a topic.

Unit Checkpoint

Lesson Overview

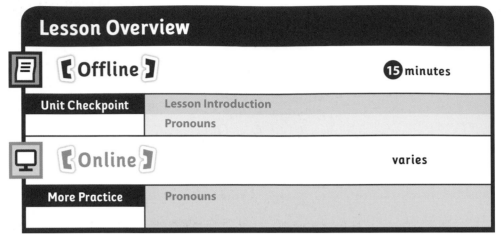

[Offline]	**15** minutes

| Unit Checkpoint | Lesson Introduction |
| | Pronouns |

[Online]	varies

| More Practice | Pronouns |

[Materials]

Supplied

- *K¹² Language Arts Assessments*, pp. WS 17–20

[Offline] **15** minutes

Work **together** with students to complete the Unit Checkpoint.

Unit Checkpoint

Lesson Introduction

Prepare students for the lesson.

1. Tell students that they are going to complete a Unit Checkpoint to show what they have learned.

2. Explain that if they miss one or more questions, they can continue to practice this grammar skill.

Pronouns

Explain that students are going to show what they have learned about identifying and using pronouns.

1. Give students the Unit Checkpoint pages.

2. Read the directions together. If needed, read the questions and answer choices to students. Have students complete the Checkpoint on their own.

Objectives

- Identify possessive pronouns.
- Recognize indefinite pronouns.
- Recognize pronouns.
- Use a capital letter for the pronoun *I*.
- Use indefinite pronouns.
- Use possessive pronouns.
- Use singular and plural pronouns.

3. Use the Answer Key to score the Checkpoint and then enter the results online.

4. Review each exercise with students. Work with students to correct any exercise that they missed.

 TIP Students who answered one or more questions incorrectly should continue to practice this grammar skill. Write several sentences and ask students to identify the pronouns in each sentence. Help them identify which nouns the pronouns replace and have them write three sentences using pronouns.

Reward: When students score 80 percent or above on the Unit Checkpoint, add a sticker for this unit on the My Accomplishments chart.

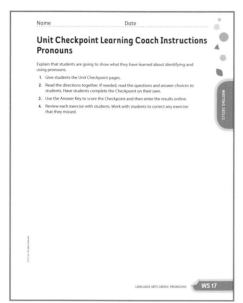

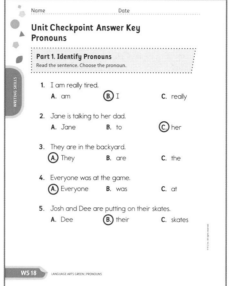

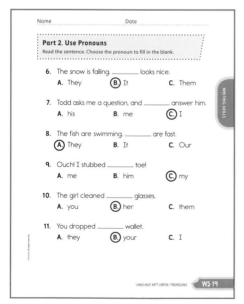

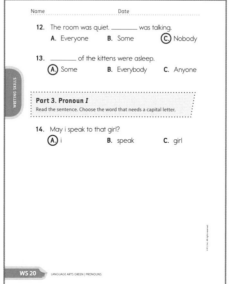

 **varies**

If necessary, work with students to complete the More Practice activity.

More Practice

Pronouns

If students scored less than 80 percent on the Unit Checkpoint, have them complete the appropriate review activities listed in the table online. Help students locate the activities and provide support as needed.

Objectives
- Evaluate Checkpoint results and choose activities to review.

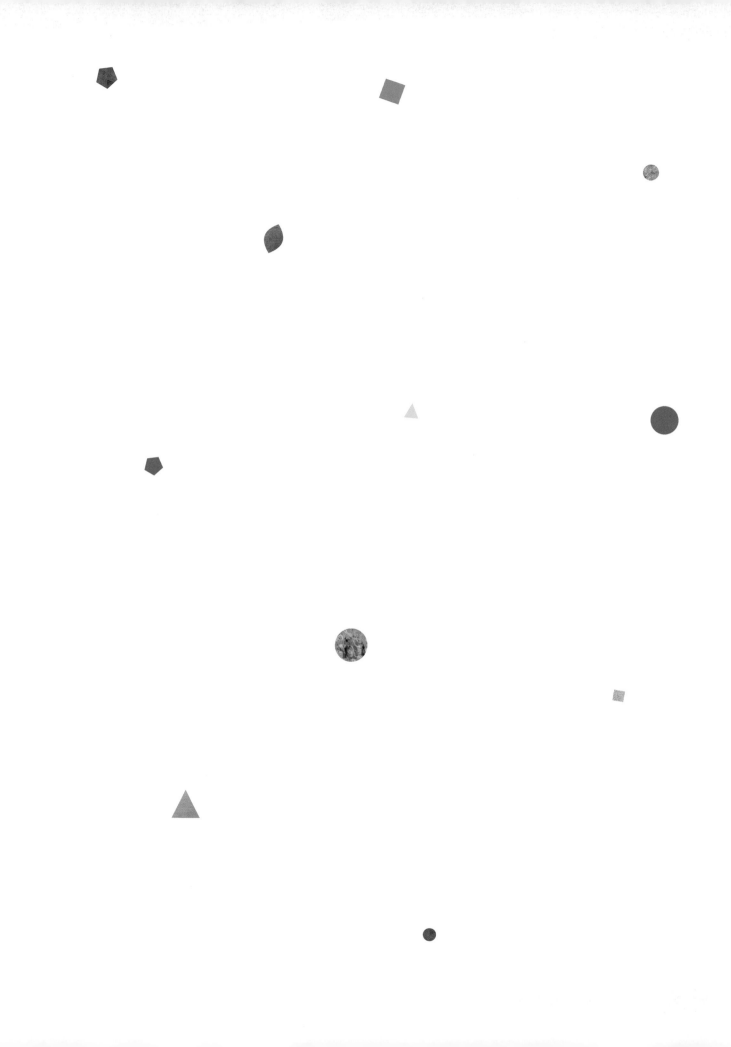

Opinion Paragraph

Unit Focus

In this unit, students will learn how to write an opinion paragraph. They will write an opinion and write a group of related sentences that give reasons to support their opinion. Students will learn how to

- ▸ Recognize the difference between an opinion and a fact.
- ▸ Write a paragraph so that all the sentences are related.
- ▸ Use transition words such as *because* to connect the ideas in a paragraph.
- ▸ Revise their writing using a checklist.

When writing about their opinions, students will use both facts and other opinions to support their viewpoint. Learning how to make a compelling argument to support an opinion is not only an important skill to develop for written communication; it is a key element of critical thinking as well. By asking students to provide reasons for their own ideas, you are teaching them to be flexible thinkers and allow for the possibility of dissent. Providing a rationale for an opinion makes a person consider that opinion more deeply. Students who are comfortable questioning their own ideas are on their way to becoming more thoughtful, and asking good questions is central to all education.

Unit Plan		〔Offline〕	〔Online〕
Lesson 1	What Do You Feel Strongly About?	15 minutes	
Lesson 2	Opinions and Paragraphs	15 minutes	
Lesson 3	State an Opinion	15 minutes	
Lesson 4	Write Your Opinion	15 minutes	
Lesson 5	Publish Your Opinion	15 minutes	varies

What Do You Feel Strongly About?

Lesson Overview

[Offline]   **15** minutes

Get Ready	Lesson Introduction
	Strong Beliefs
Try It	Freewrite: Use Your Journal

Materials

Supplied
- K[12] *My Journal*, pp. 138–139

Also Needed
- crayons

Keywords

freewrite – to write without stopping to revise, correct, or worry about proper form; a form of prewriting

opinion – a statement of belief that cannot be proven true; the opposite of a fact

Content Background

Students write in their journal to explain something they feel strongly about. What they write may be used as prewriting for the writing assignment of this unit.

Big Ideas

Journal writing is a form of freewriting. It is an opportunity to get ideas on paper without concern for correctness of the language or the format of a piece of writing.

[Offline]   **15** minutes

Work **together** with students to complete Get Ready and Try It activities.

Get Ready

Lesson Introduction
Prepare students for the lesson.

1. Explain that in this lesson, students will be writing in their journal. Remind them that their journal is a place to be creative and explore writing. They will not be judged or graded.

2. Explain that today, students will freewrite about things they have strong feelings about.

Objectives
- Define *opinion*.

Strong Beliefs

Help students prepare for the lesson by helping them talk about their own strong opinions.

1. Ask students if they remember what a **fact** is. something that can be proven to be true

2. Tell students that **opinions** are not like facts. They can't be proven to be true. Tell students that everyone has opinions. Explain that an opinion is what someone thinks or believes about something.

3. Tell students that you want to know their opinions. Explain that you are going to ask them about some of their favorite things. They are to choose what the "best" is. The "best" is their opinion. Write down their answer to each question. Answers to questions may vary.

   ▶ What is the best food?
   ▶ What is the best game?
   ▶ What is the best time of year?
   ▶ What is the best story?

4. Explain to student that the "bests" are all their opinions. Some people may disagree with their choices; others may feel the same. But these are the students' strong opinions.
   Say: Wow! Those are a lot of strong opinions.

TIP If students cannot identify a "best," make up your own questions using what you know about students' preferences to elicit a strong response. The important skill here is articulating a strong opinion.

 Try It ●

 Freewrite: Use Your Journal

Help students freewrite about their own opinions. Gather *K¹² My Journal* and have students turn to pages 138 and 139 in Writing Skills. Answers to questions may vary.

> **Objectives**
> • Generate ideas for writing.
> • Freewrite about a topic.
> • Write in a journal.

1. Ask students to think of something they really care about. Explain that you can care about a person or place. You can care about an animal or a thing. You can even care about an idea.
   Say: For example, some people really care about making sure pets get to live in a good home.

   ▶ Can you name a person you have a special relationship with?
   ▶ Do you have a favorite thing—a toy, stuffed animal, or book?
   ▶ What makes you most happy?

2. Tell students that it is important to think about why we care about things, and it is important to be able to explain why we care.

3. Read the journal prompt and have students write about something they care about.

   ▸ Explain that they are freewriting, or writing ideas on the page.
   ▸ Tell them that they can write about what they care about in any way. For example, they can write it as a list or a story or just sentences that tell why they feel the way they do.

4. If students are struggling, help by asking questions.

   ▸ When did you first start caring about this?
   ▸ Is this something you ever talk about with other people?
   ▸ What is the most important thing about this, to you?

5. Have students explain their writing to you. Do not evaluate students' writing. As long as students have written some ideas, their responses are acceptable.

TIP The amount of time students need to complete this activity will vary. Allow students to use the rest of the allotted time to complete this activity. If they have more they would like to write, you may let them complete their entry at a later time. If students are having trouble getting started, you might tell them to just list ideas or words. They may even draw a picture and describe it to you. You can transcribe their words for them.

What I Care About   Date _____

What do you care about? Write why you feel this way.

_____

_____

_____

_____

_____

_____

_____

WRITING SKILLS

138

Draw a picture.

_____

_____

_____

_____

WRITING SKILLS

139

Opinions and Paragraphs

Lesson Overview

[Offline]   15 minutes

Get Ready	Lesson Introduction
	Support an Opinion
Learn	What Is a Paragraph?
Try It	Find Supporting Sentences

Materials

Supplied
- *K¹² Language Arts Activity Book*, pp. WS 99–101
- Story Card F

Also Needed
- crayons
- household objects – book or magazine
- whiteboard (optional)

Keywords

fact – a statement that can be proven true

opinion – a statement of belief that cannot be proven true; the opposite of a fact

paragraph – a group of sentences about one topic

reason – a statement that explains why something is or why it should be

Content Background

A paragraph is a series of sentences that are connected to one another. Often, a paragraph begins with a topic sentence that states the central idea. The rest of the sentences in the paragraph relate back to that topic sentence in some way. In this unit, students will focus on writing a group of sentences that are connected. They will not learn about topic sentences or the form of a paragraph, but they will learn to write a group of related sentences.

Big Ideas

- Paragraphs should have a discrete focus.
- Writing requires organization and structure.

[Offline]   15 minutes

Work **together** with students to complete Get Ready, Learn, and Try It activities.

Get Ready

Lesson Introduction
Prepare students for the lesson.

1. Tell students that in this lesson, they will be reviewing the difference between facts and opinions.

2. Explain that today, students will learn about paragraphs.

3. Tell students that they will identify opinions in a paragraph.

Objectives
- Distinguish between fact and opinion.
- Identify an opinion.
- Identify reasons that support an opinion.

Support an Opinion

Help students understand how to support an opinion with reasons. Turn to page WS 99 in *K¹² Language Arts Activity Book.*

1. **Say:** Everyone has opinions. Everyone has likes and dislikes.

2. Remind students that an opinion is what each person thinks about something. It is not a fact.

3. Tell students that even though opinions are about personal feelings, it is still important to have reasons for opinions.

4. Read the Activity Book page with students. Begin by showing them the opinion and then show them the two reasons supporting the opinion. Explain that the first reason is a fact about apples and the second is an opinion about apples. Both can be reasons for thinking apples are a great snack.

5. Ask students for two more reasons that apples are a great snack. Have students write the two reasons on the remaining legs of the table.

6. If students disagree with the opinion that apples are the greatest snack and can't think of reasons to write, suggest responses to them.

   ▶ Apples are in apple pie. (fact)
   ▶ Apples are available all year long. (fact)
   ▶ Apples taste better than oranges. (opinion)

7. Tell students that the statement that apples are the greatest is an opinion with support. Just as the table has legs, the opinion about apples has reasons to support it.

TIP It is important for students to learn that both facts and opinions are good reasons for liking or disliking something. Students should be able to talk through their reasoning in a clear manner, which is the beginning of developing a coherent argument.

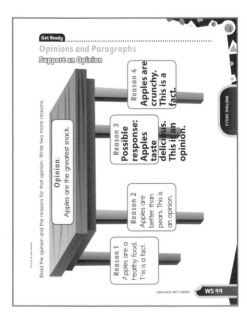

Learn

What Is a Paragraph?

Help students understand what a paragraph is. Turn to page WS 100 in *K¹² Language Arts Activity Book*. Gather Story Card F and any handy book or magazine that has paragraphs of text.

1. Open a book and point to a paragraph. Tell students that this group of sentences is called a paragraph.

2. Write *paragraph* on a whiteboard or sheet of paper and read it with students.

3. Explain to students that a **paragraph** is a group of sentences that are all related. Just as people who are related are all part of the same family, sentences that are related are all part of the same paragraph. The sentences are all about the same topic. That topic or idea is sometimes stated in the first sentence.

4. Explain that all the other sentences in the paragraph are about that one idea. They all work together to make the idea stronger. The other sentences are like the legs of a table, helping to hold the first sentence up.

5. Explain that if the first sentence is stating an opinion, the other sentences are giving the reasons for that opinion.

6. Show students Story Card F.

   ▶ What is happening in the picture? Answers will vary. Students should indicate things that are happening in the playground scene.

7. Review the Activity Book page with students. Tell students that this page goes with the story card. Have students complete the maze. The correct path through the maze is marked by sentences describing the story card. Once students have finished, help them read the connected sentences in order.

TIP It can be helpful to show different examples of paragraphs to students. Look at books and magazines to see what paragraphs look like on the page. When you read the paragraphs, talk about what the topic of the paragraph is or ask what the main idea (the idea that the sentences are mostly about) is.

Objectives

- Recognize details that support the topic sentence of a paragraph.
- Recognize the parts of a paragraph.
- Recognize what a paragraph is.
- Use details that support the topic sentence, or given focus.

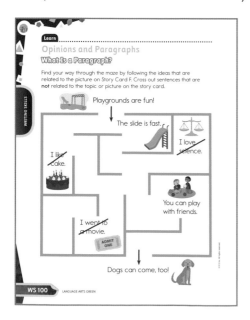

Try It ·

Find Supporting Sentences

Help students identify sentences that belong together in a paragraph. Turn to page WS 101 in *K¹² Language Arts Activity Book.*

1. Read the directions to students. Have them cross out the sentences in the paragraph that are not connected to the first sentence.

2. Provide assistance as necessary.

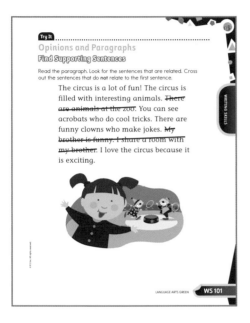

> **Try It**
>
> **Opinions and Paragraphs**
> **Find Supporting Sentences**
>
> Read the paragraph. Look for the sentences that are related. Cross out the sentences that do **not** relate to the first sentence.
>
> The circus is a lot of fun! The circus is filled with interesting animals. ~~There are animals at the zoo.~~ You can see acrobats who do cool tricks. There are funny clowns who make jokes. ~~My brother is funny. I share a room with my brother.~~ I love the circus because it is exciting.
>
> LANGUAGE ARTS GREEN   **WS 101**

Objectives
- Identify reasons that support an opinion.
- Respond to an opinion paragraph.

State an Opinion

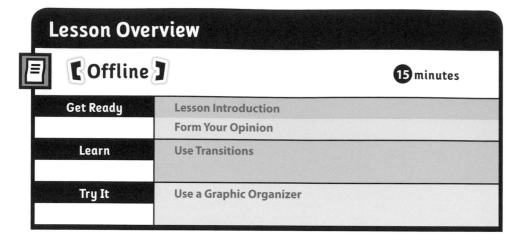

Lesson Overview

【 Offline 】 ⏱ **15** minutes

Get Ready	Lesson Introduction
	Form Your Opinion
Learn	Use Transitions
Try It	Use a Graphic Organizer

Materials

Supplied
- *K¹² Language Arts Activity Book*, pp. WS 102–103
- *K¹² My Journal*, pp. 138–139

Also Needed
- whiteboard (optional)

Keywords

opinion – a statement of belief that cannot be proven true; the opposite of a fact
paragraph – a group of sentences about one topic
reason – a statement that explains why something is or why it should be

Big Ideas

- ▸ Paragraphs should have a discrete focus.
- ▸ Writing requires organization and structure.
- ▸ Competent writers rely on a repertoire of strategies when planning, composing, and revising their texts.
- ▸ Good writers use transitions to help achieve coherence in written text.

 **【 Offline 】** **15** minutes

Work **together** with students to complete Get Ready, Learn, and Try It activities.

Get Ready ....

Lesson Introduction
Prepare students for the lesson.

1. Explain that in this lesson, students will learn how to use transitions to connect their reasons to their opinion.

2. Tell students that they will use a graphic organizer to show the connection between their opinion and their reasons.

 Objectives
- Identify reasons that support an opinion.

Form Your Opinion

Help students understand how reasons support an opinion. Gather *K¹² My Journal* and have students turn to pages 138 and 139 in Writing Skills.

1. Help students read their journal entry about what they care about.

2. Explain that they will be writing more about their opinions. Ask students if they want to write more about the opinion that they wrote in their journal or if they would rather write about a different opinion.

   ▸ If students are going to write about their journal entry, have them think about more reasons that support their opinion.
   ▸ If students are going to write about a new opinion, have them think about their opinion and the reasons for it. Have students share the new opinion and one new reason supporting their opinion.

TIP If students are having difficulty, prompt them with words such as "I like _____ because . . ." or "_____ is the best pet because . . . ."

Learn

Use Transitions

Help students understand how to use transitions when providing reasons for an opinion. Turn to page WS 102 in *K¹² Language Arts Activity Book.*

1. Read the two sentences in the example on the Activity Book page.

2. Point to the transition word *because* in the example.

3. Explain that certain words, such as *because*, are **transition words**. They work like bridges. They connect opinions and reasons together.

4. Explain that there are other transition words such as *so, that's why, therefore, also,* and *too.*

5. Tell students that transition words can connect two sentences, or they can appear at the beginning of a new sentence to connect it to the old one. Write the following sentence on a whiteboard or a piece of paper and read it with students:
   Also, you get to play outside.

6. Point to the word *also* and tell students that it is a transition word that connects this new reason for liking soccer to the old reason *It is fun.*

7. Read the Activity Page with students. Help them identify the transition words in each sentence.

Objectives

- Define *transitions.*
- Identify reasons that support an opinion.
- Identify transitions.
- Recognize the need to use transitions to connect ideas in writing.

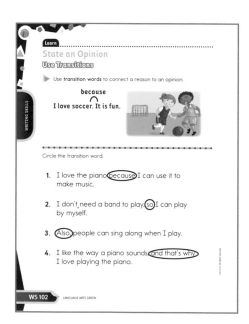

Try It
· ·

Use a Graphic Organizer

Help students use a graphic organizer to write their opinion and reasons. Turn to page WS 103 in *K¹² Language Arts Activity Book*.

Objectives

- Identify reasons that support an opinion.
- Provide reasons that support the opinion.
- Recognize the need to use transitions to connect ideas in writing.

1. Show students the graphic organizer. Explain that they are going to write their opinion and four reasons for this opinion. They can use the opinion from their journal entry or another opinion.

2. Read the directions to students. Have them write their opinion in the center bubble of the graphic organizer. Have them write their reasons in the outer bubbles.

3. Have students use the transitions words from the word bank. The transition words should be written on the lines connecting the bubbles. Students should try to use a variety of transition words, but they can use a transition word more than once.

4. Provide assistance as necessary.

TIP Keep the Activity Book page in a safe place so students can refer to it when they draft their opinion paragraph.

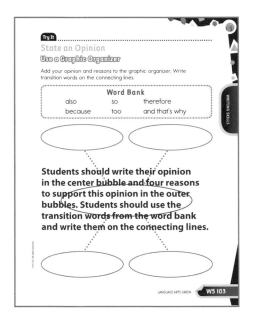

Write Your Opinion

Lesson Overview

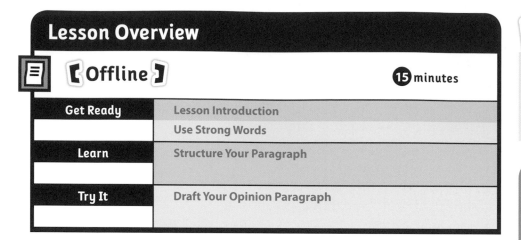

[Offline]   **15** minutes

Get Ready	Lesson Introduction
	Use Strong Words
Learn	Structure Your Paragraph
Try It	Draft Your Opinion Paragraph

Materials

Supplied

- *K¹² Language Arts Activity Book*, pp. WS 103–104

Keywords

opinion – a statement of belief that cannot be proven true; the opposite of a fact

paragraph – a group of sentences about one topic

reason – a statement that explains why something is or why it should be

Advance Preparation

Have students gather completed page WS 103 (Use a Graphic Organizer) in *K¹² Language Arts Activity Book*.

Big Ideas

- ▸ Writing requires organization and structure.
- ▸ Competent writers rely on a repertoire of strategies when planning, composing, and revising their texts.
- ▸ To be effective communicators, writers and speakers should recognize and use complete sentences.

[Offline] **15** minutes

Work **together** with students to complete Get Ready, Learn, and Try It activities.

Get Ready

Lesson Introduction
Prepare students for the lesson.

1. Explain that in this lesson, students will learn more about how to organize an opinion paragraph.

2. Tell students that they will write a draft of their opinion paragraph.

Objectives

- Identify reasons that support an opinion.
- Revise by adding or deleting text.
- Revise for clarity.

Use Strong Words

Help students understand how to use strong words when writing an opinion. Gather the completed graphic organizer.

1. Have students look at their graphic organizer. Tell them that if they want to write a strong opinion, they need to use strong words.

2. Explain that they can look at their opinions and reasons and replace some words with words that show stronger feelings.

3. Tell students certain words and have them suggest stronger words to replace them. For example:

   ▶ What is a stronger word than *like*? *love, fond of, adore, enjoy*
   ▶ What is a stronger word than *sad*? *downcast, gloomy, heartbroken, melancholic*

4. Tell students to look for two or three places on their graphic organizer where they can replace one word with a stronger word. Have them add these words to their graphic organizer.

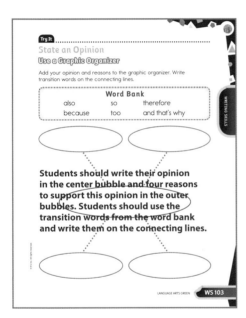

Learn

Structure Your Paragraph

Help students understand how to organize a paragraph. Gather the completed graphic organizer.

1. Tell students that there is a specific way to organize, or put together, a paragraph.

2. Explain that students should start with a sentence that clearly states their opinion. That is the first sentence in the paragraph.

3. Tell students that they are going to write four more sentences in their paragraph. The second, third, fourth, and fifth sentences are all reasons supporting the opinion. These should each have a transition word to connect the reason to the opinion.

4. The last sentence of this paragraph should be a conclusion to the paragraph. It can restate the opinion in some way.

5. Direct students' attention to their graphic organizer. Help them number their sentences. Help them write the number *1* next to the bubble in the center. **Say:** You start with your opinion, so this is the first sentence.

6. Tell students to number the rest of the bubbles on their graphic organizer, putting the reasons in a logical order.

Objectives
- Organize ideas in a logical order.

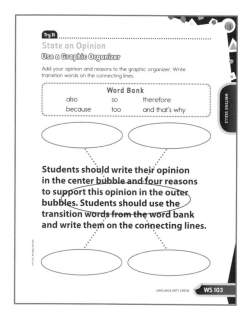

Try It

✏ Draft Your Opinion Paragraph

Help students write their opinion paragraph. Turn to page WS 104 in *K¹² Language Arts Activity Book* and gather the completed graphic organizer.

1. Have students take the opinion and reasons from their graphic organizer and write them on the Activity Book page in complete sentences.

2. Help students write a conclusion for their paragraph. Explain that a conclusion is a final sentence that helps end the paragraph. It can be used to remind the reader what the main opinion is.

3. Provide assistance as necessary.

TIP Remind students to use transitions to connect their opinions with their reasons. Keep the Activity Book page in a safe place so students can refer to it when they write the final draft of their opinion paragraph.

Objectives

- Organize ideas in a logical order.
- Provide reasons that support the opinion.
- Recognize the need to use transitions to connect ideas in writing.
- Use transitions to connect ideas.
- Write a series of related sentences.
- Write an opinion statement.
- Write complete sentences.
- Write sentences with appropriate spacing between words.
- Write a concluding sentence.

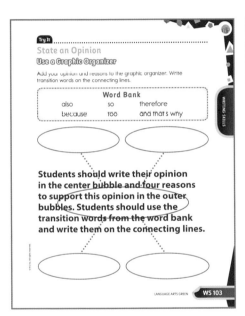

Publish Your Opinion

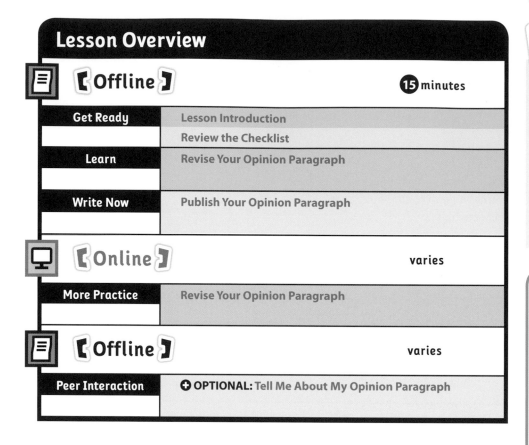

Lesson Overview

Offline — 15 minutes

Get Ready	Lesson Introduction
	Review the Checklist
Learn	Revise Your Opinion Paragraph
Write Now	Publish Your Opinion Paragraph

Online — varies

| More Practice | Revise Your Opinion Paragraph |

Offline — varies

| Peer Interaction | ⊕ OPTIONAL: Tell Me About My Opinion Paragraph |

Materials

Supplied
- *K¹² Language Arts Activity Book*, pp. WS 104–110
- Publish Your Opinion: Rubric and Sample Responses (printout)

Also Needed
- crayons

Keywords

fact – a statement that can be proven true

opinion – a statement of belief that cannot be proven true; the opposite of a fact

paragraph – a group of sentences about one topic

publish – to make your revised writing available to read.

reason – a statement that explains why something is or why it should be

Advance Preparation

Have students gather completed page WS 104 (Draft Your Opinion Paragraph) in *K¹² Language Arts Activity Book.*

Big Ideas

- ▶ Writing requires rewriting or revision.
- ▶ Writers who receive feedback during the writing process are able to apply that feedback to improve the ultimate product.
- ▶ Writers must be able to articulate a main idea and support it with appropriate details.
- ▶ The writing process is fluid and recursive. Writers improve their drafts as needed.

 **15 minutes**

Work **together** with students to complete Get Ready, Learn, and Write Now activities.

Get Ready

Lesson Introduction
Prepare students for the lesson.

1. Explain that students will be revising their opinion paragraph.

2. Tell students that before they publish their paragraph, they will use a checklist to help them decide how to improve their writing.

3. Explain that students will publish the final version of their opinion paragraph.

Objectives
- Revise using a checklist.

Review the Checklist
Help students review the opinion paragraph checklist. Turn to pages WS 105 and 106 in *K¹² Language Arts Activity Book* and gather students' draft opinion paragraph.

1. Read over the checklist with students. Tell them that they will use the checklist to revise their writing before they publish it.

2. Have students refer to their draft. Read through the checklist questions with students and have them circle their answers on the checklist.

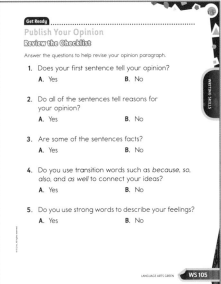

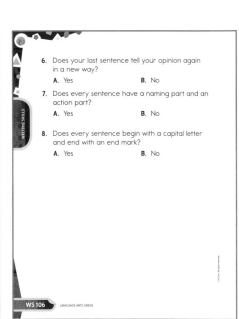

Learn

Revise Your Opinion Paragraph

Help students revise their opinion paragraph. Gather the checklist and students' draft opinion paragraph.

1. Read over students' responses to the checklist with students. Look for all the times students answered *No* to a question.

2. For each *No* answer, ask students which parts of their writing made them answer *No*.

3. Have students make notes on their draft about ways to make their paragraph better. Discuss other ways students can improve their writing. Answers to questions may vary.

   ▸ Are there stronger words you can use to describe your reasons?
   ▸ Are there more reasons you can use to support your opinion?
   ▸ Can you add more detail to any of your sentences?

Objectives
- Revise using feedback.
- Revise the draft of a paragraph.

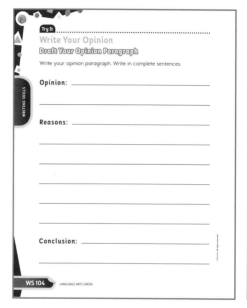

Try It

Write Your Opinion

Draft Your Opinion Paragraph

Write your opinion paragraph. Write in complete sentences.

Opinion: _____

_____

Reasons: _____

_____

_____

_____

_____

Conclusion: _____

_____

WS 104   LANGUAGE ARTS GREEN

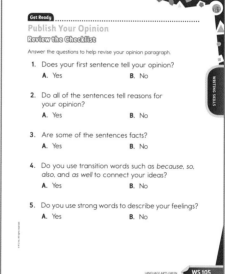

Get Ready

Publish Your Opinion

Review the Checklist

Answer the questions to help revise your opinion paragraph.

1. Does your first sentence tell your opinion?
   A. Yes   **B.** No

2. Do all of the sentences tell reasons for your opinion?
   A. Yes   **B.** No

3. Are some of the sentences facts?
   A. Yes   **B.** No

4. Do you use transition words such as *because, so, also*, and *as well* to connect your ideas?
   A. Yes   **B.** No

5. Do you use strong words to describe your feelings?
   A. Yes   **B.** No

LANGUAGE ARTS GREEN   WS 105

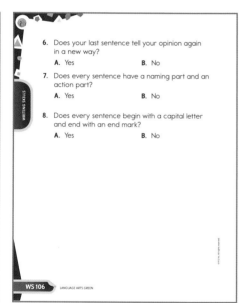

6. Does your last sentence tell your opinion again in a new way?
   A. Yes   **B.** No

7. Does every sentence have a naming part and an action part?
   A. Yes   **B.** No

8. Does every sentence begin with a capital letter and end with an end mark?
   A. Yes   **B.** No

WS 106   LANGUAGE ARTS GREEN

Write Now ••

 Publish Your Opinion Paragraph

Help students write their opinion paragraph. Turn to pages WS 107 and 108 in
K¹² Language Arts Activity Book.

1. Help students rewrite their opinion paragraph on the Activity Book pages.
   Encourage them to write clearly and legibly.

2. Use the materials and instructions in the online lesson to evaluate students'
   finished writing. You will be looking at students' writing to evaluate the
   following:

   ▶ **Purpose and Content**: The student wrote a paragraph of at least four
     sentences. The paragraph expresses an opinion, and there is evidence and
     reasons for the opinion in the supporting sentences.

   ▶ **Structure and Organization**: The writing leads with an opinion. Most of
     the other sentences express reasons that support the opinion. Most of the
     sentences contain transition words to connect the reasons to the opinion.

   ▶ **Grammar and Mechanics**: The writing mostly has complete sentences
     and makes good use of verbs, describing words, and other good word
     choices. There is some evidence of revision and proofreading.

3. Enter students' scores for each rubric category online.

4. If students' writing scored a 1 in any criterion, work with students to proofread
   and revise their work.

TIP The amount of time students need to complete this activity will vary. Students
need only work for 15 minutes.

Reward: When students complete the activity, allow them to draw a picture to show
their opinion. When students' writing achieves "meets objectives" in all three categories
on the grading rubric, add a sticker for this unit on the My Accomplishments chart.

Objectives

- Use capitalization and punctuation correctly.
- Use transitions to connect ideas.
- Write an opinion paragraph.
- Write complete sentences.
- Write sentences with appropriate spacing between words.
- Write sentences with legible handwriting.

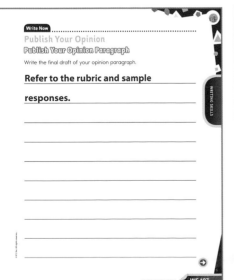

 **varies**

If necessary, work with students to complete the More Practice activity.

More Practice

Revise Your Opinion Paragraph

If students' writing scored "doesn't meet objectives" in any category, have them complete the appropriate review activity listed in the table online.

Objectives
• Evaluate writing and choose activities to review and revise.

▶ Follow the online instructions to help students revise and proofread their work.

▶ Impress upon students that revising makes their work better. Writing is a process, and each time they revise their opinion paragraph, they are making their writing stronger and better.

▶ When you provide feedback, always begin with something positive. For example, you might point out a detail students wrote (even if it's the only detail) and explain how it helps you picture the scene: "You wrote that the leaves were 'orange and gold.' That detail, the color of the leaves, really helps me picture the forest."

▶ Place the final written work together with the rubric and the sample papers in the writing portfolio. This information is useful for you to track progress, and it helps students to refer back to their own work. They can see how they improve and review feedback to remember areas that need revising.

▶ Help students locate the activity and provide support as needed.

 **varies**

If necessary, work with students to complete the Peer Interaction activity.

Peer Interaction ···

⊕ **OPTIONAL: Tell Me About My Opinion Paragraph**

This activity is OPTIONAL. It is intended for students who have extra time and would benefit from extra practice. Feel free to skip this activity.

    Students can benefit from exchanging paragraphs with someone they know or another student. This activity will work best if students exchange their paragraph with other students who completed the same activity, but you may copy the Activity Book pages and send them to someone else who is willing to give students feedback. Students should receive feedback on their paragraph. To complete this optional activity, turn to pages WS 109 and 110 in *K12 Language Arts Activity Book*.

1. Have students exchange paragraphs with other students.

2. Have students use the Activity Book pages to provide others with feedback about their writing.

3. Have students use the feedback provided from other students to revise their own paragraph.

Objectives
- Use guidance from adults and peers to revise writing.
- Collaborate with peers on writing projects.

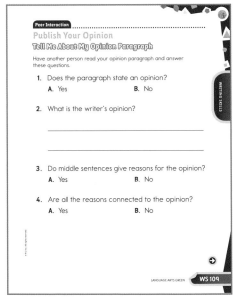

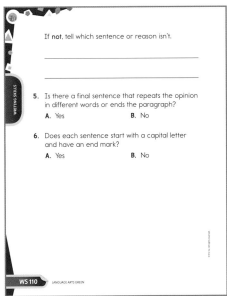

Verb Tense

Unit Focus

In this unit, students will learn about recognizing and using verb tense. Students will

- Learn to identify and use present tense verbs.
- Learn to identify and use past tense verbs.
- Learn to identify and use future tense verbs.

Correctly using verb tense is a key part of creating writing that is clear, accurate, and easy to understand. By correctly using verb tense, students will be able to convey a sense of time and order to readers.

Unit Plan		**[Offline]**	**[Online]**
Lesson 1	Present Tense	15 minutes	
Lesson 2	Past Tense	15 minutes	
Lesson 3	Future Tense	15 minutes	
Lesson 4	Review Verb Tense	5 minutes	10 minutes
Lesson 5	Unit Checkpoint	15 minutes	varies

Present Tense

Lesson Overview

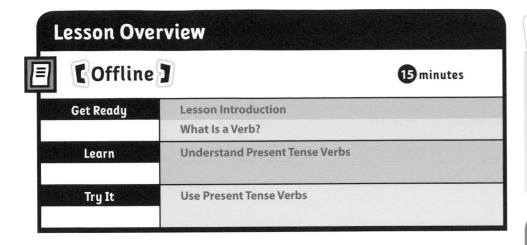

[Offline]   **15** minutes

Get Ready	Lesson Introduction
	What Is a Verb?
Learn	Understand Present Tense Verbs
Try It	Use Present Tense Verbs

Materials

Supplied
- *K¹² Language Arts Activity Book*, pp. WS 111–112

Also Needed
- whiteboard (optional)

Keywords

present tense – the verb form that tells what is happening now

verb – a word that shows action

Content Background

The tense of the verb tells the time or duration of an action. There are three simple tenses of verbs: present, past, and future. In this lesson, students will learn about the simple present tense of a verb. They will be working with action verbs such as *run*, *play*, *jump*, and *talk*.

Big Ideas

Knowing how to form verb tenses and to use them correctly helps writers and speakers express their ideas accurately.

[Offline] **15** minutes

Work **together** with students to complete Get Ready, Learn, and Try It activities.

Lesson Introduction
Prepare students for the lesson.

1. Explain that students are going to learn about verb tense.

2. Tell them that they are going to learn about the present tense of verbs.

Objectives
- Recall what a verb is.

What Is a Verb?
Help students review what verbs are.

1. Explain that students are going to use their bodies to act out words.

2. Say the following words and ask students to act them out as best they can: *run, crawl, laugh.*

3. Explain that you are going to say another group of words and that students should try to act them out: *book, dirt, shoe.*

4. Have students talk about the different groups of words.

   ▸ Which group of words was easier to act out: the first group or the second group? the first group
   ▸ Why? All the words were actions.
   ▸ What kind of word shows action? a verb

Learn

Understand Present Tense Verbs
Introduce present tense verbs to students. Turn to page WS 111 in *K¹² Language Arts Activity Book.*

Objectives
• Recognize present tense of verbs.

1. Explain to students that they are going to learn more about how to use verbs. They are going to learn about verb tense.

2. Write the following words on a whiteboard or sheet of paper and read them with students: *tense = time.*

3. Explain that a verb shows action, and the tense of the verb tells us about the time an action happened. It tells us that the action happened in the past, is happening now or happens now, or will happen in the future.

4. Write the following words in a horizontal line across the whiteboard or paper and read them with students: *Yesterday, Today, Tomorrow.*

5. Under the word *Today*, write the words *present tense*. Explain that verbs in the **present tense** are happening today or happen today.

6. Write the following words under *present tense*: *talk, smile, wave.*

7. Act out each of the words as you say them.

8. **Say:** I talk. I smile. I wave. These verbs all tell about actions that happen now. They are present tense verbs.

9. Read the Activity Book page with students. Have them complete the exercises. Provide assistance as necessary.

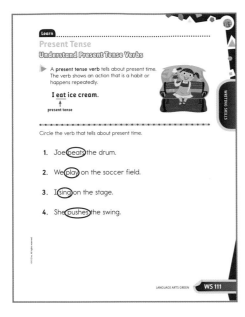

Try It

Use Present Tense Verbs

Help students practice using present tense verbs. Turn to page WS 112 in *K¹² Language Arts Activity Book*.

1. Read the instructions to students. Have them choose verbs from the word bank to fill in the blank in each sentence.

2. Provide assistance as necessary.

Objectives
• Use the present tense of verbs.

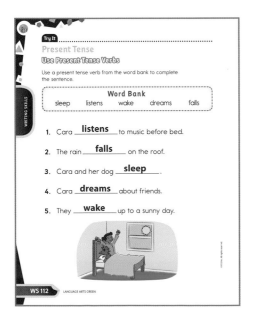

Past Tense

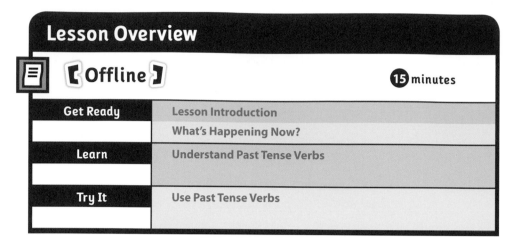

Lesson Overview

Offline | **15 minutes**

Get Ready	Lesson Introduction
	What's Happening Now?
Learn	Understand Past Tense Verbs
Try It	Use Past Tense Verbs

Materials

Supplied
- *K¹² Language Arts Activity Book*, pp. WS 113–116

Also Needed
- scissors, adult
- tape, clear
- whiteboard (optional)

Keywords

past tense – the form of the verb that tells what has already happened

verb – a word that shows action

Advance Preparation

For the Get Ready, cut out the cards on page WS 113 of *K¹² Language Arts Activity Book* and tape them on a wall. For the Learn, on a whiteboard or sheet of paper, write the words *Yesterday, Today,* and *Tomorrow*. Under the word *Today*, list the words *talk, smile,* and *wave*.

Content Background

- In this unit, students will work only with *regular verbs*. The past tense of regular verbs is formed by adding *–d* or *–ed* to the present tense form.
- *Irregular verbs* are verbs that form the past tense in other ways. Some examples of irregular verbs and their past tense are *run* and *ran, sleep* and *slept,* and *fall* and *fell*. Students will learn about irregular verbs at another time.
- Although students will be using regular verbs in this lesson, they will not learn the term.

Big Ideas

Knowing how to form verb tenses and to use them correctly helps writers and speakers express their ideas accurately.

 **[Offline]** **15** minutes

Work **together** with students to complete Get Ready, Learn, and Try It activities.

Get Ready

Lesson Introduction
Prepare students for the lesson.

1. Tell students that they will review present tense verbs.

2. Explain that this lesson will focus on past tense verbs.

3. Tell students that they will practice finding and using past tense verbs.

 Objectives
- Recall the present tense of verbs.

What's Happening Now?
Help students review present tense verbs with this physical activity.

1. Explain that students are going to play a game with present tense verbs.

   ▶ What does a verb show? action
   ▶ The present tense shows actions that are happening when? right now

2. Tell students that they are going to play a game called What's Happening Now?

3. Point to the cards on the wall. Explain that each verb written on a card is an action that is happening in the present time. Tell students that you are going to point to a card and read it, and they will act out the verb on that card.

4. Point to the card with the word *jump*.

5. **Say:** Right now, jump!

6. Repeat with the other cards, always beginning the instruction with the words *right now*. Read the cards faster and faster. For a special challenge, point to two cards at the same time.

Learn

Understand Past Tense Verbs

Introduce past tense verbs to students. Turn to page WS 115 in *K¹² Language Arts Activity Book*.

1. Remind students that the word *tense* means "time."

2. Point to the three words on the whiteboard or paper. Explain that verbs tell about something that happened yesterday, is happening today, or will happen tomorrow.

3. Under *Yesterday* write the following words and read them with students: *past tense*.

4. Explain that **past tense** verbs show actions that have already happened. The actions aren't happening now. They happened earlier.

5. Explain that when we make a past tense verb, we add *–d* or *–ed* to the end of the verb.

6. Under *past tense*, write the following verbs and read them with students: *talked, smiled*.

7. Point to the word *talk* under *present tense* and tell students that you added *–ed* to make it past tense.

8. Point to the word *smile* under *present tense*. Explain that because there was already an *e* on the end of the verb *smile*, you added just a *–d* to the word.

9. Point to the word *wave* under *present tense*.

   ▸ What should I add to this verb to make it past tense, *–d* or *–ed*? *–d*

10. Read the Activity Book page with students. Help them complete the exercises.

Objectives

- Recognize past tense of verbs.

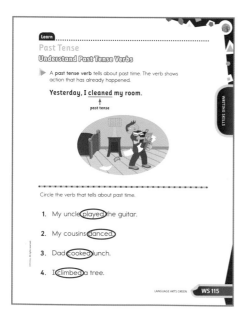

Try It

Use Past Tense Verbs

Help students practice using past tense verbs. Turn to page WS 116 in *K¹² Language Arts Activity Book*.

1. Read the directions to students.

2. Tell students they need to find the correct verb in the word bank to fill in each blank and add *–d* or *–ed* to make it a past tense verb. They will write the past tense verbs in the blanks.

3. Provide assistance as necessary.

Objectives
- Use the past tense of verbs.

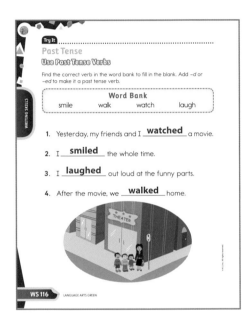

Future Tense

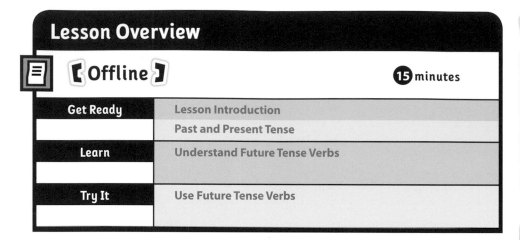

Lesson Overview

[Offline]　　　　　　　**15** minutes

Get Ready	Lesson Introduction
	Past and Present Tense
Learn	Understand Future Tense Verbs
Try It	Use Future Tense Verbs

[Materials]

Supplied
- *K¹² Language Arts Activity Book*, pp. WS 117–118

Also Needed
- whiteboard (optional)

Keywords

future tense – a form of a verb that names an action that will happen later
verb – a word that shows action

Advance Preparation

For the Learn, on a whiteboard or sheet of paper, write the words *Yesterday*, *Today*, and *Tomorrow*. Under the word *Yesterday*, list the words *talked*, *smiled*, and *waved*. Under the word *Today*, list the words *talk*, *smile*, and *wave*.

Content Background

The future tense is formed by adding *shall* or *will* to the present tense. Generally, *shall* is used with the pronouns *I* and *we*, and *will* is used with the rest of the personal pronouns. However, *will* is acceptable and will be used with all pronouns for students at this grade level.

Big Ideas

Knowing how to form verb tenses and to use them correctly helps writers and speakers express their ideas accurately.

 **15** minutes

Work **together** with students to complete Get Ready, Learn, and Try It activities.

Get Ready

Lesson Introduction
Prepare students for the lesson.

1. Tell students that they will review present and past tense verbs.

2. Explain to students that this lesson will focus on future tense verbs.

3. Tell students that they will practice finding and using future tense verbs.

Objectives
- Recognize that verbs tell the time of an action.

Past and Present Tense
Help students remember the relationship between present tense and past tense verbs.

1. Remind students that the tense of a verb tells the time of an action.

   ▸ What do verbs show? Verbs show action.
   ▸ When do present tense verbs happen? right now
   ▸ When do past tense verbs happen? before now; in the past

2. Write the following verbs on a sheet of paper: *laughed, walked, smiled, snored.*

3. Read the words with students.

   ▸ Which tense are these verbs? past tense
   ▸ How do you know? They end in *–d* or *–ed.*

4. Tell students to make the past tense verbs into present tense verbs by covering up either the *–d* or *–ed* in each verb. Have them use one finger to cover up a *–d* and two fingers to cover up *–ed*. Encourage students to say the present tense verbs aloud. *laugh, walk, smile, snore*

TIP Doing physical actions can help students remember abstract ideas. Having them cover the letters with their fingers will help them understand how to change a verb from one tense to the other.

Learn

Understand Future Tense Verbs

Introduce future tense verbs to students. Turn to page WS 117 in *K¹² Language Arts Activity Book*.

1. Remind students that verb tense tells about time. The tense of a verb explains when the action happened.

2. Point to the words *Yesterday*, *Today*, and *Tomorrow* on the whiteboard or paper. Explain that verbs tell about something that happened yesterday, is happening today, or will happen tomorrow. They tell about actions in the past, present, or future.

3. Under *Tomorrow*, write the following words and read them with students: *future tense*.

4. Explain that **future tense** verbs show actions that will happen later. They haven't happened yet.

5. Explain that to make a future tense verb, we add the word *will* before the verb.

6. Under *future tense*, write the following verbs and read them with students: *will talk, will smile*.

7. Point to the word *wave* under *Today*.

   ▸ What should I add before this verb to make it future tense? *will*

8. Write *will wave* under *Tomorrow*.

   ▸ What does the verb say? *will wave*

9. Read the Activity Book page to students. Help them complete the exercises.

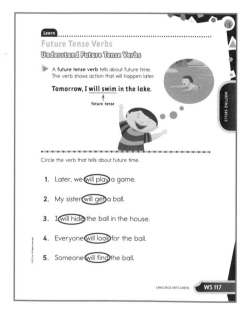

Objectives
- Recognize future tense of verbs.

Try It

Use Future Tense Verbs

Help students practice using future tense verbs. Turn to page WS 118 in *K¹² Language Arts Activity Book*.

1. Read the directions to students.

2. Tell students that they need to rewrite the end of each sentence, using a future tense verb.

3. Provide assistance as necessary.

Objectives
- Use the future tense of verbs.

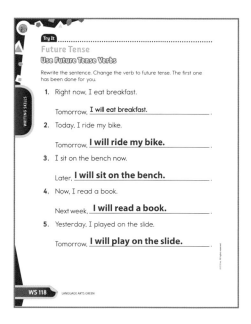

Try It

Future Tense

Use Future Tense Verbs

Rewrite the sentence. Change the verb to future tense. The first one has been done for you.

1. Right now, I eat breakfast.

   Tomorrow, **I will eat breakfast.**

2. Today, I ride my bike.

   Tomorrow, **I will ride my bike.**

3. I sit on the bench now.

   Later, **I will sit on the bench.**

4. Now, I read a book.

   Next week, **I will read a book.**

5. Yesterday, I played on the slide.

   Tomorrow, **I will play on the slide.**

WS 118   LANGUAGE ARTS GREEN

Review Verb Tense

Lesson Overview

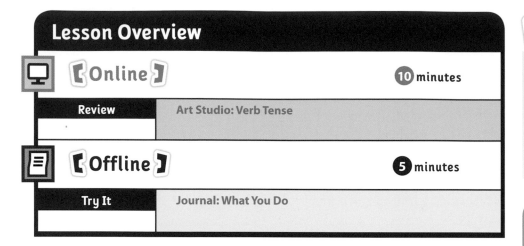

Online — 10 minutes

| Review | Art Studio: Verb Tense |

Offline — 5 minutes

| Try It | Journal: What You Do |

Materials

Supplied
- *K¹² My Journal*, pp. 140–141

Also Needed
- crayons

Keywords

future tense – a form of a verb that names an action that will happen later

past tense – the form of the verb that tells what has already happened

present tense – the verb form that tells what is happening now

verb – a word that shows action

Online — 10 minutes

Students will review what they have learned about recognizing and using present, past, and future tense verbs to prepare for the Unit Checkpoint. Help students locate the online activity and provide support as needed.

Review

Art Studio: Verb Tense
Students will work online to review what they have learned about present tense verbs, past tense verbs, and future tense verbs.

Offline Alternative

No computer access? Often, stories will include a variety of verb tenses. Look at some children's books with students. Choose some sentences and help students identify the tense of the verbs. Focus on simple present, past, and future tenses.

Objectives
- Recognize present tense of verbs.
- Recognize past tense of verbs.
- Recognize future tense of verbs.
- Use the present tense of verbs.
- Use the past tense of verbs.
- Use the future tense of verbs.

 **Offline** ⑤ minutes

Students will write on their own in their journal. Help students locate the offline activity.

Try It

∙∙

✎ **Journal: What You Do**

Students will write in their journal on their own. Gather *K¹² My Journal* and have students turn to pages 140 and 141 in Writing Skills.

1. To prepare for writing, ask students to briefly tell about an activity they like to do and one that they would like to do.

2. Read the prompt with students. Have students respond to the prompt in their journal. As necessary, remind students that there are no correct or incorrect answers.

TIP The amount of time students need to complete this activity will vary. Allow them to use the rest of the allotted time to complete this activity. If they have more they would like to write, you may let them complete their entry at a later time. If students are having trouble getting started, suggest that they just list ideas or words. They may even draw a picture and describe it to you. You can transcribe their words for them.

> **Objectives**
> - Write in a journal.
> - Freewrite about a topic.

Unit Checkpoint

Lesson Overview

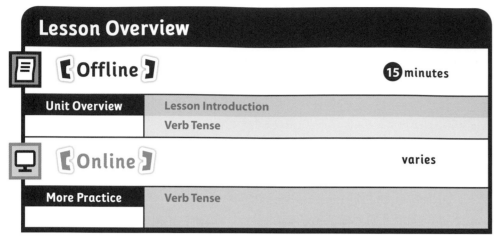

Offline		15 minutes
Unit Overview	Lesson Introduction	
	Verb Tense	

Online		varies
More Practice	Verb Tense	

Materials

Supplied

- *K¹² Language Arts Assessments*, pp. WS 21–24

Offline · 15 minutes

Work **together** with students to complete the Unit Checkpoint.

Unit Checkpoint

Lesson Introduction

Prepare students for the lesson.

1. Tell students that they are going to complete a Unit Checkpoint to show what they have learned.

2. Explain that if they miss one or more questions, they can continue to practice this grammar skill.

Verb Tense

Explain that students are going to show what they have learned about recognizing and using verb tense.

1. Give students the Unit Checkpoint pages.

2. Read the directions together. If needed, read the questions and answer choices to students. Have students complete the Checkpoint on their own.

Objectives

- Recognize present tense of verbs.
- Recognize past tense of verbs.
- Recognize future tense of verbs.
- Use the present tense of verbs.
- Use the past tense of verbs.
- Use the future tense of verbs.

3. Use the Answer Key to score the Checkpoint and then enter the results online.

4. Review each exercise with students. Work with students to correct any exercise that they missed.

 TIP Students who answered one or more questions incorrectly should continue to practice this grammar skill. Write several sentences using different verb tenses. Help students identify the verb tense in each sentence. Have them write three sentences: one with a past tense verb, one with a present tense verb, and one with a future tense verb. You may give students a sentence starter, such as "Today, I . . . ."

Reward: When students score 80 percent or above on the Unit Checkpoint, add a sticker for this unit on the My Accomplishments chart.

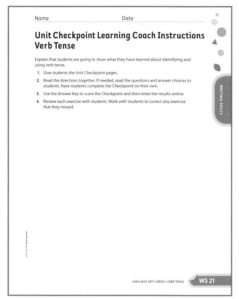

Name _____ Date _____

Unit Checkpoint Learning Coach Instructions
Verb Tense

Explain that students are going to show what they have learned about identifying and using verb tense.

1. Give students the Unit Checkpoint pages.
2. Read the directions together. If needed, read the questions and answer choices to students. Have students complete the Checkpoint on their own.
3. Use the Answer Key to score the Checkpoint and then enter the results online.
4. Review each exercise with students. Work with students to correct any exercise that they missed.

LANGUAGE ARTS GREEN | VERB TENSE   WS 21

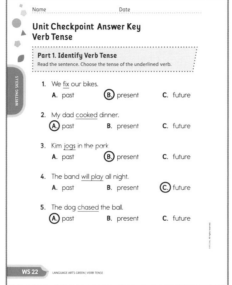

Name _____ Date _____

Unit Checkpoint Answer Key
Verb Tense

Part 1. Identify Verb Tense
Read the sentence. Choose the tense of the underlined verb.

1. We <u>fix</u> our bikes.
   A. past   **(B.)** present   C. future

2. My dad <u>cooked</u> dinner.
   (A.) past   B. present   C. future

3. Kim <u>jogs</u> in the park.
   A. past   **(B.)** present   C. future

4. The band <u>will play</u> all night.
   A. past   B. present   **(C.)** future

5. The dog <u>chased</u> the ball.
   (A.) past   B. present   C. future

WS 22   LANGUAGE ARTS GREEN | VERB TENSE

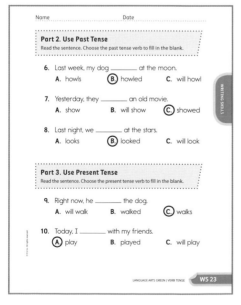

Name _____ Date _____

Part 2. Use Past Tense
Read the sentence. Choose the past tense verb to fill in the blank.

6. Last week, my dog _____ at the moon.
   A. howls   **(B.)** howled   C. will howl

7. Yesterday, they _____ an old movie.
   A. show   B. will show   **(C.)** showed

8. Last night, we _____ at the stars.
   A. looks   **(B.)** looked   C. will look

Part 3. Use Present Tense
Read the sentence. Choose the present tense verb to fill in the blank.

9. Right now, he _____ the dog.
   A. will walk   B. walked   **(C.)** walks

10. Today, I _____ with my friends.
    (A.) play   B. played   C. will play

LANGUAGE ARTS GREEN | VERB TENSE   WS 23

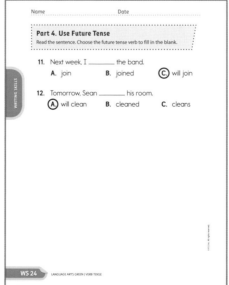

Name _____ Date _____

Part 4. Use Future Tense
Read the sentence. Choose the future tense verb to fill in the blank.

11. Next week, I _____ the band.
    A. join   B. joined   **(C.)** will join

12. Tomorrow, Sean _____ his room.
    (A.) will clean   B. cleaned   C. cleans

WS 24   LANGUAGE ARTS GREEN | VERB TENSE

 **varies**

If necessary, work with students to complete the More Practice activity.

More Practice

Verb Tense

If students scored less than 80 percent on the Unit Checkpoint, have them complete the appropriate review activities listed in the table online. Help students locate the activities and provide support as needed.

 Objectives
- Evaluate Checkpoint results and choose activities to review.

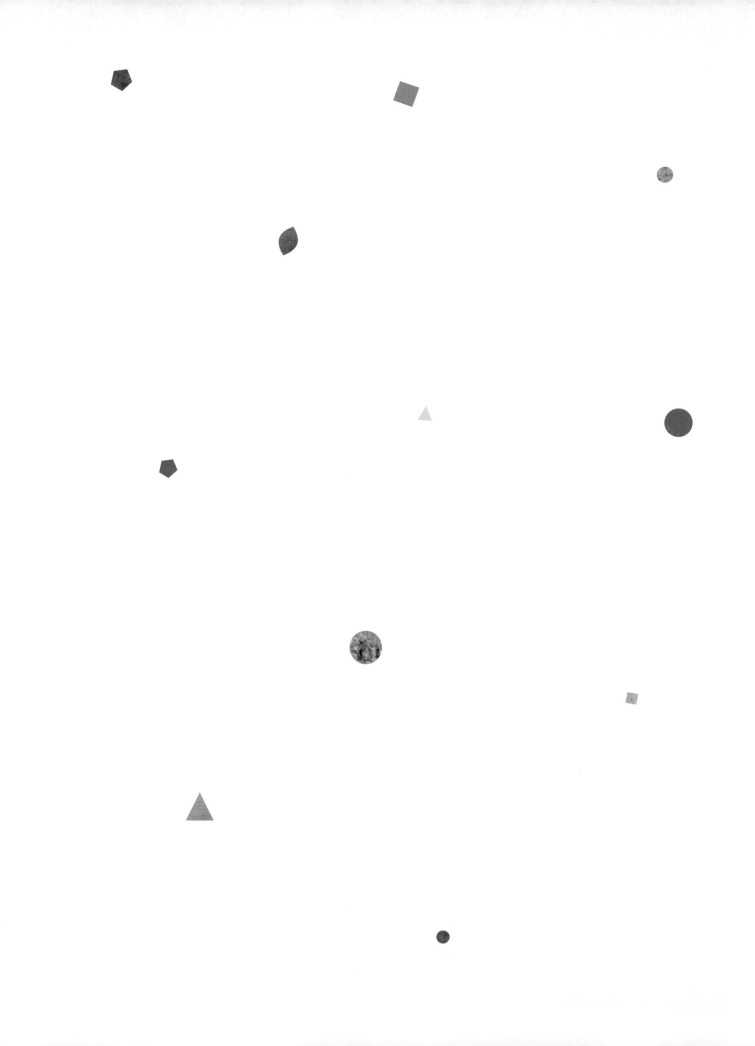

Write About Information: Heritage

Unit Focus

In this unit, students will research and write about their own heritage. Students will

▶ Use an encyclopedia and other books to research their heritage.
▶ Use the Internet to find a source for a visual aid they will create.
▶ Learn to structure their writing into a paragraph.
▶ Revise their writing using feedback.
▶ Give a presentation of their final writing.

Having students write about their family history is a great way to get them engaged with research and writing. This unit can help students understand how research and writing can have a direct effect on their life.

In this unit, students should be encouraged to follow their own interests. Let them write about the aspects of their heritage that most excite them.

Unit Plan		Offline	Online
Lesson 1	Where Do You Come From?	15 minutes	
Lesson 2	Discover and Research Your Heritage	15 minutes	
Lesson 3	Write a Draft About Your Heritage	15 minutes	
Lesson 4	Revise Your Draft and Create a Visual Aid	15 minutes	
Lesson 5	Share Your Heritage	15 minutes	varies

Where Do You Come From?

Materials

Supplied
- *K¹² My Journal*, pp. 142–143

Also Needed
- crayons
- household objects – globe or world map

Lesson Overview

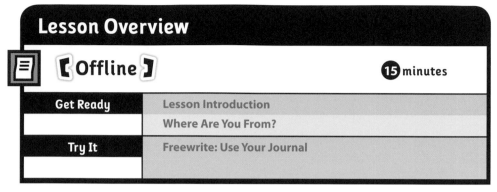

Offline		15 minutes
Get Ready	Lesson Introduction	
	Where Are You From?	
Try It	Freewrite: Use Your Journal	

Keywords

fact – a statement that can be proven true

freewriting – a way for a writer to pick a topic and write as much as possible about it within a set time limit

Advance Preparation

Gather a globe or world map.

Big Ideas

- ► Using what you already know helps you understand new information.
- ► Journal writing is a form of freewriting. It is an opportunity to get ideas on paper without concern for correctness of the language or the format of a piece of writing.

Offline 15 minutes

Work **together** with students to complete Get Ready and Try It activities.

Lesson Introduction
Prepare students for the lesson.

1. Explain that in this lesson, students will write in their journal. Remind them that their journal is a place to be creative and explore writing. They will not be judged or graded.

2. Explain that students will freewrite about what they know about their family's history—specifically, where their family comes from.

Objectives
- Generate ideas for writing.

Where Are You From?

Help students begin thinking about their heritage. Gather a globe or world map.

1. Show students the globe or map. Point to the state that you are currently in. **Say:** You live here, but you parents, grandparents, and great-grandparents may have lived somewhere else.

2. Point to places all over the globe. Explain that one person can have ancestors who came from all over the world. Point to a country in Europe, one in Asia, and one in South America.

3. Point to other parts of the United States. Explain that one person can have family members who come from different parts of the same country.

4. Point again to the state in which students live. Explain that in some families, the people have lived in the exact same place for a very long time.

5. Explain that where the members of a person's family come from is part of a person's heritage. Heritage is made up of the things that are handed down from one generation to another, such as where we come from, a language that we speak, special foods that we cook, or stories that we tell.

6. Encourage students to name family traditions or activities that are part of their heritage.

TIP If students don't know where their family comes from, have them ask a relative or family friend. Alternatively, they can pick a country they are interested in and use this country as the focus for their writing assignments.

Try It

Freewrite: Use Your Journal

Help students freewrite about where their families are from. Gather *K¹² My Journal* and have students turn to pages 142 and 143 in Writing Skills. Answers to questions may vary.

> **Objectives**
> * Generate ideas for writing.
> * Freewrite about a topic.
> * Write in a journal.

1. Explain that students are going to write about their own heritage.

   ▸ Do you know where your parents come from?
   ▸ Do you know where your grandparents come from?

2. Read aloud the prompt at the top of the page.

   ▸ Explain that they are freewriting, or writing ideas on the page.
   ▸ Tell students that they can write whatever they know about their heritage. They can pick one family member they know a lot about. Or, they can write a little bit about a few different family members.

3. Some students may not know where their families are from. Ask questions to see if you can help students discover clues to their heritage.

   ▸ Do you eat any special foods?
   ▸ Do you ever travel to visit family members?
   ▸ Does anyone in your family speak a different language?

4. Have students explain their heritage to you. Do not evaluate students' writing. As long as students have written some ideas on paper, their responses are acceptable.

5. If students don't know where their family is from, you can share facts about their heritage with them. You can tell them where parents or grandparents or other ancestors are from. Have the students write whatever they know about one of those places. If you are unable to determine a country that relates to students' heritage, have students choose a place they are interested in learning more about.

TIP The amount of time students need to complete this activity will vary. Allow students to use the rest of the allotted time to complete this activity. If they have more they would like to write, you may let them complete their entry at a later time. If students are having trouble getting started, you might tell them to just list ideas or words. They may even draw a picture and describe it to you. You can transcribe their words for them.

My Roots   Date _____

Where does your family come from?
Write what you know about that place.

142

143

Discover and Research Your Heritage

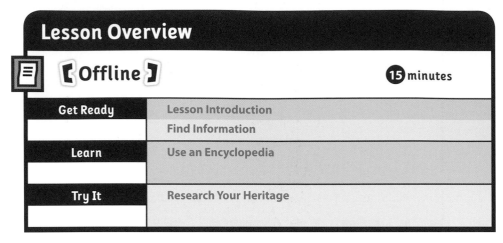

Lesson Overview

[Offline]   **15** minutes

Get Ready	Lesson Introduction
	Find Information
Learn	Use an Encyclopedia
Try It	Research Your Heritage

[Materials]

Supplied
- *K¹² Language Arts Activity Book*, pp. WS 119–120

Also Needed
- household objects – encyclopedia; globe or world map (optional)

Keywords

encyclopedia – a reference work made up of articles on many topics, usually in alphabetical order

fact – a statement that can be proven true

reference – a work that contains useful information for a writer, such as an encyclopedia, a dictionary, or a website

research – to find information through study rather than through personal experience

Advance Preparation

You will need access to an encyclopedia, either printed or online, for this lesson. You may use the Grolier encyclopedia in the online school or an encyclopedia of your own choosing.

Big Ideas

Choosing the source that best serves your needs is a good start for researching and writing.

 **[Offline]** **15** minutes

Work **together** with students to complete Get Ready, Learn, and Try It activities.

 Get Ready ....

Lesson Introduction
Prepare students for the lesson.

1. Remind students that *research* means finding information through study rather than personal experience.

2. Explain that students are going to do research on their own heritage, or family background.

 Objectives
- Define *reference*.
- Formulate questions to investigate for research.

Find Information

Help students understand the idea of research.

1. Tell students that there are different ways for them to find out about their heritage. One way is to look up facts about where their families are from.

   ▸ What can you read to find information about other places? Possible answers: an encyclopedia; a magazine; an atlas; a nonfiction book

2. Tell students that all these publications are **reference** works. A *reference* is a work that contains useful information for a writer, such as an encyclopedia, a dictionary, or a website.

3. Tell students that people can be a great source of information as well.

4. Tell students that they are going to practice getting information from you by asking questions.

5. If you know about the student's family, tell them to ask you a few questions about the topic.

6. Encourage students to ask questions that will reveal details about your topic, such as the following:

   ▸ Where is your family from?
   ▸ When did they come to the place where you live now?
   ▸ Who came here first?
   ▸ What was life like in that other place?

Learn

Use an Encyclopedia

Introduce the encyclopedia to students. Help students understand how an encyclopedia is structured and how to find information in it.

1. Tell students that they are going to research their heritage. If a student's family comes from more than one place, have them pick one of those places to learn about. Remind students that they can pick either a country or a state.

2. Show students a printed or online encyclopedia. Explain that an **encyclopedia** contains facts about many different subjects.

3. Flip or scroll through the pages and show a few entries to students. Show them that an encyclopedia has facts about people, places, things, and ideas.

Objectives
- Recognize the purpose of an encyclopedia.
- Use various reference materials to acquire information.

4. Tell students that most encyclopedias are organized from *A* to *Z*. Show them how the pages progress through the alphabet as you go through the book or the online site. (If you are using the Grolier online encyclopedia, choose the Alphabetical Browse option.)

   ▸ Where would we find information about cats? under *C*
   ▸ Where would we find information about the sun? under *S*

5. If you are using a printed encyclopedia, point to the guide words at the top of each page. Explain that they show you what the first and last words on the page are. **Say:** With guide words, you can use the alphabet to help you figure out what other words are on the page.

   ▸ Find the page with the entry for *sun* on it. Show how the word *sun* comes alphabetically between the two guide words on that page.

6. If you are using an online encyclopedia, show students the search box on the home page. Explain that they can type their topic in that box to find one or more articles on the topic.

   ▸ Type *sun* in the search box and show students the article about the sun.

7. Explain to students that the information for their heritage writing in this unit will come mostly from the encyclopedia.

Try It

Research Your Heritage

Help students research their heritage. Turn to pages WS 119 and 120 in *K¹² Language Arts Activity Book*.

1. Read the directions and questions to students. Explain that they are going to find the answers to these questions in the encyclopedia.

2. Have students answer the first question with the name of the place they are going to research.

3. Help students find the answers to Questions 2–6 in the encyclopedia and write them on the Activity Book page.

4. Help students find two more interesting facts about their topic. Have them write the facts in the space provided on the Activity Book pages.

Objectives

• Do shared research about the topic.

• Use various reference materials to acquire information.

5. If students have difficulty finding the answers to the research questions or coming up with two additional facts, feel free to substitute other questions about life in the place they are researching. For example:

- ► What kinds of jobs do people have there?
- ► What kinds of foods do people eat?
- ► What holidays or traditions are part of the culture?
- ► What language(s) do people speak?

TIP If students have a family member who knows a lot about their heritage, their research can include asking that person questions. Help students set up an interview in person, by phone, or via e-mail. They can use the interview either to answer the questions on the Activity Book pages or to find additional information for their writing. Keep the Activity Book pages in a safe place so students can refer to them when they write the draft of their heritage paragraph.

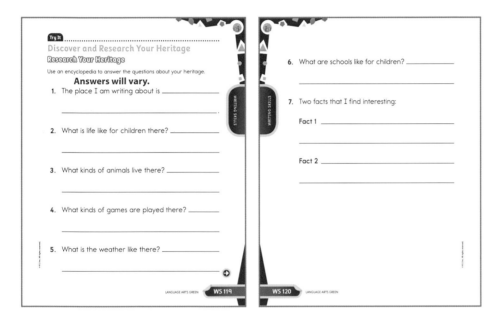

Write a Draft About Your Heritage

Lesson Overview

[Offline]   **15** minutes

Get Ready	Lesson Introduction
	Choose Your Facts
Learn	Structure a Paragraph
Try It	Write Your Draft

Materials

Supplied
- *K¹² Language Arts Activity Book*, pp. WS 119–122
- *K¹² My Journal*, pp. 142–143

Also Needed
- whiteboard (optional)

Keywords
fact – a statement that can be proven true
paragraph – a group of sentences about one topic
research – to find information through study rather than through personal experience

Advance Preparation

Gather the facts that students wrote about their heritage on pages WS 119 and 120 (Research Your Heritage) in *K¹² Language Arts Activity Book*.

Big Ideas

Competent writers rely on a repertoire of strategies when planning, composing, and revising their texts.

[Offline] **15** minutes

Work **together** with students to complete Get Ready, Learn, and Try It activities.

Get Ready

Lesson Introduction
Prepare students for the lesson.

1. Tell students that they will be putting the information about their heritage into paragraph form.

2. Explain that it is important for a paragraph to have an introduction or hello sentence, supporting ideas, and a conclusion or good-bye sentence.

Objectives
- Plan the writing.
- Use facts.
- Use details.

Choose Your Facts

Help students prepare to write a draft about their heritage. Have them pick which facts they are going to focus on. Gather students' facts about heritage on pages WS 119 and 120 in *K¹² Language Arts Activity Book* and pages 142 and 143 in *K¹² My Journal*.

1. Tell students that before they can organize their facts into a paragraph, they need to decide which facts they want to write about.

2. Have students review the facts about their heritage that they have written so far in *K¹² My Journal* and on the Activity Book pages. Tell students to pick the four or five facts that they are most excited about. Have students circle these facts or put a star next to them.

3. Explain that they are going to focus on these facts in their writing.

Try It

Discover and Research Your Heritage
Research Your Heritage

Use an encyclopedia to answer the questions about your heritage.

Answers will vary.

1. The place I am writing about is _____

2. What is life like for children there? _____

3. What kinds of animals live there? _____

4. What kinds of games are played there? _____

5. What is the weather like there? _____

LANGUAGE ARTS GREEN   WS 119

---

6. What are schools like for children? _____

7. Two facts that I find interesting:

   Fact 1 _____

   Fact 2 _____

WS 120   LANGUAGE ARTS GREEN

My Roots   Date _____

Where does your family come from?
Write what you know about that place.

142

143

Learn

Structure a Paragraph

Introduce how to structure a paragraph to students.

1. Explain that students are going to use the facts that they gathered to write a paragraph about their heritage.

2. Remind students that **paragraphs** have an introduction and a conclusion. A good paragraph also uses transitions to connect ideas.

3. Explain that students need to let readers know what they will be writing about. This is the **introduction**. It is the "hello sentence." They should make sure this sentence names the place they are writing about.

4. Have students make up an introductory or hello sentence and say it out loud. Write down what they say on a whiteboard or sheet of paper.

5. The **body** will hold almost all the information about students' heritage. Students will use order words and connecting words to build bridges between their facts.

   ▶ What are some order words and connecting words? *also, next, then, additionally, finally*

6. Explain that the **conclusion** is like a "good-bye sentence." It is the last thing students will say about their heritage. A good conclusion helps people understand that the writing is finished. Some conclusions say the same thing as the introduction but in a different way. A conclusion sums up, or finishes, the writing.

7. Have students make up a concluding or good-bye sentence and say it out loud. Write down what they say on the whiteboard or paper.

Objectives

- Plan the writing.
- Define *introduction*.
- Recognize the importance of an introduction.
- Define *conclusion*.
- Recognize the purpose of a conclusion.

Try It

Write Your Draft

Help students write a draft of their heritage paragraph. Turn to pages WS 121 and 122 in *K¹² Language Arts Activity Book*.

1. Read the instructions to students. Show them the places for the introduction, body, and conclusion in the paragraph.

Objectives

- Write a paragraph draft.
- Write an introduction.
- Write sentences about a topic.
- Organize ideas through sequencing.
- Write a conclusion.

2. Have them write an introductory sentence, four to five facts about the place they researched, and a conclusion.

- ▶ Refer to the introductory and concluding sentences that you wrote down for students. Have students write them on the Activity Book pages.
- ▶ Have students work with the four or five facts they have chosen to focus on.
- ▶ Remind them to use the order words and connecting words in the word bank to connect the facts.

TIP Keep the Activity Book pages in a safe place so that students can refer to them when they revise their draft.

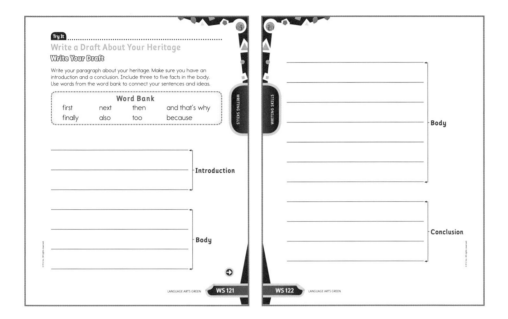

Revise Your Draft and Create a Visual Aid

Lesson Overview

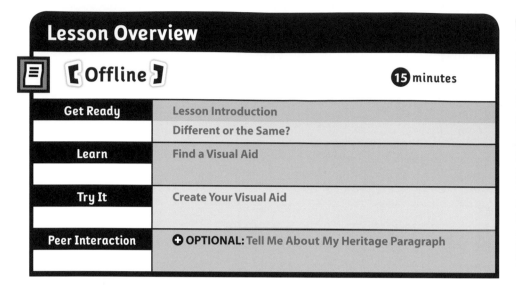

	Offline	**15** minutes
Get Ready	Lesson Introduction	
	Different or the Same?	
Learn	Find a Visual Aid	
Try It	Create Your Visual Aid	
Peer Interaction	➕ OPTIONAL: Tell Me About My Heritage Paragraph	

Materials

Supplied
- *K¹² Language Arts Activity Book,* pp. WS 121–126

Also Needed
- household objects – supplies to create visual aid (optional crayons, glue stick, coloring pencils, coloring markers, round-end safety scissors)

Advance Preparation

Have students gather their draft heritage paragraph on pages WS 121 and 122 (Write Your Draft) in *K¹² Language Arts Activity Book.*

Big Ideas

Using what you already know helps you understand new information.

 **Offline** **15** minutes

Work **together** with students to complete Get Ready, Learn, Try It, and Peer Interaction activities.

Get Ready

Lesson Introduction
Prepare students for the lesson.

1. Explain that students will be reading their draft and looking for places to make changes to make their paragraph better. They can add more information or change words.

> **Objectives**
> - Use details.
> - Make connections with text: text-to-text, text-to-self, text-to-world.

2. Tell students that they will be adding a visual aid to their writing. Remind students that a visual aid is something to look at that goes with their facts and information. It helps readers see what the writer means.

3. Explain that students will share their work so that they can receive notes for revision.

Different or the Same?

Help students add detail to their writing by finding connections between their research topic and their own life. Answers to questions may vary.

1. Tell students that writing about their heritage means that they are writing about themselves and their own history.

2. Have students think of similarities between their own lives and the lives of the people they have been researching.

   ▸ Do you eat similar foods?
   ▸ Do you play similar games?
   ▸ Is your school experience similar?

3. Have students think about the differences between their own lives and the lives of the people they have been researching.

   ▸ Is there something that seems easier about your own life?
   ▸ Is there something that seems harder?
   ▸ Is there something you admire about the lives of the people you've been researching?
   ▸ Is there something you like better about your own life?

4. Explain to students that these ideas can be part of their writing as well. When presenting their facts, they can comment on how their own lives are similar or different.

Learn

Find a Visual Aid

Help students add to their draft by finding an appropriate visual aid.

1. Explain to students that having a visual aid can make writing more engaging. It can also help readers understand the material in a new way.

2. Tell students that another way to do research is to get information from the Internet. The Internet is a great place to find pictures and videos about their topic.

Objectives

- Do shared research about the topic.
- Use a media source to do research.
- View and respond to visual media.
- Evaluate information in print and/or electronic and visual media.
- Interpret information provided by features of text and electronic media.

3. Help students go online to find an image or video that relates to their heritage paragraph. If students have trouble finding a visual, you might ask them questions to help guide their search. Answers to questions may vary.

   ▸ Can you find a map of the country or place your family is from?
   ▸ What does the flag of that country look like?
   ▸ Are there any dances or songs from that country that relate to your heritage?
   ▸ Are there pictures of food that relate to your heritage?

4. Help students decide what would make a good visual aid to go with their writing. Remind them to credit the source (to say which website they used).

TIP In addition to online encyclopedias, many other online resources can help students find a visual aid. For example, there are websites where you can create a family tree. A family tree may help students explain the different places that have been significant to their families.

Try It

Create Your Visual Aid

Help students create their visual aid. Turn to pages WS 123 and 124 in *K¹² Language Arts Activity Book* and gather the draft of students' heritage paragraph on pages WS 121 and 122.

1. Read the instructions on the Activity Book page.

2. Have students look at the draft of their heritage paragraph. Have them decide what part of their paragraph they will illustrate or expand upon with the visual aid they create.

3. Have students create a visual aid to support their writing. Students may either download an image or use what they saw on the Internet to create a drawing, collage, or prop to go along with their writing. They may draw or paste their visual on the Activity Book page if it fits.

4. Help students gather any materials they need to create their visual aid and then assist them as necessary in creating it.

Objectives
- Create a visual.
- Use a visual display to enhance facts or details.
- Write sentences about a topic.

5. On the Activity Book page, have students write an explanation of what their visual aid is and how it relates to their topic. Keep this page in a safe place for future reference.

TIP Some students may want to use their creativity to expand upon their visual aid. They might wish to create a short video, with puppets acting out a game or dance from the place they are researching. They might set up a video call with a family member far away so that the person can say hello during the presentation. They might download a song from their state or country and do a dance. If students are engaged with a particular idea, let them explore creative ways to develop their visual aid.

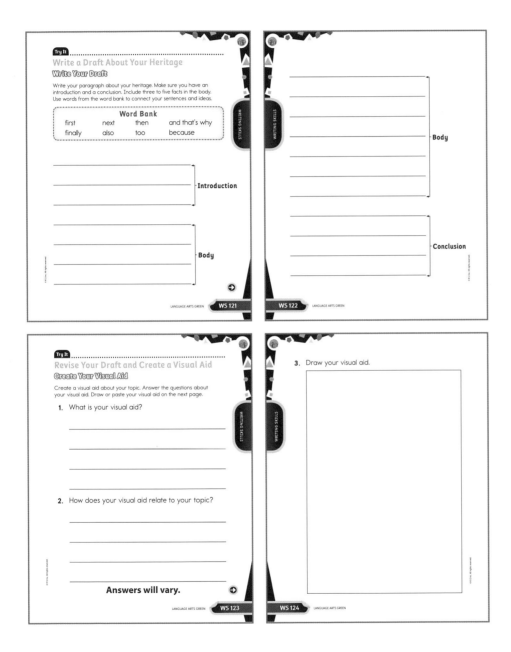

Peer Interaction

⊕ OPTIONAL: Tell Me About My Heritage Paragraph

This activity is OPTIONAL. It is intended for students who have extra time and would benefit from extra practice. Feel free to skip this activity.

Students can benefit from exchanging paragraphs with someone they know or another student. This activity will work best if students exchange their paragraph with other students who completed the same activity, but you may copy the Activity Book pages and send them to someone else who is willing to give students feedback. Students should receive feedback on the content of their paragraph. To complete this activity, turn to pages WS 125 and 126 in *K¹² Language Arts Activity Book*.

1. Have students exchange paragraphs with other students.

2. Have students use the Activity Book pages to provide others with feedback about their writing.

3. Tell students that they will use this feedback to revise their paragraph later.

Objectives

- Use guidance from adults and peers to revise writing.
- Collaborate with peers on writing projects.

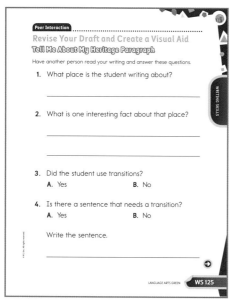

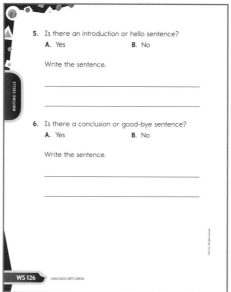

Share Your Heritage

Lesson Overview

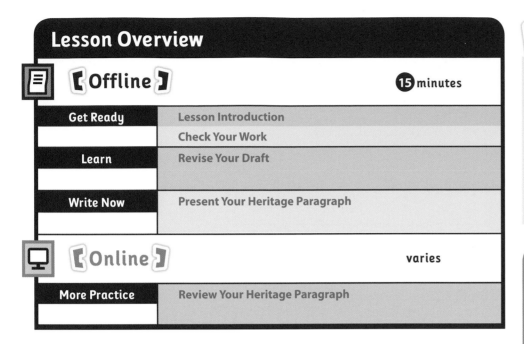

Offline — 15 minutes

Get Ready	Lesson Introduction
	Check Your Work
Learn	Revise Your Draft
Write Now	Present Your Heritage Paragraph

Online — varies

More Practice	Review Your Heritage Paragraph

Materials

Supplied
- *K12 Language Arts Activity Book*, pp. WS 121–122, 125–130
- Present Your Heritage Paragraph: Rubric and Sample Responses (printout)

Keywords

fact – a statement that can be proven true

paragraph – a group of sentences about one topic

presentation – an oral report, usually with visuals

publishing – the stage or step of the writing process in which the writer makes a clean copy of the piece and shares it

research – to find information through study rather than through personal experience

visual aid – a graphic, picture, photograph, or prop used in a presentation

Advance Preparation

Have students gather their draft heritage paragraph on pages WS 121 and 122 (Write Your Draft) and completed pages WS 125 and 126 (Tell Me About My Heritage Paragraph) in *K12 Language Arts Activity Book*. Review students' draft. Look over the checklist on pages WS 127 and 128. Be ready to give students suggestions to help them answer some of the checklist questions.

Big Ideas

Good public speakers speak clearly, make eye contact, and use appropriate expression for their subject matter and audience.

[Offline] ⏱ minutes

Work **together** with students to complete Get Ready, Learn, and Write Now activities.

Get Ready ....

Lesson Introduction

Prepare students for the lesson.

1. Explain that students will be revising their draft to make corrections, add details, and create transitions.

2. Tell students that they will add their visual aid.

Objectives
- Revise using a checklist.

Check Your Work

Help students use a checklist to revise their work. Turn to pages WS 127 and 128 and gather students' draft heritage paragraph on pages WS 121 and 122 in *K¹² Language Arts Activity Book*.

1. Read aloud the checklist on the Activity Book pages. Help students answer the questions.

2. If students answered *No* to any of Questions 1–4 or *Yes* to Questions 5 and/or 6, have them put a checkmark or a star next to the place in their paragraph where they want to add that information.

TIP Keep the Activity Book pages in a safe place so students can refer to it when they revise their draft.

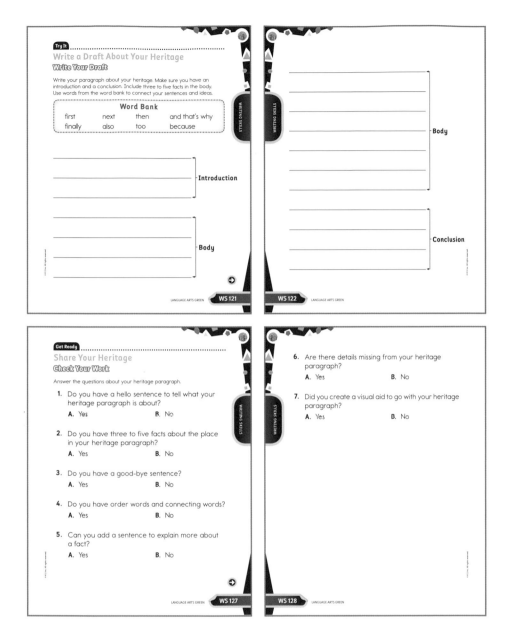

Learn

Revise Your Draft

Help students revise their writing. Gather pages WS 121, 122, and 125–128 in *K¹² Language Arts Activity Book*.

1. Tell students it is time to revise, or improve the writing. Review the Peer Interaction pages and the Get Ready checklist with them. Have students make notes and corrections in pencil on their draft heritage paragraph.

2. Help students find places to add detail to their writing. Prompt them with *how*, *which*, *where*, *who*, and *why* questions. Answers to questions may vary.

   ▸ Where do children spend their time?
   ▸ Who plays that game?
   ▸ Which special days do people celebrate?

Objectives

- Revise using feedback.
- Use details.
- Use facts.
- Organize writing with an introduction, body, and conclusion.
- Provide a sense of closure.

3. Tell students that adding order words and connecting words will help their paragraph make sense. Have them use order words such as *first, next, then,* and *finally* and connecting words such as *because, so,* and *also* to transition from one sentence to the next.

Write a Draft About Your Heritage

Write Your Draft

Write your paragraph about your heritage. Make sure you have an introduction and a conclusion. Include three to five facts in the body. Use words from the word bank to connect your sentences and ideas.

Word Bank			
first	next	then	and that's why
finally	also	too	because

Introduction

Body

Body

Conclusion

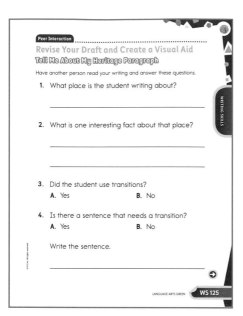

Revise Your Draft and Create a Visual Aid

Tell Me About My Heritage Paragraph

Have another person read your writing and answer these questions.

1. What place is the student writing about?

2. What is one interesting fact about that place?

3. Did the student use transitions?
   A. Yes   B. No

4. Is there a sentence that needs a transition?
   A. Yes   B. No

Write the sentence.

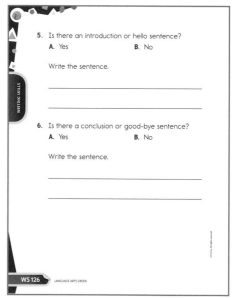

5. Is there an introduction or hello sentence?
   A. Yes   B. No

Write the sentence.

6. Is there a conclusion or good-bye sentence?
   A. Yes   B. No

Write the sentence.

Share Your Heritage

Check Your Work

Answer the questions about your heritage paragraph.

1. Do you have a hello sentence to tell what your heritage paragraph is about?
   A. Yes   B. No

2. Do you have three to five facts about the place in your heritage paragraph?
   A. Yes   B. No

3. Do you have a good-bye sentence?
   A. Yes   B. No

4. Do you have order words and connecting words?
   A. Yes   B. No

5. Can you add a sentence to explain more about a fact?
   A. Yes   B. No

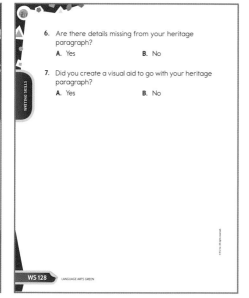

6. Are there details missing from your heritage paragraph?
   A. Yes   B. No

7. Did you create a visual aid to go with your heritage paragraph?
   A. Yes   B. No

Write Now •

Present Your Heritage Paragraph

Help students publish and present their paragraph. Turn to pages WS 129 and 130 in *K¹² Language Arts Activity Book.*

1. Help students write the final copy of their heritage paragraph on the Activity Book pages. Encourage them to write clearly and legibly.

2. When students have finished, have them present their paragraph and visual aid. Have them read their paragraph in a clear and loud voice.

3. Use the materials and instructions in the online lesson to evaluate students' finished writing. You will be looking at students' writing to evaluate the following:

   ▸ **Purpose and Content:** The paragraph is about the student's heritage or a place the student was interested in researching. Almost all the sentences are about the topic. The paragraph contains three to five facts about the place. There is a prop or visual aid that goes with the writing and has a connection to the writing.

   ▸ **Structure and Organization:** The paragraph has an introduction, a body, and a conclusion. Most sentences are connected with a transition word or follow a logical flow. The presentation includes the relevant content and makes good use of basic presentation skills.

   ▸ **Grammar and Mechanics:** The writing has mostly complete sentences and makes good use of verbs and describing words. The writer mostly uses the past and present tenses appropriately. There is evidence of proofreading.

4. Enter students' scores for each rubric category online.

5. If students scored a 1 in any criterion, work with students to proofread and revise their work.

TIP Students can publish their heritage paragraph in a variety of ways. For example, they may e-mail the final paragraph to friends and family members or make an audio or video recording of their presentation.

 Reward: When students' writing achieves "meets objectives" in all three categories on the grading rubric, add a sticker for this unit on the My Accomplishments chart.

 Objectives

- Write an informative or explanatory text.
- Write sentences with appropriate spacing between words.
- Write sentences with legible handwriting.
- Speak audibly and clearly to express thoughts, feelings, and ideas.

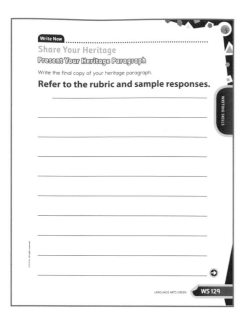

 **Online** varies

If necessary, work with students to complete the More Practice activity.

More Practice ....

Review Your Heritage Paragraph

If students' writing scored "doesn't meet objectives" in any category, have them complete the appropriate review activity listed in the table online.

> **Objectives**
> • Evaluate writing and choose activities to review and revise.

► Follow the online instructions to help students edit and revise their work.

► Impress upon students that revising makes their work better. Writing is a process, and each time they revise their paragraph, they are making their writing stronger and better.

► When you provide feedback, always begin with something positive. For example, you might point out a detail students wrote (even if it's the only detail) and explain how it helps you picture the scene: "You wrote that the heat was like an oven. That really helped me understand what the weather felt like."

► Place the final written work together with the rubric and the sample papers in the writing portfolio. This information is useful for you to track progress, and it helps students to refer back to their own work. They can see how they improve and review feedback to remember areas that need revising.

► Help students locate the activity and provide support as needed.

Adjectives

Unit Focus

In this unit, students will learn about adjectives and some of the specific kinds of adjectives. Students will

- ► Learn to recognize and use descriptive adjectives.
- ► Learn to recognize and use articles.
- ► Learn to recognize and use demonstrative adjectives.

Knowing how to properly use adjectives is a skill necessary to create strong writing. Adjectives help create pictures in the mind of the reader. They add depth, color, and character to writing. Because adjectives can be playful, students have a great opportunity to have fun when using them in their writing.

Unit Plan		[Offline]	[Online]
Lesson 1	Describing Words	15 minutes	
Lesson 2	Articles	15 minutes	
Lesson 3	Demonstratives	15 minutes	
Lesson 4	Review Adjectives	5 minutes	10 minutes
Lesson 5	Unit Checkpoint	15 minutes	varies

Describing Words

Lesson Overview

[Offline] 🕒 15 minutes

Get Ready	Lesson Introduction
	Remember Nouns
Learn	Understand Adjectives
Try It	Use Descriptive Adjectives

Materials

Supplied
- *K¹² Language Arts Activity Book*, pp. WS 131–132
- Story Card H

Also Needed
- whiteboard (optional)

Keywords

adjective – a word that describes a noun or a pronoun

Content Background

Adjectives are words that describe nouns. They often appear before the noun, as in the example *the **large** hill*. More than one descriptive adjective can appear before the same noun, as in the example *the **quiet, black** cat*. Adjectives may sometimes appear after the noun, as in this example: *The hill, **smooth** and **green**, invited picnickers.* This lesson focuses only on single adjectives that appear before the noun.

Big Ideas

Adjectives help readers visualize a scene or event.

[Offline] 🕒 15 minutes

Work **together** with students to complete Get Ready, Learn, and Try It activities.

Get Ready

Lesson Introduction

Prepare students for the lesson.

1. Tell students that they are going to be learning about adjectives.
2. Explain that adjectives are describing words.
3. Tell students that they are going to start by reviewing what nouns are.

Objectives
- Recall what a noun is.

Remember Nouns

To prepare students for learning about adjectives, use this activity to help them recall what a noun is. Gather Story Card H.

1. Tell students they are going to play a game of I Spy in which they try to find nouns.

   ▸ What is a noun? word that names a person, place, or thing

2. Show students Story Card H. Ask them to find nouns based on your descriptions. Tell them to point to the picture and name the noun.

   ▸ Point to something big that flies. What is the noun? airplane
   ▸ Point to someone with black hair in a ponytail. What is the noun? girl
   ▸ Point to a group of happy people going on a trip. What is the noun? family

3. Repeat all the nouns students found, adding the descriptive adjectives that you used.

4. **Say:** You found a big airplane, a girl with a black ponytail, and a happy family.

Learn

Understand Adjectives

Introduce adjectives to students. Turn to page WS 131 in *K¹² Language Arts Activity Book*.

1. Write the following sentence on a whiteboard or sheet of paper and read it with students:
   The dog smelled the flower.

2. Explain that the sentence gives basic information but not enough to imagine a picture.

   ▸ Can you tell what the dog looks like? No
   ▸ Can you tell what the flower looks like? No

3. Write the following words on the whiteboard or paper and read them with students:
   big, brown, pretty, yellow

4. Explain that all these words are adjectives. **Adjectives** are words that describe nouns.

5. Explain that adding adjectives to a sentence will make it easier to picture what is happening.

6. Rewrite the sentence, adding the adjectives. Read it with students.
   The big brown dog smelled the pretty yellow flower.

7. Read the Activity Book page with students. Explain that they are going to find the adjectives in each sentence. Some sentences have one adjective, and some sentences have more than one.

8. Provide assistance as necessary.

Objectives

- Recognize descriptive words known as adjectives.

TIP If you have extra time, let students add different adjectives to the first sentence on the whiteboard. Ask them to make the sentences as silly as possible, and see what adjectives they use. The more fun they have with the activity, the better they will remember how adjectives work.

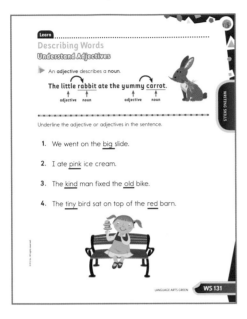

Try It

Use Descriptive Adjectives

Help students rewrite sentences using adjectives. Turn to page WS 132 in *K¹² Language Arts Activity Book*.

1. Read the instructions to students. Tell students to look at the picture.

2. Tell them to rewrite each sentence using adjectives from the word bank to make the sentence describe the picture. Provide support as necessary.

Objectives
- Use adjectives to describe someone or something.

Articles

Lesson Overview

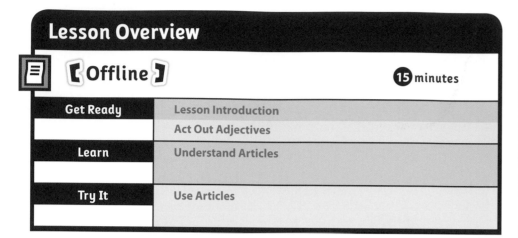

Offline		15 minutes
Get Ready	Lesson Introduction	
	Act Out Adjectives	
Learn	Understand Articles	
Try It	Use Articles	

Materials

Supplied
- *K¹² Language Arts Activity Book*, pp. WS 133–136

Also Needed
- whiteboard (optional)

Keywords

adjective – a word that describes a noun or a pronoun

article – the adjective *a*, *an*, or *the*

Content Background

A special kind of adjective is the article. The words *a*, *an*, and *the* are articles. The articles *a* and *an* refer to any noun, whereas the article *the* refers to a specific instance of a noun.

- *A* is used before a noun that begins with a consonant sound, such as in this sentence: *A dog dug up my garden.*
- *An* is used before a noun that begins with a vowel sound, such as in these sentences: *An elephant wants some food* and *An hour is a long time to wait.* Note that although *hour* begins with the consonant *h*, the sound is a vowel sound, so *an* is used.
- *The* is used before words that begin with either a vowel sound or a consonant sound. When *the* precedes a word that begins with a vowel sound, it usually is pronounced with a long *e* sound.

Big Ideas

Adjectives help readers visualize a scene or event.

[Offline] 🕒 15 minutes

Work **together** with students to complete Get Ready, Learn, and Try It activities.

Get Ready ●●

Lesson Introduction
Prepare students for the lesson.

1. Tell students that they are going to be learning about special adjectives called articles.

2. Tell students that they are going to start by reviewing what adjectives are.

> **Objectives**
> • Recognize descriptive words known as adjectives.

Act Out Adjectives
Help students remember what adjectives are.

1. Tell students that they are going to review adjectives.

   ▸ What do adjectives do? describe nouns

2. Explain that students are going to pretend to be different kinds of animals.

3. Tell students to act like a bear. Once they are pretending, tell them to act like a *slow* bear. Then tell them to act like a *fast* bear.

4. Tell students to meow like a cat. After they begin, tell them to meow like a *loud* cat. Then tell them to meow like a *quiet* cat.

5. Remind students that the words *slow, fast, loud,* and *quiet* are adjectives.

6. Ask students what kind of animal they want to pretend to be. Let them choose their own adjectives to change how the animal behaves.

TIP By using adjectives to change their behavior, students will learn that adjectives can have a big effect on a sentence.

Learn ●●

Understand Articles
Introduce articles to students. Turn to page WS 133 in *K¹² Language Arts Activity Book.*

> **Objectives**
> • Recognize the articles *a, an,* and *the.*

1. On a whiteboard or sheet of paper, write the following words and read them with students:
   the, a, an

2. Explain that these words are special adjectives called **articles**.

3. Help students understand when to use each article. **Read aloud** the following short story. Tell students to listen for the words *a*, *an*, and *the*, especially when you are talking about the animals in the story.

> One day, many birds, ants, and squirrels had a meeting in the forest. They were arguing about who should get to live in the trees. **A** bird spoke up and said, "The trees reach high into the sky, so we should get to live in them." Then, **an** ant spoke up and said, "The roots of the trees reach down into the ground where we work, so we should get to live in them."
>
> **The** bird and **the** ant who had spoken began to argue, when finally, **a** squirrel stepped forward to speak.
>
> **The** squirrel said, "The trees are so big. They reach down into the ground and all the way up into the sky. I think there is room for all of us to share." **A** bird who had been listening agreed, and so did **an** ant. Finally, **the** bird and **the** ant who had been arguing agreed as well, and all the animals lived happily together.

4. Explain to students that when any animal in the story was speaking, you used the article *a* or *an*. Explain that when you were talking about a specific animal, you used the article *the*.

5. Explain that *a* is used before nouns that begin with a consonant sound, such as *cat* or *dog*. Explain that *an* is used before nouns that begin with a vowel sound, such as *elephant* or *apple*.

6. Read the Activity Book page with students. Have them circle the articles in each sentence. Mention that some sentences have one article, and others have two. Provide assistance as necessary.

TIP If students are struggling with understanding what articles are and how they are used, look through a book they like and help them find some articles. Articles are words they use every day. Students already have an instinctual understanding of how articles work, so use writing they are interested in to help them deepen their understanding.

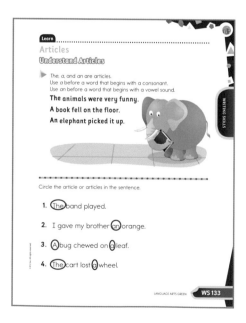

Try It

Use Articles

Help students practice using articles. Turn to pages WS 135 and 136 in *K¹² Language Arts Activity Book*.

1. Read the first set of directions to students.

2. Tell students to fill in the blanks in the sentences with the correct article, *a*, *an*, or *the*.

3. Read the second set of directions to students.

4. Tell students to use either *a* or *an* before each word.

5. Provide assistance as necessary.

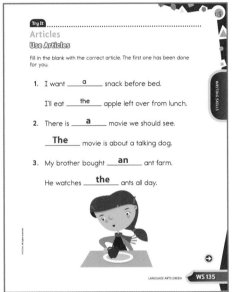

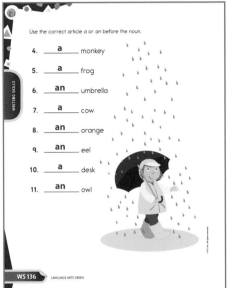

Demonstratives

Lesson Overview

	Offline	15 minutes
Get Ready	Lesson Introduction	
	Use a Lot of Description	
Learn	Understand Demonstratives	
Try It	Use Demonstratives	

Materials

Supplied
- *K¹² Language Arts Activity Book*, pp. WS 137–140

Also Needed
- scissors, adult
- whiteboard (optional)

Keywords

adjective – a word that describes a noun or a pronoun

demonstrative adjective – one of four describing words—*this, that, these, those*—that point out an object or objects

Advance Preparation

For the Get Ready, cut out the cards on page WS 137 in *K¹² Language Arts Activity Book*.

Content Background

Demonstratives are a special kind of adjective. These adjectives point out something. The demonstratives are *this, that, these,* and *those. This* and *that* are singular; *these* and *those* are plural. *This* and *these* refer to nouns that are near; *that* and *those* refer to nouns that are farther away. Although this lesson is about demonstrative adjectives, do not use the term *demonstrative* with students. Instead, refer to these words as adjectives that point out.

Big Ideas

Adjectives help readers visualize a scene or event.

 **Offline** **15** minutes

Work **together** with students to complete Get Ready, Learn, and Try It activities.

Get Ready

Lesson Introduction
Prepare students for the lesson.

1. Tell students that they are going to be learning about the special adjectives *this*, *that*, *these*, and *those*.

2. Tell students that they are going to start by reviewing what they have learned about adjectives.

 Objectives
- Use adjectives to describe someone or something.

Use a Lot of Description
Help students practice using adjectives with this sentence-building game. Gather the cards from page WS 137 in *K¹² Language Arts Activity Book*.

1. Tell students that adjectives can describe many things about a noun. Show them the word cards and explain that they are going to make a super-descriptive sentence.

2. Lay out the following cards in the order shown here.
   boy ate banana

3. Tell students that the first thing they need to do is add articles to have the sentence make sense.

4. Have students add the cards *the* and *a* before the two nouns. *the boy ate a banana* or *a boy ate the banana*

5. Tell students that now they get to make the sentence more interesting by adding adjectives. Explain that the adjectives that they add must come between the articles and the nouns.

6. Let students add the adjectives in any way they want. See what kinds of silly sentences they can make.

7. After students have made some sentences using the cards, ask them how a sentence should begin and end. A sentence should begin with a capital letter and end with an end mark.

TIP If you have extra time, let students write word cards of their own with the silliest adjectives they can think of. The more fun they have, the better they will understand how adjectives can affect their writing.

Learn

Understand Demonstratives

Introduce demonstratives to students. Turn to page WS 139 in *K¹² Language Arts Activity Book.*

1. On a whiteboard or sheet of paper, write the following words and read them with students:
   this, that, these, those

2. Hold up your pointer finger. Explain that certain adjectives work just like a pointer finger. We use them to point out nouns.

3. Explain that *this* is used to point to something nearby. Point with your finger each time you use the word.
   Say: This paper. This book. This pencil.

Objectives
- Recognize demonstrative adjectives.

4. Explain that *that* is used to point to something far away. Point with your finger each time you use the word.
   Say: That door. That window.

5. Tell students that we use *these* to point to a group of things nearby and *those* to point to a group of things faraway.

6. Read the Activity Book page with students. Have them circle the demonstrative adjectives in each sentence.

TIP Encourage students to point whenever they use these demonstratives. The physical action will help them understand the differences between the different words.

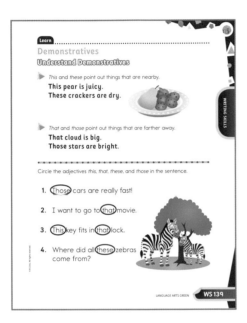

Try It

Use Demonstratives

Help students practice using demonstratives. Turn to page WS 140 in *K¹² Language Arts Activity Book*.

1. Read the instructions to students.

2. Tell students to fill in the blank in each sentence with the correct adjective. Remind them that *this* and *these* point out nouns that are nearby, and *that* and *those* point out nouns that are far away.

3. Provide assistance as necessary.

Objectives

• Use demonstrative adjectives.

Review Adjectives

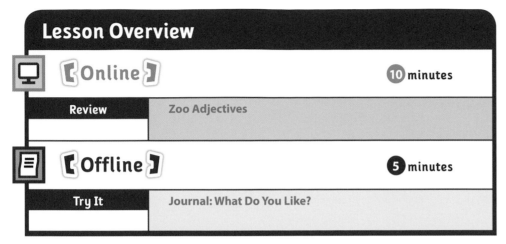

Lesson Overview

 **【Online】** 🔟 minutes

Review	Zoo Adjectives

【Offline】 🟢 minutes

Try It	Journal: What Do You Like?

【Materials】

Supplied
• *K¹² My Journal,* pp. 144–145

Also Needed
• crayons

Keywords
adjective – a word that describes a noun or a pronoun

article – the adjective *a, an,* or *the*

demonstrative adjective – one of four describing words—*this, that, these, those*—that point out an object or objects

【Online】 🔟 minutes

Students will review what they have learned about recognizing and using adjectives to prepare for the Unit Checkpoint. Help students locate the online activity and provide support as needed.

Review ••

Zoo Adjectives
Students will work online to review what they have learned about descriptive adjectives, articles, and demonstrative adjectives.

Offline Alternative

No computer access? Write out a story made up of six descriptive sentences. Have students circle all the descriptive adjectives, articles, and demonstrative adjectives in the story. Have students add three more sentences to the story. Explain that they need to use descriptive adjectives, articles, and adjectives that point out in the sentences they write.

Objectives
• Recognize descriptive words known as adjectives.
• Use adjectives to describe someone or something.
• Recognize the articles *a, an,* and *the.*
• Use the articles *a, an,* and *the* correctly.
• Recognize demonstrative adjectives.
• Use demonstrative adjectives.

5 minutes

Students will write on their own in their journal. Help students locate the offline activity.

Try It ....

✏️ **Journal: What Do You Like?**

Students will write in their journal on their own. Gather *K¹² My Journal* and have students turn to pages 144 and 145 in Writing Skills.

1. To help students prepare, have them list five adjectives to describe the room they are in.

2. Have students list five adjectives to describe the way they feel when they wake up in the morning.

3. Have students list five adjectives to describe their least favorite time of day.

4. Read the prompt with students. Have students respond to the prompt in their journal. As necessary, remind them that there are no correct or incorrect answers.

5. If students feel comfortable sharing what they wrote, allow them to share with you or their peers.

TIP The amount of time students need to complete this activity will vary. Allow them to use the rest of the allotted time to complete this activity. If they have more they would like to write, you may let them complete their entry at a later time. If students are having trouble getting started, you might tell them to just draw a picture and describe it to you. You can transcribe their words for them.

> **Objectives**
> - Write in a journal.
> - Freewrite about a topic.

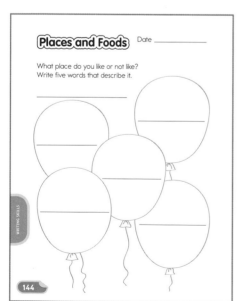

Unit Checkpoint

Lesson Overview

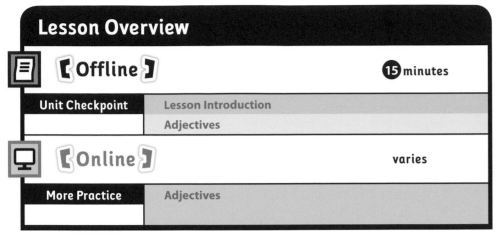

Offline		15 minutes
Unit Checkpoint	Lesson Introduction	
	Adjectives	

Online		varies
More Practice	Adjectives	

Materials

Supplied

- *K¹² Language Arts Assessments,* pp. WS 25–28

Offline   15 minutes

Work **together** with students to complete the Unit Checkpoint.

Unit Checkpoint

Lesson Introduction

Prepare students for the lesson.

1. Tell students that they are going to complete a Unit Checkpoint to show what they have learned.

2. Explain that if they miss one or more questions, they can continue to practice this grammar skill.

Adjectives

Explain that students are going to show what they have learned about recognizing and using adjectives.

1. Give students the Unit Checkpoint pages.

2. Read the directions together. If needed, read the questions and answer choices to students. Have students complete the Checkpoint on their own.

Objectives

- Recognize descriptive words known as adjectives.
- Use adjectives to describe someone or something.
- Recognize the articles *a*, *an*, and *the*.
- Use the articles *a*, *an*, and *the* correctly.
- Recognize demonstrative adjectives.
- Use demonstrative adjectives.

3. Use the Answer Key to score the Checkpoint and then enter the results online.

4. Review each exercise with students. Work with students to correct any exercise that they missed.

 TIP Students who answered one or more questions incorrectly should continue to practice this grammar skill. Write several sentences using different adjectives. Help students identify each type of adjective. Have them write three sentences. Each sentence should use a descriptive adjective and at least one article. Have them use a demonstrative adjective in at least one sentence.

Reward: When students score 80 percent or above on the Unit Checkpoint, add a sticker for this unit on the My Accomplishments chart.

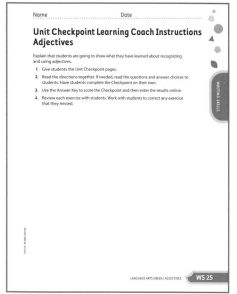

Name _____ Date _____

Unit Checkpoint Learning Coach Instructions
Adjectives

Explain that students are going to show what they have learned about recognizing and using adjectives.

1. Give students the Unit Checkpoint pages.
2. Read the directions together. If needed, read the questions and answer choices to students. Have students complete the Checkpoint on their own.
3. Use the Answer Key to score the Checkpoint and then enter the results online.
4. Review each exercise with students. Work with students to correct any exercise that they missed.

LANGUAGE ARTS GREEN | ADJECTIVES   **WS 25**

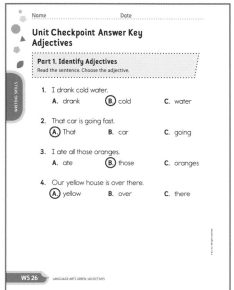

Name _____ Date _____

Unit Checkpoint Answer Key
Adjectives

Part 1. Identify Adjectives
Read the sentence. Choose the adjective.

1. I drank cold water.
   A. drank   **(B.)** cold   C. water

2. That car is going fast.
   (A.) That   B. car   C. going

3. I ate all those oranges.
   A. ate   **(B.)** those   C. oranges

4. Our yellow house is over there.
   (A.) yellow   B. over   C. there

WS 26   LANGUAGE ARTS GREEN | ADJECTIVES

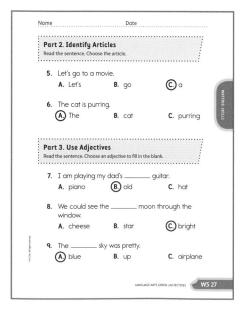

Name _____ Date _____

Part 2. Identify Articles
Read the sentence. Choose the article.

5. Let's go to a movie.
   A. Let's   B. go   **(C.)** a

6. The cat is purring.
   (A.) The   B. cat   C. purring

Part 3. Use Adjectives
Read the sentence. Choose an adjective to fill in the blank.

7. I am playing my dad's _____ guitar.
   A. piano   **(B.)** old   C. hat

8. We could see the _____ moon through the window.
   A. cheese   B. star   **(C.)** bright

9. The _____ sky was pretty.
   (A.) blue   B. up   C. airplane

LANGUAGE ARTS GREEN | ADJECTIVES   **WS 27**

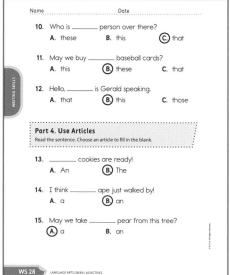

Name _____ Date _____

10. Who is _____ person over there?
    A. these   B. this   **(C.)** that

11. May we buy _____ baseball cards?
    A. this   **(B.)** these   C. that

12. Hello, _____ is Gerald speaking.
    A. that   **(B.)** this   C. those

Part 4. Use Articles
Read the sentence. Choose an article to fill in the blank.

13. _____ cookies are ready!
    A. An   **(B.)** The

14. I think _____ ape just walked by!
    A. a   **(B.)** an

15. May we take _____ pear from this tree?
    (A.) a   B. an

WS 28   LANGUAGE ARTS GREEN | ADJECTIVES

 **varies**

If necessary, work with students to complete the More Practice activity.

More Practice ···

Adjectives

If students scored less than 80 percent on the Unit Checkpoint, have them complete the appropriate review activities listed in the table online. Help students locate the activities and provide support as needed.

Objectives
- Evaluate Checkpoint results and choose activities to review.

Experience Story: Write a Story About You

Unit Focus

In this unit, students will write an experience story. They will

- ▶ Use their journal to freewrite.
- ▶ Write a beginning, middle, and end of their experience story.
- ▶ Learn how describing words make writing stronger.
- ▶ Write a draft of their experience story.
- ▶ Write a final copy of their experience story.

Unit Plan		〖Offline〗	〖Online〗
Lesson 1	Get Started on Your Story	**15** minutes	
Lesson 2	Stories with a Beginning, Middle, and End	**15** minutes	
Lesson 3	Add Strong Words	**15** minutes	
Lesson 4	Write a Draft of Your Story	**15** minutes	
Lesson 5	Revise and Publish Your Experience Story	**15** minutes	varies

Get Started on Your Story

Lesson Overview

[Offline]   15 minutes

Get Ready	Lesson Introduction
	Favorite Days
Try It	Freewrite: Use Your Journal

Materials

Supplied
- *K¹² My Journal*, pp. 146–147

Also Needed
- crayons (optional)

Keywords
freewriting – a way for a writer to pick a topic and write as much as possible about it within a set time limit

Big Ideas

Writers use various methods to plan, and novices should use what works for them: freewriting, listing, graphic organizers, or other methods.

[Offline] 15 minutes

Work **together** with students to complete Get Ready and Try It activities.

Get Ready

Lesson Introduction
Prepare students for the lesson.

1. Explain that students are going to write a story about themselves.

2. Tell them that to get started, they will write about their favorite day.

Objectives
- Generate ideas for writing.

Favorite Days

Introduce the idea that we all have favorite days.

1. Have students tell you about one of their favorite days. Answers to questions may vary.

   ▸ Do you have a favorite day?
   ▸ What makes that day so special?
   ▸ What do you remember about that day?
   ▸ What happened that was important or made you happy?
   ▸ How was that day different from a regular day?
   ▸ How did the day begin and end?

2. If students cannot think of a favorite day, ask them questions such as, "What do you like to do? What makes you smile? If you could do something again, what would it be?" Help them focus on how the day began and ended, and on the events of the day.

Try It

Freewrite: Use Your Journal

Help students freewrite about a favorite day. Gather *K¹² My Journal* and have students turn to pages 146 and 147 in Writing Skills. Read aloud the prompt at the top of the page.

1. Tell students they will write in their journal about their favorite day.

   ▸ Explain that they are freewriting, or writing ideas on the page.
   ▸ Tell them to write everything they remember about that day.
   ▸ Tell them that they can write whatever they want about that day: They can tell a story, write a list, or just jot down ideas.
   ▸ Ask students to write what happened at the beginning and end of the day, as well as what happened during the day.

2. If students are having trouble freewriting, help them by asking questions. Answers to questions may vary.

   ▸ What did you do?
   ▸ Where did you go?
   ▸ How did you feel?
   ▸ Why would you want to do that again?
   ▸ Why was that important?
   ▸ What else do you remember?

Objectives
- Generate ideas for writing.
- Freewrite on a topic.
- Write in a journal.

3. Encourage students to write as many ideas as they can.

4. If they wish, students can also draw a picture to illustrate the things they did on their favorite day.

5. Have students explain their writing to you. Do not evaluate students' writing. As long as students have written some ideas on paper, their responses are acceptable.

TIP The amount of time students need to complete this activity will vary. Allow students to use the rest of the allotted time to complete this activity. If they have more they would like to write, you may let them complete their entry at a later time. If students are having trouble getting started, you might tell them to just list ideas or words. They may even draw a picture and describe it to you. You can transcribe their words for them.

My Favorite Day   Date _____

Write about a favorite day. Tell why you liked it.

_____

_____

_____

_____

_____

_____

_____

_____

WRITING SKILLS

146

Draw a picture.

WRITING SKILLS

_____

_____

_____

_____

147

Stories with a Beginning, Middle, and End

Lesson Overview

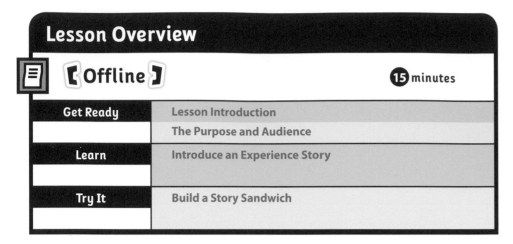

	Offline	**15** minutes
Get Ready	Lesson Introduction	
	The Purpose and Audience	
Learn	Introduce an Experience Story	
Try It	Build a Story Sandwich	

Materials

Supplied

- *K¹² My Journal*, pp. 146–147
- *K¹² Language Arts Activity Book*, pp. WS 141–147

Also Needed

- crayons – red, green
- scissors, round-end safety

Keywords

audience – a writer's readers
experience story – a story about something that happened to the writer
purpose – the reason for writing

Big Ideas

▶ Writers use various methods to plan, and novices should use what works for them: freewriting, listing, graphic organizers, or other methods.

▶ Sequencing ideas is the beginning of writing a personal narrative or experience story.

▶ Experience stories should be about a meaningful event that made a lasting impression on the writer and can be communicated to a reader.

▶ Writing requires organization and structure.

▶ Following a specific organizational structure is a useful tool for novice writers; writers require the freedom and flexibility to follow their ideas to completion.

[Offline] 15 minutes

Work **together** with students to complete Get Ready, Learn, and Try It activities.

Get Ready

Lesson Introduction
Prepare students for the lesson.

1. Tell students that they will continue working on their story.

2. Explain that they will use their ideas about their favorite day to begin to build a story.

3. Tell students that they will build their story like a sandwich, starting with the bread.

Objectives

- Identify a purpose for writing.
- Identify the audience.

The Purpose and Audience

Help students identify the purpose and audience for their story.

1. **Say:** Purpose is the reason for writing. A story has a purpose and an audience.

   ▸ Why do you read a story? Answers will vary.
   ▸ Who reads stories? children, parents, everyone

2. Have students turn to pages 146 and 147 in *K¹² My Journal* and review their journal entry about their favorite day.
   Say: Look at your journal. You wrote ideas about your favorite day. Now you are going to write a story about your favorite day.

   ▸ What is the purpose of your story? to tell about my favorite day
   ▸ Who will read your story? other students, family, friends

Learn

Introduce an Experience Story

Introduce an experience story to students and help them identify the beginning, middle, and end of their own experience story. Gather *K¹² My Journal* and the crayons.

Objectives
- Identify the beginning, middle, and end of a story.
- Plan the writing.

1. Explain that there are many kinds of stories. A good story tells about something interesting or important. Tell students that they will be writing a story that is all about one day in their life. The story tells about their experiences on their favorite day.

2. **Say:** You can read stories about lots of things. There are stories about frogs and toads and red dogs. There are stories about talking cats and best friends. And you can write stories about lots of things, too. You can even write a story that is all about you.

   ▸ Whose favorite day will you write about? mine
   ▸ Who is the best person to tell your story? me
   ▸ Why are you writing this story? to tell about my favorite day

3. Review that there are three parts to a story: a beginning, middle, and end.

4. **Say:** Think about what it means to tell a story. First, you start your story. Then, something happens in the story. And last, the story comes to an end.

   ▸ What do we call the three parts of a story? beginning, middle, end
   ▸ How many parts do you think your story will have? three

5. Have students turn to pages 146 and 147 in *K¹² My Journal* and review their journal entry about their favorite day.
   Say: Think about your favorite day and how it began. How will your story begin? Look at your journal and find what happened first on that day. Circle it with a green crayon.

6. **Say:** Think about what happened in the middle of your favorite day. What happens in the middle of your story? Look at what you wrote.

7. **Say:** Think about how your favorite day ended. How will your story end? Look at what you wrote. Find what happened at the end of the day. Circle it with a red crayon.

TIP If students do not have a beginning or ending for their story in their journal, they can add to what they have already written. If their journal page is filled, they may write on a separate sheet of paper.

Try It

Build a Story Sandwich

Help students write a beginning, middle, and end for their story, using the story sandwich graphic organizer. Turn to pages WS 141–147 in *K¹² Language Arts Activity Book* and gather the scissors.

1. **Say:** Who's hungry for a story? We are going to make a story sandwich.

2. Have students cut out the parts of the sandwich on the Activity Book pages. Help students as needed.

3. Identify the parts of the story sandwich with students.

   ▸ What are the parts of a sandwich? Look at the shapes you cut out. Can you name them? bread, meat, cheese

4. Tell students to stack the bread, meat, and cheese to make a sandwich. Students should put the meat and cheese between the two slices of bread

5. Show students how the parts of the sandwich are like the parts of a story. Point to the label on each part.

   ▸ The first piece of bread is the beginning.
   ▸ The meat and cheese are the middle.
   ▸ The second piece of bread is the end.

6. Tell students that they will use their ideas from their journal to make a story sandwich.

7. Help students write the beginning of their story on the first piece of bread.

   ▸ Have students write "My Favorite Day" next to the word *Title* on the first piece of bread.
   ▸ Help students find the part of their story that they circled in green in their journal. That will be the beginning of their story.
   ▸ Have students write the beginning of their story on the bread.
   ▸ Tell students that they do not have to write complete sentences.

8. Help students write the middle of their story on the meat and cheese.

   ▸ Remind students that the parts of their story that aren't circled in green or red are the middle.
   ▸ Have students write the middle of their story on the meat and cheese slices.
   ▸ Tell students that they can write more than one idea on a shape if they need to.

Objectives

- Write a beginning, middle, and end.
- Use a graphic organizer.
- Provide a sense of closure.

9. Help students write the end of their story on the second piece of bread.

▶ Have students find the part of their story that they circled in red in their journal. That will be the end of their story.

▶ Have students write the end of their story on the second piece of bread.

TIP Keep students' story sandwich shapes in a safe place so you can refer to them later. You can print extra copies of the pages from the online lesson, if necessary.

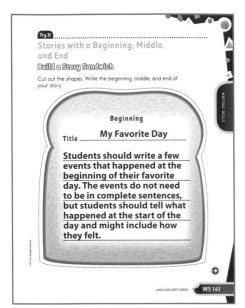

Try It

Stories with a Beginning, Middle, and End

Build a Story Sandwich

Cut out the shapes. Write the beginning, middle, and end of your story.

Beginning

Title ____ **My Favorite Day**

Students should write a few events that happened at the beginning of their favorite day. The events do not need to be in complete sentences, but students should tell what happened at the start of the day and might include how they felt.

LANGUAGE ARTS GREEN   **WS 141**

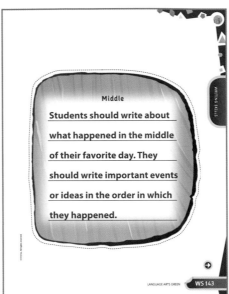

Middle

Students should write about what happened in the middle of their favorite day. They should write important events or ideas in the order in which they happened.

LANGUAGE ARTS GREEN   **WS 143**

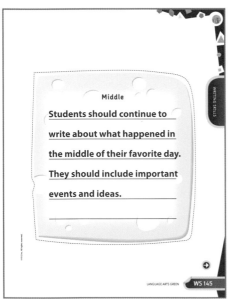

Middle

Students should continue to write about what happened in the middle of their favorite day. They should include important events and ideas.

LANGUAGE ARTS GREEN   **WS 145**

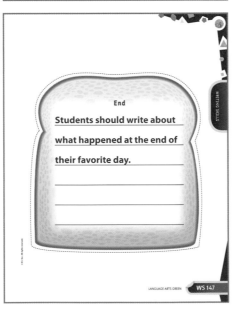

End

Students should write about what happened at the end of their favorite day.

LANGUAGE ARTS GREEN   **WS 147**

Add Strong Words

Lesson Overview

[Offline] 🕐 **15** minutes

Get Ready	Lesson Introduction
	See and Tell
Learn	Tell Me More
Try It	Write Strong Words

Materials

Supplied
- *K¹² Language Arts Activity Book*, pp. WS 141–153
- Story Card A

Also Needed
- scissors, adult
- scissors, round-end safety

Keywords
description – writing that uses words that show how something looks, sounds, feels, tastes, or smells
verb – a word that shows action

Advance Preparation

For the Learn, cut out the cards on page WS 149 in *K¹² Language Arts Activity Book*. Have students gather their completed story sandwich shapes from pages WS 141–147 (Build a Story Sandwich).

Big Ideas

▶ Good writing paints pictures with words to create a visual image of the text in the reader's mind's eye.
▶ Experience stories should be about a meaningful event that made a lasting impression on the writer and can be communicated to a reader.

[Offline] 🕐 **15** minutes

Work **together** with students to complete Get Ready, Learn, and Try It activities.

Get Ready

Lesson Introduction
Prepare students for the lesson.

1. Tell students that they will continue to work on their story about their favorite day.

2. Explain that they will learn how describing words such as strong adjectives and vivid verbs can make writing better.

3. Tell students that they will add new words to their story sandwich.

Objectives
- Use descriptive phrases.

See and Tell

Explain that using words that describe makes stories more interesting. Gather Story Card A.

1. **Say:** Pretend that you are ordering lunch. Listen to these lunch choices and tell me which one you would order.

   A tuna and cheese sandwich on a roll
   A fresh tuna and tasty Swiss cheese sandwich served on a thick, buttery roll

   Say: Which words make you hungry? *fresh; tasty Swiss; thick, buttery*

2. Show students Story Card A. Have them think of words that tell or describe what they see in the picture. Answers to questions may vary.

   ▸ What is happening in this picture? Describe what you see. Use describing words and strong action words. Be descriptive!
   ▸ What do you think that food tastes like? How does it smell?
   ▸ If I couldn't see the people in the picture, how would you tell me what they look like?

Learn •••

Tell Me More

Review descriptions with students. Gather the cards from page WS 149 in *K¹² Language Arts Activity Book*.

1. Remind students that adjectives are describing words. They describe or tell you something about a person, place, thing, or idea. They paint a picture for the reader.

2. **Say:** Listen to these two sentences.
   Grandma made a cake for dessert.
   Grandma made a delicious apple cake with white icing for dessert.

   ▸ How are the sentences different? The second sentence has describing words.
   ▸ Which words describe Grandma's dessert? *delicious; apple;* The word *white* tells about the icing.

3. Tell students that action words can also help describe.
   Say: Action words are verbs. They also tell more about what is happening.

   ▸ What is the verb, or action word, in the sentence *Grandma made a cake for dessert*? *made*

4. **Say:** What action word would be better than saying *made*? What do you do when you make a cake? *bake*

   ▸ *Grandma baked a cake* is a better or stronger sentence. You can picture Grandma wearing an apron in her kitchen and putting a cake in the oven to bake. *Baked* is a vivid verb because it helps us see a picture.

Objectives
• Use descriptive phrases.

5. Show students the cards. Explain that the words labeled *a* are adjectives and the words labeled *v* are verbs, or action words. Place the cards labeled *a* in one stack and the cards labeled *v* in another stack. If necessary, read the words to students.

   Say: Let's play a game called Tell Me More. I'll give you a sentence. You'll repeat it and then choose an *a* card or a *v* card from the top of the pile. You'll use that describing word or action word in your sentence. We'll say, "Tell me more." Then you'll choose a card from the other pile and add that word to your sentence.

   ▶ For example, my sentence is *Lily sees bugs.* I am going to pick a *v* card. The action word is *swallows.* I replace the action word *sees* with the new action word *swallows.* Now my sentence is *Lily swallows bugs.*

   ▶ You say, "Tell me more." I pick another card. This time, I choose an *a* card. The adjective is *shiny.* Now my sentence is *Lily swallows shiny bugs.*

6. Give each student a sentence. Play one round of the game so that students have a chance to add a verb and an adjective to a sentence. Use these sentences or make up your own.

   ▶ *Lily sees bugs.*
   ▶ *Matt likes frogs.*
   ▶ *Ana eats apples.*
   ▶ *Mittens has kittens.*

TIP If students are having difficulty distinguishing adjectives from verbs, ask them to tell you what they did this morning. Identify any adjectives or verbs in their response, or ask a question that will elicit examples. For instance, "What did you eat this morning? What did it look like? How did it taste? Did you gobble it or drink it?"

Try It

Write Strong Words

Help students add descriptive details such as adjectives and vivid verbs to their story. Gather students' story sandwich on pages WS 141–147 and turn to pages WS 151–153 in *K¹² Language Art Activity Book*. Also gather the scissors.

1. Review the parts of the story sandwich with students.

2. Have students cut out the lettuce and tomato shapes on pages WS 151 and 153. Help students as needed.

3. Tell students that adding lettuce and tomato to a sandwich makes the sandwich better. Adding strong words to their story makes it better, too.

4. Tell students they will now add vivid verbs and adjectives to their story sandwich. Remind them that vivid verbs tell more about what happened and that adjectives tell more about people, places, things, and ideas.

   ▸ Have students write vivid verbs on the lettuce shape. Tell them that these words should tell more about what happened in their story. For example, action words for a puppy story might be *jumped*, *wagged*, *licked*, *hugged*, and *played*. Provide support as necessary.
   ▸ Have students write adjectives on the tomato shape. Tell them that these words should describe events and details in their story. For example, for a story about getting a new puppy, the adjectives might be *cute*, *soft*, *cuddly*, and *happy*.

5. Help students if they are unable to think of action words or adjectives for their story. Ask them to tell about something in their story and then point out describing words they have just used or suggest several words. Prompt them with questions such as, "What did it look like? What did it smell like? How did it sound?"

TIP Keep students' story sandwich shapes in a safe place so you can refer to them later. You can print extra copies of the pages from the online lesson, if necessary.

Objectives

- Add descriptive details to strengthen writing.
- Use a graphic organizer.

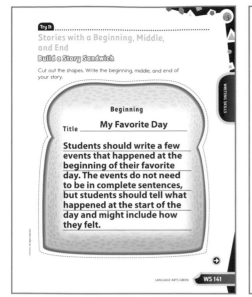

Try It

Stories with a Beginning, Middle, and End

Build a Story Sandwich

Cut out the shapes. Write the beginning, middle, and end of your story.

Beginning

Title **My Favorite Day**

Students should write a few events that happened at the beginning of their favorite day. The events do not need to be in complete sentences, but students should tell what happened at the start of the day and might include how they felt.

LANGUAGE ARTS GREEN **WS 141**

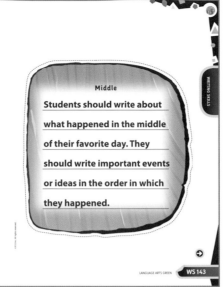

Middle

Students should write about what happened in the middle of their favorite day. They should write important events or ideas in the order in which they happened.

LANGUAGE ARTS GREEN **WS 143**

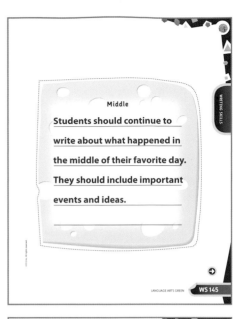

Middle

Students should continue to write about what happened in the middle of their favorite day. They should include important events and ideas.

LANGUAGE ARTS GREEN **WS 145**

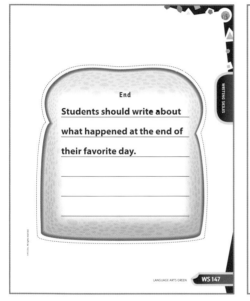

End

Students should write about what happened at the end of their favorite day.

LANGUAGE ARTS GREEN **WS 147**

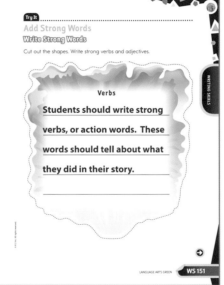

Try It

Add Strong Words

Write Strong Words

Cut out the shapes. Write strong verbs and adjectives.

Verbs

Students should write strong verbs, or action words. These words should tell about what they did in their story.

LANGUAGE ARTS GREEN **WS 151**

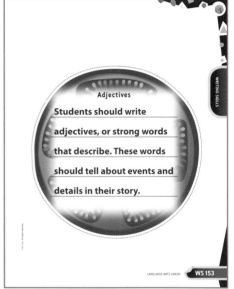

Adjectives

Students should write adjectives, or strong words that describe. These words should tell about events and details in their story.

LANGUAGE ARTS GREEN **WS 153**

Write a Draft of Your Story

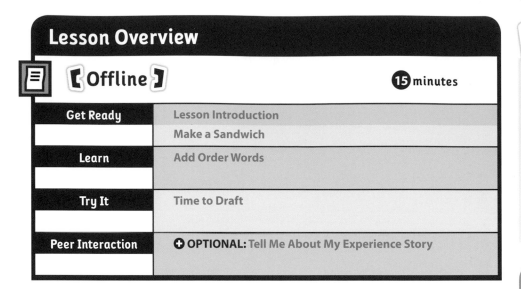

Lesson Overview

[Offline] **15** minutes

Get Ready	Lesson Introduction
	Make a Sandwich
Learn	Add Order Words
Try It	Time to Draft
Peer Interaction	➕ OPTIONAL: Tell Me About My Experience Story

[Materials]

Supplied
- *K¹² Language Arts Activity Book*, pp. WS 141–147, 151–153, 155–158

Also Needed
- household objects – hole punch; fastener (yarn, brad, or metal ring)

Keywords

drafting – of writing, the stage or step in which the writer first writes the piece

order words – words that connect ideas or a series of steps, or create a sequence, such as *first, next, later, finally*

Advance Preparation

Have students gather their completed story sandwich shapes from pages WS 141–147 (Build a Story Sandwich) and WS 151–153 (Write Strong Words) in *K¹² Language Arts Activity Book*.

Big Ideas

- ▶ Written work is never perfect in its first version. First efforts are called drafts, and they are not meant to be final.
- ▶ Experience stories should be about a meaningful event that made a lasting impression on the writer and can be communicated to a reader.
- ▶ Sequencing ideas is the beginning of writing a personal narrative or experience story.
- ▶ Writing requires organization and structure.
- ▶ Following a specific organizational structure is a useful tool for novice writers; however, writers require the freedom and flexibility to follow their ideas to completion.

 **15** minutes

Work **together** with students to complete Get Ready, Learn, Try It, and Peer Interaction activities.

Get Ready

Lesson Introduction
Prepare students for the lesson.

1. Tell students that they will put their sandwich shapes together.

2. Explain that you will review order words to help them connect ideas.

3. Tell students that they will write the draft of their story.

 Objectives
- Use a graphic organizer to tell a story orally.

Make a Sandwich
Have students put the story sandwich shapes together to make a sandwich. Gather students' story sandwich shapes on pages WS 141–147 and WS 151–153 in *K¹² Language Arts Activity Book*, hole punch, and fastener (yarn, brad, or metal ring).

1. Tell students that it's almost lunchtime—it's time to make that sandwich!

2. Have students put their story sandwich in order, with the beginning bread on top, the meat and cheese next, the lettuce and tomato after that, and finally the ending or other slice of bread on the bottom.

3. Punch a hole in the top left corner and put a fastener through the hole. The pages need to turn easily.

TIP Keep students' story sandwich in a safe place so you can refer to it later.

Learn

Add Order Words
Review order words in a story with students. Gather students' story sandwich.

1. Remind students that when they draft, they take their words and ideas from their graphic organizer and transfer them onto paper in sentences.

2. Review **order words** with students. Remind students that order words are important. They keep ideas together and in the order in which they happened. **Say:** Order words help tell a story. They tell the audience what happened first, next, and last. Remember to use order words when you write.

   ▸ What are some order words? *first, next, then, last, finally*

   Say: Listen for the order words: *First*, I wrote in my journal. *Next*, I wrote my ideas on sandwich shapes. *Last*, I wrote my draft.

 Objectives
- Use transitions to connect ideas.
- Put events in time order.

3. Have students tell their story orally, referring to their story sandwich. Listen to each story and see if the ideas make sense and if the student tells the story in the order in which it happened. Tell the student if a beginning, middle, or end is missing or unclear.

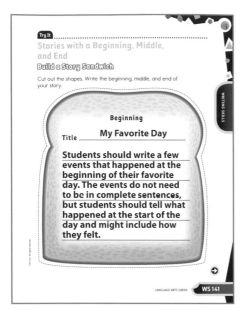

Try It

Stories with a Beginning, Middle, and End

Build a Story Sandwich

Cut out the shapes. Write the beginning, middle, and end of your story.

Beginning

Title **My Favorite Day**

Students should write a few events that happened at the beginning of their favorite day. The events do not need to be in complete sentences, but students should tell what happened at the start of the day and might include how they felt.

LANGUAGE ARTS GREEN · WS 141

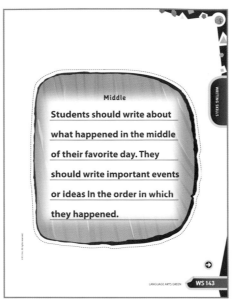

Middle

Students should write about what happened in the middle of their favorite day. They should write important events or ideas In the order in which they happened.

LANGUAGE ARTS GREEN · WS 143

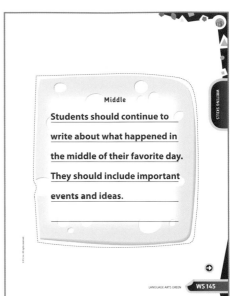

Middle

Students should continue to write about what happened in the middle of their favorite day. They should include important events and ideas.

LANGUAGE ARTS GREEN · WS 145

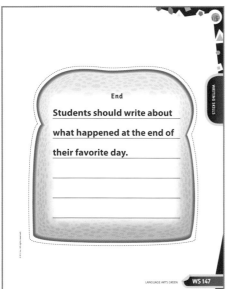

End

Students should write about what happened at the end of their favorite day.

LANGUAGE ARTS GREEN · WS 147

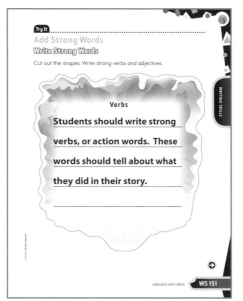

Try It

Add Strong Words

Write Strong Words

Cut out the shapes. Write strong verbs and adjectives.

Verbs

Students should write strong verbs, or action words. These words should tell about what they did in their story.

LANGUAGE ARTS GREEN · WS 151

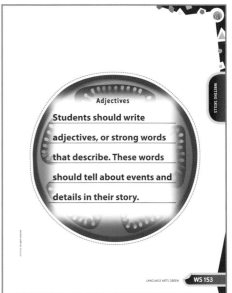

Adjectives

Students should write adjectives, or strong words that describe. These words should tell about events and details in their story.

LANGUAGE ARTS GREEN · WS 153

Try It

Time to Draft

Help students write the draft of their story. Gather students' story sandwich and turn to pages WS 155 and 156 in *K¹² Language Arts Activity Book*.

1. Tell students it's time to write the draft of their story.

2. Read the directions to students.

   ▸ Have students write the draft of their story in the order in which the events happened. Tell them to follow the order of the story sandwich. Students should write a title at the top of the Activity Book page and then write a beginning, middle, and end.

   ▸ Remind students to write in complete sentences. A complete sentence begins with a capital letter and has an end mark.

   ▸ Remind them to add the strong words on the lettuce and tomato shapes to their sentences as they write.

3. Remind students that a draft is a first attempt at writing, not a finished story. They should focus on transferring their ideas from their sandwich shapes to their draft in the correct order.

4. Provide support as necessary. If students are struggling with their sentences, have them dictate their story to you. Write their story on a separate paper that students can then refer to as they write. You should write the students' words verbatim. Do not make changes.

TIP The amount of time students need to complete this activity will vary. If students are not able to complete their writing within the allotted lesson time, you might set aside another 15-minute time block for them. Be mindful of the assignment expectations when budgeting time and remember that student writing is not adult writing. Keep students' draft in a safe place so you can refer to it later.

Objectives

- Use transitions to connect ideas.
- Put events in time order.
- Use planning ideas to produce a rough draft.
- Write a draft.
- Write a beginning, middle, and end.
- Write a brief story that describes an experience.

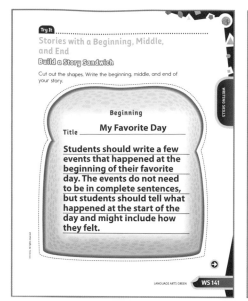

Try It

Stories with a Beginning, Middle, and End
Build a Story Sandwich

Cut out the shapes. Write the beginning, middle, and end of your story.

Beginning

Title __My Favorite Day__

Students should write a few events that happened at the beginning of their favorite day. The events do not need to be in complete sentences, but students should tell what happened at the start of the day and might include how they felt.

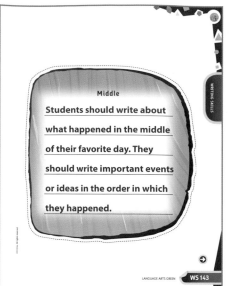

Middle

Students should write about what happened in the middle of their favorite day. They should write important events or ideas in the order in which they happened.

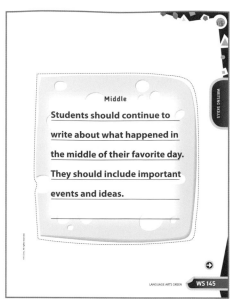

Middle

Students should continue to write about what happened in the middle of their favorite day. They should include important events and ideas.

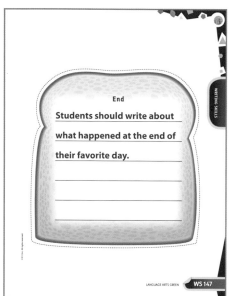

End

Students should write about what happened at the end of their favorite day.

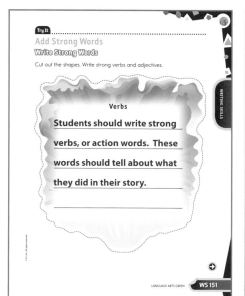

Try It

Add Strong Words
Write Strong Words

Cut out the shapes. Write strong verbs and adjectives.

Verbs

Students should write strong verbs, or action words. These words should tell about what they did in their story.

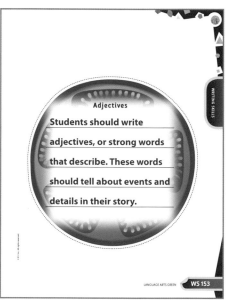

Adjectives

Students should write adjectives, or strong words that describe. These words should tell about events and details in their story.

Try It

Write a Draft of Your Story
Time to Draft

Write your story. Include a beginning, middle, and end. Use order words as you write your draft. Order words are *first, next, then, last,* and *finally.*

Students should write a draft of their story with a beginning, middle, and end. They should use complete sentences and tell the story in the order in which it happened.

Peer Interaction

⊕ OPTIONAL: Tell Me About My Experience Story

This activity is OPTIONAL. It is intended for students who have extra time and would benefit from extra practice. Feel free to skip this activity.

Students can benefit from exchanging stories with someone they know or another student. This activity will work best if students exchange their story with other students who have completed the same assignment, but you may copy the Activity Book pages and send them to someone else who is willing to give students feedback. Students should receive feedback on the content of their story. To complete this activity, turn to pages WS 157 and 158 in *K¹² Language Arts Activity Book*.

1. Have students exchange stories with other students.

2. Have students use the Activity Book pages to provide others with feedback about their writing.

3. Tell students that they will use this feedback to revise their story later.

Objectives

- Use guidance from adults and peers to revise writing.
- Collaborate with peers on writing projects.

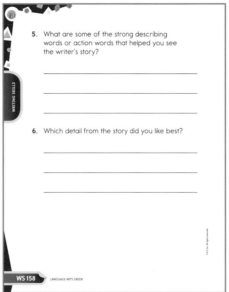

Revise and Publish Your Experience Story

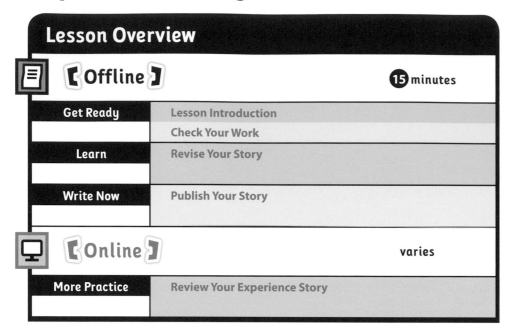

Lesson Overview

📋 [Offline]   15 minutes

Get Ready	Lesson Introduction
	Check Your Work
Learn	Revise Your Story
Write Now	Publish Your Story

🖥 [Online]   varies

| More Practice | Review Your Experience Story |

Keywords

proofreading – the stage or step of the writing process in which the writer checks for errors in grammar, punctuation, capitalization, and spelling

publishing – the stage or step of the writing process in which the writer makes a clean copy of the piece and shares it

revising – the stage or step of the writing process in which the writer rereads and edits the draft, correcting errors and making changes in content or organization that improve the piece

Advance Preparation

Have students gather their completed pages WS 155 and 156 (Time to Draft, draft experience story) and WS 157 and 158 (Tell Me About My Experience Story, feedback) in *K¹² Language Arts Activity Book*.

Big Ideas

▸ Writing requires rewriting or revision.
▸ Revision is best accomplished through discrete, focused tasks.
▸ Completed writing is a praiseworthy accomplishment. Find opportunities for students to share their work.

Offline 15 minutes

Work **together** with students to complete Get Ready, Learn, and Write Now activities.

Get Ready

Lesson Introduction

Prepare students for the lesson.

1. Tell students that they will add new ideas to their story.

2. Explain that they will revise and proofread their story.

3. Tell students that they will write a final copy of their story.

Check Your Work

Help students use a checklist to revise their work. Gather students' draft experience story on pages WS 155 and 156 and turn to pages WS 159 and 160 in *K¹² Language Arts Activity Book.*

1. Read aloud the checklist on the Activity Book pages. Help students answer all the questions.

2. If students answered *No* to any of the first four questions or *Yes* to Question 5, 6, or 7, have them circle the corresponding part of their draft.

TIP Keep the draft and checklist in a safe place so students can refer to them when they revise their draft.

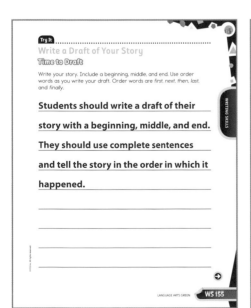

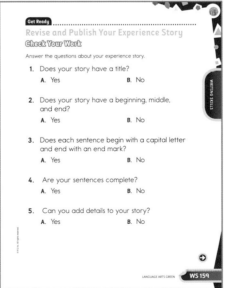

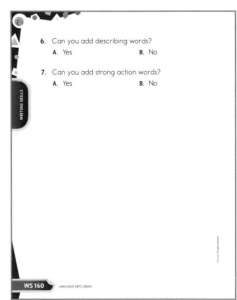

Learn

Revise Your Story

Help students revise their experience story. Gather students' draft experience story on pages WS 155 and 156, feedback on pages WS 157 and 158, and checklist on pages WS 159 and 160 in *K¹² Language Arts Activity Book*.

1. **Say:** How do you make a real sandwich taste better? Is there anything you like to add to your sandwich to make it tastier? Possible answers: pickle; onion; mustard

2. Tell students they can make their story better in the same way they would add a pickle, onion, or mustard to a sandwich.

3. Have students read their draft aloud.

4. Ask students if they have more ideas that they want to add to their story.

   ▸ Use questions to get students thinking about their story, such as "What happened after that? How did you feel when that happened?" Make your comments positive—for example, "I'd like to know more about that idea."

   ▸ Have students make notes on their draft of any ideas they might want to add.

5. Review the checklist and Peer Interaction pages with students. Using a pencil, have them make notes and corrections on their draft.

TIP Revising is a difficult step for writers at any age. All writers revise, even published authors. It is important that students do not get discouraged and think that their first attempt was wrong. Revising makes writing better, and writing a draft is only one step in the writing process.

Objectives
- Revise by adding or deleting text.
- Revise using a checklist.
- Use a checklist for editing and proofreading.
- Revise by using feedback.
- Collaborate with peers on writing projects.
- Use guidance from adults and peers to revise writing.

Try It
Write a Draft of Your Story
Time to Draft

Write your story. Include a beginning, middle, and end. Use order words as you write your draft. Order words are *first, next, then, last,* and *finally.*

Students should write a draft of their

story with a beginning, middle, and end.

They should use complete sentences

and tell the story in the order in which it

happened.

_____

_____

_____

_____

LANGUAGE ARTS GREEN   **WS 155**

Peer Interaction
Write a Draft of Your Story
Tell Me About My Experience Story

Have another person read your experience story and answer these questions.

1. Is the story about a favorite day?
   A. Yes   B. No

2. Does the story have a beginning, middle, and end?
   A. Yes   B. No

3. If the story is missing a part, which part is missing?

   _____

   _____

   _____

4. Did the writer use order words and other transitions?
   A. Yes   B. No

LANGUAGE ARTS GREEN   **WS 157**

5. What are some of the strong describing words or action words that helped you see the writer's story?

   _____

   _____

   _____

6. Which detail from the story did you like best?

   _____

   _____

   _____

WS 158   LANGUAGE ARTS GREEN

Get Ready
Revise and Publish Your Experience Story
Check Your Work

Answer the questions about your experience story.

1. Does your story have a title?
   A. Yes   B. No

2. Does your story have a beginning, middle, and end?
   A. Yes   B. No

3. Does each sentence begin with a capital letter and end with an end mark?
   A. Yes   B. No

4. Are your sentences complete?
   A. Yes   B. No

5. Can you add details to your story?
   A. Yes   B. No

LANGUAGE ARTS GREEN   **WS 159**

6. Can you add describing words?
   A. Yes   B. No

7. Can you add strong action words?
   A. Yes   B. No

WS 160   LANGUAGE ARTS GREEN

Write Now

 Publish Your Story

Help students write a final copy of their experience story. Gather students' revised draft on pages WS 155 and 156 and turn to pages WS 161 and 162 in *K¹² Language Arts Activity Book*. Also gather the crayons.

1. Help students rewrite their experience story on pages WS 161 and 162. Encourage them to write clearly and legibly.

2. Have students illustrate their story.

3. Use the materials and instructions in the online lesson to evaluate students' finished writing. You will be looking at students' writing to evaluate the following:

   ▸ **Purpose and Content:** The writing is mostly in the form of a narrative story and tells about the student's favorite day. There are some adjectives and strong verbs that provide details and add to the story.
   ▸ **Structure and Organization:** The story has a beginning, middle, and end. There are some transitions or order words used to connect ideas.
   ▸ **Grammar and Mechanics:** The story was proofread using a checklist, although a few errors may remain. Sentences are mostly complete.

4. Enter students' scores for each rubric category online.

5. If student's writing scored a 1 in any criterion, work with them to proofread and revise their work.

6. Have the students share their story with others. You might want to serve sandwiches!

TIP The amount of time students need to complete this activity will vary. Students need only work for 15 minutes. Praise students when their story is finished. This is a great achievement, and students should be proud of what they have produced. Celebrating the publishing of students' work is a way to acknowledge their success and encourage them to keep writing.

 Reward: When students' writing achieves "meets objectives" in all three categories on the grading rubric, add a sticker for this unit on the My Accomplishments chart.

 Objectives
- Write a final copy.
- Print legibly and space letters, words, and sentences appropriately.
- Illustrate a work.
- Share the story.

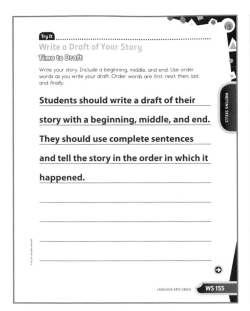

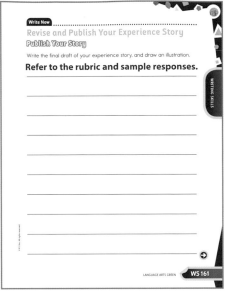

Online varies

If necessary, work with students to complete the More Practice activity.

More Practice

Review Your Experience Story

If students' writing scored "doesn't meet objectives" in any category, have them complete the appropriate review activity listed in the table online.

▶ Follow the online instructions to help students revise and proofread their work.

▶ Impress upon students that revising makes their work better. Writing is a process, and each time they revise their experience story, they are making their writing stronger and better.

▶ When you provide feedback, always begin with something positive. For example, you might point out a detail students wrote (even if it's the only detail) and explain how it helps you picture the scene: "You wrote that the heat was like an oven. That really helped me understand what the weather felt like."

▶ Place the final written work together with the rubric and the sample response in the writing portfolio. This information is useful for you to track progress, and it helps students refer back to their own work. They can see how they improve and review feedback to remember areas that need revising.

▶ Help students locate the activity and provide support as needed.

Objectives

• Evaluate writing and choose activities to review and revise.

UNIT OVERVIEW | Capital Letters and Punctuation

Unit Focus

In this unit, students will learn some rules of capitalization and punctuation. Students will learn how to

- ▶ Recognize and use apostrophes to make contractions.
- ▶ Use commas to write words in a series.
- ▶ Capitalize and punctuate a date.

Learning how to use capitalization and punctuation correctly will make students' writing clearer to the reader.

Unit Plan		**[Offline]**	**[Online]**
Lesson 1	Contractions	**15** minutes	
Lesson 2	Words in a Series	**15** minutes	
Lesson 3	Dates	**15** minutes	
Lesson 4	Review Capital Letters and Punctuation	**5** minutes	**10** minutes
Lesson 5	Unit Checkpoint	**15** minutes	varies

Contractions

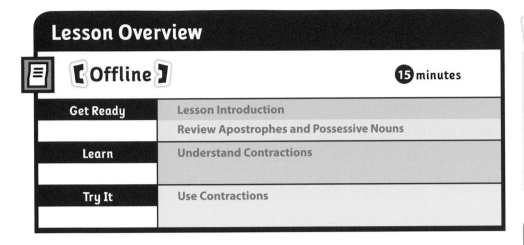

Lesson Overview

[Offline]   **15** minutes

Get Ready	Lesson Introduction
	Review Apostrophes and Possessive Nouns
Learn	Understand Contractions
Try It	Use Contractions

Materials

Supplied
- *K¹² Language Arts Activity Book*, pp. WS 163–164

Also Needed
- whiteboard (optional)

Keywords
contraction – a shortened word or words where an apostrophe replaces missing letters

Content Background

A contraction is a shortened word usually made up of two words combined into one word. An apostrophe takes the place of the missing letter or letters. Using contractions is a relatively easy way to make writing sound less formal. This lesson focuses on only those contractions formed with a verb and the word *not*.

Big Ideas

When a writer uses capitalization and punctuation correctly, the reader is better able to understand what the writer is saying.

 **[Offline]** **15** minutes

Work **together** with students to complete Get Ready, Learn, and Try It activities.

Get Ready ....

Lesson Introduction
Prepare students for the lesson.

1. Tell students that they are going to be learning about contractions.

2. Explain that a contraction usually makes one word out of two words.

3. Tell students that they are going to learn how to use an apostrophe to make a contraction.

Objectives
- Recall what a possessive noun is.

Review Apostrophes and Possessive Nouns

To prepare students to learn about contractions, remind them what an apostrophe is. Use this activity to help them remember how the apostrophe works in possessive nouns.

1. On a whiteboard or sheet of paper, write the following words and read them with students: *Jen, hat.*

2. **Say:** I want to make *Jen* a possessive noun. I want to make it clear that the hat belongs to Jen.

   ▶ What do I add to the noun *Jen* to make it possessive? an apostrophe and *s*

3. Add an apostrophe and *s* after *Jen* so the words now read *Jen's hat.*

   ▶ Can I just write an *s* after *Jen* with no apostrophe? No
   ▶ What kind of noun do I make if I write an *s* after *Jen* with no apostrophe? a plural noun

4. Point to the apostrophe in the word. Tell students that it is used to make possessive nouns. Explain that the apostrophe is also used to make another kind of word: a contraction.

Learn

Understand Contractions

Introduce contractions to students. Turn to page WS 163 in *K¹² Language Arts Activity Book.*

Objectives
- Identify contractions.

1. Explain that a **contraction** is a way to take two words and shorten them so they become one word.

2. On the whiteboard or paper, write the following words and read them with students: *do not.*

3. Tell students that sometimes two words want to work together to make one word. To do this, they need to get closer, so they get rid of a letter.

4. Under *do not*, write the following word, one letter at a time. As you write each letter, read it aloud (including *apostrophe*): *d-o-n-'-t.*

5. Explain that to get closer, the words dropped the *o* from *not*.
   Say: The words leave an apostrophe in that space so they don't forget where the *o* goes.

6. On the whiteboard or paper, write the following words and read them with students:

   ▶ *should not – shouldn't*
   ▶ *could not – couldn't*
   ▶ *is not – isn't*

7. Read the Activity Book page with students. Have students circle the contraction in each set of sentences.

8. Provide assistance as necessary.

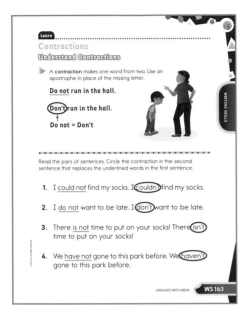

Try It

Use Contractions

Help students practice using contractions. Turn to page WS 164 in *K¹² Language Arts Activity Book.*

1. Read the instructions to students.

2. Have students make a contraction from each set of words. Then, have them write a sentence using the contraction.

3. Provide assistance as necessary.

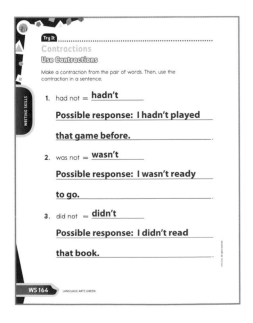

Objectives
- Form and use contractions.

Words in a Series

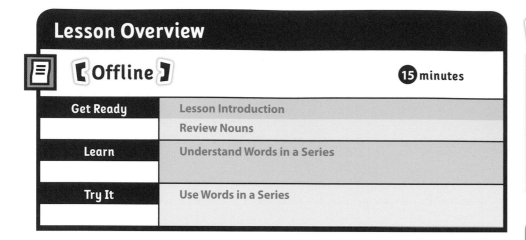

Lesson Overview

[Offline]		15 minutes
Get Ready	Lesson Introduction	
	Review Nouns	
Learn	Understand Words in a Series	
Try It	Use Words in a Series	

Materials

Supplied
- *K¹² Language Arts Activity Book*, pp. WS 165–166

Also Needed
- whiteboard (optional)

Keywords

words in a series – a list of words in a sentence that are separated by commas

Content Background

▸ Commas are used between items in a series. A comma is placed after each item, including before the word *and*. For example, this sentence uses commas correctly: *Books, puppets, and games were on the shelves in the children's room.*

▸ In newspapers and magazines, the final comma before the word *and* is usually omitted to save space. However, using this final comma helps avoid confusion. For example, in the sentence *I would like to dedicate this book to my friends, Gandhi and Abraham Lincoln,* the lack of a comma before the word *and* makes it unclear whether the writer is dedicating the book to three different people or claiming that his friends are Gandhi and Abraham Lincoln. The ambiguity is eliminated by the use of the final serial comma: *I would like to dedicate this book to my friends, Gandhi, and Abraham Lincoln.*

Big Ideas

When a writer uses capitalization and punctuation correctly, the reader is better able to understand what the writer is saying.

 **15** minutes

Work **together** with students to complete Get Ready, Learn, and Try It activities.

Get Ready

Lesson Introduction
Prepare students for the lesson.

1. Tell students that they are going to be learning about words in series.

2. Tell students that they are going to learn how to use commas to separate words in a series.

Objectives
- List nouns.
- Recall what a noun is.

Review Nouns
Use this quick exercise to review nouns and prepare students to write words in a series.

1. Review what a noun is.

   ▸ What does a noun name? a person, place, or thing

2. Explain to students that the names of different kinds of pets are nouns. Tell them that they are going to play a game in which they try to name as many pets as possible in a short amount of time.

3. On a whiteboard or sheet of paper, write the following sentence starter and read it with students: *Some great pets are* _____ .

4. Have students name as many kinds of pets as they can think of, as quickly as possible. Possible answers: cats; dogs; fish; parakeets

5. As students name pets, add them to the sentence. Instead of using a comma after each pet, write the word *and*.

6. Give students about thirty seconds to name pets and then tell them to stop. Read the sentence together.

TIP Making this list can be silly and fun. When you read the final sentence, try to say it using only one breath. Exaggerate how challenging this is. Not only might it make students laugh, it will emphasize how cumbersome the sentence is with so many *and*s.

Learn

Understand Words in a Series

Introduce words in a series to students. Turn to page WS 165 in *K¹² Language Arts Activity Book.*

1. On the whiteboard or paper, write the following sentence and read it with students: *I love popcorn and crackers and grapes and apples.*

2. Tell students that there is a simpler way to write this sentence.

3. Explain that using *and* over and over makes the sentence too long and clumsy.

4. **Say:** To make the sentence shorter, a writer can replace almost every *and* with a comma.

5. Cross out the first two uses of the word *and* and replace them with commas.

6. Explain that before the last word in the series, a comma, as well as the word *and*, is used.

7. Read the new sentence with students: *I love popcorn, crackers, grapes, and apples.*

8. Tell students that the words *popcorn, crackers, grapes,* and *apples* are called **words in a series**.

9. Read the Activity Book page with students. Have them add the missing comma to the words in a series in each sentence.

10. Provide assistance as necessary.

TIP Although words in a series are often nouns, other kinds of words, such as verbs and adjectives, can be used in a series.

Objectives

- Use a comma to separate words in a series.

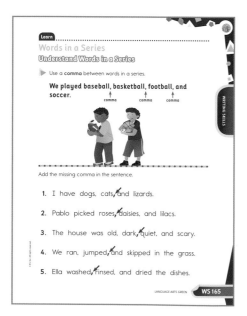

Try It

Use Words in a Series

Help students practice using words in a series. Turn to page WS 166 in *K¹² Language Arts Activity Book.*

1. Read the first set of instructions to students.

2. Tell students to add the missing commas to each set of words in a series. Sentences will be missing between one and three commas.

3. Read the second set of instructions to students.

4. Tell students to write a sentence that tells three things they like.

5. Provide support as necessary.

Objectives

- Use a comma to separate words in a series.

Try It

Words in a Series

Use Words in a Series

Add the missing comma or commas to the sentence.

1. We listen to jazz, pop, and classical music.

2. I collect worms, snails, ladybugs, and moths.

3. Everyone laughed, cried, cheered, and clapped at the show.

Write a sentence that describes three things you like.
For example, *I like bugs, plants, and rocks.*

4. **Answers must use at least three words in a series and have a comma after each word that comes before *and*.**

WS 166   LANGUAGE ARTS GREEN

Dates

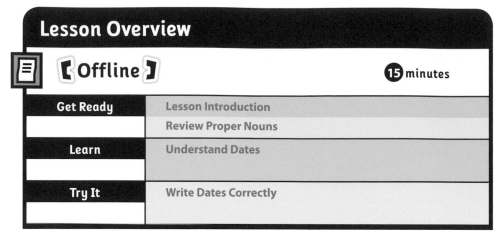

Lesson Overview

[Offline] — **15** minutes

Get Ready	Lesson Introduction
	Review Proper Nouns
Learn	Understand Dates
Try It	Write Dates Correctly

[Materials]

Supplied
- *K¹² Language Arts Activity Book*, pp. WS 167–170

Also Needed
- scissors, adult
- markers, coloring
- whiteboard (optional)

Keywords

proper noun – a word that names a specific person, place, or thing

Advance Preparation

For the Get Ready, cut out the cards on page WS 167 in *K¹² Language Arts Activity Book*, and then separate the cards *girl* and *Anne* from the rest of the cards.

Content Background

Both a capital letter and a comma are used in dates. Months are proper nouns, so they are capitalized. A comma is placed between the day and year. For example: *Spring break began on March 22, 2012.*

Big Ideas

When a writer uses capitalization and punctuation correctly, the reader is better able to understand what the writer is saying.

 **15** minutes

Work **together** with students to complete Get Ready, Learn, and Try It activities.

Get Ready

Lesson Introduction
Prepare students for the lesson.

 Objectives
- Recall what a proper noun is.

1. Tell students that they are going to be learning about dates.

2. Explain that the names of months are proper nouns.

3. Tell students that they are going to learn how to use a capital letter and a comma in a date.

Review Proper Nouns
Help students remember how to recognize and write proper nouns. Gather the cards from page WS 167 in *K¹² Language Arts Activity Book*.

1. Tell students that some nouns name something in general, but other nouns name something specific.

2. Put the word cards *girl* and *Anne* face up in front of students.

3. Point to the word *girl* and remind students that it is a common noun. Point to the word *Anne* and remind students that it is a proper noun.

   ▸ How does a proper noun always begin? with a capital letter

4. Lay out the rest of the word cards from the Activity Book page in random order. Help students match each common noun to the corresponding proper noun.

Learn

Understand Dates

Introduce writing dates to students. Turn to page WS 169 in *K¹² Language Arts Activity Book* and gather the coloring markers.

1. Explain to students that they are going to learn the proper way to write a date.

2. Tell students that when we write a date, we write the month, the day of the month, and the year.

3. Write the following date on a whiteboard or sheet of paper and read it with students: *March 4, 2012.*

   ► What kind of noun is the word *March*? a proper noun
   ► How do we begin a proper noun? with a capital letter

4. Explain that the month is always capitalized in a date. Point to the comma after the number *4*. Explain that a comma always follows the day of the month.

5. **Say:** I am going to write another date, and I need help to write it correctly.

   ► I am going to write the word *April.* How should it begin? with a capital letter

6. Write *April* on the whiteboard or paper.

   ► I am going to write the day of the month: *14.* What should come after the day of the month? a comma

7. Write *14* and a comma on the whiteboard or paper. Finish by writing the year *2012.*

8. Read the Activity Book page with students. Have them color the sections of the page that have correctly written dates.

9. Provide assistance as necessary.

Try It

Write Dates Correctly

Help students practice writing dates. Turn to page WS 170 in *K¹² Language Arts Activity Book*.

1. Read the first set of instructions to students.

2. Tell students to correct each date. Use the example as a model.

3. Read the second set of instructions to students.

4. Tell students to correctly write the date on which they were born.

5. Provide assistance as necessary.

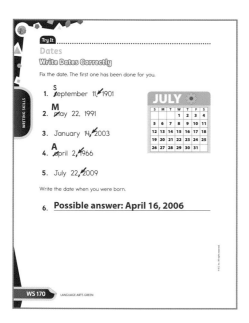

Review Capital Letters and Punctuation

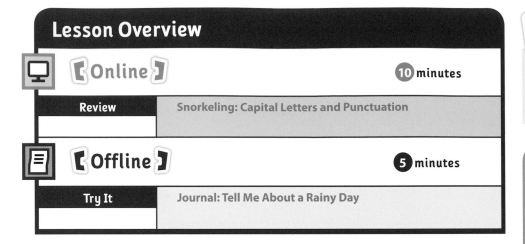

Lesson Overview

Online   🔟 minutes

Review	Snorkeling: Capital Letters and Punctuation

Offline   5 minutes

Try It	Journal: Tell Me About a Rainy Day

Materials

Supplied

• *K¹² My Journal*, pp. 148–149

Keywords

contraction – a shortened word or words where an apostrophe replaces missing letters

proper noun – a word that names a specific person, place, or thing

words in a series – a list of words in a sentence that are separated by commas

 🔟 **minutes**

Students will review what they have learned about contractions, words in a series, and dates to prepare for the Unit Checkpoint. Help students locate the online activity and provide support as needed.

Review ···

Snorkeling: Capital Letters and Punctuation
Students will work online to review what they have learned about contractions, words in a series, and dates.

 Objectives

- Identify contractions.
- Form and use contractions.
- Use a comma to separate words in a series.
- Identify correctly written dates.
- Use a capital letter and a comma in a date.

Offline Alternative

No computer access? Find a newspaper or newsmagazine. Help students find contractions, words in a series, and dates in the writing. Have them circle three examples of each. Then, have students write three sentences about something they saw in the newspaper or newsmagazine, using at least one contraction, one set of words in a series, and one date.

〖 Offline 〗 ⑤ minutes

Students will write on their own in their journal. Help students locate the offline activity.

Try It ....

 **Journal: Tell Me About a Rainy Day**

Students will write in their journal on their own. Gather *K¹² My Journal* and have students turn to pages 148 and 149 in Writing Skills.

1. Tell students that they are going to be freewriting in a journal. Remind them that there are no right or wrong answers. They just need to write what they are thinking.

2. To prepare students to write, tell them to think about the last time it rained very hard. Answers to questions may vary.

   ▸ Where were you when it was raining?
   ▸ Were you alone or with someone else?
   ▸ Did you go outside or stay inside?
   ▸ What fun things did you do?

3. Read the prompt to students. Have them write a response in their journal.

TIP The amount of time students need to complete this activity will vary. Allow them to use the rest of the allotted time to complete this activity. If they have more they would like to write, you may let them complete their entry at a later time. If students are having trouble getting started, you might tell them to just list ideas or words. They may even draw a picture and describe it to you. You can transcribe their words for them.

Objectives
- Freewrite about a topic.
- Write in a journal.

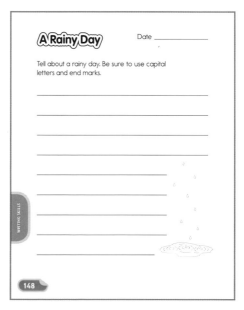

A Rainy Day   Date _____

Tell about a rainy day. Be sure to use capital letters and end marks.

148

149

Unit Checkpoint

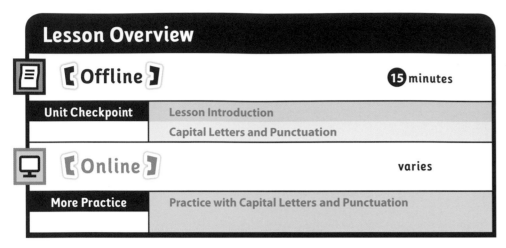

Lesson Overview

Offline — **15** minutes

Unit Checkpoint	Lesson Introduction
	Capital Letters and Punctuation

Online — varies

More Practice	Practice with Capital Letters and Punctuation

Materials

Supplied

- *K¹² Language Arts Assessments*, pp. WS 29–32

Offline — **15** minutes

Work **together** with students to complete the Unit Checkpoint.

Unit Checkpoint

Lesson Introduction

Prepare students for the lesson.

1. Tell students that they are going to complete a Unit Checkpoint to show what they have learned.

2. Explain that if they miss one or more questions, they can continue to practice this grammar skill.

Capital Letters and Punctuation

Explain that students are going to show what they have learned about capital letters and punctuation.

1. Give students the Unit Checkpoint pages.

2. Read the directions together. If needed, read the questions and answer choices to students. Have students complete the Checkpoint on their own.

Objectives

- Form and use contractions.
- Identify contractions.
- Use a comma to separate words in a series.
- Identify correctly written dates.
- Use a capital letter and a comma in a date.

3. Use the Answer Key to score the Checkpoint and then enter the results online.

4. Review each exercise with students. Work with students to correct any exercise that they missed.

 TIP Students who answered one or more questions incorrectly should continue to practice this grammar skill. Write several sentences that contain the following: words that can be made into contractions, incorrectly written dates, and words in a series that need a comma. Have students correct the errors.

Reward: When students score 80 percent or above on the Unit Checkpoint, add a sticker for this unit on the My Accomplishments chart.

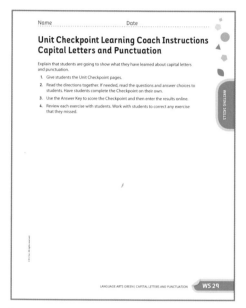

Name _____ Date _____

Unit Checkpoint Learning Coach Instructions
Capital Letters and Punctuation

Explain that students are going to show what they have learned about capital letters and punctuation.

1. Give students the Unit Checkpoint pages.
2. Read the directions together. If needed, read the questions and answer choices to students. Have students complete the Checkpoint on their own.
3. Use the Answer Key to score the Checkpoint and then enter the results online.
4. Review each exercise with students. Work with students to correct any exercise that they missed.

LANGUAGE ARTS GREEN | CAPITAL LETTERS AND PUNCTUATION   WS 29

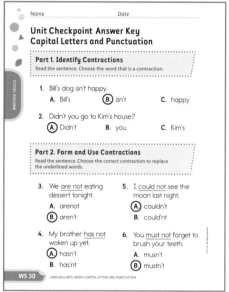

Name _____ Date _____

Unit Checkpoint Answer Key
Capital Letters and Punctuation

Part 1. Identify Contractions
Read the sentence. Choose the word that is a contraction.

1. Bill's dog isn't happy.
   A. Bill's   **B.** isn't   C. happy

2. Didn't you go to Kim's house?
   A. Didn't   B. you   C. Kim's

Part 2. Form and Use Contractions
Read the sentence. Choose the correct contraction to replace the underlined words.

3. We are not eating dessert tonight.
   A. arenot
   B. aren't

4. My brother has not woken up yet.
   A. hasn't
   B. has'nt

5. I could not see the moon last night.
   A. couldn't
   B. could'nt

6. You must not forget to brush your teeth.
   A. musn't
   B. mustn't

WS 30   LANGUAGE ARTS GREEN | CAPITAL LETTERS AND PUNCTUATION

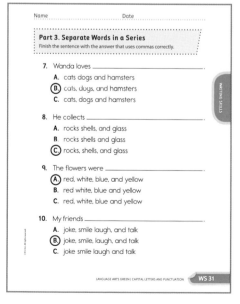

Name _____ Date _____

Part 3. Separate Words in a Series
Finish the sentence with the answer that uses commas correctly.

7. Wanda loves _____.
   A. cats dogs and hamsters
   B. cats, dogs, and hamsters
   C. cats, dogs and hamsters

8. He collects _____.
   A. rocks shells, and glass
   B. rocks shells and glass
   C. rocks, shells, and glass

9. The flowers were _____.
   A. red, white, blue, and yellow
   B. red white, blue and yellow
   C. red, white, blue and yellow

10. My friends _____.
    A. joke, smile laugh, and talk
    B. joke, smile, laugh, and talk
    C. joke smile laugh and talk

LANGUAGE ARTS GREEN | CAPITAL LETTERS AND PUNCTUATION   WS 31

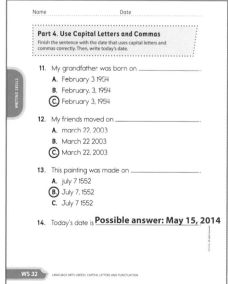

Name _____ Date _____

Part 4. Use Capital Letters and Commas
Finish the sentence with the date that uses capital letters and commas correctly. Then, write today's date.

11. My grandfather was born on _____.
    A. February 3 1954
    B. February, 3, 1954
    C. February 3, 1954

12. My friends moved on _____.
    A. march 22, 2003
    B. March 22 2003
    C. March 22, 2003

13. This painting was made on _____.
    A. july 7 1552
    B. July 7, 1552
    C. July 7 1552

14. Today's date is **Possible answer: May 15, 2014**

WS 32   LANGUAGE ARTS GREEN | CAPITAL LETTERS AND PUNCTUATION

 **varies**

If necessary, work with students to complete the More Practice activity.

More Practice

Practice with Capital Letters and Punctuation
If students scored less than 80 percent on the Unit Checkpoint, have them complete
the appropriate review activities listed in the table online. Help students locate the
activities and provide support as needed.

 Objectives
- Evaluate Checkpoint results and choose activities to review.

Write a Response to a Book

Unit Focus

In this unit, students will write a book report about a book they have read and are very familiar with. Students will

▶ Identify the author, illustrator, main characters, and setting of a book.
▶ Write a summary of the major events in the book.
▶ Write an opinion paragraph explaining their feelings about the book and their reasons for having them.

Writing a book report will help students think more deeply about the parts of a book. Separating the important events from the unimportant ones will help students understand how a story is structured. Stating a clear opinion and giving reasons for the opinion will help them think more deeply about the way a piece of writing can affect them. It will also help them structure coherent arguments by articulating a position and providing support. This kind of reading helps students develop critical thinking skills and will improve their own writing.

Unit Plan		〖Offline〗	〖Online〗
Lesson 1	What Book Have You Loved?	**15** minutes	
Lesson 2	What Is a Book Report?	**15** minutes	
Lesson 3	Write an Introduction and a Summary of Your Book	**15** minutes	
Lesson 4	Write an Opinion and Reasons	**15** minutes	
Lesson 5	Publish Your Book Report	**15** minutes	varies

What Book Have You Loved?

Lesson Overview

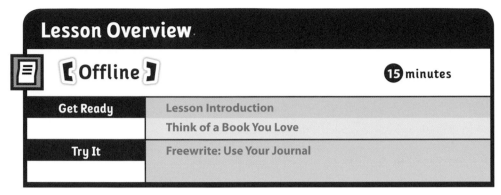

	Offline	**15** minutes
Get Ready	Lesson Introduction	
	Think of a Book You Love	
Try It	Freewrite: Use Your Journal	

Materials

Supplied

- *K¹² My Journal*, pp. 150–151
- Literature & Comprehension Support Materials

Advance Preparation

Before the lesson begins, pick out one of your favorite books. Think of one or two details you can tell students to explain why you love this book.

Big Ideas

- ▸ Writing helps build reading skills, and reading more helps improve writing skills.
- ▸ Journal writing is a form of freewriting. It is an opportunity to get ideas on paper without concern for correctness of the language or the format of a piece of writing.

Keywords

freewriting – a way for a writer to pick a topic and write as much as possible about it within a set time limit

journal – a notebook where a writer regularly records experiences and ideas

opinion – a statement of belief that cannot be proven true; the opposite of a fact

Offline **15** minutes

Work **together** with students to complete Get Ready and Try It activities.

Get Ready

Lesson Introduction
Prepare students for the lesson.

1. Explain that in this lesson, students will be writing in their journal. Remind students that a journal is a place for students to be creative and explore writing. Students' journal entries will not be judged or graded.

2. Explain that students will freewrite about a book they have read and loved.

Objectives
- Generate ideas for writing.

Think of a Book You Love

Help students prepare to write about a book they love.

1. Tell students that they are going to be writing about a book they have read and loved.

2. Explain that there are many things to love in a good book. There are memorable characters, a great story, terrific pictures, or funny things and surprising ideas that the author writes.

3. Explain that any book can be a favorite book. What matters is students' opinion—what *they* think about a book.

4. Tell students about a book that you love. Pick one or two specific details to tell students about, such as an interesting character, an exciting part of the book, or what the book taught you.

5. Tell students to begin thinking about what book they want to write about. If students have been listing books they've read on the bookmark in the Literature & Comprehension Support Materials, you might refer to this to help students think of a book that they love.

TIP When discussing a book that you love, don't try to explain everything that happens. In fact, the more specific you are about one or two small moments or details, the more students will begin to understand how to structure their own writing.

Try It •

 Freewrite: Use Your Journal

Help students freewrite about a favorite book. Gather *K¹² My Journal* and have students turn to pages 150 and 151 in Writing Skills. Read the prompt at the top of the page to students. Answers to questions may vary.

1. Explain that students are going to write about a book they love.

   ▶ Is there a book that you have read many, many times?
   ▶ Can you think of what you love about that book?

2. Explain that students are freewriting, or writing ideas on the page.

3. Tell students that they can write whatever they want about their favorite book. They can write about many different things they like about the book, or they can write about one specific thing.

> **Objectives**
> • Freewrite on a topic.
> • Generate ideas for writing.
> • Write in a journal.

4. If students are having trouble thinking of what to write, prompt them with these questions.

   ▸ Do you have a favorite picture in a book?
   ▸ Is there a person from a book you would like to meet?
   ▸ What book have you read the most?

5. Have students write about a favorite book and why they like it. Do not evaluate students' writing. As long as students have written some ideas on paper, their responses are acceptable.

TIP The amount of time students need to complete this activity will vary. If students are having trouble getting started, you might tell them to just list ideas or words. They may even draw a picture and describe it to you. You can transcribe their words for them. Students need only work for 15 minutes. If they have more they would like to write, you might want to have them complete their entry at a later time, but it is not required.

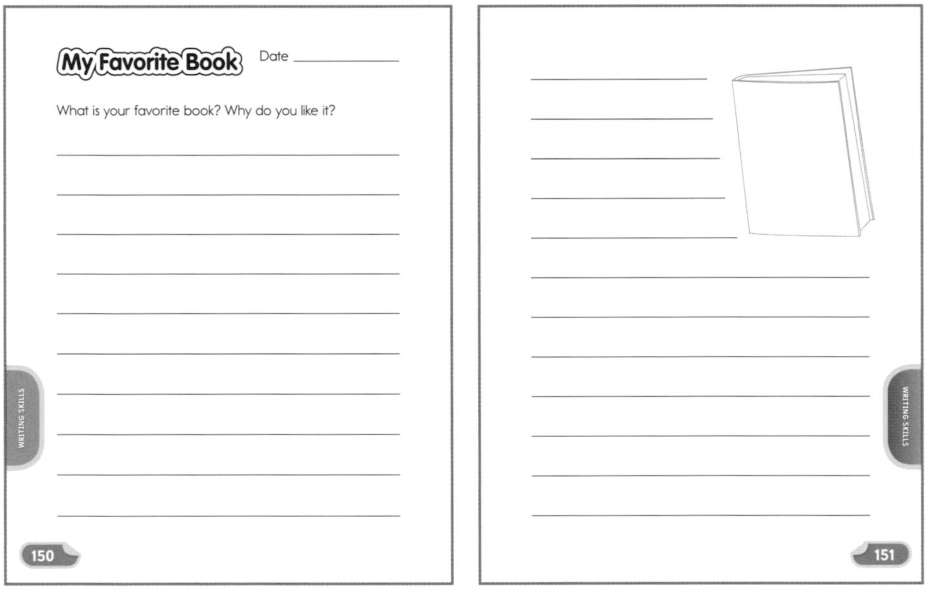

My Favorite Book   Date _____

What is your favorite book? Why do you like it?

_____

_____

_____

_____

_____

_____

_____

_____

150

_____

_____

_____

_____

_____

_____

_____

_____

_____

_____

151

What Is a Book Report?

Lesson Overview

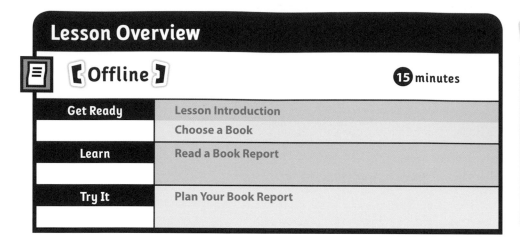

Offline — 15 minutes

Get Ready	Lesson Introduction
	Choose a Book
Learn	Read a Book Report
Try It	Plan Your Book Report

Advance Preparation

Gather a selection of books that students have read independently or heard read aloud.

Big Ideas

- Writers use various methods to plan, and novices should use what works for them: freewriting, listing, graphic organizers, or other methods.
- The study of writing models gives students opportunities to read, analyze, and emulate good writing.
- Student writers should be given good models for a particular type of writing, and the models should become the focus of the instruction.

 **Offline** 15 minutes

Work **together** with students to complete Get Ready, Learn, and Try It activities.

Get Ready

Lesson Introduction
Prepare students for the lesson.

1. Tell students that they are going to be writing a report about a book they like.

2. Explain that a book report shares information about the book.

3. Tell students that they are going to pick a book to write about. It can be the same book they discussed in their journal entry, or a different book.

 Objectives
- Identify a purpose for writing.

Choose a Book

Use this activity to help students pick a book for their book report.

1. Explain to students that a person can write to tell a lot of different kinds of information. For example, a person can write a letter about a specific event or write a journal entry about his or her heritage.

2. Tell students that another kind of writing that gives information is a **book report**. It tells about a book.

   ▸ Is there a book you want to write about?

3. Encourage students to pick a book to write about. It can be the book they wrote about in their journal or a different book. It should be a book they are very familiar with.

4. Have students tell you about the book they have chosen. Answers to questions may vary.

   ▸ What is the book about?
   ▸ Who is the main character?
   ▸ What do you like about the book?
   ▸ Does the book have pictures?

TIP Some students may have difficulty picking a favorite book. If students are struggling, show them your selection of books and ask if they would like to write a report about one of them.

Learn

Read a Book Report

Introduce a book report to students. Help students understand the structure of a book report and the information that goes into it. Turn to page WS 171 in *K¹² Language Arts Activity Book.*

1. Explain to students that the purpose of a book report is to give basic information about the book to the audience, the people who will read the report.

2. Tell students that book reports give information such as the title of the book, the author's name, the illustrator's name, and what happens in the book. A writer can also give an opinion about the book in the book report.

3. Show students the model book report on pages WS 171.

4. Read the first paragraph, which is the introduction of the model. Explain that the introduction is the opening part of the report. It's where the writer tells the audience what book the report is about and some basic information about the book.

   ▸ What is this book report about? *The Wizard of Oz*
   ▸ Who wrote the book? L. Frank Baum

Objectives
- Identify author.
- Identify illustrator.
- Identify story structure elements—plot, setting, character(s).

5. Point to the title of the book in the model. Explain that a title is underlined.

6. Point to the body of the model. Explain that the body is where the writer gives the audience a summary of the book.

   ▸ What is something that happens in the book? Possible answer: Dorothy goes to Oz. She finds the slippers. She meets three friends on the Yellow Brick Road.

7. Point to the conclusion, which is the last paragraph, in the model. Explain that the conclusion is where the writer gives his or her own opinion and reasons for that opinion. When the audience reads the conclusion, they should know that the book report is finished.

8. What does the writer like about the book? Possible answers: It is exciting; the characters are fun.

9. Look over the model book report with students and have them answer more questions about the book.

   ▸ What is the setting? the land of Oz
   ▸ Who are the main characters? Dorothy, Toto, the Tin Man, the Scarecrow, the Cowardly Lion, Glinda, the Wizard, the Wicked Witch

TIP Keep the model book report in a safe place so students can refer to it later.

Try It

Plan Your Book Report

Help students write information for their book report. Turn to pages WS 173–175 in *K¹² Language Arts Activity Book.*

1. Read the Activity Book pages with students.

2. Explain that before students write their book report, they will write down the information they are going to include.

3. Have them write the basic information about their book: title, author, illustrator, names of characters, and setting.

4. Have students list three or four events that happen in the book. They don't need to write complete sentences; they just need to make a few notes about the events in the book.

5. Have students write at least two reasons why they did or did not like the book.

TIP Keep the Activity Book pages in a safe place so students can refer to them later.

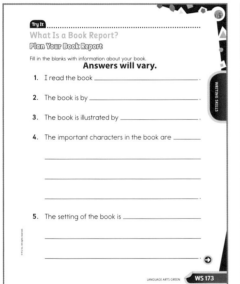

Write an Introduction and a Summary of Your Book

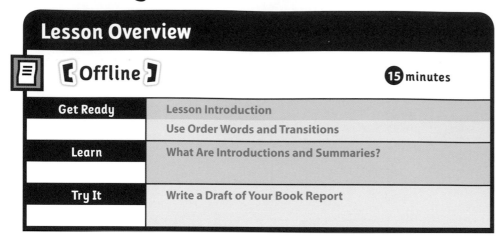

Lesson Overview

Offline   🕐 **15 minutes**

Get Ready	Lesson Introduction
	Use Order Words and Transitions
Learn	What Are Introductions and Summaries?
Try It	Write a Draft of Your Book Report

Materials

Supplied
- *K¹² Language Arts Activity Book*, pp. WS 171–179
- Story Card E

Keywords

book report – a piece of writing that gives information, a summary, and an opinion about a book

summary – a short retelling that includes only the most important ideas or events of a text

Advance Preparation

Have students gather page WS 171 (Read a Book Report, model book report) and completed pages WS 173–175 (Plan Your Book Report) in *K¹² Language Arts Activity Book*.

Big Ideas

- ▶ Writing varies by purpose and audience. The specific reason for writing and the writer's intended readers (audience) determine the form and language to use.
- ▶ Readers should be able to retell the story (or information) in their own words, not repeat what was written.
- ▶ Explicit instruction in how to summarize a text is an important element in learning how to write well.

 **Offline** **15** minutes

Work **together** with students to complete Get Ready, Learn, and Try It activities.

Get Ready

Lesson Introduction
Prepare students for the lesson.

1. Explain that students are going to write a summary of what happens in their book.

2. Tell students that they are going to use order words to explain the sequence of events in the book.

Use Order Words and Transitions
Help students prepare to write their introduction and summary by helping them remember how to use transition words. Gather Story Card E.

1. Remind students that it is important to use order words in writing. These words help the reader understand the order in which events happened.

2. Explain that the word *first* helps a reader understand how a story starts.

   ► What are other order words? *next, then, also, finally*

3. Show students Story Card E. Explain that you are going to work together to create a story about the picture.

4. **Say:** First, two girls and their mommy decided to go for a walk.

5. Have students continue telling a simple story, starting each new sentence with an order word. If students are struggling, add another part of the story yourself.

Objectives
- Define *transitions*.
- Identify transitions.
- Recognize the need to use transitions to connect ideas in writing.
- Identify story sequence.
- Sequence events in a text.
- Use time-order words.

Learn

What Are Introductions and Summaries?
Help students understand how to write an introduction and a summary. Gather the model book report on page WS 171 in *K¹² Language Arts Activity Book*.

1. Tell students that a book report has to include an introduction and a summary of the story.

2. Look at the model book report. With students, read the introduction to the book report.

   ► What kind of information is in the introduction? the title of the book, the name of the author, the name of the illustrator, the most important characters, the setting

Objectives
- Recognize the importance of an introduction.

3. Explain that a summary tells only the most important parts of a story. The author, L. Frank Baum, used a whole book to tell the story, but a summary has to tell the story in just a few sentences.
4. Look at the model book report again. With students, read the summary of *The Wizard of Oz*.
5. Explain that in a summary, the writer needs to give information about the beginning, middle, and end of the book.
   - What happens in the beginning of the book? Dorothy flies to Oz.
   - What is one thing that happens in the middle of the book? Possible answers: Dorothy gets the slippers; she meets her friends; she stops the witch.
   - What happens at the end of the book? Dorothy goes home.
6. Explain that the order words help the reader understand the order in which the events in the book happen.
   - What are the order words in this summary? *first*, *then*, *next*, and *finally*

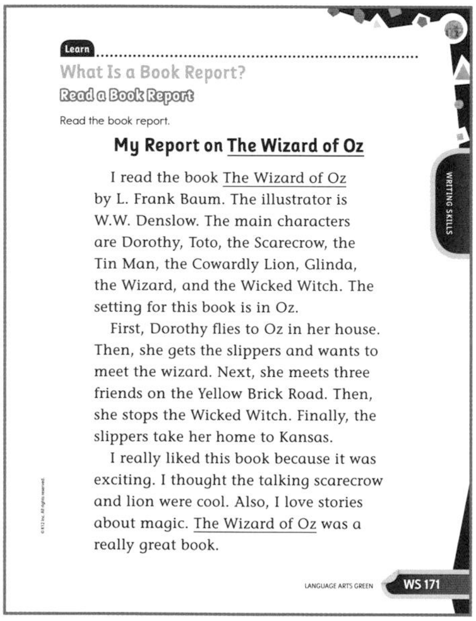

Learn

What Is a Book Report?

Read a Book Report

Read the book report.

My Report on The Wizard of Oz

I read the book The Wizard of Oz by L. Frank Baum. The illustrator is W.W. Denslow. The main characters are Dorothy, Toto, the Scarecrow, the Tin Man, the Cowardly Lion, Glinda, the Wizard, and the Wicked Witch. The setting for this book is in Oz.

First, Dorothy flies to Oz in her house. Then, she gets the slippers and wants to meet the wizard. Next, she meets three friends on the Yellow Brick Road. Then, she stops the Wicked Witch. Finally, the slippers take her home to Kansas.

I really liked this book because it was exciting. I thought the talking scarecrow and lion were cool. Also, I love stories about magic. The Wizard of Oz was a really great book.

WRITING SKILLS

LANGUAGE ARTS GREEN WS 171

Try It

Write a Draft of Your Book Report

Help students write an introduction and a summary of their book. Gather completed pages WS 173–175 and turn to pages WS 177–179 in K[12] *Language Arts Activity Book*.

1. Have students fill in the introductory information on page WS 177.
2. Have students read over the main events that they listed on page WS 174.
3. Tell students to write a four- or five-sentence summary of the book on page WS 178. Explain that the events should be written in the order that they happened in the book. Encourage students to use order words such as *first*, *then*, *next*, *also*, and *finally*.

Objectives

- Choose information for a summary.
- Write an introduction.
- Use transitions to connect ideas.
- Write a summary.
- Use time-order words.

4. Explain that students are working on only the first two parts of their draft at this time. They will work on the last part—the conclusion of their report (page WS 179)—at another time.

5. Provide assistance as necessary.

TIP When students are finished writing their introduction and summary, keep the Activity Book pages in a safe place so students can complete them later.

Try It

What Is a Book Report?
Plan Your Book Report
Fill in the blanks with information about your book.
Answers will vary.

1. I read the book _____

2. The book is by _____

3. The book is illustrated by _____

4. The important characters in the book are _____

5. The setting of the book is _____

WS 173

---

6. List three or four events that happen in the book.

First event: _____

Second event: _____

Third event: _____

Fourth event: _____

WS 174

---

7. List reasons why you like this book.

First reason: _____

Second reason: _____

Third reason: _____

Fourth reason: _____

WS 175

Try It

Write an Introduction and a Summary of Your Book
Write a Draft of Your Book Report
Fill in the information about your book to write the introduction to your book report. **Students should write a draft of their book report.**

Book report title: _____

I read the book _____

by _____

The illustrator is _____

The important main characters are _____

The setting for this book is _____

WS 177

Write a summary of the important events in your book. Use order words to tell the story.

Word Bank
first   next   then   also   finally

In this book, _____

WS 178

Write a conclusion to your book report. State your opinion about the book. Tell your reasons. Use strong describing words.

I thought this book was _____

because _____

WS 179

Write an Opinion and Reasons

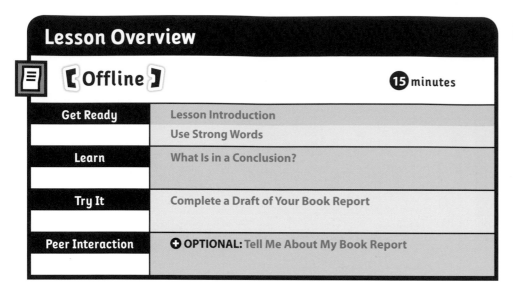

Lesson Overview

Offline   🕐 **15** minutes

Get Ready	Lesson Introduction
	Use Strong Words
Learn	What Is in a Conclusion?
Try It	Complete a Draft of Your Book Report
Peer Interaction	➕ **OPTIONAL:** Tell Me About My Book Report

Materials

Supplied

- *K¹² Language Arts Activity Book*, pp. WS 171–182

Keywords

conclusion – the final paragraph of a written work

fact – a statement that can be proven true

opinion – a statement of belief that cannot be proven true; the opposite of a fact

paragraph – a group of sentences about one topic

reason – a statement that explains why something is or why it should be

Advance Preparation

Have students gather page WS 171 (Read a Book Report, model book report), completed pages WS 173–175 (Plan Your Book Report), and partially completed pages WS 177–179 (Write a Draft of Your Book Report) in *K¹² Language Arts Activity Book*.

Big Ideas

- ▸ Readers identify the underlying implications of a text and use this information to form an opinion or make a decision.
- ▸ Writing is the communication of ideas in a structured, orderly form.
- ▸ Writers who receive feedback during the writing process are able to apply that feedback to improve the ultimate product.
- ▸ Working collaboratively with other students during various stages of the writing process can improve student writing.

 **15 minutes**

Work **together** with students to complete Get Ready, Learn, Try It, and Peer Interaction activities.

Get Ready

Lesson Introduction
Prepare students for the lesson.

1. Explain that students are going to write their opinion about their book.

2. Tell students that they are going to write reasons why they did or did not like their book.

3. Explain that students are going to practice using strong words to explain their opinion.

Use Strong Words
To prepare students to write an opinion, help them practice using strong words. Gather partially completed pages WS 177–179 in K^{12} *Language Arts Activity Book*.

1. Tell students that when a writer gives an opinion, it is important for him or her to give reasons for the opinion. It shows the audience what the writer is interested in and feels strongly about, and it helps make the writing feel personal.

2. Tell students that writing can be more interesting if the writer has strong feelings about something.

3. Tell students that when they write, they can replace some words with words that show a stronger feeling.

   ▶ What is a stronger word than *like*? *love, like a lot, adore*
   ▶ What is a stronger word than *sad*? *super-sad, heartbroken*

> **Objectives**
> - Identify reasons that support an opinion.
> - Distinguish between meaning variations in closely related adjectives. (for example, *large, gigantic, humongous*).
> - Replace ordinary adjectives with specific adjectives.
> - Distinguish between meaning variations in closely related verbs.

4. Have students look at their draft introduction and summary and think about stronger words they can use to express their opinions about their book.

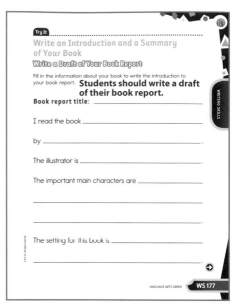
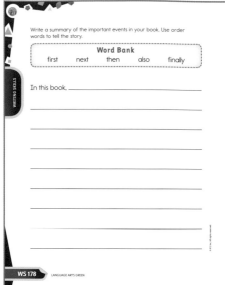

Learn

What Is in a Conclusion?

Help students write reasons to support opinions about their books. Gather the model book report on page WS 171 in *K¹² Language Arts Activity Book*.

1. Explain that a book report ends with a conclusion. The conclusion gives the audience more information and lets the audience know that the book report is finished.

2. With students, read the conclusion to the model book report.

  ▶ What does the writer include in the conclusion? an opinion and reasons for the opinion

  ▶ What reasons does the writer give for liking the story? It was exciting; the characters were cool; there was magic.

3. Explain that the conclusion in a book report is a place for writers to give their own ideas about the book.

Objectives
- Identify reasons that support an opinion.
- Provide a sense of closure.

4. Help students tell what they liked about their own book. Answers to questions may vary.

 ▸ Did you have a favorite character?
 ▸ Did you want to go to the places in the book?
 ▸ If you had to tell another person just one thing about the book, what would it be?
 ▸ What was the most exciting part of the book?

Try It

 Complete a Draft of Your Book Report

Help students write the final paragraph of their book report, stating their opinion of their book and the reasons for that opinion. Gather pages WS 173–175 and 177–179 in *K¹² Language Arts Activity Book*.

1. Help students read their opinion and the reasons for that opinion on page WS 175.

2. Explain that students are going to write a concluding paragraph for their book report. Tell students that they can use the opinion and reasons they wrote on page WS 175 or they can give new opinions with reasons.

Objectives
- Write an opinion statement.
- Identify reasons that support an opinion.
- Write a paragraph.
- Use transitions to connect ideas.
- Write a conclusion.

3. On page WS 179, have students write their opinion and at least three reasons supporting that opinion. Encourage them to use order words and connecting words when writing their sentences.

4. Provide assistance as necessary.

TIP When students are finished writing their opinion and reasons, keep the Activity Book pages in a safe place so students can refer to them later.

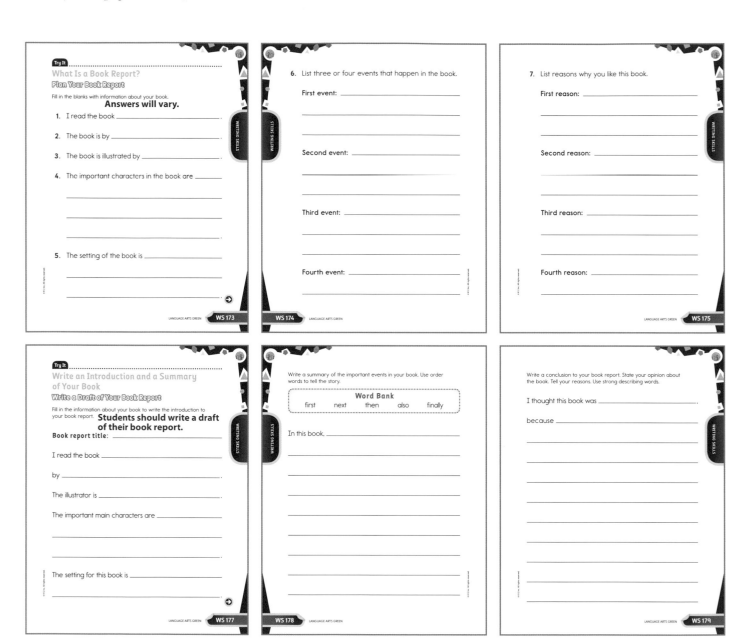

Try It

What Is a Book Report?

Plan Your Book Report

Fill in the blanks with information about your book.

Answers will vary.

1. I read the book _____

2. The book is by _____

3. The book is illustrated by _____

4. The important characters in the book are _____

5. The setting of the book is _____

LANGUAGE ARTS GREEN · WS 173

WS 174 · LANGUAGE ARTS GREEN

6. List three or four events that happen in the book.

First event: _____

Second event: _____

Third event: _____

Fourth event: _____

---

7. List reasons why you like this book.

First reason: _____

Second reason: _____

Third reason: _____

Fourth reason: _____

LANGUAGE ARTS GREEN · WS 175

Try It

Write an Introduction and a Summary of Your Book

Write a Draft of Your Book Report

Fill in the information about your book to write the introduction to your book report.

Students should write a draft of their book report.

Book report title: _____

I read the book _____

by _____

The illustrator is _____

The important main characters are _____

The setting for this book is _____

LANGUAGE ARTS GREEN · WS 177

WS 178 · LANGUAGE ARTS GREEN

Write a summary of the important events in your book. Use order words to tell the story.

Word Bank

first   next   then   also   finally

In this book, _____

Write a conclusion to your book report. State your opinion about the book. Tell your reasons. Use strong describing words.

I thought this book was _____

because _____

LANGUAGE ARTS GREEN · WS 179

Peer Interaction

⊕ **OPTIONAL: Tell Me About My Book Report**

This activity is OPTIONAL. It is intended for students who have extra time and would benefit from extra practice. Feel free to skip this activity.

Students can benefit from exchanging book reports with someone they know or another student. This activity will work best if students exchange their book report with other students who completed the same assignment, but you may copy the Activity Book pages and send them to someone else who is willing to give students feedback. Students should receive feedback on the content of their book report. To complete this optional activity, turn to pages WS 181 and 182 in *K*[12] *Language Arts Activity Book.*

1. Have students exchange book reports with other students.

2. Have students use the Activity Book pages to provide others with feedback about their writing.

3. Have students use the feedback provided from other students to revise their own book report.

Objectives

- Use guidance from adults and peers to revise writing.
- Collaborate with peers on writing projects.

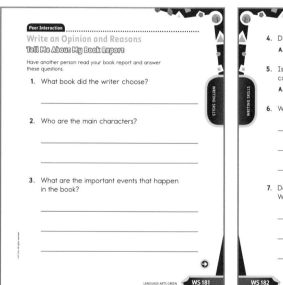

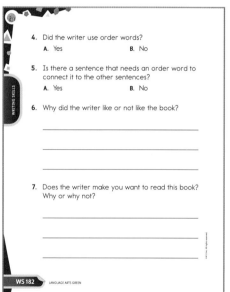

Publish Your Book Report

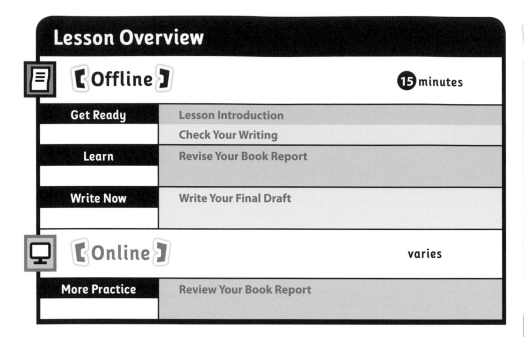

Lesson Overview

📋 [Offline]   15 minutes

Get Ready	Lesson Introduction
	Check Your Writing
Learn	Revise Your Book Report
Write Now	Write Your Final Draft

🖥 [Online]   varies

More Practice	Review Your Book Report

[Materials]

Supplied

- *K¹² Language Arts Activity Book*, pp. WS 177–186
- Write Your Final Draft: Rubric and Sample Responses (printout)

Also Needed

- crayons or markers, coloring
- paper, construction

Keywords

book report – a piece of writing that gives information, a summary, and an opinion about a book

opinion – a statement of belief that cannot be proven true; the opposite of a fact

paragraph – a group of sentences about one topic

publishing – the stage or step of the writing process in which the writer makes a clean copy of the piece and shares it

reason – a statement that explains why something is or why it should be

Advance Preparation

Have students gather completed pages WS 177–179 (Write a Draft of Your Book Report, draft book report) and WS 181 and 182 (Tell Me About My Book Report, feedback) from *K¹² Language Arts Activity Book*. Review students' draft. Look over the checklist on pages WS 183 and 184. Be ready to give students suggestions to help them answer some of the checklist questions.

Big Ideas

► Book reviews allow writers to share information about books they have read with audiences who want to know more about the books. Book reviews often include a summary or analysis of the content, an opinion about the book, and a recommendation of whether or not to read the book.

► One of the most powerful ways to improve writing is to directly teach strategies for planning and revising until students can use these strategies on their own.

 **15 minutes**

Work **together** with students to complete Get Ready, Learn, and Write Now activities.

Get Ready

Lesson Introduction

Prepare students for the lesson.

1. Explain that students will be revising their book report.

2. Tell students that before they rewrite their paragraphs, they will use a checklist to improve their writing.

 Objectives
- Revise using a checklist.
- Use guidance from adults and peers to revise writing.

Check Your Writing

Help students prepare to write a final draft of their book report. Gather students' draft book report on pages WS 177–179 and turn to pages WS 183 and 184 in *K¹² Language Arts Activity Book*.

1. Read the checklist on pages WS 183 and 184 with students. Tell students that they will use the checklist to revise their draft book report before they publish it.

2. Read the questions with students and have them circle their answers on the checklist.

TIP Keep the Activity Book pages in a safe place so students can refer to them when they revise their draft.

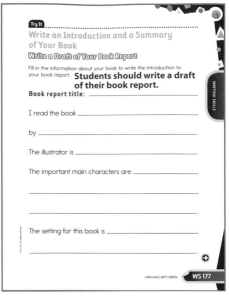

WRITING SKILLS

Try It
Write an Introduction and a Summary of Your Book
Write a Draft of Your Book Report

Fill in the information about your book to write the introduction to your book report. **Students should write a draft of their book report.**

Book report title: _____

I read the book _____

by _____

The illustrator is _____

The important main characters are _____

_____

_____

The setting for this book is _____

LANGUAGE ARTS GREEN   **WS 177**

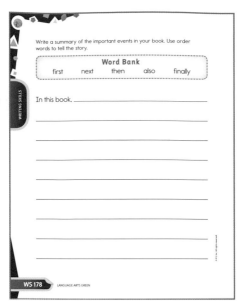

Write a summary of the important events in your book. Use order words to tell the story.

Word Bank

first   next   then   also   finally

In this book, _____

_____

_____

_____

_____

_____

_____

_____

WS 178   LANGUAGE ARTS GREEN

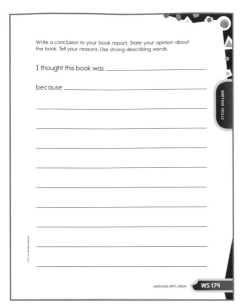

Write a conclusion to your book report. State your opinion about the book. Tell your reasons. Use strong describing words.

I thought this book was _____

because _____

_____

_____

_____

_____

_____

LANGUAGE ARTS GREEN   **WS 179**

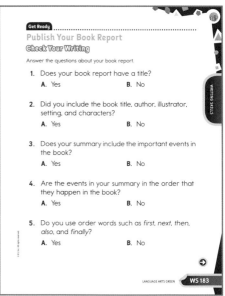

Get Ready
Publish Your Book Report
Check Your Writing

Answer the questions about your book report.

1. Does your book report have a title?
   A. Yes   B. No

2. Did you include the book title, author, illustrator, setting, and characters?
   A. Yes   B. No

3. Does your summary include the important events in the book?
   A. Yes   B. No

4. Are the events in your summary in the order that they happen in the book?
   A. Yes   B. No

5. Do you use order words such as *first, next, then, also,* and *finally*?
   A. Yes   B. No

LANGUAGE ARTS GREEN   **WS 183**

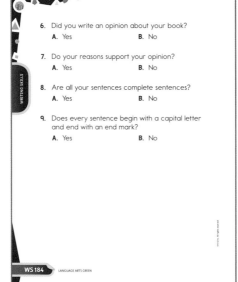

6. Did you write an opinion about your book?
   A. Yes   B. No

7. Do your reasons support your opinion?
   A. Yes   B. No

8. Are all your sentences complete sentences?
   A. Yes   B. No

9. Does every sentence begin with a capital letter and end with an end mark?
   A. Yes   B. No

WS 184   LANGUAGE ARTS GREEN

Learn

Revise Your Book Report

Help students revise their book report. Gather students' draft book report on pages WS 177–179 and the checklist on pages WS 183 and 184 in *K¹² Language Arts Activity Book*.

1. Read the checklist with students. Look for the times that students answered *No* to a question.

2. For each *No*, ask students which parts of their writing made them answer *No*.

Objectives
- Revise using feedback.

3. Help students make notes on their draft. Tell them to think about ways they can improve their writing for the final draft of their book report.

4. If there is time, have students draw a picture of a scene from the book on a piece of paper. They can add it to their report, like a cover.

TIP Keep the Activity Book pages in a safe place so students can refer to them when they revise their draft.

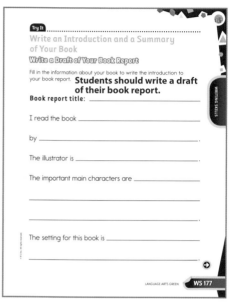

Try It

Write an Introduction and a Summary of Your Book

Write a Draft of Your Book Report

Fill in the information about your book to write the introduction to your book report. **Students should write a draft of their book report.**

Book report title: _____

I read the book _____

by _____

The illustrator is _____

The important main characters are _____

_____

_____

The setting for this book is _____

LANGUAGE ARTS GREEN   WS 177

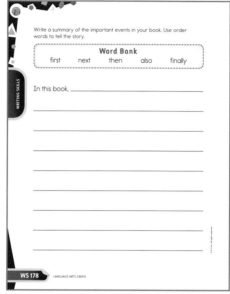

Write a summary of the important events in your book. Use order words to tell the story.

Word Bank
first   next   then   also   finally

In this book, _____

_____

_____

_____

_____

_____

_____

_____

WS 178   LANGUAGE ARTS GREEN

Write a conclusion to your book report. State your opinion about the book. Tell your reasons. Use strong describing words.

I thought this book was _____

because _____

_____

_____

_____

_____

_____

_____

LANGUAGE ARTS GREEN   WS 179

Get Ready

Publish Your Book Report

Check Your Writing

Answer the questions about your book report.

1. Does your book report have a title?
   A. Yes   B. No

2. Did you include the book title, author, illustrator, setting, and characters?
   A. Yes   B. No

3. Does your summary include the important events in the book?
   A. Yes   B. No

4. Are the events in your summary in the order that they happen in the book?
   A. Yes   B. No

5. Do you use order words such as *first, next, then, also,* and *finally*?
   A. Yes   B. No

LANGUAGE ARTS GREEN   WS 183

6. Did you write an opinion about your book?
   A. Yes   B. No

7. Do your reasons support your opinion?
   A. Yes   B. No

8. Are all your sentences complete sentences?
   A. Yes   B. No

9. Does every sentence begin with a capital letter and end with an end mark?
   A. Yes   B. No

WS 184   LANGUAGE ARTS GREEN

Write Now

Write Your Final Draft

Help students complete the final draft of their book report. Gather students' draft book report on pages WS 177–179 and turn to pages WS 185 and 186 in *K¹² Language Arts Activity Book*. Also gather the crayons or coloring markers and construction paper.

1. Help students rewrite their book report on pages WS 185 and 186. Have them fill in the basic information about the book in the first paragraph to create an introduction. Have them write their summary of the book in the second paragraph. Have them write their opinion and reasons for that opinion in the third paragraph as a conclusion.

2. Encourage students to write clearly and legibly.

3. Have students create a cover for their report or draw a picture to go with their report, if they wish.

4. Use the materials and instructions in the online lesson to evaluate students' finished writing. You will be looking at students' writing to evaluate the following:

   ▸ **Purpose and Content:** The writing contains almost all the elements listed (author, title, character or main characters, illustrator, and setting). The writing includes a summary and opinion with at least two reasons. The purpose is clear, and an audience who has not read the book can understand the main ideas.

   ▸ **Structure and Organization:** The writing has an introduction, body, and conclusion. The body contains a summary with a beginning, middle, and end. There are some order words.

   ▸ **Grammar and Mechanics:** The writing has mostly complete sentences and uses capitalization mostly correctly. The writer uses the past and present tenses appropriately. There is some evidence of proofreading.

Objectives

- Give an opinion about a book.
- Identify the main character(s).
- Organize ideas in a logical order.
- Revise the book report.
- State the title and author.
- Support an opinion.
- Use capitalization and punctuation correctly.
- Use transitions to connect ideas.
- Write a response to a book.
- Write a summary.
- Write complete sentences.
- Write sentences with appropriate spacing between words.
- Write sentences with legible handwriting.
- Write or draw a response to literature.

5. Enter students' scores for each rubric category online.

6. If students scored a 1 in any criterion, work with them to proofread and revise their work.

 TIP Students who would like to further explore their books can work on one of the book report project templates in the Literature & Comprehension Supplemental Materials.

Reward: When students' writing achieves "meets objectives" in all three categories on the grading rubric, add a sticker for this unit on the My Accomplishments chart.

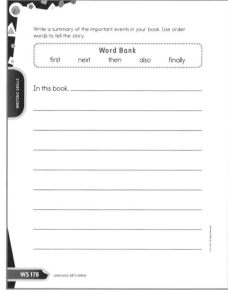

Try It

Write an Introduction and a Summary of Your Book

Write a Draft of Your Book Report

Fill in the information about your book to write the introduction to your book report. **Students should write a draft of their book report.**

Book report title: _____

I read the book _____

by _____

The illustrator is _____

The important main characters are _____

_____

_____

The setting for this book is _____

LANGUAGE ARTS GREEN   WS 177

Write a summary of the important events in your book. Use order words to tell the story.

Word Bank
first   next   then   also   finally

In this book, _____

_____

_____

_____

_____

_____

_____

_____

WS 178   LANGUAGE ARTS GREEN

Write a conclusion to your book report. State your opinion about the book. Tell your reasons. Use strong describing words.

I thought this book was _____

because _____

_____

_____

_____

_____

_____

_____

LANGUAGE ARTS GREEN   WS 179

Write Now

Publish Your Book Report

Write Your Final Draft

Use this form to write a final draft of your book report.

Refer to the rubric and sample responses.

Title: _____

Introduction: _____

_____

_____

_____

_____

_____

LANGUAGE ARTS GREEN   WS 185

Summary: _____

_____

_____

_____

_____

_____

_____

_____

_____

_____

Conclusion: I thought this book was _____

_____

_____

_____

WS 186   LANGUAGE ARTS GREEN

 **varies**

If necessary, work with students to complete the More Practice activity.

More Practice

Objectives

• Evaluate writing and choose activities to review and revise.

Review Your Book Report

If students' writing scored "doesn't meet objectives" in any category, have them complete the appropriate review activity listed in the table online.

► Follow the online instructions to help students revise and proofread their work.

► Impress upon students that revising makes their work better. Writing is a process, and each time they revise their book report, they are making their writing stronger and better.

► When you provide feedback, always begin with something positive. For example, you might point out a detail students wrote (even if it's the only detail) and explain how it helps you picture the scene: "You wrote that the heat was like an oven. That really helped me understand what the weather felt like."

► Place the final written work together with the rubric and the sample papers in the writing portfolio. This information is useful for you to track progress, and it helps students to refer back to their own work. They can see how they improve and review feedback to remember areas that need revising.

► Help students locate the activity and provide support as needed.

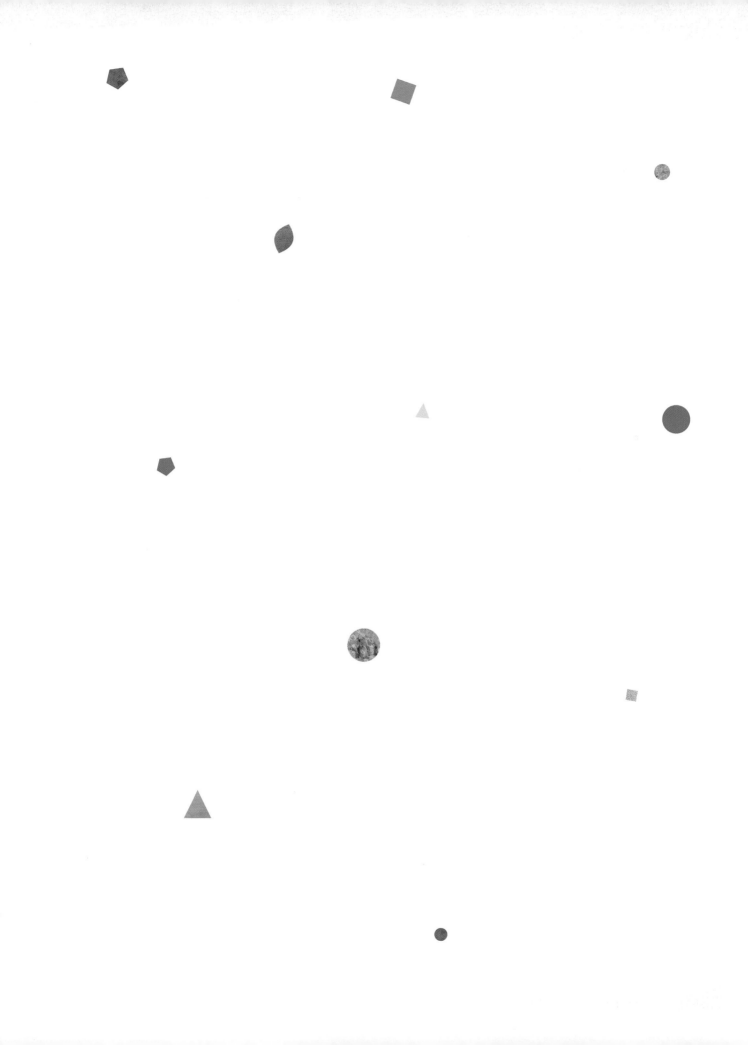

Semester Review and Checkpoint

Unit Focus

In this unit, students will

▶ Review the grammar, usage, and mechanics skills that they have learned this semester.

▶ Take a two-part Checkpoint of those skills.

Unit Plan		[Offline]	[Online]
Lesson 1	Semester Review	15 minutes	
Lesson 2	Semester Review: Sentences, Nouns, and Verbs	15 minutes	varies
Lesson 3	Semester Checkpoint: Sentences, Nouns, and Verbs	15 minutes	
Lesson 4	Semester Review: Pronouns, Verb Tense, Adjectives, Capital Letters, and Punctuation	15 minutes	varies
Lesson 5	Semester Checkpoint: Pronouns, Verb Tense, Adjectives, Capital Letters, and Punctuation	15 minutes	

Semester Review

Lesson Overview

Offline   **15** minutes

Look Back	Activity Book Pages Review

Materials

Supplied

- *K¹² Language Arts Activity Book*, pp. WS 1, 2, 5, 6, 17–22, 41, 42, 44–47, 63, 64, 67–71, 89, 90, 93, 94, 97, 98, 111, 112, 115–118, 131–133, 135–136, 139, 140, 163–166, 169, 170

Advance Preparation

Gather the following pages in *K¹² Language Arts Activity Book*:

- ▸ WS 1, 2, 5, 6 (Sentence Parts; Make Complete Sentences; Capital Letters and End Marks; Fix Sentences)
- ▸ WS 17–22 (Tell Something and Give Orders; Recognize and Write Statements and Commands; Want to Learn About Questions?; Recognize and Write Questions; Wow! Show Strong Feelings; Punctuate and Write Exclamations)
- ▸ WS 41, 42, 44–47 (Find the Nouns; Use Nouns; Common and Proper Nouns; Capitalize Proper Nouns; Find Possessives; Use Possessives)
- ▸ WS 63, 64, 67–71 (Find Action Verbs; Use Action Verbs; Singular Verbs and Singular Nouns; Use Singular Verbs; Plural Verbs and Plural Nouns; Use Plural Verbs)
- ▸ WS 89, 90, 93, 94, 97, 98 (Find Personal Pronouns; Use Personal Pronouns; Find Possessive Pronouns; Use Possessive Pronouns; Find Indefinite Pronouns; Use Indefinite Pronouns)
- ▸ WS 111, 112, 115–118 (Understand Present Tense Verbs; Use Present Tense Verbs; Understand Past Tense Verbs; Use Past Tense Verbs; Understand Future Tense Verbs; Use Future Tense Verbs)
- ▸ WS 131–133, 135–136, 139, 140 (Understand Adjectives; Use Descriptive Adjectives; Understand Articles; Use Articles; Understand Demonstratives; Use Demonstratives)
- ▸ WS 163–166, 169, 170 (Understand Contractions; Use Contractions; Understand Words in a Series; Use Words in a Series; Understand Dates; Write Dates Correctly)

 **15** minutes

Work **together** with students to complete the Look Back activity.

Look Back

Activity Book Pages Review

Work with students to review pages they completed in *K¹² Language Arts Activity Book* this semester. Gather the Activity Book pages.

1. Focus on areas students struggled with during the semester.

2. Review the grammar, usage, and mechanics rules and examples with students.

3. Ask students questions from the Activity Book pages.

4. Have students read the rules aloud and point to examples of the rules on the Activity Book pages.

Objectives
- Recall grammar, usage, and mechanics rules and explain examples.

Semester Review: Sentences, Nouns, and Verbs

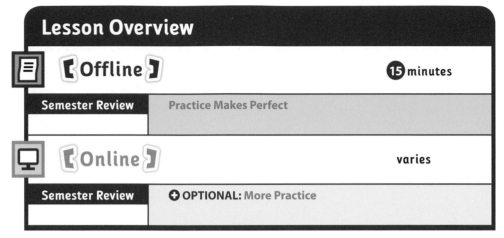

Lesson Overview

📄 **〔Offline〕**		**15** minutes
Semester Review	Practice Makes Perfect	
🖥 **〔Online〕**		varies
Semester Review	➕ OPTIONAL: More Practice	

〔Materials〕

Supplied

- *K¹² Language Arts Activity Book*, pp. WS 187–190

[Offline] ⏱ 15 minutes

Work **together** with students to complete the Semester Review activity.

Semester Review ....

Practice Makes Perfect

Help students review what they have learned this semester about sentences, nouns, and verbs. Turn to pages WS 187–190 in *K¹² Language Arts Activity Book*.

1. Read the directions to students.

2. Have students complete the exercises. Provide support as necessary.

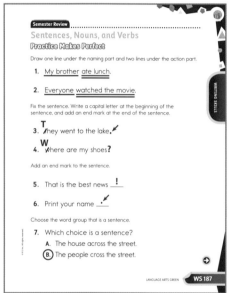

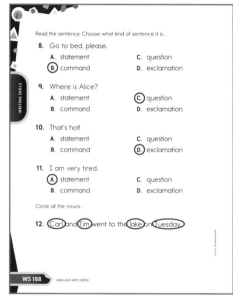

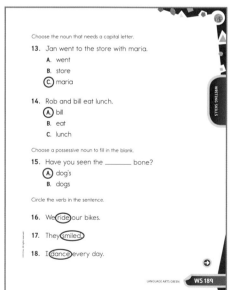

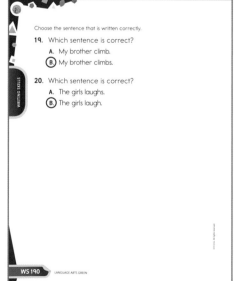

⭐ Objectives

- Identify and use possessive nouns in sentences.
- Identify predicate.
- Identify subject.
- Recognize commands.
- Recognize exclamations.
- Recognize questions.
- Recognize statements.
- Recognize word groups that are sentences.
- Use a capital letter to begin a proper noun.
- Use a capital letter to begin a sentence and an end mark to end it.
- Use action verbs in sentences.
- Use an exclamation mark to end an exclamation.
- Use a period to end a command.
- Use a period to end a statement.
- Use a question mark to end a question.
- Use a verb that agrees with its subject.
- Use nouns.

 **varies**

Students will work **independently** to complete the Semester Review activity. Help students locate the online activities and provide support as needed.

Semester Review

⊕ OPTIONAL: More Practice

This activity is OPTIONAL. It is intended for students who have extra time and would benefit from reviewing sentences, nouns, and verbs for the Semester Checkpoint. Feel free to skip this activity.

Objectives

- Identify and use possessive nouns in sentences.
- Identify predicate.
- Identify subject.
- Recognize commands.
- Recognize exclamations.
- Recognize questions.
- Recognize statements.
- Recognize word groups that are sentences.
- Use a capital letter to begin a proper noun.
- Use a capital letter to begin a sentence and an end mark to end it.
- Use action verbs in sentences.
- Use an exclamation mark to end an exclamation.
- Use a period to end a command.
- Use a period to end a statement.
- Use a question mark to end a question.
- Use a verb that agrees with its subject.
- Use nouns.

Semester Checkpoint: Sentences, Nouns, and Verbs

Lesson Overview

Offline   **15** minutes

Semester Checkpoint	Semester Checkpoint

Materials

Supplied

- *K¹² Language Arts Assessments*, pp. WS 33–38

 **15 minutes**

Students will work **independently** to complete the Semester Checkpoint for sentences, nouns, and verbs.

Semester Checkpoint

Semester Checkpoint

Explain that students are going to show what they have learned about sentences, nouns, and verbs this semester.

1. Give students the Semester Checkpoint: Sentences, Nouns, and Verbs pages.

2. Read the directions together. If needed, read the questions and answer choices to students. Have students complete the Checkpoint on their own.

3. Use the Answer Key to score the Checkpoint and then enter the results online.

4. Review each exercise with students. Work with students to correct any exercise they missed.

 Reward: When students score 80 percent or above on the Semester Checkpoint, add a sticker on the My Accomplishments chart.

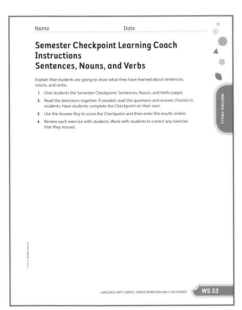

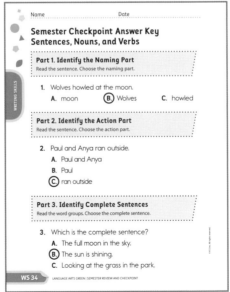

Objectives
- Identify and use possessive nouns in sentences.
- Identify types of sentences (statement, question, command, exclamation).
- Identify predicate.
- Identify proper and common nouns.
- Identify subject.
- Identify verbs in sentences.
- Recognize that a complete sentence begins with a capital letter and has an end mark.
- Recognize word groups that are sentences.
- Use a capital letter to begin a proper noun.
- Use a capital letter to begin a sentence and an end mark to end it.
- Use action verbs in sentences.
- Use an exclamation mark to end an exclamation.
- Use a period to end a command.
- Use a period to end a statement.
- Use a question mark to end a question.
- Use a verb that agrees with its subject.

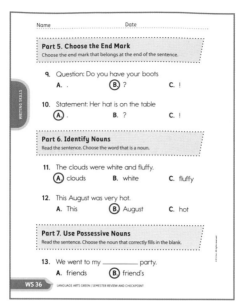

Name _____ Date _____

4. Which is the complete sentence?
   A. All of the dogs outside.
   B. Was playing in the rain.
   C. The beach is closed today.

Part 4. Identify Kinds of Sentences
Read the sentence. Choose what kind of sentence it is.

5. Please clean your room.
   A. statement   C. question
   B. command   D. exclamation

6. I won the game!
   A. statement   C. question
   B. command   **D.** exclamation

7. What time is the play?
   A. statement   **C.** question
   B. command   D. exclamation

8. The moon is full tonight.
   A. statement   C. question
   B. command   D. exclamation

LANGUAGE ARTS GREEN | SEMESTER REVIEW AND CHECKPOINT   **WS 35**

Name _____ Date _____

Part 5. Choose the End Mark
Choose the end mark that belongs at the end of the sentence.

9. Question: Do you have your boots
   A. .   **B.** ?   C. !

10. Statement: Her hat is on the table
    A. .   B. ?   C. !

Part 6. Identify Nouns
Read the sentence. Choose the word that is a noun.

11. The clouds were white and fluffy.
    A. clouds   B. white   C. fluffy

12. This August was very hot.
    A. This   **B.** August   C. hot

Part 7. Use Possessive Nouns
Read the sentence. Choose the noun that correctly fills in the blank.

13. We went to my _____ party.
    A. friends   **B.** friend's

WS 36   LANGUAGE ARTS GREEN | SEMESTER REVIEW AND CHECKPOINT

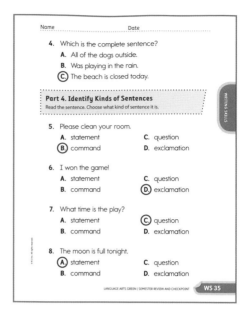

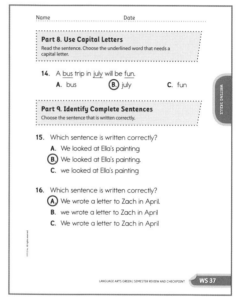

Name _____ Date _____

Part 8. Use Capital Letters
Read the sentence. Choose the underlined word that needs a capital letter.

14. A bus trip in july will be fun.
    A. bus   **B.** july   C. fun

Part 9. Identify Complete Sentences
Choose the sentence that is written correctly.

15. Which sentence is written correctly?
    A. We looked at Ella's painting
    B. We looked at Ella's painting.
    C. we looked at Ella's painting

16. Which sentence is written correctly?
    A. We wrote a letter to Zach in April.
    B. we wrote a letter to Zach in April
    C. We wrote a letter to Zach in April

LANGUAGE ARTS GREEN | SEMESTER REVIEW AND CHECKPOINT   **WS 37**

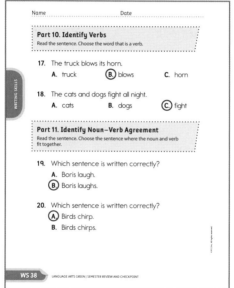

Name _____ Date _____

Part 10. Identify Verbs
Read the sentence. Choose the word that is a verb.

17. The truck blows its horn.
    A. truck   **B.** blows   C. horn

18. The cats and dogs fight all night.
    A. cats   B. dogs   **C.** fight

Part 11. Identify Noun–Verb Agreement
Read the sentence. Choose the sentence where the noun and verb fit together.

19. Which sentence is written correctly?
    A. Boris laugh.
    B. Boris laughs.

20. Which sentence is written correctly?
    A. Birds chirp.
    B. Birds chirps.

WS 38   LANGUAGE ARTS GREEN | SEMESTER REVIEW AND CHECKPOINT

Semester Review: Pronouns, Verb Tense, Adjectives, Capital Letters, and Punctuation

Materials

Supplied

- *K¹² Language Arts Activity Book*, pp. WS 191–194

Lesson Overview

📄 **【Offline】**	**⏱ 15 minutes**
Semester Review	Practice Makes Perfect

🖥 **【Online】**	**varies**
Semester Review	⊕ **OPTIONAL:** More Practice

[Offline] 15 minutes

Work **together** with students to complete the Semester Review activity.

Semester Review •

Practice Makes Perfect

Help students review what they have learned this semester about pronouns, verb tense, adjectives, capital letters, and punctuation. Turn to pages WS 191–194 in *K¹² Language Arts Activity Book*.

1. Read the directions to students.

2. Have students complete the exercises. Provide support as necessary.

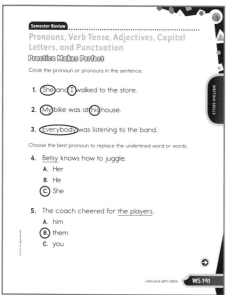

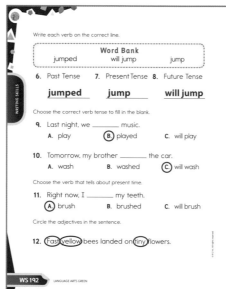

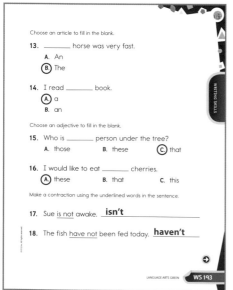

Objectives

- Form and use contractions.
- Recognize pronouns.
- Use a capital letter and a comma in a date.
- Use a capital letter for the pronoun *I*.
- Use a comma to separate words in a series.
- Use adjectives to describe someone or something.
- Use demonstrative adjectives.
- Use singular and plural pronouns.
- Use the articles *a*, *an*, and *the* correctly.
- Use the future tense of verbs.
- Use the past tense of verbs.
- Use the present tense of verbs.

 **varies**

Students will work **independently** to complete the Semester Review activity.
Help students locate the online activities and provide support as needed.

Semester Review ....

⊕ OPTIONAL: More Practice

This activity is OPTIONAL. It is intended for students who have extra time and
would benefit from reviewing pronouns, verb tense, adjectives, capital letters, and
punctuation for the Semester Checkpoint. Feel free to skip this activity.

Objectives

- Form and use contractions.
- Recognize pronouns.
- Use a capital letter and a comma in a date.
- Use a capital letter for the pronoun *I*.
- Use a comma to separate words in a series.
- Use adjectives to describe someone or something.
- Use demonstrative adjectives.
- Use singular and plural pronouns.
- Use the articles *a*, *an*, and *the* correctly.
- Use the future tense of verbs.
- Use the past tense of verbs.
- Use the present tense of verbs.

Semester Checkpoint: Pronouns, Verb Tense, Adjectives, Capital Letters, and Punctuation

Materials

Supplied
- *K¹² Language Arts Assessments*, pp. WS 39–44

Lesson Overview

Offline		**15** minutes
Semester Checkpoint	Semester Checkpoint	

Offline · 15 minutes

Students will work **independently** to complete the Semester Checkpoint for pronouns, verb tense, adjectives, capital letters, and punctuation.

Semester Checkpoint

Semester Checkpoint

Explain that students are going to show what they have learned about pronouns, verb tense, adjectives, capital letters, and punctuation this semester.

1. Give students the Semester Checkpoint: Pronouns, Verb Tense, Adjectives, Capital Letters, and Punctuation pages.

2. Read the directions together. If needed, read the question and answer choices to students. Have students complete the Checkpoint on their own.

3. Use the Answer Key to score the Checkpoint and then enter the results online.

4. Review each exercise with students. Work with students to correct any exercise they missed.

 Reward: When students score 80 percent or above on the Semester Checkpoint, add a sticker on the My Accomplishments chart.

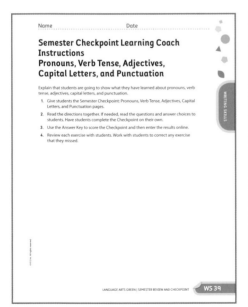

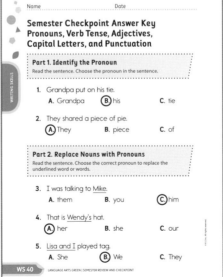

Objectives

- Form and use contractions.
- Recognize future tense of verbs.
- Recognize past tense of verbs.
- Recognize present tense of verbs.
- Recognize pronouns.
- Use a capital letter and a comma in a date.
- Use a capital letter for the pronoun *I*.
- Use a comma to separate words in a series.
- Use adjectives to describe someone or something.
- Use demonstrative adjectives.
- Use indefinite pronouns.
- Use possessive pronouns.
- Use singular and plural pronouns.
- Use the articles *a, an,* and *the* correctly.
- Use the future tense of verbs.
- Use the past tense of verbs.
- Use the present tense of verbs.

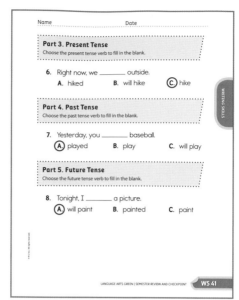

Name _____ Date _____

Part 3. Present Tense
Choose the present tense verb to fill in the blank.

6. Right now, we _____ outside.
   A. hiked   B. will hike   **C.** hike

Part 4. Past Tense
Choose the past tense verb to fill in the blank.

7. Yesterday, you _____ baseball.
   A. played   B. play   C. will play

Part 5. Future Tense
Choose the future tense verb to fill in the blank.

8. Tonight, I _____ a picture.
   A. will paint   B. painted   C. paint

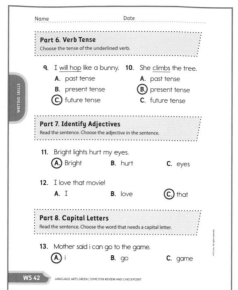

Name _____ Date _____

Part 6. Verb Tense
Choose the tense of the underlined verb.

9. I will hop like a bunny.
   A. past tense
   B. present tense
   C. future tense

10. She climbs the tree.
    A. past tense
    B. present tense
    C. future tense

Part 7. Identify Adjectives
Read the sentence. Choose the adjective in the sentence.

11. Bright lights hurt my eyes.
    A. Bright   B. hurt   C. eyes

12. I love that movie!
    A. I   B. love   **C.** that

Part 8. Capital Letters
Read the sentence. Choose the word that needs a capital letter.

13. Mother said i can go to the game.
    A. i   B. go   C. game

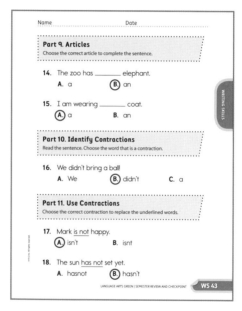

Name _____ Date _____

Part 9. Articles
Choose the correct article to complete the sentence.

14. The zoo has _____ elephant.
    A. a   **B.** an

15. I am wearing _____ coat.
    A. a   B. an

Part 10. Identify Contractions
Read the sentence. Choose the word that is a contraction.

16. We didn't bring a ball!
    A. We   **B.** didn't   C. a

Part 11. Use Contractions
Choose the correct contraction to replace the underlined words.

17. Mark is not happy.
    A. isn't   B. isnt

18. The sun has not set yet.
    A. hasnot   **B.** hasn't

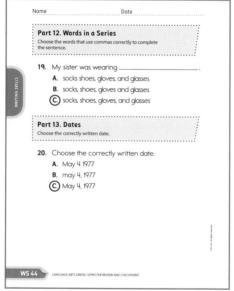

Name _____ Date _____

Part 12. Words in a Series
Choose the words that use commas correctly to complete the sentence.

19. My sister was wearing _____.
    A. socks shoes, gloves, and glasses
    B. socks, shoes, gloves and glasses
    C. socks, shoes, gloves, and glasses

Part 13. Dates
Choose the correctly written date.

20. Choose the correctly written date.
    A. May 4 1977
    B. may 4, 1977
    C. May 4, 1977

Write Your Own Story

Unit Focus

In this unit, students will write their own creative story. Students will learn how to

▸ Use a story map to plan a story.
▸ Write a story with a clear problem and solution.
▸ Use dialogue to tell a story.
▸ Revise a story using feedback.

When students create their own story, they discover that writing allows them to express their thoughts and create what exists in their imagination. Although it is important for students to learn about the structure and format of a story, it is equally important that they have fun while they are writing. They should be encouraged to see story writing as an exploration and adventure that they can revisit at any time.

Unit Plan		〖Offline〗	〖Online〗
Lesson 1	The Best Characters	**15** minutes	
Lesson 2	Create a Story Map	**15** minutes	
Lesson 3	Draft a Story	**15** minutes	
Lesson 4	Keep Writing Your Story	**15** minutes	
Lesson 5	Illustrate and Publish a Story	**15** minutes	varies

The Best Characters

Materials

Supplied
- *K¹² My Journal*, pp. 154–155

Lesson Overview

Offline		**15** minutes
Get Ready	Lesson Introduction	
	What Makes a Great Character?	
Try It	Freewrite: Use Your Journal	

Keywords

character – a person or animal in a story

fiction – make-believe stories

freewriting – a way for a writer to pick a topic and write as much as possible about it within a set time limit

Content Background

In this lesson, students will get to choose between two freewriting prompts in their journal. One prompt asks students to write about a character they like from a book. The other prompt is more open and invites students to begin creating ideas for their own stories. Some students will respond well to the structured prompt; others will respond better to the open-ended prompt. Help students choose the prompt that will work best for them.

Big Ideas

- ► Writing helps build reading skills, and reading more helps improve writing skills.
- ► Writing varies by genre. Different kinds of writing, whether creative, academic, or personal, vary in form and structure.
- ► Imaginative writing, in the form of stories and poems, allows writers to access their creativity while entertaining an audience.

[Offline] 🕐 minutes

Work **together** with students to complete Get Ready and Try It activities.

Get Ready ....

Lesson Introduction
Prepare students for the lesson.

Objectives
- Identify the main character(s).

1. Explain that in this lesson, students will be writing in their journal. Remind students that their journal is a place for them to be creative and explore writing. They will not be judged or graded.

2. Tell students that today they will prepare to write a story of their own. They will either freewrite about characters from a story or start to create their own story.

What Makes a Great Character?
Help students prepare to write about characters.

1. Tell students to think of a book or story that they like.

2. Explain that great stories usually have great characters. Help students think about the characters in their favorite story. Answers to questions may vary.

   ▸ Who is your favorite character in the story?
   ▸ What do you like about that character?
   ▸ Is that character funny? Exciting? Brave?
   ▸ What does that character say or do that makes you like him or her?

3. Tell students to think of three things they like most about the character from their favorite story.

TIP The purpose of this exercise is to prepare students to write their own story. Some students may struggle when trying to think of character traits, so you might encourage them to think of important events from the story and how the character acted or what he or she said.

Try It

Freewrite: Use Your Journal

Help students freewrite either about a character from a book or about a story that they want to write. Gather *K¹² My Journal* and have students turn to pages 154 and 155 in Writing Skills. Read the prompts at the top of the pages to students.

Objectives

- Generate ideas for writing.
- Freewrite about a topic.
- Write in a journal.

1. Explain that students get to choose what to freewrite about. They can either write about a favorite character from a book or write ideas for their own story.

2. If students want to write about a character from a book, turn to page 154 in the journal. If students want to write their own story, turn to page 155.

3. Explain that all students will be writing a fiction story in this unit, even if they choose to focus on a character from a favorite book for this activity.

4. Explain that they are freewriting, or writing ideas on the page.

5. Tell students that they can write any reason for liking a character. If students are writing ideas for an original story, they can write about any part of the story that they want.

6. Note that some students may struggle with both prompts. If students are writing about a character, help them think of specific details to answer the prompt.

   ▸ Docs your character remind you of anyone?
   ▸ Would you ever want to be your character?
   ▸ What did the character say or do that made you like him or her?

7. If students are writing ideas for their own story, help them think of specific details to answer the prompt.

   ▸ Where does your story take place?
   ▸ Who is your story about?
   ▸ Is there a problem that needs to be solved?

8. Have students explain their writing to you. Do not evaluate students' writing. As long as students have written some ideas on paper, their responses are acceptable.

TIP The amount of time students need to complete this activity will vary. Allow students to use the rest of the allotted time to complete this activity. If they have more they would like to write, you may let them complete their entry at a later time. If students are having trouble getting started, you might tell them to just list ideas or words. They may even draw a picture and describe it to you. You can transcribe their words for them.

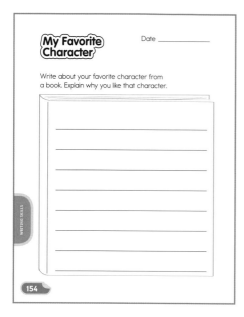

Create a Story Map

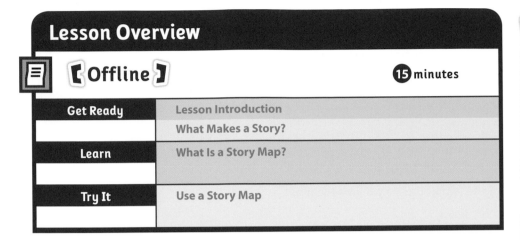

Lesson Overview

[Offline]   🕐 **15** minutes

Get Ready	Lesson Introduction
	What Makes a Story?
Learn	What Is a Story Map?
Try It	Use a Story Map

Materials

Supplied
- *K¹² Language Arts Activity Book*, pp. WS 195–196
- *K¹² My Journal*, pp. 154–155
- Story Card E

Keywords

character – a person or animal in a story

main character – an important person, animal, or other being who is central to the plot

problem – an issue a character must solve in a story

setting – when and where a story takes place

solution – how a character solves a problem in a story

Big Ideas

▶ Writers use various methods to plan, and novices should use what works for them: freewriting, listing, graphic organizers, or other methods.

▶ Engaging students in prewriting activities improves the quality of writing.

 🕐 **15** minutes

Work **together** with students to complete Get Ready, Learn, and Try It activities.

Get Ready

Lesson Introduction

Prepare students for the lesson.

1. Tell students that they will be creating a story map, which is a plan for writing.

2. Explain that students will be filling in information about their characters, setting, problem, and solution.

Objectives
- Identify the main character(s).
- Describe story structure elements—problem and solution.
- Identify setting.

What Makes a Story?

Help students understand what parts are needed to create a good story. Gather Story Card E.

1. Explain that to write a good story, a writer needs certain pieces, like the pieces of a puzzle.

   ► What is a **character**? a person in the story
   ► What is the **setting**? where the story takes place

2. Explain that characters can be main characters, the people who the story is mainly about or the most important people in the story. Or they can be other characters who just appear in the story.

3. Show students Story Card E. Look at the picture with them and help them create the elements of a story to go with the picture.

   ► Who are the main characters? the family; the woman and the girls
   ► What is the setting? on the street
   ► Who could some other characters be? a taxi driver, a police officer, another person on the street

4. Explain that the other key piece of a story is the problem. Tell students that the **problem** is what happens to the main characters. Usually the main characters have to find a **solution** to the problem. They need to figure something out or get something done.

5. Have students make up a problem and a solution to go with Story Card E. The story can have any problem at all, as long as there is a solution to go with it.

TIP Encourage students to be very imaginative. Anything can happen in a story. For instance, maybe an alien spacecraft lands on the street, or one of the little girls learns how to fly. Tell students that in their stories, anything is possible.

Learn

What Is a Story Map?

Help students understand a story map. Turn to page WS 195 in *K¹² Language Arts Activity Book*.

1. Explain to students that they are going to use a story map to help plan their own story.

2. Look at the Activity Book page with students. Explain that the words in the word bank are labels for different parts of the map. They are going to use these labels to identify the different parts of the map.

   ► If students are ready to write on their own, allow them to do so.

Objectives
- Identify character(s).
- Identify examples of problem and solution.
- Identify title.
- Identify setting.
- Identify the main character(s).

3. **Say:** This is a story map for *Peter Pan*.

   ▸ How should we label the box with the words *Peter Pan*? Title
   ▸ How should we label the box with the words *Peter, Wendy, Captain Hook,* and *Tinkerbell*? Main Characters
   ▸ How should we label the box with the words *the Lost Boys, Michael, John, Tiger Lily,* and *the pirates*? Other Characters
   ▸ How should we label the box with the word *Neverland*? Setting
   ▸ How should we label the box with the words *The pirates kidnap the Lost Boys and the Darling family*? Problem
   ▸ How should we label the box with the words *Peter rescues everyone, and the Darling family decides to go home*? Solution

4. Explain to students that they will create a story map like this one for their own story.

TIP If students are struggling with any of these terms, use *Peter Pan* to help explain what each means. Some students may have trouble with the difference between main characters and other characters. The most important thing to understand is who the story is primarily about.

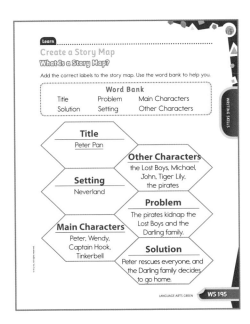

Try It

🖉 **Use a Story Map**

Turn to page WS 196 in *K¹² Language Arts Activity Book* and gather *K¹² My Journal*.

1. Read the instructions on the Activity Book page to students. Tell students that they are going to fill in the boxes on the story map with ideas for their own story.

2. Explain that this map is a tool to help students plan their story. They can make any changes that they want to when they actually write their story. This is a first draft of their ideas that they will revise while writing.

3. Note that some students may have only main characters in their story. This is fine as long as students know all the other elements of the story.

4. If students used their journal entry on page 154 or 155 to begin their story, they may refer back to that entry while working. If students used their journal entry to write about a character, have them use this story map to help generate ideas to write about.

5. Have students fill in the story map. Provide assistance as necessary.

TIP Some students may have a hard time with this activity because they have many ideas to write about. Encourage them to pick just one idea or problem and fully explore it with the story map. Tell them that letting ideas change and grow is a key part of being a writer. It is useful to either start with a character and decide what happens to that character, or start with a problem and figure out who will solve it and how it is solved. Keep the Activity Book page in a safe place so that students can refer to it later.

Objectives

- Use a graphic organizer.

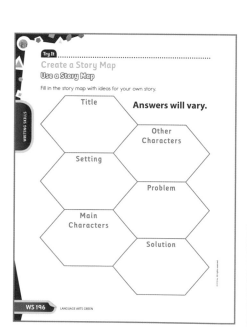

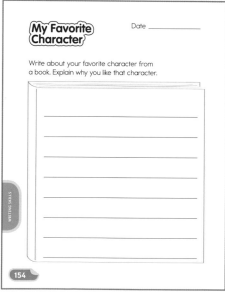

Draft a Story

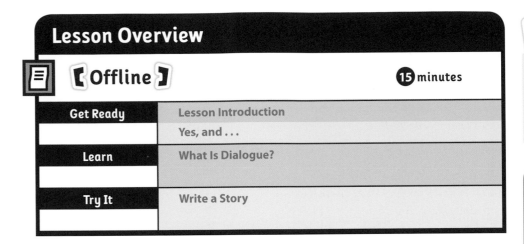

Lesson Overview

Offline — **15** minutes

Get Ready	Lesson Introduction
	Yes, and . . .
Learn	What Is Dialogue?
Try It	Write a Story

Materials

Supplied

- *K¹² Language Arts Activity Book*, pp. WS 196–200

Keywords

character – a person or animal in a story

dialogue – the words that characters say in a written work

main character – an important person, animal, or other being who is central to the plot

problem – an issue a character must solve in a story

setting – when and where a story takes place

solution – how a character solves a problem in a story

Advance Preparation

Have students gather their completed page WS 196 (Use a Story Map, story map) in *K¹² Language Arts Activity Book*.

Big Ideas

- ▶ Written work is never perfect in its first version. First efforts are called drafts, and they are not meant to be final.
- ▶ Dialogue adds realism and interest to a story.
- ▶ Good writers use transitions to help achieve coherence in written text.

 **Offline** **15** minutes

Work **together** with students to complete Get Ready, Learn, and Try It activities.

Get Ready

Lesson Introduction
Prepare students for the lesson.

1. Explain that students will begin writing their story.

2. Tell students that they will use their story map to create characters, a setting, a problem, and a solution.

3. Explain that students are going to use dialogue, or the words that characters say, to help tell their story.

Objectives
- Generate ideas for writing.

Yes, and . . .

Play a game to get students ready to write their own story.

1. Tell students that when creating a story, writers should let their imagination go anywhere. A writer should say *Yes* to any idea.

2. Explain that you are going to play a game to help students begin to say *Yes* to their imagination.

3. Tell students that the game is Yes, and . . . . Explain that you are going to begin to act out a story by explaining one thing that is happening. Students will then add on to the story by saying "Yes, and . . ." and adding one thing that is happening.

4. Stand up and begin acting out one idea.

    Say: We are on a boat. [pause] Yes, and [pause] the boat is flying through the air! Now you try it.

5. Have students say "Yes, and . . ." and add one idea, acting it out with you. For example, students might say, "Yes, and the boat is landing in a tree!" When they have finished, add your own *Yes, and . . .* idea and act it out.

6. Take turns adding statements and acting them out. The only rule is that no one can say *No* to an idea.

TIP Some students can find it very difficult to start writing, rejecting every idea as it comes to them. This game will help them realize how much fun it can be to make up a story if they just let their imagination wander.

Learn

What Is Dialogue?

Help students understand how to write dialogue. Turn to page WS 197 in *K¹² Language Arts Activity Book*.

1. Tell students that one of the best ways to tell a story is through the words of the characters. Remember that we learn about **characters** by what they say, what they do, and what others say about them. A good writer shows the audience who the characters are by what those characters say.

2. Read the rule and the example passages on the Activity Book page with students.

3. Explain that both passages give information about the story, but the second passage shows the information through the character's own words.

4. **Say:** When a character in a story speaks, it is called dialogue.

Objectives

- Describe characters by what they do, what they say, or what others say about them.
- Recognize quotations in dialogue.
- Use dialogue.

5. Point to the quotation marks in the second passage. Explain that these marks show you where the words a character speaks begin and end. Point to the word *said* in the second passage. Explain that this word is another clue that a character is speaking.

6. Explain that **dialogue** lets us hear more about the characters' thoughts and feelings.

   ▸ Which paragraph shows us how Jack is feeling? the second one

7. Read the exercise on the Activity Book page. Have students rewrite the sentence so that the information is given through dialogue.

TIP It doesn't matter if students punctuate their dialogue correctly. The important thing is to get them to use the character's own words to tell the story.

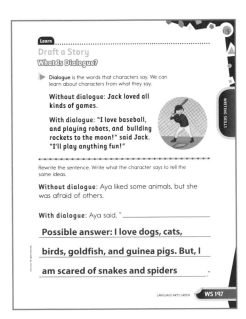

> **Learn**
>
> **Draft a Story**
> **What Is Dialogue?**
>
> ▸ **Dialogue** is the words that characters say. We can learn about characters from what they say.
>
> **Without dialogue:** Jack loved all kinds of games.
>
> **With dialogue:** "I love baseball, and playing robots, and building rockets to the moon!" said Jack. "I'll play anything fun!"
>
> Rewrite the sentence. Write what the character says to tell the same ideas.
>
> **Without dialogue:** Aya liked some animals, but she was afraid of others.
>
> **With dialogue:** Aya said, "_____
>
> Possible answer: I love dogs, cats, birds, goldfish, and guinea pigs. But, I am scared of snakes and spiders ."
>
> LANGUAGE ARTS GREEN   WS 197

Try It •

✏ **Write a Story**

Help students begin to write their own story. Gather students' completed story map from page WS 196 and turn to pages WS 199 and 200 in *K12 Language Arts Activity Book.*

1. Read the instructions and word bank on the Activity Book page with students. Remind them that order words and connecting words help the reader understand what is happening in a story.

2. Have students begin writing their story on the Activity Book pages.

Objectives
- Write a story.
- Write dialogue.
- Use transitions to connect ideas.
- Write a narrative with a beginning, middle, and end.

3. If students are struggling, encourage them to focus on specific details in their story. Answers to questions may vary.

   ▸ What are three ways that you can describe the setting?
   ▸ Does your main character remind you of anyone? Can you describe that person? What does he or she say or do?
   ▸ What time is it in your story? Day? Night?
   ▸ Can your story take place in a really silly place, such as in the ocean or on the back of a running elephant?
   ▸ What happens to your character?

4. If students still can't write, try having them write automatically without thinking too much. Tell them that they have to write for one minute without ever stopping, no matter what words come out. For one full minute, their pen or pencil has to be constantly moving. Tell students that it doesn't matter if the words make sense at all; they can revise later.

5. Note that students may write on the front and back of the Activity Book page, but they don't have to use both sides. Their story can be as long or as short as they want, as long as it contains all the necessary story elements.

TIP Keep the Activity Book page in a safe place so that students can refer to it later.

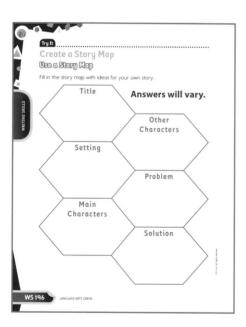

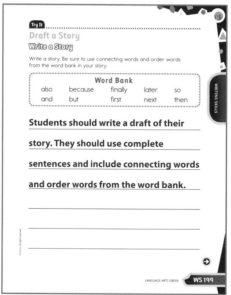

Keep Writing Your Story

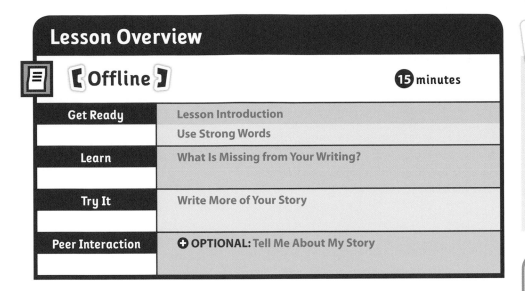

Lesson Overview

Offline		**15** minutes
Get Ready	Lesson Introduction	
	Use Strong Words	
Learn	What Is Missing from Your Writing?	
Try It	Write More of Your Story	
Peer Interaction	⊕ **OPTIONAL:** Tell Me About My Story	

Materials

Supplied
- *K¹² Language Arts Activity Book*, pp. WS 196, 199–202
- *K¹² My Journal*, pp. 154–155

Also Needed
- pencils, coloring

Keywords

character – a person or animal in a story

dialogue – the words that characters say in a written work

main character – an important person, animal, or other being who is central to the plot

problem – an issue a character must solve in a story

setting – when and where a story takes place

solution – how a character solves a problem in a story

Advance Preparation

Have students gather completed page WS 196 (Use a Story Map, story map) and partially completed pages WS 199 and 200 (Write a Story, draft story) in *K¹² Language Arts Activity Book*.

Big Ideas

- Good writing paints pictures with words to create a visual image of the text in the reader's mind's eye.
- The writing process is fluid and recursive. Writers improve their drafts as needed.
- Competent writers rely on a repertoire of strategies when planning, composing, and revising their texts.
- Writers who receive feedback during the writing process are able to apply that feedback to improve the ultimate product.
- One of the most powerful ways to improve writing is to directly teach strategies for planning and revising until students can use these strategies on their own.
- Working collaboratively with other students during various stages of the writing process can improve student writing.

[Offline] 15 minutes

Work **together** with students to complete Get Ready, Learn, Try It, and Peer Interaction activities.

Get Ready

Lesson Introduction

Prepare students for the lesson.

1. Explain that students will continue to work on their story.

2. Tell students that they will finish writing the draft of their story and then look over their writing to see how they can make it better.

> **Objectives**
> - Create mental imagery using sensory and descriptive language.
> - Identify language that shows, not tells.

Use Strong Words

Help students strengthen their writing.

1. Tell students that a story should be exciting and interesting and should make a reader feel something.

2. Explain that it is very important to use strong words to communicate clearly with the audience.

3. Explain that students will play a game to help them use strong words. You will say a word, and students will say a stronger word or phrase in response. And they will not only say the word or phrase; they will act it out as well.

   ▸ What is a stronger word than *good*? Possible answers: *excellent; fantastic*
   ▸ What is a stronger word than *unhappy*? Possible answers: *heartbroken, super angry; volcano mad*

4. Continue giving students mild words and having them suggest and act out stronger words.

Learn

What Is Missing from Your Writing?

Help students examine their story so far. Gather completed page WS 196 and partially completed pages WS 199 and 200 in *K¹² Language Arts Activity Book*. Also gather the coloring pencils.

1. Have students read over what they have written so far.

2. Tell students that, as they continue to write, they should be sure that their stories make sense. Answers to questions may vary.

   ▸ Do your characters seem like real people? Do they act the same way throughout your story, or do they suddenly change?
   ▸ Do you have a clear problem?
   ▸ Does your solution fix the problem?
   ▸ Are all the parts of your story connected to the main problem, or do some parts seem out of place?
   ▸ Do you use dialogue? Do you tell the story through the characters' own words?

3. Tell students to come up with their own questions about their story. If there are parts of the story that don't feel right to them, have them ask questions to figure out why.

4. Have students make notes on their draft with coloring pencils so that they can fix problems as they continue to write.

TIP The key idea in this lesson is to have students examine their own writing with a critical eye. Any ideas they have about how to improve their writing will be helpful. Encourage them to ask as many questions as possible about their writing as they are working.

Objectives

- Generate ideas for writing.
- Revise for clarity.
- Revise for logical order or sequence.
- Revise by adding or deleting text.

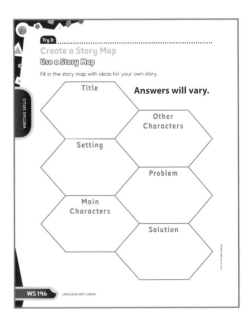

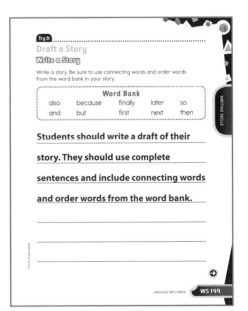

Try It

Write More of Your Story

Have students continue to write their story. Gather completed page WS 196 and partially completed pages WS 199 and 200 in *K¹² Language Arts Activity Book*.

1. Have students continue to write and revise the draft of their story. Students should refer to their story map as they work.

2. Encourage students to use showing language, dialogue, order words, and connecting words to tell their story.

3. Tell students that they need to find an ending for their story.

   ▸ How is your problem fixed?
   ▸ Does your main character learn anything?
   ▸ Does your main character have a question that was answered?
   ▸ What has changed in your story?

Objectives

- Use transitions to connect ideas.
- Write a story.
- Write dialogue.
- Write a narrative with a beginning, middle, and end.

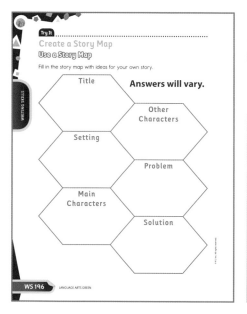

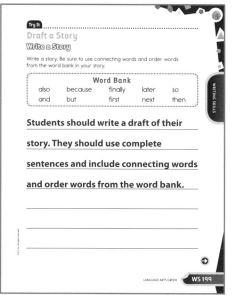

Peer Interaction

✚ OPTIONAL: Tell Me About My Story

This activity is OPTIONAL. It is intended for students who have extra time and would benefit from extra practice. Feel free to skip this activity.

Students can benefit from exchanging stories with someone they know or another student. This activity will work best if students exchange their story with other students who completed the same assignment, but you may copy the Activity Book pages and send them to someone else who is willing to give students feedback. Students should receive feedback on the content of their story. To complete this activity, turn to pages WS 201 and 202 in *K¹² Language Arts Activity Book*.

1. Have students exchange stories with other students.

2. Have students use the Activity Book pages to provide others with feedback about their writing.

3. Have students use the feedback provided from other students to revise their own stories.

Objectives
- Use guidance from adults and peers to revise writing.
- Collaborate with peers on writing projects.

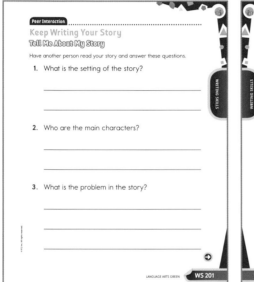
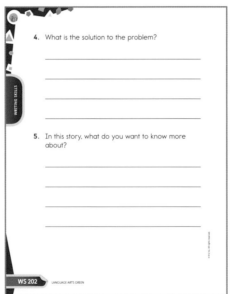

Illustrate and Publish a Story

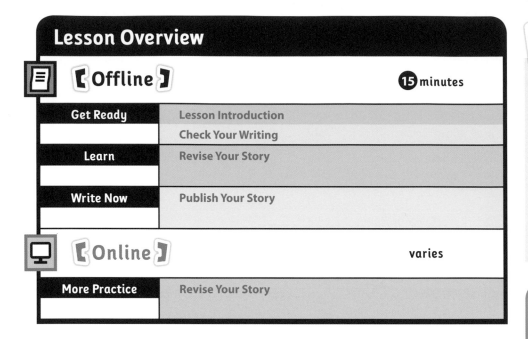

Lesson Overview

Offline · 15 minutes

Get Ready	Lesson Introduction
	Check Your Writing
Learn	Revise Your Story
Write Now	Publish Your Story

Online · varies

More Practice	Revise Your Story

Materials

Supplied
- *K¹² Language Arts Activity Book*, pp. WS 196, 199–207
- Publish Your Story: Rubric and Sample Responses (printout)

Also Needed
- crayons or markers

Keywords

proofreading – the stage or step of the writing process in which the writer checks for errors in grammar, punctuation, capitalization, and spelling

publishing – the stage or step of the writing process in which the writer makes a clean copy of the piece and shares it

revising – the stage or step of the writing process in which the writer rereads and edits the draft, correcting errors and making changes in content or organization that improve the piece

Advance Preparation

Have students gather completed pages WS 196 (Use a Story Map, story map), WS 199 and 200 (Write a Story, draft story), and WS 201 and 202 (Tell Me About My Story, feedback) in *K¹² Language Arts Activity Book*. Review students' draft. Look over the checklist on pages WS 203 and 204. Be ready to give students suggestions to help them answer some of the checklist questions.

Big Ideas

▶ Revision is best accomplished through discrete, focused tasks.
▶ Teaching the writing process encourages students to organize their ideas before they write and to revise their work after they write.
▶ The writing process is fluid and recursive. Writers improve their drafts as needed.
▶ Competent writers rely on a repertoire of strategies when planning, composing, and revising their texts.

 **15** minutes

Work **together** with students to complete Get Ready, Learn, and Write Now activities.

Get Ready

Lesson Introduction

Prepare students for the lesson.

1. Explain that students will revise their story.

2. Tell students that before they rewrite their story, they will use a checklist to improve their writing.

Check Your Writing

Help students do a final review of their writing before publication. Gather students' draft story on pages WS 199 and 200 and turn to page WS 203 in *K¹² Language Arts Activity Book*.

1. Read the checklist on page WS 203 with students. Tell them that they will use the checklist to revise their writing before they publish it.

2. Read the questions with students and have them write their answers on the checklist.

TIP Keep the draft and checklist in a safe place so students can refer to them when they revise their draft.

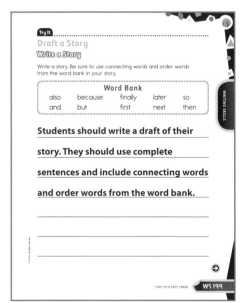

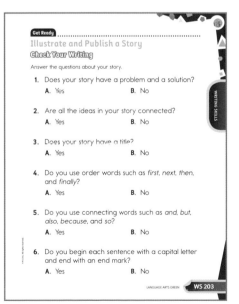

Learn

Revise Your Story

Help students revise their story. Gather students' story map on page WS 196, draft story on pages WS 199 and 200, feedback on pages WS 201 and 202, and checklist on page WS 203.

1. Help students revise their draft story. Students should refer to their story map, feedback, and checklist.

2. Tell students that they should also use feedback that they have received from adults and peers to make revisions to their story.

3. Ask students if they have more ideas that they want to add to their story. Tell them to think about ways they can improve their writing for the final draft of their story.

4. Review the checklist and feedback with students. Have them use a pencil to make notes and corrections on their draft.

TIP Revising is a difficult step for writers at any age. All writers revise, even published authors. It is important that students do not get discouraged and think that their first attempt was wrong. Revising makes writing better, and writing a draft is only one step in the writing process.

Objectives

- Revise by adding or deleting text.
- Revise using a checklist.
- Use a checklist for editing and proofreading.
- Revise using feedback.
- Use guidance from adults and peers to revise writing.

WRITING SKILLS

Try It ....
Create a Story Map
Use a Story Map

Fill in the story map with ideas for your own story.

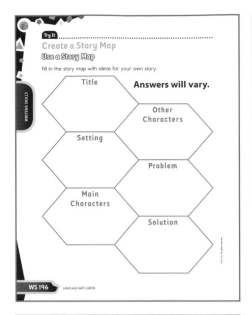

Title

Answers will vary.

Other Characters

Setting

Problem

Main Characters

Solution

Try It ....
Draft a Story
Write a Story

Write a story. Be sure to use connecting words and order words from the word bank in your story.

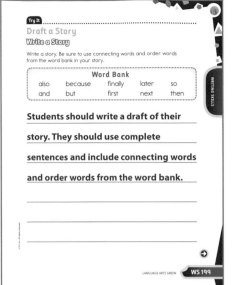

Word Bank				
also	because	finally	later	so
and	but	first	next	then

Students should write a draft of their

story. They should use complete

sentences and include connecting words

and order words from the word bank.

_____

_____

Peer Interaction ....
Keep Writing Your Story
Tell Me About My Story

Have another person read your story and answer these questions.

1. What is the setting of the story?

   _____

   _____

2. Who are the main characters?

   _____

   _____

3. What is the problem in the story?

   _____

   _____

   _____

---

4. What is the solution to the problem?

   _____

   _____

   _____

   _____

5. In this story, what do you want to know more about?

   _____

   _____

   _____

   _____

Get Ready ....
Illustrate and Publish a Story
Check Your Writing

Answer the questions about your story.

1. Does your story have a problem and a solution?
   A. Yes   **B.** No

2. Are all the ideas in your story connected?
   A. Yes   **B.** No

3. Does your story have a title?
   A. Yes   **B.** No

4. Do you use order words such as *first, next, then,* and *finally*?
   A. Yes   **B.** No

5. Do you use connecting words such as *and, but, also, because,* and *so*?
   A. Yes   **B.** No

6. Do you begin each sentence with a capital letter and end with an end mark?
   A. Yes   **B.** No

Write Now

 Publish Your Story

Help students write a final copy of their story. Gather students' draft story on pages WS 199 and 200 and turn to pages WS 205–207 in *K¹² Language Arts Activity Book*.

1. Help students rewrite their final, revised story on the Activity Book pages. Students should refer to their draft. Encourage them to write clearly and legibly.

2. When students have finished, have them draw a picture to illustrate their story.

3. Use the materials and instructions in the online lesson to evaluate students' finished writing. You will be looking at students' writing to evaluate the following:

   ▸ **Purpose and Content:** The writing is a made-up story with characters and descriptions from the writer's imagination. There is a problem and a solution.

   ▸ **Structure and Organization:** The writing has a clear beginning, middle, and end. There are order words to provide structure, and the ideas are connected with transitions.

   ▸ **Grammar and Usage:** The writing has complete sentences and uses capitalization correctly. The writer uses the past and present tenses appropriately. There is evidence of proofreading.

4. Enter students' scores for each rubric category online.

5. If students scored a 1 in any criterion, work with them to proofread and revise their work.

TIP The amount of time students need to complete this activity will vary. Students need only work for 15 minutes. Praise students when their story is finished. This is a great achievement, and students should be proud of what they have produced. Celebrating the publishing of students' work is a way to acknowledge their success and encourage them to keep writing.

 Reward: When students' writing achieves "meets objectives" in all three categories on the grading rubric, add a sticker for this unit on the My Accomplishments chart.

 Objectives

- Organize ideas in a logical order.
- Use capitalization and punctuation correctly.
- Use transitions to connect ideas.
- Write a story.
- Write complete sentences.
- Write sentences with appropriate spacing between words.
- Write sentences with legible handwriting.

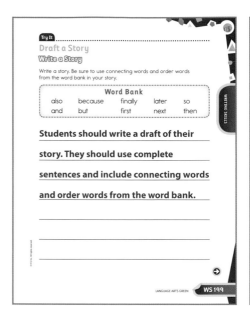

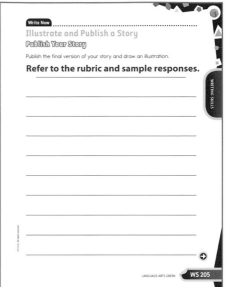

 varies

If necessary, work with students to complete the More Practice activity.

More Practice

Revise Your Story

If students' writing scored "doesn't meet objectives" in any category, have them complete the appropriate review activity listed in the table online.

Objectives
- Evaluate writing and choose activities to review and revise.

- ▶ Follow the online instructions to help students edit and revise their work.
- ▶ Impress upon students that revising makes their work better. Writing is a process, and each time they revise their paragraph, they are making their writing stronger and better.
- ▶ When you provide feedback, always begin with something positive. For example, you might point out a detail students wrote (even if it's the only detail) and explain how it helps you picture the scene: "You wrote that the heat was like an oven. That really helped me understand what the weather felt like."
- ▶ Place the final written work together with the rubric and the sample papers in the writing portfolio. This information is useful for you to track progress, and it helps students to refer back to their own work. They can see how they improve and review feedback to remember areas that need revising.
- ▶ Help students locate the activity and provide support as needed.